THE MODERN WORLD-SYSTEM III

The Second Era of Great Expansion of the
Capitalist World-Economy, 1730–1840s

ENCYCLOPÉDIE,

OU

DICTIONNAIRE RAISONNÉ

DES SCIENCES,

DES ARTS ET DES MÉTIERS,

PAR UNE SOCIÉTÉ DE GENS DE LETTRES.

Mis en ordre & publié par M. *DIDEROT*, de l'Académie Royale des Sciences & des Belles-Lettres de Prusse ; & quant à la PARTIE MATHÉMATIQUE, par M. *D'ALEMBERT*, de l'Académie Royale des Sciences de Paris, de celle de Prusse, & de la Société Royale de Londres.

Tantùm series juncturaque pollet,
Tantùm de medio sumptis accedit honoris! HORAT.

TOME PREMIER.

A PARIS,

Chez {
BRIASSON, *rue Saint Jacques, à la Science.*
DAVID l'aîné, *rue Saint Jacques, à la Plume d'or.*
LE BRETON, Imprimeur ordinaire du Roy, *rue de la Harpe.*
DURAND, *rue Saint Jacques, à Saint Landry, & au Griffon.*
}

M. DCC. LI.
AVEC APPROBATION ET PRIVILEGE DU ROY.

Diderot's *Encyclopedia* is considered the quintessential intellectual expression of the Enlightenment and has long symbolized for many the triumph of scientific rationalism as the reigning ideology of the modern world-system. Written by Denis Diderot with the aid of Jean Le Rond d'Alembert for the mathematical part, it was published originally from 1751 to 1780, in 35 volumes in folio, of which 21 were text, 12 contained plates, and 2 contained tables constructed by P. Mouchon.

THE MODERN WORLD-SYSTEM III

The Second Era of Great Expansion of the
Capitalist World-Economy 1730–1840s

WITH A NEW PROLOGUE

Immanuel Wallerstein

UNIVERSITY OF CALIFORNIA PRESS

Berkeley   Los Angeles   London

University of California Press, one of the most distinguished university
presses in the United States, enriches lives around the world by advancing
scholarship in the humanities, social sciences, and natural sciences. Its
activities are supported by the UC Press Foundation and by philanthropic
contributions from individuals and institutions. For more information,
visit www.ucpress.edu.

University of California Press
Berkeley and Los Angeles, California

University of California Press, Ltd.
London, England

Previously published in 1989 by Academic Press, Inc.

ISBN 978-0-520-26759-6 (pbk. : alk. paper)

The Library of Congress has catalogued an earlier edition
of this book as follows:

Library of Congress Cataloging-in-Publication Data

Wallerstein, Immanuel Maurice, Date.
   The second era of great expansion of the capitalist world-economy,
1730s–1840s / Immanuel Wallerstein.
      p.   cm.
   Bibliography: p.
   Includes index.
   ISBN 0-12-785925-X (hardcover) (alk. paper)
   ISBN 0-12-785926-8 (paperback) (alk. paper)
   1. Economic history—1600–1750.   2. Economic history—1750–1918.
3. Europe—Economic conditions—18th century.   4. Europe—Economic
conditions—19th century   5.Capitalism—History.   I. Title.
II. Series.   III. Series: Wallerstein, Immanuel Maurice, Date Modern
world-system ; 3   IV. Series: Studies in social discontinuity.
HC51.W28   1974 vol. 3
[HC52]
330.94'02 s —dc19
[330.94'0253]   88-10457

Manufactured in the United States of America

20   19   18   17   16   15   14   13   12   11
10   9   8   7   6   5   4   3   2   1

This book is printed on 50# Enterprise, a 30% post consumer
waste, recycled, de- inked fiber and processed chlorine free.
It is acid-free, and meets all ANSI/NISO (Z 39.48) requirements.

To Beatrice

CONTENTS

LIST OF ILLUSTRATIONS

The illustrations were selected and annotated with the assistance of Sally Spector.

ACKNOWLEDGMENTS

A number of colleagues have consented to give a critical reading to one or more chapters of this book. Though many of them demur on some major propositions, they each gave me the courtesy of identifying errors or quarreling over emphasis. I thank them each for their valuable assistance and absolve them of all those matters on which I declined their good advice: Perry Anderson, Sabyasachi Bhattacharya, Rondo Cameron, Ferenc Fehér, Walter Goldfrank, Patrice Higonnet, Keith Hitchins, Eric J. Hobsbawm, Terence K. Hopkins, Charles Issawi, Reşat Kasaba, Hans-Heinrich Nolte, Patrick K. O'Brien, Madhavan K. Palat, Donald Quataert, George Rudé, and Charles Tilly.

Part of Chapter 2 appeared in *Thesis XI* (1986), and an earlier version of Chapter 3 appeared in *Studies in History* (1988).

PROLOGUE TO THE 2011 EDITION

There are three controversial questions in my treatment of the period running from 1730 to the 1840s. For many analysts, perhaps the majority, this
period represents the great turning point of the modern era, the moment
when capitalism as a system, or modernity as a mode of existence, came
into being. Readers of the first three volumes will know that I do not agree,
since I think the great turning point was in the "long sixteenth century."

The second controversial question concerns the concept of "incorporation" into the capitalist world-economy of zones that were previously part of
what I have been calling the "external arena." This assumes that a distinction
can be made between the modern world-system (which is a capitalist world-
economy) and other parts of the globe, especially in the period 1500–1750.
It further assumes that there is a significant difference between being a zone
outside the capitalist world-economy and being a peripheral zone within the
capitalist world-economy.

A third issue is the concept of cyclical processes within the *longue durée,*
and their role in explaining historical processes. These cyclical processes are
what are called in French *conjonctures* (and cognate words in other Romance
languages as well as Germanic and Slavic languages; the main exception to
this usage is English, in which the word *conjuncture* is very much not a *conjoncture*). The principal economic cycle is what is often called Kondratieff
long waves—a concept employed in this volume, but one whose very existence is often contested by others.

It is perhaps useful to restate the basic arguments for all three concepts—
the absence of a turning point in this period, the process of incorporation
into the modern world-system, and the nature of the Kondratieff long
waves. This is particularly important since I believe there has been considerable misunderstanding of what I have been trying to argue.

1. The Great Turning Point

Social scientists of all kinds like to designate turning points. It is a device
that clarifies immensely the story they are trying to tell. It becomes a basic
building block of their analyses of the immediate phenomena they are
studying. The choice of turning points constitutes a basic framework within
which we all operate. But choosing different turning points can change entirely the logic of the analyses. What are considered to be the "turning points"
can mislead as readily as they can clarify.

If one reads the major works of the historical social sciences over the past
two centuries, one will readily see that a strong favorite in the collective lit-

erature for what is the major turning point in the past five hundred (or five thousand) years has been precisely the period 1730–1840s. Whether one is using the framework of "modernity" or "capitalism" or "industrialism" or "Western dominance of the world," most persons have dated its true onset to this period—or at least most persons until the last forty years or so, during which there has come to be a growing questioning of this period as the "great turning point." This entire work revolves around a rejection of this period as that turning point in favor of the "long sixteenth century" as the moment of the creation of the "modern world-system" as a "capitalist world-economy."

In a sense, the entire first three volumes make this case. But allow me to repeat the argument in condensed form. We have argued that the essential element of capitalism as a system is not, as is often contended, proletarian wage labor or production for the market or factory production. For one thing, all of these phenomena have long historical roots and can be found in many different kinds of systems. In my view, the key element that defines a capitalist system is that it is built on the drive for the *endless* accumulation of capital. This is not merely a cultural value but a structural requirement, meaning that there exist mechanisms within the system to reward in the middle run those who operate according to its logic and to punish (materially) those who insist on operating according to other logics.

We have argued that, in order to maintain such a system, several things are necessary. There has to be an axial division of labor, such that there are continuous exchanges of essential goods that are low-profit and highly competitive (i.e., peripheral) with high-profit and quasi-monopolized (i.e., core-like) products. In order to allow entrepreneurs to operate successfully in such a system, there needs in addition to be an interstate system composed of pseudosovereign states of differing degrees of efficacy (strength). And there also have to be cyclical mechanisms that permit the constant creation of new quasi-monopolistic profit-making enterprises. The consequence of this is that there is a quite slow but constant geographical relocation of the privileged centers of the system.

All of this did occur in the modern world-system, which was initially located primarily in most (but not all) of Europe and in parts of the Americas. It was, in Braudel's words, *a* world and not *the* world. But by its internal logic, the capitalist world-economy expanded its boundaries as a system. It did this most spectacularly in the period treated in this volume, and we have tried to tell this story, describing which new regions this involved and why they came to be submitted to this expansion.

There are two forms of arguing against this position. One is to assert a process of gradual expansion in the globe of intercourse of various kinds (trade, communications, culture, conquest). This is seen as a multimillennial process, in which case neither the long sixteenth century nor the turn of the nineteenth century is so dramatic a moment as to constitute a turning point per se. Recent arguments about the long-standing centrality of China in the trade patterns of the Eurasian landmass are a variant on this argument. Capitalism as a concept largely drops out of the discussion when the issue is framed in this manner.

Or one can argue that the emergence of an industrial bourgeoisie and landless industrial workers, engaged in class conflict with each other, is the crucial defining characteristic, and that this appears only in this period and only in a few countries (perhaps only in England). That makes this period the "turning point." The interstate system and the existence of core–peripheral exchanges largely drop out of this discussion. This argument can be formulated either in "Marxist" language or in "Weberian" language. Either version essentially dismisses the notion of a world-system and its mode of constraining action.

2. Incorporation into the World-System

In volume 1, we distinguished between the external arena and the peripheral zones of the modern world-system. While parts of the external arena engaged in trade and other forms of interaction with the capitalist world-economy, the trade, we argued, was largely in "luxury" goods and was therefore not essential to the functioning of either party. As a result, the trade was relatively equal in the sense that each side was exchanging items that it considered of low value for items that it considered of high value. We might call this a win-win situation.

We suggested that peripheral products were traded with corelike products in a form of unequal exchange in which there was a complicated but real transfer of surplus value from the peripheral zones to the core zones. The exchanges were in essential goods, which each side needed to maintain itself. This trade could not be cut off without negative consequences for one or both sides. It was, however, possible for short periods to establish blockages to the free movement of goods, and we discussed the political circumstances in which such "protectionism" was practiced.

The cyclical processes within the capitalist world-economy led repeatedly to situations in which, in order to maintain the low production costs of peripheral goods, it was necessary to involve new regions within the world-economy—that is to say, to "incorporate" them within the division of labor.

Of course, the process of incorporation might receive resistance. It was argued, however, that the technological development of the capitalist world-economy, itself a process internal to that system, led over time to strengthening the military capacity of strong states of the world-economy compared with the military capacity of parts of the external arena. Hence, for example, whereas in the sixteenth century pan-European military strength was perhaps insufficient to "conquer" India, by the late eighteenth century this was no longer true.

Finally, how much expansion occurred at any given time was a function of how much new territory the capitalist world-economy was able to integrate at any given moment. It was also a function of how distant and therefore how difficult it was to incorporate *manu militari* certain regions. Hence, it is argued in this volume that whereas what we now call India was incorporated during this period, this was not true of China, which would be incorporated at a later time.

We then argued that incorporation was a process. It did not occur in a day or even a decade, but over a substantial period of time. However, we tried to show, by comparing four different regions—Russia, India, the Ottoman Empire, and West Africa—how "peripheralization" was a homogenizing process. That is, although these four zones were quite different from each other at the beginning of the process, the pressures of the world-system acted to make them more similar in their characteristics. For example, these pressures weakened the state structures in some zones and strengthened them in others, so that they would perform optimally in terms of the modalities of the modern world-system.

There have been two forms of arguing with this distinction. One has been to assert that the process of incorporation is a much more gradual one, with multiple stages. I am perfectly willing to entertain this amendment to the argument, the result of more empirical research into the matter.

The second has been to cast doubts on the distinction between luxury goods and essential goods. It has been asserted that what are often thought of as luxury goods are essential, at least as prestige items. It is further argued that the perspective on luxuries is culturally grounded and different peoples would define it differently.

I agree that this is a difficult distinction. But the fact that the concept of luxury is culturally grounded is part of my own argument. And although peacock feathers may seem essential to some groups, I find it difficult to accept that this is the same kind of necessity as the need of grains for human consumption. Furthermore, grains are bulk goods, and diamonds take up very little space in transportation. This seems to me to make a lot of practical difference.

So, I persist in feeling that the "equal" exchanges of two regions external to each other and the "unequal" exchanges within the capitalist world-economy constitute a crucial theoretical distinction. The capitalist world-economy is by its very mode of functioning a highly polarizing system. This is its most negative feature and, in the long run, one of its fatal flaws. Capitalism as a system is very different from the kinds of systems that existed before the long sixteenth century. It is not helpful analytically to lose this basic reality from view.

3. Kondratieff Cycles

Kondratieff cycles are named after Nikolai Kondratieff, a Russian economist who described them in the 1920s. He was not in fact the first scholar to have described such cycles. And his descriptions of both how the cycles work and when they first occurred are no longer widely accepted. But the most widely used name for such cycles continues to be his. My own view of how they operate derives from my understanding of how producers in a capitalist system make profits from their enterprises and thereby are able to accumulate capital.

Capitalism is a system in which the endless accumulation of capital is the raison d'être. To accumulate capital, producers must obtain profits from their operations. However, truly significant profits are possible only if the producer can sell the product for considerably more than the cost of production. In a situation of perfect competition, it is absolutely impossible to make significant profit. Perfect competition is classically defined as a situation with three features—a multitude of sellers, a multitude of buyers, and universally available information about prices. If all three features were to prevail (which rarely occurs), any intelligent buyer will go from seller to seller until he finds one who will sell at a penny above the cost of production, if not indeed below the cost of production.

Obtaining significant profit requires a monopoly, or at least a quasi-monopoly, of world-economic power. If there is a monopoly, the seller can demand any price, as long as he does not go beyond what the elasticity of demand permits. Any time the world-economy is expanding significantly, one will find that there are some "leading" products, which are relatively monopolized. It is from these products that great profits are made and large amounts of capital can be accumulated. The forward and backward linkages of these leading products are the basis of an overall expansion of the world-economy. We call this the A-phase of a Kondratieff cycle.

The problem for capitalists is that all monopolies are self-liquidating. This is because there exists a world market into which new producers can enter, however politically well defended a given monopoly is. Of course, entry is not easy and takes time. But sooner or later, others surmount the obstacles and are able to enter the market. As a result, the degree of competition increases. And when competition increases, prices go down, as the heralds of capitalism have always told us. However, at the same time, profits go down. When profits for the leading products go down sufficiently, the world-economy ceases to expand, and it enters into a period of stagnation. We call this the B-phase of a Kondratieff cycle. Empirically, the A- and B-phases together have tended to be fifty to sixty years in length, but the exact lengths have varied. Of course, after a certain time in a B-phase, new monopolies can be created and a new A-phase can begin.

A- and B-phases of Kondratieff cycles seem, therefore, to be a necessary part of the capitalist process. It follows that they should logically be part of its operation from the very beginning of the existence of a capitalist world-economy. In the argument of this work, this means that they should be found from the long sixteenth century forward. And indeed, economic historians have regularly described such *conjonctures* during all this time, as can be seen in the many references to such descriptions in this and other volumes. To be sure, these economic historians did not call them Kondratieff cycles. But they may be found as a regular phenomenon in the system as a whole within the geographic boundaries we have been insisting were those of the capitalist world-economy in this period.

A few economic historians have described such cycles for the late Middle Ages in Europe, although this is a more contentious proposition. Were it to be established, it would give some support to those who wish to date the beginning of the modern world-system to an earlier date than the long sixteenth century.

1

INDUSTRY AND BOURGEOISIE

Although Joseph Wright of Derby (1734–1797) began his career as a portrait painter, he is most famous for paintings which express his interest in science and technology. His participation in the Lunar Society, a group of enlightened industrialists and scientists whose meetings were held when there was sufficient moonlight for making one's way along dark country roads, inspired his interior scenes illuminated by moonlight or artificial light. The family setting of the "Experiment with the Air Pump (1768)," emphasizes the egalitarian attitude that scientific concepts and discoveries could be presented to those outside the laboratory such as women and children.

The tale grows with the telling.
—Eric Kerridge[1]

We are accustomed to organizing our knowledge around central concepts which take the form of elementary truisms. The rise of industry and the rise of the bourgeoisie or middle classes are two such concepts, bequeathed to us by nineteenth-century historiography and social science to explain the modern world. The dominant view has been that a qualitative historical change took place at the end of the eighteenth and the beginning of the nineteenth centuries. This was an age of revolutions when both the "first"[2] industrial revolution in Great Britain and the "exemplary"[3] bourgeois revolution in France occurred. No doubt there have been voices to challenge this consensus. And there has been incessant quibbling about the details. Nonetheless, the imagery of these two revolutions remains deeply anchored in both popular culture and scholarly thought.[4] These concepts are in fact the lodestars by which we usually navigate the misty and turbulent waters of modern historical reality. Indeed, as I shall indicate, the two lodestars are but a single one.

The term "revolution" connotes for us sudden, dramatic, and extensive change. It emphasizes discontinuity. There is no doubt that this is the sense that most of those who use the concept of "industrial revolution" intend.[5] Coleman speaks of a "comparatively sudden and violent change which launched the industrialized society,"[6] and Landes of "a far more drastic break with the past than anything since the invention of the wheel."[7] Hobsbawm similarly insists: "If the sudden, qualitative, and fundamental

[1] Kerridge (1969, 468).

[2] See, for example, among very many others, Mathias (1969) and Deane (1979).

[3] Poulantzas (1971, I, 187).

[4] Charles and Richard Tilly put it well: "Belief in *the* Industrial Revolution is so widespread and tenacious among us that we may call it the principal dogma and vested interest of European economic historians" (1971, 186).

[5] The original use of the term has been traced by Bezanson (1922, 345–346) to a comparison in 1798 with the French Revolution, a comparison that has remained implicit ever since. Williams suggests that its usage as the instituting of a new order of society rather than as mere technical change should be traced to Lamartine in the 1830s (1976, 138). It is used in this sense subsequently by Adolphe Blanqui, Friedrich Engels, John Stuart Mill, and Karl Marx (Mantoux, 1928, 25, fn. 1). Heaton suggests Arnold Toynbee took the term from Marx and put it "into academic circulation"(1932, 3).

We should note as well that contemporaries seemed little aware of the phenomenon. M. S. Anderson (1979, 192) observes that in the "best book of the time," George Chalmer's *An Historical View of the Domestic Economy of Great Britain and Ireland from the Earliest to the Present Times*, published in Edinburgh in 1812, there is much discussion of trade, population, and public revenues, but that "industry receives scarcely any attention."

[6] Coleman (1956, 20). Responding to usages of the term, "industrial revolution," which he considers too loose, Plumb responds vigorously: "Between 1760 and 1790 it was crystal clear there were two worlds [in Britain], the old and the new. . . . Nor could the process of change be gradual. . . . Compared with the centuries which had gone before, the changes in industry, agriculture, and social life in the second half of the eighteenth century were both violent and revolutionary" (1950, 77).

[7] Landes (1969, 42).

3

transformation, which happened in or about the 1780's, was not a revolution, then the word has no common-sense meaning."[8]

Of what is this revolution supposed to consist? Toynbee (to whom we owe the classic analysis of the industrial revolution as such), writing in 1884, finds its "essence" in the "substitution of competition for medieval regulations."[9] Hartwell, writing 80 years later, defines its "essential character" somewhat differently: "the sustained increase in the rate of growth of total and per capita output at a rate which was revolutionary compared with what went before."[10]

The two emphases—freedom from "medieval" constraints (or social revolution) and the rate of growth (or economic revolution)—are, to be sure, not incompatible. Indeed, the heart of the traditional argument has been that the former led to the latter. But in recent years it has been the rate of growth that has been the focus of attention, with one after another factor invoked to explain it. Nor is this surprising. The continued development of the capitalist world-economy has involved the unceasing ascension of the ideology of national economic development as the primordial collective task, the definition of such development in terms of national economic growth, and the corresponding virtual "axiom . . . that the route to affluence lies by way of an industrial revolution."[11]

The two "essential" elements—growth and freedom—remain too vague. Each must be translated into more specific concepts. Growth seems very closely linked conceptually to the "application of mechanical principles . . . to manufacturing,"[12] what the French often call "machinisme,"[13] and the "revolution" of mechanization has usually been attributed to "a cluster of innovations in Schumpeter's sense of the term."[14]

[8] Hobsbawm (1962, 46).

[9] Toynbee (1956, 58). This emphasis on social or sociological change as the heart of "revolution" was put forward already in 1844 by Friedrich Engels: "On the surface it may appear that the century of revolution has passed England by. . . . And yet since the middle of the [eighteenth] century England has undergone a greater upheaval than any other country, an upheaval which has had consequences all the more far-reaching for being effected quietly and which is therefore more likely to achieve its goal in practice than the French political revolution or the German philosophical revolution. . . . Social revolution is the only true revolution, to which political and philosophical revolution must lead" (1971, 9).

[10] Hartwell (1967a, 8). Cannadine (1984) sees *four* different and successive interpretations of the industrial revolution; as negative social consequences (1880–1920), as cyclical fluctuation (1920–1950), as economic growth (1950–1970), and as limit to growth (1970–).

[11] Deane (1979, 1).

[12] Hughes (1968, 253); see also Dobb (1946, 258) and Landes (1969, 41). Landes elaborates this into three improvements: the substitution of machines for human skill, of inanimate for animate power, and of mineral for vegetable or animal substances as raw materials. Cipolla calls this the substitution of mechanical for biological "converters" of energy (1961, 529).

[13] See Ballot (1923). To translate "machinisme" by "mechanism" is to lose its usage as a concept.

[14] Deane (1979, 106). In seeking to justify his argument that British industrialization was "unique," Mathias argues that it was unique "in the extent of the dominance of a single national economy in the crucial matrix of cheap coal, cheap iron, machine-making, power and mineral fuel technology, engineering skills." And, he adds, it was "first, and therefore unique" in that sense too (1979a, 19); cf. a similar argument of conjuncture in Rostow (1971, 33).

The argument of conjuncture is taken to its

The analysis of mechanization places the development of the forces of production in the foreground. The increase of "freedom" (or social revolution) refers, on the other hand, primarily to the relations of production: who may produce what, who may work for whom, and on what terms. Two phenomena are central to this part of the discussion: the factory (locus of concentration of the machines) and the proletarian or wage laborer (employee of the factory). The modern factory is said to have "originated in England in the last third of the eighteenth century."[15] For many authors, it is the factory, and all that it implies in terms of the organization of the work force, that is thought to be the crucial innovation in the organization of work, requiring a salaried work force. Hobsbawm insists that the industrial revolution "is not merely an acceleration of economic growth, but an acceleration of growth because of, and through, economic and social transformation."[16] The transformation refers, above all, to the rise of an urban proletariat, itself the consequence of a "total transformation of the rural social structure."[17]

Much of the discussion on the industrial revolution, however, *assumes* both the processes of mechanization and the process of "liberation"/ proletarianization and concentrates instead on the question: what made these processes occur "for the first time" in Great Britain, what made Britain "take off"? Take off is, in fact, an image which aptly reflects the basic model of the industrial revolution, however much Rostow's detailed hypotheses or periodization may have been the subject of sharp debate. To this question, a series of answers, which are not by any means mutually exclusive, have been given, although various authors have insisted on the centrality of a given factor (which other authors have in turn duly contested). Placing them in an order of chronological immediacy, and

logical extreme by Wrigley. In seeking to refute the idea that "modernization" (or "rationality") leads "ineluctably" to "industrialization" (or "sustained economic growth"), since in that case Holland which was more "modern" than England in the eighteenth century should have been the first to industrialize, Wrigley insists that the series of technical innovations were "the product of special, local circumstances," what he terms a "happy coincidence." It follows that "what is explained is not simply why the Industrial Revolution occurred in England earlier than elsewhere, but why it occurred at all." He concludes on the thought that "it is quite possible for a man to have, say, a one-in-fifty chance of hitting the jackpot and yet still win it" (1972, 247, 259). This is logically similar to Hartwell's argument that the industrial revolution must be seen "as a discontinuity in its own right rather than as a residual result of the rise of capitalism" (1970b, 10).

[15] Mantoux (1928, 25), who adds that "the distinctive characteristic of the factory system is the use of machinery" (p. 38). See also Toynbee (1956, 63).

[16] Hobsbawm (1968, 34). Furthermore, this transformation was seen from the beginning as a "crisis." Saint-Simon, in his apostrophe to the king in *Système industriel* published in 1821 wrote: "Sire, the march of events continues to aggravate the crisis in which society find itself, not only in France but throughout the large nation formed by the peoples of western Europe." Cited in Febvre (1962, 514).

[17] Saville (1969, 251). Once again the argument is that Great Britain is unique: "Nowhere save in Britain was the peasantry virtually eliminated *before* acceleration of economic growth that is associated with the development of industrial capitalism, and of the many features of early industrialization in Britain none is more striking than the presence of a rapidly growing proletariat in the countryside" (p. 250).

working backward, these are the factors of increased demand (which is said to make mechanization and proletarianization profitable), the availability of capital (which in turn makes the mechanization possible), demographic growth (which makes the proletarianization possible), an agricultural "revolution" (which makes the demographic growth possible), and a preexisting development of land-tenure patterns (which makes the demographic growth possible). Furthest in the rear, and most difficult to pin down, is a presumed attitude of mind (which ensures that there will be entrepreneurs who will take advantage of all the many opportunities this revolutionary process offers at its many junctures, such that the cumulative effect is "revolutionary"). Obviously, this chronology of factors is a bit abstract, and various authors have argued a different sequence.

Demand, as the explanation of innovation, is an old theory ("necessity is the mother of invention") and Landes makes it central to his analysis: "It was in large measure the pressure of demand on the mode of production that called forth the new techniques in Britain."[18] But which demand? There are two candidates: foreign trade and the home market. The argument for exports centers on the fact that their growth and acceleration were "markedly greater" than those of domestic industry in the second half of the eighteenth century."[19] Against this, Eversley argues that, in the "key period" of 1770–1779, it is "incontrovertible" that the export sector declined but nonetheless there was "visible acceleration" in industrialization, which reinforces the thesis that "a large domestic market for mass-produced consumer goods" is central to industrialization.[20] Hobsbawm suggests the inevitable compromise—both foreign trade and a large

---

[18] Landes (1969, 77). See also Plumb (1982, 284). "After all, the new industrial methods began in the consumer industries—textiles, pottery, the buttons, buckles and pins of Boulton and Watt." Deane argues in a similar vein: "It is only when the potential market was large enough, and the demand elastic enough, to justify a substantial increase in output, that the rank and file of entrepreneurs broke away from their traditional techniques. . . . There is no evidence to suggest that . . . the majority of producers were any more ready to innovate in 1815 than they had been in 1750" (1979, 131). Deane and Cole have, however, vacillated on the source of demand. Having located it in foreign trade in the first edition of their book in 1962, they wrote in the preface to the second edition: "Were we to write this book again today we might be tempted to take our stand on somewhat different ground, notably, for example, on the role of foreign trade in eighteenth-century growth" (1967, xv).

[19] Whitehead (1964, 74). Crouzet calls the eighteenth century "the Atlantic stage of European

economic development," asserting that, for France before the Revolution, trade with the Americas was "the most dynamic sector of the whole economy" (1964, 568). Boulle adds a locus of demand not usually included. He notes that in the slave trade the assorted goods used to pay for slaves had become quite standardized. "Thus all the demand factors ordinarily identified at the beginning of the Industrial Revolution—importance of the market, standardization of merchandise, bonus for the artisan producing on schedule—were all to be found in Africa" (1975, 312).

[20] Eversley (1967, 248, 211); see also Bairoch (1973b, 571). Eversley places himself in the Rostow tradition, arguing that the 1770–1780 period, during which the domestic market was said to be favorable was "crucial as the 'warming-up' period just before the take-off [1780s] into sustained growth (p. 209). Rostow, however, *refutes* Marczewski's arguments about eighteenth-century French economic growth on the grounds that France's *foreign* trade was insufficient to permit take-off: "The difference between Prof.

domestic market were necessary, plus "a third, and often neglected, factor: government."[21]

There are those who doubt that demand rose significantly. They put their emphasis rather on "supply not demand related processes."[22] For some, the question of the supply of capital has loomed large. Hamilton, in 1942, explained the "revolutionary" character of the industrial revolution by the "profit inflation" of the last half of the eighteenth century, resulting from the wage lag, the gap between the rise of prices and the rise of wages,[23] an old standby which Hamilton had previously used to explain the economic expansion of the sixteenth century.[24] Ashton found the heart of his explanation of the industrial revolution in "relatively cheap capital,"[25] coming from the fall in the rate of interest. A generation later, and after reviewing the literature covering the theme of capital formation, Crouzet would take his stand on a more modest position: the "relative abundance" of capital was a "permissive factor," neither necessary nor inevitable, but one historically true of England in the eighteenth century.[26]

But was fixed capital even important? There are a growing number of skeptical commentators who argue that "the capital needs of early industrialization were modest."[27] In the face of these arguments, the proponents of capital's importance have retreated to surer, because less provable, ground. "It was the flow of capital . . . more than the stock that counted in

---

Marczewski and him [Rostow] was a simple one. In assessing French evolution, Prof. Rostow said that he had decided . . . that the development of a modern textile industry for the home market alone did not have a sufficient scale effect to act as a basis for sustained growth. For textiles to serve that function, the lift which foreign trade gave was also necessary. This was an arbitrary judgment which led him to deny that the early nineteenth-century cotton industries in France and Germany could have acted as leading sectors in take-off" (Hague, 1963, 359).

Markovitch, Marczewski's associate, inverts the argument, doubting that the growth of the English cotton industry in the late eighteenth century, which he admits was "exceptional," could be "the central pivot which pulled the British industrial machine into the orbit of the Industrial Revolution," since in 1770 cotton was only 5% of British textile production, and all textiles only 10% of the national revenue, whereas wool represented a third of British industrial production and was equally significant in France (1976a, 645). Cameron uses these same precentage figures about cotton to confront Hobsbawm's assertion (1968, 40) that "whoever says Industrial Revolution says cotton" with the retort: "Insofar as the statement is accurate, it also reveals the inadequacy and pretentiousness of the term [industrial revolution]" (1985, 4).

[21] Hobsbawm (1968, 42).

[22] Mokyr (1977, 1005). For a critique of Mokyr and a defense of Elizabeth Gilboy's argument of change of taste as the basis of expanded demand, see Ben-Schachar (1984). Another supply-side theorist is Davis who sees the impetus precisely in "technical change in the manufacture of cotton" (1979, 10). For the argument of technological innovations as the single, sufficient explanation of the industrial revolution, see Gaski (1982); and for devastating criticism, see Geary (1984).

[23] Hamilton (1953, 336). Landes (1969, 74) attacks Hamilton on the grounds that profit inflation was as high on the continent of Europe in that period but only Britain had the industrial revolution. See also Felix (1956).

[24] See Wallerstein (1974, 77–84).

[25] Ashton (1948, 11).

[26] Crouzet (1972a, 68). "Evidence of Britain's wealth in the eighteenth century is overwhelming" (p. 40). Crouzet also agrees that there were in this period "extremely high net profits" (1972b, 195; cf. Pollard, 1972a, 127–129).

[27] Hartwell (1976b, 67). Chapman also uses the word "modest" (1970, 252). Pollard says the speed of growth of fixed capital has been "often exaggerated" (1972a, 143). See also Bairoch on the low capital costs involved (1974, 54–65).

the last analysis."[28] A variant on this theme is the suggestion that what
mattered was not a change in the "relative size" of capital stock (that is, the
size "relative to the national income") but the change in the "content of the
capital stock," that is, the diversion of investment "from traditional to
modern forms of capital accumulation."[29] Emphasis on the flow of capital
leads immediately to a concern with credit facilities. A standard view is that
Great Britain differed from other countries precisely in the amount of
credit facilities available to industry.[30] This view, of course, assumes that
capital investments were limited by frontiers. Lüthy, however, believes that,
already in the mid-eighteenth century, western and central Europe constituted a "zone of exchange" characterized by "ease in banking transactions
and the flow of capital" and speaks of the virtual absence of obstacles to this
flow.[31]

Another group of authors gives pride of place to demographic shifts.
Population growth presumably provided both the demand for industrial
products and the work force to produce them. Britain's "unprecedented
growth of population"[32] is said to be particularly remarkable because it was
sustained, long term, and went along with a growth in output.[33] Plumb
adds the twist that the key element was the survival of more children of
"middle and lower middle class" parents, for "without a rapidly expanding
lower middle class with sufficient education and technical background, the
Industrial Revolution would have been impossible."[34]

---

[28] Landes (1969, 78). He seems to feel this thrust
will hurt primarily the Marxists. "So much," he
adds, "for the preoccupation with primitive accumulation."

[29] Deane (1973b, 358–359). Insofar as this means
a shift from investment in land to investment in
industry, Crouzet's caution is salutary: "Landlords
put their power of borrowing on the security of
their estates at the disposal of transport improvements. But, as far as industry is concerned, one is
tempted to keep to Postan's view that 'surprisingly
little' of the wealth of rural England 'found its way
into the new industrial enterprises'" (1972a, 56).
The reference is to Postan (1972) who argues that
"apart from the inner circle of merchants and
financiers, the habit of investing has grown only in
the nineteenth century" (p. 75).

Crouzet also notes that "in the eighteenth and
even at the beginning of the nineteenth century,
[agriculture, transport, and building] absorbed
much more capital than was invested in British
industry" (1972b, 163).

[30] See Gille: "[Credit facilities] were much lower
on the continent, perhaps because the larger banks
. . . got a larger proportion of their profits from
government financing" (1973, 260). Chapman,
however, does not believe that capital was all that

available from the banks for the English cotton
industry. "All indications are that before the advent
of the joint-stock banks and the coincident spread
of acceptance houses [in the 1830s], the institutional support for northern manufacturers was
weak" (1979, 66).

[31] Lüthy (1961, 25). Morineau similarly argues
about investment patterns in eighteenth-century
Europe: "Capitalism didn't worry about frontiers"
(1965, 233).

[32] Deane & Cole (1967, 5).

[33] See Deane (1979, 21). Habakkuk observes:
"The growth [in English population] which started
in the 1740's was not reversed. It was not only not
reversed; it accelerated" (1971, 26).

[34] Plumb (1950, 78). Krause provides the ac-
companiment of the reassuring hypothesis that the
"poorer groups" possibly had the lowest reproduction rates, unlike the situation in the contemporary
peripheral countries where they have the highest.
He admits the assertion is on "treacherous ground"
but argues that had the Western poor not limited
the size of families, following closely it seems the
good advice of Pastor Malthus, "it is difficult to see
how the West could have avoided the poverty which
is found in India today" (1969, 108). Thus, from
theory, we infer empirical data.

There are, however, two questions to be posed: was there really a demographic revolution, and what in fact caused the rise of population (which, of course, then bears on whether it is cause or consequence of the economic changes)? The question of the reality of the demographic revolution is in turn two questions: were the changes "revolutionary" in relation to what went before and after, and was the pattern in England (or Great Britain) significantly different from that in France and elsewhere? Given a curve which is logarithmic, some authors see no reason to designate the late eighteenth-century segment as somehow singular.[35] To be sure, the rate of population growth in the second half of the eighteenth century was greater than in the first half. But it has been argued that it is the first half which was exceptional, not the second. Tucker argues, for example, in the case of England, that "the growth of population over the eighteenth century *as a whole* was not very much more than an extrapolation of earlier long-run trends would have led us to expect."[36] Morineau makes exactly the same point for France. The demographic growth at the end of the eighteenth century was not revolutionary but should be considered more modestly as "a renovation, a recuperation, a restoration."[37] And Milward and Saul reverse the argument entirely in France's favor. The French population pattern was the unusual one (because its birth rate went down before or simultaneously with the reduction of the death rate). "But in the circumstances of nineteenth-century development a more slowly growing population made increases in *per capita* incomes easier to achieve and thus gave the French advantages rather than disadvantages in marketing."[38]

Even, however, if the population rise (uncontested) were not to be considered revolutionary, and even if it were not necessarily peculiar to England, the "core of the problem"[39] remains whether the population growth was the result of the economic and social changes, or vice versa. "Did the Industrial Revolution create its own labor force?" as Habakkuk puts it.[40] To answer this question, we have to look at the debate concerning whether it was a declining mortality rate or a rising fertility rate that accounts for the demographic increase. For the majority of analysts, there seems little doubt that the declining mortality rate is the principal explanation, for the very simple reason that "when both rates are high it is very

[35] See McKeown: "Since the modern rise [of population since the late seventeenth and early eighteenth centuries] is unique [in its size, continuity, and duration], it is quite unsatisfactory to attempt to explain separately its initial phase" (1976, 6). For Garden, the late eighteenth- and early nineteenth-century demographic pattern was that of "a very slow evolution, not a revolution," the true revolution occurring in "the second half of the twentieth century" (1978d, 151, 154).

[36] Tucker (1963, 215).
[37] Morineau (1971, 323).
[38] Milward & Saul (1973, 314).
[39] Drake (1969, 2).
[40] Habakkuk (1958, 500). Habakkuk's own answer was that "the most reasonable interpretation of the increase in agricultural output in the late eighteenth century is that it was a *response* to the growth of population rather than the initiator of that growth" (1971, 33).

much easier to increase the population by reducing the death-rate than by increasing the birthrate,"[41] and of course when both are low the reverse is true.

Why then would the death rate decline? Since a death rate that is high is "chiefly attributable to a high incidence of infectious diseases,"[42] there are three logically possible explanations for a reduced death rate: improved medicine (immunization or therapy), increased resistance to infection (improvement in the environment), or decline in virulence of the bacteria and viruses. The last may be eliminated if there is reduced mortality from multiple diseases simultaneously (which there seems to have been), since it is not credible that all of them could be due to "fortuitous change in the character of the [disease-causing] organisms."[43] This leaves us with the true debate: better medicine or a better socioeconomic environment. Better medicine has long been a favorite explanation. It still has its strong defenders, who give as the most plausible explanation of declining mortality rates "the introduction and use of inoculation against smallpox during the eighteenth century."[44] This thesis has been subjected to a careful and convincing demonstration that the medical influence on the death rate was rather insignificant until the twentieth century and can scarcely therefore account for changes in the eighteenth.[45] By deduction, this leaves us with the conclusion that it must be "an improvement in economic and social conditions" that led to demographic expansion and not vice versa.[46]

The role of fertility has received a major boost in the monumental population history of England by Wrigley and Schofield. They see a rising fertility rate via the lowering of the percentage of non-marriers. This is tied to a model in which the increased availability of food is the key ingredient in a process that leads to the possibility of founding a household. Their data are over a very long period (1539–1873), in which they find that, except for a short interval (1640–1709), births, deaths, and marriages all increase but there are consistently more births than deaths. Thus they seem to be arguing a long-standing pattern of English demographic history. Yet they also wish to argue that somewhere between the early eighteenth

---

[41] McKeown & Brown (1969, 53).

[42] McKeown & Brown (1969, 53).

[43] McKeown (1976, 16).

[44] Razzell (1969, 134). The key argument is that since the English middle and upper strata also show a rise in their life expectancy, "an explanation in terms of increased food supplies is inappropriate." In a later article, Razzell (1974, 13) makes his argument more general: "It was an improvement in personal hygiene rather than a change in public health that was responsible for the reduction in mortality between 1801 and 1841."

See also Armengaud (1973, 38–43), who, however, believes this factor was combined with

higher agricultural productivity which led to better-fed populations, more resistant to disease.

[45] The disease-by-disease analysis is to be found in McKeown (1976, 91–109). He admits that hard data are only available after 1838, but argues that if this data show that "immunization and therapy had little influence on the trend of mortality in the hundred years after [1838 in Great Britain], it would seem to follow that they are very unlikely to have contributed significantly in the century that preceded it" (p. 104).

[46] McKeown & Record (1962, 122). See also Bairoch (1974, 30), Le Roy Ladurie (1975, 386–390), and Post (1976, 35).

century and the late nineteenth century England broke with the "preventive-check cycle" and the link between population size and food prices.[47]

In addition to the contradiction in the Wrigley and Schofield logic (a long-standing pattern as explanatory versus a break in a pattern as explanatory), there is the further problem of reconciling their emphasis on increases in marriage rate (and/or lowering the marriage rate) as explanatory of economic "take-off" with the directly opposite argument by Hajnal. Hajnal has argued that there is a unique western European (note: *not* English alone) marriage pattern as of the first half of the eighteenth century which consists of a later marriage age and a high proportion of non-marriers. Hajnal finds that it is this pattern of *lower* fertility (lasting until the twentieth century) which serves economic development by "stimulating the diversion of resources to ends other than those of minimal subsistence."[48]

One last demographic factor, less frequently discussed but probably of great importance, is the increase in population transfer from rural peripheral zones in Europe to urban and industrializing areas. But this is, of course, the result both of increased employment opportunity and improved transportation facilities.[49]

Increasing attention has been drawn in recent years to changes in the

[47] For the periodization, see Wrigley & Schofield (1981, 162); for the change in demographic pattern, see p. 478. On p. 245, they seem to date the moment of change more precisely as 1751, after which they say there was a clear "dominance of fertility in changing the intrinsic growth rate."

Goldstone seeks to modify this thesis a bit, by arguing that, whereas in the sixteenth century it was the increase in the numbers of those who married that accounted for increases in fertility, in the period 1700–1850, it was primarily the lowering of the marriage age. "What was crucial was that in England industrialization and the growth of markets for foodstuffs occurred in the context of an agricultural sector that was already significantly proletarianized, and becoming more so" (1986, 28).

Another argument for emphasis on increased fertility is drawn from the presumed Irish example of earlier marriages as of the 1780s due to the earlier and more extensive "settlements" on young rural adults, due in turn to a shift from pastoral to arable cultivation. See Connell (1969, 32–33). The shift to arable cultivation is, of course, a consequence itself of the expansion of the world-economy, as Connell himself recognizes: "By [the 1780s], *because of* the growth of England's own population she was no longer an exporter of corn and she could look with less jealousy upon its production in Ireland."

Drake is skeptical, however, on the whole age of

marriage argument in the Irish case, because of the possibly inverse relationship of male and female ages at marriage. He prefers to credit the spread of potato cultivation (1963, 313). Connell indeed does not rule this explanation out: if our "insecure statistics" err and the population increase in fact began in the 1750s or 1760s, "it may well have followed hard upon the generalization of a potato dietary" (1969, 38).

Even if Ireland were in fact characterized in the early eighteenth century by a high death rate and low birth rate, McKeown and Brown doubt that a population rise could be explained by a lowered age of marriage. They point out that if an older husband in times of late marriage take a younger wife, the impact of an earlier marriage date (for the male) may be small. They point out furthermore that the greatest alleged difference is in the number of children per family, but that a high death rate, which increases with the size of the family, would have a counteracting effect (1969, 62). And Krause adds that, on the other hand, "even late marriage can lead to exceedingly high birthrates" (1969, 108).

[48] Hajnal (1965, 132).

[49] Le Roy Ladurie makes this point in terms of the migration of people from Auvergne and the Pyrenees to Paris and other northern cities in the eighteenth century (1975, 407), and Connell argues the same for Irish migration to England (1950, 66).

agricultural sector as a prelude to and determinative of changes in the industrial sector. (That such an emphasis has implicit policy directives for contemporary peripheral countries is not without a link to the increased concern and is often explicitly stated.) In addition to the industrial and demographic revolutions, we are now adjured to locate and explain the agricultural revolution. This turns out to be a big topic. First of all we must remember that, even for Great Britain and even through the whole of the first half of the nineteenth century, "agriculture was the premier . . . industry."[50] Therefore, if there is to be any meaning to the idea that an economic revolution occurred and in particular that there was an agricultural revolution, there must have been somewhere, and for the total of some entity, an increase in yield. We immediately run into the question of whether we mean yield per hectare cultivated (which in turn may mean yield per seed input, yield per unit of labor input, or yield per capita) or total yield. There seems little doubt that total arable production went up in the European world-economy as a whole in the 100 years that span the eighteenth and nineteenth centuries.[51] If, however, there was a transfer of part of the work force from arable production to other kinds of production (and in particular to industry), then there must have been, it is argued, either an increase in yield per seed input or in yield per unit of labor input (combined with an expansion of the cultivated area).[52] If there was, furthermore, an improvement in the general standard of living, it is argued, then there must have been an increase in yield per capita. There is no necessary reason, however, why an increase in yield per capita need accompany an increase in yield per seed input or labor input, and it is the latter two which are defining elements of an expansionary period of the world-economy.

Might an increase in yield have come about through the mechanization of farm implements? While there seems to have been some increase in the use of iron in plows (and horseshoes for horses),[53] it can scarcely be argued that there' was significant mechanization of agriculture before the nine-

---

[50] Deane (1979, 246).

[51] For example, Slicher van Bath suggests that this whole period constituted "a time of agricultural boom" (1963, 221) in terms of overall price levels (despite the relative decline after 1817), of expansion of cultivated area, and of new methods.

[52] See, for example, Bairoch (1974, 83), who sees an increase in agricultural productivity as not merely "the determining factor in the initiation of industrialization," but as something which in turn requires the beginning of these processes. Wyczánski and Topolski, however, specifically deny the need for increased agricultural productivity to free labor for industry given the "considerable latent reserve of labor force" in the countryside (1974, 22).

[53] The strongest case is made by Bairoch (1973a,

490–491), who argues that these usages of iron plus the increased number of plows in use (resulting from the extension of land clearance and the diminution of fallow) account for a significant increase in the overall demand for iron.

[54] O'Brien asserts that, in general, "mechanization in farming proceeded more slowly than mechanization in industry because agricultural operations are more separated in time and space than industrial processes" (1977, 171). Deane says that, even for England, "we can find nothing to suggest that there was a substantial increase in the stock of farming capital or in the rate of agricultural capital until the end of the eighteenth century; and even then the expansion appears to have been modest in relation to the growth of agricultural incomes at this period" (1972, 103). Indeed, Deane attributes

teenth century.[54] The advances came primarily through the more intensive cultivation of the soil by the use of fodder crops.[55] There were two main systems, that of alternate husbandry (called at the time the "Norfolk system") and that of convertible husbandry (or ley farming). Both variants eliminated the need for fallow by using the roots (turnips, potatoes) to eliminate weeds and the grasses (clover, sainfoin, ryegrass) to nutrify the soil.[56] The resulting continuous cropping permitted livestock to have food in winter with their manure serving as an additional nutrient to the soil.

Neither system was new, but the late eighteenth century was a moment of considerable expansion of their use. While, no doubt, these systems made great headway in England, it is doubtful whether this can be said to be exceptional. Slicher van Bath speaks of a "general shift from three-course rotation . . . to convertible husbandry" in western Europe after 1750 in response to higher wheat prices.[57] What was nonetheless new in this spread of the use of fodder crops was that it permitted the shift to increased arable production without the sacrifice, as previously, of pasturage.[58]

Even this advance, if analyzed as output per capita, has been challenged by Morineau. He argues that a significant increase in yield occurred only in the mid-nineteenth century.[59] He sees agricultural "progress" in the late eighteenth century, no less than previously, as obeying a "logic of poverty." Crop innovation tended, he argues, to coincide with conjunctural declines in living standards. These phases of decline were attended by food

to the limitations of agricultural mechanical technique the fact that until the middle of the nineteenth century, most of the new techniques "were suitable only to the light sandy soils" and it was not yet possible "to drain the clay soils and the fens" (1979, 41). Chambers and Mingay also minimize the role of mechanical innovation and point out that Jethro Tull's famous drill which permitted constant tillage, although "described . . . in 1733, and with a long history before that, was not generally used for sowing corn before well into the nineteenth century" (1966, 2).

[55] See Timmer: "The leguminous crops not only increased soil fertility directly but supported larger herds of livestock which produced more, and richer, manure" (1969, 382–383).

Slicher van Bath, however, reminds us that "more intensive cultivation does not necessarily mean a higher yield" (1963, 245), but he means here yield per seed input. It is still possible to get greater yield per hectare cultivated by reduction of fallow. In terms of yield per seed input, it was possible also to get greater output through heavy manuring which, however, had previously to be brought in largely from the outside and was, therefore, too expensive by and large.

[56] The difference between the systems was that alternate husbandry could be used only on light

soils. On heavier (but still well-drained) lands, it was necessary to avoid root-break and to keep the pasture down (a ley) for a number of years. On wet and cold clays, neither system would work, until the development of cheap underdrainage in the mid-nineteenth century. See Chambers & Mingay (1966, 54–62), and Deane (1979, 38–42).

[57] Slicher van Bath (1963, 249–250). "The Norfolk system, in different forms, was followed by enlightened landowners in various European countries at the end of the eighteenth century and the beginning of the nineteenth" (p. 251).

[58] Chambers and Mingay say that the new husbandry broke medieval farming's "vicious circle of fodder shortage which led to soil starvation" (1966, 6).

[59] See Morineau (1971, 68–87). He endorses the view of Ruwet that a critical prerequisite of yield per seed input was the development of chemical fertilizer (p. 69, fn. 129). He proceeds, however, to doubt Ruwet's view that yield per capita went up since the mid-seventeenth century by the increase of quantity of seed sown (presumably made possible primarily by reduction of fallow). Similar doubts on the increase in yield per labor input of the Norfolk system are to be found in Timmer (1969, 392), who sees, however, some increase in yield per seed input.

shortages, and the crop innovations "contributed to maintaining them."[60]
While Morineau's analysis centers on the French data, and he accepts the
argument that England had certain advantages over France, he doubts that
even England had "a substantial increase in productivity" before 1835.

> The take-off of the Western economy did not plunge its roots in an 'agricultural
> revolution.' Is not this latter concept, inappropriate to designate, even in the case
> of England, such a somnolent progress, frightened away at the first frost?[61]

Even if the changes in husbandry could be said not to have resulted
immediately in any dramatic increase in yield per capita, might not the
changes in the social relations of production on the land have been an
essential element in the process of industrialization, either because they
made available manpower for industrial work (through higher yield per
labor input, permitting intersectoral labor flows, or through greater total
yield, permitting demographic expansion) or because they were a prerequisite to the technical innovation which would eventually lead to higher
yield per seed input, or, of course, both? Was not, in short, enclosure a key
element in the whole process?

There are three separate, not inevitably linked, processes that are
discussed under the heading of enclosure. One is the elimination of "open
fields," the system which transformed individual units of arable production
into common grazing land between harvest time and sowing time. The
second is the abolition of "common rights," which were the equivalent of
open fields on the land that was harvested by the lord of the manor, or
were "waste lands" (waste, that is, from the point of view of arable
production). Both of these changes reduced or eliminated the ability of the
person who controlled little or no property to maintain livestock. The third
change was the consolidation of scattered property, necessary to realize the
economies of scale which the end of open fields and common rights made
possible.

Enclosure presumably made mixed husbandry more profitable, both by
increasing the size of the units and by protecting those who planted fodder
crops against free riders.[62] The prime object of the landlords was "the

---

[60] Morineau (1971, 70–71; see also 1974b, 355).
When Le Roy Ladurie describes the diversification
in Lourmarin of agricultural production (no longer
wheat alone; on the eve of the French Revolution,
half the land was devoted to vineyards, orchards,
mulberries, gardens, and irrigated leys), he explains: "There it is, the true agricultural revolution,
adapted to the conditions of the French Midi"
(1975, 402). Morineau criticizes this specific excla-
mation, accusing Le Roy Ladurie of "seductive
reasoning" which has an insecure quantitative basis

and which "interprets, extrapolates, and is involun-
tarily circular" (1978, 383). Le Roy Ladurie responds in kind. He says that Morineau's work is
"paradoxical and brilliant" but still wrong: "I do not
think, in fact, one can deny the agricultural progress of the eighteenth century" (1978, 32). All
revolves, as we shall see, around what is meant by
progress. Le Roy Ladurie tends to the view that
inequalities diminish whereas Morineau sees them
as increasing.

[61] Morineau (1971, 76, 85).

increase in rents resulting from the technical improvements which were facilitated by enclosure and consolidation."[63] Whether in fact enclosures did achieve increased yield is, however, less clear. Chambers and Mingay, who claim that enclosure was the "vital instrument" in greater output, nonetheless admit that the evidence for eighteenth-century England is at best "circumstantial."[64] O'Brien is even more skeptical. "There can no longer be any easy presumption" that the massive enclosures between 1750 and 1815 "had any really significant impact on yields."[65]

Enclosures, of course, started long before 1750. What accelerated their pace and visibility was the new role of Parliament in Britain in the process.[66] It is this political intervention which accounted for the "massiveness" of the development. Still, it would be an error to believe that Britain alone was enclosing. The careful analyses of Bloch indicate that considerable enclosure of one form or another had occurred in France, and that there too it accelerated after 1730.[67] In fact, the relative expansion of what Bloch calls "agrarian individualism" was a Europe-wide phenomenon in the eighteenth century.[68] If the success of the movement was greater in Great Britain than on the continent, the difference was clearly in the strength of the state machinery in Britain which offered the large landlords weapons that were less available in France, both before and after the French Revolution.[69]

[62] On the increase of size of unit, see Chambers & Mingay (1966, 61). But Yelling says that "the environments favorable or unfavorable to large-scale farming do not correspond in distribution to regions of enclosure" (1977, 97). On the free rider problem, see Fussell (1958, 17).

[63] Dovring (1966, 628).

[64] Chambers & Mingay (1966, 34, 37).

[65] O'Brien (1977, 170). This is given some confirmation by the estimate of Deane and Cole that "it would appear that output per head in British agriculture increased by about 25 percent in the eighteenth century, and that the whole of this advance was achieved before 1750" (1967, 75). They even add in a footnote that "it would appear that agricultural productivity may actually have fallen in the third quarter of the century and recovered thereafter."

[66] See Mantoux (1928, 170–172). E. L. Jones suggests the history of enclosure was more gradual than generally acknowledged because of the exclusion from consideration of enclosure by agreement. "The apparently rapid upswing represented by the parliamentary enclosures of the second half of the eighteenth century would not be steam-rollered out of existence by the inclusion of other evidence, but it would be somewhat flattened" (1974b, 94). Yelling similarly suggests that a considerable amount of engrossment of common fields had occurred in the late seventeenth and early eigh-

teenth centuries. He denies wishing to replace the post-1760 period with the earlier one as the "decisive and revolutionary era that broke with the medieval past." Rather, he argues, "it is unlikely that such an apocalypse ever occurred" (1977, 111).

[67] "In a large number of provinces—Champagne, Picardy, Lorraine and the Three Bishoprics, Bourgogne and Bresse, Franche-Comté, Berry, Auvergne, Toulousain, Béarn—beginning in the sixteenth and seventeenth centuries, but especially from about 1730, successive temporary measures were taken such that, each time there was a drought, a frost, or floods, the access to open fields (*la vaine pâture sur les prés*) before the second growth of grass was, if not always abolished, at least restricted in the subsequent year" (Bloch, 1930, 341). See also page 332 for a discussion of the various kinds of enclosure gradually established in various areas.

[68] "The movement was general, because it responded both to a doctrine that was professed everywhere and to needs, more or less clearly felt, by the most powerful elements among those who cultivated the land" (Bloch, 1930, 511).

[69] "Faced with enclosure, the village [in Britain] had no choice; Parliament having decided, it simply had to obey. In France, the strong constitution of peasant tenure seemed incompatible with such rigor" (Bloch, 1930, 534).

The mere enclosing (fencing-in) of the land was not enough, given the historical legacy of scattered holdings. Like enclosing, the consolidation of holdings, and the consequent decline of the small farmer (whether owner or tenant), was a secular process, which probably accelerated in the eighteenth century, both in Britain and in France.[70] Whether compactness of land in fact significantly increased yield has also, however, been more assumed than demonstrated.[71]

Finally, there is the view that the agricultural social rearrangements led to the elimination of persons from employment on the land, and their consequent availability as urban, industrial manpower. It is in this sense too that an agricultural revolution has been said to be a prerequisite for an industrial revolution. Dobb, for example, argues that the enclosures in England in the late eighteenth century "dislodg[ed] . . . the army of cottagers from their last slender hold on the fringes of the commons, . . . which coincided with a new epoch of industrial expansion."[72] This standard Marxist thesis has been the subject of much refutation, both on the

[70] On the disappearance of the English yeomanry, see Wordie (1974, 604), and Chambers and Mingay (1966), who observe: "This tendency [to consolidation] was encouraged by enclosure but in no sense dependent on it" (p. 92). For France, see Laurent (1976a, 660) and Vovelle (1980, 60–61), who measures a clear decline of "intermediate categories" of landholders in Chartres. That is, let us be clear, we are talking here of the disappearance of that category of landholders whose units were large enough to sustain their families but no larger. See, however, for reservations about France, Meuvret (1971d, 196).

Dovring gives this explanation for the pressure for land consolidation: "Under the system of the heavy ox-plough, strip farming may have had some technical advantages since the length of the strip was more essential than the compactness of a field. (This point must not be overemphasized since the strips were, in fact, not always as long as the ox plough required, nor were heavy wheel-ploughs the rule even in areas of dominant arable farming.) But the new iron ploughs, drawn by a horse or two, were believed to work better on consolidated lots with more breadth and less length than the strips of the old open field system; and the new rotations are also assumed to have been easier to apply on consolidated holdings. . . . No less important than these technical advantages was the fact that the eighteenth century witnessed a rising tide of population increase in Europe's peasant villages which inevitably carried with it more and more intense fragmentation of the land" (1966, 627).

[71] Yelling, who has done one of the most careful studies of the history of enclosure in Great Britain, concludes: "Changes in the compactness and convenience of farms were one of the central benefits of enclosure, one of the most confidently asserted by its proponents and least attacked by its critics. For all that, it is not easy to demonstrate the results that were achieved . . . . [The problem] is the inability to see how any advantage was translated into concrete economic terms as some sort of improvement in productivity" (1977, 144). Having said this, Yelling lists the hypothetical potential for improvement and asks us not to underestimate it "because it is difficult to find sufficient evidence to confirm [the] effects [of the hypothetical advantages]" (p. 145).

O'Brien takes another tack. Given that over time Great Britain developed different forms of land tenure than many continental countries, ones that were less "feudal" in their arrangements, it has been argued that they furthered productivity by encouraging investment and innovation. "But, *a priori*, there is no reason to expect that the British pattern of landlord–tenant relations would necessarily produce markedly higher rates of investment than peasant proprietorship, Prussian-style feudalism, or even certain forms of métayage" (1977, 168). If Britain had an advantage, he argues, it was because it had reached the geographical limits of extensive growth earlier such that "small additions to the stock of farm capital . . . could produce quite marked increments to output" (p. 169). He places greatest emphasis on the higher ratio of animals per cultivated acre.

[72] Dobb (1946, 239).

question of how much this process was a violent and repressive one,[73] and how much quantitative dislodgement there was at all.[74] The latter argument is twofold. On the one hand, it is said that the new husbandry required "more rather than less labour."[75] On the other hand, since there seems to be an unquestioned reduction of the percentage of families in agriculture and an increase in the numbers in industry,[76] it is argued that it is population growth which explains the source of the increased urban laboring population.[77] Of course, the two theses—forced eviction and demographic overflow—are by no means incompatible. But it is seldom observed that both hypotheses run against the argument of British exceptionalism. If it were demographic growth that led to the expansion of an urban labor force, wherein lay the special advantage of Great Britain in the eighteenth century? And if forced eviction explains Britain's advantage, how do we account for the absence of evidence of a labor shortage in continental industries?[78] As the French like to say: of two things, one. Either there was a different outcome in Britain than on the continent (the "first industrial revolution") which is then explained by a factor or set of factors peculiar to Great Britain; or the process is a more general one, in which case we must look more closely at how different the outcome was.

[73] Tate, for example, contends that "a remarkable feature of the eighteenth-century enclosure movement is the care with which it was carried out and relatively small volume of organized protest which it aroused" (1945, 137). When Tate published his arguments later in book-length form, a reviewer, Richardson, described him aptly as "a historian who almost choked with indignation upon reading L. L. and B. Hammond's *The Village Labourer*" (1969, 187).

[74] The classic argument is found in Clapham, who asserts that the increase in the ratio of laboring families and entrepreneur families between 1685 and 1831 was from 1.74 : 1 to 2.5 : 1. "The increase seems small and this [article] is not a demonstration; but for any larger increase there is no evidence at all" (1923, 95). Lazonick suggests that Clapham's mode of calculation underestimates the change (1974, 37–38).

Following the line of Clapham, we find Chambers: The enclosure movements had the effect of further reducing, but not of destroying, the remaining English peasantry. . . . The cottage-owning population seems actually to have increased after enclosure" (1953, 335, 338).

[75] Deane (1979, 45). See Chambers: "To any one acquainted with the varied and time-consuming process of turnip farming—the careful preparation of the soil, the sowing, singling, holing, gathering, slicing, feeding to stock—the thought that it could

be identified with any form of labor-saving comes as a surprise" (1957, 37). See also Mingay (1977, 50).

This argument has been given a Marxist twist by Samuel: "In agriculture, cheap labor rather than invention was the fulcrum of economic growth, and the changes inaugurated by the agricultural revolution were accompanied by a prodigious increase in the work force, as well as by an intensification of their toil" (1977, 23).

[76] Mathias shows this by comparing data collected by King in 1688, Massie in 1760, and Colquhoun in 1803. See Mathias (1979d, 189, Table 9.3) which shows a clear shift between 1760 and 1803.

[77] See Chambers (1953, passim).

[78] See, for example, Lefebvre on northern France: "The great industry of the North was to recruit the laborers (*manoeuvriers*) of the countryside and thus resolve the agrarian question" (1972, 547). Indeed, the reasoning of Hufton would lead us to think that the advantage lay with France. Speaking of social polarization in western Europe as a whole in the late eighteenth century, he says that Great Britain had the best "overall social balance" in the rural areas because of the existence of "a solid middling farmer grouping." France, he suggests, represented the opposite extreme. 60% of the rural population (and in some regions, 90%) "did not have enough to live on" (1980, 30). If this were so, then why were these rural poor not the obvious candidates for an urban proletariat?

The same thing is true if we push the argument one step backward, in terms of an agricultural revolution which precedes an industrial revolution. We find ourselves, as we have already suggested, before the two questions: to what degree did the phenomenon take place; and to the extent that it did, how different was Great Britain?

We have mentioned Morineau's acute skepticism on the theme of an agricultural revolution in eighteenth-century France. An equally thunderous denunciation of received knowledge about English agriculture has been made by Kerridge, who has suggested that the agricultural revolution took place there much earlier, in the sixteenth and seventeenth centuries, and that "in their truly modest proportions, the agricultural advances of the eighteenth and nineteenth centuries fall nicely into place as things secondary in importance to the revolutions in industry and transport."[79] Strangely, however, in his riposte, Mingay (who is one of Kerridge's main targets) salvages the late eighteenth century by enclosing it as a segment of an agricultural revolution that was "a long drawn-out process of gradual technological and institutional change" running from the later seventeenth to the nineteenth centuries,[80] an argument which considerably reduces the case for a "revolution" more localized in time.

Dovring suggests a similar skepticism for western Europe as a whole in the eighteenth century. He too finds no changes in agriculture "at anything resembling the scale and pace of the industrial revolution." He has, however, a simple explanation for why we have believed there was an agricultural revolution in Britain. He suggests that the changes that did occur there were "better publicized" than those on the Continent, and that "this, plus the seductive analogy of industrial and agricultural revolution, may have led us to exaggerate the depth no less than the originality of what took place."[81]

If the specificity of British demography and British agriculture are thrown into doubt as explanations of the industrial revolution, there remains one explanation of some weight that could be put forward: British culture, or some element therein that would explain the existence of a greater entrepreneurial spirit. Instead of arguing this with the circular reasoning of the somewhat ethereal realm of national character, let us look at it in terms of its presumed institutional expression: the existence of a more liberal state structure (derived from history and considered to be the outcome of a cultural thrust).

---

[79] Kerridge (1969, 474). On the "unparalleled achievement" of the sixteenth and seventeenth centuries in England, see Kerridge (1967, 348, and passim). See also O'Brien: "There appears to be nothing extraordinary about the British achievement in agriculture from 1700 to 1850" (1977, 173). Kerridge says, in a plaint redolent of Morineau: "Nowadays . . . the myth [of the English agricultural revolution between 1750 and 1850] has been disproved. But disproving a myth does not kill it" (p. 469).

[80] Mingay (1969, 481).

[81] Dovring (1969, 182).

The orthodox view, if one may be permitted to call it that, is that the industrial revolution in Great Britain "occurred spontaneously, without government assistance,"[82] or, more strongly, "without any help."[83] There are some who are less categorical, and who are willing to acknowledge a role for government in the establishment of the "market environment" itself, through the creation of such prerequisites as political stability, administrative unification, the common law, and a sympathetic attitude toward business interests. Supple, for example, concludes: "The state did play an important, albeit indirect, role in the pioneer Industrial Revolution." Still, he adds: "The fact remains, however, that the role *was* indirect."[84]

If one looks more closely at the presumed liberalism of the British state in the eighteenth century compared to others (and particularly to France), it comes down to two theses: the British state regulated less and it taxed less. However, the major role of Parliament in the enclosures of land can scarcely be offered up as an instance of the absence of state intrusion into the economy. Indeed, it is clear that, in agriculture, the British state excelled in regulating the social relations of production. It may be preferred that this regulation was aimed at removing the shackles of customary constraints, but clearly more was involved than a simple act of legal permissiveness of market transactions. This is equally true with the removal of the market-constraining role of guilds. Once again, state intrusion was essential. Indeed, Milward and Saul offer us as an alternative general hypothesis about Europe as a whole that "where the central government was *most* powerful after 1750 the guilds and corporations were weakest."[85] Once again, however, this is a regulation presumably aimed at freeing the market.

There was, however, more direct intervention, less in the home market than in the world market. Protectionism played no small role even in that epitome of the newer and freer of industries, cotton production in Great Britain. Mantoux is quite categoric on the subject.[86] Furthermore, it would be a mistake to see the government's regulatory role limited to protection. For as the protection became less necessary, intrusion at home into the production process became a growing reality. Brebner doubts even that there was ever a moment of true laissez faire in Britain: "As the state took its fingers off commerce during the first half of the nineteenth century, it simultaneously put them on industry and its accompaniments."[87]

---

[82] Deane (1979, 2).
[83] Crouzet (1972b, 162).
[84] Supple (1973, 316).
[85] Milward & Saul (1973, 36).
[86] See Mantoux (1928, 262–263). A half-century later, Cain and Hopkins made the same point (1980, 473).

[87] Brebner (1966a, 252). See also Ashton: "The truth is that at all times some measure of rivalry has existed in industry and trade; and at all times have men sought to tame and control the focus of competition" (1924, 185).

Indeed the same Phyllis Deane who writes of the "spontaneity" of the industrial revolution, nonethe-

Finally, it is not the case that the state was absent as a source of financing for industrial enterprise in Great Britain. No doubt the money did not come directly from state banks but, in practice, as Pressnell has noted, "a considerable volume of public money swelled the funds of private bankers, and in this indirect fashion helped to fructify private enterprise."[88]

If the British state was less of a model of noninterference than it is often asserted or even assumed to be, what are we to say of the view that it was the relative thinness of the British bureaucracy and consequent lower tax load that accounts for British advantage, once again especially over the French?[89] This truth, once sanctified by every textbook, has recently come under a heavy barrage from both sides of the Channel—by Mathias and O'Brien in Great Britain and by Morineau in France. In each case, a close look at the fiscal and budgetary data of the two countries in the eighteenth century leads them to invert the traditional hypothesis. Mathias and O'Brien find that the British tax burden was "rising more rapidly than the French" throughout the whole of the eighteenth century, although, up to the 1790s "not dramatically so." However, after that, the British tax burden pulled far ahead.

> Thus, in Britain the increasing pace of industrial growth, urbanisation and population growth after 1775 . . . were processes taking place in a context of a steeply rising real burden of taxation. And the rate of increase of this burden was much faster than in France.[90]

Morineau's comparison, using a somewhat different French data base than Mathias and O'Brien, locates the discrepancy even earlier than 1790. Comparing the two countries between 1725 and 1790, he finds British tax receipts to have risen faster, absolutely and relatively, such that

> the subject of the United Kingdom paid higher taxes than the subject of the Most Christian King from the first quarter of the eighteenth century: 17.6 livres

less notes: "The fact was that as industrialization proceeded the state was intervening more deeply and more effectively in the economy than it had ever done before. . . . The real objective of the philosophical radicals . . . turned out to be not less freedom from government but freedom from inefficient government; and efficiency meant effective and purposeful intervention in the economic system as opposed to ineffectiveness and aimless intervention" (1979, 231–232).

[88] Pressnell (1953, 378), who notes that the "retention of traditional methods of tax-collection, which permitted the collectors of taxes to employ them for their own private gain" was one of the elements that "assisted the growth of country (i.e., provincial) banking." For a general explanation of British growth (in comparison to France) based on

the absence of government interference with entrepreneurs, see Hoselitz (1955a) and the devastating response by Gerschenkron (1955).

[89] A recent article that has pulled together all the arguments for this viewpoint is Hartmann (1978).

[90] Mathias & O'Brien (1976, 606–607). For further evidence on English levels of taxation from 1660 to 1815, see O'Brien (1988). Riley expands on the Mathias/O'Brien argument, asserting that the frailty of France's finances "may be attributed to the failure . . . to tax a growing volume of wealth in the economy." He goes even further asserting that, between 1735 and 1780, the peacetime tax burden in France not only failed to increase "when measured against output," but that it even declined (1987, 211, 236).

tournois, after conversion, against 8.1 (ratio of 2.17 to 1) and *a fortiori* on the eve of the last decade: 46 livre tournois against 17 (ratio of 2.7 to 1).[91]

This dramatic reversal of received truths does not stop there. Traditionally, one thought British tax burdens not only less heavy than French in the eighteenth century, but more equitable. The argument was that the French fiscality gave a greater role to direct taxation, and that direct taxation is inherently less just because it is less progressive. This was thought to be particularly so in the French case because of the taille, with its exemptions for the nobility and the clergy and even for some bourgeois. But, as Morineau notes, the fiscal role of the taille was not that central. Indeed, it diminished in the eighteenth century and represented only 15% of all receipts in 1788.[92] The indirect British taxes were, in turn, scarcely progressive, falling as they did mainly "upon consumption and demand, rather than upon savings and investment."[93]

What conclusion is to be drawn from this? For Morineau, it is that equality existed neither in Great Britain nor in France, and even more important that the two modes of taxation (which he explains largely in terms of historical possibilities) had "almost the same level of efficacity, *mutatis mutandis,* in relation to taxable revenue."[94] Mathias and O'Brien are willing to go further and "raise the possibility" that, both in terms of direct and indirect taxes, French taxation "might on investigation turn out to be less regressive" than British.[95]

If this is so, then one question remains: whence the misperception? The main answer to this question has been in terms of the absence of formal exemptions in Great Britain which "produced less resentment," and the fact that the direct taxes "remained 'invisible' when passed on as an element in rents."[96] This is to analyze the misperception as historical in origin. But

[91] Morineau (1980b, 320). See also similar figures by Palmer (1959, I, 155) for 1785, which show the British rate as one and a half times higher than the French.

[92] See Morineau (1980b, 321), who also argues: "No one in England would dare be sure that the Land Tax was actually paid by the landowners and not, in the last analysis by the actual producers: by the farmers and the tenants. There were many sharp practices" (p. 322).

Mathias and O'Brien argue somewhat differently, but with the same conclusion, that "there is no doubt that British direct taxation was generally 'progressive'—which is doubtless why it formed so small a proportion of the total public revenue" (1976, 614).

[93] Mathias & O'Brien (1976, 616), who thereupon note: "Arguments about the structure of demand encouraging the faster growth of industry

in eighteenth-century England (particularly the thesis which stresses the importance of 'middling incomes' in this process) need to take these important transfers involved in indirect taxation into account" (p. 621). Mathias, in an earlier publication, sums up Britain's taxation as "highly regressive" because of the fact that two-thirds of the revenue yield from indirect taxes came from commodities in mass demand (1969, 40).

[94] Morineau (1980b, 322–323).

[95] Mathias & O'Brien (1976, 633).

[96] Mathias & O'Brien (1976, 636). Goubert gives a similar explanation for French self-perception of the late eighteenth century: "The expenses of the king and the crown have been exaggerated: they were much greater under Henry IV than under Louis XIV, and under Louis XIV than under Louis XVI; but these latter expenses suffered from a less good press (*une autre publicité*)" (1973, 139).

perhaps it is historiographical, especially if we notice Dovring's suggestion of a parallel misperception in agriculture.

We have taken a long detour through the "causes" of the "first industrial revolution" without attending to the explicandum. We must now look at the nature of the beast itself. What industrial revolution? The answer is, of course, that a series of innovations led to the flourishing of a new industry in cotton textiles, primarily in England. This industry was based on new and/or improved machines and was organized in factories. Simultaneously, or soon thereafter, there was a similar expansion and mechanization of the iron industry. What is said to have made this process different from that associated with any previous set of innovations in production was that it "trigger[ed] a process of cumulative, self-sustaining change."[97] The problem with this latter concept is not only that it is difficult to operationalize, but that it is also controversial to date. It is, for example, a central thesis of this work that cumulative, self-sustaining change in the form of the endless search for accumulation has been the leitmotiv of the capitalist world-economy ever since its genesis in the sixteenth century. We have specifically argued that the long stagnation of the seventeenth century, far from being a break in this cumulative process, was an integral part of it.

Let us therefore look more closely at the social reorganization that may be attributed to those innovations. The innovations of this epoch do not seem to have affected fundamentally the capital–labor ratio in existence for a long time before. Some innovations were labor saving, but many others were capital saving. Even the railroads, which come at the very end of this period, while capital intensive, were capital saving for the economy as a whole because the improved transport permitted manufacturers to reduce stocks and thereby bring down their capital–output ratio "in spectacular fashion."[98] This seems to be what Deane means when she insists that in the period 1750–1850 there was "capital widening" as opposed to "capital deepening" in production.[99]

What permits this capital widening, the "gains in aggregate output"? Landes has an answer: "the quality of the inputs," that is, "the higher productivity of new technology and the superior skills and knowledge of

[97] Landes (1969, 81), who argues: "For it took a marriage to make the Industrial Revolution. On the one hand, it required machines which not only replaced hand labor but impelled the concentration of production in factories. . . . On the other hand, it required a big industry producing a commodity of wide and elastic demand [that is, cotton textiles] such that (1) the mechanization of any of its processes of manufacture would create serious strains in the others, and (2) the impact of improve-

ments in this industry would be felt throughout the economy."

[98] Milward & Saul (1973, 173).

[99] She adds "at least up to . . . the railway age." Deane defines capital widening as the provision of resources that permit "an increase of population, extension of the market, or exploration of new and latent natural resources" as opposed to "capital deepening, that is, adoption of more capital-intensive techniques of production" (1973b, 364).

both entrepreneurs and workers."[100] No doubt, this is true, but it is always true of a phase of expansion in the world-economy that the leading industries are high-profit industries precisely because of higher productivity which translates into lower costs, and is made possible by a temporary market monopoly of "skills and knowledge." The question remains whether there was anything very special about this period.

Was there then a scientific or technological breakthrough? The historians of science have seldom credited this particular period as being some sort of turning point. The seventeenth or the twentieth centuries would seem better candidates than the 1750–1850 period in this regard. Furthermore, the historiographic debate on the relative role of science and technology in the industrial revolution seems to have been concluded strongly in favor of technology.[101]

There must then have been a technological breakthrough. The list of actual inventions is familiar: from Jethro Tull's seed drill in 1731 to the threshing machine in 1786; from Kay's fly shuttle in 1733 to Hargreaves's jenny in 1765, Arkwright's water frame in 1769, Crompton's mule in 1779, culminating in Roberts's fully self-acting mule in 1825; from Darby's coke-smelted cast iron in 1709 to Cort's puddling in 1784; and perhaps, above all, Watt's steam engine in 1775.[102] This series of inventions represents the heart of the case for British exceptionalism. These machines were invented in England and not in France or elsewhere.[103] They are what account for Britain's triumph in the world market in cotton and iron.

The story of cotton comes first. Until the late eighteenth century, textiles

---

[100] Landes (1969, 80).

[101] See Mathias: "[The critical technical blockages] lay in engineering rather than in science" (1979b, 33). Also: "Judging the effectiveness of the contributions of science by results, *ex post facto*, rather than by endeavor, is to greatly reduce their importance" (1979c, 58); see also Gillespie (1972). A rear guard defense of science is made by Musson, who insists that "applied science played a considerably more important role than has been generally realized" (1972, 59). Landes typically uses the greater importance of technological change as a stick with which to beat the French. "Nor is it an accident" that, in thermodynamics, the French devoted their efforts to "the reduction of technique to mathematical generalization" whereas the entrepreneurial English continued "to lead the world in engineering practice and innovation" (1969, 104).

[102] Let no reader be upset about the dates suggested. I have found in comparing a series of histories of technology and basic texts that there are many discrepancies about the dating of this or that invention. The problem lies in the fact that there

often was a difference between the year of invention, the year of first use, and the year of patent. Furthermore, when a particular machine had several successive slightly different forms, different authors call different forms *the* invention. For the purposes of this discussion, it matters little if slightly different dates had been listed.

[103] There are a few dissenting voices, even on the question of the numbers and significance of invention. See McCloy: "France, if she was behind Britain—and I am reluctant to think that she was—was certainly not far behind" (1952, 4). The book argues this for every field, including textiles and steam engineering. The author often notes how disturbances resulting from the French Revolution interrupted the process. Sometimes the inventor went into exile; sometimes the government's interest and attention were distracted. See also Briavoinne on the French reaction to British superiority in mechanical processes: They "promptly seized what remained to them to balance this superiority; they turned to chemistry" (1839, 194).

meant first of all wool and secondly linen. Cotton textiles were manufactured, but in terms of total production they represented a relatively small percentage of the whole, and furthermore a large part of what was supplied to the European market was manufactured in India. Indeed, this latter fact provided a considerable impetus to innovations in cotton textile technology: "machines—which alone could effectively compete with Indian textile workers," says Braudel.[104] For the new cotton technology was, above all, labor saving.[105]

Since it was woollen textiles and not cotton that was the main industry of western Europe in the early eighteenth century, and since the eighteenth century prior to the 1770s was a time of significant *expansion* of the woollen textile industry,[106] it may be asked—it often has been asked—why the technical innovations did not occur first in woollen textiles.

There are various explanations offered for this conundrum. One traditional explanation is the greater freedom of cotton (as opposed to wool and linen) textiles from guild supervision.[107] But, as Landes says, "the argument will not stand scrutiny,"[108] since wool was free in England and

---

[104] Braudel (1984, 572). In his remarkable book written in 1839, the Belgian analyst, Briavoinne, sees this conquest of the cotton market by Europe over India as the major "political" consequence of the industrial revolution, a locution he uses: "Europe was for centuries dependent on India for its most valuable products and for those of most extensive consumption: muslins, printed calicoes (*indiennes*), nankeens, cashmeres. Each year she imported a considerable number of manufactures for which she could only pay in specie, which was forever buried in regions which had no opportunity to send it back our way. There was hence impoverishment for Europe.

"India had the advantage of a less expensive and more skilled workforce. By the change brought about in the mode of fabrication, the state of things is no longer as it was; the balance of trade is henceforth in our favor. The Indian workers cannot compete with our steam engines and our looms. . . . Thus Europe has, for most textiles, supplanted in the world market the Indian manufacturers (*fabricants*) who had had for centuries the exclusive market. England can buy in India cotton and wool which she then sends back as manufactured cloth. If the latter country remains stationary, she will return to Europe all the money she has received from her. This evident consequence promises an increase of wealth to our continent" (1839, 202–203). How right he was.

Briavoinne pursued his insights (remember he was writing in 1839) to warn about the other side of

this political coin: "But among the political results, there is one to be feared and which the statesman must, as of now, foresee. Work, organized on a new basis, renders the body less of a slave, and leaves more freedom for intelligence. If one doesn't hasten to offer them a solid education as a guide, there is in that a permanent source of agitation, from which may emerge one day new political commotion. Experience teaches us; workers grouped together can become an element of sedition, and most industrial crises will take on a social character. This point of view is worthy of serious attention."

[105] On what the new machines meant in terms of improved quality, see Mann (1958, 279); on how they saved labor, see Deane (1979, 88–90).

[106] Deane points out that in England, real output of woollen textiles increased 2½ times between 1700 and 1770, at a rate of 85 per decade in the first four decades, and then at 13–14% in the period 1741–1770 (1957, 220). Markovitch describes a "global growth" for the French wool industry in the eighteenth century of 145% which he says is close to the hypothetical rate of 150% found in Deane and Cole (1967) for the same period. "The French woollen industry did not therefore fall behind English industry in the eighteenth century. In both cases, the woollen industry seems to have attained an overall annual average (geometric) rate of growth of 1%" (1976a, 647–648). (If these statistics are not totally consistent, it is not my doing.)

[107] See Hoffmann (1958, 43).

[108] Landes (1969, 82).

cotton not so new. Landes offers in its stead two others: cotton was easier to mechanize,[109] and the market for cotton goods was more elastic. But ease of mechanization runs against the grain of the hypothesis of a technological breakthrough,[110] and ignores the fact that in the early eighteenth century some progress was in fact being made in wool technology, and indeed in France.[111]

An argument of elasticity of market raises the question of why this should be so, especially if we remember that one of the reasons for the success of English new draperies (wool) in the sixteenth century was also the elasticity of its market.[112] Elasticity of market usually refers to the potential market of new customers at lower prices. But if the idea is extended to the ability to acquire new markets by the political elimination of rivals, it may well be that cotton textiles were more "elastic" than woollen textiles at this time from the point of view not only of British but of all of western Europe's producers. For in wool they competed against each other and were fairly certain that innovations could and would be rapidly copied. In cotton, however, western Europe (collectively) competed against India[113], and was eventually able to ensure politically that innovations did not diffuse there.

The other great arena of innovation was iron. Iron was, of course, like textiles, one of the traditional industries of the European world-economy. The main utility of iron hitherto had been in ironwares, both in the household and in armaments. In the late eighteenth and early nineteenth century, two additional outlets of consumption for iron became significant: machinery and transport. Each of the three outlets is said to have played a role in turn in Britain's economic expansion. Davis attributes to the growing demand of the North American colonies for ironwares in the first three quarters of the eighteenth century the pressure to seek economies of

---

[109] "[Cotton] is a plant fibre, tough and relatively homogeneous in its characteristics, where wool is organic, fickle, and subtly varied in its behavior" (Landes, 1969, 83).

[110] See Lilley: "In summary, we may say that, apart from the one really novel idea of drawing out by rollers, the cotton-spinning inventions up to about 1800 were essentially a matter of connecting together in new combinations the parts of the spinning wheel which had been familiar for centuries. These were 'easy' inventions to make in the sense that they required no specific qualifications or training. They could be made by any intelligent man who had sufficient enthusiasm and sufficient commercial vision" (1973, 194). Lilley argues that they broke through no technological barriers and were not conditions for expansion, but "consequences of the new incentives and opportunities which more rapid expansion created" (p. 195). See

also Chapman: "The longer one looks at the early cotton industry under the microscope, the less revolutionary the early phases of its life-cycle appear to be" (1970, 253).

[111] See Patterson (1957, 165–166). Furthermore, innovation is not the only way of increasing competitiveness. Transfer of the site of production is a second method, and a quite standard one. Furthermore, Davis notes that this is exactly what was done in the case of the English woollen and linen industries which "were able for a time to lower costs by moving into low-wage areas of Scotland, Ireland and the north of England" (1973, 307).

[112] See Wallerstein (1974, 279–280).

[113] Hoffmann gives the British parliament's actions against Indian calicoes as the second of the two circumstances that explain the innovations, the other being (as previously noted) freedom from guild control (1958, 43).

scale which, once achieved, lowered costs and thereby in turn "stimulate[d] demand further."[114] Bairoch makes the case that it was the growing use of iron, first in agriculture, then in textile machinery, which is this further demand.[115] And, of course, it would be the railroads in the 1830s that would provide the base for the true expansion of the iron and steel industry, its transformation into the leading industry of the nineteenth-century world-economy. The development of railroads is in turn linked to the massive expansion of mining operations in coal and iron which made the heavy capital investment in transport worthwhile,[116] first in canals,[117] then in railways.

Hence, the rise of coal as the basic fuel of energy production is intertwined with the expansion of the iron industry and its technological advances. Coal too was nothing new. It was, however, in the eighteenth century that it became a major substitute for wood as a fuel. The reason is very elementary. Europe's forests had been steadily depleted by the industrial production (and home heating) of previous centuries. By 1750, the lack of wood had become "the principal bottleneck of industrial growth."[118] England's shortage of timber had long been acute and had encouraged the use of coal already in the sixteenth century, as well as a long-standing concern with coal technology.[119] A new technology was needed that would change high-cost industry into a low cost one. The "efficient" use of coal, along with the steam engine to convert the energy, was the solution.[120]

Landes says, quite correctly, that the "use [of coal and steam], as against that of substitutable power sources, was a consideration of cost and convenience."[121] In seeking to explain why Darby's method of coke smelting, invented in 1709, was not adopted by others in England for half a century, Hyde suggests the explanation was purely and simply "costs."[122]

[114] Davis (1973, 303).

[115] See Bairoch (1974, 85–97). Mantoux argues the general relationship between iron and machinery. Early, largely wooden, machines had "irregular motion and rapid wear." Watt's engine, however, required Wilkinson's metal cylinders "of perfectly accurate shape" (1928, 316).

[116] Wrigley sums up succinctly the reason why: "Production [of mineral raw materials] is punctiform; [production of vegetable and animal raw materials] areal . . . The former implies heavy tonnages along a small number of routeways, whereas the latter implies the reverse" (1967, 101).

[117] In the case of the majority of the canals built in Great Britain between 1758 and 1802, the "primary aim was to carry coal" (Deane, 1979, 79); cf. Gayer *et al.*: "The Duke of Bridgewater's early link between Worsley and Manchester halved the price of coal in the latter town" (1975, 417).

[118] Chaunu (1966, 600).

[119] See Nef (1957, 78–81).

[120] See Forbes: "Scarcity of charcoal and limitation of water-power were economic threats to the iron industry of the eighteenth century. Many attempts were made to break this tyranny of wood and water" (1958, 161). A very clear exposition of the technological problems and their historical solutions is to be found in Landes (1969, 88–100). See also Lilley (1973, 197–202).

[121] Landes (1969, 99).

[122] "It was cheaper to use charcoal rather than coke in the smelting process until around mid-century, so ironmongers were rational in shunning coke-smelting and continuing to use the older technique. The costs of making pig iron with coke fell significantly in the first half of the century, while charcoal pig iron costs rose sharply in the 1750's, giving coke-smelting a clear cost advantage" (Hyde,

This throws some light on the question of why coal technology was not similarly developed in France in the eighteenth century. Landes seems to think that Britain's choice was "indicative of a deeper rationality," whereas France "obdurately rejected coal—even when there were strong pecuniary incentives to switch over to the cheaper fuel."[123] Milward and Saul see it, however, as a "proper reaction" to an "expensive process producing poorer iron" which made no sense as long as the French were not confronted by the acute shortage of wood faced by Britain.[124]

In this picture of the two great industrial expansions—cotton and iron—one of the subordinate but important debates has been which of the two was the "crucial" one. There are some important differences in structure between the two industries and their technologies. The inventions in cotton textiles were mechanical in nature and essentially labor saving. Those in the iron industry were largely chemical and improved both quantity and quality of output without immediately diminishing the use of labor.[125] The changes in textile technology led to the end of the putting-out system and the use of factories, but factories had already been the mode for the iron industry since the sixteenth century.[126]

These differences are linked to what we think of as "revolutionary" in the "first industrial revolution." The rise of the British cotton textile industry involved essentially two changes. First, it meant a major shift in the organization of work (the relations of production) in the then prime industry of the world. Second, it was integrally and visibly linked to the structure of the world market. The raw materials were entirely imported and the products "overwhelmingly sold abroad." Since, therefore, control of the *world* market was crucial, Hobsbawm draws the conclusion that there was room for only one "pioneer national industrialization," which was that of Great Britain.[127] Cotton textiles were crucial precisely because they restructured this world-economy. Lilley, however, is skeptical of the importance given to cotton. Looking ahead, he argues that one can "imagine" sustained growth without cotton textiles, but "without an expansion in iron it would have been inconceivable."[128] This debate is revealing

---

1973, 398). If then one wonders why the Darbys used it, Hyde argues that they used it *"in spite* of the higher costs of the new process because they received higher than average revenues for a new by-product of coke pig iron—thin-walled castings." And this casting technology was a "well-guarded industrial secret" (pp. 406–407).

[123] Landes (1969, 54). In 1786, the Bishop of Landoff, Richard Watson, was less harsh on the French in a debate in the House of Lords concerning the Eden Treaty. He said: "No nation ever began to look for fuel under ground, till their woods were gone" (*Parliamentary History of England*, XXVI, 1816, 545).

[124] Milward & Saul (1973, 173). Curiously, at a later point in his book, Landes says virtually the same thing: "Even nature's bounty hurt, for the *relative* abundance of timber seems to have encouraged retention of the traditional technique" (1969, 126).

[125] See Mantoux (1928, 304).

[126] See Deane (1979, 103).

[127] Hobsbawm (1968, 48–49).

[128] Lilley (1973, 203). Landes rightly suggests this is perhaps being anachronistic for an analysis of the late eighteenth century, giving the iron industry "more attention than it deserves. . . . Not in number of men employed, nor in capital invested, nor

of the fluidity (or the fuzziness) of the way the concept of industrial
revolution has been employed.

A key example is the commonplace argument that the industrial
revolution in Britain in the late eighteenth and early nineteenth centuries is
revolutionary in that it marked the creation of the factory as the framework
for the organization of work in industry. But on the one hand we know that
there had been factories (in the sense of physical concentration under one
roof of multiple workers paid by one employer) before this time.[129] On the
other hand, the extent of the introduction of the factory system at this time
can easily be overstated, even for Britain.[130]

Of course, there was a shift in textiles from rural to urban sites of
production. (The same shift had, let us recall, also occurred in the sixteenth
century only to shift back in the seventeenth.) Whether there was at this
time truly a shift in manpower allocation is more doubtful. Whereas
previously a rural worker spent part of his time on agriculture and part on
textile production, now there was greater specialization. But the "global
time" devoted to agriculture and industry by British workers may at first
have remained approximately the same.[131] Since, in addition, these early
factories were "not invariably that much more efficient,"[132] we must ask
why the shift occurred at all, especially since the entrepreneur was losing
that great advantage of the putting-out system, the fact that the workers
were not only "cheap," but also "dispensable."[133] Landes himself gives us
the key explanation. At a time of a "secularly expanding market," the
entrepreneur's major concern was not dispensing with his workers but
expanding his output, at least extensively, and countering "the worker's

value of output, nor rate of growth could iron be
compared with cotton in this period" (1969,
88–89).

[129] The examples are many. The most notable
example of their extensive earlier use is in the
Italian silk industry. Carlo Poni has been doing
much research on this subject.

Freudenberg and Redlich prefer to call these
structures "protofactories" or "centrally controlled
consolidated workshops," involving increased control of production but not necessarily an increased
division of labor" (1964, 394). The degree to which
the late eighteenth-century cotton factories differed significantly from the earlier ones, however,
is a subject on which there has been insufficient
research.

[130] "The move to factory production was less
universal than it is commonly held to have been"
(Bergier, 1973, 421). See also Crouzet: "The most
widespread form of organization in the large British industries at the beginning of the nineteenth
century was outwork, the combination of commer-

cial capitalism and domestic labor; it is in this form
that capitalist concentration developed" (1958, 74).

See also Samuel on the British cotton industry:
"Now is it possible to equate the new mode of
production with the factory system. . . . Capitalist
growth was rooted in a sub-soil of small-scale enterprise" (1977, 8). In emphasizing what he believes to
be the "slow progress of mechanization" (p. 47),
Samuel observes that: "In manufacture, as in agriculture and mineral work, a vast amount of capitalist enterprise [in early nineteenth-century Britain]
was organized on the basis of hand rather than
steam-powered technologies" (p. 45).

[131] See Bairoch (1974, 108).

[132] O'Brien & Keyder (1978, 168).

[133] Landes (1969, 119). Landes refers us to Hirschman (1957) for an explanation of why this
theoretically should be so. Since Hirschman is writing of the twentieth-century peripheral zone of the
world-economy, we are thereby reminded that
putting-out is still a major feature of the organization of work in the capitalist world-economy.

predilection for embezzlement," especially when, because of rising prices, "the reward for theft was greater."[134]

We must now face up to the central assertion about the "first industrial revolution": that there was one in Great Britain and not one in France (or elsewhere). From the mid-nineteenth century to the mid-twentieth century, this was widely accepted as an elementary truism by world scholarship. Paul Mantoux published an elegy to the industrial revolution in Britain, and Henri Sée wrote that "machinism" in France at the end of the *Ancien Régime* was "sporadic" and "at its beginnings" and that "only a few industries . . . [had begun] to be transformed,"[135] all this by comparison with Great Britain.

Superior British economic growth has traditionally been the subject not of demonstration but of explanation. Kemp's version of explanations is archetypical. Economic growth on a broad front is "conditioned in large part by an aptitude" which the British had, while the French, even in the nineteenth century, continued to suffer from the "historical carry over" of a socioeconomic structure which "inhibited" them.[136] Recently, however, a number of scholars have begun to throw doubt on the truism of British superiority. They start with an alternative truism: "France was in the seventeenth and eighteenth centuries the premier industrial power in the world."[137] Furthermore, it is argued that industrial product surpassed agricultural product earlier in France than in Great Britain.[138] If one can use such a concept as "take-off," the argument continues, it occurred in France "towards the middle of the eighteenth century" or "at the very latest, about 1799," but more probably at the earlier date.[139] This whole line of argument is supported by an accumulation of considerable quantita-

---

[134] Landes (1969, 57).

[135] Sée (1923a, 191, 198). In that same year, however, Ballot's book on "machinism" was posthumously published. In the preface, Henri Hauser wrote that "machines, in pre-1789 France, were more widely diffused than one ordinarily believes" (1923, viii).

[136] Kemp (1962, 328–329; cf. Cameron, 1958, 11; Kranzberg, 1969, 211; Henderson, 1972, 75).

[137] Markovitch (1976b, 475), who argues that France was not only "superior to England in industrial strength under the *Ancien Régime*" (1974, 122), but remained so "even in the beginning of the nineteenth century" (1966c, 317). See, however, Léon, whose formulation is more prudent: "[The period 1730–1830 in France] shows itself to be, despite everything, as more and more dominated, in spite of the persistent inferiority of its techniques, by a wave of industrialization and growth which, if not massive, is at least real and highly significant" (1960, 173; cf. Garden, 1978c, 36).

See, finally, Wilson whose summary view of the whole period 1500–1800 is that "England did not deviate from the normal European pattern so much as was once thought" (1977, 151).

[138] Marczewski says it occurs "before 1789" in France but only between 1811 and 1821 in Great Britain (1965, xiv). He, however, acknowledges that Britain is superior in the growth of the physical product in the nineteenth century, "especially in agricultural production" (p. cxxxv).

[139] Marczewski (1961a, 93–94). Markovitch says it is hard to talk of a "take-off" since the whole industrial history of France from the mid-eighteenth century to now has been that of "an almost uninterrupted secular economic growth" (1966c, 119). Milward and Saul date the French "industrial revolution" as occurring between 1770 and 1815, although they say that if one uses the take-off criteria, a take-off did not occur until the mid-nineteenth century (1973, 254–255).

tive data which bear directly on the key period under debate.[140] From these data O'Brien and Keyder are led to reject the whole concept of French "relative backwardness" and to conclude rather that "industrialization in France simply took place in a different legal, political and cultural tradition."[141]

There are two ways to challenge the concept of a "first industrial revolution" in Great Britain. One is to suggest, as we have just seen, that the differences between Great Britain and France at that time was small, or at least smaller than is required by the concept. The second, however, is to raise the question of whether there was an industrial revolution at all. There is the suggestion that there were earlier industrial revolutions—in the thirteenth century[142] or in the sixteenth.[143] There is the contrary suggestion that the really revolutionary changes came later, in the mid-nineteenth century, or even in the twentieth.[144] The most extreme of these suggestions is the argument that technological revolutions occurred in the period 1550–1750, and after 1850, but precisely *not* in the period 1750–1850.[145]

---

[140] See, for example, Marczewski (1961b), wherein the tables demonstrate that there was a steady rate of growth in France from 1701 to 1844 (except for short periods) characterizing both agriculture and industry and that the dominant factor of this growth was an intensive and extensive industrialization dominated by a tremendous development of the cotton industry.

[141] O'Brien & Keyder (1978, 21). Another way of putting it is to say that the question about England's primacy is "misconceived" and "unanswerable," since to the question of whether England was "self-evidently superior" in the eighteenth century, the answer can only be "a resounding 'no.'" The inference of superiority has been drawn merely from England's "ultimate primacy" (Crafts, 1977, 434, 438–439). Crafts suggests that "the question, 'why was England first?' should be distinguished from the separate question, 'Why did the Industrial Revolution occur in the eighteenth century?'" (p. 431). Milward and Saul similarly call for a shift from the question "why Britain?" to a "pan-European perspective" (1973, 30–38); see also Braudel, who says we can find on the Continent "examples more or less close to the English model", and wishes to see both the agricultural and industrial revolutions as "a European phenomenon" (1982, 282).

[142] See Carus-Wilson (1954). Abel (1973, 51, n. 1) writes that the description of the thirteenth and early fourteenth centuries as the period of the first industrialization of Europe was first made either by Schmoller or by F. Philippi who, in 1909, published *Die erste Industrialisierung Deutschlands.*

[143] See Nef (1954). While Carus-Wilson argues that there was an industrial revolution in the thirteenth century (that is, the fulling-mill), she omits any comparison, in terms of importance, with that of the late eighteenth century. Nef, by contrast, in vaunting the period 1540–1640 in Great Britain, suggests that its "rate of change was scarcely less striking" than that of the latter period (p. 88). See, however, Deane's reply that there was a difference nonetheless in "the sheer scale of industrial development" between the two periods and also in the "wider" impact of its "organisational and technical changes" (1973a, 166).

[144] Garden, for example, warns that "one ought not . . . to confound hastily the eighteenth century and the industrial revolution: the British truth was itself belated and limited; everywhere there was the survival of—indeed, even, the development of—traditional forms throughout the eighteenth century" (1978a, 14). See also Williamson who says that before the 1820s, British growth was "modest at best" (1984, 688).

[145] Daumas calls the period 1550–1750 one of "fundamental transition" in technology (1965, v). He calls the idea that there was a technological revolution between 1750 and 1850 "one of the principal errors" in our understanding of the history of technology (1963, 291). He then offers to salvage the period 1750–1850 by acknowledging its achievements outside his specialty, in the social organization of the economy. See Daumas (1965, xii) and Daumas & Garanger (1965, 251).

Similarly, Lilley asserts: "The early stages of the Industrial Revolution—roughly up to 1800—were

The suggestion that there were earlier and later industrial revolutions blends easily into the suggestion that there was a longer one. Already, in 1929, Beales, in reviewing the literature, argued that the extensions backward and forward had eliminated the "cataclysmic character" attributed to the industrial revolution.[146] The consequent acerbic comment of Heaton seems pertinent: "a revolution which continued for 150 years and had been in preparation for at least another 150 years may well seem to need a new label."[147]

The concept of "protoindustrialization" serves virtually as a belated response to Heaton's appeal. By creating a new term for "a first phase which preceded and prepared modern industrialization proper"—that is, the phase of "market-oriented, principally rural industry"—Mendels has attempted to retain the specificity of a more narrowly delimited and time-enclosed industrial revolution while accepting simultaneously the emphasis on the gradualness of the process.[148] He is even able to argue that the use of this concept can resolve the debate on the superiority of British to French industry in this period by reducing it to a semantic quarrel.[149] What he cannot answer thereby is Garden's query: "is the vigor of change a consequence of the strength of the industrial sector, or on the contrary of its structural weakness in the eighteenth century?"[150]

based largely on using medieval techniques and on extending these to their limits" (1973, 190). See also Braudel: "If there is a factor which has lost ground as a key explanation of the industrial revolution, it is technology" (1984, 566).

[146] "The conventional narrative . . . makes too much of the coming of the great inventions." Beales says that with the "quieter interpretation" of the inventor as "mouthpiece of the aspirations of the day [rather] than as the initiator of them," what the concept of industrial revolution loses in "dramatic quality, . . . it gains in depth and in human significance" (1929, 127–128). See also Hartwell, for whom the industrial revolution needs no "explanation" since it is "the culmination of a most unspectacular process, the consequence of a long period of slow economic growth" (1967b, 78); and Deane and Habakkuk, for whom "the most striking characteristic of the first take-off was its gradualness" (1963, 82; cf. Hartwell, 1970b).

[147] Heaton (1932, 5).

[148] Mendels (1972, 241), who accounts for the shift to the second phase of "modern, factory, or machine industrialization" by the fact that protoindustrialization results in the accumulation of capital in the hands of merchant entrepreneurs with the necessary skills for factory industrialization, and in the creation of markets for agricultural goods which led to increasing geographic specialization.

Bergeron calls attention to the "reintegrative" character of the concept of protoindustrialization, which "insists on the continuities, more than on the ruptures, in the organization of production and work between the 'pre-' and 'post-' periods of the technological revolution" (1978a, 8).

[149] Mendels points out that Markovitch's revisions of standard beliefs concerning the relative backwardness of French industry in the late eighteenth and early nineteenth century (as well as similar views of Crouzet) are dependent on the inclusion into his category of industry and crafts of "handicrafts in their broadest possible meaning, even including household industrial work for home consumption." He concludes: "One's interpretation of French economic development could thus be drastically changed, depending on the place which is given to 'pre-industrial industry'" (1972, 259).

Jeannin, in his critical note on protoindustrialization, of which he reviews a more recent version, that of Kriedte *et al.* (1977), argues that the concept of protoindustrialization is "at once a bit inflated, incorporating non-specific elements, and too narrow because too specific to poor industries" (1980, 64).

[150] Garden (1978a, 14), who calls this "the fundamental question."

There are other ways to respond to the argument of gradualism. One is that of Landes, who says it is an artifact of surface descriptions and of unchanging nomenclature.[151] A second is that of Hobsbawm, who singles out a period of "triumph" within the longer, more gradual process.[152] A third is that of Schumpeter, who says that both the thesis of revolution and of evolution are correct here (as always), since it is merely a matter of a microscopic versus a macroscopic perspective.[153]

And yet one wonders whether all this does not add up to putting in doubt the heuristic value of the concept of the industrial revolution. Nef takes a strong negative position:

> There is scarcely a concept in economic history more misleading than one which relates all the important problems of our modern civilization to economic changes that are represented as taking place in England between 1760 and 1832. There is scarcely a concept that rests on less secure foundations that one which finds a key to the understanding of the modern industrialized world in those seventy-two years of English economic history.[154]

[151] "One must not mistake the appearance for the reality. . . . As described by occupational data, the British economy of 1851 may not seem different from that of 1800. But these numbers merely describe the surface of the society—and even then in terms that define away change by using categories of unchanging nomenclature. Beneath this surface, the vital organs were transformed; and though they weighed but a fraction of the total— whether measured by people or by wealth—it was they that determined the metabolism of the entire system" (Landes, 1969, 122). But this leaves us uncertain of how to identify "vital organs" and "metabolism"; and even more important, whether the difference 1800–1850 is significantly greater than that of any previous 50-year period.

[152] The years 1789–1848 mark the "triumph not of 'industry' as such, but of *capitalist* industry; not of liberty and equality in general, but of the *middle class* or '*bourgeois*' *liberal* society. . . . They mark not the existence of these elements of a new economy and society but their triumph; . . . not the progress of their gradual sapping and mining in previous centuries, but their decisive conquest of the fortress" (Hobsbawm, 1962, 17, 19). Hobsbawm's period barely squeezes into Marx's periodization. Marx writes of a rather late moment of decisive conquest, even for Great Britain: "The complete rule of industrial capital was not acknowledged by English merchant's capital and moneyed interests until after the abolition of the corn tax [1846], etc." (1967, 327, n.).

[153] "A revolution can never be understood from itself, i.e., without reference to the developments that led up to it; it sums up rather than initiates. . . . [This is the] difference between the mi-

croscopic and macroscopic points of view: there is as little contradiction between them as there is between calling the contour of a forest discontinuous for some and smooth for other purposes" (Schumpeter, 1938, 227).

[154] Nef (1943, 1). McEvedy goes further, saying the concept of the industrial revolution "has, in fact—no mean achievement for a historical theory —done a lot of practical harm" (1972, 5–6). Cameron (1982; 1985) has been similarly pursuing the argument that the term "industrial revolution" is a "misnomer."

Schumpeter makes the same essential charge: "The writer concurs with modern economic historians who frown upon the term, the industrial revolution. It is not only outmoded, but also misleading, or even false in principle, if it is intended to convey the idea that what it designates was a unique event or series of events that created a new economic or social order, or the idea that, unconnected with previous developments, it suddenly burst upon the world in the last two or three decades of the eighteenth century. . . . We put that particular industrial revolution on a par with at least two similar events which preceded it and at least two more which followed it" (1939, 253). He designates 1787–1842 as a Kondratieff cycle and says: "We have reason to believe that this long wave was not the first of its kind" (p. 252). Coleman responds to Schumpeter by reiterating that the term industrial revolution should be reserved for that of Great Britain in the late eighteenth century which, "in the long focus of history, was the comparatively sudden and violent change which launch[ed] the industrialized society into being" (1966, 350).

I share Nef's view that the concept of the "industrial revolution" and its almost inevitable correlate, that of the "first industrial revolution" of Great Britain, is profoundly misleading. No amount of patchwork, by extending it in time, by making it into a two-stage process, by distinguishing between slow quantitative accretion and qualitative breakthrough, will salvage it, because it starts from the premise that what explains British "advantage" is a constellation of traits which are absolute when what we need to locate is a constellation of positions which are relational within the framework of a world-economy. It is the world-economy which develops over time and not subunits within it.

The question is not why Great Britain outdistanced France or any other country (to the degree that it did, and, however, one measures the "outdistancing"), but rather why the world-economy as a whole developed in the way that it did at any particular point in time (and here we take the period 1730–1840), and why at this time there resulted a greater concentration of the most profitable economic activities within particular state boundaries (and why more capital accumulated therein) than within other state boundaries.

Briavoinne in 1839 stated more simply than we do now what was going on:

> The sphere of labor grew larger; the means of production (*exécution*) were in the process of being multiplied and simplified each day a bit more. Population grew consequently through the diminution of the mortality rate. The treasures found in the earth were exploited better and more abundantly; man produced and consumed more; he became more rich. All these changes constitute the industrial revolution.[155]

If you then ask Briavoinne what accounts for this revolution, he explains it by three key inventions: firearms, the compass, and the printing press.[156] We are thus referred back to a previous moment in time, the moment precisely of the creation of a capitalist world-economy several centuries earlier.

The "first industrial revolution" and the French Revolution refer presumably to event-periods coterminous in time. This has often been noted and the expression, "the age of revolutions," has sometimes been used to designate this period. The temporal linkage is in fact reinforced by a conceptual linkage, which has been less frequently discussed. To be sure, many authors have remarked that the locution "industrial revolution" emerged out of "a very natural association"[157] of the rapid industrial changes with the political changes of the French Revolution. But the converse is also true. Our perceptions of the French Revolution have come to be framed centrally by our perceptions of the industrial revolution.

---

[155] Briavoinne (1839, 185–186).
[156] Briavoinne (1839, 188).

[157] Bezanson (1922, 343).

The French Revolution incarnates all the political passions of the modern world, more so perhaps even than its only real rival as a symbolic event, the Russian Revolution. It is perhaps the one theme of modern history about which so many historiographies have been written that it is time for someone to do a historiography of the historiography. We shall concentrate here on the question which seems to have been central to the whole debate since the Second World War: was the French Revolution a bourgeois revolution?[158]

Soboul, who came to be the principal spokesman of the social interpretation of the French Revolution, which he calls the classical interpretation of the French Revolution, asserts that for Jaurès, whom he considers the founder of this school, "the Revolution was but the outcome of a long economic and social evolution which made of the bourgeoisie the mistress of power and the economy." After Jaurès, says Soboul, came Mathiez and Lefebvre, then Soboul and Rudé.

> Thus bit by bit the social interpretation of the French Revolution was perfected by a more than century-long progression. By its constant recourse to erudite research . . . , by its critical spirit, by its attempt at theoretical reflection, by its global vision of the Revolution, it alone merits being considered truly scientific.

This global vision of the Revolution is itself part of a global vision of modern history in which,

> the French Revolution is only an episode in the general course of history which, after the revolutions of the Netherlands, England, and America, contributed to bringing the bourgeoisie to (or associating it with) power, and liberated the development of a capitalist economy.[159]

That the social interpretation of the French Revolution hides fundamentally a Whig interpretation of history, the same which produced the concept of the "first industrial revolution" in England, can be seen in the conclusion Lefebvre came to in the synthesis of his thought he wrote to commemorate the 150th anniversary of 1789:

> The Declaration of the Rights of Man remains . . . the incarnation of the whole revolution. . . . America and France, as England before them, are in parallel ways tributary of a current of ideas whose success reflects the rise of the bourgeoisie and which constituted a common ideal in which is resumed the evolution of Western civilization. In the course of centuries, our West, shaped by Christianity, but heir

---

[158] Schmitt (1976), in his historiography of the literature since 1945 on the French Revolution, lists this question as one of six, but the other five seem to me all to be avatars of this one question. The other five are: the French Revolution—myth or reality?; the problem of the "Atlantic Revolution"; was there a "feudal reaction"?; were there one or three revolutions in 1789?; the Jacobin dictatorship—highpoint of the French Revolution?

[159] Soboul (1974, 41–42, 44).

also to the thought of Antiquity, has concentrated its efforts, overcoming a
thousand visissitudes, on realizing the liberation of the human person.[160]

It is perhaps most useful therefore if we begin by spelling out the
arguments of the social interpretation in some greater detail.[161] There are
three fundamental claims in this perspective. The revolution was a revolution against the feudal order and those who controlled it, the aristocracy.
The revolution was an essential stage in the transition to the new social
order of capitalism on behalf of those who would control it, the bourgeoisie. The bourgeoisie could succeed in the revolution only by appealing for
the support of the popular classes who, however, were at best its secondary
beneficiaries and were at worst its victims. Furthermore, it is argued that
these three statements not only summarize (French) historical reality but
they are statements about a particular event-period beginning in 1789 and
ending in 1799.[162] This event-period is "revolutionary" in that it marked a
sudden, qualitative social transformation as opposed to being merely a
segment of a secular ongoing sequence of social development.

"At the end of the eighteenth century," we are told, "the structure of
French society remained essentially aristocratic." The French Revolution
marks "the advent of bourgeois, capitalist society" in that it achieved "the
destruction of the seigneurial system and the privileged orders of feudal
society."[163] Soboul's assessment of French society is curiously close to that
of Landes, except that the difference they both see between Britain and
France in the eighteenth century continues to exist for Landes in the
nineteenth (and perhaps even the first half of the twentieth) centuries:

[160] Lefebvre (1939, 239–240).

[161] It may be objected that we shall rely too heavily on the Soboul (or more generally a Marxist version) of this social interpretation, and that Lefebvre's views (not to speak of those of Mathiez) were different in several respects. But since, as Ferro has noted "[history in France] (as well as the history of France) is one of the prime loci of civil war" (1981, 32), this may be justified, given the following plausible assessment by Grenon and Robin: "Curiously, 1789 still remains a fundamental line of cleavage between the right and the left in France; the Revolution as a myth can still arouse emotion. This is because, in the writing of history, the two concepts of the classical interpretation of the French Revolution and the Marxist interpretation have always been casually superimposed upon one another. The classical interpretation is none other than the progressive reading of the Revolution" (1976, 6).

[162] 1799 is the terminal date Soboul used in his short history (1977a). One can, to be sure, choose

other terminal dates, say 1793, or 1792, or 1815. One can also choose other starting dates, say 1787 or 1763. To do so is to change the interpretation. To choose the dates 1789–1799 is not, however, necessarily to agree with Soboul in all aspects. Agulhon chooses precisely those dates in order to argue that 1830 marks the resumption of the "revolution" which he argues is a revolution of "liberalism," whereas 1800–1830 represents counter-revolution "in two successive forms"—that of the Napoleonic dictatorship and that of an authoritarian, clerical monarchy (1980, 15).

[163] Soboul (1977a, 1, 3). The old order must be called "feudalism, for lack of a better name" (Soboul, 1976a, 3). Indeed, if any thing, this negative side of the Revolution is more important than its positive side. Speaking of the "aristocratic reaction" of the eighteenth century, Soboul says: "From this angle, the Revolution was perhaps not bourgeois, but it was surely anti-aristocratic and anti-feudal" (1970b, 250).

The effect of these forces [aristocratic snobbery, bourgeois aspiration, the pressure of literary and artistic opinion] was a general atmosphere [in France] that can best be termed anticapitalistic. The medieval concept of production for use and not for profit, of a static as opposed to a dynamic society, never lost its validity.[164]

In eighteenth-century France, a France that was not merely "feudal" but said to be undergoing an "aristocratic reaction," the bourgeoisie found itself deeply frustrated, especially in terms of investment in manufacture because of restrictions imposed on "the elementary capitalist freedoms: the freedom to have labor, the freedom to produce, and the freedom to buy and sell." The freedoms, it need hardly be added, were presumed to be widely available to the British, who utilized them to launch an industrial revolution. Thus the stage was set, it is argued, for the bourgeoisie to make "its entry on the revolutionary stage."[165]

The French bourgeoisie had fortune thrust upon it in 1789, taking (of two possible paths from feudalism to capitalism) the one Marx designated as the "really revolutionizing path."[166] If one asks why the bourgeoisie took this path, Soboul attributes it to the "obstinacy of the aristocracy" (which refused to make concessions) and to the "relentlessness of the peasant masses" (the antifeudal *jacqueries* of 1789–1793), but not at all to the bourgeoisie "which had not sought the ruin of the aristocracy."[167] Soboul does not tell us if these are the same reasons why the English bourgeoisie took the same "really revolutionizing path." Nor does he tell us if those countries who followed the other path, the "Prussian path," were blessed by a less obstinate aristocracy or had a less relentless peasantry.

It is at this point that the exposition becomes a little hazy. Soboul argues quite conventionally that the English revolution was "far less radical" than the French, which was "the most dramatic" of all bourgeois revolutions, indeed the "classic bourgeois revolution."[168] This said, we are left with Hobsbawm's "gigantic paradox," that, "on paper" (that is, in accordance with this explanatory model), France was "ideally suited to capitalist development" and should have soared ahead of its competitors. Yet, in fact, its economic development was "slower" than that of others, most particularly than that of Britain. Hobsbawm has an explanation: "the French Revolution . . . took away with the hand of Robespierre much of

[164] Landes (1949, 57).

[165] Rudé (1967, 33).

[166] Marx (1967, I, 334). This is the path by which "the producer becomes merchant and capitalist," as opposed to the one by which "the merchant established direct sway over production."

[167] Soboul (1976d, 16; 1977b, 38). Apparently, the monarchy was more foresighted than the aristocracy. It tried to resolve the differences between

the aristocracy and the bourgeoisie in the *Ancien Régime* by creating a "trading aristocracy" and by "ennobling the merchants." But the experience was a "failure" and demonstrated "the impossibility, under the conditions of the *Ancien Régime*, of a veritable fusion" of the two groups (Soboul, 1970b, 279, 282).

[168] Soboul (1977a, 160–161, 168).

what it gave with the hand of the Constituent Assembly."[169] If, however, the Jacobins, representatives *par excellence* of the bourgeois revolution, created by their actions an "impregnable [economically retrogressive] citadel of small and middle peasant proprietors, small craftsmen and shopkeepers" which "slowed [the capitalist transformation of agriculture and small enterprise] to a crawl,"[170] one wonders in what sense this was indeed a *bourgeois* revolution, or if bourgeois, in what sense a revolution?[171]

It is thus that we come to the most delicate part of the perspective, the role attributed to popular forces. Chateaubriand's aphorism, "the patricians began the Revolution: the plebeians completed it,"[172] is now accepted truth. Where then do the bourgeois come in? Presumably by confounding both: taking the leadership away from the aristocracy in 1789 with the (solicited) support of the popular forces,[173] but checking the popular forces by Thermidor, by the defeat of the popular insurrections of Year III, by putting down the Conspiracy of the Equals, and ultimately (perhaps also) by the 18th Brumaire.[174]

The picture of class forces is one with bourgeoisie in political control everywhere. The Girondins, the Jacobins (Dantonists or "Indulgents,"

---

[169] Hobsbawm (1962, 212–213), who explains his aphorism thus: "The capitalist part of the French economy was a superstructure erected on the immovable base of the peasantry and petty bourgeoisie. The landless free laborers merely trickled into the cities; the standardized cheap goods which made the fortunes of the progressive industrialist elsewhere lacked a sufficiently large and expanding market. Plenty of capital was saved, but why should it be invested in home industry?" Hobsbawm refers us (p. 381, n. 19) to the "locus classicus" of this argument: Lefebvre's article of 1932 (see Lefebvre, 1963).

Soboul answers Hobsbawm's paradox by arguing that the peasant revolution was "incomplete." Had the radical sectors of the peasantry won out, there would have been "a restructuring of landed property in favor of small producers" which later would have resulted in "concentration" and no paradox (1977b, 42–43). Poulantzas answers Hobsbawm's paradox in a different way. The "paradox" demonstrates that the revolutionary state "is not the state of a bourgeois revolution which is politically successful at this moment and in this conjuncture, but rather the state of a bourgeois revolution which is politically *held in check*. At this precise moment it is not in fact the state of a hegemonic bourgeoisie, but that of the peasantry and the petty-bourgeoisie, as Tocqueville rightly saw. This state anyway failed to last" (1973, 176).

[170] Hobsbawm (1962, 93).

[171] We can, of course, reply that it was a revolution less in the realm of the economy in the narrow sense and more in the realm of values. "The chief result of the Revolution in France was to put an end to aristocratic society. . . . The society of postrevolutionary France was bourgeois in its structure and values. It was a society of the parvenu, i.e., the self-made man" (Hobsbawm, 1962, 218, 220).

If so, George V. Taylor suggests, this was an unintended consequence. "The revolutionary state of mind expressed in the Declaration of the Rights of Man and the decrees of 1789–91 was a product —not a cause—of the crisis that began in 1787" (1972, 501). Taylor's case is based on his reading of the *cahiers de doléance*.

[172] Cited in Lefebvre (1932, 40).

[173] "There weren't in 1789 three revolutions, but a single one, bourgeois and liberal, with popular (particularly peasant) support. There was no *dérapage* of the Revolution in 1792, but a determination of the revolutionary bourgeoisie to maintain the cohesion of the Third Estate thanks to the alliance of the popular masses, without whose support the gains of 1789 would have been forever compromised" (Soboul, 1974, 56).

[174] Soboul asserts that the French Revolution twice "transcended its bourgeois limits" in revolutions of "the peasants and the masses"—in Year II, and in the Conspiracy of the Equals (1977a, 168).

Robespierrists, Hébertistes), the sans-culottes were all "bourgeois" forces
(or in the case of the sans-culottes an alliance of forces led by petty-
bourgeois shopkeepers and artisans). These political factions represented
increasing degrees of revolutionary militancy, and, to a limited extent,
decreasing degrees of bourgeois rank.[175]

The masses who took so active a role did so under (petty) bourgeois
leadership; this was true not only of the sans-culottes, but even of the
peasantry, insofar as one means by petty-bourgeois leadership, the leadership of better-off peasants.[176] On the one hand, these petty producers
(urban and rural) are said to be the vanguard of the revolution and
"uncompromisingly antifeudal,"[177] (unlike, I presume, other bourgeois
who were prone to compromise). On the other hand, it is precisely the
concessions that were made to this petty bourgeois group and which
proved so durable that are used to explain Hobsbawm's paradox: the slow
pace of nineteenth-century French industrial development and hence the
global failure of the French bourgeoisie.

This classical model was disquieting to many in part because of its
political implications and usage, in part because of the lack of theoretical
rigor behind the facade of a straightforward account, in part because it was
thought to be inconsistent with some of the empirical realities. In any case,
it has been subjected to a massive attack on all fronts since the 1950s: from
the proponents of the Atlantic thesis (Godechot, Palmer), from the skeptics
about the role attributed to the bourgeoisie in the Revolution (Cobban,
Furet), and from those who have been undertaking to reassess the
traditional descriptions of eighteenth-century France, in particular, of the
role of the aristocracy in the functioning of the economy.

The Atlantic thesis is essentially that the French Revolution is one part of
a larger whole, that "great revolutionary movement which affects the whole
Western world." This larger whole includes, notably, the American Revolution but also the various Latin American revolutions, that of Haiti, and
revolutions in almost every European country in the late eighteenth
century. The French Revolution is said to be "of the same nature" as these
others, only "infinitely more intense."[178] Having made this assertion, the
proponents of the Atlantic thesis are less revisionist of the classical

---

[175] "The vanguard of the revolution was not the
commercial bourgeoisie. . . . The real force behind the Revolution was the mass of direct petty
producers" (Soboul, 1977a, 154–155). See also Kaplow: "Just as a revolution without the bourgeoisie
to set it in motion was unthinkable, so was the
formation of the sans-culottes without the participation of the master artisans impossible. The sans-
culottes as an entity were not synonymous with the
laboring poor of the old regime. They were rather
one of the provisional forms, in this case principally

a political one that grew out of the disintegration of
that regime as carried on by the Revolution" (1972,
163).

[176] "The bourgeois revolution, by suppressing
finally all feudal rights by the law of July 17, 1793,
liberated the direct producer, the petty merchant
producer henceforth independent" (Soboul,
1976d, 15).

[177] Soboul (1977a, 168).

[178] Godechot (1965, 114).

interpretation than is sometimes thought.[179] This singular revolution of the West is defined by the Atlanticists as a " 'liberal' or 'bourgeois' " revolution,[180] a "democratic" revolution, in which "democrats" were fighting against "aristocrats."[181] Furthermore, the Atlanticists interpret the Jacobin phase conventionally as the "revolutionizing of the revolution,"[182] a revolution which was, however, "radical at the very beginning."[183] Jacobin radicalism is explained, at least in part, by the "class struggle."[184]

Given that the Atlantic thesis utilizes the key premises of the social interpretation—that the revolution was one of the bourgeoisie against the artisocracy, that it was a necessary mode of transition, that the Jacobins incarnate its most radical form—why does Soboul hurl anathema upon it and charge that it "empties [the French Revolution] of all specific content,"[185] especially since the Atlanticists present a sympathetic picture of the Revolution? The answer seems very clear: the Atlanticist version "dissociates" the French and Russian Revolutions, seeing the one as indigenous and the other as reactive (to "backwardness"), one as part of the eighteenth-century "Revolution of the Western world" and the other as part of the twentieth-century "Revolution of the non-Western."[186] Atlanticism, therefore, ends up more as an implicit reinterpretation of the Russian Revolution than of the French.

This concern with the Russian Revolution is, of course, not far from the minds as well of those who challenge the concept of a "bourgeois revolution," but they go more for the jugular. "Everything is derived from Cobban," it has been said.[187] It is more reasonable to argue that everything

[179] This is less surprising when one remembers that Jacques Godechot, the foremost proponent of the Atlantic thesis, is a disciple of Mathiez and Lefebvre and has never, to my knowledge, renounced this heritage. Of Lefebvre, he says that "his works occupy a cardinal (*capitale*) place in the historiography of the French Revolution" (1965, 257). On Godechot's close relation to Mathiez, see Godechot (1959). The other major Atlanticist, R.R. Palmer, has translated Lefebvre into English.

[180] Godechot (1965, 2).

[181] Palmer (1959, passim, but esp. 13–20).

[182] Palmer (1964, 35–65), who attributes this revolutionizing to "the infusion of popular and international revolutionism" (p. 44).

[183] Palmer (1959, 446). If the American revolution was less revolutionary than the French, it was because "[America] did not know feudalism. . . . In France and in Europe, . . . the efforts to reach the same revolutionary ideal came up against the implacable opposition of classes that were dispossessed or threatened with being so" (Godechot & Palmer, 1955, 227, 229).

[184] Godechot & Palmer (1955, 229). The concept of the alliance of classes is also there: "The peasants, like the 'bourgeois,' or upper stratum of the third estate, saw the nobility as their enemy. This convergence of interests . . . is what made possible the French Revolution of 1789" (Palmer, 1971, 60).

[185] Soboul (1974, 44).

[186] Palmer (1959, 13). Soboul specifically invokes the charge that the Atlantic thesis is a consequence of the "cold war," noting its appearance in the mid-1950s (1974, 43). This assertion is not without justification. The long joint communication of Godechot and Palmer to the 1955 International Congress of Historical Sciences turns around the question: is there something which might be called an Atlantic civilization? The sympathies of the authors seem clearly in favor of a positive response. They end on the plaintive note that: "America, this former colony, believes more than does Europe, it seems, in the reality or the possibility of an 'Atlantic civilization' " (1955, 239).

[187] Mazauric (1975, 167, n. 53). See also Schmitt: "The name 'Cobban' has become in its controversy virtually a code-word (*Reizwort*)" (1976, 50).

is derived from Tocqueville's basic sense that "the Revolution did not overturn, it accelerated."[188] The key operation is to insist upon looking beyond the event-period of the French Revolution itself to the longer sweep, backward and forward, of the sixteenth to nineteenth centuries, which encompasses "a slow but revolutionary mutation" resulting from the "plurisecular" development of capitalism.[189] Furet makes the telling point that, given the premises of the tenants of the social interpretation, they should welcome rather than resist this reorientation of temporal perspective. "If one insists on a conceptualization in terms of 'mode of production', one has to take as the object of study a period infinitely vaster than the years of the French Revolution by themselves."[190]

The central case against considering the French Revolution a bourgeois revolution is that by the eighteenth century France was no longer a feudal country in any meaningful sense. Cobban quotes a legal treatise of the time to argue that seigniorial rights were merely "a bizarre form of property." It follows then that the push to increase seigniorial dues which constituted the largest part of the feudal or aristocratic "reaction" was "much more commercial than feudal."[191]

The argument consists of two parts. The first is to assert that many seigniors, even most seigniors, functioned in the economic arena as bourgeois, and that it is "scarcely stretching terminology" to define the nobility as "successful bourgeois."[192] Against the "false" traditional picture of the provincial French noble as "indolent, dull and impoverished," he should be seen as being more often than not an "active, shrewd, and prosperous landowner,"[193] whose improving role in agriculture has been

[188] This is not a quote from Tocqueville but Tilly's very apt summary of his position (1968, 160). What Tocqueville said himself was: "At one fell swoop, without warning, without transition, and without compunction, the Revolution effected what in any case was bound to happen, if by slow degrees" (1955, 20). See, in a similar vein, Le Roy Ladurie: "The fact that an event like the French Revolution was unique does not make it a necessary event. Or at least it is difficult to prove that it was. . . . It is the expression of the behavior of a society that has come to be exasperated. . . . The French Revolution, in the rural zones, is the direct result of the expansions of the century, even and especially when they were compromised by the economic difficulties of the 1780's. It represents rupture and simultaneously continuity" (1975, 591).

[189] Richet (1969, 22). Richet argues elsewhere that public law in France follows this same trajectory, thus seeking to eliminate one of the key arguments of Soboul and others, that a revolution was essential to the transformation of the legal

superstructure that had been constraining the rise of capitalist forces. Rather, says Richet: "the Revolution broke out in a country that was in the midst of a process of legislative modernization" (1973, 36). Choulgine similarly argues that the constraints on the growth of large enterprises, deriving from guild restructions, has been vastly overstated, since "the great importance of rural industry limited the influence of the guild system [in the *Ancien Régime*]" (1922, 198–199).

[190] Furet (1978, 158).

[191] Cobban (1963, 155–156). See also Roberts: "Most of the 'feudal' forms abolished in the August [1789] decrees were fictions covering a simply reality of cash transactions" (1978, 28).

[192] Chaussinand-Nogaret (1975, 265), who continues, "commercial capitalism is, in its most modern aspects, in the hands more of the nobility than of the bourgeoisie" (p. 274). The other side of the coin is to note, with Bien, that "a very large part of the grand bourgeoisie were nobles in 1789" (1974, 531).

[193] Forster (1961, 33).

"too often depreciated" in comparison to the "sometimes exaggerated" role of the English noble.[194] Thus, there were "nobles who were capitalists," and these were to be found in the "highest ranks" of the nobility.[195] If one analyzes carefully seigniorial balance-sheets, it will be seen that feudal dues, as opposed to capitalist profit, "counted *strictō sensū* often [only] for a small part òr even a very small part" of total income.[196] It was indeed, as Bloch argued quite early, the extension of capitalism in the seventeenth and eighteenth centuries that had revalidated economically "feudal" privilege:

> In a world more and more dominated by an economy that was capitalist in form, privileges originally accorded to the heads of a few small involuted village communities, came little by little to take on a previously unsuspected value.[197]

Nor was this capitalist activity of the nobility limited to agriculture. Goubert argues that "a large proportion" of the nobility became significantly interested in manufactures in the eighteenth century, thus "installing themselves early on in the economy of the future and preparing its 'take-off'."[198]

The second part of the argument is to insist that the "aristocratic reaction" has been mislabeled. What observers term a "reaction" reflects primarily the improvement in the market position of "lessors (*bailleurs*)

---

[194] Forster (1957, 241). Furthermore, "personal estate management not only was the best way of assuring a *gentilhomme campagnard* a good income but it was also recognized as his profession, and, in contrast to retail trade and purely commercial speculation, a perfectly respectable noble enterprise" (p. 224).

[195] Taylor (1967, 489), who asserts therefore that the term bourgeois is "inadequate and misleading," if by bourgeois we mean a "nonnoble group playing a capitalist role in the relations of production" (p. 490). He draws therefrom these conclusions about the French Revolution: that "we have no economic explanation for the so-called 'bourgeois revolution,' the assault of the upper Third Estate on absolutism and aristocracy" and that the Revolution is "essentially a political revolution with social consequences and not a social revolution with political consequences" (pp. 490–491). Taylor receives indirect support for this line of argument from the recent attempt to reinterpret the industrial revolution in England by Cain and Hopkins, who introduce the concept of "gentlemanly capitalism," based on "landed wealth" and argue for this period: "our aim is not to deny what is irrefutable, namely that Britain industrialized, but rather to suggest that non-industrial, though still capitalist, activities were much more important before, during, and

after the industrial revolution than standard interpretations of economic and imperial history allow" (1986, 503–504).

Vovelle, however, finds that Taylor's inferences about the French Revolution go beyond what his "useful remarks" on "noncapitalist wealth" permit. "To enroll this old-style bourgeoisie at the end of the *Ancien Régime* in the ranks of a fully constituted elite is like pulling the grass up by its shoots in order to make it grow" (1980, 136–137).

[196] Le Roy Ladurie (1975, 430), who sees feudal privilege, like all political power, as an "indirect generator of monetary profits." For large estates, "with a capitalist vocation," the French state served as the same kind of "sugardaddy" that it had for Colbertian manufacturers (p. 431).

[197] Bloch (1930, 517). As Bloch points out, sometimes it was a matter of reinterpreting feudal privileges, but sometimes merely a matter of exercising them. Moore calls this "a penetration of commercial and capitalist practices by feudal methods" (1966, 63).

[198] Goubert (1969, 234; see also 181–182). This is in fact similar to the description by Jones of English landlords, who he says "cashed the industrial potential of their territories [in the eighteenth century]" (1967, 48).

vis-à-vis lessees (*preneurs*)."[199] It was, in addition, the result not of backwardness but of technological progress. Improved methods of surveying and cartography permitted the seigniors to benefit from "a sort of perfecting of management techniques."[200] Far from there being a "closure" of the nobility, the problem was its "opening, too great for the cohesion of the order, too narrow [nonetheless] for the prosperity of the century."[201] And far from this being a period of great frustration for the French bourgeoisie, the proper theme of the eighteenth-century French history is "the rise of the Third Estate."[202]

One can hear the response of the advocates of the social interpretation. These bourgeois who "rose" in the *Ancien Régime* sought to "aristocratize" themselves as rapidly as possible. Their ideal was *vivre noblement*. It was only after 1789 that a new kind of bourgeoisie emerged, one ready to live as reinvesting bourgeois (one is almost tempted to add the refrain, one that was infused with a Protestant ethic).

Three kinds of answers are given to this retort. First, *vivre noblement* was not necessarily incompatible with continuing a profit-oriented mercantile activity. [203] Second, the implicit group of comparison, British bourgeois (even British industrialists), also shared the ideal of *vivre noblement*.[204] Third, the pattern did not change in France after the Revolution.[205]

---

[199] Le Roy Ladurie (1975, 435), who continues: "It is true—and herein enters the subjective element—that the lessor sometimes took a while to realize that the market had shifted in favor of the property-owners; in a case of this sort, once the awareness of advantage came, the lessor went twice as fast (*met les bouchées doubles*); he sought, with all the more energy, to give an assist to the *conjoncture*, and to pressure the lessees (*fermiers*), whom he had hitherto spared through negligence."

[200] Goubert (1974, 381).

[201] Furet (1978, 145). Furet further notes that the blockage was not from commoner to noble, but between the "small" noble of the sword and the "grand" but parvenu nobles of the court who constituted the ruling class. It is, he argues, the "small" nobles who were behind the edict of 1781, the *loi Ségur* (p. 140). Godechot, whose analysis once again is close to that of the classical interpretation, explains the presumed attempt by the nobility to monopolize government positions in the eighteenth century by the fact that the nobility found it difficult "to live off their revenues, given the constant increase in prices since 1730" (1965, 115).

Doyle, on the other hand, doubts there was any such monopolization of posts: "In social terms, most institutions in France seem to have become less, nor more, exclusive in their recruitment as the century went on" (1972, 121). Gruder's research on

royal intendants tends to confirm this argument. By comparing the social origins of intendants in the reign of Louis XIV with those in the reigns of Louis XV and XVI, Gruder finds that, far from there being an increase in aristocratic monopolization, if anything "the reverse was true" (1968, 206). Of course, the commoners who were ennobled in the eighteenth century did not go "from poverty to riches; the road to the top did not begin at the bottom" (p. 173). For Gruder the proper characterization of this governing class was "an aristocracy embodying a plutocracy" (p. 180).

[202] Cobban (1963, 262).

[203] This is Boulle's argument about the ennobled slave traders of Nantes who remained in commerce (1972, 89).

[204] See Crouzet: "We must not . . . overemphasize the frugality of these early British industrialists. Once they had built up their businesses and secured their fortunes, they nearly always relaxed somewhat, withdrawing more money and adopting a more comfortable way of life. Some of them bought landed estates and built themselves large mansions (1972b, 189). See also Jones: eighteenth-century English urban entrepreneurs "sought a final safebank in the purchase and embellishment of landed estates" (1967, 48).

[205] Cobban sees "*nouveaux riches*" replacing "the cultured upper bourgeoisie of the *ancien régime*."

If it is indeed "not possible to discern a fundamental cleavage at this time between the bourgeoisie and the nobility,"[206] what then explains the French Revolution, since surely *something* occurred in 1789? This argument thus far has eliminated class antagonism as an explanation, since the economic roles of the social categories, noble and bourgeois, are considered to have been highly congruent.[207] Tocqueville also eliminates as an explanation a difference in political rights—"neither [aristocrat nor bourgeois] had any"; and a difference in privileges—"those of the bourgeoisie [in the *Ancien Régime*] were [also] immense." This leaves only the difference that nobility and bourgeoisie led "separate [social] lives."[208] Tocqueville concluded nonetheless that the Revolution was the "natural, indeed inevitable, outcome" of the various particular aspects of the *Ancien Régime*, "so inevitable yet so completely unforeseen." The Revolution occurred through the coming together of the two "ruling passions" of eighteenth-century France, the "indomitable hatred of inequality" and the "desire to live . . . as free men."[209]

The recent Tocquevillians in France have continued this explanatory model, combining an amorphous melange of particulars[210] and the emphasis on a change in values.[211] But they have made one major change in the argument. The Revolution is no longer seen as "inevitable." It has now become an "accident," the coincidental result of the telescoping of three

---

He says disdainfully: "We can call it the triumph of the bourgeoisie if by this term we mean the venal officers, lawyers, professional men, proprietors, with a few financiers and merchants, who invested their money, for the most part, in land or *rentes*, after venal offices were no longer available. . . . In their way of life they were the heirs of the obsolescent *noblesse*, and if they were bourgeois their aim was to be *bourgeois vivant noblement*" (1963, 251, 264–265). Of course, this undoing of the social interpretation serves in turn as grist for the mill of arguments such as those of Landes. But that no doubt was not something that would have perturbed Cobban.

[206] Lucas (1973, 91): "The middle class of the late Ancien Régime displayed no significant functional differences from the nobility, no significant difference in accepted values and above all no consciousness of belonging to a class whose economic and social characteristics were antithetical to the nobility."

[207] As Palmer says, "it is one of the puzzles of the Revolution that class animosity, or antagonism between noble and non-noble, should have been so little in evidence in 1787 and much of 1788" (1959, 457).

[208] Tocqueville (1953, 361–362).

[209] Tocqueville (1955, 1, 203, 207–208).

[210] See Furet & Richet (1973, 19–27). As Anderson remarks of a similar melange drawn up by Althusser about the Russian Revolution, such a melange is "mere empirical pluralism," conjuring up many circumstances and currents, but failing to establish "their material hierarchy and interconnection" (1980, 77).

[211] See Richet: "The Revolution of 1789 resulted from a double awareness (*prise de conscience*) of the elites achieved through a long journey. Awareness, first of all, of their autonomy vis-à-vis the political order, of their consequent need to limit its power. An awareness that was shared by all, wherein the nobility played the role of initiator and educator, but which was enlarged to include wealth, property, and talent. It was the Enlightenment. However this common will aborted momentarily on the terrain of the homogeneity of the ruling group" (1969, 23). Hence, Tocqueville's final explanation recurs.

It should be noted, here a divergence with Cobban who is more hostile to the *whole* of the Revolution. "The end of the eighteenth century may truly be said to have witnessed a partial transformation from an individualist to a collectivist view of society. . . . The Revolution ends the age of individualism and opens that of nationalism. . . . In all this can be seen not the fulfillment but the frustration of the Enlightenment" (1968a, 25).

revolutions (that of the Assembly, of Paris and the towns, and of the countryside) into a single time period; it was "the popular intervention that transformed the rhythms of the revolution."[212] The shift in emphasis is important analytically but understandable politically. Tocqueville was seeking to persuade conservative forces to accept the Revolution, which was not as bad, he said in effect, as they thought, whereas his successors were seeking to persuade liberal intellectuals that all was not virtue in the Revolution (the Girondins *sí*, Robespierre *no*). As Furet himself says, "for almost 200 years, the history of the Revolution has never been other than an account of causation, thus a discourse about identity."[213]

By renouncing the concept of a bourgeois revolution, Furet and Richet wish to identify instead with a "liberal revolution," a revolution they say began earlier in 1789. They are quite explicit about what is to them the most significant intellectual question concerning the French revolution:

> Let us dare ask the question: as a result of what accidents did the liberal revolution fail in the short run, that revolution which was launched (*enfantée*) in the eighteenth century, and would be finally achieved decades later by the French bourgeoisie?[214]

August 10, 1792 marks for them the date that began the great *"dérapage"*[215] from the path of liberalism which reached its apogee during the Terror, that "brief parenthesis and counter-current" in the "immense thrust of liberalism" spanning the period 1750 to 1850.

It was, it seems, the patriotic fervor of the masses which undid liberalism.[216] Furet and Richet reproach Soboul for analyzing Year II as an "annunciation" of 1871 or 1917.[217] But is not their analysis equally a certain reading of the history of the twentieth century? In any case, they

---

[212] Furet & Richet (1973, 102; cf. Furet, 1963, 472). Calling the role of the popular revolutions "accidental" in terms of the long-term structural evolution does not apparently mean they were unimportant, since we are also adjured to "restitute to the revolutionary fact itself, to the *event*, its creative role of historical discontinuity" (Furet & Richet, 1973, 8).

Nonetheless, we are now so far from Tocqueville's word "inevitable" that Furet makes "the necessity of the event" one of the two main implausible presuppositions of the concept of bourgeois revolution—the other being the "rupture of time" (1978, 36).

[213] Furet (1978, 18–19).

[214] Furet & Richet (1973, 126).

[215] Furet & Richet (1973, 10). In the English translation of Furet and Richet, the chapter titled "Le dérapage de la révolution" was called "The revolution blown off course." This is a reasonable (if perhaps too nautical) a translation, but has the

inconvenience of changing the noun into a verb and making it difficult therefore to refer later to the concept of "dérapage" in English. Higonnet, for example, translates it differently in two sucessive pages as "deviation" and "slide" (1981, 4–5). I prefer therefore to keep the French term in English, since it seems to me the central term of the entire analysis by Furet and Richet.

[216] "Against a king suspected of treason, against the generals who refuse to fight, against the Brissotins who hesitate between power and the opposition, there is unleashed a firm popular reflex which has at least found its name—patriotism. . . . It is a second revolution. . . .

"Revolutionary patriotism became [on August 10, 1792] a religion. It already had its martyrs. It would soon get, after the military setbacks, its Inquisition and its stakes" (Furet & Richet, 1973, 129, 157).

[217] Furet & Richet (1973, 204).

draw one conclusion from their analysis of this period which is impeccably Soboulian—that, after Year II, the bourgeoisie rediscovered its true objectives: "economic freedom, individualism in property, limited suffrage."[218] But if that is the case, the critique of the concept of a bourgeois revolution loses some of its force. To be sure, the dating of Furet's "liberal" revolution is somewhat different, somewhat longer, than Soboul's "bourgeois" revolution. It is less political, more "cultural" perhaps. And the two analyses are in profound disaccord about the interpretion of Year II. The implications once again for the study of the *Russian* Revolution are different. But the revisionist and the social interpretation of what this historic turning point represents for France are less antithetical than all the fanfare might lead one to believe.

That this is so can be seen by the numerous attempts to find a mode of reconciling the two analyses. These attempts share a common characteristic: they seek to incorporate what seems correct in the critique of the concept of the bourgeois revolution without incorporating the political implications that have been drawn from this critique.

Robin accepts the critique of Furet that, if one is analyzing a change in the mode of production, it is necessarily an analysis that must be made about a long term. A social revolution cannot transform the "rhythm of productive forces; it can only render such a transformation possible." It was not the social revolution but the industrial revolution which permitted the passage from a formal to a real subsumption of labor, and this industrial revolution was "clearly posterior to the social revolution."[219]

Furthermore, it is true that the difference between the nobility and the bourgeoisie in economic roles in the eighteenth century had become relatively minor. Both were "mixed classes,"[220] and most seigniors were transforming themselves into capitalist landlords. Once one asserts that France was following neither the English path nor the "Prussian path" but represented an in-between case, and that France was in a typical stage of "transition" from feudalism to capitalism going on for several centuries *before and after* the French Revolution,[221] it is no longer dif-

---

[218] Furet & Richet (1973, 258).

[219] Robin (1970, 52).

[220] Grenon & Robin (1976, 28).

[221] Robin (1973, 41–43). A full-scale rebuttal of Robin is to be found in a book edited by Soboul. Guibert-Sledziewski argues that Robin poses the problem as the existence of two alternative modes of transition—either through disintegration of feudal forces or through their incorporation into capitalism—and says that this formulation eliminates "a fundamental aspect of the problem: the problem of the necessity of the French Revolution." The true alternative is rather between the "reactionary recuperation of capitalist tendencies" by feudalism or

the "entry into force of capitalist relations of production in revolutionary France" (1977, 48–50). The latter occurred via the Revolution, thus saving France from following the Prussian path (pp. 66–75). (This argument is similar to that of Moore, 1966, passim.)

Finally, Guibert-Sledziewski accuses Robin of sliding into a position no different from that of Richet: "[Robin's] desire to pose a 'problematic of this transition' [from feudalism to capitalsim] leads her to make the transition a specific stage of the bourgeois revolution, a stage which would not have the panache of 89–94, but which would indicate as much as the violent phase the necessity of a decisive

ficult to reconcile the perspective of the long term and a Marxist analysis.[222]

There is a second mode of reconciling the two. Zapperi asserts that it is correct to say that the quarrel between the Third Estate and the nobility was merely a quarrel between competing elites, both of which for Zapperi were, however, precapitalist elites. The French Revolution was not a bourgeois revolution because France was *still* in a precapitalist stage of its history. To see the "vulgar polemics" of an urban mercantile stratum quarreling with a landed aristocracy as a class struggle requires a "strong dose of imagination." The bourgeoisie do not deserve the merit of attributing to them a "revolutionary path"; they achieved their ends "over long centuries" by expanding their role in civil society. To designate the French Revolution as a social revolution is to project backwards by analogy the proletarian revolution, whereas the bourgeoisie had not yet even created a situation in which the working class lived entirely off the sale of its labor force. The Soboulian scenario turns out to be a myth for Zapperi too, but one perpetrated by the Abbé Siéyès more than by Marx, although Marx played into the hands of "mercantile prejudices."[223]

There is a third way to accept the critique of the concept of bourgeois revolution without necessarily endorsing liberalism. It is to remove the bourgeoisie from its pedestal in favor of other groups whose actions are considered more consequential and which may be then said to define the true historical meaning of the event-period. Guérin made this case with some force already in 1946. The French Revolution had a "double character." It was both a bourgeois revolution *and* "a permanent revolution in its internal mechanism," which "bred an embryonic proletarian revolution," that is, an anti-*capitalist* revolution.[224]

confrontation between the rival modes of production. Thus the revolutionary 'phenomenon', as its appellation would indicate, would be merely a manifestation, a vicissitude of this vast confrontation: and what a vicissitude! A fulfillment of what Denis Richet calls the 'slow but revolutionary mutation' of nascent capitalism. . . . But it seems to us that any problematic of transition leads necessarily to a problematic of revolution" (Guibert-Sledziewski, 1977, 68).

[222] This is confirmed by the analyses of two orthodox Marxist historians, Manfred and Dobb.

Manfred: "Capitalism first emerged in France about the sixteenth century. Advancing slowly and gradually within feudal society, it reached its full development and maturity in the last third of the eighteenth century. The contradictions between the new productive forces and the dominant feudal order led to a period of ever sharper conflict. These contradictions then exploded all over the place" (1961, 5).

Dobb: "The industrial revolution . . . and the appearance on the scene of bourgeois relations of production do not coincide in time. . . . This requires an explanation and one that is able to cover a long time period (in England an interval of several centuries) going from the earliest appearances of bourgeois relations of production . . . to the industrial revolution. . . .

"The industrial revolution requires the maturation of a total situation. . . . It requires a long process of complex and prolonged development which in the end has a foreseeable outcome. . . . To speak of the concomitance of a certain number of factors does not, however, imply that it is a fortuitous 'unique event', one that is 'accidental'" (1961, 458–460).

[223] Zapperi (1974, 13–15, 83–86, 91–92).

[224] Guérin (1968, I, 17, 23, 27, and passim).

Guérin managed to unite Soboul and Furet in opposition to him. They both reject this perception of the role of the sans-culottes, this implicit reading of twentieth-century history. For Soboul, Guérin mistakes for a proletarian avant-garde what is largely "a rear-guard defending their positions in the traditional economy." The sans-culottes furthermore, says Soboul, were united with the bourgeoisie "on the essential matters, the hatred of the aristocracy and the will to be victorious."[225]

For Furet and Richet, too, the sans-culottes were largely rear-guard forces indulging in "Rousseauian" reminiscences, in search of "reactionary" utopias of a past golden age. If, during Year II, the sans-culottes quarreled with the government, it was the doing of their cadres, "a sort of sub-intelligentsia [a petty bourgeoisie] which had emerged out of the stalls and shops," who were jealous of those who had gained positions during the Revolution. Far from this being a class struggle, embryonic or otherwise, it was a mere power struggle, "a matter of rivalry between competing teams."[226]

It is clear now how the Guérin critique bypasses the Soboul–Furet quarrel in an opposite way from those of Robin and Zapperi. The latter agree with Furet that the French Revolution was not a bourgeois revolution in the way Soboul thinks it is, because the full social revolution occurred or was fulfilled *after* the French Revolution. Guérin however agrees with Soboul that Year II was no "*dérapage*" because the Jacobins were really no different from the Girondins. This was not, however, because they represented the high point of bourgeois radicalism but because they represented the high point of bourgeois political deception of the masses.[227] Robespierre may not incarnate "*dérapage*" but neither is he a hero for

---

[225] Soboul (1958a, 10, 1025). Kaplow echoes Soboul's riposte with this argument: "The [laboring] poor were not capable of sustaining their anger because they did not—could not—place it in a larger context. I submit that they were incapable of thinking in longer terms . . . because all their disabilities . . . had led them into the blind alley of the culture of poverty. . . . The revolutionary bourgeoisie began to destroy the psychological and social core of the culture of poverty by putting forth the idea that it was possible, not to say legitimate, to challenge the established order" (1972, 170). A curious argument for a Marxist to assert; it seems to imply that the proletariat can only emerge from its false consciousness via the example and the ministrations of the (revolutionary) bourgeoisie.

[226] Furet & Richet (1973, 206, 212–213).

[227] See Guérin: "Robespierre, of all the personalities of the Revolution, was the most popular. He had not yet revealed his true image. The *bras nus*

had not yet caught him *in flagrante delicto* of 'moderationism' " (1968, I, 411). Higonnet makes a similar point. Against the "traditional Marxist interpretation" that Jacobin ideology represents "the genuine and immediate expression of the real material goals which unified several classes," and first of all that of the "revolutionary bourgeoisie," he suggests that a "better explanation of the origins and functions of Jacobin ideology holds instead that the Jacobin world-view was, as it were, a progressive form of 'false consciousness'. . . . Within a week of the 'entire' destruction of feudal seigneurialism, the Constituents began their efforts to salvage as many feudal dues as they could in the name of bourgeois property. Sans-culottes and *honnêtes gens* began to part ways. Unable to accept this fully, the Revolutionary bourgeoisie, and the Jacobins in particular, were forced into a number of blind alleys" (1980, 46–48).

Guérin. The sans-culottes and Babouvism thus become even more central to his story than to that of Soboul (and Cobb, Rudé).[228]

The Guérin position emphasizes the role of the embryonic proletariat and thereby downplays the extent to which the French Revolution can be defined as primarily a bourgeois revolution. In parallel fashion, others emphasize the role of the peasantry not merely as a set of actors in an additional revolution side by side with the bourgeois revolution but as those who left the strongest mark on the French Revolution, which can be defined as the "first successful peasant revolution of modern times."[229] The peasants were the only group, it is argued, whose gains were not taken away in the Restoration of 1815.

This emphasis has been used to criticize Soboul[230] and to criticize Furet.[231] But the most important point is that its results in a perspective that sees the French Revolution as an anti-*capitalist* revolution. Le Roy Ladurie asks whether it would not be better to designate the "revolutionary antiseigniorialism" of the last years of the *Ancien Régime* as an "anticapitalist reaction," given the fact that it was against the enclosers, the irrigators, the modernizers that the peasants were reacting, and that where such improving landlords were lacking, as in Brittany, where there was no "penetration in depth" of capitalism, peasants were passive.[232] In a similar fashion, Hunecke sees precisely in the rise of laissez faire and the end of the control of bread prices the explanation of "the revolutionary mentality of the masses" which took the form of a "defensive reaction" against free trade and the laws of the market.[233]

---

[228] Guérin conceded in 1968 that Soboul and Rudé had "revised considerably their Robespierrist dogmatism and are more ready to admit that the decapitation of the Paris commune, the destruction of democracy at the base constituted a mortal blow to the Revolution" (1968, II, 524). As for Cobb, he has adopted a large part of "my criticisms of Robespierre and Robespierrism" but he is "rarely consequent with himself" (p. 534). In any case, Soboul and Cobb, however "inequitable they are in their criticisms of my work, have implicitly confirmed and completed it" (p. 536).

See Higonnet on the role of Babouvism: "Clearly, the importance of Babouvism depends on the place that one gives to socialism and class-war in the world-historical place of things. If the French Revolution is seen as a *Ding an sich,* Babeuf does not count for much. If it is seen as the first act of the People-versus-Capitalism, Babouvism matters a great deal" (1979, 780).

[229] Milward & Saul (1973, 252); cf. a more restrained version by Moore: "It is fair, therefore, to hold that the peasantry was the arbiter of the Revolution, though not its main propelling force" (1966, 77).

[230] See Mackrell: "The Marxist view that the Revolution saw both the overthrow of feudalism and the advent of capitalism to France hardly squares, among other facts, with the important part that the peasants took in the overthrowing of 'feudalism'" (1973, 174).

[231] See Hunecke who attacks "revisionist' historians (Cobban, Furet & Richet) on the grounds that the peasant revolution "announces the future more than it remembers the past" (1978, 315). Gauthier wants to see the peasants as playing a "progressive" role in the development of capitalism. "The peasantry was not opposed to capitalism in general, but to a form of capitalism favorable to the seigniors" (1977, 128).

[232] Le Roy Ladurie (1975, 568, 575). For a review of recent literature that attacks the view that peasants were somehow "retrograde" and emphasizes their anti-bourgeois role, see David Hunt (1984).

[233] Hunecke (1978, 319). "At the heart of the revolution of the poor peasants were two demands that were in no way whatsoever antifeudal: they wanted land to cultivate and the restoration of rights to the commons (*usi collectivi*)." The peasants were rebelling "not only against those with [feudal]

The centrality of the lord–peasant struggle (in the tradition of Barrington Moore) finally leads Skocpol also to insist that the French Revolution was not a "bourgeois revolution" and that it was not comparable to the English Revolution. It was rather the expression of "contradiction centered in the structures of old-regime states." It was as much or more a "bureaucratic mass-incorporating and state-strengthening revolution as it was (in any case) a bourgeois revolution." In this sense, the appropriate comparison is to the Russian and Chinese revolutions of the twentieth century. But neither was it then part of a liberal revolution since the political result of the peasant revolts in the French Revolution was a "more centralized and bureaucratic state, not a liberal-parliamentary regime."[234]

What then is this whole argument about? Clearly, the French Revolution did occur and was a monumental "event" in terms of its diverse and continuing consequences for France and the world. It is also undoubtedly a "myth" in the Sorelian sense; to this day it remains politically important, and not only in France, to capture this myth and harness it.

"The revolution," Clemenceau said in 1897, "is a bloc." For Cobban, this is the "real fallacy" behind all the particular myths of the French Revolution, the idea that there is a something, one thing, "which you can be for or against."[235] Lefebvre is quite right to retort:

> The convocation of the Estates-General was a 'good tidings'; it announced the birth of a new society, in accordance with justice, in which life would be better; in the Year II, the same myth inspired the *sans-culottes*; it has survived in our tradition, and as in 1789 and in 1793, it is revolutionary.[236]

It is because this myth is so powerful that Cobban, instead of denouncing the Revolution as evil in the fashion of the nineteenth-century opponents,

privileges but also (and probably primarily) against the 'revolutionary bourgeoisie'" (pp. 313–315). Similarly, see Moore: "The radical thrust behind the Revolution based on the *sans-culottes* and sections of the peasantry, was explicitly and strongly anticapitalist" (1966, 69).

Cobban also sees the French Revolution as "a revolution not for, but against, capitalism" (1964, 172). In this version, however, the triumph is not that of the peasants alone but of "the conservative, propertied, land-owning classes, large and small" (p. 170). This is in fact said to be one of the features that put "the economic development of English society . . . so far in advance of that of France" (p. 146).

[234] Skocpol (1979, 29, 41, 181). "Social revolutions . . . have changed state structures as much or more than they have changed class relations, societal values, and social institutions" (p. 29). A strange argument: *social* revolutions are defined primarily not by *social* changes but by changes in the primary modern *political* institution, the state. What then are *political* revolutions? And if it is not a social revolution that changes class relations, societal values, and social institutions, is that because the latter are changed only gradually, never in a "revolutionary" manner? Perhaps then it is the very concept of "social revolution" that needs to be reexamined.

[235] Cobban (1968d, 108).

[236] Lefebvre (1956, 345). Furet pours scorn on this analysis because it is imbued with faith: "It would not be difficult to demonstrate that [Lefebvre, a great historian] had, as his synthetic vision, . . . nothing more than the conviction of the *cartel des gauches* or the Popular Front" (1978, 22). This does not seem to me a very telling argument.

seeks to undermine the myth of attacking its credibility, an attack which even a defender of the classical model of the bourgeois revolution like Vidotto admits has been relatively "persuasive." As Vidotto says, however, to respond to these criticisms by widening the definitions, as some defenders of the concept do, leads to "terminological indeterminacy" and makes the whole explanation incomprehensible. Therefore he finds the concept of the bourgeois revolution in its classical form "an unrenounceable heritage for those who move in a Marxist orbit, and not only for them."[237]

But is this heritage unrenounceable for those who wish to hail the "good tidings"? As we have seen, time and again, the interpretations of the French Revolution serve as commentaries on the twentieth century. But may it not be possible that some of our confusions about the twentieth century are due to our misinterpretations of the eighteenth? If so, then to perpetuate models because they represent an "unrenounceable heritage" is to ensure strategic error in the interests of maintaining the form of sentiments that were once useful (but may no longer be so) for collective cohesion. I don't believe we should try to preserve the image of the French Revolution as a bourgeois revolution in order to preserve that of the Russian Revolution as a proletarian one. But I also do not believe we should try to create the image of the French Revolution as a liberal one in order to tarnish that of the Russian Revolution as a totalitarian one. Neither category—bourgeois nor liberal—classifies well what did in fact go on.

Furet says, "the Revolution incarnates *the illusion of politics;* it transforms objective reality (*le subi*) into subjective consciousness (*en conscient*)." He reminds us that Marx considered that Thermidor represented the "revenge of real society."[238] He draws from this anti-voluntarist conclusions. But by insisting on reanalyzing the French Revolution in the context both of long-term social change (with its transmutations of the very concept of the bourgeoisie) and of a rupture in the dominant political ideology, he gets closer to the spirit of historical materialism than he believes. I am sometimes tempted to classify Furet as a closet Marxist revolutionary, while identifying Soboul, by his exaltation of Year II and his reification of concepts like bourgeoisie and aristocracy into sociological categories, as a double agent of rampart bourgeois liberalism. By refusing the concept of bourgeois revolution on the grounds of the fluidity of the categories themselves, the "revisionists" of the classic interpretation may be making it possible to see how a process of class polarization actually operates—

[237] Vidotto (1979, 51).

[238] Furet (1978, 43, 84). But who is "real society"? Barber notes that "the bourgeoisie who suffered most . . . were those of the middle bourgeoisie, who aimed at legal, political, military, or ecclesiastical careers. . . . It was very difficult to legislate either the great financiers or the leading intellectuals out of existence" (1955, 143).

through long, sinuous, persistent restructuring in which the French Revolution plays its role but is not a *decisive turning point* (drums roll!).

Marx had one major fault. He was a little too Smithian (competition is the norm of capitalism, monopoly a distortion) and a little too Schumpeterian (the entrepreneur is the bearer of progress). Many twentieth-century Marxists no longer share these prejudices, but they think that this is because capitalism has evolved. Once, however, one inverts these assumptions, then the use of a dialectical and materialist framework for analysis pushes one to a very different reading of the history of the sixteenth to eighteenth centuries, even of the nineteenth, than Marx himself made for the most part.

But surely, I can hear the objection, the French Revolution spoke the language of anti-feudalism. Serfdom was finally abolished; guilds were finally forbidden; the aristocracy and the clergy finally ceased to be privileged orders. Yes, all this is more or less true. It is certainly the case that, in the *Ancien Régime*, at a time when the ideology of "orders" was dominant, even the wealthiest of *haut-bourgeois*, insofar as they were not ennobled, suffered from social disdain and material discrimination. Nor was it enough to purchase nobility. In 1781, the *loi Ségur* rendered it necessary to be a noble of the fourth generation to become an army officer. Whether this was merely a passing snobbism of the aristocracy of the sword, which would have soon been revoked or ignored, we shall never know. It was nonetheless a fiercely felt irritation by the upper strata of the Third Estate as well as by the recently ennobled nobility of the robe.

And then came the French Revolution. For a few years, on the streets, people were actually stopped and aggressively asked, "Are you of the Third Estate?" and the answer had better be yes. This difficult moment was followed by Thermidor and Napoleon and the Restoration and things were back to normal somewhat. *Haut-bourgeois* once again sought to obtain noble titles, at least until 1870. And after that, they continued to seek signs of formal social status, as successful bourgeois have since the emergence of capitalism as a world-system.

If, then, anti-feudalism is not what the French Revolution was about, why then the language of anti-feudalism? Braudel has an excellent answer:

> Might is not be thought that it was at least partly because the language of capitalism had not found the vocabulary to handle a new and surprising situation, that the French peasant reverted to the familiar old language of anti-feudalism?[239]

But if this is the answer for the peasantry, how can we explain that the notables of the Third Estate also came to use the same language? One answer is that the noisy quarrel of the "bourgeoisie" and the "aristocracy"

---

[239] Braudel (1982, 297).

was a gigantic diversion, in the two senses of the word diversion: fun and games; and displacement of the attention of others, in this case, the peasants and the sans-culottes.[240]

Yet, of course, something did change in 1789, and even more in 1791–1793. As Anderson has said, "the whole ideological world of the West was transformed."[241] The transition from feudalism to capitalism had long since occurred. That is the whole argument of these volumes. The transformation of the state structure was merely the continuation of a process that had been going on for two centuries. In this regard Tocqueville is correct. Thus, the French Revolution marked neither basic economic nor basic political transformation. Rather, the French Revolution was, in terms of the capitalist world-economy, the moment when the ideological superstructure finally caught up with the economic base. It was the consequence of the transition, not its cause nor the moment of its occurrence.

The grande bourgeoisie, transposition of the aristocracy in a capitalist world, believed in profit, but not in liberal ideology. *La carrière ouverte aux talents,* universal truth, the categorical imperative are first of all ideological themes in the narrow sense. They are instrumental, diversionary creeds, not meant to be taken seriously whenever they interfere with the maximal accumulation of capital. Nonetheless, the ideology *also* reflects the structural endpoint of the capitalist process, the final bourgeoisification of the upper classes, where all advantage will be derived from *current* position in the economic structure rather than from *past* position. And the proclamation of the instrumental ideology is itself an important factor in the structural unfolding of this process. What was meant as a screen became over time a constraint.

The French Revolution had, in addition, one further meaning, and this is the sense in which it announced the future. The French Revolution represented the first of the antisystemic revolutions of the capitalist world-economy—in small part a success, in larger part a failure. But the "myth" that it represents is not a bourgeois myth but an anti-bourgeois myth.

---

[240] See Chaussinand-Nogaret: "It is only as of the moment that the popular forces enter the scene for reasons that have nothing to do with the revolution desired by the notables that a fault appears which will eventually widen the ditch between nobility and bourgeoisie. For it now became a question of saving one's hide, and to that end any maneuver is legitimate. Threatened just as much as the nobility, the bourgeoisie played a major trump card, the comedy of scandalized virtue; it shouted alongside the people and displaced onto the 'aristocracy' the tempest which threatened to sweep them away. . . . And in post-revolutionary society, the two orders, having reconciled their differences, once again shared power" (1975, 277).

[241] Anderson (1980, 36). He actually says this transformation results from the two revolutions—the French and the American. See also Lynn Hunt who says that one of the "most fateful consequences" of the French Revolution was "the invention of ideology," which represented a "new political culture" (1984, 12, 15). Similarly, Sewell speaks of "the idea of revolution itself" being one of the "unanticipated" outcomes of the French Revolution (1985, 81).

The concept of the bourgeois revolution serves ultimately the same function as the concept of the industrial revolution. The latter purports to explain why Great Britain captured a disproportionate amount of world surplus in this particular period, particularly vis-à-vis its chief rival, France. The concept of the bourgeois revolution explains the same phenomenon, using French rather than British data. It tells us why France lost out. France had its "bourgeois revolution" more than a century later than Great Britain, and a "bourgeois revolution" is presumed to be the prerequisite to an "industrial revolution."

We are in no sense denying that, in the period 1730–1840, Great Britain (or more exactly the bourgeoisie who had their territorial base in Great Britain) gained a major competitive edge over France. We shall now seek to explain how this happened, without having recourse to either of these two interlinked misconceptions, the industrial and the bourgeois revolutions.

2

STRUGGLE IN THE CORE— PHASE III: 1763–1815

The English printmaker, James Gillray (1757–1815), produced some 1500 satirical prints on contemporary political issues. Pitt and Napoleon were two of his favorite subjects. In this engraved cartoon, "The Plumb-pudding in danger: —or—State Epicures taking un Petit Souper," published on February 26, 1805 by H. Humphrey, Pitt with a trident fork in the Atlantic Ocean cuts the globe west of Britain from the pole to the equator, obtaining the West Indies. Napoleon, using his sword as a knife, cuts France, Spain, Swiss, Italy, and the Mediterranean from Europe, but misses Sweden and Russia. A subtitle reads: " 'The great Globe itself, and all which it inherit' (*Tempest*, IV, 1), is too small to satisfy such insatiable appetites. . . ."

The Treaty of Paris in 1763 placed Great Britain in an advantageous position to accomplish what it had been seeking to do for a century already—outdistance France decisively at all levels, economically, politically, and militarily.[1] It was not, however, until 1815 that this task was accomplished, and it was not easy.

This third and last phase of the continuous and open struggle between the two claimants to hegemony occurred under circumstances of a renewed expansion of the capitalist world-economy, itself the result of the restructuring of this world-economy during the long stagnation of the seventeenth century (which I analyzed in Volume II). This renewed expansion created what Labrousse has called "the great century of prosperity . . . from the 1730's to just before 1820."[2] Labrousse was speaking primarily of France, but the description applies as well to Great Britain, and indeed for the world-economy as a whole, as we shall see. To be sure, one must always ask, prosperity for whom? Furthermore, the concept of a long upswing does not exclude the existence of cyclical phases within this long upswing, as indeed there were. But during this long period we can nonetheless talk of "a continuous movement of rising production, prices, and revenues."[3]

Morineau denounces what he believes is a prevalent "good fairy" explanation of this price rise. He prefers to see it not as one long-term phenomenon but rather as a succession of short-term price rises resulting from poor harvests, linked to each other by an "inertia" that operated against price reductions following each spurt of higher prices (cherté), "which thus had a cumulative effect."[4] This observation, however, does not deny the trend; it is rather a particular mode of explaining it.

To understand this story more clearly, we must begin with the so-called crises d'Ancien Régime, of which this period has been said to be the "last" historical moment—for Europe and perhaps for the whole capitalist world-economy. The crise d'Ancien Régime, as described classically by Labrousse, was a phenomenon of the harvest, of the short term. Its operation depended on the centrality of cereals as a staple of the diet and

[1] "In 1762 the Peace of Paris sealed the defeat of Louis XIV, as the Peace of the Pyrenees in 1659 had sealed the defeat of Philip II" (Dehio, 1962, 117).

[2] Labrousse (1954, vii). In an earlier work, Labrousse was even more precise, speaking of "the long surge of prosperity observed for France between 1733 and 1817" (1944, xi). Léon (1966, 20) similarly speaks of the 100 "decisive" years between the end of the Regency (1723) and the beginnings of the July Monarchy (1830s).

[3] Soboul (1976a, 4). P. K. O'Brien says: "We have no real data for rising production; only price data" (personal communication). Labrousse, in his classic work on prices offers similar indices for French prices—1733:100, 1789:192, 1816:254—and for European: 100, 177, 269. He calls this rise in prices "unique . . . in its amplitude" since the movement 300 years earlier (Labrousse, 1933, 143–144.) Sée calls it "a replica of the famous rise of the sixteenth century" (1933, viii). See also Lüthy (1961, 12). Abel (1973, 269–270) calcualtes a 163% increase in wheat prices for France from 1740 to 1810, a 250% increase for England, and overall in Europe a doubling at least of prices, thus making France one of the relatively less inflationary countries. Deane and Cole (1967, 14) speak of the "tendency for the price level to rise" in Great Britain, beginning "a little before the mid-century," but reserving for the 1790s the description of "violent inflationary disturbances."

[4] Morineau (1978, 386).

the rapid response of market prices to shifts in local supply, bread being
essential to survival for the mass of the population, and transport being
slow and costly. For large producers, a food shortage meant a sudden rise
in prices and hence usually a dramatic rise in profits, even if their stock
diminished. But for the mass of small producers, the same situation
offered not profits but disaster, which at first sight seems paradoxical. The
reason is that the harvest of a small producer was divided into multiple (of
course, unequal) parts: one part for seed for the following year, one part
for tithe, one part (sometimes) for rent in kind, one part for subsistence,
and one part for sale on the market. Whenever the harvest was bad, it was
the last part which largely or entirely disappeared (as well as perhaps a
segment of the part for subsistence). Thus, the sale prices may have been
high but the small producer usually had nothing to sell under the
circumstance of a poor harvest. Perhaps, even worse, he himself needed to
buy in order to eat, and to buy when prices were high.[5]

For the other small consumers, of course, high prices were equally
disastrous. Their expenses suddenly expanded at precisely the point in
time when unemployment increased, since a large percentage of salaried
work was in fact part-time agricultural work, the need for which diminished precisely because of the same poor harvest. Furthermore, textile
producers tended simultaneously to slow down production because of a
reduction in their short-term demand caused by the bad harvest, which
further increased the degree of unemployment.[6]

This scarcely sounds like prosperity, which is Morineau's point.
However, it was also not something new in the eighteenth century. The
short-term harvest crises had always functioned this way to the extent that
the agrarian sector operated with a significant number of small peasants
(whether proprietors or tenants), with staples as a large part of the popular
diet, and with a high cost of transport of staples. What was less usual was
that there was some stickiness in the prices in the years when harvests were
good. The advantage to the large landlords (and merchants) of poor
harvest years should normally have been compensated by the advantage to
the small peasants of good harvest years. In fact, however, as agricultural
prices climbed after 1730, so did "rent," rent owed in one form or another
by the small producers to the larger landowners.[7]

What explains this? A succession of years of bad weather?[8] We are often

---

[5] See Danière (1958a, 318–319). Landes argues,
however (1958a, 335) that this effect of harvests on
business activity is restricted to "extreme" (that is,
famine) situations.

[6] There are many descriptions in Labrousse's
writings and elsewhere of this phenomenon. Perhaps the most lucid brief statement is in Labrousse
(1945, iv–v).

[7] This is, of course, the central empirical finding

of Labrousse's work. See in particular Labrousse
(1933, II, 379, 399, 444).

[8] The "real crisis of French agriculture, at the
end of the reign of Louis XV, and occasionally
throughout the reign of Louis XVI, [was] the crisis
caused by a worsening of climatic conditions" (Morineau, 1971, 67; see also 1969a, 419). But see below
on the problems of "good weather."

inclined to fall back on this kind of "tempting" explanation, as Vilar calls it. The real question, as he reminds us, is located, however, "at the point of arrival, in the social arena" (that is, at the point of distribution of revenues and payments), and "not at the point of departure, in the climate."[9] This is, of course, absolutely correct, but had the "social arena" changed so much from the previous century that it had created a different economic profile from that of earlier times?

One of the issues that gets lost in this discussion of the *crises d'Ancien Régime* is one to which, nonetheless, Labrousse himself drew attention early on. While short-term price rises had convulsive effects, and in particular were associated with reduced production, long-term price rises had the opposite significance, "the same significance as today,"[10] for they led to long-term increases in production. And this had to do with the difference in the mode of operation of local markets on the one hand (domain, par excellence, of the small producer, though not of him alone), and regional or world-economy-wide markets on the other (domain primarily of the large producer). *Crises d'Ancien Régime* were phenomena of the *local* markets. Production for the larger, more distant markets were "orthodox" capitalist phenomena, which operated on the simple principle that higher prices reflected some unfulfilled effective demand in the world-economy and therefore a potential long-term profit for those who were ready to expand production. In relation to this larger arena, climate played a secondary role, even in agriculture. What was crucial rather was the general rate of accumulation of capital.

We have previously argued[11] that, in the long stagnation of the seventeenth century, the core countries reacted by attempting to concentrate all the major sources of capitalist profit within their frontiers: world-market oriented cereals production, the new metallurgical and textile sectors, the new transport infrastructure, and the entrepôts of Atlantic trade. They more or less succeeded in this. Furthermore, in the intracore struggle, the United Provinces, which did best by far initially, was eventually undercut by English and French competition. Between England and France, the struggle was more even and, as of the turn of the eighteenth century, neither could be said to have been significantly stronger than the other within the world-economy. The slow restructuring of the production processes within the core led to some redistribution of revenue within each of these countries such that one could speak of some increased "home" demand and the tentative beginnings of a further expansion of the frontiers of the world-economy. In short, most of the processes we associate with the period after 1750 (technological changes in agriculture and industry, geographical expansion, growing demand within the core)

[9] Vilar (1974, 40).
[10] Labrousse (1944, xvi).

[11] See Wallerstein (1980, especially 259–275).

were already occurring in the century previously, albeit at a slower pace.[12] However, with the economic expansion of the world-economy, there came to be renewed geographic differentiation of production (specialization) and increased mechanization in the core (the "industrial revolution").

The main achievement of the long seventeenth century, from the point of view of the core countries, had been the ability of the capitalists of these countries to corner such profits as there were to be had. The main drawback had been the limited overall demand, one of whose signs was the stagnation of population growth. The elimination of marginal producers throughout the world-economy plus the limited redistribution of revenues (primarily in core zones) laid the base for a new era of expansion, which began somewhere in the first half of the eighteenth century, and reached a high level in the second half, culminating in that period of profitable turbulence, the Franco–British wars of 1792–1815.

The traditional correlate of economic expansion (both its evidence and its consequence) is a population upsurge, and there seems to be general agreement that one began circa 1740, give or take 10 years.[13] In the previous chapter, we have indicated why the explanation of demographic rise in terms of socioeconomic transformations seems plausible: whether it be via mortality decrease (through better hygiene and more food far more than through better medicine, at this time), or via increased fertility. It is the explanation of fertility that is given pride of place by the majority of current scholars. Flinn is representative when he argues that while mortality remained largely "in God's sector," fertility was "entirely in man's [sic!] sector,"[14] the key variable being the age of marriage of women.[15] To the

[12] "This habit of playing down technological change before the mid-eighteenth century and conversely exaggerating its novelty in the second half of that century has a long history" (Jones, 1970, 49).

[13] Deane says the usual date for England is the 1740s, and that even if the upsurge was "modest" before the 1780s, it was the case that "the growth that appears to date from the 1740s, was not reversed" (1979, 214). Chambers says that the usual dates for the "demographic revolution" in England are 1750–1800, and that even if Tucker (1963) is correct that this is compensatory for the "low rates" of 1720–1740, "the side effects on the demographic and economic situation that followed were profound" (1972, 122). Similarly, Wrigley and Schofield have a chart (1981, 207) that shows a sharp upturn from 1750 (but dated as of 1740, on pp. 210–211). For France, Le Roy Ladurie's synthetic overview (1975, 364–365) is: "After 1717, there is the beginning of an upturn (*reprise*) and soon a sharp rise (*essor*)!" He speaks of 1737–1745 as "a pause, a momentary stagnation," after which the growth "resumes beginning in 1745–1750" and soon "breaks through the ceiling." Toutain says that

"about 1720 already, the [French] population was growing" (1963, 17).

To be sure, as Helleiner (1965, 86) reminds us, this was not "unique," but comparable to earlier demographic expansions. Wrigley and Schofield make the same point (1981, 211), as does Morineau, who adds a skeptical note about "the demographic progession of the eighteenth century, to the degree that it has been established" (1971, 85). Flinn (1981, 76) evinces a similar skepticism in his emphasis on contrasting the whole of the sixteenth to eighteenth centuries with the nineteenth in which "growth rates in most European countries were substantially greater."

[14] Flinn (1981, 18).

[15] See Flinn (1981, 21) and Lee & Schofield (1981, 27). Wrigley and Schofield, however (1981, 247–248) indicate that, while this was true for England, a fall in mortality played a major role in certain other countries such as Sweden. France is cited as an in-between case. Habakkuk (1953, 133) too says that "in pre-industrial society," the largest variation will come from the age of marriage and therefore the effect on the birth rate.

evidence of lowered marital age some analysts add the deduced and negative evidence of the decline of the (inferred) rate of contraception (by coitus interruptus) which is believed to have occurred in seventeenth-century England and France as a reaction by the peasantry to hard times.[16]

In effect, by the reduction of the population in the previous century, the survivors ate better, with the "real wage" level thereby slowly rising. Eventually, this "psychology" of austerity bred its own undoing. When, then, there was a "run of good harvests,"[17] which seems to have been the case for the period 1715–1750 (a run itself the consequence in part of improving techniques?), it is easy to see why such a run could ignite the increase in fertility observed.

If England was perhaps a bit more productive as the century began, the literature on England also emphasizes a setback, resulting precisely from this advantage, somewhere in the second quarter of the century: the so-called "agricultural depression," which was a classic case of a price decline resulting from the good harvests.[18] Two important points should be noted, however. One is that the price changes at this time did not seem to disrupt the growth in agricultural output either in terms of labor productivity or per capita production.[19] The second is no doubt in part the explanation of the first—the consensus that the 1730s and the 1740s saw a tendency for rents to fall (plus more frequent arrears on rents), and "the granting of various concessions by the landlord to the tenants,"[20] such that the period could be considered "a golden age for the agricultural laborer."[21]

The low prices of cereals, a phenomenon that spread across Europe from circa 1620 and lasted until circa 1750, thus saw one of its most acute expressions at the end of this period, and particularly in the country which was the largest grain exporter at that point, England. But this long-term

[16] See Wrigley (1969, 181) for arguments based on Colyton and Chaunu (1972a, 295–296) for arguments concerning Normandy. Chaunu includes a discussion of how neo-Augustinian moral theology favored an ascetic Malthusianism via a view of coitus interruptus as a "lesser evil."

Le Roy Ladurie (1969, 1600) reminds us, in addition, that there is a biological link between acute famines (of which there were many in the seventeenth century) and temporary sterilization. "It is as if the organism suppresses its function of reproduction, and this becomes a luxury if the price is the sacrifice of the vital function."

[17] Deane (1979, 49). The literature on France does not acknowledge this directly, but it does talk of the end of famines. See Meuvret (1971e, 275).

[18] The dating as usual is subject to much controversy. Mingay (1956, 324) places it at 1730–1750, but especially to 1745. Chambers talks of 1720–1750 (1972, 143), Little (1976, 5) of "the second quarter" but also of the 1730s and 1740s.

P. K. O'Brien, however says: "There is no decline in agricultural prices, merely stability up to the 1740's. The John view is not backed by data" (personal communication).

[19] Crafts (1981, 3) asserts: "Agriculture . . . was emphatically not a declining enterprise—indeed, in the second quarter of the century the much greater pressure of demand on its limited supplies drove up agricultural prices relative to industrial prices." Cole (1981, 48) similarly argues: "The new estimates undoubtedly provide powerful quantitative evidence for the Johns-Jones view . . . that the rising agricultural productivity was the major factor in the growth of the economy as a whole in the early part of the eighteenth century." See, however, the reserves of Ippolito (1975, 311) on the "magnitude" of the contribution of this period to the "forthcoming industrial revolution."

[20] Mingay (1956, 324).

[21] Little (1976, 18–19).

decline in prices itself helped to create the sources of new demand (in better distribution of revenue) which gave impetus to the demographic reprise. It also encouraged agricultural capitalists in the core to search for new sources of profit. First, they intensified their efforts to concentrate cash-crop production in their hands and to reduce the share of the direct producers. Second, they sought to capture new sources of profit via innovation in industry, which in turn led to an intensification of the conflict over world markets. Each story needs to be told in turn.

The story of agriculture in the eighteenth century is normally recounted in very different languages in the cases of France and of Great Britain. In France, the reigns of Louis XV and Louis XVI were marked, it is said, by a "seigniorial reaction," which in turn is said to have been one of the factors (the key factor?) which explains the outbreak of the French Revolution. In Great Britain, beginning circa 1750, there is said to have occurred a (new) wave of great enclosures, which in turn is said to have been one of the factors (the key factor?) which explains the "first" industrial revolution. But were the "seigniorial reaction" and the "wave of enclosures" so different? I think not.

The eighteenth-century effort to increase rental income and to expand control over land and production in the core countries began, in my view, as a modest response to declining profit by large agricultural landowners (akin to the response of eastern European seigniors at the beginning of the seventeenth century). With the demographic upsurge, it became a source of considerable profit in and of itself. That is to say, supply having been at one point excessive became subsequently deficient, and grain prices rose, first slowly, then with momentum, everywhere in the European world-economy, particularly after circa 1750.[22]

One natural response to a supply gap is normally an effort to increase production through technological improvements. And, indeed, as Abel notes, after 1750 "agriculture became so suddenly the center of interest of cultivated circles that even contemporaries were surprised."[23] But the fact is that, despite the efforts at developing the new techniques of production —constant tillage, new crop rotations, mixed husbandry[24]—the results were far less dramatic than the "very misleading"[25] term, "agricultural

[22] Slicher van Bath (1969, 173–174) calls 1755 the "turning point in the price ratios." He notes that the average price of wheat in Europe from 1760 to 1790 was 30–40% higher than from 1721 to 1745, and constituted "a serious increase after an unusually long period of constant prices since about 1660 (with the exception of the period of the War of the Spanish Succession)." O'Brien (1977) dates the rise from 1745.

[23] Abel (1973, 281). Bourde (1967, III, 1571) dates the period of first great "intensity in the production" of agronomic manuals in France as 1750–1770.

[24] See, inter alia, Deane (1979, 38).

[25] Hufton (1980, 23). The principal polemics on this subject, cited previously, are Kerridge (1967) and Morineau (1971). Goy and Head-König revise downward Toutain's estimate of rise in eighteenth-century French agricultural productivity (1969, 263); see also Le Roy Ladurie (1975, 395). O'Brien (1977, 175) does not find British "capacity for change" in the period 1745–1820, "all that impressive." He reminds us that this is precisely the period when the classical economists invented the law of diminishing returns.

Turner similarly argues that such productivity

revolution," implies. Obviously, it was not the case that there was no increase in production cr productivity at all. But it can very well have been the case that the population increase outstripped the food supply increase by just enough to provide a base for significant profit but not by so much that the traditional "Malthusian" checks intervened. This would entail, to be sure, a decline in real income of the working strata, and for this there is considerable evidence.

What was the so-called seigniorial reaction in France? It has usually been defined by two central elements: the renewed enforcement of seigniorial dues and privileges which had fallen into disuse or into reduced usage; and the appropriation of common fields by these same seigniors and/or other local large landlords. While, in legal terms, the first operation appealed to a jurisprudence that derived from medieval feudal society (and, therefore, it could perhaps justify the analytic label of "refeudalization"), the second operation went in direct opposition to this same jurisprudence.[26] Therefore, even on the face of it, the assertion that the seigniorial reaction represented the last gasp of a feudal regime faces an elementary contradiction. Furthermore, as Forster has suggested, the "reaction" has in fact been "too narrowly understood."[27] It occurred within the context of an expanding world market, to which it was a "comprehensive" reaction, which included as well modern estate management (e.g., accounting, surveying, improved supervision), stocking, speculation, foreclosure, and support for the Physiocratic theory of prices—in short whatever might be expected of entrepreneurs.

The keystone of this "reaction" was located in rent. Rent should not be confused with seigniorial dues, which also expanded during this period, but which only accounted for a small percentage of the total revenue increase. Le Roy Ladurie's summary of French regional analyses indicates that in a comparison between the 1730s and the 1780s, the largest real increase was in land rent proper—51% in deflated prices, using a weighted index of all agricultural prices. The closest other increase was for tithes paid in money (35%). Revenue from interest on loans also rose significantly, despite an important fall in the interest rate. The weakest sources of increased agricultural revenue, although each still a small increase, were in taxes, tithes paid in kind, and seigniorial dues.[28]

change as occurred did so largely before 1770 and therefore was permissive of the demographic rise rather than a response to it. He argues that "productivity [in England], measured by greater yields, stood still from c. 1770 or before, until after 1830, and this at the time of the demographic revolution" (1982, 506).

[26] It should not be inferred that all reassertion of feudal rights was legal. Henri Sée (1908, 181–184) long ago spelled out how much of this reassertion involved legal abuses.

[27] Forster (1963, 684).

[28] See Le Roy Ladurie (1975, 434–437). Meyer (1966, II, 1248) find the same thing even in such a redoubt of feudal privilege as Brittany. "In reality, seigniorial rights properly speaking, however high they were, represented a rather small percentage of the revenue of the nobility. The importance of the 'feudal' system lay much more in the high cost of the irregular 'fees' (*casuels: lods et ventes, rachats*), of the tithes attaching to fiefs, and, most of all, in the arbitrary social power that it accorded to its holder, whether nobleman or commoner."

Who profited from this dramatic rise in agricultural income over a 60-year period? In terms of the rising price level,[29] the answer is simple. The winners were those "in command of a marketable surplus" and the losers those "forced to be a purchaser even for part of the year."[30] But in addition to the 80% of the benefit which derived from increased prices, there was the 20% of the benefit that derived from "the extortion of supplementary surplus-value."[31] It is this 20% which reflects the process of transformation of the internal social structure.

At the top of the hierarchy were the large landowners. For the most part, they were noblemen, but in fact, the whole of the seventeenth and eighteenth centuries in France were marked by the relative "ease of transition"[32] from the status of commoners to noblemen, for those who were wealthy enough to be large landowners. And in this period in particular, it was the status of large landowner which counted the most in terms of real revenue.[33]

While the feudal dues played a limited role in direct terms, they could be turned into capitalist profit via the indirect mechanism of farming-out (*affermage*). For it was not only the central government which had tax farmers; seigniors also "farmed out" their feudal dues. That is to say, the seigniors would each contract with one of more *fermiers* to pay annually a predetermined sum, which the *fermiers* in turn collected from the direct producers in kind. It was these *fermiers* then who actually sold the produce thus collected on the market, which in an era of rising prices, meant that any rise in the prices "benefited the *fermier*."[34]

Side by side with the increased rent which the landlord obtained directly and indirectly went his attempt to increase the size of his domains.[35] The

[29] See summary in Labrousse (1933, II, 361–362).

[30] Hufton (1980, 26, 28).

[31] The phrase and the percentage estimates are those of Le Roy Ladurie (1975, 434).

[32] Goodwin (1965a, 358). See also Gruder (1968, 226, 228): "It seems probable . . . that in the last decades of the [eighteenth] century the bourgeoisie, especially the wealthy, upper bourgeoisie, were not cut off from relations with those above them nor from professional and social advancement. . . . Status was not unalterable; birth no longer predetermined careers. [The bourgeois] could advance along the accepted paths if he had the tools required for success: ability and money. Moreover, he too wanted to become a noble." Was it so different in eighteenth-century England? The wealthy commoner became a Member of Parliament, and from there he could hope to be ennobled. "By 1784 the House of Commons was universally regarded as the high road to the House of Lords" (Namier, 1957, 14).

[33] "[The landowning class] increases in strength

more than the seigniorial nobility as such (seigniorial rights), than the Church as such (tithes), than the State as such (taxes)" (Le Roy Ladurie, 1975, 584).

[34] Aberdam (1975, 75). Since, furthermore, the *fermier* could subfarm out to someone who could then sub-subfarm out, the category of "*fermier*" was a large one.

[35] This is in addition to the *quality* of his lands. As Léon (1966, 18) points out for southeastern France, the large landowners had "the best cereal-growing lands, and especially the best vineyards and fields, loci of the most substantial profits."

We should, of course, always bear in mind Marc Bloch's caution (1930, 513) about the intentions of the seigniorial class: "It would be very artificial to speak . . . of the agrarian policy of the seigniorial class, conceived of as a bloc; this would be to give to its action a unanimity in the conception of its interests, a sureness of view . . ., a class consciousness . . . which it was far from having to that degree. But we can at least discern overall certain tendencies."

main efforts were first the attempts to eliminate the rights of common of shack (*vaine pâture*), and its extension to neighboring lands, the *droit de parcours*, which permitted the common feeding of animals on the stubble after the harvest as well as on fallows and waste land[36]; and second the attempts to divide the commons (*communaux*) and permit enclosures.

In these efforts, which had at least as long a history in France as in England,[37] large landholders in France in the period after 1750 were notably less successful than their English counterparts. A weaker state-machinery in France and a politically weaker peasantry in England led to quite different political results in the two countries. But the converse was also true. English landlords in the period after 1750 were less successful than their French counterparts in the degree to which rents could be raised. The entrenched "rights" of the English tenants to renewal prevented the rapid turnover of tenants, a practice which was "legend" in France.[38]

If one asks why this were so, one explanation, quite the opposite of the standard one, might be the combination of the greater spread of capitalist values in France (the sanctity of the entrepreneur's rights of disposition) and its converse, greater endurance of traditional values in England (acquired rights of a sitting tenant) on the one hand, and the weaker ability of the French state (compared to the British) to impose change, on the other. As Forster notes, the efforts by French large-scale tenant farmers engaged in cereals production to obtain tenure security, longer lease terms, and rebates for insurance were considered "unwarranted interference in the freedom of contract."[39]

The overall picture on English enclosures is rather clear. There was a considerable acceleration of the pace of enclosures after 1750, largely achieved not through private contract but through Parliamentary decree (that is, via the state). No doubt we are aware today that this is merely the culmination of a three-century-long trend.[40] And we are aware today that

---

[36] Bourde (1967, I, 538, n. 1) points out that the key feature of the *droit de parcours* which involves the reciprocal right to send animals to feed in a neighboring parish is that it was "an extension, *by mutual consent* [of the two parishes], of the zone of *vaine pâture*." See the legal definition in the *Répertoire de jurisprudence* cited in Sée (1913, 265).

[37] See Bloch (1930).

[38] Forster (1970, 1610). "Less successful" does not mean that rents did not rise. But more frequently English landlords resorted to enclosure as the mode of increasing their rentals. See Mingay (1960, 377). See also Parker (1955) who wishes to emphasize the gradualness of the rent rise and the degree to which it was a less cataclysmic phenomenon than often asserted.

Of course, the powers of the bureaucracy in France were rising, but not as much as in Great Britain. While the French state was not in a position (unlike the British state) to achieve much enclosure, it was strong enough to take over many functions which had previously justified the seignior's collection of dues. By thus "destabilizing" the function of the seignior as collector of feudal dues, it contributed to turning the seigniory into a "business" (Root, 1985, 680–681).

[39] Forster (1970, 1614).

[40] Kerridge (1967, 24) goes the furthest in seeking to debunk its novelty. "All in all, it might be roughly estimated that in 1700 about one quarter of the enclosure of East and West remained to be undertaken. The hoary fable of the supreme importance of parliamentary enclosures should be relegated to limbo."

the long-existing prior system of open fields and scattered strips had not been based merely on the persistence of irrational folly.[41] Nonetheless there was an extra spurt of enclosure in the late eighteenth century, occurring primarily on land that lent itself *less* to the process than the land that had been enclosed previously.[42] It is this spurt we have to explain. There is a further problem. As Dahlman argues, if enclosure had been primarily the result of technological change, we should have seen less of it previously than was in fact the case. We consequently need an explanation in terms of a "gradually developing element of change." He offers us one: "the extent of the market and the influence of relative prices" which require a degree of "specialization" inconsistent with the open field system.[43] And if one asks why parliamentary intervention was needed, Deane has a most plausible response: "It is reasonable to suppose that private enclosures proceeded more slowly than in the period before 1760, because the incentives to resist dispossession were *strong* when the price of food was high."[44]

Spurred on by the high prices, agricultural production did advance, if not perhaps quite at the rate of population growth. But it may be considered nonetheless a "heavy and slow" sector in the eighteenth century. The sectors which eventually "galloped"[45] were rather industry and commerce. At the beginning of the eighteenth century, the industries of England and France (the Northeast, Languedoc), but also of the Austrian Netherlands (Belgium), and Switzerland enjoyed a "rough parity" of development in terms of the internal ratio (about 2 : 1) of agriculture to industry.[46] They all were exporters, but the bulk of their industrial production was still sold within their frontiers. These industries all tended,

[41] The system was both more "flexible" than originally thought, permissive of more "advances" than thought, and subject to more "increasing differentiation and engrossment" than thought. See Yelling (1977, 146). Dahlman develops a whole case for the economic rationality of the system, as long as production was primarily for nearby markets. He reminds us (1980, 178) that the wheel is a great invention, but not for snow transport. "The open field system was adapted to cope with the problem of producing two different classes of output [arable and pastoral] with the same resources, under conditions of few exogenous changes and consequently greater stability."

[42] Early enclosures had occurred "in those districts least favorable to arable agriculture" (Yelling, 1977, 58) and which therefore required greater technological and organizational efforts to produce at a given level.

[43] Dahlman (1980, 154). "The enclosed farms were adopted once specialization became profitable and greater flexibility in production was desirable"

(p. 178). Cohen and Weitzman (1975, 321), though criticized by Dahlman, give a basically similar explanation: "The main force behind the enclosure movement was an urge to maximize profits from the land." They see this as a "break from medieval values" (p. 304) that presumably occurred at this time, but this runs against the strong evidence for earlier enclosures. The explanation of E. L. Jones (1981, 84) also goes in the same direction: "The main incentive to enclose was perhaps external— the fairly rapid rise in farm produce prices after mid-[eighteenth]century. . . . The efficiency gains are easily exaggerated." Finally, Abel (1973, 283–284) assents to this view, pointing out: "In the unanimous view of contemporaries, the immediate cause of the extraordinary multiplications of enclosures was the rise in cereals prices. . . . France offers the same spectacle."

[44] Deane (1979, 44); see also Hill (1967, 269).

[45] Labrousse (1970, 698).

[46] Hufton (1980, 31).

therefore, to advocate protectionist policies.[47] Industrial production began to rise parallel to cereals production, and earlier in France, perhaps circa 1715,[48] than in England, where the more usual date is 1740.[49] It is clear, in any case, that the global expansion, as one would expect, was a cumulative process. Hartwell argues:

> What good harvests facilitated, general economic expansion after 1750 sustained. . . . Thus after 1750 investment on a broad front—in agriculture, industry, trade and communications—set the stage for the great technological breakthrough of the 1770's and 1780's which created profit opportunities in key industries of such magnitude that enterprises responded quickly by rapidly increasing output.[50]

For Hartwell, however, as for many, this is a description only of England. We must look more closely at the degree to which this "sequence" was only an English phenomenon, and to the extent that it was, by what process it became so. that is to say, why was it true that after 1790, English costs of production fell sufficiently fast such that English producers were able "to invade successfully the large markets of Europe"? If it is true, as Habakkuk and others argue, that most of the inventions of the time can "more plausibly be ascribed to the pressure of increasing demand"[51] than to random chance, or to change in factory prices, or to Schumpeterian innovators, then why did not demand have the same effect in France? And did it not?

In addition, economic expansion meant not only increased production but also increased trade. Both England and France expanded their foreign trade after 1715, but not to the same degree in all markets. The British, Crouzet notes, "on the whole did not do well in the European markets, where they came up against protective tariffs and French competition."[52]

[47] See, for example, Ashton (1924, 104) on the English iron industry in the early eighteenth century: "English iron thus sold in the home market in rivalry with a foreign product. The competition was felt more keenly in that the demand for iron was . . . highly inelastic. . . . Small wonder, therefore, that the harassed English ironmaster was highly protectionist." The inelasticity of iron would change with the expansion of the world-economy.

[48] Marczewski speaks of a rise after 1715 (1963, 137), Fohlen of one after 1715–1720 (1973, 12). Léon (1954, 200), for the Dauphiné, speaks of 1732, closer to Labrousse's general date of 1733 for French renewed economic expansion.

[49] Deane and Cole (1967, 58; also Deane, 1973a, 170) have become the leading advocates of dating the English "industrial revolution" from the 1740s. They have been subject to criticism by those who consider the industrial developments from 1740–

1780 as relatively minor and wish, like Rostow, to emphasize the importance of the 1780s as a period of "take-off." See Whitehead (1964, 73).

[50] Hartwell (1968, 11–12).

[51] Habakkuk (1955, 150).

[52] Crouzet (1967b, 147). Davis's data (1979, 21, Table 10) show a steady *decline* in the value of the exports of woollen goods from England to north and northwest Europe between 1699–1701 and 1784–1786, whereupon they begin to turn up again, all this within a context of rising overall woollens exports. See also Butel (1978c, 112–113) on Germany and northern Europe as the "center of gravity" of *French* foreign trade. Deane and Cole (1967, 86) note that Britain's foreign trade shifts dramatically in the eighteenth century. At the beginning, four-fifths went to Europe, at the end, one-fifth. The reason was simple—the "protected markets of [Britain's] European rivals." Conversely,

This situation would change only circa 1785 with the new innovations which proved to be the British lever into this market. But conversely, throughout the eighteenth century, the British had a far larger colonial market than the French and were able, unlike the French, to penetrate extensively the markets of other colonial powers.[53]

This British edge in colonial trade was given even more importance by the growing role in the world-economy of the Americas trade.[54] Furthermore, it is precisely this colonial trade which supplied the income-elastic products that permitted Britain to expand trade at all with Europe in the period of expansion after the 1750s (and before the later post-1785 cotton goods breakthrough).[55] Still, on the whole, the growth of English exports was not "remarkably fast"[56] before the 1780s. Thus it is this final spurt that will need the explanation.

Similarly, the famous "home market" may turn out on closer examination to be less of a difference between England and France than is regularly asserted by its advocates. There are two issues here. One, did English producers have a significantly larger "total effective demand" within their frontiers—political frontiers, customs-free frontiers, low transport cost frontiers—than did France? Two, was the home market, however defined, significantly more of a dynamic stimulus than the "foreign" market (that is, one traversing the "frontiers") for either country or both?

In terms of political frontiers, which presumably define the limits of the immediate impact of state policy, we know that France was far larger than England, or even than Great Britain (the effective entity after the Act of Union), although if we add in the empires, the ratio of France's "internal" market to Great Britain's diminishes. In terms of customs-free frontiers, to the extent that it was a major price consideration internally (which is doubtful),[57] England was about the size of the Five Great Farms. In terms

Britain's trade with North America, the West Indies, Ireland "formed a virtually closed system from which competitors were rigidly excluded."

[53] See Davis (1973, 306). The British North American market was particularly important, given the tenfold increase in population between 1700 and the beginning of the American Revolution in 1775 and given the high wages current in those colonies. See Butel (1978a, 64). Ireland was a further important market for Great Britain, similar to British North America. See Davis (1969, 107).

[54] Milward and Saul (1973, 104) argue: After [the Treaty of Utrecht in 1713] the expansion of trade between Europe and other continents became ever more important and that trade grew much more rapidly than trade within the confines of Europe."

[55] See Deane (1979, 55).

[56] Crouzet (1980, 50). One element of uncertainty is what smuggling would add to the picture.

Cole (1969, 141–142) argues that "the legal and illegal branches of England's import [and export?] trade tended to move in opposite directions in the eighteenth century," and that, therefore, allowing for smuggling would dampen down the recorded fluctuations. He estimates smuggled goods as a quarter or a fifth of total value. Mui and Mui (1975) criticize Cole's data. In any case, we do not have a comparison with France.

[57] Braudel (1984, 347) concludes from his mappings that "by the end of the seventeenth century, France was indeed on the way to having a tightly-knit network, which could properly be called a national market." Similarly, Louise Tilly finds a "trend . . . towards a national market [in grains in France] as early as the end of the seventeenth century" (1971, 43). Le Roy Ladurie (1978, 389) speaks of the "development of the internal market" of France as a major element of the expansion of

of low transport cost frontiers, the eighteenth century was a period of internal improvements for both countries, no doubt more for England than for France (but how much more?).[58] In any case, improvement in internal transport facilities served "foreign" trade as well, making it far less of a port-to-port affair.

The question thus is was there more purchasing power available in the one place than the other? One should in this regard distinguish between the size and prosperity of the middle strata and the degree to which the lower strata had available cash for purchases which, although individually small, could have a meaningful impact given their numbers in the population.

In the previous discussion on the developments in the period 1650–1750,[59] we distinguished between the larger landlords, the prosperous (medium-size) producers, the nonprosperous (small) producers, and the landless laborers. Of the two middle categories (which we noted could not be distinguished from each other in terms of tenure rights) we saw the prosperous (medium-size) stratum prospering in that period at the expense of the nonprosperous (small) producers, both in England and northern France. This, in fact, probably *reduced* overall purchasing power, the increased incomes of the prosperous stratum being more than compensated for by the decreased incomes of the other. This shift moved many of the latter in the direction of engaging in cottage industry and rural wage work, the phenomenon partially analyzed in recent years under the label of protoindustrialization.[60]

The smaller producers in the long period of stagnation having been undermined, so to speak, it would now be those who had been relatively more prosperous in that earlier period who were most hard hit by the

agriculture in the eighteenth century (1975, 398). Morineau (1978, 379) cautions, however, that the unification of prices signals less a unified market (given "difficult and costly long-distance transport") than a "blocking of transactions, the creation by their inhabitants of economic defense zones of local sources of supply." See also Bosher (1965, 577–578).

[58] In terms of canals, England built many more and was consequently far ahead of France in navigable water per head or per kilometer. However, the French ones represented more of an engineering achievement, particularly the Languedoc canal which laid the "technical basis . . . for the vast expansion of the canal system of Europe which took place in the succeeding period of industrial development" Skempton (1957, 468). The literature on England emphasizes the "revolution" in transport in terms of economizing on costs of stockage, reduction of theft because of reduction of transport time, etc. See Deane (1979, 85–86); see also Girard

(1966, 216–217) and Bagwell (1974, 25, 43, 55). Letaconnoux (1909, 282–283), reflecting on French water transport, suggests that economies were overstated, the losses during transport and brigandage often being overlooked in the calculations of the analysts.

Canals and rivers were better than roads; Girard (1966, 223) claims a reduction of cost of carriage by one half to three-quarters. Arbellot (1973) notes, however, a great improvement in French roads in the eighteenth century. On the revolution in transports everywhere in France, see Le Roy Ladurie (1975, 397).

[59] Wallerstein (1980, 85–90).

[60] See the summary of the evidence on the growth of nonagricultural work in rural areas after 1650 throughout western Europe in Tilly (1983, 126–128), such that "important parts of the eighteenth-century European countryside teemed with non-peasants and hummed with manufacture."

concentration, usurpation, and high rents of the post-1730–1740–1750 period of economic expansion. Chambers concludes about the English enclosures of the late eighteenth century that "it was *not* the smallest type of owner, but the intermediate type, those paying more than 4s. but less than £10, who were 'swallowed up' "[61] The increase in rents in France in this period, which exceeded gains in production and productivity, led many peasants who hadn't done so before "to seek a second job (*métier*) merely to acquit themselves of the annual payments for their land. . . . The extra work, undoubtedly, served in such cases barely to maintain the previous standard of living, to keep it from declining further."[62]

To this somber picture, one that seems to go against the idea of a growing home demand, must be added the picture of wage income, affecting both rural and urban areas. There seems little doubt that real wages declined in the period 1750–1815, though how much is subject to debate.[63] The famous Hobsbawm–Hartwell *et al.* controversy (to be discussed later), over whether the industrial revolution raised or lowered workers' real incomes, concerns primarily the period after 1815. If home demand expanded in the period 1750–1815, it seems most likely that this may have been as much a function of increased population as of increased per capita income.[64]

The same may well be true at the level of the world-economy. Thus, although Cole speaks of the "unprecendented expansion" of Britain's trade in the late eighteenth century as taking place "in spite of, rather than, because of" conditions in foreign trade, he is quick to add that a large part of the growth was due to the "rapid increase in sales in the North American market," and speaks of England's ability to invade the "relatively sluggish markets" of the rest of Europe at this time.[65]

When thus the Treaty of Paris brought the Seven Years' War to an end, it was by no means obvious that England was economically performing at a level significantly different from France. What does seem obvious is that each had different advantages in commerce. Great Britain was growing weaker in its competition with France on the continent and compensating

[61] Chambers (1940, 119). He contends (p. 123) there was actually an increase in the "smallest type of owner" explaining it "by the fact that those squatters and cottagers who had not been recognized as liable to land tax now came in for the first time."

[62] Morineau (198, 385); see also Le Roy Ladurie (1975, 584).

[63] See Gilboy (1930, 612–613; 1975, 7, 16–17), Tucker (1975, 32), Deane (1979, 31), Labrousse (1933, II, 491, 600, 610), and Morineau (1978, 377).

[64] Indeed, Labrousse (1944, xviii) makes just this point: "If real wages declined [in the eighteenth century], the number of wage workers increased, and the amount of employment available augmented alongside the [expansion of] the mass of productive capital."

[65] Cole (1973, 341–342; cf. Minchinton, 1969, 16–17). The "balanced" view—it was both home and external demand—has become quite popular. See Landes (1969, 54), Cole (1981, 45), and Crafts (1981, 14). The question, however, remains not the comparison of France and England to peripheral zones, but to each other. What made the difference between the two?

for this decline with an improvement in its relative position "overseas." This was very clear to the perspicacious Dutch author, Accarias de Sérionne, who, writing in 1778, analyzed British difficulties in terms of internal price and wage rises which made her production too expensive to compete with France (and Holland) on the continent. Her difficulties pushed her to "triumph" elsewhere in the world, and, of course, also to the innovations which would soon recreate a competitive position for Britain in Europe. But this "triumph" in the rest of the world must be analyzed carefully, as Braudel insists:

> It is easy to see how by and large England pushed her trade to these outer margins. In most cases, success was achieved by force: in India in 1757, in Canada in 1762 or on the coasts of Africa, England shouldered her rivals aside. . . . Her high domestic prices . . . drove her to seek supplies of raw materials . . . from low-cost countries.[66]

What Choiseul had sought in the Seven Years' War was to prevent just this, to stop England from creating "a despotic power over the high seas."[67]

Although Great Britain emerged victorious from the war, she stopped short of total victory.[68] Pitt, who saw as clearly as Choiseul that the struggle over world trade was critical at that moment, was ousted from office after the death of George II in 1760. Peace was made, too soon for Pitt and his friends, who deplored the return of Guadeloupe and Martinique to France, as well as the fishing rights on the Grand Banks off Newfoundland. In the debate of the Treaty, Pitt, supported, by the City merchants, thundered:

> The ministers seem to have lost sight of the great fundamental principle that France is chiefly if not solely to be dreaded by us in the light of a maritime and commercial power.[69]

---

[66] Braudel (1984, 575–578), who cites Accarias de Sérionne; see also Frank (1978, 214–218). Deane (1979, 10) confirms Accarias de Sérionne's analysis indirectly in her comparison of English and French living standards in the 1770s. "There seems little doubt that the average Englishman was appreciably better off than his French counterpart." This inability to compete on the Continent is the negative side of such home market advantage as Britain had.

[67] Cited by Meyer (1979a, 211). Meyer says France's policy was to insist on the neutrality of the high seas during wartime. But an objective of neutrality itself is a measure of military weakness.

[68] "The Peace of Paris established Britain as, with the exception of Spain, the greatest colonial power

in the world. . . . [However,] Britain's colonial and maritime predominance over France . . . was [not] as yet beyond challenge" (Anderson, 1965, 252).

[69] Cited in Plumb (1956, 104); see also Barr (1949, 195). If one wonders how it was possible that Pitt's views and those of the City merchants did not prevail, one must remember that there were other interests at play. J. R. Jones (1980, 222) observes: "British merchants and West Indian proprietors showed no enthusiasm for the annexation of conquests in the Caribbean, since the result would be increased competition in a protected foreign market; Martinique and Guadeloupe could undercut the prices charged by British plantations, and Cuba formed potentially an even more efficient large-scale producer."

Those who concentrated their attention on the appropriate role of the state in the competitive struggles within the capitalist world-economy seemed as frustrated in Britain at this point as they proved to be shortly in France:

> All seemed within their grasp, but they failed, because they lacked political power. In defeat, they directed their attention to the institutions and methods of government. The day of the bourgeois radical dawned.[70]

If, however, France's overseas economic base was not yet destroyed, as Pitt and his friends had hoped, Britain at least emerged with key strategic assets—Canada, Dominica, St. Vincent, Minorca, parts of the Senegal coast, plus, of course, Bengal. France tried immediately to reduce the effect by invoking the balance of power mechanism in European diplomacy.[71] The annexation of Corsica in 1768 helped redress the situation in the Mediterranean.[72] But this was insufficient to counter the undermining of the French economy in two critical spheres, an undermining that would be its undoing.

In the first place, the Seven Years' War broke the upward élan of the commerical–industrial complexes of the Atlantic coast of France, that link between the triangular trade, the slave trade, and cotton manufactures which we know worked so well in Britain. In the 20 years before the Treaty of Paris, it was French port cities like Nantes, which had been at the "forefront" of "modern economic development."[73] The war, however, was "disastrous," the blockade affecting the "fastest growing sector," and the end of the war saw the emergence of "a more cautious spirit," the war thus marking "a turning point" for the economy.[74]

Second, it was the war which "perturbed" fundamentally the finances of the state, permanently breaking the equilibrium between current receipts and ordinary expenses. Thus the state went down the dangerous path of living off future income which it could only obtain through ever greater

---

[70] Plumb (1950, 115).

[71] See McNeill (1982, 157); and Anderson (1965, 254 ff.). But France's diplomatic position had been considerably weakened by the defeat in 1763. "On ceremonial occasions at the courts of Europe, British diplomatic representatives demanded and received, as a result of the Seven Years' War, precedence over France, a practice which sometimes led to exceptionally humiliating exhibitions" (Bemis, 1935, 9).

[72] See Ramsey (1939, 183). But Choiseul was ousted in 1770 when he was ready to risk a new war rather than cede the Falklands (Malouines) to Britain, since the islands controlled access to the Straits of Magellan and Cape Horn. See Guillerm (1981, II, 451).

[73] Boulle (1972, 109), who argues (p. 93): "Thanks to the slave trade, cheapness and quantity, the two motors of modern industry, were available in Nantes. And so was capital, accumulated by the slave-trading oligarchy."

[74] Boulle (1972, 103, 106, 108, 111). Dardel (1963, 52) reports the same kind of economic reversal for Rouen, but gives 1769 as the date of the turnaround. Bergeron (1978e, 349) says that the idea that the maritime economy of France was marginal to the true France based on artisans and peasants is "simplist" and insists on the "multiple and vital organic links" between the two in the late eighteenth century. But then, it follows all the more that the damage done to Atlantic France would have severe repercussions elsewhere.

concessions to its creditors.[75] This proved to have for the French state, as for many others in similar situations, a spiral effect.

The period following the Seven Years' War saw a general slowdown in world trade, a sort of Kondratieff-B period from which the world-economy would not fully emerge until about 1792.[76] It would, however, be Great Britain that would be in the best position to seize the advantage of the upturn rather than France and this would become clear by the 1780s. We shall now look at the developments in agriculture and industry which comprise this seizing of advantage. It would be well, however, to bear in mind how fundamental to the upsurge were the politico–strategic advantages Britain had secured in the long struggle with France for the growing overseas markets, the import of which Habakkuk expresses well:

> The acceleration of English exports in the 1780's is, of course, to some extent, the *result* of technical improvements. But at least in cotton textiles these improvements were in some measure the result of the fact that in the preceding decades England had been linked to markets which . . . were growing rapidly. The textile industries of the Continent . . . served markets where the growth of demand was much slower, and for this reason they were not faced with the same need to improve their techniques and methods of organization.[77]

It seems to be at this point, in the 1760s, the French elites—the intellectuals, the bureaucrats, the agronomists, the industrialists, and the politicians —began to express the feeling that they were somehow "behind" Great Britain, and began to thrash about for ways to "catch up." In light of our current knowledge, such an impression was probably exaggerated, but that does not efface its impact on the social and political behavior of the time. In agriculture, this meant three major sociopolitical efforts: land clearance, "freeing" grain prices, and agronomic improvements.

Land clearance took two forms: the division of the commons and the abolition of collective servitudes (in particular, obligatory *vaine pâture*).

[75] Morineau (1980b, 298). Lüthy called the impact of the Seven Years' War on French finances a "1914 of the eighteenth century." Cited in Bergeron (1978b, 121). See also Price (1973, I, 365) who sees the Seven Years' War as "a turning-point in the fiscal history of eighteenth-century France."

[76] The Seven Years' War itself had been one of the motors of the previous expansion of world trade, since the servicing of overseas armies became itself a significant cause of increased exports. Some of this effect carried over into peacetime. Davis (1969, 114) wonders "how much of the enhanced [British] export to America in the [post-1763] years resulted from the demands of garrisons which were maintained on a much larger scale than before the war in the colonies."

In any case, this carryover effect was insufficient. There was a turndown in commerce, though there is some debate as to whether this started in the 1760s (Cole, 1981, 39–43; Crafts, 1981, 16; Crouzet, 1980, 50–51; Fisher, 1969, 160; Frank, 1978, 170–171) or only as of 1770 (Labrousse, 1944, xxiii; Davis, 1979, 31–32).

[77] Habakkuk (1965, 44). See also Cole (1981, 41) who speculates on what England might have been like had she been a closed economy: "Instead of being well on the road [in 1800] to becoming an industrial nation, [she] would not yet have begun the trip."

Because of the legal weaknesses of the French state, this effort at reform had to proceed province by province. Despite this complication, there were successive authorizations by provincial edict for the division of the commons between 1769 and 1781, and for the end of *vaine pâture* between 1766 and 1777. The monarchy added its support in various ways. Fiscal incentives were provided to clear waste land which further encouraged land usurpation. Bloch calls the effort "grandiose," pointing out that it was in part a deliberate attempt to imitate Parliamentary procedures in England. Yet, as he observed, the reformers came up against "unexpected difficulties," and a "wave of timidity and discouragement" brought it to an early end.[78] The failure of these reforms is not in question.[79] But should we attribute it to a mere cult of tradition? No doubt, the reforms evoked fears reflecting a desire to maintain certain "feudal" privileges (such as hunting zones), but the main source of the opposition was clearly one of menaced material interests.

The division of the commons was generally supported by larger land-owners who could obtain a third of the land through the *droit de triage*. The landless laborers or those who had very little land could also see some advantage in a division, but only if the shares were not proportional to existing property size. It was the *laboureurs* in general who tended to be most strongly opposed, since what they could add in land scarcely matched what they would lose in grazing rights, and the land that went to the poorest elements, albeit small, was enough to threaten to remove the latter from the labor market of the *laboureur*. The French *laboureur* was thus being led in the same direction of proletarianization as the English yeoman. Indeed, Le Roy Ladurie tells us, speaking of eighteenth-century France and not of England, "proletarianization replaced the cemetery."[80]

When, however, the issue was the suppression of collective rights (*vaine pâture, droit de parcours*), the political lineup was different. The landless laborer or very small owner drew no advantage from this whatsoever. Elimination of such rights meant that he would have no grazing land for the very few animals he had.[81] It was precisely the *laboureur*, especially the

---

[78] Bloch (1952, I, 226). In his earlier article (1930, 381), Bloch underlined the same theme: "Timidity was decidedly the dominant note of the agrarian policy of the last years of the *Ancien Régime*." On peasant resistance as one of the "difficulties," see Gauthier (1977, 59–60).

[79] See Sutton (1977, 256): "Set against the total area of wasteland and against the total French agriculture production, the addition of 300–350,000 ha. could only represent a very limited success for the government policy of land clearance." See also Le Roy Ladurie (1975, 582) who says that in the eighteenth century, unlike in England and Prussia, the peasant's small plot (*lopin*) is only "marginally threatened." The descriptions

by Sée (1923b, 49; cf. 1908, 1913), however, indicate that, despite the slowdown of state intervention, seigniorial usurpations "only worsened as we approach the years of the Revolution."

[80] Le Roy Ladurie (1975, 440; see also 415–416); and see Bloch (1952, I, 229–235).

[81] This was true even if the commons were not divided, since as Bloch (1930, 523) notes, "almost nowhere did the commons suffice." See also Meuvret (1971b, 179) on the doubtful advantages of reciprocity on good fields. Therefore, "unanimous in their resistance, the [laborers (*manoeuvriers*)] formed everywhere the shock troops of the rural opposition" (Bloch, 1952, I, 228); see also Sée (1923b, 76).

one who had good fields, who, being the loser in the "reciprocity" of the existing arrangements, could benefit by enclosure.[82] On this question, however, the large landowners were of a divided mind. Wherever the units that belonged to the large landowners were scattered, these collective rights were as useful to them as to those peasants with very little or no land, if not more useful. But if their lands .were concentrated, they lost by *vaine pâture*.[83]

But does this description of the situation differ from one we could make for England? Yes, in one fundamental respect: the degree of scattering of the land units was far greater in France,[84] which as we see, can affect the attitude of the large landowners. But why did the French landowners not then simply seek to regroup land by legislative edict, an action that was frequent in English enclosure acts? Bloch supplies the answer:

> Natural in a country where the largest segment of landholdings (*tenures*) had not at all been able to achieve perpetuity, was such a constraint [regrouping] conceivable in France? The economists, the administrators did not even envisage the possibility.[85]

Once again, it turns out that the strong rules governing existing property rights in France was France's "disadvantage" vis-à-vis Great Britain where property rights were *less well* anchored. It enabled better resistance to usurpation in France.

When we turn to the picture of the freeing of grain prices, we discover another irony. It was France, not England, which first tried to implement Smith's *Wealth of Nations,* even before it was published. It was in the Declaration of May 1763 and the Edict of July 1764 that the French government broke the provisioning tradition and established "grain liberalism." The Declaration created free circulation throughout France, and the Edict permitted the free export of grain and flour.[86] These decrees were in large part a response to the "humiliating, . . . demoralizing and disorganizing" defeat of 1763. They constituted "a sensational event," marking a "decisive rupture" with a long tradition. It did not last long, ending with the onset of economic difficulties in 1770, when a decree

---

[82] See Bloch (1930, 531), and Meuvret (1971b, 179).

[83] See Bloch (1952, I, 230). He notes that large landowners were particularly strong in favor of the *droit de parcours*. Speaking of Franche-Comté where, abusively, they had gained the right to maintain almost unlimited flocks on the commons and fallow land, Bloch observes: "These farms had become all the more lucrative since the transformations of the economy ensured that the stockraisers had precious outlets while at the same time opening all the doors to a capitalist style of operation."

Meuvret (1971d, 195–196) insists that one should distinguish between *vaine pâture* on fallow land and on cultivated fields, since in fact fallow land was used for sheep and cultivated fields for horned animals. It was not in the large landowner's interest to suppress *vaine pâture* on the fallow land, given his large sheep flocks and the profitability of wool.

[84] See Meuvret (1971d, 196).

[85] Bloch (1952, I, 236).

[86] Kaplan (1976, I, 93) cites a distinguished Breton magistrate of the time who, in language that seems remarkably avant-garde, said the Edict marked the entry of France into "the common market of Europe."

once again prohibiting import was proclaimed, appropriately enough on July 14.[87]

If grain liberalism was intended to lower prices, equalize them regionally, or reduce annual variations, it did not succeed notably in these objectives during its short history. Labrousse accounts for its "feeble influence" by the objective economic constraints caused by transport "difficulties."[88] But this assumes that we take the Physiocratic claims as the political explanation. Kaplan reminds us, however, that, though the program surprised by its "radicalism," it drew its support from very "traditional and conservative-minded" landowners, who were not concerned with the ideology of liberalism but with immediate profits from the grain trade.[89] Is it a total accident that grain liberalism was proclaimed during exactly the years (1763–1770) designated by Labrousse as those in which the advantages in leasing land went against the owner and in favor of the tenant? Grain liberalism could be seen as a measure to maintain profit levels by expanding total sales, which became less necessary in the period 1770–1789 when rents were rising while the profits of the direct producers were going down. The brief reemergence of grain liberalism under Turgot in 1774 encountered strong popular reaction this time, the *guerre des farines*,[90] without the necessary political support from the landowning classes. In 1776 Turgot tried to extend free trade in grains even to Paris which had previously been exempted. Turgot fell from office.

But was this failure of reform in this field a sign of the strength of feudal forces? One would not think it to hear Labrousse on the "happy landed patriciate," whose principal revenue, rental income, was "rising, rising violently."

> Landed capitalism does not merely play the role of a powerful sheltered sector of society. It attacks, it advances at a record pace, and, before it, peasant profit declines enormously.[91]

No wonder then we have a return to interest in land proprietorship and investment.[92]

[87] Kaplan (1976, I, 145, 163).
[88] Labrousse (1933, 122, 124).
[89] Kaplan (1976, II, 687). Grain liberalism had also been supported by the king's advisors who thought it would lead to price rises and hence higher taxes. This, however, "proved to be a grisly error" (Hufton, 1983, 319).
[90] "Against a crazy price of cereals regulated by supply and demand which was what the Physiocrat Turgot wanted, the mass of ordinary workers (*manoeuvriers*), especially the artisans, demanded in the name of 'the moral economy of the crowd' a just price" (Le Roy Ladurie, 1975, 388). Riley considers grain liberalism (and also curtailing peacetime tax-

ation) as an "experiment in stimulating economic expansion," an experiment that proved "hazardous" (1987, 237).
[91] Labrousse (1944, xxxv). See also Saint-Jacob's description (1960, 428, 569) of the same period for Burgundy. He describes the increasing role of the *fermier*, true author of the seigniorial reaction. "From that point on, in the eyes of the peasant, the seigniory is the *fermier*." However, this successful emergence of the non-noble capitalist farmer is what will undo the seigniory. "The *fermier* who became an arrogant entrepreneur of the fief ended by discrediting it."
[92] See Bourde (1967, III, 1609).

How different was the reality (as opposed to the legality) of grain freedom in France as compared to Britain? As Morineau suggests, in the "absence of statistics," we cannot really be sure about comparative grain export figures. But in any case, as he says, the problem is not "correctly posed" if one ignores the fact that the excess-supply provinces of France (e.g., Brittany and Languedoc) were shipping to the deficit-supply provinces,[93] and consequently foreign trade figures alone are not the appropriate basis for comparison.

If we turn to the third arena of reform, that of economic improvements, first prize is usually given to Great Britain. Indeed, Bourde concludes his study of the influence of England on the French agronomists in the eighteenth century by asserting that the consequences in agronomy proper were few, and the influence "less a fact of economic history than a fact of the history of ideas."[94] Nonetheless, there are three remarks to be made. First, the advances in English agronomy, while real, were (as already suggested) less of a "revolution" than it has often been argued.[95] Second, English soil lent itself better than French to the new fodder crops.[96] Third, the new husbandry in England did *not* increase yield per worker, but merely yield per land unit.[97]

There are thus various ways one can interpret the lack of success of attempted Physiocratic reforms in French agriculture in the period 1763–1789. The real differences between France and Britain have been exaggerated. To the extent that they were real, French hesitations on the part of the landowning/large *fermier* sector reflected rational concerns to optimize immediate profit possibilities. The French lower strata were more successful in opposing certain aspects of the further extension of capitalist exploitation than the British lower strata. Perhaps all three propositions are true.

How did the picture present itself in the industrial arena? There too, there is a widespread view that the French were falling behind—a view of the actors at the time, of the analysts since. How accurate is this view? The rise of the British cotton industry is the centerpiece of such analysis. We

[93] Morineau (1971, 325–326; cf. Lefebvre, 1939, 115–116).

[94] Indeed, Bourde (1953, 217–218) exculpates "feudalism" as the explanation by arguing that French agronomic backwardness continued in the nineteenth century. He offers therefore an explanation that subordinates the "traditional mentality of the French peasant" to the "geographical conditions peculiar to France."

[95] Bergeron (1978c, 226–227) reminds us: "Finally, if there was an 'agricultural revolution', was it English? In the eighteenth century, England was merely overcoming a lag in this field in relation to Flanders and Holland," Furthermore, of course,

France after 1760 did make many of the same innovations in northern France. See Slicher van Bath (1963, 279–280).

[96] See O'Brien and Keyder (1979, 1293–1294), who also argue that the greater density in France led to devoting more territory to cereals production and labor-intensive techniques.

[97] See Timmer (1969, 392). He argues: "The agrarian revolution [in England] apparently did not supply surplus labor for an industrial army of workers. It did provide food for the rapidly growing population from which an increased agricultural and industrial labor force were recruited" (pp. 384–385).

should start by remembering that, for a good portion of the eighteenth
century, the cotton industry was not only larger in France than in England,
but that in the years 1732–1766 the French cotton industry doubled in size.
England's tiny industry had been stimulated into growth by the protectionist anti-Indian legislation of 1700 but its growth "accelerated *only* in the
mid-1760's after the Seven Years' War."[98] Many authors would mark a
significant British spurt only as of the 1780s.[99]

We should also remember that Europe, beginning in the seventeenth
century and continuing into the nineteenth century, saw a vast multiplica-
tion of small rural industries based on small to medium accumulations
of capital.[100] Milward and Saul remind us that, as of 1780, the "most
industrialized landscapes" of Europe were still to be found not in Britain
but in "the country areas around Lille, Rouen, Barcelona, Zurich, Basel
and Geneva."[101] And Tilly, summarizing the now vast literature on
so-called protoindustrialization, suggests that from 1650 to as late as 1850,
"large units and big capital may well have experienced a relative decline."[102]

In this context, what is usually called the industrial revolution should in
fact be thought of as the reurbanization and reconcentration of the leading
industries alongside an effort to increase scale. By definition, then, only
one or two zones could be the locus of such an effort. What was at stake
between France and Britain was which country could succeed in chan-
neling this countermovement whose benefits would be high precisely
because of the new expansion of the world-economy.

It is far from sure that Britain even started the process ahead of

[98] Davis (1973, 311); cf. figures on British cotton–wool import from 1697 to 1831 in Rostow (1971, 54).

[99] See Nef (1943, 5): "The rate of industrial change from abut 1735 to 1785 was no more rapid in Great Britain than in France. . . . What is striking in eighteenth-century economic history is less the contrasts than the resemblances between Great Britain and the continent, both in the rate of economic development and in the directions that development was taking." Nef also argues (1968, 971) that in the period 1735–1785, overall production, particularly in the iron industry, grew more rapidly in France than in Britain. See also Wadsworth & Mann (1931, 193), Bairoch (1974, 24), O'Brien & Keyder (1978, 57–60), Cole (1981, 36), and Crafts (1981, 5).
Cole and Deane (1966, 11) assert that "At the outbreak of the revolution (and perhaps for the whole of the preceding century, [France] was lagging behind [Britain] in average productivity. But [they add] the gap was not wide by modern standards." Furthermore, they see France as being in a "position of advantage" based on their "strong

scientific tradition." Cf. Mathias (1979, 54–55). See also Léon (1974, 407) who talks of eighteenth-century France as being traversed by "powerful, active forces of renewal." He asserts that "the reality of industrial progress, of industrial growth no longer needs to be demonstrated in a country which affirms, in both these domains, a vocation which places it in the top rank of European states."

[100] See Wallerstein (1980, 193–200).

[101] Milward & Saul (1973, 94). See Le Roy Ladurie & Quilliet (1981, 375) on what they call the "Oberkampf model" in France.

[102] Tilly (1983, 130). One of the reasons for this was the partial incorporation of the putting-out system into the new factory system. A "textile entrepreneur might be what we can call a service station. . . . Dyers and finishers might work on cloths belonging to merchants; worsted combers or spinners might take in wool and send back combings or yarn. The putting-out system thus showed remarkable powers of adaptation, with the mill-operator rather than a domestic craftsman as a 'puttee'" (Heaton, 1972, 86).

France.[103] As for the size of industry, in the eighteenth century, it was France, not Britain, that housed more "large-scale units."[104] Nonetheless, it is the case that, in the period 1780–1840, Britain was able to achieve the position of the central locus of the larger scale, relatively more mechanized, relatively high-profit[105] industrial sector of the world-economy, at the expense of everyone else, and most immediately at the expense of France.[106] How did this in fact happen?

It seems clear there was a sudden rise in British relative efficiency of production in the cotton industry in the 1780s—the consequence of the famous "wave of gadgets," a wave that was greater in Britain than in France.[107] One can attribute this, if one wants, to greater "imagination."[108] But one other factor which surely helped was the fact that at this point the British had an edge in access to markets.[109] This coincided with a rather "classical phenomenon of transfer of a pole of development—from France to Spain—perhaps complicated by the effect of full maturity in certain provinces with outdated equipment like Brittany."[110]

[103] Roehl (1976) argues the opposite, even intimating that this earlier start was its disadvantage. Marczewski (cited in Garden, 1978a, 16), counting all transformation industries, asserts that industry represented in 1780–1790 42.6% of all value produced in France. For a review of recent revisionist literature on French economic growth, see Cameron & Freedeman (1983). For a position in between the early writers and the revisionists, see Crafts (1984). For a critique of Roehl and his reply, see Locke (1981) and Roehl (1981).

[104] However, "in the eighteenth century what Gille has called 'big capitalist enterprise' was brought into being not in textile production, which accounted for from 60 to 65 percent of French industrial activity, but in mines, metallurgical industries, canals, and chemical plants" (George V. Taylor, 1964, 493).

[105] The Fourth Edition of the *Encyclopedia Britannica*, published in 1810, exults over this aspect: "East India cotton wool has been spun into one pound of yarn worth five guineas; and when wove into muslin and afterwards ornamented by children in the tambour, has extended to the value of £15; yielding a return of 5,900 percent on the raw material" (Anon., 1810, 695).

[106] "Exports of cotton goods, almost negligible in 1770, accounted for nearly half of all exports of British produce during the first half of the nineteenth century. The transformation of their role in export trade was virtually completed in 1800, having taken no more than a single generation" (Davis, 1979, 14). See also Crouzet (1980, 92) on the striking change in the pattern of British exports between 1782 and 1802.

[107] The story has been told many times. See

Landes's summary observations (1969, 84–88). Crompton's mule, which Lévy-Leboyer (1964, 7) asserts to have been "decisive" dates from 1779. On increase of British productivity see also Hoffmann (1955, 32), Nef (1968, 967), Crouzet (1980, 65), and Crafts (1981, 8).

One says "greater" in Britain because it is not the case there were no innovations in France in this period. Ballot (1923, 22) speaks of 1780–1792 as a period of "renovating activity" in French industry, including "the definitive implantation of the mechanical working of cotton."

[108] This is the phrase of Lévy-Leboyer (1964, 24).

[109] "Both countries were dependent to some extent on the markets [for cotton goods] in Africa and America, and here the course of events from 1720 onward favored the English industry at the expense of France" (Wadsworth & Mann, 1931, 208). "The enormous colonial and naval expansion of Britain in the eighteenth century provided a larger colonial market for cotton cloth than France had and it was in the cotton industry that the major mechanical innovations occurred" (Milward & Saul, 1973, 97). The 1780s combined thus an historically acquired edge in access to certain markets, a "product that gave her a competitive edge in major markets" (Cain & Hopkins, 1980, 474), and favorable market conditions in the trading area, which had been "only slowly ripening before 1780" (Berrill, 1960, 358). The end of the American War (de facto, 1781) was an important stimulus to British foreign trade in its "great leap forward" (Perkin, 1969, 100). On the difficulties faced by France in colonial commerce in the 1780s, see Clark (1981, 139) and Stein (1983, 116–117).

[110] Morineau (1978, 411–412).

There is one other consideration concerning markets. Much has been made by historians of the impact of the British home market. This has always seemed curious to me in two respects. Why would this account for technological advance in an industry which found so large a part of its outlet in foreign trade (and was so dependent on foreign imports, tied in turn to having something to sell in return)? And was not the French home market large or larger? Léon gives what seems to me a far more plausible answer to the question why, precisely at this point, there occurred this leap in British productivity. "Might one not think that the attraction of the [French] home market came to bear with all its force against any profound modification of the dynamics of foreign trade?"[111] That is to say, precisely because of profit levels at home, there was less pressure to be competitive abroad—which is why the Treaty of 1786, to which we shall soon come, was so important.

Although "decreasing costs and expansible markets" were no doubt of "strategic importance in the [further] acceleration of technical progress,"[112] Britain had one last advantage—a state-machinery that was ready to interfere actively in the market. I can scarcely do better than reproduce the early, and often forgotten, analysis of Mantoux:

> Nothing is less accurate than to say that the English cotton manufacture grew up without artificial defence in the face of foreign competition. . . . The import of printed cottons from whatever source remained forbidden. No protection could be more complete, for it gave the manufacturers a real monopoly of the home market. . . . And not only was the home market reserved for them, but steps were taken to help them gain markets abroad. A bounty was given on every exported roll of calico or muslin (21 Geo. III, c. 40 [1781] and 28 Geo. III, c. 21 [1783]. . . . Stern measures were enacted to prevent [the] exportation [of new machinery] to foreign countries. . . . If it be true that the history of the cotton industry can provide arguments for the doctrine of *laissez-faire,* these will certainly not be found during [the] early period.[113]

Nonetheless, even given all this, the British edge was not all that large. As Lévy-Leboyer puts it, "the English could not expect to maintain for very long their technological and financial edge." Nonetheless they did, and for longer than seems reasonable. To what extent is the explanation to be located in the French Revolution, which Lévy-Leboyer wishes to call "from this point of view . . . a national catastrophe"?[114]

If we look at the set of political events which led to the French

[111] Léon (1974, 421).
[112] Deane & Cole (1967, 35).
[113] Mantoux (1928, 262–264). See Thompson (1978a); See also Jeremy (1977, 2–5) who notes that the period of maximal legislative prohibition of technological export in Great Britain was the 1780s to 1824.

[114] Lévy-Leboyer (1964, 25, 29). This viewpoint is shared by Pugh (1939, 312) who saw Calonne's "New Deal" of 1783–1787 as steps to develop capitalism in France. "The Revolution interrupted [Calonne's] work and enabled England to forge so far ahead in industrial development that France was never able to catch up."

Revolution, there is widespread agreement that it was the convening of the Estates-General that set the immediate process in motion, and that the decision to convene the Estates-General was the result of a sort of "crisis of the monarchy." Lefebvre offers a straightforward explanation of this crisis:

> The government crisis went back to the American war. The revolt of the English colonies may be considered the principal direct cause of the French Revolution, both because in invoking the rights of man it stirred up great excitement in France, and because Louis XVI in supporting it got his finances into very bad condition.[115]

This explanation leads to two immediate questions. Why was there not the same ideological impact on Great Britain? What about the finances of the British state? Once again, we must return to the turning point of 1763. France perceived herself as "falling behind" Britain. There were basically two solutions discussed: strengthen the French state—financially, socially (vis-à-vis centrifugal forces, whether geographical or class based), and militarily—or "open" the country economically. Both were seen as movements of "reform." The one proposed using state resources to strengthen France's economic position by supporting its entrepreneurs and the other proposed using state resources to strengthen France's economic position by forcing France's entrepreneurs to be more "competitive." This kind of national debate has become a familiar one in the last century. It is the debate between the protectionist interventionists and the "liberal" interventionists. France after 1763 oscillated between the two, with poor results, and a high potential for the political explosion which in fact occurred.

The oscillation began with the Duc de Choiseul, who

> willed the end, which was the re-establishment of French power in the world and a war of revenge against England; he did not will the necessary means, which was the restoration of royal authority inside France and the reforms of royal finances, without which all other reforms would be in vain.[116]

It continued with Vergennes who served as Foreign Minister from 1774 to 1786, and with the succession of men who controlled France's finances: Turgot (1774–1776), Necker (1776–1781), Fleury (1781–1783), and Calonne (1783–1787). Each wrestled with the same problems. Each came up with solutions (diverse ones) which were unpopular. Each failed to strengthen France's basic economic position in the world-economy. Had the absolute monarchy been more absolute, it might have been able to overcome the crisis, but all the projects for financial reform from 1715 to 1789 "broke on the rock of the opposition of the *parlements.*"[117]

---

[115] Lefebvre (1939, 24).

[116] Cobban (1963, 91).

[117] Cobban (1968c, 74). Robin (1973, 53) similarly speaks of "the decisive role played by the judiciary (*magistrature*) in the blocking of all possi-

bilities, all attempts at compromise." As Behrens (1967, 177) reminds us, "until the end of the 1780s, the struggle for reform had never been between the third estate (or any section of it) and the nobility."

The key issue throughout remained state finances. If the long expansion of the world-economy involved a steady accumulation of capital by the landowning producers, primarily via the mechanism of rent, this concentration of capital involved not merely obtaining more surplus-value from the direct producers but reducing the role of the state as a redistributive center. Whereas state revenue as a percentage of national product had risen steadily in the seventeenth century and until at least 1715, from 1730 on it was on the decline.[118] The situation had been aggravated by the system of the Company of General Farms, which in the eighteenth century (at least until 1774) had been the principal agency of tax collection, to the great profit of the tax collectors.[119] "The monarchy lost its independence [to the Company]." Necker may have reduced the Company's role, but "it required nothing less than a revolution to bring it down."[120]

It was, however, the American war that transformed a steady trend into an acute problem, by dramatically increasing state expenditure in an era of declining state revenue.[121] The American war was supposed to serve

[118] See Le Roy Ladurie & Quilliet (1981, 387–388). Of course, in absolute terms, state revenue was increasing (see Price, 1973, I, 375, Table IV), but much less than either national product or government expenditures.

[119] In the eighteenth century, 40% of state revenue came via the General Farms. But this figure does not tell the whole story. "Delay reigned everywhere. It was almost structural, giving the low coherence of the [fiscal] system, the intentional bad will of many, the real difficulties of transport . . . and a whole complex of habitually slow behavior" (Goubert, 1973, 147).

[120] Chaussinand-Nogaret (1970, 266). "The Terror straightened out the matter. On May 8, 1794, out of 36 general farmers who were arrested or imprisoned, 28 were executed. The confiscation of their goods was the occasion, to the profit of the Republic, of the last financial operation of a Company which had become synonomous with royal finances."

These financiers were at the same time "bourgeois" and "aristocrats." Their rise "was the rise of a bourgeoisie, of this dynamic bourgeoisie, with few scruples and often enlightened, constituted by 'la marchandise'. . . . The financiers formed in fact an oligarchy of which one couldn't tell whether it was founded on fortune or heredity" (Chaussinand-Nogaret, 1970, 270). "The power of these families, founded on money, quickly obscured their origins and the conditions of their rise in status. . . . Finance penetrated the nobility, aristocrats concerning themselves with it just as much as financiers an industrial entrepreneurs" (Soboul, 1970b, 228). This fusion of interests was based on the common accumulation of capital. As Bosher (1970, 309) notes, "the National Assembly, in large majority,

did not like the financial system precisely because it was in the hands of profit-making capitalists—they used that word—and in this respect the debt seemed to them to be the worst feature of a bad system."

[121] On the increasing gap between government expenses and ordinary revenues, see Guéry (1978). For Morineau (1980b, 318), it was not merely one war but the succession of wars which created the problem. "The most powerful impact, as one might suspect, came from the cumulation of the Debt after each period of hostilities." Still even Morineau acknowledges (p. 311) that it was with the resignation of Necker in 1781 that "French finances entered a period of anguish. . . . [Borrowing] ate away from within ordinary revenue [the French system distinguished between ordinary and extraordinary revenue] by the growth of the service on the debt (*charge des intérêts*)." This is all the more noteworthy in that, in the American war, the French did not need, as in previous Franco–British wars, to maintain large land armies in Europe. See Anderson (1965, 266).

It is for this reason that Skocpol's argument (1979, 64) that it was "its unquenchable penchant for war [that] carried the eighteenth-century Bourbon monarchy into an acute financial crisis" seems to me off the mark. The "penchant" seems to me no greater in France than in Britain, probably less. "Who would not understand . . . the fears of a Turgot" when he learned of the outbreak of the American war? (Morineau, 1980b, 309). As for Necker, Grange (1957, 29) notes that it was "the American war which he hated [which] kept him from realizing most of his projects." It was Pitt, let us remember, who bemoaned the Peace of Paris.

French interests, and in many ways it did. After all, it represented a secession by that colonial zone of Great Britain which was its most important client for exports. And indeed the war did hurt Britain, causing a "sharp interruption"[122] in foreign trade and a decline in its total value. For France, it was a "war of revenge"[123] and the ideological implications were ignored.

Although Great Britain lost the American war, the French advantage turned out to be chimerical. Lüthy denounced retrospectively this "unnatural alliance" that derived from Choiseul's conception of a revenge in the New World, and points out that no sooner was peace concluded than "the English and the Americans found themselves once again in tête-à-tête to liquidate their family quarrel on the backs of those foreigners (Latins and Papists) who had intruded without being invited."[124] Why did this happen? In large part, for all the reasons which explain the parallel resumptions of commercial links between excolonizer and excolonized after the so-called decolonizations of the twentieth century: it is far simpler—in terms of existing commercial, social, and cultural networks—for the excolonized to resume their old ties (in somewhat altered form) than to transfer this relationship to other core powers.[125]

Indeed, by 1796, an astute French analyst, Tanguy de la Boissière, reflecting on Franco—American commercial relations since 1775, could write that

> Great Britain, in losing the ownership of the land of its colonies, has lost nothing, since she immediately became the owner of its usufruct. She has the benefits at present which are provided by an immense commerce without having, as in the past, the costs of administrations. . . . It is thus obvious that England, far from having suffered a loss, has gained from the secession of 1774.[126]

Such an analysis was not unknown in Britain. It undoubtedly underlay Burke's opposition to George III's policies and his view that this "disaster" represented "a departure from the traditions established by the Great Revolution of 1689."[127] Nor was Burke alone. Josiah Wedgwood, a great

---

[122] Mathias (1969, 44). Deane and Cole (1967, 47) see the American War as a "disastrous interlude" in what was otherwise a "period of rapid growth" in British foreign trade since the 1740s. Ashton also speaks of the "disaster" of 1775 (1948, 148).

[123] Meyer (1979a, 187).

[124] Lüthy (1961, 592). On the disappointment of the French concerning their hopes for an expanded North American trade, see Godechot (1980d, 410): "Instead of an active commerce with the United States [1778–1789], bringing prosperity to both countries, . . . it was a stagnant or worse a unidirectional, commerce which took from France her cash without bringing her any profit."

[125] A typical situation can be found in the ques-

tion of the export of naval masts from the United States. Bamford (1952, 33–34) wonders why France, in the period 1776–1786, failed to import such masts in quantity, thus depriving the French navy "of a great forest resource on which Britain had long depended and on which she was left free to draw with little hindrance from the French." His answer: "the ignorance and conservatism of many French naval officers regarding American foreign resources" plus some instances of irresponsibility of American merchants which confirmed French prejudices.

[126] Tanguy de la Boissière (1796, 19).

[127] Plumb (1950, 135).

entrepreneur "typical of his time and class," was also opposed to the war. He "blessed his stars and Lord North when America achieved its independence."[128]

This advantage to Britain of decolonization existed, however, primarily because of the dominant position in world commerce that Britain had already achieved as of 1763. Under such circumstances, to keep British North America as a colony represented a burden without sufficient concomitant advantage, even if not all British officials immediately realized it at the time. In hindsight it is evident (but is it only in hindsight?) that "commercially the secession of the colonies worked out almost to the advantage of the motherland."[129]

It was thus that the American war, intended by France to be the "knell of British greatness," turned out to have as its price "a French revolution."[130] France's state debt doubled as a result of the war.[131] Within five years the monarchy had become "no longer credit-worthy."[132] In 1788, the service on the debt reached 50% of the budget.[133] The state was approaching "bankruptcy."[134]

But was the British state in the 1780s in so much better a situation? Debt service in Great Britain in 1782 was even greater as a percentage of public revenue than in France—the France even of 1788, not to speak of the France of 1782. The difference was not in where they were at the time of the peace treaty in 1783, but in "what took place after."[135]

---

[128] Plumb (1956, 129).

[129] Dehio (1962, 122). It is not only France that was "deceived" by this development. In Holland, the two anti-stadhouder groups, the Regents (liberal grand bourgeois) and the Patriots (radical democrats) "were persuaded that the British defeat in America would wield a fatal blow to English commerce and that the interest of their country was henceforth to ally itself to France. . . . [However,] the commerce between Holland and the United States did not [after 1783] become as significant as had been hoped by the merchants, because the American ports renewed their ties with England" (Godechot, 1965, 108–109).

France also lost economically in northern Europe (as did Britain, but who lost more?) because of the American war, since the Franco–British naval struggle created a commercial void partially filled by the "neutral commerce" of these countries. See Meyer (1979a, 213–214).

[130] Cobban (1963, 122).

[131] See Morineau (1980b, 312–313), who says the debt reached 1000–1300 million livres. How much of a role the desperate selling of life annuities (*rentes viagères*) during the American war, without regard to the age of the purchaser, played in this process is a matter of debate. Riley (1973, 742) finds it "costly"; Harris (1976, 256) says "it has yet to be proved that these loans were catastrophic." But

rentes viagères precisely were not "loans," unlike *rentes perpetuelles*. See Taylor (1961, 959–960).

Furthermore, the state loans offered "unusual speculative profits," drawing in capital from Geneva, Amsterdam, London, and Genoa. The result was that by 1786, "prices and credits were dangerously inflated." This led to a fear of state insolvency, threatening the "whole structure of French commercial capitalism, to say nothing of foreign financial centers." The link to the Revolution can be clearly seen in the fact that the National Assembly in 1789 made three explicit guarantees of these state loans. And "it was Talleyrand, bishop and agioteur, who led the fight to restore governmental solvency by nationalizing the property of the Church." As we know, this only postponed the evil day. Eventually, the assignats and the Convention in 1793 "destroyed speculative wealth" (Taylor, 1961, 956–957).

[132] Roberts (1978, 8).

[133] See Le Roy Ladurie & Quilliet (1981, 386).

[134] Hobsbawm (1962, 79–80).

[135] Morineau (1980b, 329). Nor was it a difference between the system of *financiers* in France and the existence of the Bank of England in Britain, a difference which is "somewhat overstated" (p. 332). They both served as "monetary breeding-grounds" (*viviers d'argent*) (p. 332) for their respective governments.

The British–French disparity grew suddenly. First of all, the British raised additional revenue, thereby reducing debt service perceptibly.[136] But this was not enough, especially since the British had a further problem resulting from the steady repatriation of Dutch investment in the 1780s.[137] That is, their debt could no longer be rolled over. Yet we know that between 1783 and 1790 or 1793, the French debt kept mounting while the British debt was largely liquidated.[138] Davis has an explanation—"the plunder of India in the decades after Plassey"—which, even if it wasn't the basis of capital investment in industry, could be said to have "supplied the funds that bought the national debt back from the Dutch and others."[139] Once again, Britain's advantage derived from a position acquired as of 1763. When we compare the happy decade of industrial growth in Britain in the 1780s which culminated in the "veritable boom of 1792, on the eve of the [renewed Franco–British] war,"[140] with the unhappy "pre-revolution" in France, we must put this in the context of a very different situation of state finances. This financial–fiscal difference could have been merely a "passing annoyance,"[141] had it not resulted in an

---

[136] See Morineau (1980b, 326). This was unlike the period following the Seven Years War. See Ward (1965, 549–550). But in that earlier period, Great Britain had a different advantage (over France), that of its favorable balance of trade with British North America which enabled it "to remain solvent" during the Seven Years' War (Andrews, 1924, 109). In the case of France, the "unforeseen costliness of the war" led to a pair of policy decisions which, combined, created the fundamental dislocation of state finances. On the one hand, France decided in 1755–56 "to fund the war from credit rather than taxes." This was essentially because of the strength of the *parlements* in opposition to higher taxation. On the other hand, France decided in 1764, unlike in 1714, "to preserve the sanctity of the . . . debt," preferring to free grain and to reduce taxes. Too much *laissez faire*, we note once again. The first decision fostered a significant growth in debt, while the second "asssured that the debt would be allowed a free rein in exercising its influence on the polity, the economy, and the finances" (Riley, 1986, 160, 230–231).

[137] On the importance of Dutch holdings in eighteenth-century Britain, see Eagly and Smith (1976, 210–211); see also Wallerstein (1980, 279–280). On the repatriation, see Mathias (1969, 4), and Davis (1979, 54–55).

[138] See Morineau (1980b, 324–325).

[139] Davis (1979, 55).

[140] Crouzet (1965, 73).

[141] On October 25, 1786, an astute British diplomat in Paris, Daniel Hailes, dispatched this analysis to Lord Carmarthen in London: "According to M. Necker's calculation, the public debts of England

and France, by great singularity of accident, at the end of the war, amounted to nearly the same sum. France had been, taking all circumstances together, full as great a sufferer as Great Britain by the war, and she had nothing to console herself with but the unproductive gratification of seeing America politically separated from her parent country, without any increase of commercial advantage to herself; and that for reasons evidently existing in her inability to furnish those articles of first necessity of which America stands in need, either so good, so cheap, or at so long credit as England. Disappointed then in those hopes (if she really had entertained any) of securing the trade of the United States to herself, it might have been expected that she would have turned her eyes inward upon her own domestic condition, and, after having seen the mischief she had brought upon herself in common with her enemy, that she would have taken some effectual steps toward the contracting her expenditure, and have applied to her wounds the only medicament from which she could expect relief, that of economy. Great Britain, by setting that example, made such a conduct doubly necessary; each country being accustomed, and with reason, to measure its own wants and distress by the advantages and resources of its rival. But France, at the present moment, seems to have lost entirely sight of that policy; and your Lordship will have observed that I have particularly dwelt, in the course of my correspondence, upon those operations of finance which I have thought most likely to throw light upon a conduct so opposite to what might have been expected.

"Although I have always been in the perfect

explosion and thus an eventual considerable magnification of the Franco–British disparity."[142]

Thus it was that the accumulated advantages of Britain in the world-economy that were hers after 1763 increased in the 1780s to become definitive by 1815. The French state's desire to "catch up" with Britain was very important in the 1780s in creating the conditions for an explosion. A mounting state debt can only be solved by cutting expenditure, or by increasing revenue, directly or indirectly. The French state chose the path of trying to increase it indirectly.

In 1776, Louis XVI wrote on the margin of a memorandum of Turgot: "There is the great complaint of M. Turgot. For the lovers of novelty, we need a France more English than England."[143] Louis XVI seemed dubious. Necker tried to move in the other direction, the direction of increasing the state's share in the extraction of surplus value. He failed. The 1780s would offer the chance again to those who wished to "open" France to the fresh winds (their opponents thought wild gales) of "novelty" and of competition. On the one hand, those who profited well from cornering the rent, especially in the 1780s, may be thought to have "sawed off the branch on which they were sitting."[144] On the other hand, the monarchy, reacting against its frustrations (inability to reform the internal fiscal system) and turning thereupon to the solution of open frontiers (and consequent increased customs dues) as a source of revenue, may be said to have joined in the sawing. For the monarchy thereby caused to turn against it yet another section of the capitalist strata, those who feared an eventual "semiperipheralization" of France in a British-dominated world-economy.

The first sign of the new policy was the decree of August 30, 1784 opening the French colonies to free foreign trade. This was an attempt to encourage trade between the now-independent North American states and the French West Indies, a move which turned out to benefit Britain at least as much as France.[145] Already, at this point, the great port merchants of

persuasion that the systems of reform proposed, and begun indeed, in this reign, by Mons. Turgot and Mons. Necker are as impracticable as they are inapplicable to the government of this Monarchy, and altho' it be evidently necessary that that powerful class which stands between the throne and the people should be supported by a part of the revenues of the country, yet (if I may be allowed the expression) the wise management of venality, and the economy of corruption and favour, by not heaping, as is the case in the present day, too many honours and emoluments on the same persons, offer such great resources as to constitute, perhaps, the only essential and practicable superiority of a good over a bad administration of the finances. It is to the Court, my Lord, that you must look for the source of the present evil" (Browning, 1909, 144–145).

[142] Morineau (1980b, 334).
[143] Cited as Item No. 7623 in Osler (1978, 680).
[144] Le Roy Ladurie (1975, 422).
[145] Calonne and his minister of colonies, Castries, whose decree it was, quarreled over whether the colonies should be open to *all* foreigners or only to the North Americans. Castries won, arguing that *de facto*, via the most favored nations clause, a concession to the North Americans meant a concession to everyone. Calonne thereupon sought to compensate French cod fishers by raising the duty on imports and giving bounties for cod exports. See Pugh (1939, 294–295); see also Habakkuk (1965, 39).

Tanguy de la Boissière, writing in 1796 (p. 22), saw the decree as the result of blind hopes in their future commercial relations with North America. "The cabinet in Versailles . . . believed at the time

France protested vigorously.[146] One of the justifications of the government was that the monopolies had already been undermined by an extensive contraband trade. The 1784 decree thus recognized and sought to capitalize upon a reality of economic life.[147] It was this logic that led to the fateful Eden Treaty of 1786 which, Braudel argues, "proved," rather than brought on, France's failure in the struggle for hegemony.[148] But did one have to demonstrate it so glaringly? And was it not itself in many ways the last nail in the coffin?

What caused France not merely to sign the Anglo–French Commercial Treaty of 1786 but to take the lead in seeking it?[149] It seems quite evident that the hope was to kill two birds with one stone: both to resolve the financial crisis of the French state by being able to tax what was previously a contraband trade (and indeed to expand this trade globally)[150] and to

that nothing was too much for the Americans." Tanguy (p. 5) cited with approval the text of Arnould (1791, I, 233): "The Americans obtain, against France, a net balance of payments with which they confound English industry. That is then the *nec plus ultra* of a commerce, the hope for which contributed to the sacrifice by France of hundreds of millions [of livres] and several generations of men." For Arnould, the reason this decree did not pay off was twofold: poor quality of French merchandise and active competition (in the North American market) of other European states (see p. 235). Even the Dutch begged Louis XVI to revoke the decree, saying that it was the English who profited from it, at their expense as well as at that of the French. See Morineau (1965, 225).

[146] See Godechot (1980a, 81).

[147] See Habukkuk (1965, 39).

[148] Braudel (1984, 379).

[149] Vergennes and Rayneval, the principal French negotiators, "wanted to have a policy of 'clearing' à la Briand, settling the differences which separated the two neighboring peoples. The hour was furthermore grave from a financial point of view; a new war might provoke an internal collapse. A long peace was necessary to restore the throne and the national economy. . . . One thing is sure. Negotiation was the result of French insistence" (Cahen, 1939, 258). Indeed the French initiative "was greeted with profound suspicion by the younger Pitt, who suspected the French even when they appeared to bring gifts" (Cobban, 1963, 111). If the British agreed to negotiate, it was no doubt because both governments "were influenced by considerations of a practical character since both urgently needed to increase their revenues" (Henderson, 1957, 105). In addition, the French put pressure on the British to negotiate by means of the decree of July 17, 1785, restoring prohibitions on English manufactures and by engaging in negotiations with Holland for a new commercial treaty. See

Dumas (1904, 30–35). They also threatened to annul (Dumas, 1904, 36) the Treaty of Utrecht of 1716, that is, the treaty of navigation and commerce signed the same day as the peace treaty. See Ehrman (1962, 30, n. 4). It is useful to remember that, in 1716, the British parliament had rejected clauses 8 and 9 of the Treaty, which would have opened trade widely between the two countries because at that time French industry "still inspired such dread among English industrialists that they felt incapable of sustaining a struggle against it" (Dumas, 1904, 3). Briavoinne made this same point in 1839 (p. 193). The French had been thereupon stuck with the "disadvantages" of Article V (English navigation having access to French ports) without the "advantages" of Articles VIII and IX. See the complaints of de Rayneval in his memo to Calonne (1784, 2066) urging the beginning of negotiations.

[150] Dupont de Nemours, generally credited with being the chief intellectual advocate of the treaty and of freer trade, is quite clear on this. He argued (1786, 36 bis), in his longest memorandum on the subject, in favor of a controlled, reciprocal trade between Britain and France that would replace the contraband trade which, since neither country had been able to suppress it, had deprived both of them of "the benefits of the returns to be furnished for the merchandise each received." that is, the customs duties. He returned to this theme in his justificatory pamphlet two years later, complaining of the "customs of Our Nation" which had sustained the contraband and arguing that the Treaty had "shifted to the profit of the state . . . the money previously expended for insurance premiums to sustain an illicit trade" (Dupont de Nemours, 1788, 49, 72). See also Anisson-Dupéron (1847, 16).

The French analysis of Dupont de Nemours is quite close to that of the British diplomat, Daniel Hailes: "In Great Britain, His Majesty's Ministers, with uncommon wisdom, vigilance, and perseverance, have, at last, found means to carry into effect

resolve the long-term structural difficulties of French production by forcing innovation via market pressures.[151] There was furthermore a conjunctural factor that played in favor of a French initiative from France's perspective. There was the dramatic fall of agricultural prices in the period after 1778,[152] which made the large landowners all the more resistant to any mechanism that would shift surplus from them to the state. The route of increased customs duties must have seemed all the more attractive.

The treaty involved a trade-off with the British. Freer trade meant (crudely) more British cottons (and pottery, wool, hardware) in the French market against more French wine (and other agricultural products, but also silk, linens, glassware) in the British. But how much more? The answer depended on the economic calculations. The French negotiators no doubt underestimated the impact of British manufactures[153] and overestimated their ability to compensate French manufacturers for any losses.[154] But

the revenue laws, which had been so long eluded. . . .

"It seems, therefore, probable, that the French Government felt its own inability to give effect to its prohibitory laws against the importation of British manufactures, and in that respect, at all events, they may be said to have been the gainers by the treaty.

"But I think I can take upon me to assure your Lordship that there exists another, and no less principal cause, of the eagerness of France to conclude the commercial arrangements. I mean that of the immediate relief of the Trésor Royal by the increase of the revenue, an increase which, it may be presumed, will prove immense from the sudden influx of all sorts of British Merchandise paying the legal duties, as soon as the Treaty shall take effect." (Dispatch to Lord Carmarthen written on October 25, 1786, in Browning, 1909, 149–150).

[151] Stourm (1885, 31), explaining the motives of Dupont de Nemours, Vergennes, and others, points out that the Treaty was not the only effort along this line. "The heroic remedy of English competition followed a series of measures taken with the same objective over the previous several years: enrollment of shop foremen (*chefs d'atelier*) from England, promises to inventors, the import at the expense of the state of foreign machines piece by piece as well as advantages accorded to various machine-builders, favors given for commerce with the colonies, a police embargo on English workers to keep them [in France] for the full term of their contract, exceptional benefits accorded to foreign manufacturers (*fabricants*) who wished to settle in France, etc." Lefebvre (1932, 14) saw it as a "good idea in principle. . . . By opening brusquely the frontiers to English industry whose superiority was overwhelming [dixit Lefebvre], a brutal shaking would be induced." Landes (1969, 139) shares this

view. The Eden Treaty of 1786 "opened the French market to British cottons and made modernization a matter of survival."

[152] Labrousse (1944, 417) talks of a fall of 45–50%. "The advance obtained since 1760 was thus lost."

[153] It is striking to note that when Eden was appointed by Pitt as the chief British negotiator, then and only then did Vergennes write to the French chargé d'affaires in London, M. de Barthélemy, asking for such elementary information as whether or not the British government paid bounties on exports. See Ségur-Dupeyron (1873, 386–387). Rayneval was equally ignorant. See Dumas (1904, 27). They both might have been able to draw on the knowledge of Holker, who was English by birth but had become an inspector-general of French manufactures, and who warned Rayneval on December 29, 1785 that the English "could provide France with cotton cloth of all types at 30% cheaper than we can." (Cited in Boyetet, 1789, 86–87.) But Holker died a few days before Eden arrived in Paris. The merchants of Manchester were said to be overjoyed on learning of his death, not only because it deprived de Rayneval of a precious advisor but because they expected his own cotton factories in Rouen to collapse with his death. See His de Butenval (1869, 65, 70).

[154] In his open letter to the Chamber of Commerce of Normandy, written in 1788 in reply to their complaints about the effects of the Eden Treaty, Dupont de Nemours (1788, 8) said that he had long supported government aid to French industry. "I told the Minister, wrote him, forcefully repeated to him that he had to try to render bearable and even advantageous the competition which he thought necessary to permit. He recognized this necessity. . . . [However,] the suspen-

worst of all, they seemed to welcome a new semiperipheral role for France. Chaptal, in his memorandum to Napoleon in 1802, speaking of the Treaty, thought that France had banked on "the advantages and prosperity of her agriculture" and said that the products of English soil "had nothing that were either special or rare."[155] Nonetheless, Rayneval, it has been argued, seemed ready to make any concession, "provided there were a lowering of duties on [France's] agricultural products."[156] Indeed, Rayneval wrote to M. Adhemar, French Ambassador in London in 1786, just before the signing of the Treaty:

> Doubtless, we are introducing into England principally the products of our soil, in exchange for English products. But I have always believed, and still do, that an agricultural producer is the most interesting person from the point of view of the state.

Nor did de Rayneval stop there. For, as a further justification of the Treaty before the Conseil d'Etat on May 21, 1786, he argued:

> Suppose the results are other than those we predict, is it preferable to seek the prosperity of a few iron and steel manufacturers, or that of the kingdom? To increase the number of manufacturers, or the number of agricultural producers? And suppose that we are inundated with English hardware, could we not resell them in Spain or elsewhere?[157]

Thus did Rayneval appear to contemplate with great equanimity the possibility that France would play the conveyor-belt role in the world-economy that had been the glorious fate of Spain and Portugal for two centuries already. No wonder Pitt could say in defense of the Treaty in Parliamentary debate: "It was in the nature and essence of an agreement between a manufacturing country and a country blessed with peculiar [sic!] productions, that the advantages must terminate in favor of the former."[158]

Was this an inevitable strategy for the French state, at the very moment of the apogee of economic growth under the *Ancien Régime*?[159] It is striking that Britain was trying to negotiate commercial treaties between 1785 and 1793 with Portugal, Spain, Russia, England, Prussia, the Two Sicilies, and Holland alongside its negotiations with France. There was also preliminary talk about negotiations with Sweden, Turkey, and the Austrian Nether-lands. Thus, the Marquis of Carmarthen could speak in 1786 of "the

sion of the Assembly of Notables has had the effect, along with the frequent changes within the Ministry, of retarding regretfully the execution [of this intent]."

[155] Chaptal (1893, 86).
[156] Dumas (1904, 78).
[157] Both quotes are cited in His de Butenval

(1869, 57, 70). One can see why Weulersee terms the Treaty of 1786 "a brilliant success" for the Physiocrats (1985, 33).
[158] Cobbett (1816, 395).
[159] Marczewski (1965, xcv) marks the apogee as 1780–1786.

present Rage for Commercial Treaties." None of the other negotiations
came to anything. "The success [of the French treaty] was unique."[160] The
pressure on the French government was no doubt great—the state of
government finances, the crisis in the wine trade[161]—but so was the
decision, symbolically and in reality. The French state seemed to be opting,
under the guise of reform, for a partial deindustrialization which would
serve the interests of certain agricultural entrepreneurs but which compromised the interests of its manufacturing classes. The "reforms" seemed
similar to those advocated by the International Monetary Fund in the
twentieth century for indebted governments with balance of payments
difficulties.

It is thus understandable that British objections to the Treaty, though
real, were easily overcome. Pitt defended the treaty on the basis of
commercial advantage. Fox opposed it on purely political grounds, that
"France was the natural foe of Great Britain."[162] In any case, the British
had various good, immediate economic reasons to support the treaty. They
had the same incentive as the French to find new sources of state revenue,
and thus to legalize a smuggling trade, thereby rendering the Franco–
British exchanges taxable.[163] They were worried about potential losses of
markets to France in North America (because of the postwar treaty), in
Spain (because of the Family Accord), and in Portugal (which had just
accorded France most-favored-nation status), and thereby welcomed markets in France itself.[164] But most of all, they knew that the heart of the
competition was in cotton. Not only were they confident of their ability to
sell in the French market[165] but they were also concerned to maintain

[160] Ehrman (1962, 175). The Carmarthen quote
is on p. 2.

[161] See Labrousse (1944, 78–82), Slicher van
Bath (1963, 235–236). The support of the wine-
growers for the Treaty was still strong in retrospect
in 1802 when the Conseil de Commerce de Bordeaux sent the Minister of the Interior Chaptal a
memo in defense of the Eden Treaty. See His de
Butenval (1869, 107).

[162] Cobbett (1816, 398). It is true that The Morn-
ing Herald, an opposition paper, argued that
French cotton manufactures were superior to British and that taxes in Britain were higher. See His de
Butenval (1869, 134) and Dumas (1904, 107). But,
as Dumas suggests (p. 121), this was doubtless
political propaganda designed to frighten British
manufacturers—without success, in fact. Ehrman
(1962, 65) considers that it was "perhaps the weakness of such [economic] arguments that [led the
Opposition] to concentrate on the treaty's diplomatic implications."

Dull gives this some credence by arguing that for
Vergennes the treaty was "an 18th-century version
of Nixon & Kissinger's Russian policy" (1983, 11).

Mantoux believes, however, there was a division
among British manufacturers, the older industries
favoring protection and opposing the treaty, the
newer ones realizing that "their main interests lay in
obtaining cheap raw materials and free markets for
the sale of their goods" (1928, 400).

[163] See Browning (1885, 354).

[164] See Dumas (1904, 14–15).

[165] "The weight of the cotton, iron, and pottery
interests was . . . strongly thrown in favour of
Government policy. . . . For all these trades had
much to gain by a wider entry into the French
market, which none had cause to be afraid of
serious competition from French manufactures"
(Ashton, 1924, 171).

Two Manchester calico printers, Joseph Smith
and Robert Peel, saw the advantage of the English
cotton trade in their cost-saving machinery. "It is
impossible to say how soon foreign countries may
obtain these machines, but even then, the experience we have in the use of them would give us such
an advantage that I should not fear competition"
(Cited in Edwards, 1967, 51).

access to cotton imports from outside the British colonies, which at the time provided less than 30% of their needs.[166] From that point of view, vulgar protectionism would not do.

The economic consequences of the treaty for France were felt almost immediately, especially (as a 1788 French government memorandum indicates) in the field of "ordinary cloth" as opposed to "good cloth," that is, all the kinds that were used for the consumption of "the people" rather than of "rich persons."[167] The treaty led to a massive import, a "veritable deluge,"[168] of cotton manufactures from Britain (and other manufactures as well). It was an "economic revolution,"[169] one of the "turning-points in the industrial history of France."[170] British goods "inundated" the French market, Arnould wrote in 1791.[171] But it did not take five years for the French to become aware of this. These effects were a matter of political discussion almost immediately. It has often been argued since that this was an error in popular perception, since the economic decline began in 1786 or even in 1785, before the actual date of entry into effect of the Treaty which was July 1, 1787.[172] This seems to me to miss the point. Objectively, the effect may have been most acute after 1787, but one factor that in part explains the difficulties of 1786 was probably the anticipation of the treaty. In any case, it is the perception and not the reality which governed the political response.[173]

Of course, the French manufacturers and others recognized that British cloths were selling well because they were selling cheaper than French cloth

[166] See Bowden (1919, 25–26).

[167] A.E. 46, 1788, 239.

[168] Morineau (1978, 411). This is otherwise known as a "formidable competition" (Furet & Richet, 1973, 26).

[169] Dardel (1963, 71).

[170] Markovitch (1966c, 130). Schmidt (1913, 270) cites a *mécanicien* who in 1788 spoke of the "commercial Revolution in which we are caught."

[171] Arnould (1791, 181–183). See also Chaptal (1819, I, 95–96), Dumas (1904, 150–151), Schmidt (1908, 91–92), Mantoux (1928, 263), Sée (1930, 308), Labrousse (1933, II, 320), Acomb (1939, 42), Guérin (1968, I, 64–65), Tilly (1968, 215–222), and Morineau (1971, 331).

A few scholars argue that, since French industry was already in difficulty prior to the treaty, the latter's role should not be overstated. See Gaillardon (1909, 151), and Murphy (1966, 578). What seems more just to me is to say, as does Bouloiseau (1957, liv), that, although the difficulties of the industry existed since at least 1780, it was the treaty that "revealed the amplitude of the problem"— revealed its amplitude, accentuated it, and threatened to institutionalize it.

[172] Cahen (1939, 275), for example, talks of the fact that the "whole responsibility" for grave economic crisis was "by confusion . . . attributed to the treaty." Henderson (1957, 110) depreciates the advantage to Britain, arguing that the doubling of British exports to France between 1787 and 1792 "may merely have represented a transfer to legitimate channels of trade in goods that had formerly been smuggled."

[173] "Contemporaries attributed a large role to the treaty of 1786" (Lefebvre, 1939, 118). See also Heckscher (1922, 22). In August 1788, a caricature was circulating in Paris. A person called Commerce was being hanged in a public square. The strangling cord was called discount houses. A weight was hanging from his bare feet, called "export duties." His hands were tied with a band reading "trade treaty." See Schmidt (1908, 78).

That these perceptions of the time were not hysteria but based on material conditions is confirmed by Tarrade who points out that, as soon as the treaty was signed, English manufacturers, in anticipation of profit, speculated on cotton. This led to a "rapid" price rise, "prejudicial to French enterprises at the moment that they had to face up to English competition" (1972, II, 691).

in the French market,[174] an advance caused by greater mechanization, which in turn could provide the solution. But how, and how fast? A French encyclopedia published in 1789 wrote:

> We have just made a commercial treaty with England, which may enrich our great-grand-nephews, but which has deprived of their bread 500,000 workers in the kingdom and undermined 10,000 commerical houses.[175]

In the meantime, the French perceived the British government as aiding a process of dumping.[176] They worried about effects that would be "difficult to undo" such as the emigration of unemployed skilled workers.[177] By the time of the *cahiers de doléance*, the treaty was so unpopular that complaints about it were to be found in the *cahiers* even of provinces "less immediately affected."[178] "The general desire was the total abolition of this treaty."[179]

Writing in 1911, Mourlot argued what many had felt at the time. The treaty made of France an "economic province" of England; it was a sort of "new Revocation of the Edict of Nantes."[180] Politically, the effect was dramatic. The manufacturing sector felt abandoned by the state-machinery precisely when they thought they needed it most. It must have seemed as if the king's men were ready to accept the semiperipheralization of France under the guise of liberalism and the beneficence of competition. No doubt, in some sense, "the game had already been lost . . . [and] England had already gained control of the worldwide economy."[181] But the Treaty seemed the act that might make this irreversible, a view which could lead to a strong reaction, particularly in light of how well things seemed to be going in England.

---

[174] A Glasgow manufacturer, writing in 1786 or 1787, relates how he met Holker at Rouen, and how Holker admitted to him that, while French manufacturers paid lower wages, they also had lower productivity because of indiscipline, and therefore in fact costs were higher. See Auckland (1861, I, 516–517).

[175] Jacques Peuchet, *Encyclopédie méthodique* (Jurisprudence, IX, Police et Municipalitiés, *v°* agriculture), cited in Bloch (1900, 242, n. 1).

[176] "[The English sell their products] at very low prices, even below those which French speculators, who bought their goods in England, can sell them without loss, which leads me to believe that they are aided sub rosa by the government. We know that such is their method to crush the industry of countries into which they have procured the admission of the goods" (A.E. 46, 236). It is curious that no later scholar has pursued this matter to see whether or not this French perception of the time is justified by the evidence.

[177] Letter, written in 1788, cited by Mourlot (1911, 106).

[178] See Picard (1910, 156, 161). Of course, "the

cahiers of the *bailliages* of the industrial regions were unanimously hostile to the treaty" (Dumas, 1904, 182). To be sure, some agricultural districts saw the treaty in an opposite light (p. 186).

[179] Champion (1897, 164) and Sée (1931a, II, 950, n. 1) agree, first that the treaty was "harmful," the provinces of Champagne, Picardy, and Normandy suffering in particular, and second that "in France the complaints wee unanimous against this treaty and against the manner of English application," as could be seen in the *cahiers*.

Nor did the hostility stop in 1789. On the contrary. "In the misery and turmoil of 1789–93 that treaty appeared to be the prelude of Pitt's deep-laid conspiracy to enrich England at the expense of France. . . . The premature attempt of 1786, made under the old monarchy, and the reaction which it caused under the republic, have done much to identify in France a prohibitive or strictly protective policy with popular government" (Rose, 1893, 705).

[180] Mourlot (1911, 105).

[181] Braudel (1984, 381).

There were immediate and "clear benefits" for England. State revenue rose, export opportunities expanded, and the balance of trade "veered sharply" in favor of Britain.[182] But there was more. The Eden Treaty, by opening the French market, permitted the economies of scale to the British manufacturers which enabled the British to cut their prices in the United States (and presumably elsewhere). As early as 1789, a British Consul noted that there was a result "a sensible check to the progress of the cotton manufactory at Philadelphia."[183]

It had been expected that the French disadvantage in cotton would be somewhat compensated by the French advantage in wine. It was not to be. The English, while they bought more French wine, did not buy all that much more.[184] The "crisis" caused by the Eden Treaty presumably caused a decline in the internal French market. Therefore, although the wine producers were naturally[185] and factually[186] supporters of the open-trade policies incarnated in the treaty, their situation did not materially improve. Wine prices had been declining since 1777 and indeed reached their nadir in 1786, the low levels persisting until 1791. When the violent price rises of cereals occurred in 1788 and 1789, there resulted a squeeze on winegrower revenue resulting in a 40% decline in purchasing power.[187] They turned for relief to a campaign against the tithe and seigniorial dues. It is no wonder that this "terrible" crisis of the manufacturing sector, coinciding with very high prices of cereals and bread, "would provoke the Revolution."[188]

How does one "explain" a complex "event" like the French Revolution? It does not much matter if one defines the French Revolution as what happened on July 14, 1789 or what happened between 1789 (or 1787) and 1793 (or 1799 or 1815). Whatever the time scope of the event, no explanation of one event in terms of another event can ever be very satisfying. Two events provide a sequence, and their linkage may be plausible, but still other "events" of course intervened, and the question always immediately arises as to how essential such other events might have been to the sequence. Nor can one ever reasonably eliminate other sequences that did not occur as not having been equally likely. To claim a sequence as a causal chain is almost surely to argue *post hoc ergo propter hoc*.

It is, however, equally unsatisfying to explain an "event" by the *longue durée*. The *longue durée* explains large-scale, long-term structural change, but it is not possible to demonstrate that such change could occur only through particular events. Much of the debate about the French Revolution is at this ultimately pointless level. A major event is the result of a

[182] Ehrman (1962, 206).
[183] Cited in Cain & Hopkins (1980, 472).
[184] "The taste of the English in wine was not materially changed . . . ; whereas English hardware and linen found an immediate sale in France' (Browning, 1885, 363).
[185] "Wine is a product of an open economy, a market-oriented product. . . . The wine economy is international" (Labrousse, 1944, 207, 211).
[186] See Labrousse (1944, 586–588).
[187] See Labrousse (1944, 579–580).
[188] Dardel (1948, 62).

conjuncture (in the English sense of the word, meaning a joining point), of *conjonctures* (in the French sense, that is, of intermediate-length cyclical phases), and the event may be called major because of its consequences more than because of its causes. In this sense, the French Revolution is without doubt a "major event" of the modern world.

Two "objective" *conjonctures* have been widely used as the "explanation" of the outbreak of the French Revolution: the economic *conjoncture*[189] and the *conjoncture* in the state-machinery, specifically the growing deficit in state finances. It should be obvious from what has been said thus far that these *conjonctures* did exist, and did in fact play a major role. If these two *conjonctures*, however, were the whole story, there might well have been a French Revolution of sorts,[190] but it is hard for me to believe that it would have been such a central event in the history of the modern world-system.

The centrality of the French Revolution is a consequence of the centrality of the Franco–British struggle for hegemony of the world-economy. The French Revolution occurred in the wake of, and as a consequence of, France's sense of impending defeat in this struggle.[191] And the French Revolution had the kind of impact on the world-system that it did have precisely because it occurred in the country that had lost the struggle for hegemony. The French Revolution, which many had hoped would reverse the tide of British victory, may be said to have been, on the contrary, decisive in ensuring an enduring British victory. But precisely because of this geopolitical, geoeconomic defeat, the French revolutionaries in fact achieved their long-run ideological objectives.

Let us then look at the history of the French Revolution primarily in terms of its consequences rather than of its imputed causes. First of all, what were the actual economic policies of the early revolutionary governments in two key domains: the structure of agricultural production and the role of the state in relationship to industrial production?

[189] On economics, Lefebvre (1947b, 89) says authoritatively: "It is therefore beyond dispute that the economic distress [*crise*] should be included among the immediate causes of the Revolution." To be sure, there are at least three versions of the economic crisis: a crisis of "poverty" (see, *inter alia*, Labrousse, 1944, xlii); a crisis of "growth" (LeRoy Ladurie, 1976, 29–30); or a "J-curve" crisis, that is, a phase of improvement followed by a sudden fall (Tocqueville, 1955, 176–177).

[190] I do, however, agree with the case, argued persuasively by Higonnet (1981), that such an "event" was not inevitable, even if probable.

[191] This is not a popular thesis. As Hartwell and Engerman observe (1975, 193): "Historians might argue that the Napoleonic Wars were the outcome of capitalist–imperialist rivalries, in the way in which historians have argued that the First World War was the outcome of competing imperialisms; but they have not."

As if to prove this point, Furet cried out soon thereafter (1978, 92): "Of course, one can see how one could make of [the Wars from 1792–1815] the culmination of the old Franco–English commercial rivalry. But to go further, and enlarge this aspect of the conflict, the principal content and the 'objective' cause of the interminable war, requires a leap that no historian of the French Revolution, except Daniel Guérin, has been willing to make."

But this is a red herring. No one requires herculean leaps. What is needed is simply a recognition that what Dehio (1962, 139) says of the military conflict—"the Revolution entered the great struggle not with a sense of its own strength but rather with the courage of despair"—applies *mutatis mutandis* to the whole last phase of the struggle for hegemony over the world-economy.

A long time ago, Marc Bloch put forward a view that, in its emphases, goes against the simplistic perception that the Revolution represented the downfall of the large agricultural domain:

> Everyone knows how the seigneurial edifice crashed in ruins between the years 1789 and 1792, taking with it a monarchical regime with which it had become identified.
>
> For all that he liked to see himself as the head of his peasantry, the new-style lord had really became once again primarily a large-scale manager; as had similarly many ordinary bourgeois. If we can imagine, which is of course absurd, the Revolution breaking out around the year 1480, we should find that land relieved of seigneurial charges was reallocated almost without exception to a host of small occupiers. But the three centuries between 1480 and 1789 saw the rehabilitation of the large estate. It was not, as in England and Eastern Germany, all-embracing. Large tracts of land, in total larger perhaps than those covered by the great estates, were still left under peasant proprietorship. But the victory was a sizeable one, though its completeness varied noticeably with the region. The Revolution was to leave the large estate relatively unimpaired. The picture presented by the rural France of our own day—which is not, as is sometimes said, a land of petty proprietors but rather a land where large and small proprietors coexist in proportions which vary considerably from province to province—is to be explained by its evolution between the fifteenth and eighteenth centuries.[192]

How then have we gotten the impression that the role of peasant production in fact rose as a result of the French Revolution? One reason is that there were indeed some dramatic juridical acts affecting the "traditional" rights of the seigniors. The National Assembly did formally abolish, on the famous night of August 4, 1789, the "feudal regime," including the tithe and certain (but not yet all) seigniorial rights.[193] The remaining seigniorial rights would, however, be abolished in turn and without indemnity on July 17, 1793. Furthermore, the Rural Code adopted on September 28, 1791 did authorize enclosure of commons. The law of August 28, 1792 did authorize the division of the commons. The lands of the clergy were nationalized and eventually sold.

Yet, all this was less than it seems. For one thing, no more than the agrarian reformers of the last decades of the *Ancien Régime* did the revolutionary governments abolish either *vaine pâture* or the *droit de parcours*. (Indeed, *vaine pâture* was only to be abolished in 1889, and even then its abolition was subject to local consent.[194] It was unconditionally abolished only following the First World War.) And the law permitting the division of the commons was suspended in 1797.

---

[192] Bloch (1966, 149). I have corrected the translation of the second sentence, which was seriously incorrect.

[193] See Hirsch (1978). Lefebvre (1972, 407) considers this abolition of the tithe "the most important consequence of the agrarian revolution." Sewell goes further. He sees the night of August 4 as "the crucial turning-point of the Revolution both as a class struggle and as an ideological transformation. . . . [It] was a holocaust of privilege" (1985, 69).

[194] See Bloch (1930, 549). For a detailed account of the fate of *vaine pâture* in the nineteenth century, see Clère (1982).

Second, and more importantly, such "gains" as were made by some peasants were largely gains by those who had a certain amount of property, the reasonably well-off *laboureurs,* and were as often as not gains at the expense of the small tenants, small sharecroppers, and landless laborers.[195] To be sure, the various reforms created administrative order in France.[196] But, as Bourgin somewhat sourly suggests, it was "an administration much more coordinated than one believes . . . placed at the service of a legislation much more conservative than one thinks."[197]

Lefebvre attributes our scholarly misperceptions of the radicalness of agrarian reform under the Revolution to the "violent" and "obstinate" quality of the peasant revolt and the "noise" created by the night of August 4 concerning the abolition of feudal rights. Rather than being radical reform, he argues, the legislation was no more than a "compromise." He does add that we shouldn't despise it as such because, if it slowed down

---

[195] The general consolidation of property rights actually slowed down enclosure, despite the formal authorization. As a consequence, Milward and Saul (1973, 263) note "a sharp upward shift [in the revolutionary period] in the income of many peasants." This no doubt explains the political consequence Labrousse (1966, 62) observes: "The land reform of the Revolution and the tradition it established always found in the countryside, in spite of Royalist movements (*les chouanneries*), numerous and ardent defenders."

But, as Chabert remarks, the resulting agricultural prosperity under the Consulate and the Empire was more profitable for the larger proprietors (1949, 91). It thereby increased, not decreased, rural polarization: "The revoluionary event, more than anything else, confirmed the strong in their strength, whilst emptying the pocketbooks of the small *laboureurs* seeking assiduously to round out their plot (*clos*). It increased the gap more than ever between the latter and the large estate. The Revolution hardened the dominant traits of each regional space" (Perrot, 1975a, 38–39).

Bloch's harsh conclusion (1930, 544) seems justified: "In their agricultural policy, the legislatures, not only the Constituent Assembly . . . but even the Convention, far from destroying . . . the reforms enacted by the monarchy, followed in their footsteps. . . . New traits do characterize the work of the revolution. If [the revolutionary legislatures] sacrificed deliberately the landless laborers (*manoeuvres*) just like the *Ancien Régime*, being rid of the need to appease the privileged sectors, it could devote itself much more closely to the interests of the medium-sized owners." The result was particularly harsh in the north of France, as Soboul suggests (1976a, 63) via the disintegration of the peasant community: "The poor peasants, rapidly

proletarianized, furnished the manpower necessary for modern agriculture and large-scale industry."

Such limited damage as was done to the large aristocratic estate during the Revolution was more or less undone in the Napoleonic era, where "one witnessed the reconstitution of the land-based wealth of the former nobility" (Tulard, 1970, 643). See also Chabert (1949, 330); Meyer (1966, II, 1254); Laurent (1976a, 643); Soboul (1976b, 126, 132), and Gauthier (1977, ch. 5 & Part III, passim).

[196] The second new trait of agricultural policy under the Revolution that Bloch noted (1930, 544) was that: "Less timid [than the *Ancien Régime*] and essentially unitarist, it proceeded by measures that applied to the whole national territory."

[197] Bourgin (1911, 192). "The economic and juridical innovations served primarily to consolidate the situation of previous owners, or of new men who, taking advantage of the exceptional circumstances, entered the ranks of the new society" (p. 185). Mackrell is even more acerbic (1973, 176–177): "Once the names were dropped . . . feudal and seigneurial rights became respectable. . . . Successive governments were only too eager to hasten the assimilation of former dues to property rights. Feudal rights in their new form did not so much survive as prosper."

Root sees in the failure to transform agriculture a continuity of the limitations of a weak French state: "The revolutionary government had to abandon its commitment to agrarian reform because of fiscal priorities rather than of threatened peasant resistance. . . . Both before and during the Revolution, the French state, preoccupied with international wars, fiscal chaos, and administrative weakness, proved incapable of promoting agricultural growth" (1987, 241).

economic progress, it also "caused less suffering and was more humane" than British agrarian changes.[198] This is one way to describe what happened, but it sounds a bit too voluntaristic for my taste. The "compromise," as we shall see, was the outcome of a ferocious class struggle that was between those who were gaining from the development of the capitalist world-economy and those who were losing.[199] The "humaneness" of the outcome was the result of the strength of anti-capitalist forces.[200]

If we now turn to the state's role in promoting industrial production, we shall see that the accomplishments of the Revolution in this arena were at least as significant as, probably more so than, in the arena of agrarian reform. Chaptal, writing in 1819, and looking back at the comparative situation of British and French industrial production as of 1789, saw Britain as having a distinct advantage in terms of the geographic width of its market, the quantity of goods sold, and lower prices. He put forward a number of explanations for British advantage, the first of which was "the system followed by England, for more than a century, of allowing into its internal market only the products of its own factories, and rejecting those of foreign producers by means of prohibitions or by customs duties which have the same effect."[201]

---

[198] Lefebvre (1963, 355, 366–367). We can note another less than humane aspect of British economic transformation. The British shift to coal (so often lauded) led directly to "the life-bond of Scottish coal mines" in the eighteenth century. The coalmasters "found labour difficult to recruit" and hence got the state to impose a form of serfdom (Duckham, 1969, 178).

[199] If one looks at it in this fashion, one can integrate more easily the thorny problem of western France's "counter-revolution." LeGoff and Sutherland (1974, 101) point out that under the *Ancien Régime*, Brittany was very lightly governed by the Center, which was kept "at a healthy distance" by the rural communities. The Revolution brought a more activist Center. In their centralizing disposition, the revolutionary legislatures did not take account of the peculiarities of the system of leaseholding there known as *domaine congéable*, which had the effect of considerably increasing the precarity of the position of reasonably well-off tenant farmers. We have already seen that elsewhere in France it was this stratum that did well as a result of the agrarian reform. LeGoff and Sutherland (1983, 75) estimate that in the west of France, the net consequence of the reforms varied from zero effect to an *increase* of 40% in the burdens of the peasantry. They therefore suggest (1974, 109) that it would make sense to pull out of the works of Bois, Faucheux, and Tilly an underdeveloped common theme, that "in general the mass of the poor who inhabited the French countryside profited little if at all from the Revolution, and that in counterrevolutionary areas it was such people who gave desperation, and sometimes force of numbers, to discontent and risings." One can thus interpet the *chouanneries* as peasant revolutions (in the guise of popular royalism) against the urban-based authority of "men whose backgrounds were identical with the class of bourgeois landlords who had taken power in the elections of 1790 and retained it thereafter" (Le Goff & Sutherland, 1983, 86). In this interpretation, counterrevolution looks suspiciously revolutionary. In the face of this argument, Mazauric drops the appelation "counter-revolutionary" for the more anodine mode of labeling the popular oppositions merely "anti-revolutionary" (1985, 239).

[200] For the version of a liberal who argues that French "timidity in the face of obvious opportunity" throughout the nineteenth century was the consequence of the fears of peasants that the "revolutionary land settlement" might be reversed, see Grantham (1980, 529). He deplores (p. 527) the inadequacy of the French capitalist ethos: "Had landownership in France been more concentrated it is certain that individual landowners would have worked harder to secure consolidation of their holdings."

[201] Chaptal (1819, I, 90). The other six explanations are similar to prevailing contemporary scholarly literature: absence of constraining regulations, mechanization, abundance of coal and internal canals, technical division of labor, colonial pos-

The return to protectionism was clearly one of the immediate concerns of a large segment of those who made the revolution and/or came to power as a result of it. "There is no doubting the unpopularity of the [1786 Anglo–French Commercial] treaty among the members of the [Constituent] Assembly and in the country as a whole."[202] In 1793 the treaty was formally renounced by the Convention.

This was in no way in contradiction with the other main economic decision that affected industrial production, the abolition of internal tariffs, thereby achieving at last the dream of Colbert.[203] For this latter act (as well as the abolition of guilds) the Revolution receives the plaudits of Heckscher, who celebrates its "negative result" of dismantling the "irrational monstrosity" of the industrial legislation of the *Ancien Régime*. Heckscher calls this "a tremendous work of reform."[204] Soboul, who in principle, should agree, since he sees the Revolution as the triumph of bourgeois liberalism, does observe nonetheless about the various protectionist measures (tariffs, the *Exclusif*, the navigation act of 1793) that: "The bourgeoisie of the Constitutent Assembly, faced with the dangers of foreign competition, compromised on their commercial liberalism." He calls this "another proof of the realism of the men of 1789."[205] But why was this a "compromise"? It was only a compromise if one assumes that capitalists by definition favor free trade and a minimal role for the state.[206]

The whole point of the French Revolution for many was to expand, not

sessions and supremacy of the seas, sympathetic government working to find external markets and to stifle foreign competition (pp. 91–93). As Crouzet says: "There were indeed few factors which modern observers have called forth in order to explain England's economic growth during the eighteenth century, of which French observers and writers of that period had not caught a glimpse at least" (1981, 72).
[202] Milward & Saul (1973, 167). In a Foreign Office memo written by M. Theremin in 1797, analyzing the 1786 treaty, the author argues that the British sought "reciprocity" because they had two advantages in the market. First, they were more efficient producers at that point in time; and second they were in effect opening an English market of 8 million people in exchange for a French market of 30 million (A.E. 46, 287.) A few years later, a further memo by a M. Arnould (A.E. 46, 331 bis) argued against a renewal of the treaty of 1786 on the following grounds: "Public opinion seems very satisfied to have avenged the national interest of the harm that it had been caused by the treaty of 1786 which is recognized to have been *disastrous*, especially by our manufacturers."
Crouzet (1962, 217), however, warns against Jouvenel's assumption (1942, 127–128) that it was

only France's economic resistance to Britain that led to the rupture of the Treaty of Amiens in 1802 by Bonaparte. Crouzet points to an 1802 British memo that suggests British reticence about reviving the 1786 treaty. However, there are many reasons why Britain in 1802 may have been reticent, among which are that it might have given the wrong geopolitical signal and that the disruption of the French economy might have made the trade resumption less tempting.
[203] See Cobban (1963, 176).
[204] Heckscher (1934, I, 456–459).
[205] Soboul (1976a, 14).
[206] Pitt at least had no such illusions about the role of the French state. Another of the latter's aggressive actions was the "opening" of the Scheldt, which had been closed since the Revolt of the Netherlands in the sixteenth century. See Wallerstein (1974, 185–186; 1980, 53–54, 198). This was seen as "a direct threat to British trade and military security. When French warships forced the river, it meant that Antwerp, the proverbial 'pistol' pointed at the heart of England, could now be used as an anti-British naval or even invasion base. No single act did move to drive the reluctant Pitt away from his policy of neutrality" (Ascherson, 1975, 90).

to contract, the role of the state. Who wanted this and why? Rousseau in fact posed the problem clearly in his distinction between the general will and the will of all, that is, the common interest versus the sum of particular wills.[207] The modern state within the interstate system is precisely the battleground of this unending tension. Strengthening the state obviously means reducing (not eliminating) the ability of particular wills to prevail over some more general will which seeks to optimize the advantages of the state and its citizen–beneficiaries (which is a category smaller than that of all citizens) in the world-economy relative to the citizen–beneficiaries of other states. The state can thus become the mechanism whereby the collective interests of the bourgeois located in a given state prevail (when they do) over the particular interests of particular bourgeois. This is a continuing issue, to be sure, but one that becomes at times acute. The issue tends to become acute, and thus some movement is forced, whenever one or more other states are about to make a surge forward in relative position vis-à-vis the state in question. This, as we have seen, was precisely France's dilemma in the 1780s.[208]

As Lüthy put it, in the juridical "jumble" of the *Ancien Régime,* "there was no established group . . . who did not have privileges to defend," and thus every royal administration of the eighteenth century, whether neo-Colbertist, liberal, or Physiocratic, "had to become revolutionary or else be bogged down." All "progressive" tendencies put their hopes in an "enlightened despotism."[209] The French Revolution plus Napoleon provided precisely that enlightened despotism in terms of the administrative structure of the state, as Tocqueville, that prudent conservative, was to recognize and to a considerable extent deplore.[210]

Still, the fact is there is no truly general will, only a state will or consensus that is based on a more or less stable political coming together of particular wills. It is now commonplace to recognize that the breakdown of this "stability" in France (that is, the Revolution) took two different forms: a breakdown among the privileged strata and a conflict between the privileged strata and those without privilege. Put blandly like this, almost no one will disagree. It is around the effort to attach conceptual terminology

---

[207] Rousseau (1947 [1762]), Book II, ch. III.

[208] The floodgates seemed to be opening in all directions. It was not merely a question of such direct problems as the economic consequences of the Eden Treaty. Note Lefebvre's account (1947b, 32–33) of the indirect diplomatic consequences of the crisis of French finances: "For want of money the French government had to let the Prussians intervene in Holland [in 1788] in support of the Stadholder against the Dutch bourgeoisie; the Stadholder broke his alliance with France and joined with the English."

[209] Lüthy (1961, 14–15).

[210] "The same conditions which had precipitated the fall of the monarchy made for the absolution of its successor. . . . Thus there arose, within a nation that had but recently laid low its monarchy, a central authority with powers wider, stricter, and more absolute than those which any French King had ever wielded. . . . Napoleon fell but the more solid parts of his achievement lasted on; his government died, but his administration survived, and every time that an attempt is made to do away with absolutism the most that could be done has been to graft the head of Liberty onto a servile body" (Tocqueville, 1955, 205, 209).

to these two struggles that the historiographic battles of the French Revolution (and through it the basic political struggles of the modern world-system) have been fought.

The "class" terminology which almost everyone uses to describe the political actors in this debate—aristocrats, bourgeois, sans-culottes, peasants, and (sometimes) proletarians—is embedded in a series of political codes which have come to render the real struggles very opaque. Let me therefore outline my views on the three debates which I think are crucial: (1) What was, in fact, the relationship between the "aristocracy" and the "bourgeoisie" in this period? (2) What was, in fact, the role and the objectives of "popular forces" (urban and rural) in the French Revolution? (3) Who were the Jacobins?

That the aristocracy and the bourgeoisie were distinct sociojuridical categories under the *Ancien Régime* is unquestionable. What is under debate, however, is whether they were members of different *classes*. The readers of this work will know how skeptical I am that these kinds of sociojuridical categories tell us much, if anything, about the economic roles of these groups, in France or elsewhere, since the emergence of a capitalist world-economy in the sixteenth century. If they do not, and if the members of the categories tend to overlap heavily as *de facto* capitalist entrepreneurs, then the triumph (if we may call it that) of the "bourgeoisie" over the "aristocracy" in the French Revolution is neither the prerequisite, nor the correlate, nor the consequence of a transition from feudalism to capitalism in France, but rather the expression of an acute intra-"elite" struggle (or if you will, an intrabourgeois struggle) over the constitution and the basic policies of the French state.

Can such a view be upheld? To argue that the Revolution began as an upper class internal quarrel we do not have to invoke Chateaubriand or Lefebvre or any other later commentator. It was stated well by Robespierre himself: "Thus it was that in France the judiciary, the nobles, the clergy, the rich, gave the original impulse to the revolution. The people appeared on the scene only later."[211] Indeed, it is one of the more ironic facts in this great drama that one of the elements in the British "example" which attracted attention and admiration in France in the period before the Revolution, and thereby contributed to the readiness to enter a "revolutionary" path, was the political and economic strength of the British *aristocracy*.[212] It is, after all, never to be forgotten that one of the countries

[211] Cited by Cobban (1963, 137).

[212] "In the eighteenth century the political predominance and economic fortunes of the British nobility had excited on the continent, and particularly in France, the same admiration and envy as the British Constitution itself. . . . Such impressions, though based on limited experience of the inner workings and conventions of English political life and distorted by political prejudices, were not wholly erroneous" (Goodwin, 1965b, 368).

This admiration of the French for the role of the British aristocracy was to be sure just part of a wider sense of French deficiency vis-à-vis Britain in this period that covered virtually all domains. See Crouzet's survey (1981) of French eighteenth-century writings in this regard. This admiration of

in which the "aristocracy" as such retained the largest role the latest into the modern era has been precisely Great Britain, symbolic heartland for so many of modern capitalism.

The so-called social interpretation of the French Revolution (the Revolution as preeminently a "bourgeois revolution") has been under much systematic attack in recent years, as we have already discussed. But some of the doubts about the description of the revolution as the work of a bourgeoisie which was in structural need of it for its own interests (against those of a feudal aristocracy) can be found by reading the analyses of the tenants of the social interpretation themselves. Mathiez starts his main work by acknowledging that, in 1789, the situation was that the real powers of the absolute monarchy were limited, the seigniors had lost all public power to the state, serfdom had already virtually disappeared and feudal rents had become a minor phenomenon, and the bourgeoisie "despite the shackles of the corporative regime, [were] nonetheless less opposed than we have believed," since, despite all the constraints, "commerce and industry had grown throughout the [eighteenth] century."[213] Where then the structural need of a revolution?[214]

Lefebvre, in his analysis of the Declaration of Rights of Man, explains the absence therein of an insistence on the right of property by the fact that it seemed unnecessary to the drafters "because it was a right which the Old Regime did not question. On the contrary, ministers and administrators of the eighteenth century always spoke of property with respect, in an altogether bourgeois manner."[215] And it is Vovelle and Roche who argue persuasively that in eighteenth-century France the term "bourgeois," although it denoted a commoner to be sure, nonetheless was "restricted to nonactive categories." Indeed, far from allowing this group to triumph, "the French Revolution dealt a mortal blow to this social class."[216]

But is this all a "trivial quibble," as Barrington Moore would have it, since the "ultimate outcome" was a Western parliamentary democracy, and since "the destruction of the political power of the landed aristocracy constitutes the most significant process at work in the course of French modernization"?[217] Quite the contrary: it is scarcely a quibble, for two reasons. If, in

---

the role of the British (landed) aristocracy may not have been displaced. Perkin argues that it was precisely "the domination of government and society by the landed aristocracy jealous of the Crown" that enabled Britain to take the "decisive step toward industrialism." He sees them as creating the political preconditions for a take-off (1969, 63–64).

[213] Mathiez (1923–1924, 9).

[214] Mathiez (1923–1924, 47) does proceed to recount the social injuries suffered by the bourgeoisie. But to attribute the revolution to the search to redress amour propre is less than a social interpretation. Furthermore, he concludes his opening *mise en scène* with this somewhat startling observation:

"If Louis XVI had mounted his horse [on June 25, 1789], if he had taken personal command of his troops, as Henry IV would have done, perhaps he could have succeeded in holding [the troops] to their duty and thereby bring to fruition his show of force. But Louis XVI was a bourgeois."

[215] Lefebvre (1947b, 175).

[216] Vovelle & Roche (1965, 26).

[217] Moore (1966, 105–106). Or, in a milder form: "Whoever won the Revolution, the noble landlord lost" (Forster, 1967, 86). See similar statements in Rudé (1964, 288, 290), Shapiro (1967, 510), Tilly (1968, 161), and Hirsch (1980, 330).

fact, the French Revolution is to continue to be interpreted as primarily an anti-feudal revolution of the capitalist bourgeoisie, we really should spend more attention on why it failed in so many ways to achieve more significant economic transformation than it did. Hobsbawm, puzzling over this "paradox," blames it essentially on the peasantry.[218] But that of course only leads us to ask whether a successful "bourgeois revolution" depends on a politically weak peasantry? And if the "classical" bourgeois revolution "failed" to accomplish its bourgeois objectives, wherein is the utility of the concept?

This then brings us to the second reason why this is no quibble. The emphasis on the centrality of the bourgeois struggle against the feudal order had led to a very distorted, and when all is said and done, a very subordinated, view of the revolt of the popular classes, even (if not especially) among the partisans of the social interpretation, most of whom think of themselves as advocates of the popular classes. And this is true despite the incredible amount of scholarly effort that has been invested of late in the study of the sans-culottes and of the peasants.[219]

Thus we must turn to our second question on the role and the objectives of these "popular forces." These popular forces are those who Mathiez calls the "Fourth Estate," and they were, of course, in numbers largely rural. All the talk of an alliance between the bourgeoisie and these popular forces founders on one basic fact, to which Mathiez points:

> The propertied bourgeoisie became suddenly aware of the fierce face of the Fourth Estate. It could not permit the nobility to be expropriated without fearing for itself, for it held a large part of the noble lands and received from the villagers seigniorial rents.[220]

Rather than an alliance, there seems to have been from the beginning an independent action of the popular classes, to which the capitalist strata (on whichever side of the political in-fighting) responded with varying degrees of ferocity or fear.

Let us start with the "peasant revolution," which in fact refers to a series of struggles that, even for Soboul, are "at the heart of the French Revolution."[221] If one looks at them as comprising an ongoing conflict that

---

[218] Hobsbawm (1962, 212–213) speaks of the "gigantic paradox" of mid-nineteenth-century France. It should have developed fastest there, since France possessed "institutions ideally suited to capitalist development." Yet its development was "distinctly slower" than elsewhere. He explains the paradox in terms of the history of the French Revolution. "The capitalist part of the French economy was a superstructure erected on the immovable base of the peasantry and petty-bourgeoisie."

[219] Here I think Furet (1982, 74) is absolutely on target: "It is precisely what is not bourgeois in this revolution, and what is furthermore exciting—the peasants and the urban popular masses—that is the best known: proof perhaps that the concept of the bourgeois revolution is not all that operational, since it has not launched a domain of research for social history."

[220] Mathiez (1923–1924, 59).

[221] Soboul (1976a, 17).

stretches across the eighteenth century, merely culminating in the more dense violence of the years 1789–1793,[222] it seems reasonable to perceive this peasant unrest as resistance to the "capitalist offensive," in Saint-Jacob's phrase,[223] which in many areas (especially the Northeast, the East, and the Center-East of France) sought, and often largely succeeded in obtaining, the destruction or diminution of the "collective rights" of French peasants. The peasants responded with "defensive action."[224]

The convening of the Estates-General came after decades of such defensive action. In addition it took place, as we know, in a moment of a particularly acute food crisis. The extra agonies of the rural poor compounded and interacted with their fears (which were also those of the stratum of somewhat better-off peasants) about their "collective rights." In this struggle against the "capitalist offensive," both the better-off peasants and the rural poor often made less distinction between the "aristocracy" and the "bourgeoisie" than either the latter themselves or subsequent scholars have been wont to do.[225] To rural workers, both aristocrats and bourgeois were part of the "privileged classes."[226]

If then peasant revolts are to be seen as "the crucial insurrectionary ingredient"[227] in the French Revolution, we need to explain what rendered these revolts so explosive. It was, it seems to me, the coming together of resistance to a long-term process of proletarianization with a short-run but

---

[222] "Between a seigniory which was gradually 'physiocratizing' itself and becoming more urban-based, on the one hand, and on the other peasant minorities, ever more educated, who refused to sacrifice their hopes on the seigniorial altar of an English-style capitalist revolution, there were skirmishes and vanguard combats throughout the eighteenth century. In 1789, the revolutionary event brought these conflicts, theretofore minor or suppressed, unexpectedly to the fore" (Le Roy Ladurie, 1974, 22).

"The hatred of the peasants for the lords was not a thing of yesterday. . . . Yet if they were brought to a state of general rebellion in 1789 one reason is to be found in the convocation of the Estates-General" (Lefebvre, 1947b, 143).

[223] Saint-Jacob (1960, 572). See also Lefebvre: "The intrusion of capitalism in agriculture took place under the cloak of feudal rights which rendered them even more unbearable. It perverted their nature, for they had been invested to sustain a seignior who lived amidst his peasants and they now fell into the hands of capitalists who thought only of deriving profit from them" (1963, 352).

[224] This phrase of Charles Tilly is used in his analysis of East Anglia between 1500 and 1900 (1982, 30), but what he describes seems equally true of France: "The peasant version of subsistence farming—in which land-controlling households de-

vote a portion of their product to the market—expanded under the early phases of capitalism and statemaking, before declining under the later phases of the same processes" (p. 9). It was the resistance to this later phase, more successful in France than in England, that we find in the eighteenth and nineteenth centuries in France.

[225] "Desperate with hunger, the peasant was an inevitable threat to the aristocracy. The bourgeoisie itself was by no means secure. Their share of taxes, too, remained unpaid; they held a good number of seigneuries; they provided the lords of the manor with judges and *intendants*; as tax-farmers, they took over the collection of feudal dues. Great landowners, wealthy farmers and corn merchants all profited just as much as tithe-collectors and seigneurs from the king's agricultural policy which restricted the *droits collectifs*, so dear to the peasant, and which by its insistence on commercial freedom increased the price of food. As the people had no wish to die of hunger, they saw no reason why the rich, whoever they might be, should not put their hands in their pockets on behalf of the poor. Lawyers, *rentiers*, merchants, farmers and, in Alsace, Jews were threatened just as much as priests and nobles. They too had reason to be afraid" (Lefebvre, 1973, 32–33).

[226] Lefebvre (1973, 40).

[227] Skocpol (1979, 112–113).

very intense demand for bread.[228] Marie Antoinette was not alone in
misperceiving this. A large part of the "revolutionary" bourgeoisie as well
seemed to have misunderstood that for the popular masses the Revolution
was "as much a revolution for bread as for the political rights of man."[229]

A look at the sequence of events of the Great Fear will illustrate the
dynamic of these popular sentiments. In the rural areas, the "growing anarchy" of 1788–1789 inspired the "conjunction of nobles and
bourgeois in an attempt to protect their property from the 'fourth estate'."
If July 14 shook this alliance, "during the subsequent troubles it reappeared in the provinces far more frequently than is realized."[230] After July
14, when the Great Fear spread over vast areas of rural France, the
revolutionary bourgeois blamed the "aristocrats' plot" and the provincial
aristocrats in turn blamed the revolutionary bourgeois. Lefebvre has
dispelled both theories in his detailed picture of what actually happened.
What is clear is that, after July 14, the peasants began to implement their
demands, ceasing to pay tithes and dues, resuming collective rights they
had lost. "The peasant population took its own cause in hand."[231] The
Great Fear stirred the pot considerably, and by doing so "it played its part
in the preparations of the night of 4 August."[232] The so-called abolition of
feudalism on August 4, 1789 was not the program of the revolutionary
bourgeois. It was pressed upon them by the insurgent peasantry. The
National Assembly spent its own energy attempting to limit the reality of
this institutional transformation.[233]

In some sense this story was to be repeated for the next four years: the
government and legislature taking "radical" action only under direct
pressure of the popular masses, and always in some sense trying to limit
it.[234] One can interpret this, as do Soboul and many others, as the peasants

[228] "When all is said and done, the inescapable
conclusion remains that the primary and most
constant motive impelling revolutionary crowds
during this period was the concern for the provision of cheap and plentiful food" (Rudé, 1967,
208). On why, traditionally in France, the bread riot
was primarily a phenomenon of the area of *grande
culture* (from the Channel to the Loire, except Brittany) and the area of viticulture, but not the zone of
petite culture, see Hufton (1983). This has some
correlation with primary zones of support for the
French Revolution.

[229] Rose (1956, 171). Criticizing the "historians
favorable to the Revolution" for their belief in the
parallel interests of the bourgeoisie and the "popular masses," Lefebvre (1937, 324) argues that "hunger played a more important role" than these
historians have admitted.

[230] Lefebvre (1973, 46, 49).

[231] Lefebvre (1973, 101).

[232] Lefebvre (1973, 211). See also Aulard (1913,
200–201).

[233] See the discussion in Zapperi (1972). See also
Soboul (1976d, 268): "Feudalism was destroyed in
its institutional and juridical form; it was maintained as an economic reality." But was it feudalism
or capitalism that was maintained? As Lefebvre
(1963, 356) writes, reviewing the actions of the
National Assembly and the Convention from 1789–
1793, the sum total of what was achieved seems
clear: "For the wishes of the immense majority of
peasants, the Revolution had no regard."

[234] "When the Viscount of Noailles, on the eve-
ning of 4 August 1789, invoked the demands of the
communities and proposed that one show the people 'that we don't oppose it in what it's interesting
for it to preserve,' did he not seek to circumscribe
the popular assault on the field of 'privileges' and
the feudal system and to save for some years yet the
privilege of property. One must be aware of the
threat to understand the shouting" (Hirsch, 1980,
327–328).

Furthermore, a large part of the "recuperation"
of rights by the peasantry was done by their direct

and sans-culottes forcing the timid bourgeois to pursue the logic of the bourgeois revolution.[235] It seems more straightforward and obvious to me to see the peasants and sans-culottes pursuing their own revolution, one against the "privileged classes" in their language, the capitalist strata in mine.[236] This opposition grew greater, not less, in the period 1789–1793, since the elimination of the "aristocrat" and the church as rural rent-receiver often merely intensified the class struggle in the rural areas between rural worker and rural beneficiary of surplus value.[237]

The famous problem-issue of how to interpret the Vendée and the *chouannerie* becomes less difficult from this perspective. Even Mazauric, close in his interpretation to Soboul, asserts that they were "first of all anti-bourgeois."[238] Paul Bois locates the essential cause of these revolts on the deceptions of the participants that the French Revolution brought no real benefit to the rural cultivator. "Under one title or another, he had to continue to pay."[239] Charles Tilly not only concludes the same thing about

action between 1789 and 1792, to be legitimated only later by the laws of 28 August 1792 and 10 June 1793. See Gauthier (1977, 149–150, 163–166); see also Hunt (1983, 137).

[235] "The peasant revolt was also chronic in a large part of France from 1789 to 1793. It constituted, which is often not realized, the dynamic force of the Revolution. . . . If the French Revolution is bourgeois, that doesn't mean it was the work of the bourgeoisie alone" (Soboul, 1973, 86–87).

Ado (1977, 127) goes even further and reprimands the masses because they got ahead of the bourgeoisie: "The general problem posed at the beginning of this essay was what was the historical content and significance of this peasant egalitarian program in the bourgeois revolution at the end of the eighteenth century? Was this program anticapitalist and therefore [sic!] retrograde, conservative from an economic standpoint? . . . In the majority of instances, the answer must be yes."

[236] "In destroying the *Ancien Régime*, the peasant wished also to react against the process that was leading society towards economic freedom and competitive individualism, towards the capitalist society. Along with the artisan, he opposed free trade in grains and demanded price controls (*la taxation*). Everywhere he repossessed customary rights of which he had been deprived" (Lefebvre, 1978, 242).

[237] "Many historians imply that, when the revolutionary alliance of the peasants and the bourgeoisie had finally laid low the feudal system, rural questions were seen to be settled, and the peasants wanted only to enjoy their newly-acquired benefits in the restored order. It was nothing of the kind. The elimination of the feudal and ecclesiastical rival, the rising prices of agricultural products, all that whetted the appetite of the landowners. As they

most often controlled the municipalities, it was easy for them to transform these traditional defenses of the peasantry into arms against those who worked the land" (Aberdam, 1975, 73). Aberdam further notes the emergence of the expression, the "bourgeois tithe" (p. 88), and adds (p. 89): "The share-croppers of the Revolution, heirs to three centuries of antifeudal struggle by resisting their masters, defended essentially a disguised wage."

[238] Mazauric (1965, 71). He gives much detailed evidence for this, but then concludes (p. 75): "In sum, the *chouannerie* developed wherever the bourgeoisie was seen to be parasitic, wherever it compromised with the feudal system instead of introducing the revolutionary processes of the division of labor and capitalism, when it gave the example of an historic 'failure.'" And once again he condemns (p. 66) the peasants for being ahead of their time. "[If a historian] conceives the French Revolution to mark progress, he cannot consider the *chouannerie* to be 'legitimate', even if he finds moving its popular underpinnings and its rich collections of miseries and individual grandeurs." Elsewhere, Mazauric (1967, 364) reminds us of the view of Jaurès, "It is the people who imposed their views and saved the bourgeois revolution of the Enlightenment." Hence without "the people," the bourgeois revolution would have failed. But when "the people" in the west of France opposed the revolutionary government, they were being "illegitimate."

[239] Bois (1971, 347). "It was in those areas where the greatest desire to shake off all forms of domination was displaced that the distrust of an eventual takeover by the town bourgeoisie was the deepest" (p. 344). See Sutherland (1982) on the class basis of the rural *chouannerie* (tenant farmers as opposed to independent peasant proprietors). While Sutherland says this is not the whole story, he merely

the peasants,[240] but finds the counterrevolutionary forces to have a strong base as well among workers in manufactures.[241] Why not therefore simply consider the Vendée as part of the France-wide peasant anti-bourgeois struggle?

The story was not very different in general in the urban areas, most notably in Paris, where the sans-culottes may be said to provide the urban parallel to the small peasants with some land (in particular, the *laboureurs*), that is, oppressed workers but not indigent ones. Just as the peasants fought against the "privileged classes" (which included indistinctly aristocrats and bourgeois), so did the urban workers struggle against an "aristocracy" defined to refer not merely to noblemen but

> to the rich and idle, to large landowners and capitalists, to speculators, to Girondins, to those who paid insufficient wages to workers, to those who wore their hair long and powdered, to those who frequented priests who had not sworn loyalty to the republic, to those with moderate political opinions of any description, even to those who were merely indifferent to politics.[242]

With such a definition, it is not surprising that the sans-culottes and the revolutionary government were at least as often at odds with each other as they were allies. The sans-culottes were most angry about the depreciation of the *assignat*[243] and about the price of grain, both of which caused a virtual "rupture" between the government and them.[244] Their demand for

modifies the argument in detail. Mitchell also sees the Vendée as a "manifestation of popular discontent" (1974, 117).

[240] "From the beginning of the Revolution [the peasants] resisted and resented the efforts of the bourgeoisie to gain control of the commune" (Tilly, 1968, 281).

[241] "In fact, a great many incidents of the so-called Peasant Revolt of 1789 in the West turn out, on close inspection, to involve nuclei of rural or semiurban workers rather than peasants. . . . It may be more than coincidence that three of the most turbulent series of popular outbursts of the entire Revolution—the 'agricultural' revolutions of Maine and the Norman Bocage in 1789, the Chouan guerrillas of Maine, Normandy, Brittany, and northern Anjou from 1793 on, and the Vendée itself—broke out in the West's area of rural textile production" (Tilly, 1968, xi). Remember that many of these textile workers would have lost work when textile production fell in the wake of the Eden Treaty.

Faucheux argues that both the urban and rural insurgents were "moved primarily by material concerns" (1964, 384). The Vendée had known worse famine conditions than the rest of France for years

(p. 191). Bendjebbar notes that the bocage zones were oriented to the market and that "the *assignat* destroyed the circuit of meat for butchery" (1987, 95).

[242] Sewell (1980, 111). This usage was, in Sewell's words, "closely linked to the sans-culotte's notion of the place of labor in society. . . . For the sans-culotte, useful labor . . . was performed only by those who had worked with their hands."

[243] Fehér (1987, 40) demonstrates quite convincingly, based on the work of Falkner (1919), that the history of the *assignat* was not one of accidental misfortune but of policy choice, in which the "constant devaluation grants the political and temporal priority of budgetary needs, even if at the cost of those living on wages."

[244] Soboul (1958a, 259). "The hostility of the sans-culottes against commercial capital was primarily symbolized by the persistence of their demands against trade in currency" (p. 475). It was precisely because of their distrust of the government that they never "ceased to lay claim to the approval of laws by the people" (p. 510).

So strongly did the sans-culottes feel this antagonism that they were precisely ready to cut themselves off even from the smaller bourgeois. "Popu-

the maximum was accorded to them by the Jacobin bourgeoisie not freely, but "only constrained and forced," as Soboul says.[245] But why then talk of the "ambiguous position of the sans-culotterie," as Soboul does?[246] Fehér seems to be far more correct in calling Parisian direct democracy "the most striking instance of anti-capitalist political will in early modern history."[247] What other attitude was to be expected vis-à-vis a government that forbade the workers to organize at work (*loi Le Chapelier*) and, on the eve of Thermidor, was denouncing their demonstrations and strikes as "criminal maneuvers"?[248]

One side issue often confuses the discussion on the class struggle between the urban workers and the bourgeoisie: the presumed nonproletarian character of the sans-culottes. Most analysts seem to agree on the occupational description of that essentially political term. It was a "concertina word"[249] that included small shopkeepers, petty traders, craftsmen, journeymen, laborers, vagrants, and the city poor.[250] However, their "heart and core"[251] were artisans. Salaried workers were only a minority,

---

lar violence alienated from the *sans-culotterie* movement the sympathies of a mass of small *bourgeois*, householders, small shopkeepers, people *ayant pignon sur rue*, who, while belonging to much the same social category as the upper crust of the *sans-culotterie*, were thoroughly alarmed and disguested by the destruction of property. . . . The average Jacobin could not fail to condemn a movement which appeared to offer no guarantee of civil peace; the *ancien régime* had been brought down because it had been unable to maintain internal order, and the Paris shopkeeper had not denounced the predatory violence of the French *seigneurs* . . . to find himself exposed to the blind fury of half-starved women" (Cobb, 1959, 64).

[245] Soboul (1958, 11).

[246] Soboul (1954, 55). This "ambiguity" explains, says Soboul, "certain errors in perspective" such as those of Daniel Guérin.

[247] Fehér (1987, 82–83). To be sure, Fehér insists on a negative side to this, asserting that this "anticapitalist political will . . . was inextricably bound up with the idea of terror." Even if this were true as a description of 1793, I cannot agree with any inference that it must inevitably be so.

Tønnesson (1959, 347) too, in discussing the insurrections of Germinal and Prairial, Year III (1795), reminds us that it is "this hatred of the sans-culottes for the rich . . . which gives to the insurrections their character as a class conflict," adding that this attitude "was no less conscious on the other side of the barricades." On the sans-culottes as both the have-nots and the political militants, see Burstin (1986, 45–46). For the debate as to whether the sans-culottes should be seen

primarily as a social or as a political movement, see Rudé (1962, 370–372) and Zacker (1962, 384).

[248] Kaplan (1979, 75), who adds: "Was that so different from the imputation of workers' agitation by the police of the Consulate to the doings of the 'English committee'? Was it very different from the thesis of a conspiracy which permitted Turgot to deny the popular and spontaneous character of the wheat war? What had been the crime of insubordination in the Ancien Regime became, by an almost unconscious transference, the crime of counter-revolution. One was not less subversive nor infamous than the other."

Furthermore, the Revolution could be said to have been in part even a means by which the bourgeoisie reduced the class pressure of the urban workers. Garden (1970, 592) describes the acute "class struggle" of silk manufacturers and their workers which was particularly acute in the last years of the *Ancien Régime*, but "paradoxically, the history of the Revolution in Lyon is marked by a retreat in workers' demands and a weakening of their position. It would take many years for the Lyon workers to recover their cohesiveness and strength, to try and shake off once again the ties of dependency in which they were kept by the merchant-manufacturers."

[249] Williams (1968, 19).

[250] This is the list of Rudé (1967, 12).

[251] Williams (1968, 20). But see Sonenscher who argues that the sans-culottes were in fact more the journeymen than the artisans, and that if their political language assimilated the two categories, "it was an incorporation which rested very much upon the terms set by the journeymen" (1984, 325).

"one element amidst others."[252] Soboul wishes to deny even to this minority
the status of true proletarians by calling them "wage workers of the old
style,"[253] which presumably means they worked in small shops and not
large factories.

No doubt this is all true descriptively. Implicit, however, in the description is a presumed sharp contrast with workers' movements in truly
industrialized countries, composed differently. Is this so sure? Has it not
been true subsequently of the majority of workers' movements that their
strength and their cadres have been drawn from a segment of the working
population which was somewhat "better off," whether this segment were
technically independent artisans or more highly paid skilled (and/or craft)
wage workers? The search for those who truly had nothing to lose but their
chains led us at the time of the French Revolution to the *indigents* and leads
us today to what is variously called the subproletariat, the lumpenprole-
tariat, the unskilled (often immigrant) workers, the marginal, the
chronically unemployed. If we are to argue, as does Soboul, that a true
"class spirit is missing"[254] from the urban popular masses because they
followed the lead of the artisans (even if this were always so during the
French Revolution, which it was not), what are we to say of the class spirit of
the working class of twentieth-century industrialized countries?

Before we conclude, let us turn to the last debate, the nature and role of
the Jacobins. The discussion here is more heavily overlain with contemporary political implications than any other. For a large part of the
participants in the debate, "Jacobins" tends to serve as code language for
Third International Communists, in power in the U.S.S.R. and elsewhere.
This code discussion, scarcely veiled, makes a dispassionate analysis of the
role the Jacobins actually played very difficult. There seem to be, nonetheless, basically two positions which cut across other lines in a curious fashion.
Either the Jacobins represented something radically different from those
in power previously—not only the *Ancien Régime* but the Girondins as
well—or they were one more variant of the same ruling group. The camp
of those who believe the differences were great unites Soboul and Furet,
symbols otherwise of sharply opposed views, and also includes Fehér. The
other camp is smaller but includes such diverse persons as Tocqueville,
Guérin, and Higonnet.

[252] Tønnesson (1959, xviii). See also
Chaussinand-Nogaret (1981, 548).

[253] Soboul (1968, 192). Contrast this view with
Garden's description (1970, 595) of Lyon: "Before
1789, in a city where the nobility plays only a
limited role, it is surely a class society that is being
constructed throughout the eighteenth century,
despite the force of traditions. In more than one
way, Lyon society of the eighteenth century pre-
sages that of the nineteenth: the domination of the

bourgeoisie over the industrial work force was
already its essential feature." See also the debate
"among Marxist historians" of using the term "pre-
proletariat" to describe the sans-culottes (Rudé,
1962, 375–377; Lotté, 1962, 387–390; Soboul,
1962, 392–395).

[254] Soboul (1981b, 356). Tønnesson similarly
talks of the *indigents* becoming "the political clien-
tele of sans-culotte patrons" (1959, xv).

Mathiez stated the position of the partisans of the social interpretation quite explicitly:

> Between Girondins and the Mountain, the conflict was profound. It was almost a class conflict. . . .
> June 2 [1793] . . . was more than a political revolution. What the sans-culottes overthrew was not merely a party; it was up to a point a social class. After the minority of the nobility which fell with the throne, it was now the turn of the upper bourgeoisie. . . .
> Robespierre was, beginning with the Constituent Assembly, the most popular revolutionary of the class of artisans and small proprietors whose total confidence he held. He was the uncontested leader of the sans-culotterie, especially after the death of Marat.[255]

To be sure, Furet and Richet mark the turning point of the Revolution more on August 10, 1792 (the constitution of the Revolutionary Commune of Paris) than on June 2, 1793 (the arrest of the Girondin deputies).[256] And they argue that the turning point had to do more with political values than with class struggle:

> After August 10, 1792, the Revolution was dragged by war and the pressure of the Parisian crowd out of the great path traced by intelligence and wealth in the eighteenth century. . . . Beyond the Revolution which Jaurès understood so well, there was the revolution instinctively sensed by Michelet: that of the obscure forces of misery and anger.
> Obliged to come to terms with them the politicians of the Mountain gave in to all their demands: conscription, price control, terror. But they conserved what was essential to them: power.[257]

Beyond the fact that for Mathiez the Jacobin period was a great positive and for Furet and Richet a great negative, they in fact combine to agree that it was profoundly different from the "first phase" of the Revolution and that the Jacobins and the popular masses were basically on the same side.

Fehér presents a somewhat different twist on the same viewpoint. For him the Jacobins do indeed represent politically the sans-culottes and other popular masses. They do this not, however, as the advanced representatives of a radical bourgeoisie, but rather as "anti-bourgeois and anti-capitalist."[258] But for Fehér, as for Furet and Richet, the Jacobin experience is negative. For the latter, it was negative because it was a *dérapage* from the liberal, parliamentary road, the British road, which the Enlight-

---

[255] Mathiez (1923–1924, 262, 383, 405). And that is why it is an "ironic tragedy" (p. 577) when the "misguided sans-culottes" turn against Robespierre in the end.

[256] "June 2, 1792 is far from having the same importance in the history of the Revolution as Aug, 10, 1792," even if nonetheless it did mark a "rupture," a "defeat for Parliamentary government," and therefore a "defeat of the Revolution" (Furet & Richet, 1973, 201–202).

[257] Furet & Richet (1973, 253).

[258] Fehér (1987, 131).

enment had embraced. Fehér, by contrast, sees not only it, but also, behind
it, a whole tradition of Enlightenment thought, as representing precisely
the rejection of the British "solution" of capitalism.[259] If the Jacobin period
was negative for Fehér, it is because he believes socialism to be more than
mere anti-capitalism, and that terror can be no part of socialism.[260]

Tocqueville never explicitly discusses this issue, but his whole emphasis on the continuities weighs against any sense of a basic midway
turning point in the Revolution. The conflicting passions for equality and
liberty were there already under the *Ancien Régime*, and the struggles
merely continued afterward, with ups and down. "Radical though it may
have been, the Revolution made far fewer changes than is generally
supposed." Rather, very quickly, the Revolution accomplished "what in any
case was bound to happen, if by slow degrees."[261]

Guérin is in many ways an orthodox member of the social interpretation
school. The French Revolution of the Assemblies was a bourgeois revolution, and remained bourgeois, as Rudé says, "even at the height of the
Jacobin democracy."[262] Except that it was not even then for Guérin a
"democracy" but rather a "bourgeois dictatorship,"[263] struggling against a
second, separate proletarian revolution. Robespierre was not the agent of
this second revolution but its most clever opponent. He "dreamed up a
bold plan . . . : make concessions to the *bras nus*, without giving in on
anything crucial."[264]

Higonnet comes to these questions from a standpoint much closer to the
Cobban–Furet rejection of the concept of a bourgeois revolution (objectively, if not subjectively) than to the social interpretation, but he still
arrives at conclusions not all that different from Guérin. For Higonnet sees
the period 1792–1793 as one of "opportunistic anti-nobilism" in which the
Terror was a "strategic gesture . . . designed to harness 'the people' to the
bourgeois Revolutionary cause." In effect, the persecution of nobles (by
both the Girondins and the Mountain) was "opportunistic, tactical, and

---

[259] Fehér (1987, 54–55) insists on the degree to
which Jacobinism was a conscious effort to exclude
the "British development, or at least the Jacobin
perception of this development." He cites the
speech to the Convention on May 10, 1973, of
Robespierre (*Oeuvres*, IX, 499): "Witness England,
where the gold and the power of the monarch
constantly weight the scales to the same side . . . ; a
monstrous form of government, whose public vir-
tues are merely a scandalous show in which the
shadow of liberty annihilates liberty itself, the law
consecrates despotism, the rights of the people
openly traded, where corruption is uncurbed by
shame."
[260] See Fehér (1987, 149–154) on "learning from
Jacobinism," learning that anti-capitalism and socialism are not identical.

[261] Tocqueville (1955, 20). A recent empirical
study which reinforces this thesis is Brugière (1986)
who demonstrates the continuity of French finances
from Louis XVI through the Revolution and Napoleon to afterwards, not only in structures and
policies, but even to some degree in personnel.
[262] Rudé (1954, 247).
[263] Guérin (1968, II, 11).
[264] Guérin (1968, I, 405). It is often argued
against Guérin, as does Rebérioux (1965, 197–198),
that he does not take into account "the impossibility
in 1793–1794 of making a truly socialist choice."
But even if this were so, this argues about the
wisdom of what the urban masses sought, and not
about what they did in fact seek.

demagogic" because it served essentially to deflect popular complaint from their real object, the "bourgeois, individualist, and capitalist world order" in which nobles, *officiers*, and bourgeois alike had already long been involved.[265]

What can we conclude about the Jacobins? From any viewpoint of the *longue durée*, it seems clear to me that the Tocquevillian continuities dominate the balance sheet of French political and economic structures, and hence Guérin and Higonnet are more nearly right about the Jacobins than the others. To turn Robespierre into a proto-Lenin (whatever one may think of Lenin) seems to me clearly to misread his role, as he and his contemporaries viewed him. It further seems to me that the theory of a bourgeois revolution cannot withstand the fact that the realities of capitalism in France as elsewhere in Western Europe long predated 1789.

What then the French Revolution? Much ado about nothing? Surely not. The French Revolution was three things, three very different things, but all three deeply intermeshed. First, it was a relatively conscious attempt by a diverse group of the ruling capitalist strata to force through urgently needed reforms of the French state in light of the perceived British leap forward to hegemonic status in the world-economy. As such, it continued under Napoleon, and while the reforms were achieved, the objective of preventing British hegemony was not. Indeed the French revolutionary process probably increased, as we shall see, the British lead.

Second, the Revolution created the circumstances of a breakdown of public order sufficient to give rise to the first significant antisystemic (that is, anti-capitalist) movement in the history of the modern world-system, that of the French "popular masses." As such, it was, of course, a failure, but as such it has been the spiritual basis of all subsequent antisystemic movements. This is so not because the French Revolution was a bourgeois revolution but precisely because it was not.

Third, the Revolution provided the needed shock to the modern world-system as a whole to bring the cultural–ideological sphere at last into line with the economic and political reality. The first centuries of the capitalist world-economy were lived largely within "feudal" ideological clothes. This is neither anomalous nor unexpected. This sort of lag is normal and indeed structurally necessary. But it couldn't go on forever and the French Revolution, which in this sense was only one part (but the key part) of the "world revolution of the West," marked the moment when feudal ideology would at last crumble. The proof is in the intellectual reaction—of Burke and of Maistre. One needs to defend "conservative" ideas explicitly only when they are fundamentally questioned and no

[265] Higonnet (1981, 39, 91, 112, 131). Higonnet's arguments enable us to easily explain the severity of some of the actions of the Convention as when, on March 13, 1793, it decreed the death penalty for "anyone who proposed the agrarian law" (which meant the forcible redivision of landed property). See Rose (1984, 113).

longer accepted by the majority. And until 1789 that was not true.[266] This was an exciting change, and is what excited many. But it marks not the beginning of a bourgeois, capitalist era but the moment of its full maturation.

Let us therefore return now to the story of the Franco–British competition for hegemony in the world-system, in this last crucial phase which ran from 1792 to 1815, a period normally identified in the literature on Kondratieff cycles as an A-phase of economic expansion.[267] Serge Chassagne cautions us, in his study of the French wool industry from 1790 to 1810, that this period is simultaneously one which "revealed long-existent weaknesses and . . . accelerated inevitable revolutions." Therefore, he says, let us not overstate the accidental features of the revolutionary period and confuse them with profounder "structural transformations," thereby seeking either "to glorify of vilify the Revolution."[268] Still, was the Revolution merely an accidental factor, even in narrowly economic terms? Our argument heretofore leads us to doubt this. It broke out, in large part, precisely in response to the structural transformations going on in the world-economy and would, by its dynamic, as Chassagne himself notes, "accelerate" the evolutions.[269] Whether or not these evolutions were otherwise "inevitable" we shall never know. What we do know is that they occurred.

The key policy element of this phase of Franco–British rivalry that was different from the previous phases was the virtually automatic involvement of both states, on opposite sides, of every "revolutionary" struggle that occurred. Properly speaking, this difference didn't start in 1789 but under the *Ancien Régime* in the 1770s.[270] As we know, Great Britain ultimately prevailed globally in military terms. Thus it can indeed be said that "within a *conjoncture* that was generally favorable, Great Britain created politically, sometime militarily, its own *conjoncture*."[271] It was these politico–military

[266] See Western (1956, 603–605) on British conservative ideology as "a product of the French Revolution."

[267] For Great Britain, see Gayer *et al.* (1975, 486–500, 623–658, and Vol. II, *passim*); for France, see Labrousse (1965, 480–494).

[268] Chassagne (1978, 164–165). See also Markovitch (1976a, 484).

[269] This can be illustrated by an elementary statistic on the comparative growth in metallurgy. Between 1720 and 1790, England grew 100%, while France grew 468%. Between 1720 and 1830, however, the percentage for England was 2608 but for France only 908. See Léon (1960, 179; cf. Lévy-Leboyer, 1964, 326–332; Birch, 1967, 47–56).

[270] "The revolutionary struggle . . . was inseparable from the struggle between England and

France. The British government opposed every revolutionary effort. . . . The French, on the other hand, under both the Bourbon and ensuing republican governments, patronized virtually all revolutionary disturbances" (Palmer, 1954, 9–10).

[271] Morineaù (1976b, 69). Hobsbawm makes the same case. "Whatever the British advance was due to, it was not scientific and technological superiority. . . . [Britain] possessed an economy strong enough and a state aggressive enough to capture the market of its competitors. In effect the wars of 1793–1815 . . . virtually eliminated all rivals from the non-European world, except to some extent the young U.S.A." (1962, 47, 51).

Nef (1957, 86) goes even further, by suggesting, counterfactually, that in the absence of the Revolution, France might have surged ahead of Great Britain: "[In the eighteenth century] technological

victories that critically increased the economic gaps—in agriculture, in industry, in trade, and in finance.

In agriculture, the key difference was that while, in France, the political strength demonstrated by the peasantry in the Revolution slowed down (even halted) the process of concentration of ownership,[272] the wartime period actually accelerated concentration in Great Britain,[273] thereby accentuating the gap and creating Britain's long-term nineteenth-century advantage in terms of yields on arable land.[274]

In industry too, the war seems to have had a clear impact on production in the crucial textiles industry. On the one hand, the most recent revisions in the data on British economic growth, particularly in the cotton industry, suggest that the previous picture of "spectacular acceleration" in the period starting in the 1780s seems exaggerated,[275] and that instead one should talk of a "steady acceleration" both of per capita income and of total

development, in imitation of England, became a watchword among the French. . . . By the end of the century they had in many cases begun to improve them. Had it not been for the French Revolution and the Napoleonic wars, it is conceivable they might at this time have forged ahead of Britain even in the technological development that owed its strength to the use of coal fuel." But this, of course, relegates political developments to the realm of the accidental, if not the irrelevant.

Hartwell, on the other hand, is skeptical, since he claims England also suffered. He argues that, had there been no wars, "the situation would have been the same; England would have been ahead, with France and Germany industrializing a little later" (1972, 373). McNeill, on the other hand, scoffs at the idea that the war made little economic difference for Britain. He points to increased government expenditures as increasing internal demand, subsidies as increasing external demand, not to speak of war expenditures as paving the way for exports. Without all this, "it seems impossible to believe that British industrial production would have increased at anything like the actual rate" (1982, 211).

[272] See Bergeron (1970, 490), Tulard (1970, 645–646), and Milward & Saul (1973, 262–263). Crouzet, in a debate with Soboul, argues, as a devil's advocate, that the suppression of the feudal levies "was not necessarily a factor of growth," since it may have diminished demand. To Soboul's response that the peasants lived better in the Napoleonic era, Crouzet responds: "I agree entirely; but the fact that they lived better signifies an increase in subsistence consumption, and in addition, there was probably an increase in hoarding with an eye to land purchase. From the point of view of economic

analysis, this represented a break in growth" (1971, 556–557).

[273] Cole (1952, 42) says that the pace of various agricultural changes that had been going on in eighteenth-century Britain was "speeded up prodigiously" by the wars. John (1967, 30) notes that the higher prices resulted in "a quickening of enclosing activity," half of all the enclosures between 1727 and 1845 occurring in the period 1793–1815. Hueckel (1976a, 343) notes that the advantages of the price rises went to the landlords as "unearned increment" in inelastic land, as opposed to the tenants who provided only their own labor and capital. While these tenants could increase their absolute profits by investments in new techniques, the "rates of return on capital above the customary level were short-lived," since agriculture was a "competitive industry."

[274] See O'Brien and Keyder (1978, 136–138), who note that "French retardation [in the nineteenth century] . . . [stemmed] from the limited capacity of small units of ownership and cultivation to generate an investible surplus," a situation they attribute to the fact that the "Revolution checked the rehabilitation of large estates." Grantham (1978, 311) attributes the delay in the adoption of intensive mixed husbandry in northern France to "the slow growth in demand for meat and dairy products before 1840," but this surely was due at least in part to the very lack of concentration in agriculture with the consequent greater degree of subsistence production.

Laurent nonetheless asserts (but without comparison to Great Britain) a continuous improvement in French wheat and rye yields from 1815 to 1880 (1976b, 683).

[275] Crafts (1983, 186).

productivity.[276] Furthermore, previous impressions of a major role in this acceleration for large-scale industry[277] or for steam power [278] seem equally overstated for this period. Finally, Chapman argues that the distinction between British "mass-produced" and French "fashion and design-conscious" products "cannot be sustained after 1790."[279]

Yet we know that, on the other hand, Britain had as of 1815 an "unquestionably increased economic advantage" in the cotton industry over the continent in general, and over France in particular.[280] How could this be? Gayer insists that we cannot infer that British expansion "would have been less rapid at a time of peace."[281] Perhaps this is true, although the war clearly increased the share of cotton relative to linen and wool textile production because of the greater availability of the former's sources of supply under wartime conditions.[282] What seems to be the case is less that British expansion was so much more rapid than previously than that there was "a noticeable slowing-down" of the pace of French industrialization.[283]

A close look at the timing indicates exactly what happened in France, and by extension, in the rest of continental Europe as it came under French control. The growth rate for the Revolutionary and war periods in fact can be subdivided into a period of low growth from 1790 to 1800, a period of relatively higher growth from 1800 to 1810, and a new low period from 1810 to 1815.[284] The first period was that of the self-imposed disruption of

---

[276] Harley (1982, 286). It is striking that two such similar revisions "downward" of the extent of British economic growth in the late eighteenth century—Harley and Crafts (1983)—should have been published within a year of each other in the two leading journals of economic history in the United Kingdom and the United States.

[277] Chapman (1971, 75) who concludes: "Indeed, the longer one looks at the early cotton industry under the microscope, the less revolutionary the early phases of its life cycle appear to be" (p. 76).

[278] See Chapman (1972, 18–19) and Crouzet (1958, 74). On the continuing importance of the hydraulic engine up to 1840 (as opposed to the less economical steam engine), see Bairoch (1983) and Endrei (1983). See also Gille (1959, 28), Robinson (1974, 101), Musson (1976, 416–417), and von Tunzelmann (1978, 6).

[279] Chapman (1972, 22).

[280] Gayer et al. (1975, 649). See the figures in Godechot (1972, 370, Table 53).

[281] Gayer et al. (1975, 649).

[282] Edwards (1967, 33), who points out that cotton's advantage in the British home market in the 1790s was abetted by the rise of Beau Brummel as the arbiter of male fashion, with his emphasis on laundering and starch. "Calicoes and muslin were

well fitted for these tasks" (p. 35), and servants could imitate them.

[283] Fohlen (1973, 69). See also Crouzet (1967a, 173) and Lévy-Leboyer (1968, 282). Even Godechot, who reproaches Lévy-Leboyer for exaggerating the negative effects of the French Revolution on French industry, admits that it is "incontestable" that the revolutions "not only kept" continental Europe from reaching the level of British industry "but even accentuated the gap" (1972, 370). In the case of France in particular, he says that the Revolution "seriously perturbed the evolution of industrialization" (Godechot, 1972, 362). In addition, there was the effect on particular regions of France. Crouzet (1959) asserts that 1793 marks the turning point for southwest France from a region not less industrialized than other zones of France to one that was deindustrialized, and would remain so after 1815.

[284] Marczewski (1963, 127) suggests a trough in 1796 and a second break point in 1812. Soboul (1976a, 4) blames the *assignat* and inflation for creating a "rupture" from 1790 to 1797 "which broke growth for a time and brought about irremediable social consequences." Crouzet (1962, 214) speaks of a "slump during the Directory and at the beginning of the Consulate" which he attributes to

the Revolution. The third was that of the disruption imposed by the British. Napoleon's valiant efforts, in between, did not suffice.

One further difference between Britain and France should be noted with respect to the cotton textile industry. While this period was that of the liquidation, more or less, of the putting-out system in the British textile industry and the urbanization of its productive activities, it was by contrast the period of the veritable creation of a putting-out structure in French textiles, one that would last until 1860. Chassagne calls this a "dualist process of industrialization" which separated physically as of the 1790s the "concentrated very capitalistic" mechanical spinning processes based on hydraulic power and the countryside activities where the weaving was done.[285]

If one asks why this should have happened, a clue is suggested by Schmidt and has to do precisely with the impact of the Revolution. Remembering that one concern of the French was the catching-up with the new mechanical spinning advances of Great Britain, Schmidt points out that to do this rapidly and inexpensively required the use of factory buildings that were already in existence. The nationalization of church property was in this regard a windfall, large numbers of convents, church schools, and abbeys being given to manufacturers gratis or at low price by the revolutionary government for the purpose of installing spinning mills.[286] This property, however, had to be taken where it was found, which was most often in rural areas. Along with this went the sentiment that a putting-out system was an "excellent guarantee of social order,"[287] itself a reaction to the strong antisystemic thrust of the French working class during the Revolution.

No doubt, the element that had the greatest impact on both agriculture and industry was the impact of the wars on interstate trade, the key growth sector at this point. In the last two decades of the eighteenth century, almost 60% of Britain's "additional industrial output" was exported.[288] It was just at this point that France's external trade which had played a key role in French economic growth in the last decades of the *Ancien Régime* suggered a "catastrophic decline"[289] because of, first, the Revolution,[290] second, the loss of Saint-Domingue,[291] and third, the Napoleonic wars.

"the loss of foreign markets by French industry." Bergeron (1970, 504–505) says that the good years of 1800–1810 "fell between two disastrous episodes, the disorganization of the prospect of the *Ancien Régime* by the first years of the Revolution and war and the relative failure of the policy of the Blockade and the defeat of Napoleon."

[285] Chassagne (1979, 104). While Chassagne notes that this ruralization of French cotton textiles had started already in the last years of the *Ancien Régime*, "the Revolution accelerated this socio-economic 'revoluton'."

[286] See Schmidt (1914, 51).
[287] Chassagne (1979, 107).
[288] Crafts (1983, 199).
[289] Marczewski (1965, lx), who argues that not until 1855 would France again reach the level of external trade of 1787–1789.
[290] Braudel says that "the external [trade] collapse of revolutionary France, even before the dramatic events of 1792–1793, has weighed very heavy upon her history" (1982, 219).
[291] Saint-Domingue furnished by itself in the last years of the *Ancien Régime* one-third of France's

The case seems clear then that it was the wars that allowed the "spectacular change"[292] in Britain's exports of cotton textiles while it simultaneously "imposed a curb on France,"[293] thereby creating for Britain a "permanent trading advantage in world markets."[294] To be sure, Napoleon attempted to reverse this situation. Indeed, in the very month he came to power (Brumaire, Year VIII), a French government internal memorandum observed: "The existence of England is due solely to its trade and its credit. If one or the other is made to totter, she is ruined, she is lost."[295] And yet we know that, despite Napoleon's best efforts, he could never make foreign trade reach the level it had had in 1789.[296]

external trade. "As long as France still had 'the Islands', and especially the 'pearl of the West Indies' [Saint-Domingue], the economic system of *Ancien Régime* France remained intact." But this was "the first part" of the *Ancien Régime* "to collapse" (Lüthy, 1961, 596). As Bergeron continues: "From that point on, the French economy, amputated of its most dynamic sector, found itself exposed to the temptations of ruralization, or at least was required to face the transition to the industrial era under less favorable conditions" (1970, 476).

[292] Deane & Cole (1967, 30). See also Schlote (1952, 42, Table 8), Crouzet (1958, 178–192), Deane & Habakkuk (1963, 77), and Edwards (1967, 27–29). Even an author like Davis (1974, 66) who emphasizes technology as opposed to demand as the factor explaining the expansion of cotton textile production in Britain notes a rapid rise in exports in the 1790s, which suffered what he calls a "distortion" of trade patterns caused by the wars. The term "distortion" in my view distorts reality. Habakkuk and Deane (p. 78) are more correct in arguing: "To the extension of the market which took place in the 1790's and early 1800's the power of the British navy contributed at least as much as the inventiveness of British industrialists."

[293] Fohlen (1973, 13). Lévy-Leboyer (1964, 246–247), noting that in the first half of the nineteenth century, "the struggle for the seas was almost exclusively fought out among the Anglo-Saxons," something "scarcely foreseeable" earlier on, particularly in the case of France. "The cut-off of 1793 and the appearance of new sources of supply was to deal a fatal blow to [French and Dutch maritime] traffic." See also Crouzet (1962, 215): "What France lacked at the beginning of the Consulate was external markets, and not productive capacity which, despite the losses suffered during the Revolution, was still largely underemployed." Ellis (1981, 102) precisely confirms Crouzet's findings (1962)—about the crucial role of the lack of markets for their industries (as opposed to the lack of industrial capacity) in this period—for the case of Alsace.

[294] Deane (1973a, 208). See also O'Brien and Keyder (1978, 76) who remind us of Adolphe

Thiers's explanation: "We didn't win the battle of Trafalgar. We aren't the masters of the seas, and we don't have 200 million consumers, as does England. That is the whole secret of our inferiority." Morineau (1978, 416) points to the sequence: Britain's traditional outlets, to which were added those gained on the Continent as a result of "France's forced abstention," to which were added the expansion into South America. "After which, things were en route, the game was over." Crouzet (1980, 72) notes that, of "additional exports" from Britain between 1783 and 1812, 60% were to the New World, 23% to continental Europe.

Even Landes (1969, 145), whose principal emphasis is on what he called the local determinants of industrial growth, speaks of "secondary effects" caused by the delays in continental industrialization as a result of the Revolutionary upheaval: "In particular, the gap between continental and British industrial equipment had increased, and while such a spread may mean in theory a greater incentive to modernization, it constituted in fact an obstacle." He gives two explanations. One is that the increased capacity meant that the latest equipment was "less suitable to the post-Waterloo continental market" (p. 146), but this of course was because Britain now commanded access to the non-European market. The second reason is the increased "initial lump of investment" (p. 147) now necessary. Landes therefore talks of continental industry engaging in "voluntary obsolescence," which he admits "helped maintain Britain's competitive advantage in third markets." But how voluntary is an economic structure created in large part by a politico-military dominance? Landes is in fact describing the situation of "hegemony." See in this regard Milward & Saul (1973, 307–309).

[295] A.E. 46, f° 326. In 1847, a German author wrote: "This war [between France and Britain, 1792–1815]—will posterity believe it?—was proclaimed as a crusade against sugar and coffee, against percales and muslins" (Schlegel, cited in Lingelbach, 1914, 257).

[296] Soboul (1976b, 105) says this "underlined once again the importance of large-scale colonial

Napoleon's policies, of course, did not really start with Napoleon. They started with the return to protectionism in 1791, continued with the French navigation act of 1793, the banning of British merchandise arriving on neutral vessels in 1798, and merely culminated in the decrees of Berlin and Milan of 1806–1807 organizing the Continental Blockade.[297]

The Blockade itself seemed primarily directed against British cotton textile production, which was "menaced with overproduction because of a too rapid expansion,"[298] especially between 1799–1802, years in which Napoleon was experiencing his first commercial crisis.[299] The Blockade was a "serious" menace, because Great Britain was indeed "vulnerable."[300] Napoleon hoped to affect British trade on many fronts: closing of outlets for manufactured products in Europe, blocking raw materials imports, and impairing British financial credit (by creating a negative balance of payments leading to exhaustion of bullion and therefore a collapse of confidence in the paper money).[301]

The only one of these objectives achieved even partially was the closing of outlets in Europe.[302] Denying Great Britain raw materials imports foundered on the fact that Napoleon's power, in Captain Mahan's acerbic prose, "ceased, like that of certain wizards, when it reached the Water."[303] As for Britain's financial credit, it remained good because the financial links with the continent were never really broken,[304] not to speak of the fact that Britain was the steady recipient of a bullion inflow as the haven for the flight of capital, first from the Revolution, then from Napoleon's Continental System.[305] Britain's state finances were kept in balance, at first by income from the expanded foreign trade,[306] and, when the costs of war escalated, by borrowing[307] and by imposing the increased tax burden

---

trade at the end of the *Ancien Régime* and the irremediable consequences of its ruin."

[297] See Bergeron (1978e, 358) and Rose (1893, 704). As for Britain's blockade, Meyer argues that the British pressure on the Dutch as early as 1778 to renounce their commercial treaty with France was "one of the distant antecedents of the English 'continental' blockade during the Revolution and the Empire" (1979a, 213, fn.).

[298] Crouzet (1958, I. 86).

[299] See Butel (1970) who notes that the improved situation in 1802 with the Peace of Amiens was quickly reversed in the summer of 1803 with the resumption of the maritime war. Still, at this point, the British blockade was "still very tolerant" in that the British permitted "indirect trade with the colonies via neutral intermediaries, particularly the Americans" (p. 546).

[300] Crouzet (1958, I, 203).

[301] Crouzet (1958, I, 57–63, 91–97, 102, 122–123).

[302] Crouzet (1958, I, 126–152).

[303] Mahan (1893, II, 279). For 1806, Mahan speaks of "that supremacy and omnipresence of the British navy, which made it impossible for vessels under the enemy's flag to keep at sea" (p. 308). Mahan's conclusion: "By the mastery of the sea, by the destruction of the French colonial system and commerce . . . [Britain] drove the enemy into the battleground of the Continental System where his final ruin was certain." (400–401).

[304] See Fugier (1954, 236).

[305] See Lévy-Leboyer (1964, 708). Braudel speaks of "a large-scale flight of capital" from revolutionary France (1982, 219).

[306] See Sherwig (1969, 12).

[307] "The early practice of borrowing to pay for the war was of more benefit than is generally recognized, both in maintaining employment levels and in preserving the momentum of advance during a possibly critical period in British economic development" (Anderson, 1974, 618).

disproportionately on the agricultural sector, thereby protecting industry and trade.[308]

Although Napoleon was using the power of the state to encourage, indeed subsidize, industry,[309] the British were just as actively aiding theirs,[310] and trying with some success to deny French and continental industries their raw materials.[311] Crouzet insists that the Continental Blockade was not "inefficacious" economically. It did seriously affect British economic activity, but Napoleon could not apply it long enough to succeed in his objectives, for essentially political and military reasons.[312] On the one hand, the French encountered political, nationalist resistance within their empire.[313] On the other hand, in this fertile atmosphere, Britain was buying allies through its considerable subsidies.[314] Under the counterpressure Napoleon began in effect to retreat in the economic arena as early as 1810, when he reopened the ports of France to colonial products via licenses. He did thereby absorb into the state treasury the profit margin of the smugglers, but this only aggravated political resistance within Europe, since it amounted to a covert economic deal with the British at the expense of other Europeans. It thus added one more element fostering the reversal of alliances that would occur.[315]

[308] See Deane (1979, 52), and John (1967, 47).

[309] There were three main forms of state aid: (1) rental or sale at low prices of church properties to manufacturers (whose implications for the long-term structure of industry we noted previously); (2) government encouragement of new machinery derived from British models; (3) modest subsidies to those installing such machinery (used especially to help employers otherwise threatened by bankruptcy). See Bergeron (1978b, 213–214). Leleux says of the great industrialists in Napoleon's empire—Dollfus, Oberkampf, Richard-Lenoir, Ternaux, Bauwens—that "they felt understood, assisted, supported" (1969, 122). See also Chassagne (1980, 336).

[310] The British were actively protectionist of their technological advantage. They enacted various legislation, which was consolidated in a general act of 1795 that forbade the export of machinery (including tools, and sketches or models of machines) as well as the emigration of skilled workers, with severe penalties for violation (loss of British citizenship, confiscation of property). To be sure, such laws were not 100% successful. Nonetheless, they were effective and were repealed only in 1824, and then only partially, complete abolition occurring only in 1843. See Clough (1957, 1346).

[311] See Cobban (1965, 52) and Godechot (1967b, 167–168). Bouvier (1970, 512) attributes France's industrial crisis of 1810–1811 to "difficulties in obtaining supplies of raw materials" because of the Blockade. See also Fugier (1954, 237–238).

[312] Crouzet (1958, II, 855–860).

[313] See Godechot (1967a, 180–200) on resistance in Spain, Germany, and Italy. Crouzet (1958, I, 408) notes that the results of the Blockade in Spain were "disastrous" for France. France would now finally see significant displacement in the Spanish market by the British. See Broder (1976, 310). See also Dupin (1858, 160) who shows that the sale of British products in the Iberian peninsula quintupled between 1807 and 1812.

The nationalist resistance to Napoleon had an economic as well as political base. See Pollard on Napoleon's intent: "Other countries on [France's] edge, notably Italy, were to become suppliers of certain raw materials and markets for its manufactures. The rest of Europe, in as much as it entered the picture at all, was to become a dependency, to be flooded by the protected and pampered industries of France while the manufactures produced there were wholly excluded from the metropolitan market. The French vision was that of exclusive nationalism" (1981, 24).

[314] Subsidies began with the Prussian threat of 1794, and grew increasingly generous "under the pressure of events." By the winter of 1806–1807, subsidies were being "doled out . . . by the spoonful" (Sherwig, 1969, 181). By 1812–1814, such subsidies amounted to circa 14% of Britain's total tax yield (p. 354). The total amount for the period 1793–1816 was "upwards of £57,000,000" (Clapham, 1917, 495).

[315] See Jouvenel (1942, 399–417). Ellis (1981,

Was, therefore, the whole effort of the Revolutionary governments and Napoleon to undo the growing relative advantage of Great Britain over France one enormous failure? Probably not entirely. Crouzet argues that "by 1800, Central Europe was threatened by pastoralization and the fate of India in the nineteenth century."[316] This threat did not materialize. Nonetheless, Britain was much further ahead in 1815 than in 1793,[317] and further ahead precisely because of the effects, direct and indirect, of the Revolutionary and Napoleonic eras.

There is, however, one further factor to take into account, the course of the state-level class struggles in France and in Great Britain. In France, we have already recounted the antisystemic thrust of the urban masses in the revolutionary years. We know that the Enragés or Jacquesroutains as well as the Babouvistes, failed, and decisively, as political movements.[318] The planned reforms in social policy which the popular masses had been able to extract from the revolutionary government were never enacted. Nonetheless, the ideal of Jacobin *bienfaisance*—the rights of those below the poverty line to social assistance—left a political legacy which "should not be belittled,"[319] and this legacy was felt in the Napoleonic era.

Napoleon preserved all the legal reforms instituted by the Revolution and indeed codified them.[320] Of course, that did not necessarily mean more security and rights for the wage earner, who was not better off under Napoleon, probably worse.[321] But nonetheless the economic conditions of the popular masses improved considerably under Napoleon. His was an era dominated by a "rise in wages." This improvement in material conditions was "unquestionable," so much so that, after the economic downturn of 1817, peasants and urban workers looked back upon the Empire "as a sort of golden age."[322] No doubt, the *conjoncture* served Napoleon well. But it was not automatic that this meant popular support. It is pertinent to compare the atmosphere in France with that in Great Britain in this same *conjoncture*.

The French Revolution aroused considerable sympathy in the beginning from what might broadly be called the left half of the British political spectrum. While more moderate supporters began to fall away during the Jacobin phase, there remained a faithful group of so-called English Jacobins, whose politics were in fact closer to that of the sans-culottes than to that of the Jacobins. Their strength was among the artisan class and they

---

266) argues that one of the explanations of the failure of Napoleon's economic policies was their "deliberate one-sidedness" vis-à-vis the rest of continental Europe. Instead of promoting a Continental *Zollverein*, Napoleon created "a vast 'Uncommon Market' geared to French interests."

[316] Crouzet (1964, 579).

[317] See Crouzet (1958, II, 872).

[318] See Tønnesson (1959), Markov (1960), Soboul

(1963), Rose (1965, 1972, 1978), and Higonnet (1979).

[319] Forrest (1981, 172).

[320] See Soboul (1970a, 335), who speaks of Bonaparte respecting "the social accomplishments" of the Constituent Assembly. See also Godechot (1970, 795–796).

[321] Lefebvre (1969, 153).

[322] Tulard (1970, 659–661).

maintained a "root-and-branch opposition" to monarchy, the aristocracy, the state, and taxation.[323] But once the war broke out, the members of these popular societies came to be "isolated" politically from more mainline Whig groups.[324]

Nonetheless, the government found them quite threatening, fearing "any form of popular self-activity," because it seemed to menace not only traditional authority but the "new ideology of political economy."[325] The result was a serious and relatively effective repression, such that British radicals during the 1790s "believed that they were experiencing a reign of terror,"[326] which included the suspension of habeas corpus.

The two most significant new policies in relation to the control of labor during this period were the Speenhamland "allowance system" of 1795 and the Anti-Combination Acts of 1799. Speenhamland loosened the old Act of Settlement of 1662, whose effect Thorold Rogers asserted to have been "to annex the labourer to the parish of his residence, and to make him a serf."[327] The revised Poor Law system provided in effect for a minimum wage (through government subsidy) tied to the cost of living plus a family allowance system.

Three questions should be asked about Speenhamland. Was it better for the workers? Was it better for the employers (largely of agricultural labor)? Why was it enacted? It clearly had some advantages for the workers in that it meant that even in bad years they "could count on escaping outright starvation."[328] Was it better for the employers? By subsidizing what in fact were "substandard wages," the effect was that, between 1795 and 1824, it "depressed agricultural wages." Blaug, however, argues that these subsidies to employers were in effect paid by them through the rate system, the "link" between the two being close.[329]

Then cui bono? What it did effectively was to prevent unemployment by spreading underemployment in a still largely agricultural country.[330] If we ask then why it was done, the motivation seems clearly and immediately political, "the fear of popular uprising,"[331] the spectre of the French Revolution as an anti-capitalist revolution. In this regard Speenhamland succeeded.[332] It only did so, however, because it was coupled with the

---

[323] Thompson (1968, 171–172). On the leading role of artisans in English working-class radicalism of this time, see also Gareth Stedman Jones (1974, 484), Prothero (1979), and Calhoun (1982, 7).

[324] Goodwin (1979, 26).

[325] Thompson (1971, 129).

[326] Emsley (1981, 155). In addition to prosecutions for treason and sedition, there was considerable "personal victimization" (p. 174). Lefebvre (1968, 616) notes the widescale use of what in France was called the "guillotine sèche," that is deportation.

[327] Rogers (1884, 434).

[328] McNeill (1982, 209). It did this to be sure by a system which eliminated all incentive to productivity. In Polanyi's words (1957, 79–80), this "amounted to the abandonment of Tudor legislation not for the sake of less but of more paternalism." In the long run, he says, "the result was ghastly.'

[329] Blaug (1963, 162, 168, 176).

[330] See Blaug (1963, 176–177).

[331] Mantoux (1928, 448).

[332] See McNeill's analysis (1982, 209): "In the absence of the poor law help, rural laborers in time of dearth and in the seasons of the year when work

Anti-Combination Laws, "but for which Speenhamland might have had the effect of raising wages instead of depressing them as it actually did."[333] Plumb points out that the Anti-Combination Laws accomplished two things simultaneously: it kept down wages despite rising food costs, but it also enabled the government "to eradicate one of the best breeding grounds for subversive propaganda."[334]

Thus the policies vis-à-vis the popular masses were in the end harsher in Great Britain than in France, probably because the antisystemic thrust in France, although repressed, had been more efficacious. One piece of evidence in this regard is the actual level of wages and food supply in the two countries during the war period. Whereas we saw that French workers felt that the Napoleonic era has been a period of increased real wages, Britain in this period saw a fall.[335]

When this was combined with years of scarce bread, such as 1809–1811, the difficult situation led to serious rioting, which was in some ways comparable to what occurred in prerevolutionary France, except that it expressed itself not in anti-government sentiment, but in anti-employer, anti-machine sentiment, Luddism.[336] Yet the net result was not, or not yet, to be a revolutionary upsurge.[337] Despite worsening conditions in the war period, British workers were held in check—in part by government repression, in part no doubt (as has often been claimed) by Methodism,[338] but also in part by the harnessing of nationalist (anti-French) sentiment to

on the land was slackest would have had no choice but to flee into town. . . . Crowds of just such people had flooded into Paris because of bad harvests in 1788–89." After 1795, however, the like could scarcely occur in England, Polanyi (1957, 93) cites Canning's conviction that "the Poor Law saved England from a revolution."

This leads one to take with a grain of salt the conclusion by Chambers and Mingay (1966, 109–110) that "it was basically a humanitarian policy which helped keep alive a swelling rural population at the expense of farmers' profits and landlord's rents."

[333] Polanyi (1957, 81). "Between 1793 & 1820, more than 60 acts directed at repression of working-class collective action were passed by Parliament. By 1799, virtually every form of working-class association or collective action was illegal or licensable by the justices of the peace" (Munger, 1981, 93).

[334] Plumb (1950, 158). Mantoux (1928, 456) similarly argues that the Act was inspired by "the fear of a revolution, such as was taking place in France."

[335] Mantoux (1928, 436) characterizes the fall as sharp. "The nominal rise of wages . . . bore no proportion to the rise of prices due to the war." See also Foster (1974, 21), Jones (1975, 38), and von Tunzelmann (1979, 48). O'Brien and Engerman

(1981, 169, Table 9.1) show something closer to a stable level of real wages, with a dip nonetheless in the middle.

[336] On food rioting, see Stevenson (1974). On 1809–1811 England as comparable to 1786–1789 France, see Cunningham (1910, 75–77). On Luddism as a response to worker's acute distress, see Thomis (1972, 43–46).

[337] Nairn (1964, 43) has a somewhat different overall impression: "The early history of the English working class is . . . one of revolt, covering more than a half century, from the period of the French Revolution to the climax of Chartism in the 1840's." I do not disagree, but feel that the French revolt was the more successful, largely because of their early successes as an anti-*bourgeois*, anticapitalist force. They became hardier, the bourgeoisie in France somewhat less hardy than their British counterparts, and the French workers became more difficult to coopt by a bourgeoisie who had less surplus to spare with which to do it.

[338] The most complete argument is made by Semmel who assembles the evidence to argue (1973, 7) that "Methodism may have helped to block a violent English counterpart to the French Revolution by preempting the critical appeal and objective of that Revolution." See also Kiernan (1952, 45), and Thompson (1968, 419).

the cause of political stability.[339] All that remained for the British ruling class was to begin to transfer a piece of the pie to their lower strata. But this had to await the new hegemonic era (and even then it was slow in coming).

With the end of the wars, Britain was finally truly hegemonic in the world-system. It consolidated its world power by acquiring a set of maritime bases, which added to what it already had, and meant that it now circled the globe strategically. Between 1783 and 1816 Britain acquired, in the Atlantic Ocean area, St. Lucia, Trinidad, Tobago, Bathurst, Sierra Leone, Ascension, St. Helena, Tristan da Cunha, and Gough Island; in the Indian Ocean, the Cape Colony, Mauritius, the Seychelles, the Laccadive Islands, the Maldive Islands, Ceylon, the Andaman Islands, and Penang; in Australasia, New South Wales, New Zealand, Macquarie Islands, Campbell Islands, Auckland Island, Lord Howe Island, and Chatham Island; and in the Mediterranean, Malta and the Ionian Islands.[340]

Furthermore, Britain had in the process of the war been able to end the last vestige of Holland's one-time hegemony, her role as a financial center of Europe.[341] Through her dominance in commerce and finance, Britain now began to earn massive invisible credits—earnings of the merchant marine, commercial commissions, remittances from technicians and colonial officials abroad, earnings from investments—which were enough to compensate a continuing, even expanding, trade deficit, one that existed despite the size of her export trade. Britain, therefore, could maintain a constantly favorable balance of payments.[342] She commenced too her new role as the "schoolmaster of industrial Europe,"[343] while nonetheless still maintaining her high protectionist barriers.[344]

In this period, the sense of French backwardness in relation to British industry became accepted truth. A French industrialist in the 1830s explained British superiority by the greater specialization of British industry, which meant the British could produce faster and cheaper.[345] Chaptal's explanation at the time as to why this should be so emphasizes

[339] See Anderson (1980, 37–38). "The sense of *national* community, systematically orchestrated by the State, may well have been a greater reality in the Napoleonic epoch than at any time in the previous century. . . . The structural importance of [counter-revolutionary nationalism], general and durable, was certainly more than the more local and limited phenomenon of Methodism. . . ." But see Colley who arguest that the British state was strong enough not to feel the need to "promote and exploit national consciousness" (1986, 106).
[340] See Graham (1966, 5), Shaw (1970, 2), and Darby & Fullard (1970, 12–13).
[341] See Graham (1966, 7) and Braudel (1982, 395).
[342] See Imlah (1958, 40–42).

[343] Henderson (1972, 212).
[344] British industrial protectionism ended only in 1842. See Imlah (1958, 16, 23). The British Navigation Acts were repealed only in 1849. See Clapham (1966, 169–170). See also Lévy-Leboyer (1964, 213–214) and Deane (1979, 203). Of course, French protectionism lasted even longer. See Lévy-Leboyer (1964, 15), Broder (1976, 334–335), Daumard (1976, 155–159), Léon (1976a, 479), Chassagne (1981, 51); and on Europe in general, Gille (1973, 260).
[345] Cited by Gille (1959, 33). See Stearns (1965) for an analysis of the sense by French industrialists between 1820 and 1848 of "the overwhelming superiority of British industry" (p. 53).

low French wages as a disincentive to mechanization.[346] This seems dubious, however, in light of recent data that workers in French industries at the time "achieved higher levels of productivity than their counterparts" in Britain.[347] It is even more dubious if we remember that the data on lower wage rates in France than in Britain is not necessarily a statement about "average levels of earnings," given a different household income structure, "and therefore [about] welfare in the two countries."[348]

One of the clear outcomes of the final British surge forward and France's defeat in the wars was the emergence of a quite different demographic pattern for the two countries. Le Roy Ladurie somewhat dramatically calls the French Revolution France's "demographic Islam,"[349] meaning that because of it birth control became widespread in the countryside. Reinhard, more soberly, suggests that France's pattern was merely the "prototype" of what would later occur everywhere.[350] McNeill, however, looks at it quite differently, seeing the Napoleonic wars as a way of "ameliorating social tensions arising from rapid population growth" in the eighteenth century.[351]

Could we not, therefore, see the post-1815 demographic pattern as an adjustment to economic and political reality? The British, having gained the upper hand in the world market, needed to expand their labor force to maximize their advantage. They did this by encouraging high rates of natural increase, by immigration, and by encouraging a shift to higher ratios of waged to nonwaged labor.[352] France, unable to support an expanded work force through an income from international trade, foreign investment, and mercantile services in general as could Britain, settled for supporting a parallel domestic output per head of population by "restraints on fertility."[353] In this case, it would not be the slow population growth that explains slow mechanization[354] but the inverse. If such were the case, Frenchmen might be forgiven for believing that "successful mercantilism, not the factory system . . . [was] at the centre of British superiority for a century after Waterloo."[355]

[346] Chaptal (1819, II, 31). Landes (1969, 161–164) agrees. Crouzet (1972c, 286), however, cites a "cheap and clever workforce" as one of France's few *advantages* vis-à-vis Great Britain in the post-1815 period.

[347] O'Brien & Keyder (1978, 174; see also Table 4.3, p. 91). The authors do note that this is an "unorthodox finding."

[348] O'Brien & Keyder (1978, 74).

[349] Le Roy Ladurie (1975, 378). Sédillot says the same thing more soberly. He asserts that between 1789 and 1815, population rose 9% in France, 23% in Great Britain, which "contributed to reducing the gap in population size and to preparing the ditch which would be built" (1987, 37).

[350] Reinhard (1965, 451).

[351] McNeill (1982, 201). Dupâquier (1970, 340–341) seems to share this perspective.

[352] See the discussion in Tranter (1981, 209–216) who argues that the largest part of the increase in the labor force from 1780 to 1860 derived from natural increase. See also Reinhard (1965, 458). On Ireland's role in the growth of England's population, see Connell (1969, 39).

[353] O'Brien & Keyder (1978, 75).

[354] This view is reflected in Gille (1959, 40), Léon (1976a, 478), and Sewell (1980, 153).

[355] O'Brien & Keyder (1978, 75).

It is in this light that we should read the long-standing controversy over the standard of living of the British working class. It is, in fact, a debate largely centered about what happened between circa 1815 and 1840. Ashton launches the post-1945 debate by asserting that, given the fall in prices and the rise in imports into Britain, "it is difficult to believe that the workers had no share in the gain." Hobsbawm conversely suggests that, given the rise of mortality rates and unemployment, the scattered evidence "support a pessimistic rather than a rosy view." Hartwell in turn suggests improvement occurred "slowly during the war, more quickly after 1815, and rapidly after 1840." And Hobsbawm retorts that there are improvements in national income, but was there more equal distribution? Taylor continues by suggesting that "the progress of the working class lagged behind that of the nation at large."[356]

It does not seem hard to reconcile the actual empirical findings reported. This much seems difficult to contest. Prices fell considerably, although, because of the Corn Laws, they fell less for bread than they otherwise would have.[357] The real wages of those who were employed at wage labor rose somewhat. But this is not necessarily the case for agricultural labor, nor for the unemployed and partially employed in the towns. Nor does it exclude the likelihood that for their real wage increase, the wage laborer and his family worked longer and harder hours than previously. That is, the real wage per annum could go up without the real wage per hour going up. Finally, it is clear that profits in the cotton industry (and elsewhere in industry) were "well-maintained" despite falling prices, and that one of the reasons was that industrialists "enjoyed an almost inexhaustible low-priced labor supply."[358] Materially, a segment of the British working class got a slightly increased portion of the pie. But looked at from the point of view of the world-economy as a whole, this is perfectly consistent with the assertion that the *world-economy-wide* working class got a diminished portion of the same pie.

We should remember a double movement was occurring at just this point

---

[356] Ashton (1949, 28), Hobsbawm (1957, 52), Hartwell (1961, 412), Hobsbawm (1963, 126), and Taylor (1960, 25). See also Imlah (1958), Hartwell (1963; 1970a), Williams (1966), Neale (1966), Gourvish (1972), Flinn (1974), Hartwell & Engerman (1975), Hueckel (1981), O'Brien & Engerman (1981), Crafts (1983), and Lindert & Williamson (1983).

It is fascinating to read the reflections of Briavoinne on this issue in 1838: "That there is material profit is clear. But a result which up to now seems less proven, although it is no longer doubted by many distinguished persons, is to know whether the new industrial system tends to inspire in the working man a surer sense of his dignity, more regular work habits, a livelier penchant for savings, a purer morals. The existence of savings banks is cited. To this material evidence one can easily counterpose the birth registration records and those of asylums for abandoned infants which reveal a sad state of disorder within families; and criminal statistics, which show a steady increase of misdemeanors and felonies. The questions is not yet ripe; there is not yet sufficient data to permit a clear analysis" (1838, 98). One wonders, even today, if the question is "ripe."

[357] Deane (1979, 208) says that, between 1815 and 1846, the Corn Laws were "a symbol of the conflict between rich and poor."

[358] Deane (1979, 99–100).

in the world-economy. There was a significant incorporation of new zones into the world-economy, new peripheries which were suffering a significant *decrease* in their standard of living. However, Western Europe generally (and particularly France, Belgium, western "Germany," and Switzerland) and also the northern states of the United States, having been pushed behind Great Britain, were nonetheless proceeding to "industrialize" and would be able to (re)emerge as strong core zones in the mid-nineteenth century. In the meantime, the resistance of their working classes to capitalist development may have earned them similar *small* increases in real living standards.

Both of these developments will be the subject of detailed analysis later. But a few preliminary observations are in order here to complete the Franco–British comparison. In the period 1815–1840, France was able to "modernize" its textile industry in particular and thus "overcome its backwardness"[359] vis-à-vis Britain. Note carefully nonetheless how this was done and what market was served. France turned to a specialization in quality textiles along with, as we have already noted, a ruralization of location.[360] One of the key reasons was the size of the market. Deprived of the world, France had to reconstruct to serve France, which it would do by restructuring and industrial relocation.[361] While, therefore, this was a period of deindustrialization in the periphery, in Europe, this "evil, not unknown, was less profound," and that was so because the states were still strong enough to intervene actively to counter the threat.[362] But was it not also the case that Britain did not need the deindustrialization of Europe? Quite the contrary, perhaps. Given the widened market of the periphery, Britain would need a second layer of industrializing countries coming in behind her, to take up the slack as she would progress to new technological advances. Or so it would work for at least 50 years.

We must stop this story, however, for the moment at 1830/1832, a political turning point. July 1830 in France was "more than a riot, and certainly less than a revolution."[363] It played in many ways the function vis-à-vis the French Revolution that the Glorious Revolution of 1688–1689 played in England vis-à-vis the English Revolution. It represented an ideological compromise among the ruling classes that in some sense laid to rest the bitterness of the ideological quarrels caused by the extreme violence of the previous revolution. It ensured that the internecine quarrels among the upper strata would henceforth be fought in "normal" (if not always constitutional) political form. By so doing, it in fact liberated the workers from their conceptual dependence on bourgeois thinkers. The

[359] Lévy-Leboyer (1964, 144–145, 169–171, 342, 411–414).

[361] See Crouzet (1964, 586). This shift from the seaboard inward started of course during the wars and involved all of ex-Lotharingia: northeast France, Ghent, Verviers, Liège, Aachen, Alsace.

[362] Lévy-Leboyer (1964, 186–191).

[363] Montgolfier (1980, 7).

workers "took up the language of the Revolution and reshaped it to fit their own goals."[364]

The French Revolution of 1830 had an immediate echo in Great Britain and led to the Reform Act of 1832.[365] Indeed, a violent outbreak there in 1832 was "averted only at the eleventh hour."[366] The Reform Act of 1832 then turned out to be a sort of ideological coda to 1688–1689, including the industrialists within the political game, who had been excluded previously "not because their property was industrial but because it was petty."[367] This coda served the same function for Britain that 1830 did for France. It liberated the working class terminologically. Now British workers could begin to talk the class-conscious action they had long since begun to perform.

[364] Sewell (1980, 281), who also says: "Class consciousness first emerged in France during the agitation that followed the Revolution of 1830." But, as I argued above, class consciousness was already there. What had been missing was the theorizing, which would now begin.

[365] See Thompson (1968, 911).

[366] Thompson (1978b, 46–47) who adds this very pertinent historiographical comment: "If it had not been, then it is reasonable to suppose that revolution would have precipitated a very rapid process of radicalization, passing through and beyond a Jacobin experience; and whatever form a counter-revolution and eventual stabilization might have taken it is unlikely that many eighteenth-century institutions could have survived—the House of Lords, the Established Church, the monarchy, and the juridical and military elite would probably have been swept away, at least temporarily. Now if it had happened in this way, the model-builders at least would now be satisfied; 1832 would be *the* English bourgeois revolution, and 1640 would have fallen into neglect, as a 'premature' outbreak, a sort of amalgam of Huguenot wars and the Fronde. The tendency to imply some kind of 'feudal' society existed in Britain until the eve of 1832 (as witness the quaint notion that peeps from the edges of some Marxist interpretations of the French Revolution, that 'feudalism' prevailed in France in 1788) would have been reinforced."

[367] Thompson (1978b, 50).

3

THE INCORPORATION OF VAST NEW ZONES INTO THE WORLD-ECONOMY: 1750–1850

   The engraving illustrates one part of the elaborate process of receiving a European envoy at
the Ottoman court—the ceremonial dinner offered by the Grand Vizier in the hall of the
Divan after the exchange of credentials with the Grand Vizier and immediately preceding the
presentation of the envoy to the Sultan. The etching was made by Bénoist in 1785 (probably
M.-A. Bénoist, who worked in Paris 1780–1810), and was completed by Delvaux (probably
Rémi Delvaux, 1750–1832). It appeared as an illustration in one of the first major
presentations of Ottoman customs and history to a European public. This book, *Tableau
général de l'Empire Othoman,* was written by Ignatius Mouradgea d'Ohsson, who had been
chargé d'affaires of Sweden at the Sublime Porte, and was published in French in Paris in
three volumes in 1787, 1790, and 1820.

In the course of the renewed economic expansion (and monetary inflation) of the period 1733–1817 (more or less), the European world-economy broke the bounds it had created in the long sixteenth century and began to incorporate vast new zones into the effective division of labor it encompassed. It began by incorporating zones which had already been in its external arena since the sixteenth century—most particularly and most importantly, the Indian subcontinent, the Ottoman empire, the Russian empire, and West Africa.

These incorporations took place in the second half of the eighteenth and the first half of the nineteenth centuries. The pace, as we know, then accelerated and, eventually by the end of the nineteenth century and the beginning of the twentieth, the entire globe, even those regions that had never been part even of the external arena of the capitalist world-economy, were pulled inside. The pattern of this process of incorporation into the existing ongoing process of capital accumulation was set with these four zones. Although the incorporation process of each was somewhat different in detail, the four processes occurred more or less simultaneously and exhibited substantial similarities in their essential features.

Incorporation into the capitalist world-economy was never at the initiative of those being incorporated. The process derived rather from the need of the world-economy to expand its boundaries, a need which was itself the outcome of pressures internal to the world-economy. Major and large-scale social processes like incorporation are furthermore not abrupt phenomena. They emerge from the flow of ongoing continuous activities. While we may give them dates retrospectively (and approximately), the turning points are seldom sharp and the qualitative changes they incarnate are complex and composite. Nevertheless, they are real in their impact and eventually they are perceived to have occurred.

Previously in this work we have sought to distinguish systematically those zones which (in the long sixteenth century) were in the periphery of the world-economy and those which were in its external arena. We suggested then that there were three principal differences between the way Russia (in the external arena) and eastern Europe (in the periphery) related to western Europe: "(a) a difference in the nature of the trade, (b) a difference in the strength and role of the state-machinery, and (c) as a consequence of the two prior points, a difference in the strength and role of the indigenous urban bourgeoisie."[1]

The question we are dealing with now is the nature of the process by which a zone which was at one point in time in the external arena of the world-economy came to be, at a later point in time, in the periphery of that same world-economy. We think of this transition as a period of medium duration and we denominate it the period of "incorporation." Hence, the model we are using involves three successive moments for a "zone"—being

---

[1] Wallerstein (1974, 302).

in the external arena, being incorporated, and being peripheralized. None of these moments is static; all of them involve processes.

Incorporation means fundamentally that at least some significant production processes in a given geographic location become integral to various of the commodity chains that constitute the ongoing divisioning of labor of the capitalist world-economy. And how will we know if a particular production process is "integral to" this divisioning of labor? A production process can only be considered to be thus integrated if its production responds in some sense to the ever-changing "market conditons" of this world-economy (whatever the source of these changes) in terms of efforts by those who control these production processes to maximize the accumulation of capital within this "market"—if not in the very short run, at least in some reasonable middle run. As long as this cannot be said to be happening by and large, as long as the vagaries of the particular production processes can be accounted for by considerations other than those which permit the maximal accumulation of capital in the world-economy, then the zone in which these particular processes are located must be considered to remain in the external arena of the world-economy, despite the existence of trade links, and no matter how extensive or profitable the ongoing "trade" seems to be.

Of course, however much defining the difference in this way might clarify the issue theoretically, it is of little utility as an empirical indicator of the correct description of a particular situation. To find such indicators, we must turn to some of the empirical consequences of such integration. And here we must make a distinction between the moment (however long) of "incorporation" and the subsequent moment of "peripheralization." If an analogy may be permitted, incorporation involves "hooking" the zone into the orbit of the world-economy in such a way that it virtually can no longer escape, while peripheralization involves a continuing transformation of the ministructures of the area in ways that are sometimes referred to as the deepening of capitalist development.

Perhaps if we ask ourselves the simple question of what is required in order that a local production process respond in some sense to the ever-changing market conditions of a world-economy, we may locate the criteria we need. It seems clear that the ability to respond is a function in part of the size of the decision-making unit. A larger unit is more likely to have an impact *on itself* and its own prospects for capital accumulation by altering its production decisions in light of what it believes to be altered conditions in some market. It follows that, for enterprises in a zone to begin to respond in this way, they may have to become larger. The creation of such larger units of decision making may occur either at a site of direct production (e.g., by creating a "plantation") or at a site of mercantile collection of production, provided that the collector, that is, the merchant, has some mechanism of controlling, in turn, the activities of multiple petty producers (e.g., debt obligation). Second, decisions, most simply those of expanding of contracting production, must be possible in terms of the ability to acquire (or rid oneself of the responsibility for) the elements that enter into the production process—the machines, the materials, the capital, and above all, the human labor. Human labor must be "coercible" in some way. Third, those who control production processes are more likely to respond if the political institutions that have relevant power and authority permit, abet, and subsidize such responses than if they do not. Finally, responses require an institutional infrastructure of reasonable security and appropriate currency arrangements.

It follows from this that to analyze whether the production processes of a given zone are integrated in the larger divisioning of labor of a world-economy, we should enquire into the nature of the structures of economic decision making, the ways in which labor is differentially available for work in these productive processes, the degree to which governance units relate to the requirements of the political superstructure of the capitalist world-economy, and, finally, the emergence of the necessary institutional in-frastructure, or rather the extension of that which already exists in the capitalist world-economy to cover the zone being incorporated. It is this story we shall seek to tell in this chapter.

Let us begin by reviewing in what sense these four zones were *not* incorporated in the long period 1500–1750 during which all four might be said to have been in a constant trading relationship with the European world-economy as part of its external arena.

There was, first of all, the nature of the trade. The specificity of trade between two zones not within a single division of labor revolves around the distinction, in the language of earlier times, between the "rich trades" and the trade in "coarse" or "gruff" goods. Today we speak of the distinction between "luxury goods" on the one hand and "bulk goods" or "necessities" on the other. A luxury is of course a term whose operational definition is a function of normative evaluation. We know today that even such a seemingly physiological concept as the minimum standard of living for survival is socially defined. If for no other reason, this is so because we have to put into the equation the length of time over which one is measuring the survival. It is difficult to decide that any particular products—spices or tea or furs or indeed slaves—are or are not, in a given context, luxury exports, not to speak of the special case of bullion. I say luxury *export*, because in an economic sense there is little meaning to the idea of a luxury *import*. If an item is bought on a market, it is because someone feels subjectively a "need" for that item, and it would be fatuous for the analytic observer to assert that the "need" was not real. In the classical expression of the Thomases, "if men define situations as real, they are real in their consequences."[2] To be sure,

---

[2] Thomas & Thomas (1928, 572).

some items are expensive per unit and others not, but what is relevant to the merchant is the rate of return for the totality sold multiplied by the quantity of sales.

Luxury export may, however, have a more analytic definition. It refers to the dispositon of socially low-valued items at prices far higher than those obtainable from their alternative usages. This is a concept that can only apply if one is dealing with the trade between two separate historical systems which then can conceivably have different measures of social value. Hence, the concepts "luxury" and "external arena" go hand in hand. If we now look at the literature we find that authors have frequently used the language of "luxury" trade in the descriptions of India and West Africa. Kulshresthra, for example, notes: "'The objects of oriental traffic were splendid and trifling,' says Gibbons. And this is particularly true for the sixteenth and seventeenth centuries."[3] Northrup, speaking of the development of Atlantic commerce in the Niger Delta observes that at first the Aro traded in "luxury items—slaves, horses and cattle for ritual purposes and beads"[4] and that such commerce was not conducted in the local markets.

But what makes the luxury a luxury? Amin finds the crucial variable to be ignorance. He links the "rarity" of the goods in "long-distance trade" with the fact that such trade is based on the exchange of commodities "for which each is unaware of the other's cost of production."[5] If ignorance is a crucial element, we see immediately in what way such luxury trade can be self-liquidating. As the trade expands, the basis of the ignorance may disappear. This brings us then to the second crucial element, the one raised by Karl Polanyi, and illustratively applied particularly to the case of Dahomey in the eighteenth century. It is the concept of "port of trade," which we may reconceptualize as the political mechanism by which the "ignorance" is safeguarded.

---

[3] Kulshresthra (1964, 220). Das Gupta specifically criticizes the argument (of Leur) that Indian Ocean trade prior to 1750 was "luxury" trade, saying the argument is "untenable" since, although some of the trade was in "luxuries," this part of the trade was "marginal to the mass of the commerce in textiles which was overwhelmingly in the coarse varieties" (1974, 103). But let us be careful about systemic boundaries here. Das Gupta is talking of the intra-Indian Ocean trade which is not what is at issue, but rather the trade between the Indian Ocean zone and the European world-economy.

See a similar argument by Raychaudhuri about interregional trade by which he means, however, trade between different "regions" of the Indian subcontinent: "Despite the heavy expense of land transport . . . the trade in foodstuffs and a wide range of textile products, some of which surely cannot be described as luxuries, were the most important components of the inter-regional trade of the [pre-1750] period" (1982b, 329). When it

comes, however, to what Raychaudhuri calls "international trade" in textiles, he notes that European purchases were "a mere fraction of the total trade" (1982b, 331).

[4] Northrup (1972, 234).

[5] Amin (1972b, 508). For North (1985), such ignorance would be defined as an increased "transaction cost" which would be a departure from the efficiency of competitive markets.

Chamberlain (1979, 421) contrasts "bulk export trade" in West Africa, which he says is what so-called legitimate trade was about to "luxury-export trade," defining the latter as "high value per pound commodities." While the pound/value ratio works in a lot of cases, it does not seem to me essential. In some parts of the world and in some contexts, the export of elephants for use in court ceremonies was a quintessential "luxury" product—costly, non-essential, gathered rather than produced, and rare, but quite heavy nonetheless.

As Rosemary Arnold spelled out the functioning of Dahomey's "port of trade," Whydah, the key was in the "drastic institutional separation of the trading organization and the military organization" of the kingdom of Dahomey.[6] Institutional, and spatial as well—because the wars were located "inland" but the trade at the coast, which meant that the kingdom's military objectives, including slave raiding, could be pursued "without interference from the traders, whether European or Dahomean."[7] But what interference? Clearly, Arnold is thinking not of military but of economic interference, and economic interference implies knowledge of market conditions.

In order to maintain this knowledge monopoly, the concept "port of trade" is linked to the trade monopoly of the ruler, the merchants serving merely as the ruler's employees or agents.[8] In addition to physical separation and royal monopoly, Austen adds a third element: "a system of *gathering* international trade commodities which remained separate from the *production* of goods for internal African use."[9] This assumes, which may not be incorrect, that the infrastructural base of "gathering" as opposed to "producing" is much thinner and that, therefore, the costs of expansion and contraction of the quantity of gathering activities is significantly less than that involved in productive activities.

To be sure, the Polanyi–Arnold argument has not been unchallenged as empirical description of the kingdom of Dahomey. In particular, the royal monopoly on the slave trade seems not to have been total. However, Argyle, who launched this critique, does observe that the king's power was sufficient to require both African slave raiders and European merchants to do business first with the king before dealing with others, to sell to the king at "fixed prices," and to buy from him at prices higher than "they gave to the other dealers."[10] Manning's form of criticism is perhaps more apt. He suggests that the Polanyi–Arnold model, by confounding three different centuries is thereby "distorted and ahistorical."[11] Thus the description may

---

[6] Arnold (1957a, 174).

[7] Arnold (1957a, 175).

[8] Polanyi (1966). See also Elwert (1973, 74, and passim).

[9] Austen (1970, 268).

[10] Argyle (1966, 103). Law pursues Argyle's view of the slave trade being shared between the kind and other sellers and calls the concept of a royal commercial monopoly "essentially mythological" (1977, 556). However, Law proceeds to note that: "The kings of Dahomey do not appear to have allowed traders from the hinterland states to deal directly with the European merchants at Whydah" (p. 564). Therefore, in place of the concept of a royal monopoly standing between and physically separating the slave raiders and the European traders, Law is substituting a monopoly shared between the king and Dahomean private traders. In terms of blocking the flow of information, this may

not make much difference. See Peukert who also emphasizes the role of private Dahomean traders (1978, xiii–xiv), but who seeks to balance his criticism of Polanyi's argument about Dahomey as a "substantive economy" with an equally strong rejection of "Eurocentric world-historical analysis" (p. 224).

[11] Manning (1982, 42). Yet in the end Manning himself pleads historical ignorance: "One cannot yet say to what degree the state was content to regulate and protect the slave trade, and to what degree it actually conducted the collection and merchandizing of slaves. For example, if most slaves were captured in war, a mechanism must have existed to transfer slaves from the state, who presumably claimed them upon capture, to the merchants who exported them. On this and on the key details, contemporary European observers pleaded ignorance" (p. 43).

only have been true for the earliest period. Furthermore, the port of trade, established to prevent integration, may nonetheless have led to other modes of dependence equally integrating. For the port of trade required a stronger state form, a feature of West African involvement in the slave trade that has been frequently noted, and to which we shall return. And the very survival of the stronger state may come to depend on maintaining the trade links.[12]

The strength of the state machinery in the external arena turns out to be a critical variable but one whose impact on incorporation is more complex than we have been wont to recognize. In terms of initial contact with another world-system, strong state-machineries can guarantee that trade is conducted as an equal exchange between two arenas external to each other. The very process of such trade may strengthen some state-machineries on each side, as we know it did in this historic case. The increased strength of some states in the external arena thereupon provoked the power-holders in the European world-economy to invest in the relationship still more force in order to break down this "monopolistic" barrier to incorporation. In a sense, the states in the external arena went from strength to greater strength to relative weakness.

Nolte argues against my previous distinction between Poland, already incorporated and peripheral in the sixteenth and seventeenth centuries, and Russia, which I assert was still then in the external arena. His argument hinges on the extensiveness of Russian trade with western Europe. He does admit that Russia's "process of integration" began later than Poland's. This happened, however, he says, "more for political and social reasons than for economic ones."[13] But this is precisely my point.[14]

---

[12] Consider what happened in the later period of the kingdom of Dahomey. In the late eighteenth century, the Dahomean authorities curtailed the slave trade. This was partly to reduce dependence on what was seen as a depressed and unstable market (presumably a "port of trade"-inspired kind of reasoning) and partly to appease the kingdom of Oyo, which at this point was nominally Dahomey's suzerain and was also her competitor in furnishing slaves. However, this curtailment had sufficient negative consequences for various groups in the kingdom that in 1818, there was a sort of coup d'état, installing G(h)ezo as king. Indeed, today, Gezo is regarded as one of the great historic leaders of Dahomey. What did he do? "Gezo revived a stagnant slave trade and inaugurated an era of territorial expansion and economic growth. . . . His kingdom's economy was stimulated by the labour of captives forced to work on plantations in Dahomey, by the revenue from the sale of slaves through the market at Whydah, and by the trade monopoly Dahomey established over the newly conquered territories" (Yoder, 1974, 423–424).

This particular mode of involvement in the world-economy, for that is what it had become by this time, seems to have evolved directly out the strong state structure designed to prevent the involvement. It was ended only by the active British blockade of the Whydah slave trade as of 1843.

Law is skeptical that Dahomean authorities ever curtailed the slave trade. But he sees the strong state as something created as "a solution to the problems of order posed by the slave trade" (1986, 266).

[13] Nolte (1982, 47).

[14] In addition, I agree totally with the inference Nolte draws: "Furthermore, it is an open question whether the delay of Russia's incorporation into the world-system was an advantage or a disadvantage in the long run. Economically, this delay led to the development of Russia's own manufactures. It had advantages in politics, too, from the Tsar's point of view, since the fight against Sweden legitimated absolutism" (p. 48). Once again, this is precisely my point. Ultimately, the argument comes down to whether Russia was "incorporated" after 1750

Nor should we be deceived by mere cultural borrowings. The reign of Sultan Ahmed III in the Ottoman Empire (1718–1730) came to be known as the "Tulip Age" because of the presumed infatuation of the Court with tulips imported from Holland. Hogdson adjures us not to perceive this Western cultural borrowing by the Ottoman Empire as "display of exotic luxury" (which fits in with our insistence that imports are never luxuries), but rather as an attempt by the Ottoman rulers "to restore absolutism" against the regional decentralization which had been occurring. And when the opponents of this absolutism invoked the values of Islam to inveigh against "the infidel (and commercially-competitive) luxuries of the court," Hodgson says they were striking "knowingly" against those trade links with the Occident "which might have increased the court's power."[15]

Similarly, the recent scholarship on the Indian Ocean era tends to reduce not augment our perception of Portuguese oceanic dominance in the sixteenth century. (There has never been any question of belief in significant land dominance on the Indian subcontinent by any Western power before the second half of the eighteenth century.) The Portuguese, notes Digby, competed "with only qualified success" for a share in the so-called country (i.e., intraregional) trade, and to get even that they had to reach "accommodations with other holders of power" in the region.[16]

Finally, there is the familiar story of the emergence of new kingdoms and strengthening of old ones in the zones along or just inland from the West and Central African coast in the process of the slave trade. The result was,

(symbolically under Catherine II) or was already incorporated under Peter the Great or perhaps even earlier. We discuss the dating issue below.

See, for example, Blanc's evaluation of Peter the Great: "Peter was a convinced protectionist. . . . Governments following Peter's reign were occasionally more liberal than his. The tariffs of 1731, or even the benefits granted the English following the treaty of 1734, mark a definite progress which brings out, by contrast, the indisputable 'mercantilism' of Peter the Great" (1974, 29).

[15] Hodgson (1974, II, 139–140). Rustow (1970, I, 677) points out that: "The idyll of the Tulip Era at Istanbul was rudely shattered by the Ottoman-Russian War of 1182–8/1768–74" and not before. "In the peace treaty of Küchük Kaynarja, the Sultan was forced to cede the Crimea—the first Muslim land yielded by Ottomans to Christians." The Age of Tulips was "short-lived," says Heyd (1970, I, 363). True enough, but we should see it as part of a last-ditch effort to resist the pressure for incorporation.

Sometimes, as evidence of Ottoman weakness and implicitly of its incorporation earlier than 1750–1850, the ouster of Ottoman subjects by the Portuguese from their role in the Indian Ocean trade is cited. Hess (1970, 1917–1918) says this is a

very Portugalocentric viewpoint. "By the standards of [the sixteenth] century and according to the institutions that formed their society, the Ottomans successfully met the external naval challenges in their frontiers. . . . The contours of the Mediterranean and not the open areas of the Indian Ocean were the main boundaries for the sixteenth-century Ottoman navy."

[16] Digby (1982, 150). See also Marshall (1980, 19): "In the western Indian Ocean, Portuguese naval power was largely exerted in default of effective opposition; further east it was increasingly contested."

Japan's ability in 1637 to close out all Western trade except a small amount via the "port of trade" in Nagasaki in the mid-seventeenth century is notorious. "After the order of exclusion was enforced, the 'Bakufu' or the Shogun's government . . . developed into an organized bureaucracy, under a council of elders. Thus with the restoration of peace after a long period of internal strife and a strong central government, Japan was able to face the world without fear" (Panikkar, 1953, 87). Similarly, "the substitution of the effete Mings by a vigorous new dynasty strengthened China at a very important time" (p. 77).

for the most part, a situation "where the Africans called the tune,"[17] especially in terms of shaping the general working of the trading system in West Africa—that is to say, the Africans who governed these intermediary kingdoms and not those of the regions being pillaged. One should, of course, bear in mind that the strength of the kingdoms went hand in hand with the strength of a local trading class.[18]

There is a fourth feature to the trade of these external arenas with the European (and capitalist) world-economy that is striking—the persistent long-term imbalance of trade.[19] The outflow of bullion to the Indian subcontinent in the pre-1750 period has long been noted. Chaudhuri calls it a "paradox" that even the increase in India's demand for Europe's imports in the period 1660–1760 was insufficient to overcome "the fundamental structural imbalance."[20] There are two ways to think about this phenomenon. One can see it as the purchase by these zones of a necessary commodity, bullion, which, therefore, becomes a sign not of being in the external arena but precisely of the opposite, of being integrated into the European world-economy. This is the path Chaudhuri takes in talking of it as "essentially due to the rising liquidity created by the working of American gold and silver mines"[21] which created "a relative difference in international production costs and prices."[22] Perlin goes further in arguing that the import of bullion was "a trade in commodities, which in Sraffa's terms enters . . . into the production of all commodities."[23] This is the same line of argument Nolte uses about precious metals going to Russia: "They were essential for the circulation of money."[24]

But why then all the fuss about the outflow of precious metal? If, in fact, bullion is just another commodity, then there can never be a meaningful distinction between trade within one world-system as opposed to trade between two world-systems (that is, separate and probably differing economic structures). And why then was this outflow so dramatically

[17] Martin (1972, 14). This description is of the Loango Coast but the same statement could easily be made of other areas. Martin points out the two main conditions that made this true: "one was the intensive European competition, the other was that no European gained a permanent footing ashore" (p. 115). Of course, in West Africa, eventually, the second condition was violated by the establishment of forts, and efforts were made to reduce the competition. Still it would not be until events in Europe took another turn (as of, say, 1815) that competition could be significantly constrained.

[18] On the role of the so-called Luso-Africans, especially in the sixteenth and seventeenth centuries, see Boulègue (1972).

[19] On the outflow of silver to India, the Ottoman Empire, and Russia in the seventeenth century, see

my previous discussion (Wallerstein, 1980, 106–110).

[20] Chaudhuri (1978, 159). "The foundation of the East Indian trade as carried on by the maritime nations of northwestern Europe largely rested on an exchange of Western precious metals for Asian manufactured goods" (p. 97).

[21] Chaudhuri (1981, 239).

[22] Chaudhuri (1978, 456). Western Europeans had to pay for Indian goods with bullion, says Chaudhuri, because they "were not able to market Western products at prices that would generate a large demand for them." This is scarcely convincing. How does the United States sell computers to India today?

[23] Perlin (1983, 65).

[24] Nolte (1982, 44).

altered in the case of India? "The import of bullion . . . was stopped after 1757."[25]

An alternative way to think about the outflow is to see it as being, from the point of view of the European world-economy, the outflow of a dispensable surplus (hence a "luxury" export) during the European world-economy's long contraction of the seventeenth century (when the bulk of the outflow occurred), an outflow which then ceased to be dispensable upon the renewed expansion of the European world-economy after circa 1730–1750. Ergo, from the point of view of the European world-economy, the links with these external arenas had either to be transformed or to be cut. Since there were other motives as well that pushed for incorporation as the solution, the process was launched.

From the point of view of the zones external to the European world-economy—the Indian subcontinent, the Ottoman Empire, Russia—the fact that they in effect insisted on receiving bullion indicates that other European products held insufficient attraction for them, which can be translated as meaning that they were not involved in the integrated links that constituted the commodity chains of the capitalist world-economy. The difficulties of the Europeans in selling as opposed to buying has long been noted. For example, the Portuguese first and later the Dutch and English had to engage in the "country" (or "carrying") trade in the Indian Ocean area in order to finance their purchases.[26] This turns out to have been the case initially in the Ottoman Empire[27] and West Africa as well.[28]

Somewhere around 1750, all this began to evolve rapidly and the Indian subcontinent, the Ottoman Empire (or at least Rumelia, Anatolia, Syria, and Egypt), Russia (or at least the European part), and West Africa (or at least its more coastal areas) were incorporated into the ongoing set of linked productive processes (the so-called division of labor) of the capitalist world-economy. This process of incorporation was completed by 1850 (perhaps somewhat later in West Africa). In terms of the production processes, there were three main changes, which we shall discuss successively: a new pattern of "exports" and "imports"; the creation of larger economic "enterprises" (or economic decision-making entities) in the four zones; and a significant increase in the coercion of the labor force.

The new pattern of "exports" and "imports" was to be one that replicated

[25] Datta (1959, 318).

[26] As late as the 1730s, there "seems to be no doubt that it is only the English country-shipping which increases" (Furber, 1965, 45).

[27] "The demand of the Balkan peoples [in the eighteenth century] for the goods of Europe was smaller than the demand of the west for the goods of the Balkans" (Stoianovich, 1960, 300). The European carrying trade continued in the Ottoman Empire well into the nineteenth century. See Issawi (1966, 1980a).

[28] "To obtain the gold and ivory (as well as pepper) they needed for the home market, the Portuguese had to expend a good deal of energy as middlemen, carrying goods along the western coast" (Northrup, 1978, 22). He concludes: "The arrival of the Portuguese . . . necessitated no abrupt changes in the trading life of [the Niger Delta] region; they were instead accommodated within well-established patterns of commercial organization" (p. 29).

the core—peripheral dichotomy that constituted the axial division of labor in the capitalist world-economy. This meant essentially at that time the exchange of peripheral raw materials against core manufactures. In order that the four zones concentrate on raw materials exports, there had to be changes in their productive processes in two directions: in the creation or significant expansion of cash-crop agriculture (and analogous forms of primary sector production) destined for sale on the market of the capitalist world-economy; and in the reduction or elimination of local manufacturing activities. Of the two, the first was primary in time and probably in importance, but eventually the second had to occur as well. In turn, the creation of cash-crop (and analogous) exports involved more than establishing a series of land units on which a particular crop, say cotton, was grown. If these land units were used for cotton, it generally meant that they were no longer used for food crops. It followed that, as a larger and larger percentage of the land area specialized in growing specific crops for "export," other land units had to begin to specialize in growing food for sale to the workers on the first set of land units. And, as economic rationality moved toward the creation of hierarchies of work forces, perhaps under the authority of property owners, still other areas began to specialize in exporting people to work on both the cash-crop land units and the food-crop land units. The emergence of a three-tiered spatial special-ization within a zone—"export" cash crops, "local market" food crops, and "crops" of migrant workers—has been a telltale sign of incorporation of an erstwhile external arena into the ongoing divisioning of labor of the capitalist world-economy.

After 1750, the trade of both Great Britain and France—the two major economic centers of the capitalist world-economy of the time—expanded significantly into all four zones we are analyzing. For both countries, the Napoleonic Wars put a crimp in this trade, and after 1815 France's role became significantly less than that of Great Britain, but it still did not disappear completely (except perhaps in India). Everywhere, the exports of these four zones to western Europe expanded at a faster pace than the imports, but nonetheless the balance of payments was no longer closed by means of bullion exports from western Europe. A rapid overview will confirm how consistent this picture was.

The most familiar story, no doubt, is that of the Indian subcontinent. In the century before this, 1650–1750, the older centers of oceanic trade—Masulipatnam, Surat, and Hugli—declined in importance, beginning to cede place to new centers linked to European trade, like Calcutta, Bombay, and Madras.[29] The period 1750–1850 is neatly marked off by two political

---

[29] Watson (1980a, 42) who notes as well the degree to which English private traders were sup-planting a part of the indigenous merchant class. Whether those who survived were those who coop-erated with the English, as suggested by Das Gupta (1970), "still requires an answer," says Watson.

events which had a direct impact on the pattern of trade. The East India Company's unconstrained combination of political and economic control in India ran from 1757 to 1813. Chaudhuri argues that, nonetheless, in this period, the trade "continued to flow along the traditional channels" and with the same composition.[30] Datta agrees, though he makes the turning point 1793 (the Permanent Settlement of Cornwallis), which seems a more plausible date.[31]

Still, there was already one great difference between the period 1757–1793 and the earlier period—no bullion was exported.[32] There were two ways in which this balance of trade gap was covered without bullion export from Europe. One was using the newly acquired state revenues of the Bengal Presidency which seemed to be enough in this period to cover the administration of Bengal, the costs of British conquest and administration elsewhere on the subcontinent, and still leave some over to be used to purchase the items exported to Britain.[33]

The second was the system which dates from 1765 known as hypothecation. The East India Company sold bills in London on the Indian Presidencies, and bought bills in India upon England. The Indian goods exported through the Company to English mercantile houses were "hypothecated" as collateral security for the Company's loans in England with which the Company bought the British exports to India. The Company meanwhile advanced money to sellers of goods in India, which loans were repaid with goods serving as Indian exports to Britain. Bullion flows were in such cases not needed, and the Company received in addition the shipping profit plus any differential on higher interest rates on its Indian loans than on its London borrowings.[34]

While the plunder of the Bengal Presidency could provide a transitional link, we can talk of incorporation only with the "dramatic expansion" after 1757 of trade along the Ganges linked via Calcutta to the world-economy,[35] and a parallel expansion in south India after 1800.[36]

By the first half of the nineteenth century, four raw materials products dominated exports, accounting for some 60% of the total: indigo, raw silk, opium, and cotton.[37] While the first two items went westward to Europe, cotton and opium went at this time primarily to China. We shall discuss

---

[30] Chaudhuri (1983a, 806).

[31] The Permanent Settlement had the effect of removing barriers to land being "a commodity to be bought and sold on a market" (Cohn, 1961, 621).

[32] See Datta (1959, 317–318).

[33] See Bagchi (1976c, 248), Ganguli (1965), Arasaratnam (1979, 27). N. K. Sinha says: "The stock of silver in Bengal in 1757 was not only not replenished but much of it was drained away in various ways" (1956, 14).

[34] See Sinha (1970, 28–29), Chaudhuri (1966, 345–346).

[35] Kessinger (1983, 252). "By the end of the eighteenth century there were high prices and a growing demand for certain cash crops such as sugar cane, opium, and indigo" (Cohn, 1961, 621).

[36] Bhattacharya (1983, 359).

[37] Chaudhuri (1983a, 844), who gives further details in (1966, 348–349). See also Sovani (1954, 868–870).

below the reasons for this and the significance of this Indian–Chinese–British (so-called) triangular trade.

The immediate impetus to the first European indigo factories, established in either 1778 or 1779, seems to have been the American Revolution, which cut Britain off from its previous North American supply.[38] This shortage in world-economy supply was later reinforced by the elimination of Santo Domingo's supply because of its revolution[39] and the virtual abandonment by Spanish America of its cultivation at the turn of the century.[40] Thus, the production of indigo, which had already been significant commercially in Mughal India, expanded three to four times in absolute terms under British rule.[41]

Cotton also was an old Indian production, primarily of Gujarat. But before 1770 Gujarati cotton had never been exported other than to Sind, Madras, and Bengal,[42] and the production had been shrinking for a century.[43] As of 1775, a cotton export trade from India to China was launched by the British.[44] After 1793, with war in Europe, there came to be a market in Europe as well, although this was a "small affair" compared to United States exports.[45] The increased world demand seems to have been a factor in annexing Surat in 1800.[46] The expansion of silk production was also linked to Napoleon's Continental system, which deprived the British market of its Italian supply.[47] Only the expansion of opium production had no direct link with shifts in production elsewhere in the world-economy but was rather a function of the Company's needs in the China trade.[48] In the long run, none of these four commodities would last as a central Indian contribution to the world-economy's division of labor (although cotton remained of significance in India's export production for a very long time), but they provided the mode by which India could be incorporated in the period 1750–1850.

The story of the Ottoman Empire is similar. The volume of trade suddenly increased circa 1750. For example, France's trade, which dominated the Ottoman arena throughout the eighteenth century, quadrupled in the second half of the century.[49] Over this same period, there was a steady shift in exports from "manufactured or partially-treated goods [to]

[38] See Marshall (1976, 153).
[39] See Dutt (1956, 280).
[40] Sinha (1970, 1).
[41] See Habib (1963, 44).
[42] See Guha (1972, 2).
[43] See Habib (1963, 39–40).
[44] See Nightingale (1970, 128). This was originally only from western and north central India. Southern India began to export cotton to China as of 1803. See Ludden (1985, 137–138).
[45] Harlow (1964, II, 292). Siddiqi (1973, 154) links the decline in production after 1820 to United States competition. By the 1850s, "cotton was a

subordinate crop in India grown mainly for internal consumption" (Tripathi, 1967, 256). Cotton got a momentary boost during the American Civil War (1861–1865), but even then British policy towards cotton cultivation remained "half-hearted" (p. 262).
[46] See Nightingale (1970, 160).
[47] See Sinha (1970, 2).
[48] See Guha (1976, 338–339). For an overview of the Indian cash-crops and their regional location at this time, see Dutt (1956, 272–285).
[49] See Frangakis (1985, 152). See also Davis (1970, 204).

raw materials"—mohair yarn instead of camelots, raw silk instead of silk stuffs, cotton in place of cotton yarn.[50]

In the Balkans, it was the expansion of staples production that was most noticeable,[51] in particular cereals after 1780 whose increase has been called "spectacular."[52] Cotton was now also very important in Balkan production,[53] as well as in western Anatolia. In the late eighteeneth century, it was the key source of raw materials for the French cotton industry, to the point that the Chamber of Commerce of Marseilles in 1782 could say that "the Levant's destiny is to nourish . . . French industry."[54] A "link between production in Ankara and export abroad in Izmir was firmly established" at this time.[55]

The British as well as the Austrians replaced the French as the main direct partners in the nineteenth century. The role of Anatolian cotton declined, faced (as was the case in India) with American competition,[56] as well as in this case with Egyptian competition.[57] Nonetheless, cotton export would have a renewed temporary boost during the American Civil War.[58] Furthermore, the relative decline of Anatolian cotton exports to Britain was more than compensated by the steady increase in this same period of Ottoman Balkan wheat exports to Britain and Austria, the Balkans competing with southern Russia as an export zone.[59]

In the case of Russia, too, its trade with western Europe had a "remarkable upturn" in the period 1750–1850.[60] In this period, the composition of its exports changed rather dramatically as well, coming to be 95% primary products.[61] Russia's primary exports at this point in time were hemp and flax, "vital raw materials for British manufacturing

[50] Frangakis (1985, 241–242); cf. Karpat, 1972, 246). On the expansion of export-oriented cotton production in south Syria/Palestine, see Owen (1981, 7).

[51] See McGowan (1981a, 32) who notes that this starts as an inter-Ottoman trade.

[52] Stoianovich (1976, 189). Keith Hitchens doubts that is true for Wallachia and Moldavia before the 1830s (personal communication).

[53] Stoianovich (1983, 349). Paskaleva also speaks (1968, 275) of a "great expansion" in the cotton exports of the Balkans.

[54] They continue: "We take from it only raw materials; we exploit it with the manufactured goods of the kingdom." Cited in Masson (1911, 431–432). Masson says the Levant played the same role for France at this time that Mantoux attributes to the East Indies for England (see p. 434).

[55] Frangakis (1985, 248).

[56] See Issawi (1966, 67).

[57] See Richards (1977, 17). The Egyptians at this

time pushed forward with long-staple cotton which had many advantages.

[58] In 1862, Farley wrote: "As very great anxiety . . . is felt at the present moment with regard to the future supply of this important article [cotton], it will not be out of place if I direct the attention of those interested to the facilities which exist for the growth and improvement of that plant in the Ottoman empire" (p. 55).

[59] See Puryear (1935, 1; see also 132–139, 180–226). Puryear notes that toward the end of this period, the British increasingly turned away from Russian wheat for political reasons, and consequently toward Balkan wheat (see pp. 215–217, 227).

[60] Gille (1949, 154). On the rapid growth of Anglo–Russian trade after 1750, see Newman (1983, 96).

[61] Gille show (1949, 156) that from 1778–1780 to 1851–1853, the percentage of "primary" plus "food" exports went from 71 to 95%, while export of manufactures declined from 20 to 2.5%.

industries,"[62] and at first for French as well.[63] It was the quality of Russian hemp, "treated with deference" by its cultivators and with a "slow and meticulous" processing that made it so useful, features attributed by Crosby to Russia's "cheap labor and practice."[64]

In the late eighteenth century, Russian iron (which was processed in Russia) was still an important export because Russia (along with Sweden) had the two essential elements of a quality product based on a charcoal technology—large forests and rich mines[65]—and in addition, as we shall see, servile labor. When new British technology caused the collapse of the Russian iron export industry in the early nineteenth century, a new major export replaced iron—wheat.[66] By 1850, wheat exports reached 20% of an average harvest. Russia primarily exported the expensive variety of wheat, "which scarcely entered into national consumption."[67] To be sure, Russia was responding to the steady rise in world wheat prices, at least until the 1820s,[68] after which the main sellers, the Russian nobility, were so far committed to wheat production that they had little choice.[69]

It is worth noting that Russia's main trade partners at this time were not only England (and in the late eighteenth century, France) but two semiperipheral zones, which were able to build strength on Russia's incorporation. These were Scotland and the United States. In the case of Scotland, the "truly dramatic" economic progress of the late eighteenth century was "particularly" marked by the increase in Russian trade, Russia becoming the "leading continental exporter" to Scotland by the 1790s.[70] In the case of the United States, its economy "to an appreciable extent . . . prospered because it had access to the unending labor and rough skill of the Russian muzhik."[71]

As for West Africa, here as elsewhere, incorporation into the capitalist

[62] Kahan (1979, 181), who continues: "it is warranted to conclude that Russia's voluminous raw material exports to expanding British industries significantly helped to maintain the growth and demand for labour" (p. 182). This was also the somewhat self-interested view at the time of Mr. Foster, the Agent of the Russia Company, who in 1774, testified to Parliament that without Russian imports, "our navy, our commerce, our agriculture, are at end." Cited by Dukes (1971, 374). When Napoleon's Continental System interfered with Russian exports to Great Britain, the British found, however, that all these imports in general were replaceable or secondary, except hemp. See Anderson (1967, 73–74).

[63] See Besset (1982, 207–208).

[64] Crosby (1965, 20–21).

[65] Crosby (1965, 16).

[66] The Russian government's restrictions on wheat exports were in force until the second half of the eighteenth century. When Catherine II ac-

quired the Black Sea ports, "central exports began to mount" (Blum, 1961, 287). Later, after the repeal of the British Corn Laws in 1846, there was another major leap forward.

[67] Regemorter (1971, 98).

[68] See Confino (1963, 22, fn. 1).

[69] On the dependence of the Russian nobility on foreign trade to maintain their style of life, see Crosby (1965, 36).

[70] Macmillan (1979, 168–169). In an earlier article, Macmillan discusses Scottish use of "long-term credits to Russian merchants and producers" to stimulate this trade, and concludes that the importance of this trade to Scotland's growth is "undeniable" (1970, 431, 441).

[71] Crosby (1965, 24). Between 1783 and 1807, American trade with Russia grew into "a business of no small importance." Americans purchased particularly iron and hemp and "their purchases made some impression on prices in St. Petersburg" (Rasch, 1965, 64).

world-economy was not something sought by those being incorporated. As Walter Rodney says, "historically, the initiative came from Europe."[72] Often, it is said that the shift from the slave trade to so-called legitimate trade is what brought about this incorporation. This is not correct. The initial impetus was the expansion of the slave trade itself. With this expansion, slave raiding passed the barrier from providing a luxury export of gathered "surplus" to being a veritable productive enterprise that entered into the ongoing division of labor of the capitalist world-economy.[73] The shift may be considered to have occurred in the eighteenth century with the steady rise in slave prices[74] reflecting the combination of the increased demand for slaves, the increased competition among European slave traders, and the increased difficulty in expanding supply at the same pace,[75] all typical phenomena of a period of overall expansion in the world-economy. The peak of the slave trade seems to have occurred in the decade prior to 1793,[76] the Franco–British wars causing a decline in this as in all other oceanic trade, and subsequently, the combined effect of abolition and the Haitian revolution kept the figures from ever going as high again, although they remained significant until at least the early 1840s.[77]

One of the more passionate and less well-posed questions that has haunted the discussion on the slave trade in this period is the argument about the so-called "profitability" of the slave trade. One would have thought that any trade that flourished over a long period of time must have

[72] Rodney (1970, 199).

[73] For example, Gemery and Hogendorn (1978, 252–253) note the technological change in what they call merchandizing: reorientation and regularization of long-distance networks, establishment of transfer camps and of depots, new ships, using slaves to double as porters.

[74] Curtin speaks of the "steep eighteenth-century rise in real prices of slaves" (1975a, 165). The abolition of the slave trade in the early nineteenth century, by increasing the costs of the persistent trading, drove prices even higher. See Argyle on Dahomey after Ghezo comes to power in 1818: "A number of slave ships were still getting through to Whydah, and were paying very high prices for slaves, so that revenue from these was not much less, even though fewer slaves, so that revenue from these was not much less, even though fewer slaves were exported" (1966, 42). See also Le Veen: "[The British Navy's role] forced the prices of newly imported slaves to Brazil and Cuba to rise as much as twice what they would have been without interference" (1974, 54). Of course, eventually, as the demand for slaves was shut off, "slave prices fell substantially" (Manning, 1981, 501), but this was probably much later.

[75] See Martin (1972, 113). There were, to be sure, yearly fluctuations due largely to "the incidence of war" (Lamb, 1976, 98).

[76] The Loango Coast was at its peak between 1763 and 1793. See Martin (1972, 86). Measured in Europe, the slave trade of Nantes was "particularly important" in the period 1783–1792, "surpassing— and by far—the great burst of prosperity from 1748 to 1754 (Meyer, 1960, 122). Because of the expansion in the world sugar market, the French government in the second half of the eighteenth century offered bounties for slave ships and additional payments if these ships landed in the French West Indies. See Hopkins (1973, 91). Northrup says that "trade in slaves reached a dominant position in the commerce of the Bight of Biafra only in the mid-eighteenth century" (1978, 50). Curtin (1969, 266) locates the overall peak in the Atlantic slave trade in the 1790s.

[77] See Eltis (1977), Manning (1979), and Northrup (1976). Indeed, although perhaps not reaching the figures of the 1790s, Flint argues that, because of the demand from Brazil, Cuba, and United States, "the slave trade actually increased [in West Africa] from 1807 until about 1830, despite British and French abolition" (1974, 392).

been profitable to someone. Otherwise, it is hard to conceive that private traders, under no legal compulsion to indulge in the trade, would have continued to do so. This debate originated as an exercise in cultural decolonization. Faced with the standard and traditional picture of the British abolitionists as great humanitarians, to be found most notably in the classic work by Coupland (1964, but first edition 1933), Eric Williams (1944) sought to debunk this overly self-satisfied picture by arguing the economic motives that underlay the banning of the slave trade. His thesis was that, as a result in large part of the American War of Independence and the industrial revolution, Britain's sugar colonies in the West Indies became "increasingly negligible for British capitalism."[78] This led British capitalists to succeed in imposing a triple successive reform—against the slave trade in 1807, against slavery in 1833, and against sugar duties in 1846. "The three events are inseparable."[79] The reason for these actions was that, with the loss of the British West Indian "monopoly" and competitive edge, the main problem was the "overproduction" of sugar, and the solution was in these legislative enactments.[80]

In point of fact, this ostensibly central thesis of the book, which has been subjected to a technical attack that is less than devastating,[81] is not at all what aroused the passion. For the more fundamental thesis is that the slave trade plus slave-labor sugar plantations were a major source of capital accumulation for the so-called industrial revolution in Britain. This is, of course, an early version of the dependency thesis, more daringly stated than solidly sustained. Anstey's countercalculations lead him to conclude that the contribution of the slave trade to British capital formation was "derisory."[82] Thomas and Bean go one better by alleging that, theoretically, given the perfectly competitive market of the slave trade, the slave traders were "fishers of men." As in fishing, so in slave trading, profits were

---

[78] Williams (1944, 132). See, however, the critique by Drescher whose line of argument is that "abolitionism came not on the heels of trends adverse to slavery but in the face of propitious ones" (1976a, 171). Asiegbu, on the other hand, argues that it was "the great promise of a vast labor advantage over [Britain's] rivals which international abolition had held out to planters [that] largely explain West Indian actions in 1807, when the colonials joined the mother country in subscribing to the act of abolition" (1969, 38).

[79] Williams (1944, 136).

[80] See Williams (1944, 154–168). Hancock sees them as linked, too, but in error: "But the left hand of British idealism as too little aware of what its right hand was doing. The removal of the sugar duties, following on the abolition of slavery, had the effect of exposing West Indian sugar to a shattering assault by the slave-grown sugar of Cuba. The Cuban demand for African labor pushed up the

profits [those profits, again!] of the illicit slave-trade, and thereby caused a new high-level export for West Africa. It is not surprising that the 'legitimate trade' languished" (1942, 160).

[81] The most direct attack on Williams by Anstey concludes more prudently than one would expect: "And yet, even though the economic argument, in respect of 1833, may seem persuasive, whereas in respect of 1807 it is demonstrably vulnerable, it remains unproven" (1968, 316).

[82] Anstey (1974, 24). See Robinson who criticizes Anstey for restricting his analysis of profits to those who "quite literally handled slaves . . . [He seems not to] understand that profits could be made from speculation on commodities, the circulation of money, the multipliers of credit expansion, slaving-demonstration projects, and any number of forms of capital (for example insurance)" (1987, 134–135).

necessarily too low, the prices of slaves were too low, and consequently the price of plantation commodities was too low. The only beneficiaries of this apparently economically absurd enterprise were "the consumers of tobacco, sugar, indigo, rice, cotton, etc."[83]

This ingenious argument has only three defects: slave trading was far from perfectly competitive, as we shall see; the principal "consumers" of the raw materials were European manufacturers (thereby reinforcing, not weakening, the case of Williams); and slave trading was sufficiently attractive in the second half of the eighteenth century to attract some investors *away from* textile production.[84]

The real rejoinder, however, is the unimportance of the exact percentage. As we have been trying to show, the late eighteenth century was a period of global expansion of the capitalist world-economy. Each product from a given zone could only be a small percentage of the whole. The whole was eminently profitable, and did in fact lead to considerable capital accumulation which eventually was concentrated, for reasons we have already discussed, more in Britain than in France or elsewhere in western Europe. There is no need to argue that profits from the slave trade were exceptionally large[85] to conclude that they were a central part of the picture and constituted West Africa's contribution, as it were, to the global accumulation of this period.[86]

[83] Thomas & Bean (1974, 912). The Thomas-Bean article led to an attack and defense series of responses: Inikori (1981), Anderson & Richardson (1983), Inikori (1983), Anderson & Richardson (1985), and Inikori (1985).

[84] See Boulle: "It may be that the decline in textile production in Rouen between 1763 and 1783, with the exception of *indiennes* [which were exported to West Africa in exchange for slaves] was less the result of bankruptcies than of deliberate transfers of capital from a declining sector to another more promising one. In this case, the slave trade may be said to have enabled Rouen and its region to make one more step in the direction of the industrial revolution" (1975, 320–321). Viles points out that "the slave trade . . . was considered [in France] to be a more rewarding variant of the West India trade" (1972, 534).

[85] Boulle points out that the high profits per successful voyage must be tempered by considering the length of time taken to realize the profits, making them "not as markedly different from those obtained for non-maritime investments as appears at first" (1972, 83). See also Richardson who says that, after all the appropriate adjustments, the rate of return, "while not spectacular . . . was . . . solid and apparently reasonable (1975, 305).

In any case, as Darity says: "It was not profitability or profits from the slave trade that were essential in William's theory, but that the American colonies could not have been developed without slavery" (1985, 703).

[86] The terms of this argument have been presented clearly in the colloquy between Sheridan and Thomas. Sheridan argues: "Rather than being millstones around the neck of the mother country, the West Indian colonies thus became a vital part of the British economy in the eighteenth century. . . . [They] contributed in no small way to the growth of the metropolitan economy" (1965, 311).

Thomas responds: "The contribution of a colony . . . to the economic growth of the overall economy is precisely the difference (positive or negative) earned by the resources employed there relative to what they would have earned in their next best alternative. . . . [It can] be simply a huge misallocation of resources" (1968b, 31).

Sheridan's rejoinder is that "Thomas is, in effect, speculating on what would have happened in the event that something else had happened which could not have happened" (1968, 60).

To which Thomas insists that unless Sheridan "can show that Great Britain's total benefits exceeded her costs sufficiently to cover the return that the capital invested in the West Indies would have earned in its next best alternative, he has failed to come to grips with the question he originally asked" (1968b, 47).

That there were economic motives in the abolition of the slave trade by the British may be seen a bit more dispassionately by looking at the Danish and French debates. The Danes in fact anticipated the British (and deliberately). The then Danish Minister of Finances appointed a commission to advise him in 1791. Their main finding which led him to propose the edict of abolition was that their slave population in the West Indies could sustain itself without a new supply after a transitional period and after the introduction of certain social improvements.[87] In the French case, the slave trade had been abolished during the Revolution,[88] restored later, then outlawed in the Treaties of Vienna in 1815. The de facto resistance was nonetheless enormous.[89] The reason was simple. The French interpreted the imposition as "the Machiavellian invention of England which wished to ruin our colonies by depriving them of the servile manpower indispensible to their prosperity."[90] Thus did the analysis of the time anticipate Eric Williams by 125 years.

It is true nonetheless that the abolition of the slave trade eventually had its effect. Slaves declined as exports to be replaced by raw materials exports. The shift occurred largely in the 1800–1850 period, although the two export trades were not per se antithetical. As Rodney reminds us, "slaves were never the exclusive export of West Africa."[91] What did change in this period is that, for the first time, exports were no longer "foraged" items (such as ivory, gold, gum, dyewoods, and, of course, slaves) but had become agricultural products that were "commonplace, low value-to-bulk" items like palm oil and peanuts.[92] If the total value of these exports was still low (the period after 1817 in the world-economy was deflationary), the quantities were more impressive; indeed the increase was "staggering," going up by "a factor of six or seven."[93]

Why is it meaningful to use as a unit of assessment "Great Britain's total benefits"? The entrepreneurs operated in their own interests and were presumably rational. The British government could have in practice many objectives other than optimizing Great Britain's total benefits. Finally, in all this counterfactual history, we must ask why the "next best alternative" was not in fact taken.

[87] See Green-Pedersen (1979, 418).

[88] On the reluctance of the Constituent Assembly to vote abolition, see Quinney (1972) on the pro-planter role of the *Comité des Colonies* and Resnick (1972, 561) who shows that, even for the *Société des Amis des Noirs*, "slavery remained . . . a very derivative concern." See also Dubois and Terrier (1902, 29). In 1789, even the derivative concern of the *Société des Amis des Noirs* in abolition led to their being accused of being "instruments of a foreign power" (that is, England) which was seeking to "poison" the sustenance of the French empire. Cited by Vignols (1928a, 6).

[89] "The crumbling of the French colonial system did not end the French slave trade as much as modify it. Technically, the trade was outlawed in 1814–1815, but in reality it continued until the second half of the nineteenth century" (Stein, 1979, 198). See also Daget (1975, 131–132).

[90] Debbasch (1961, 315–316). "Abolition had been imposed, [by the victor] on the vanquished" (Daget, 1971, 57). In 1838, Chateaubriand, writing about the Congress of Verona in 1822, commented on "all these Tories, who had been opposed for 30 years to Wilberforce's proposal, [but had suddenly] become passionate advocates of liberty for Negroes. . . . The secret of these contradictions lies in the private interests and commercial genius of England." Cited by Escoffier (1907, 53–54).

[91] Rodney (1970, 152).

[92] Munro (1976, 48). See also Coquery-Vidrovitch & Moniot (1974, 297–298).

[93] Newbury (1971, 92). See his further comments: "The most remarkable feature of early nineteenth-century West African trade is the increase in bulk imports and exports from fairly low base lines. The 'official' evaluations in British and French trade statistics of trade with Africa before

Basically, the pattern of exports from West Africa to the European world-economy during the period of incorporation went through three phases: (1) an increase in and continued concentration on slave exports, in absolute and probably in relative terms, from circa 1750 (especially) to 1793; (2) a maintenance of significant slave export along with a steady increase in so-called legitimate trade, from the 1790s to the 1840s; and (3) the virtual elimination of the Atlantic slave trade and a steady expansion of primary products export (particularly palm oil and peanuts), from the 1840s to the beginning of the full-scale colonial era in the 1880s.

It is important to bear in mind that, although it is true that slave raiding and cash-crop production are indeed incompatible in the long run, since combining the two tends to create an impossible conflict over the use of labor power, this was not true in the short run. Both exports could flourish simultaneously and did for some 30 to 40 years. Indeed, as Northrup argues, one of the very factors explaining the rapidity of the growth of palm-oil production—given, of course, the indispensable (and new) European demand for fats and oil for industrial lubrication, personal hygiene, and candle power—was the previous massive growth of the slave trade which had stimulated African demand for foreign goods, expanded the network of trading communities, and (which is frequently overlooked), expanded "the economic infrastructure of markets, roads, and currencies."[94] Furthermore, slaves could be used directly in the production of "legitimate" goods—first of all as porters in both directions,[95] and second, as workers on plantations (most notably in Dahomey, between the 1830s and 1860s).[96] Both uses served to reduce the costs of production.[97]

Still, palm oil eventually began to displace slave raiding as the major productive enterprise. Its expansion began as early as the 1770s in the Niger Delta region.[98] By the 1830s, it was a steadily growing traffic along the coast, "in spite of fluctuations in prices."[99] Of course, the overall

the 1850's must be ignored as underevaluations; the quantities of manufactured exports provide a more reliable guide" (1972, 82).

[94] Northrup (1976, 361). See also Manning: "Slave commerce constricted the commodity exchange system because of war and the export of slaves; on the other hand it expanded the commodity exchange system through the circulation of imported manufactures and imported money" (1982, 12). Latham, however, bases his argument for compatibility of slave export and palm-oil production on the grounds that the latter required little labor and, therefore, only "a small shift in leisure preference" (1978, 218).

[95] See Adamu (1979, 180) and Martin (1972, 118).

[96] See Manning (1982, 13). See Reynolds (1973, 311) on the use of slave labor on Danish plantations in the Gold Coast at the beginning of the nineteenth century.

[97] Manning argues that "the economies achieved [in the plantations] probably had more to do with working the slaves long hours than with any increased technical efficiency" (1982, 54). No matter! Economies are economies.

[98] See Northrup (1978, 182). This was, of course, precisely what some people had feared. In 1752 the Board of Trade refused permission to the Company of Merchants Trading to Africa to start sugar cultivation in Africa, saying: "There was no saying where this might stop. The Africans who now support themselves by war would become planters." Cited by Rawley (1981, 424). The Board of Trade felt that it would be more difficult to control sugar plantations in West Africa than in the West Indies since, in West Africa, Englishmen "were only tenants in the soil which we held at the good will of the natives."

[99] Metcalfe (1962, 116), who is referring specifically to Cape Coast and surrounding areas.

improved prices on the European market after the 1840s gave it further economic incentive.[100]

The French were culturally resistant at first to palm-oil products, unlike the British, Germans, and Americans, but this ended in 1852 with the discovery of a chemical method to whiten yellow soap.[101] Indeed, the origin of the peanut trade lay precisely in this French consumer's resistance to yellow soap. The Marseilles soapmakers had discovered in the first half of the nineteenth century that peanut oil plus olive oil made a blue marble soap.[102] The peanut trade began in the 1830s and confirmed the decision of the French to stay in Senegal despite the end of the slave trade, this "economic basis for further involvement" coinciding with various internal French pressures for a "more active" colonial policy.[103]

The link between cash-crop production and the expansion of market-oriented food production has been largely neglected, especially in terms of the process we have been calling incorporation. Still, there seems to be some evidence of it that has been observed in the Indian and West African cases. Habib finds that the critical difference in terms of agricultural production between Mughal India and British India was less in the "production for distant markets" than in the "considerable geographic concentration of particular crops in certain tracts," allowing the soil to be used for purposes for which it was "best suited."[104] The self-sufficiency of the region was ceding place to the self-sufficiency of the world-economy. Gough analyzes how, in Madras, in the first half of the nineteenth century, alongside the cash-crop areas (for cotton, indigo, pepper, tobacco), other zones began to specialize in grain for the regional market,[105] while still others began to send out indentured laborers, at first only to southern India, but eventually to Ceylon, Burma, Malaya, Mauritius, and finally the West Indies.[106] And Bayly makes the important point that a new expansion of "fragile" town economies emerged in indigo and cotton cash-crop areas as the result of housing "chains of dependent intermediaries on a small group of cash-crops."[107]

As for West Africa, Rodney reminds that the "victualling" of slave ships has received "no serious treatment."[108] But it is clear that it required a

[100] See Newbury (1961, 43). England had already lowered the previous high duty in 1817.

[101] See Schnapper (1961, 118–128). On the earlier unsuccessful efforts of the French Ministry of Colonies in the late 1820s to stimulate cash-crop production, see Hardy (1921, 215–216, 231–249). In the interim, the French continued to make money out of the gum trade, using slaves to collect the gum. See Charles (1977, 29) and Hardy (1921, 353–354).

[102] Martin A. Klein (1968, 36–37).

[103] Klein (1972, 424). Klein's dates for peanut production onset are 1833 for (British) Gambia and 1841 for (French) Senegal. Brooks (1975, 32) says

that peanuts were first commercialized in Gambia in 1829 or 1830.

[104] Habib (1963, 56, 75).

[105] Gough (1978, 32).

[106] Gough (1978, 35).

[107] Bayly (1975, 499).

[108] Rodney (1968, 282). See also Johnson (1976, 26). Northrup says: "By the early nineteenth century the cultivation of [food] crops was said to have ceased entirely at Bonny" (1978, 89). This was because of their full involvement in the slave trade. Obviously, they then had to buy food from somewhere. He himself points to slave-based food production for palm-oil areas (p. 220).

tremendous amount of food and that many slaves were deployed into the local production of food to feed the other slaves en route to the Americas. Latham, for example, notes that there was a large settlement of slaves east of Calabar between 1805 and 1846 who were not, however, engaged in palm-oil production. He speculates that this was probably "to grow food for Calabar."[109] Finally, Newbury notes the close linkage of "bulking centres" with the growth of local food markets because of the considerable migration into these loci of the trade networks.[110]

The other, second half of the reconstruction of the pattern of export–import that was imposed by incorporation was the decline of the manufacturing sector in the zones being incorporated. This theme has been so long associated with the experience of the Indian subcontinent that it may be somewhat enlightening to realize that it was by no means peculiar to India. Let us start, nonetheless, with the Indian case. It is clear that, before 1800, the Indian subcontinent was, by world standards, a major locus of textile production. Indeed, Chaudhuri argues it was "probably the world's greatest producer of cotton textiles."[111] The decline was precipitous. Although the early years of the Napoleonic wars actually saw a brief export boom, the Berlin decrees plus English competition "meant the end of the export of Surat piece-goods to London."[112] As for Bengal's cotton piece goods, they "practically disappeared" from the East India Company's export list circa 1820 and soon thereafter from that of the private traders as well.[113] For a while, there remained (or began) a textile export trade to China, but this too then disappeared, so that the statistics show a continued decline, export value of cotton piece goods diminishing by a further 50% between 1828 and 1840 from an already much-reduced base.[114] Furthermore, by observing the sharp decline in Bihar production in the nineteenth century, an

[109] Latham (1973, 92). See also Dike (1956, 156). A further use of food-crop specialization was political. Latham argues that the Efik traders in palm oil "invested the profits of the new [palm oil] trade in slaves, which they settled in the newly discovered agricultural areas, to serve as self-maintaining retainers essential to their masters' security in interward politics" (p. 146).

[110] Newbury (1971, 96).

[111] Chaudhuri (1974, 127). Morris argues this was less than it seems: "There is a widespread notion that India was a great preindustrial manufacturing nation. It is much more likely that in the eighteenth century India had achieved a technology that was at the productive levels of late medieval Europe. . . . While India produced fine textiles and a few examples of remarkable craftmanship, we must not mistake manual dexterity for productivity nor assume that dexterity implied the presence of sophisticated tools and manufacturing techniques. In fact, the reverse was true" (1968, 5–6).

Raychaudhuri responds to Morris: "Such a view

does scant justice to the fact that India was *the* major supplier of textiles—not just fine clothes, but everyday wear for the masses—to the whole of South East Asia, Iran, the Arab countries and East Africa. . . . [Furthermore,] except for an insignificant amount of luxury goods, . . . India imported *no* manufactured metal products before the nineteenth century" (1968, 85). Nonetheless, Raychaudhuri does admit: "In striking contrast to India's pre-eminence as an exporter of manufactured goods, her technology was remarkably backward in comparison with other advanced civilizations of the period, especially Europe and China" (1982a, 291). He adds: "A level of manual skill which bordered on the fantastic served as a substitute for sophistication of techniques and instruments" (p. 294).

[112] Nightingale (1970, 233).

[113] Sinha (1970, 4). Export value went from 61 lakh rupees in 1792–1793 to 14 lakh in 1819 to 3 lakh in 1823 (p. 3).

[114] Chaudhuri (1968, 34). At the same time, cotton yarn imports rose by 80% and cotton goods by 55%.

area which never exported to Europe, we see the impact on the "internal" market as well.[115]

One explanation is simply Britain's new technological, and hence, competitive edge. Smelser gives the self-actor (or self-acting mule) the credit for Britain's "final conquest" of the Indian market.[116] One wonders then why, if this is so, the British had nonetheless to resort to political measures to guarantee their market supremacy. In 1830, Charles Marjoribanks testified before the House of Commons:

> We have excluded the manufactures of India from England by high prohibitive duties and given every encouragement to the introduction of our own manufactures into India. By our selfish (I use the word invidiously) policy we have beat down the native manufactures of Dacca and other places and inundated their country with our goods.[117]

He also explained why trade with China was going less well: "We do not possess the same power over the Chinese as we do over the Indian empire." As late as 1848, as Parliamentary Committee argued the non-"necessity" of India's import of clothing, justifying thereby the removal of duties on the import of sugar into Britain, in these terms: "If you take India's market for her sugars, you in the same ratio, or in a greater ratio, destroy England's market for her manufactured goods."[118] In any case, it is rather difficult to deny the thesis of the deliberate deindustrialization of India, when the chairman of Britain's East India and China Association boasted of it at the time. In 1840, George G. de H. Lampert testified:

> This Company has, in various ways, encouraged and assisted by our great manufacturing ingenuity and skill, succeeded in converting India from a manufacturing country into a country exporting raw produce.[119]

The Ottoman Empire did not become a British colony in this period, as did the Indian subcontinent. Nonetheless, the story is remarkably parallel and the timing even earlier. In the first half of the eighteenth century, the Ottoman Empire was still exporting silk cloth and cotton yarn to Europe. In 1761, the French placed a high protective duty on imports of cotton yarn from the Ottoman Empire and this duty plus English machine

---

[115] See Bagchi (1976a, 139–141).

[116] Smelser (1959, 127, fn. 5). See, however, Mann: "The self-actor was acclaimed as an almost perfect machine, but it did not spread quickly. By 1839 the profits had not exceeded £7000" (1958, 290).

[117] Cited in Sinha (1970, 11). Sinha's own views are that the duty of cotton piecegoods being exported to "foreign Europe" as well as the United States plus inland customs "helped perhaps to kill the Indian cotton industry more speedily and effec-

tively than the competition of cheap British piece-goods alone would have done" (p. 7).

Note also, in regard to silk manufacture, when the ban on Indian exports to France was briefly lifted in the 1830s, British export to France almost disappeared while Indian export rose spectacularly. See the table on p. 12.

[118] British Parliamentary Papers (BPP), Reports from Committees (1848b, 10).

[119] BPP, Reports from Committees (1840b, 24).

spinning closed off the west European market.[120] Genç locates the peak of the industrial sector in the 1780s, and says that after this point, the hitherto parallel paths of west European and Ottoman textile production diverged and Ottoman industry started to decline, not only in terms of export but even in terms of "the levels of production it had achieved in its own past."[121] Despite a whole series of political and economic countermeasures attempted by the Sublime Porte beginning with the measures of Selim III in 1793–1794,[122] by 1856 one English author talks of the fact that manufacturing industry has "greatly declined" in Turkey and that Turkey now exported raw materials which later returned there in a manufactured form.[123] By 1862, another British author's comment has an even more decisive tone: "Turkey is no longer a manufacturing country."[124]

The story is the same if we shift our optic from the Anatolian heartland to outlying Egypt and Syria. Despite Mohammed Ali's attempt at "forced industrialization" in Egypt,[125] he failed. Not least of the reasons was the fact that the provisions of the Anglo–Turkish Commercial Convention were forced on him in 1841 and this "brought rust and ruin to his factories on the Nile."[126] As for Syria, a "catastrophic decline" of manufactures started in the 1820s[127] and by the 1840s, the process was completed in both Aleppo and Damascus.[128]

Was Russia better equipped to stem the tide? A little bit, but not much. The first half of the eighteenth century had been a high point of Russian industry. The Urals metal industry had a period of rapid expansion from 1716 onwards.[129] Under Tsaritsa Elisabeth, and especially from 1745 to 1762, there was a "*second* burst of industrialization," reaching a "golden age" under Catherine II,[130] when exports to England grew "briskly."[131] It is no wonder that the Russian historian, Tarle, argued in his 1910 textbook that, in the eighteenth century, "Russian backwardness does not appear very great when placed in a general European context."[132]

Yet, after 1805, Russia began to fall behind Britain in the production of cast iron, and once coke smelting became the dominant technology,

[120] Issawi (1966, 41).

[121] Genç (1976, 260–261). Issawi (1966, 49) dates the turning point as 1815–1820. Köymen (1971, 52) says the crisis began in 1825.

[122] These are spelled out in Clark (1974) who has no good explanation of the final collapse by the 1850s. He does note in passing that, with the Anglo–Turkish Commercial Convention of Balta Limann in 1838, the Ottoman government was required to lift all export–import controls.

[123] M. A. Ubicini, in a book, *Letters on Turkey* (London: 1856, II), reprinted in Issawi (1966, 43). Ubicini is not talking only of cotton goods but also of steel and arms, as well as silk, gold thread, tanning leather, pottery, saddlery, and all kinds of textiles.

[124] Farley (1862, 60).

[125] Issawi (1961, 6).

[126] Clark (1974, 72).

[127] Smilianskaya in Issawi (1966, 238). See also Chevallier (1968, 209).

[128] Polk (1963, 215).

[129] See Koutaissoff (1951, 213); see also Goldman (1956, 20).

[130] Coquin (1978, 43, 48).

[131] Portal (1950, 307). The American War of Independence plus the revolutionary Napoleonic wars were of some assistance in this. Portal notes that: "Russian metallurgical production, in its great expansion phase after 1750, was . . . in large part oriented to export" (p. 373).

[132] Cited in Dukes (1971, 375).

Russian production was at a disadvantage.[133] In addition, under Nicholas I (1825–1855), the leading officials became "lukewarm" or even "hostile" to industrial growth, fearing social disturbances. Still, despite the drastic decline of the exports of the principal industry, pig iron, the Russians were able to maintain an internal market for their textiles by a combination, after the 1830s, of high tariff protection and some import of technology. They were also able to create a beet sugar refining industry.[134] This limited ability to resist total deindustrialization, to which the continued relative strength of the Russian army was not an insignificant contributing factor, explains in part their ability to play a different role in the world-economy at the beginning of the twentieth century from either India or Turkey.

Lastly, we do not often think of West Africa as having had industry. And indeed textiles were being imported into West Africa already in the eighteenth century.[135] Still, one shouldn't exaggerate. Prior to 1750, Rodney notes, local cottons on the Guinea coast "withstood competition" of English manufactures.[136] And Northrup, speaking of the Niger Delta in the eighteenth century, observed that imports such as iron bands still required significant processing "and thus had a multiplier effect on the internal economy."[137] It is only after the Napoleonic wars, and the withdrawal of British ships from slaving after 1807, that the "nature and quality of imports change."[138] This is true not only of textiles but of iron products. West African blacksmithing and iron smelting were "ruined" by the cheap European imports of the early nineteenth century.[139]

Large-scale, export-oriented primary production, as we have already explained, can operate effectively if it is market-responsive, and this can really be the case only when the effective decision-making bodies are large enough such that a change in their production and merchandizing decisions can really affect their own fortunes. The self-interest of the insignificant actor is not necessarily in "adjusting" to the market, or in any case is far less so than that of the large-scale actor.

There are two primary loci where one can create large nodes of decision-making bodies. One can group primary production in large units—what we might call the "plantation" solution. Or one can create large nodes at a stage after the initial production zones in the commodity chain. For example, some large "merchants" (what the French called

[133] See Baykov (1974, 9–13).
[134] See Falkus (1972, 36–39). The first boom of sugar refining begins in the 1820s.
[135] In fact, Indian textiles were going there via European traders as early as the seventeenth century. See Furber (1965, 12). Boulle (1975, 325) even argues that the West African market was "of great significance" (*de taille*) in terms of English and French exports in the mid-eighteenth century. In the 1760s, for example, of all English cloth exported, 43% went to Africa and only 39% to the

Americas. Metcalf observes that textiles were a more attractive import than firearms and that these textiles "were for mass consumption rather than finery for elites" (1987, 385).
[136] Rodney (1970, 182).
[137] Northrup (1978, 149).
[138] Northrup (1978, 175). See also Johnson (1978, 263). Curtin (1975a, 326) dates it a bit later for Senegambia, in the 1830s.
[139] Flint (1974, 387).

négociants as opposed to *traitants* or *commerçants*) can station themselves at bottlenecks of flows. It is not enough then, however, to create a quasimonopoly or oligopoly of merchandizing. It is also crucial for this (let us call him) large-scale merchant (or merchant–banker) to establish a dependency upon him on the part of a mass of small producers. The simplest and probably most efficient way to do this is debt bondage. In this way, when the large-scale merchant wishes to "adjust" to the world market, he can rapidly alter patterns of production in ways he finds profitable.[140] The creation of these large-scale economic units—either plantations or large-scale merchant bottlenecks—is a primary feature of incorporation.

In this period, Indian export centered around four main crops—indigo, cotton, silk, and opium. Of the four, indigo was the most plantation-oriented. In the last quarter of the eighteenth century, responding to the faltering Western Hemisphere supply, a number of English private traders created plantations.[141] In addition, they granted credit to small-scale producers. The credit was rapidly called in "at the earliest sign of a recession" and this led to land forfeitures, further concentrating the land.[142] The putting-out system,[143] which was crucial in this process, came into use in indigo production only in this period.[144] In either case—direct production or a system of advances to petty producers—the indigo planters kept the basic production decisions in their hands, using either "petty oppression" or "debt servitude" to realize their objectives.[145]

Similarly, in the production of raw cotton, as it became more export-oriented, there came to be an "increasing grip of usury and trading capital over production," as the "real burdens of rent and interest became . . . heavier."[146] In the case of opium, the fact that it was a state merchandizing monopoly (via the East India Company) served the same purposes of controlling quantity and quality of production, setting price levels, and in effect monitoring the international competition for the Chinese market.[147]

---

[140] "Advance contracting" also minimizes the ability of the direct producer to control prices and enables the large merchant to stabilize his supply market (Chaudhuri, 1978, 143).

[141] See Furber (1951, 290–291).

[142] Siddiqi (1973, 151).

[143] Chaudhuri says this "European" concept "obscures as much as it reveals" (1974, 259). Perhaps so. Then let us find another term. Arasaratnam cites this Chaudhuri view with approval but goes on nonetheless to admit the essential point of the system in regard to a weaving community: "Though there was this freedom to dispose of the final produce, the restrictive nature of access to the market and the near monopoly conditions in the purchase of goods existing in many remote weaving villages made this freedom rather an empty one" (1980, 259).

[144] See Raychaudhuri (1965, 756; see also 1962, 180–181).

[145] Fisher (1978, 115). On page 118, Fisher weighs the disadvantages of each system: direct cultivation was more expensive; a system of advances was more likely to arouse peasant discontent.

[146] Guha (1972, 18, 28).

[147] See Richards (1981, 61). The state monopoly used the same system as private large-scale merchants for other products: "The entire process, from preparing the ground for [opium] seed, to the final auction at Calcutta, was based upon an elaborate system of advance payments" (Owen, 1934, 26).

In 1848, F.W. Prideaux testified before a House of Commons Select Committee that "nothing is cultivated in India without advances, sugar, indigo, and everything which is cultivated to be exported from that country."[148] Yet, despite the absence for the most part of European "planters" as in the West Indies, it is nonetheless true, as Clapham argues, that most of these exports goods had "something of what he called a plantation or colonial character of the old sort."[149] Rothermund catches the shift from external arena to incorporation precisely in the changing functions, as he describes them, of the (trading) factory: it went from buying and selling aboard ships to placing special orders to financing these orders by advances to using the advances to stimulate production to organizing production via a putting-out system and operating workshops.[150]

The rise of plantation-type *çiftliks* in the Ottoman Empire has been a matter of discussion for some time. *Çiftlik* is a legal term denoting a form of land tenure. The origin of the word is the reference to a *çift* (or pair) or oxen, ergo the amount of land that a pair of oxen could plow in one day.[151] Some confusion has therefore arisen, since it was primarily those *çiftliks* that were far larger than a *çift*, and which came closer to the usual meaning of plantation, that seem to have been directly linked to export-oriented cash-crop production.

Stoianovich directly links the spread of the *çiftlik* (in particular of the larger *hassa-çiftlik*) to the "diffusion of cultivation of new colonial products: cotton and maize" from the 1720s in the Balkans.[152] Gandev similarly sees their growth in northwestern Bulgaria as the emergence of large-scale cash-crop land units, which were the subject of capital investment and capital accumulation.[153] Peter Sugar too emphasizes their market orientation, the cultivation of new crops, and the debt-bondedness of their villagers.[154] McGowan notes that they were located near the sea and that their development in the later Ottoman Empire was "almost always linked . . . with foreign trade in commodities."[155] Finally, İnalçık too connects the larger *çiftliks* with market orientation and "plantation-like structures"

[148] BPP, Reports from Committees (1848a, 21).
[149] Clapham (1940, 232).
[150] See Rothermund (1981, 76).
[151] See Gandev (1960, 209); Stoianovich (1953, 401), and Busch-Zantner (1938, 81).
[152] Stoianovich (1953, 403). "The new textile factories of Austria, Saxony, Prussia, and Switzerland required the wool and cotton of Macedonia and Thessaly, and rising French, German, and Italian demands caused the cotton production of Macedonia to treble between 1720 and 1800" (Stoianovich, 1960, 263). See also Stoianovich (1976, 184).
[153] See Gandev (1960, 210–211).

[154] See Sugar (1977, 211–221).
[155] McGowan (1981a, 79). Still McGowan cautions that "the sector of Ottoman agriculture aimed at exporting must . . . have grown only slowly during the period [of the seventeenth and eighteenth centuries]," (p. 170) and that "the average Balkan *chiftlik* was a rental operation, far closer in its character and its scale to the *Grundherrschaft* past from which it evolved than to the *Gutsherrschaft* character which has been frequently imagined for it" (p. 79). Nonetheless, he distinguishes between the larger *çiftliks* oriented to foreign trade and the average-size ones less likely to be (see 1981b, 62).

which spread, he says, particularly in conjunction with land reclamation and improvement in marginal waste lands (mîrî).[156]

As for Egypt, it is clear that the rise of cotton production was directly linked to the creation of large estates in the course of the nineteenth century.[157] Already in 1840, John Bowring explained why in his testimony to the House of Commons. He talked of the reluctance of the fellah to produce cotton, for fear of being cheated, for fear of taxation, because it involved only one crop a year. The solution?

> Of late many tracts of land have been transferred to capitalists who have consented to pay the arrears due, and who in consequence employ the fellahs as day laborers, taking from them the responsibility of discharging the land-tax, and of declining the stimpulated quantity of produce at the prices fixed by the pacha.[158]

In Russia, of course, there had already been considerable land concentration in the hands of the aristocracy. What happened during incorporation was the strengthening of this process and the intensification of its link to cash-crop production. As Blum notes, the seigniors were "by far the chief suppliers of the market," producing up to 90% of the market's grain, for example.[159] It is this same period during which we have the major agronomic innovation of three-course crop rotation.[160]

In the late eighteenth century thus, the "rural economy took on an ever-more mercantile character."[161] The shift in the pattern of serfdom— away from obrok (or payment in kind and money) to barshchina (or payment in labor, i.e., corvée)[162]—a shift we shall discuss below in terms of labor coercion, should also be viewed as a mode of land concentration. It is not that the ownership was being concentrated, since it already was, but that the decision-making procedures in production were, and this was crucial to a commercialized agriculture. And in those estates where obrok remained, the seigniors often encouraged and protected those peasants who became merchant entrepreneurs (despite the law's restrictions) because this not only permitted such peasants to pay larger obrok but enabled the seigniors to use them as "guarantors for the less prosperous members of the village commune."[163]

---

[156] İnalcık (1983, 116). In western Anatolia, it was precisely the "high productivity and high value of land . . . [which] accounted for the smaller size of çiftliks" (p. 117). The acquisition of rights to land by reclamation is already a feature of the classical period of the Ottoman Empire, and had no legal link with the size of the unit being reclaimed. It was now, however, used to create large çiftliks.

[157] See Baer (1983, 266–267).

[158] Reproduced in Issawi (1966, 387).

[159] Blum (1961, 391–392).

[160] See Confino (1969, 39). This was especially the case in the North and Center nečernozem zone and the northern part of the black soil lands.

[161] Kizevetter (1932, 637).

[162] On the difference, see Confino (1961b, 1066, fn. 2). The shift to barshchina began already in the mid-seventeenth century but expanded in the mid-eighteenth century, especially in the nečernozem zone. This was in part counterbalanced by the decline of percentage of peasants on private estates, since those on state or court estates normally paid obrok.

[163] Blum (1961, 289). Many of these entrepreneurs were recruited among the persecuted Old Believers. Their theology may not at all have been "Protestant" but the factor of persecution led to a need for reading texts, a need for money to defend

The picture in West Africa once again bears a greater resemblance than chance would suggest. We start with slave marketing which, far from encouraging infinite competition, led to merchandizing bottlenecks. Everywhere we find the existence of "restrictive trade associations and practices, sometimes official, sometimes private, and sometimes involving collaboration between the two."[164] Furthermore, the shift toward cash crops such as palm oil was accompanied by attempts to create plantation structures. Indeed, the abolitionists themselves directly supported this as a means, they thought, of giving legitimate trade a solid economic basis.[165] Plantations were primarily successful in Dahomey and Yorubaland. The combination of strong monarchs, slave labor, and presumably capital, meant that the monarchs were able to export palm oil from a considerable distance inland, which was otherwise too expensive.[166] But where transport was less of a problem, the technology of palm oil (and peanut) production made it available to small-scale farmers.[167]

However, as Law notes, speaking of the erosion of the dominant position of the king and military chiefs in the production process, as the shift was finally made from the slave trade to palm oil, "the beneficiaries of this change, however, included substantial merchants as well as small farmers."[168] In other words, the locus of concentration had simply shifted from one product collection point to another, a point we miss if we concentrate on the relatively small unit of palm-oil extraction. Indeed, the link between state power and mercantile concentration was particularly great during this period of incorporation. Newbury presents this phenomenon clearly:

> The trading states of Dahomey or the Niger Delta . . . [provide good] examples of African rulers supported by income from trade. . . . Rulers such as Ja Ja of Opobo or Nana of Warri were astute merchants, rather than African bureaucrats milking traders.[169]

themselves, and a need for secret writing, all, of course, relevant training for a merchant class. See Gerschenkron (1970, 35–37).

[164] Lovejoy & Hogendorn (1979, 232). Hogendorn further notes: "The taking of slaves was an expensive propositon taken against people who knew how to defend themselves. It was as if the fish [those of Thomas & Bean] could fight back" (1980, 480). Sundström reinforces the same theme: "One of the most striking aspects of African external trade is the strong position, often amounting to a monopoly, held by the middlemen. . . . The commercial monopoly was in part founded on the exclusive control of river transportation;; (1974, 254–255). See also van Dantzig (1975, 264) who stresses the capital intensity of slave trading, and hence the tendency to larger scale operations.

[165] See Ajayi & Oloruntimehin (1976, 211). On the Danish attempts to establish post-abolition plantations, see Nørregard (1966, 172–185). Müller argues that, at least among the Igbo in densely populated areas, palm-oil export production began in a zone already "producing oil and other items for exchange" (1985, 58).

[166] See Manning (1969, 287).

[167] See Hopkins (1973, 125). Augé (1971, 161), however, describing southern Ivory Coast palm-oil production in the second half of the nineteenth century, notes the difficulties in recruiting laborers from the lineage and the consequent recourse to captive labor. This then presumes somewhat larger-scale units.

[168] Law (1977, 572).

[169] Newbury (1969, 74–75).

To understand what was going on, we must be aware of the emergence of a multitiered structure of traders. At the Atlantic ports there were merchants, or exporter–importers, who represented European firms and were usually Europeans. These merchants dealt in turn with large-scale brokers or intermediaries (in French, the *négociants*), who in turn dealt with other intermediaries who were itinerant traders (in French, the *traitants*), and it was they who normally dealt with direct producers. It is usually at the level of the brokers that we have concentration wherever there was small-scale production. It is these brokers who would later be absorbed and replaced by the European firms, as the zone fell under colonial rule.[170]

The process of incorporation, we have argued, led to the creation of one or another kind of relatively large-scale decision-making units, self-interested in responding to the changing requirements of the world market. The size of these units served in part to motivate them, since changes they made had significant impact on their possibilities of accumulation, but served in part as well to increase their ability to respond, since they controlled sufficient capital and commodities to make some impact in turn on the world market. There remains one element to discuss in terms of the ability to respond, which is the capacity to obtain sufficient labor at a price which would render the product competitive.

For a worker, especially an agricultural worker, involvement in cash-crop production, particularly but not only within plantation-like structures, offered little intrinsic attraction, since it inevitably reduced the time for and physical availability of all sorts of subsistence practices which offered guarantees of survival and even of relative well-being. It should not be surprising, therefore, that, at least at first and for a long time thereafter, the labor supply needed by market producers in a zone undergoing incorporation had to be coerced, directly or indirectly, to work in the appropriate places at the appropriate rhythm. This coercion involved two elements which should be conceptually distinguished: the ways in which the worker was made to work harder (more efficiently?) and longer (per day, per year, per lifetime); and the formal rights or juridical status of the worker, and, therefore, the range of his options in relation to his work.

Mughal India is one of the few areas about which we have some data on standards of living of working strata prior to its incorporation into the world-economy. Four kinds of comparison exist. Habib argues that per capita agricultural output in 1600 was not less than the same area in 1900, and also was not less than that of western Europe in 1600.[171] Spear argues

---

[170] On the multiple tiers, see Chamberlin (1979, 422–423) and Newbury (1971, 100). On the distinction between *négociants* and *traitants*, see Hardy (1921). By and large, at this time, the lower level of itinerant trade was unregulated, competitive, and conflictual. The three areas where this was not so—the Cross River basin (Old Calabar), the Niger Delta (Opobo), and Dahomey—were precisely the areas of political concentration and maximal export production. See Chamberlin (1979, 434).

[171] See Habib (1969, 35).

that the average person in Mughal India ate better than his European counterpart.[172] And Desai has accumulated quantitative data to support the thesis that the "mean standard of food consumption. . .[was] appreciably higher" in Akbar's empire than in the 1960s in India.[173] Yet, as soon as we have the beginnings of incorporation after 1750, we hear of (British) complaints about the "indolence" of the Bengal peasant.[174] A solution to this "indolence" was soon found, one to which we have previously adverted, the system of "advances." We find this phenomenon suddenly emerging in all the cash-crop areas as the principal mechanism of coercion.

At this time, two systems of land tenure evolved, *zamindari* and *ryotwari*, both defined or rather redefined to mean ownership with quiritary rights. This direction of evolution of tenurial forms is a hallmark of involvement in the capitalist world-economy, since quiritary rights are indispensable to the commercialization of land, itself a necessary element in the liberation of all factors making possible the endless accumulation of capital. The *zamindari* system was instituted in Bengal by the Permanent Settlement of 1793.[175] In this system, the *ryots* (or peasants) living on their land were considered tenants to the *zamindars* and therefore subject to rent-enhancement or ejectment. As a result, "rents rose, and ejectments were common."[176] But also, new crops were grown and new laborers were acquired.[177]

The *ryotwari* system, by contrast, presumably eliminated the *zamindar* as an intermediary by conferring the quiritary rights on the *ryot* himself. This was touted as being "more sound in theory, expedient and beneficial in practice, and more in accordance with the native institutions, customs and manners of the people."[178] The system was initially applied in Madras and is often thought to be southern Indian, but it was utilized in the north as

[172] See Spear (1965, II, 47), who continues: "Taking it all in all Mughal India, with an estimated hundred million inhabitants, had for a century and a half a standard of life roughly comparable with that of contemporary Europe. . . . The peasant had a little more to eat, the merchant less opportunity of spending."

[173] Desai (1972, 61). This is supported by Moosvi (1973, 189). There is a rebuttal by Heston (1977) whose recalculation, he says, "certainly weakens [Desai's] contention that real wages declined since Akbar" (p. 394). Desai in turn rebuts Heston, doing some recalculation and concluding that there were both "higher crop yields" and "higher purchasing power of urban wages in terms of food grains" in Akbar's time compared to the 1960s (1978, 76–77).

[174] See the discussion in Sinha (1962a, II, 217–218), who points out that given fertile soil, three hard months labor, plus a few additional weeks at harvest time sufficed to produce one rice crop that maintained this reasonable standard of living. This

amount of labor would not suffice, however, to produce cash crops for the world market.

The Bengal situation, and the consequent view of the peasant's "indolence" was surely exacerbated by the "disastrous" famine of 1770 which intensified the scarcity of the labor force and no doubt thereupon increased the bargaining power of those who survived. See B. B. Chaudhuri (1976, 290–292).

[175] Of course, there had been *zamindars* under Mughal rule, but they did not have quiritary rights, and in any case, except for "pockets," their role in the system of agrarian exploitations had been "a secondary one" (Moosvi, 1977, 372).

[176] Neale (1962, 69).

[177] See Bhattacharya (1983, 308) on the use of tribal labor by the Bengali *zamindars*. B. B. Chaudhuri (1976, 320–323) also describes the recruitment of immigrant labor, both tribals and Muslims.

[178] S. C. Gupta (1963, 126).

well, even in Bengal. In reality, the *ryots* who obtained the quiritary rights turned out in most cases to be the higher-caste village leaders. These *ryots* were cultivators, of course, but they were also intermediaries (albeit smaller scale ones than the *zamindars*), since they were in many cases overseers of lower-caste direct laborers.[179]

What is important for us to note is that in both systems the combination of quiritary rights plus the system of advances made possible considerable compulsion. As a British Parliamentary Report of 1861 on indigo production put it:

> Where the planter has zemindary rights, the ryot has probably but little option. . . . The influence is perhaps best to be described as moral compulsion, and the apprehension of physical force.[180]

But, in fact, indigo was cultivated more frequently under the *ryotwari* system. It was not, however, any better for the direct producer:

> Even in the best of seasons cultivation of indigo barely paid at the rate which indigo planters would allow. . . . Advances were forced upon ryots [by the indigo planters] and the ryots could not furnish the quota of land demanded for indigo cultivation. . . . It would not be wrong to describe the system of indigo cultivation as indigo slavery.[181]

No wonder the indigo planters were thought to be "conspicuous for their oppression."[182]

Cotton weavers were not much better off than the peasants growing indigo. In the Regulations for Weavers, promulgated in Bengal in July 1787, once a weaver accepted advances from the East India Company, he was required to deliver cloth to the Company, and it became illegal to sell this cloth to anyone else. The Company was given the right to impose guards over the weavers to see that they fulfilled their contracts.[183] The result, of course, was a "visible deterioration in their economic conditions," and the weavers eventually were "pauperized out of their occupation."[184] The Company extended their policy to southeastern India. Once the East India Company was able to shut out their Dutch and French competitors, as of the 1770s, they made their merchants "draw hard bargains with the weavers."[185] The workers' real income declined in terms of direct receipts and in addition because of their inability under the new conditions to carry on their weaving "side-by-side with cultivating the fields."[186] As for cotton

---

[179] See Mukherjee & Frykenberg (1969, 220).

[180] BPP, Accounts of Papers (1861, xv).

[181] Sinha (1970, 21–22).

[182] Sinha (1956, I, 199).

[183] See Embree (1962, 105–108).

[184] Hossain (1979, 324, 330). Over time, she adds, there was "a progressive squeezing of the productive organization, and a strengthening of the hierarchical structure promoted by it" (p. 345).

[185] Arasaratnam (1980, 271).

[186] Arasaratnam (1980, 262). "The drift of the changes introduced by the English Company was to make the weaver a wage worker" (p. 280).

growing itself, we have the telling 1848 testimony of J. A. Turner of the Manchester Commercial Association, asserting that "India, with its cheap labor, will at all times be able to compete with the slave labour of America."[187]

Salt production presented even worse conditions for the worker. Given the poor pay and working conditions, it was "obvious" that salt manufacture could not be carried on "without coercion." The use of advances took an extra twist here. Once a man was employed, even if on a voluntary basis, he was "liable to be seized" in the future; furthermore his descendants were also bound "in perpetuity." Under such circumstances, one can imagine the reluctance to accept the advances. The latter were, therefore, frequently thrown before the door of a potential worker. "The mere sight of the money rendered him liable to be sent down to the *aurangs*."[188] A similar forcing of advances on the workers is recorded for saltpetre production in Bihar after 1800.[189] In general, this system of advances produced long-term coercion. As Kumar says, one of the reasons that "serfdom" proved "so durable in practice" was the "burden of indebtedness" created by these advances.[190]

In Russia, as we have already noted, the more oppressive form of serfdom, *barshchina* (corvée obligation), grew at the expense of *obrok* (quit-rent obligation), rather than the reverse (which has too readily been assumed to be the case in the past), particularly during the period between 1780–1785 and 1850–1860.[191] Confino gives as the explanation for this slide toward *barshchina* precisely the development of the capitalist market and capitalist doctrine, despite the fact that, superficially, *obrok* seems more compatible. He sees the crucial turning point in 1762, at which time (and then in an accelerated fashion after 1775), the nobles began to return to their lands, a phenomenon linked directly to the rise in cereals prices on the world market. It seems that *barshchina* was, in most cases, "more advantageous" to the cash-crop growing landlord than *obrok*.[192] Kahan notes a second factor favoring *barshchina*. The "Westernization" of the

---

[187] BPP, Report from Committees, (1848a, 83).

[188] Serajuddin (1978, 320–321).

[189] Singh (1974, 283).

[190] Kumar (1965, 75–76). To be sure, she adds that the other explanatory factor of durability was the caste system. But this does explain then why the bondage increased at this time nor why similar bondage occurred elsewhere without a caste system. Perhaps the form the caste system took in this period and later is a consequence rather than a cause of the bondage.

[191] See Confino (1963, 197). He is referring to the 20 *guberniya* of European Russia. *Barshchina* went from 50% in the 1790s to 70% in the 1850s. See Yaney (1973, 151), and Kizevetter (1932, 636). Dukes (1977) makes the case that such serfdom in

early nineteenth-century Russia was in fact comparable to slavery in the United States at the same period—morally, politically, and economically.

[192] Confino (1963, 229). Blum dates the shift a bit earlier than 1762. It was, beginning with Peter the Great, that the "rulers intensified the bonds of serfdom" (1961, 277). *Barshchina* was particularly pervasive in blacksoil Russia, White Russia, the Ukraine, the Volga area, and the Eastern steppe. The end of the eighteenth century marked "the height of the development of the serf economic system." At that time, "it consumed the preponderant part of the working time of the serf [i.e., 5 to 6 days a week] leaving him an insignificant portion of time in which to provide his own subsistence" (Lyashchenko, 1970, 277, 314).

gentry led to a considerable increase in imports, which required "a substantial increase" in the real income of the nobles and therefore led to increased pressure by them on the serfs.[193] The increase in *barshchina* permitted an expansion of estate lands at the expense of peasant plots, estate lands being "more flexible and more capable of reaping short-term gains from the changing market situations."[194]

It is not that *barshchina* became the only form of rural labor. Confino, in fact, argues the merits of a form of mixed *barshchina–obrok* obligations, which offered the lord the assurance of an estate labor supply plus some liquid income from *obrok* in poor harvest years. This combined form indeed became more frequent during this era.[195] It was a matter of priorities. Given the fact that the domains had acquired the character of an "economic enterprise," the disadvantages of the *obrok* system seemed greater than its advantages. When the landlords sought to raise rents on the *obrok* serf, he frequently sought employment elsewhere to meet the *obrok* obligations. Thus, by the end of the eighteenth century, an *obrotchnik* was thought of as someone who no longer tilled the soil and the word was often "employed in the pejorative sense of 'vagabond.' "[196] To produce the wheat, which remained their basic source of income, the landlords needed *barshchina*.

Furthermore, we must dispense with the myth that corvée labor was necessarily inefficient labor.[197] In fact, the zone that saw the greatest increase in *barshchina*, the blacksoil zone, also saw the most agronomic innovations (e.g., the introduction of potatoes as a garden crop.) In any case, both the expansion of arable land and the rise in yields took place primarily on the estates and not on the land of *obrok*-peasants.[198]

Finally, we must bear in mind that this intensification of coerced labor was not accidental but the result of policy decisions. The increase in cereals production was facilitated by the abolition of internal customs in 1754 and the authorization of grain exports in 1766. The acquisition of the southern steppes and the Black Sea ports also furthered grain exports and hence integration into the world-economy. And the manifesto of 1762, freeing

---

[193] Kahan (1966, 46).

[194] Kahan (1966, 54). As for the decline of burden on the serfs which Kahan sees from the 1730s to the 1790s, Longworth argues that, even for this period, the picture is "unsatisfactory" as the calculations are only based on the quitrents and polltaxes, "taking no account of labor-services, indirect taxation, land resources, peculation, nor the effect of accumulating poll-tax arrears" (1975b, 68, fn. 14).

Even so, Kahan's point still holds. There was a decline in quitrents and polltaxes. But this is precisely what led to a reaction: "By the 1760s' landlords felt they were in a bad squeeze: grain prices and the cost of living were rising, while revenues

remained stable or declined relative to purchasing power. They believed the solution to their plight lay in the greater availability of grain, either to lower purchase prices or to provide agrarian marketable surplus for a bigger profit. . . . They believed that one way of increasing income was to force the peasants to stay in the countryside and to till the soil in preference to any other occupation" (Raeff, 1971a, 97).

[195] See Confino (1961b, 1079, 1094–1095).

[196] Laran (1966, 120).

[197] See Blum (1961, 343) for pertinent criticisms.

[198] See Kahan (1966, 50).

the lords from bureaucratic service, gave them the liability to become agricultural, capitalist entrepreneurs.[199]

Furthermore, the process of increased land concentration was greatly assisted by the comprehensive land survey ordered by Catherine II in 1765, since, by validating all existing boundaries unless specifically contested, the state acquiesced in previous seizures of both state lands and empty tracts and "ratified the spoliation of free peasants and petty serf owners."[200] Le Donne sees in Catherine's great administrative reform, the establishment of the *guberniya*, the creation of "an apparatus capable of facilitating the utmost exploitation of serf labor."[201] And it was under Catherine, too, that the legal categorization of serfdom was finally fully developed, ratifying a de facto situation but also excluding almost all the peasants from a so-called personal legal status. As a result, de facto free peasants became "potential serfs and could be made into actual ones whenever the government wanted to use them."[202]

One of the most interesting aspects of Russian incorporation was the way in which iron manufacture played the transitional role to a more conventional emphasis on cash-crop exports, somewhat parallel to the role of slave trade in West Africa and cloth export in India. The significant rise of the Urals iron manufacture industry occurred in the mid-eighteenth century and owed its real take-off to the increased demand caused by the European wars of 1754–1762, as a result of which both the purchases of the Russian government and the English market became major outlets.[203] This manufacturing export role was in the long run not to last and was furthermore based heavily on coerced labor.

Work in the Urals factories was arduous and not well paid. For many, the "conditions and treatment were frequently far worse than those of agricultural serfs."[204] This was, of course, particularly true of the unskilled apprentices and the "youth of the mines," that is, the very young children engaged in auxiliary tasks.[205] The skilled workers were, in part, foreigners (recruited on attractive terms, one presumes), in part, metallurgists recruited from central Russia, and, in part, local artisans.[206] They were industrial wage earners. The skilled workers not only had a cash salary but in many cases a small plot of land that often brought in as much income as the wage received from the factory.[207]

However, the unskilled workers were "ascribed" peasants who per-

[199] See Confino (1963, 21–22).
[200] Raeff (1971b, 168).
[201] Le Donne (1982, 164).
[202] Yaney (1973, 135).
[203] See Portal (1950, 131, fn. 1, and passim, 131–174). To be sure, the origins of the industry were in 1716, when Peter the Great founded industrial enterprises in the far-off Urals, because the Northern Wars had cut him off from the previous supplier, Sweden, with whom he was at war. But the government soon lost interest, and the survival of

the industry is due to a few private entrepreneurs, notably Nikita Demidov. See Portal (1950, 26, 34, 52–130).
[204] Falkus (1972, 25).
[205] The ratio of skilled to unskilled was about 1:3, or for each 12 specialists and 20 skilled workers, there were 50 apprentices and 50 "youth of the mines." See Portal (1950, 258–259).
[206] Portal (1950, 44).
[207] See Portal (1950, 251–252). Lyashchenko (1970, 288) points out that many manufacturers

formed multiple auxiliary tasks—felling trees, burning charcoal, and transporting both the raw materials and the finished products. Initially, the "ascribed" peasants were merely local settlers, doing this work in payment of their taxes.[208] But such local settlers were not enough. A law of 1721 permitted factory owners to buy whole villages of serfs, who were then known as possessional serfs, attached to the factory and not to its owner.[209] There were, in addition, fugitives from domains of the state who volunteered for the factories and were then reintegrated into the feudal system as possessional serfs.[210] Finally, there were also *obrok* serfs in the factories, who were, however, located more in textile than in metallurgical factories. They were "detached" from their villages, and were relatively freer than the other serf workers, having a better bargaining position vis-à-vis the factory owner.[211] This added up to a system that, from the point of view of the factory owners, provided "flexible and cheap labor,"[212] but, from the point of view of the worker, was "repugnant."[213]

Given the oppressive conditions, the owners had to resort to considerable force and they maintained estate prisons to punish drunkards, quarrelsome types, and even lazy or incompetent workers.[214] Needless to say, coerced labor, bad conditions, and disciplinary punitiveness added up to conditions provoking rebellion. Already in the mid-eighteenth century, troubles began in the Urals.[215] When Pugachev would begin his great revolt in 1773, the industrial peasants of the Urals as well as the agricultural serfs would rally to him.[216] They were not the only ones as we shall see.

were composed of scattered units and included the possibility of part-time work at home by the *kustars* (or petty households).

[208] See Koutaissoff (1951, 254).

[209] See Falkus (1972, 24–25), Portal (1950, 47). These possessional serfs came to number 30% of the total. In 1736, a decree attached them "forever" to the factories. See Koutaissoff (1951, 255). In 1734, Tsaritsa Anna Ivanovna decreed that anyone starting one iron mill would get 100–150 families of state peasants assigned to the plant for each blast furnace and 30 families for each forge. See Blum (1961, 309). Blanc speaks of the "progressive subjugation of labor in the second quarter of the eighteenth century" (1974, 364).

As the industry grew more important, the situation of the workers continued to worsen. See Portal (1950, 366). In 1797, Paul I gave further judicial consecration to the idea of possessional workers. In 1811, the Ministry of Finance formally distinguished private enterprise and possessional factories, the latter having the right to receive from the state either peasants or land, forests, and mines. See Confino (1960a, 276–277).

[210] It was, as Portal says, merely "a provisional conquest of liberty, by flight, one to which the State

rapidly put an end" (1950, 233). See also Blum (1961, 311).

[211] See Portal (1950, 236–237).

[212] Tscherkassowa (1986, 26).

[213] The system provided formally for the possibility that the serf could replace himself with a substitute, a possibility that could only be realized in the Southern Urals where a free Bashkir population existed as potential substitutes. See Portal (1950, 272–273). "The high indemnities the peasants agreed to pay their replacements are strong testimony to their repugnance to work in the factory" (p. 277).

[214] See Portal (1950, 243).

[215] See Portal (1950, 290). The immediate factors were a combination of the sudden worsening of peasant conditions by the redefinition (upward) of seigniorial rights, by the increasing percentages of peasants assigned to the factories (where, in addition, salaries for possessional and other ascribed serfs were lower than for contract workers doing the same task), by increased surveillance, and by rising food prices. See Portal (1950, 278–290) and Lyashchenko (1970, 279–280).

[216] See Blum (1961, 313) and Portal (1950, 337–341).

The existence of "slavery" within West Africa has been a subject of much debate in which there has appeared confusion about dating and definitions, and, therefore, about its social causes and meaning. Slavery turns out to be a concept whose empirical content runs at least as wide a gamut as that of wage labor. If we define it very minimally as some kind of indefinitely lasting work obligation of one person to another from which the worker may not unilaterally withdraw (and to that extent at least the slave is at the mercy of the master), then no doubt there were forms of slavery in West Africa, or at least in parts of West Africa for a long time. There was surely in many regions some form of so-called domestic slavery, which might be seen as involving the compulsory integration of non-kin into a relatively low-status family role as pseudokin. This seems a significantly different phenomenon from the process of enslavement for sale to others, or from the use of slaves as "field" laborers. Even in this last case, the term has been used to cover not only plantation slaves but also persons who owed their master a rent in kind or a rent in labor (in which case the term is being used quite loosely, since the latter persons in a European context have been historically called serfs and not slaves). We shall not try to sort out this definitional maze at this point, but instead concentrate on seeing what were the trends as West Africa first came into Europe's external arena and then subsequently was incorporated into the capitalist world-economy.

It seems rather clear that there was a sequence, more or less imperfectly followed everywhere, from a period of the predominance (if not virtual exclusive existence) of some form of domestic slavery (and not even that everywhere) to a period when slave raiding became the dominant phenomenon (and these slaves were then sold via commercial networks) to a third period when increasingly the slaves were used on productive enterprises within West Africa itself. The slave raiding took on importance initially when West Africa was in the external arena, and continued (even grew in importance) as a mode of incorporation, giving way during incorporation to a form of so-called legitimate trade that in practice involved significant slave labor in West African cash-crop production itself, a phenomenon that would only slowly taper off. In the late eighteenth and nineteenth century, thus, there were large numbers of slaves within West Africa, for one reason because those who sold the captives "kept some for their own purposes."[217] As Kopytoff puts it with simple clarity, "in case after African case, when the possibility of profiting from the labor use of acquired persons rises, such use increases."[218] But as we have seen this was not a phenomenon peculiar to Africa.

[217] Rodney (1967, 18). On the sequence from domestic slavery to the slave trade to cash-crop slavery within West Africa, see Aguessy (1970, 76) and Meillassoux (1971a, 20–21, 63–64). As Aguessy insists, the three periods were not "radically separated" (p. 90).

[218] Kopytoff (1979, 65–66).

The first shift, therefore, was when Africans began to conceive of the "slave" not as someone given into bondage for crimes or because of "dire necessity" and thus as pseudokin in a new family but as a "vendable commodity," a concept which seems to have originated with the export trade in slaves.[219] Furthermore, there seems to have been a clear correlation between being a slave-selling people and being a slave-using people, a correlation which emerged over time. The sequence is not sure, but it is more probable that the selling preceded the using than vice versa.[220]

As the transition to a greater emphasis in cash crops began, particularly in the decades following the British proclamation of abolition, the slave-selling states faced economic difficulties, losing some outlets for their slaves, and, in addition, losing some of the trade profits from the resale of European products. Where they couldn't delay the effects, they thereupon reacted "by diverting the slaves they could not sell into producing alternative crops." Hence, Ajayi insists, abolition led, in fact, directly to "more extensive and intensive use of domestic slaves."[221]

[219] Johnson (1976, 38, fn. 31; cf. Martin, 1972, 104). See, however, Fage who insists that internal slavery went along with state development and "was already well advanced before European sea trade with West Africa began in the fifteenth century" (1969, 397). Uzoigwe insists, however, that the massive serf class to which the slave trade gave rise was new. To the extent that such slaves were known before then, "the numbers had been insignificant" (1973, 205). Lovejoy in a sense goes even further insisting that, as late as the seventeenth and eighteenth centuries, "despite the increase in enslavement, slave exports, and domestic slavery, the areas where slaves were central to the economy and society were still relatively restricted . . ." (1979, 36). See Manning as well: "The immense extent of slavery in the nineteenth century was a recent phenomenon for almost the entirety of the continent, which cannot be projected backward in time" (1981, 525–526). Finally, Rodney insists that the "late eighteenth-century situation on the upper Guinea Coast was quantitatively and qualitatively different" from domestic slavery (1975a, 293–294).

[220] Van Dantzig reminds us that, in general, peoples were either slave producing (that is, the objects of slave raids), slave raiding, or slave selling. "As soon as a state became predatory or engaged in the sale of slaves, its future seemed assured" (1975, 267). One consequence was that its population grew—by prosperity, by not losing persons to slavery, perhaps by "immigration" to a flourishing area, and very probably by enslavement. Rather than slave selling being "a palliative of an overpopulation" (p. 266) as, for example, suggested in

Fage (1975, 19), slave-selling zones had dense populations as a result of the slave trade.

See also Rodney: "It is a striking fact that the greatest agents of the Atlantic slave-trade on the Upper Guinea Coast, the Mande and the Fulas, were the very tribes who subsequently continued to handle the internal slave trade, and whose society came to include significant numbers of dispriv-ileged individuals laboring under coercion" (1966, 434).

[221] Ajayi (1965, 253). I think, however, the adjective "domestic" is a bit misleading, because we are really referring to such activities as gum or palm-oil production. See Catchpole and Akinjogbin (1984, 53) who note the high correlation of "export commodities" and such "domestic slavery." Similarly, in Freetown and Bathurst, which early fell under successful pressure to cease involvement in the Atlantic slave trade, Fyfe notes that "an internal slave trade was still needed to supply labour to harvest the vegetable produce. No longer exported across the Atlantic to work directly for Europeans, slaves were now sold within coastal West Africa to work indirectly for the European market" (1976, 186).

Klein and Lovejoy, responding to my 1976 article, assert: "We revise Wallerstein's thesis to take account of the intensive use of slaves in West Africa. This suggests that the process of 'peripheralization' was more advanced in the eighteenth and nineteenth centuries than Wallerstein allows" (1979, 211, fn. 103). The point is well taken in regard to that article, except that I would denote what was going on as "incorporation" rather than as "peripheralization."

It is this more extensive and intensive use of slavery within West Africa which is the mark of incorporation into the world-economy and which, therefore, represents a more decisive transformational break than the rise of slave trading per se.[222] In addition to being for sale as workers on enterprises integrated into the commodity chains of the world-economy, slaves had become, in addition, objects of financial investment—a capital good, a store of wealth, and an object of speculation.[223]

This increased coercion for mercantile production also took the other form in West Africa that it took elsewhere—debt linkage. This started with the European ships making advances to African brokers;[224] the practice then moved inland from brokers to itinerant traders. For example, in the Niger Delta, the development of the *Ekpe,* a secret society with a debt-collecting role, dates from the period of the rapid expansion of the slave trade in the mid-eighteenth century. The *Ekpe* was, in Latham's words, an "elementary capitalist institution."[225] The next step was easily taken: European imports advanced on credit "against seasonal provision of staples." Newbury regards this as "a major structural innovation arising from the new bulk produce trade."[226]

If the Ottoman literature discusses the increase of work obligations at this time less, this may simply be the result of scholarly neglect. We do have hints along these lines. Discussing the Ottoman tax structure, Stoianovich estimates that the Peloponnesian peasant in the last part of the eighteenth century had to provide "at least 50 percent more labor" than a French peasant of the time.[227] McGowan notes that Macedonia is subject to increased peonage: of the stick via debt; of the carrot via the garden plot. He also speaks of Romania and the southern Danube of the ways in which the government collaborated with the local lords "to bring almost the entire peasant class, the *clacaşi,* into complete subjection, legislating progressively more oppressive corvée requirements."[228] And Issawi notes for Syria the transformation of the peasant proprietors into sharecroppers, and observes that cash-crop production led the landlords to the increased use of corvée labor.[229] Sharecropping was also common in Anatolia.

We have tried to establish that incorporation involved the integration of

---

[222] See Aguessy (1970, 89) for a similar view.

[223] See Latham (1971, 604).

[224] "For Christians the advantages of lending to Africans in spite of the risks [given that loans were beyond cultural boundaries and beyond the jurisdiction at first of "civilized" governments] was not only the interest payments but the fact that loans gave the lender a competitive advantage over other buyers. The practice of lending in order to secure a quasimonopoly over the business of debtors was suggested by the Gambia station of the Royal African Company as early as 1677" (Curtin, 1975a, 303). See also Martin (1972, 103).

[225] Latham (1973, 29). Indeed, Drake credits the ability of the Niger Delta to sustain a large interior network to its credit system built upon the *Ekpe,* "which, though traditional in origin, was apparently capable of being employed as a debt-collecting agency" (1976, 149).

[226] Newbury (1971, 97–98; see also 1972, 85).

[227] Stoianovich (1976, 177).

[228] McGowan (1981a, 72–73).

[229] Issawi (1966, 236).

the production sphere into the commodity chains of the capitalist world-economy and that this integration tended to require, in the period of incorporation, both the establishment of larger units of economic decision making (including often, but not always, plantations) and the increased coercion of the labor force. Sometimes, confusing counterexamples are offered which are not necessarily relevant. This is because a secondary phenomenon occurred which has often been insufficiently distinguished from incorporation.

As a given zone is incorporated into the world-economy, this often led to an adjacent further zone being pulled into the external arena. It is as though there were an outward ripple of expansion. As India was incorporated, China became part of the external arena. As the Balkans, Anatolia, and Egypt were incorporated, parts of the Fertile Crescent area and the Maghreb came into the external arena. As European Russia was incorporated, Central Asia (and even China) moved into the external arena. As coastal West Africa was incorporated, the West African savannah zone became an external arena.

From the point of view of the capitalist world-economy, an external arena was a zone from which the capitalist world-economy wanted goods but which was resistant (perhaps culturally) to importing manufactured goods in return and strong enough politically to maintain its preferences. Europe had been buying tea in China since the early eighteenth century but found no acceptable payment other than silver. The incorporation of India offered some alternatives for Britain which were better for her and yet still acceptable to China. This was the origin of what has come to be called the India–China–Britain triangular trade.

The triangular trade was an invention of the East India Company. As early as 1757, the Company began shipping Bengal silver to purchase tea in China.[230] Over the next 70 years, the Company's purchases in China (90% of which were tea) expanded five times.[231] The cost in silver would have been very high. The Company was under great pressure to do something to avert this.[232] There was a solution that arranged two matters simultaneously. On the one hand, as we have already seen, a process was underway to reduce cotton cloth manufactures in India which had found a market in western Europe and of course in various parts of the Indian subcontinent, and to substitute British cloth imports. But this process created a problem of what to do with Indian cotton production, since it was not really economical at this point to ship it to Europe. China, it turned out, needed

[230] Sinha (1956, I, 222). At this point the British began to penetrate Tibet as well (in 1772–1774) "to keep open the land route to China" (Hyam, 1967, 124). This was necessary because the Gurkhas were threatening to close it. See Marshall (1964a, 17).

[231] Chung (1974, 412).

[232] "It irked ambitious manufacturers [in Britain]

to see India and China goods being imported into London on a massive scale with a corresponding export, and the blame was laid exclusively at the door of East India House" (Harlow, 1964, II, 489). It was the contention of many that the Company's monopolistic practices constrained private traders from expanding the trade network.

more raw cotton and, unlike Indian cloth manufactures, those of China were not being exported to Europe, and posed, therefore, no competitive threat. Indian cotton exports to China thus provided a suitable market outlet[233] from Britain's point of view and simultaneously eliminated the need for British silver exports to China.[234]

Cotton exports nonetheless posed a problem since China produced cotton herself and imports from India were merely supplementary. The price of Indian cotton in China varied with the success of the Chinese annual crop which made profits uncertain and led the Company to prefer to act as commission agents in China rather than as principals and to shift the economic burden of crop variation on the Hong merchants by means of long-term contracts. The 1820s were particularly difficult as Chinese demand was depressed.[235]

The British then found a substitute for cotton—opium, grown in Malwa and Bengal. Although, in theory, the Chinese Emperor forbade its import, the combination of "a corrupt Mandarinate and naval weakness" opened Chinese ports to the opium trade.[236] The import levels became so high that, reversing the original situation, China began to *export* silver to pay for the opium. As of 1836, the Emperor sought to enforce the ban on opium more seriously. This led to the Opium War in 1840 and, with the Treaty of 1842, China would start on the path of being herself incorporated.[237] But that is another story.

The incorporation of India into the world-economy induced changes in its production patterns (decline of cloth manufactures) which created problems for cotton producers in Gujarat which were solved by finding an outlet (China) in the external arena. Similarly, the incorporation of coastal West Africa in the world-economy induced changes in its economic patterns (ultimately, the end of the slave trade) which created problems for the slave-selling zones. Some reconverted to cash crops sold in the capitalist world-economy. Others, for various reasons, were unable to do so at this point in time. They found new outlets for new products in the new external arena, savannah West Africa.

---

[233] "By 1789 raw cotton had ceased to be exported in any quantity from Gujarat to Bengal, but it went instead in bulk to China. The great increase in the trade began about 1784 when Pitt's Commutation Act [of duties on tea] caused the East India Company to increase enormously its purchase of tea at Canton" (Nightingale, 1970, 23). See also Mui & Mui (1963, 264).

[234] While Sinha (1956, I, 222) dates the end of silver export to China as sometime in the 1790s, Greenberg (1951, 10) gives 1804 as the date. Marshall says that by the end of the eighteenth century, the growth of Indian trade [with Britain had become] inexplicable without reference to the demands and opportunities created by Canton" (1964a, 16).

[235] See Greenberg (1951, 80–81, 88).

[236] Greenberg (1951, 111). Whereas cotton profits were low and uncertain, "no other commodity could be as profitable as opium, which needed little investment" (Chung, 1974, 422). See also Sinha (1970, 27). By 1821, opium overtook tea as the prime item of the triangular trade (Chung, 1974, 420), and by 1840, Indian exports of opium to China were over three times her exports of cotton (Fay, 1940, 400). See also Owen (1934, 62 ff).

[237] See Greenberg (1951, 141, 198–206, 214).

The size of Saharan commerce—a phrase which covers the trade of the savannah or Sahelian zone of West Africa both northward to the Maghreb and southward (westward) to the forest and coastal zones of West Africa— had a "recrudescence" and "sharp growth" between 1820 and 1875.[238] Asante, a major slave-selling state in the forest zone in the late eighteenth century, significantly expanded its export of kola northward to Hausa areas as a "response of the Asante Government to the decline in the Atlantic slave trade in the early nineteenth century."[239] But the most remarkable change was in the savannah zone itself, which was marked by two central phenomena: the spectacular expansion of major Islamic reformist and expansionist state-building movements, most notably those of Uthman dan Fodio, Al Hajj Umar, and Samory, and the equally spectacular expansion of the phenomenon of slavery.

In the case of the Islamic movements, the story started essentially with the revival of the Sufi orders throughout the Islamic world in the late eighteenth century which was undoubtedly linked to the sense of threat posed by (Christian) European expansion and the decline of the three major Islamic political entities of the time—the Mughal, Safavid, and Ottoman Empires.[240] In West Africa, the continued disruptions in the interior caused by the Atlantic slave trade no doubt gave this sense of malaise further basis.[241] Major religious movements cannot be reduced to merely instrumental politics, as so many of the commentators have insisted.[242] But it also clear that political transformations, which is what these religious movements brought about, can only be explained in the larger context of social and economic transformations. We shall discuss these political

[238] Meillassoux (1971a, 13, 57). It reached its height in the 1870s, and was of a value equal to that of coastal West Africa's palm-oil trade in the 1860s. See Newbury (1966, 245).

[239] Wilks (1971, 130). Hausa links with the coast went back to the beginning of the eighteenth century (Colvin, 1971, 123), but they grew considerably in the nineteenth century.

[240] See Martin (1976, 2–3).

[241] For example, describing the situation in Kayor and Boal (located in contemporary Senegal/Mali), Becker and Martin observe: "A strong link existed between the slave trade and the disorders in the interior which the sources describe emphatically" (1975, 272). They continue: "The examination of these peasant resistances . . . show that it wasn't primarily a question of internal political problems, but reactions specifically to the consequences of participation by the chiefs in the Atlantic trade. The objective of the revolts was to end the 'pillage' and slave-raiding" (pp. 291–292, fn. 31).

[242] Waldman (1965) discusses how Uthman dan Fodio attracted support by pulling many motivations together, only one of which was that of the

oppressed against the oppressors, the factor emphasized by Hodgkin (1960, 80). Last (1974, 10) insists that peasants and traders were "little involved" in the jihad. Hiskett, however, spells out (1976, 136–139) the social and economic background to the jihad including the "violent process of enslavement" and the cowrie inflation caused by the influx of European shells on the coast.

As for Al Hajj Umar who came along 75 years later, Oloruntimehin (1974, 351–352) criticizes Suret-Canale (1961, 191–192) for arguing that Al Hajj Umar mobilized his followers on the basis of an anti-aristocratic struggle and insists on the "religious factor." Last says that Al Hajj Umar's struggle with the French was "not central to his jihad" (1974, 21). Hiskett again is somewhat more tolerant of the social thesis, but only up to a point. The jihad "took place during the full tide of French colonial penetration into West Africa. In consequence, it has often been presented as a movement of African resistance against European colonialism. Such an interpretation, although not entirely invalid, is too simple" (1976, 155).

changes in themselves shortly. Let us, for the moment, concentrate on the economic changes.

Why did slavery expand so notably in the savannah at this time? The answer is in one sense simple. The demand for slaves increased in adjacent regions both southward and northward, and within the savannah itself.[243] I have already described the sources of the southward demand. The growth of large-scale production created "labor-intensive economies which relied on increased numbers of slaves."[244] The export of slaves northward to Tripoli, and beyond to Egypt, Cyprus, and Constantinople, doubled in comparison with the eighteenth century. This was because of the economically "booming" nature of the nineteenth century. This trade nonetheless remained largely one in female slaves, hence still reflecting a domestic "luxury" expenditure.[245]

Finally, a significant number of slaves were retained for use in the savannah zone on the new plantation structures which were used to produce for the regional economy.[246] In a sense, the ripple effect of the incorporation of coastal West Africa caused, in nineteenth-century savannah West Africa, the same phenomenon which had occurred on the coast when it was still an external arena in the early eighteenth century: the rise of slave-selling states and the expansion of the use of slaves for local-regional production.

Incorporation into the world-economy means necessarily the insertion of the political structures into the interstate system. This means that the "states" which already exist in these areas must either transform themselves into "states within the interstate system" or be replaced by new political structures which take this form or be absorbed by other states already within the interstate system. The smooth operation of an integrated division of labor cannot operate without certain guarantees about the possibility of regular flows of commodities, money, and persons across frontiers. It is not that these flows must be "free." Indeed, they are hardly ever free. But it is that the states which put limitations on these flows act within the constraint of certain rules which are enforced in some sense by the collectivity of member states in the interstate system (but in practice by just a few stronger states).

[243] See Lovejoy (1979, 42).

[244] Tambo (1976, 204), who is describing the Sokoto caliphate as the main source of slaves for the Bights of Benin and Biafra at this time. See also Klein & Lovejoy: "In the forest areas, too, large-scale production was common by the nineteenth century. Plantations were found around Kumasi in Asante, and many thousands of slaves were used in gold mining. . . . In Dahomey and the Yoruba states, the government was equally involved in large-scale production that depended upon slave labor in both agriculture and trade. . . . In the new agricultural lands of northeastern Igboland,

yam plantations were common. As the central Igbo country was planted with palm trees, the northern frontiers became an important source for foodstuffs. A similar pattern emerged in the immediate hinterland of Calabar" (1979, 197).

[245] Austen (1979, 60–61, Table 2.7). Boahen (1964, 128) estimates the women slaves at 60%, children under 10 as 10%, and says the men were mainly used as eunuchs. See also M'Bokolo (1980).

[246] See Lovejoy (1979, 1267–1268; see also 1978). Meillassoux reports (1971b, 184–186) a similar phenomenon further west in the savannah zone.

From the point of view of the existing interstate system, the ideal situation in an area undergoing incorporation is the existence of state structures which are neither too strong nor too weak. If they are too strong, they may be able to prevent necessary transfrontier flows on the basis of considerations other than that of maximizing the accumulation of capital in the world-economy. And if they are too weak, they may not be able to prevent others within their territory from interfering with these flows. At the end of the process of incorporation, one should expect to find states, which internally, had bureaucracies strong enough to affect directly in some ways the production processes, and which were linked externally into the normal diplomatic and currency networks of the interstate system.

The transformation that is involved is splendidly caught up in Meillassoux's discussion of the relationship of West African states to traders in the nineteenth century:

> [It is not] established in any clear way that trade was everywhere encouraged by the existence of state systems. The militarism of the latter was opposed to the pacifism of the traders. . . . According to nineteenth-century travelers the most dangerous regions, avoided by the caravans, were found in the territory of the most centralized of the states due to the wars they fought among themselves. . . .
> The state starts playing a positive role in furthering trade when the means of its administration (transport, currency, public order) becomes the means of commerce. This tendency leads to the integration of the trader as a subject of the state and removes his 'stranger' status. This phenomenon is mostly to be found in the Gulf of Guinea where the slave trade prevailed.[247]

As a zone became incorporated into the world-economy, its transfrontier trade became "internal" to the world-economy and no longer something "external" to it. Trade moved from being at great risk to something promoted and protected by the interstate system. It is this shift of which we are speaking.

Of course, the prior political situations in the four regions we have been analyzing had been quite different from one another. The details of other political transformations that were required were therefore considerably different. Nonetheless, as we shall see, the outcomes at the end of incorporation turned out to be less different than the starting points, although the particularities of each region were never effaced entirely.

Let us start the analysis this time with the Ottoman Empire. The Empire had been under steady pressure at all its edges since the unsuccessful siege of Vienna in 1683. The successive wars, primarily with Austria and Russia, involved a slow but steady loss of territory throughout the eighteenth (and then nineteenth) century whose ultimate outcome would be the republic of Turkey, which in its present frontiers, is essentially reduced to Anatolia, the original core of the Ottoman Empire. The physical retrocession of the Ottoman Empire was, for a long time, matched by the steady retrocession

---

[247] Meillassoux (1971a, 74).

of its ability to control politically its empire with the institutions it had
created in the era of its expansion. Specifically, the state was seeing a
serious diminution of its ability to control the means of production, of
circulation, of violence, and of administration.[248]

The end of the territorial expansion of the empire had been a severe
blow to a foundation block of its structure, the *timar* system, in which newly
acquired land was distributed to intermediate officials (*sipahis*) who served
as local representatives of the central state and in particular as its tax
collector. As the same time that the central state was losing its ability to
reward retainers with land, it underwent a long decline in its ability to
maintain revenue levels—in part because of price inflation (the impact of
being in the external arena of the world-economy and the recipient of a
silver outflow from this world-economy), in part because of the diversion of
once lucrative trade routes (because of the rise of the new Atlantic and
Indian Ocean networks of the European world-economy in the sixteenth
and seventeenth centuries). To solve this problem, the state turned to tax
farming which ultimately resulted in the quasiprivatization of imperial
land.

There was a parallel decline in the detailed control of mercantile activity
via the *hisba* regulations. The ability of the government to control all trade
transactions so as to give priority to the provisioning of the Ottoman center
gave way to a system where European currencies circulated with ease in the
Empire and money lending to the bureaucracy became widespread.

In the military domain, the empire found itself beginning to fall behind
the Europeans by the turn of the seventeenth century. To remedy this, the
central government authorized provincial administrators to create mercenary units (*sekban* troops), and it expanded its own mercenary force (the
janissaries). Given the growing financial difficulties, the growth in the
military mercenary forces simply meant, over the long run, a growing body
of servitors both difficult to control and restive.

Finally, the empire saw the power of provincial officials and local
notables (the *ayans*) grow, as they acquired income from tax farming and
military power from *sekban* troops.[249] By the time we get to the "disastrous
peace treaty"[250] of Küçük Kaynarca in 1774, following defeat in the war
with Russia, the *ayans* had emerged as "*de facto* rulers of various areas" and
were in a position to "contend for power."[251]

This rise of regional power occurred everywhere within the Ottoman
empire—in Rumelia (the Balkans), in the Fertile Crescent, in Egypt, and in
North Africa. It took its most dramatic form in Egypt, with the virtual
secession of Mohamed Ali whose de facto new state emerged in the

---

[248] This subject is treated in considerably more
detail in Wallerstein & Kasaba (1983, 338–345).
[249] On the rise of *ayans* as a function of the
decline of *timar*, see Sucéska (1966).

[250] Heyd (1970, 355).
[251] Karpat (1972, 355).

aftermath of the Napoleonic invasion. But Egypt's autonomy was not merely a function of internal Ottoman decline which was its precondition. If it were that alone, Mohamed Ali might have succeeded in creating a new powerful counter empire. In the context of the process of incorporation, the world war between Great Britain and France initially permitted his secession; but, later, Britain constrained (over 40 years) his ability to consolidate such a new imperial structure.[252]

The rise of virtual "autonomies" in the Balkans is equally striking. By the end of the eighteenth century, Ottoman control over the Balkan provinces had become "purely nominal"[253] Such figures as Pasvanoğlu Osman Pasha in Serbia and Ali Pasha in Janina had become "semi-independent." Their base was, to be sure, in the class of large landowners but they received support as well from the local merchant classes, who "had every interest in creating a strong governmental structure which could check the anarchy that the Sublime Porte could no longer do anything about."[254] The emerging strong structures were, however, being created within the framework of medium-size units larger than the *sandjak*s of the Empire.

Sultan Mahmud II's reforms aimed at ending this frittering of central power. And ultimately he was able to abolish both the *ayan*s and the janissaries.[255] His achievement was that he "founded an absolute monarchy, supported by a centralized bureaucracy and a state army recruited from among commoners and formed with a new secular and progressive orientation."[256] But there was a price for this consolidation. In a sense, in the long run, he did succeeed by creating a modern "state with the interstate system," but only within a zone smaller than the whole of the previous Ottoman Empire.

Mahmud II's attempts at reform and recentralization in the early nineteenth century became the "immediate cause of the Greek rising,"[257]

[252] See Abir: "The authority and power of the Ottoman central government rapidly declined in the second half of the eighteenth century and the beginning of the nineteenth. . . . Among the *valis* who tried to consolidate their autonomy at the expense of the central government, Mohamed Ali of Egypt was exceptional. . . . Mohamed Ali's expansion was facilitated by the weakness and uncertainty which prevailed in the Ottoman Empire. It coincided, unfortunately for him, with the growing British interest in the region" (1977, 295, 309).

[253] Skiotis (1971, 219). The *ayans* were now posing "the most dangerous challenge to the Ottoman state" (Jelavich & Jelavich, 1977, 16). For the same phenomenon in the Fertile Crescent, see Hourani (1957, 93–95).

[254] Buda (1972, 102). On a parallel joint base of local power (landlords and merchants) in Damascus, Aleppo, and the Holy Cities, see Hourani (1968, 52–54).

[255] See Karpat (1972, 243–256).

[256] Berkes (1964, 92).

[257] Braude & Lewis (1982, 19). They continue: "During the late eighteenth and early nineteenth centuries, Greek maritime and merchant communities had prospered greatly. The Ottoman flag, neutral during some of the crucial years of the revolutionary and Napoleonic wars, had given them considerable commercial advantages; the loose and highly decentralized administration of the Ottoman Empire in the period allowed them the opportunity to run their own administrative, political, and even military institutions. The local rulers and dynasts who governed much of Greece were for the most part Muslims. They presided, however, over largely Greek principalities, were served by Greek ministers and agents, and even employed Greek troops. The attempts by Mahmud II to restore the direct authority of the Ottoman central government thus represented in effect a

the first successful true secession. Although the Greek cause would eventually take a classically nationalist form, built around common language and creed,[258] its wider base as resistance to Ottoman recentralization can be gauged by the important role "Bulgarians" played in the early days both in the Greek war and in political resistances in Romania.[259]

It is within this context of the attempt to stem the decline of centralized power and to ward off external military pressure that the Ottoman Empire became "the first non-Christian country to participate in the European state system and the first unconditionally to accept its form of diplomacy."[260] If the first Western "diplomat," an Englishman named William Harborne, arrived in Istanbul as early as 1583,[261] Ottoman unilateralism and contempt for European states was still unbridled at that time and would largely remain so until the end of the eighteenth century. Nonetheless, the Treaty of Karlowitz in 1699, which was the first step in the Ottoman geographical recession in Europe, marked the beginning of at least episodic acquiescence in negotiations and rule recognition, and, therefore, a new Ottoman view of diplomacy.[262]

A similar evolution was beginning in the role of the "consul." The "capitulations" were originally a privilege granted to foreign nationals belonging to a non-Moslem religious community, a *millet*, whose representative was the "consul." As late as 1634, the Sultan "appointed" the French ambassador without waiting for word from Paris. But once geographical recession began after 1683, capitulations became something the Sublime Porte could trade for European "diplomatic support" against other European powers.[263] In 1740, the French received just such a reward for their assistance in the peace negotiations with the Russians at Belgrade in 1739.

---

severe curtailment of liberties which the Greeks already enjoyed."

It should be noted that it took Mahmud II a while to pursue his reformist schemes. Due to the large role played in his coming to power in 1807 by the *ayan* of Rusçuk, Alemdar Mustafa Pasha, Mahmud II in fact began his reign by issuing in 1808 the Senedi İttifak which granted the *ayan*s considerable freedom in their domains in Rumelia and Anatolia and is considered by Karpat a "humiliating act of concession" (1974, 275).

[258] See Dakin (1973, 56).

[259] See Todorov (1965, 181).

[260] Hurewitz (1961a, 455–456; 1961b, 141), who adds: "The Ottoman realization of full diplomatic reciprocity with Europe thus constituted a major step in the transformation of the European state system into a world system."

[261] See Anderson (1984, xv).

[262] At Karlowitz, a Venetian participant, Carlo Ruzzini, noted specific changes in the ways the Ottomans negotiated. He stressed their acceptance of the "equality of the participants," their willingness to submit differences to "method," and their "deliberateness in the formalities of negotiation." This was not, however, the Ottoman self-image. They sought "to make sure that none of the Allies could have claimed a change in the 'ancient' procedures of negotiation of dictation of terms" (Abou-el-haj, 1974, 131, 134).

In the treaty, the Ottomans gave up Hungary, Transylvania, recognized the conquest of Morea and Dalmatia, returned Podole and (in 1702) Azov (see Sugar, 1977, 200). This meant that boundaries had to be demarcated, a process completed by 1703. Fluid frontiers were no longer legitimate and the "stabilization of the borders required a readiness on the part of the [Ottoman] state to exercise direct restraint on [Tatar] frontier elements until a change in their mode of living had been effected" (Abou-el-Haj, 1969, 475).

[263] İnalçık (1971, 1180, 1185).

This led to a considerable increase in French trade with the Ottoman Empire.[264] .

But most importantly, in this new arrangement with the French, the Ottomans redefined the meaning of "capitulations," extending the certificates of protection (the *berats*) beyond the foreign nationals to non-Muslim Ottoman subjects who were accepted to be under the aegis of the foreign consul.[265] This would result in a profound change in the overall social composition of the commercial classes, from a situation in which Moslems had been "either the majority or a strong minority" in most regions to one in which in finance, in industry, and in foreign trade the non-Muslims (Greeks, Armenians, Jews, Levantines), linked via the capitulations to foreign consuls, would predominate.[266]

When the Treaty of Küçük Kaynarca in 1774 forced upon the Ottomans the "bitter fact" that they were in no position to defend themselves militarily without assistance, they "drew the obvious conclusion" that they had to integrate themselves into the "complicated mechanism" of the European interstate system.[267] It is in the reign of Selim III (1789–1807) that the Ottoman Empire made its first "experiment with reciprocal diplomacy,"[268] while seeking at the same time to "reduce abuse" in the administration of the capitulations. The latter effort, however, was successfully opposed by the European ambassadors and consuls "who saw in every

[264] See Paris (1957, 93–101). But when, in the 1768–1789 period, France could no longer aid effectively against the Austro–Russian offensive, commercial links with France diminished and England began to rise as a trade partner (see pp. 104–106).

[265] See Hodgson (1974, III, 142).

[266] Issawi (1982, 262). And even in agriculture, although Muslims predominated (Turks in Anatolia, Arabs in West Asia), the *millets* were important, especially in cotton, which had become "the most rapidly expanding sector of agriculture" (p. 263).

[267] Heyd (1970, I, 356). Gibb and Bowen argue that prior to this time the leaders of the governing class of the Ottoman Empire felt no sense of inferiority to Europe. "It was only with the experience of two disastrous wars, lasting one from 1767 to 1774 and the other from 1788 to 1792, that induced a change in attitude" (1950, 19).

In addition to the military implications of Küçük Kaynarca, Karpat reminds us of its economic consequences: "The opening of the Black Sea to the Russians and through the peace treaties of Küçük Kaynarca and Jassi in 1774 and 1792, coupled with the loss of territory along the north shores of the same sea, deprived the Ottoman state of its major economic base. The Black Sea had been an exclusive Ottoman trade area, which compensated for

the French and British domination of Mediterranean commerce" (1972, 246).

[268] Hurewitz (1961a, 460). In 1792, the first permanent embassy was sent abroad. France was the logical choice. "However, on consideration, it was feared that this move would offend those other European states who were at war with France and who might therefore refuse to accept an Ottoman envoy" (Naff, 1963, 303). The embassy was opened instead in London, followed by Vienna in 1794, Berlin in 1795, Paris in 1796. See also Shaw (1971, 187–189, 247–248).

Diplomatic reciprocity involved as well the end of Ottoman ill-treatment of ambassadors during their audiences with the Sultan. The British Ambassador reported in 1794 that "instead of that sullen and contemptuous dignity with which former Sultans are said to have given audience to the ministers of crowned heads, I met with a reception from the reigning prince as generous and attentive as I could have expected from any other sovereign in Europe" (cited in Hourani, 1957, 116).

Diplomatic reciprocity between western Europe and China was only in place in 1875, with Japan in 1870, with Persia in 1862. "By contrast, all the major European powers and a number of the lesser ones maintained diplomatic missions at Istanbul before the end of the eighteenth century" (Hurewitz, 1961b, 144–145).

reform only a new attempt to reduce the profits" which they and the merchants protected by them obtained via these "abuses."[269]

This new atmosphere did not stop the European powers from lending support to the decentralizing thrusts within the Empire. Bonaparte invaded Egypt, thus ending definitively the prudent reserve of the *Ancien Régime* which had feared that such intrusion would only redound to the advantage of Russia and Britain,[270] which indeed turned out to be the case.[271] The British would support de facto the Greek struggle for independence, with Lord Byron singing its romance.[272]

Selim's reforms were insufficient because Ottoman diplomacy lacked an organizational basis in terms of a permanent specialized bureaucracy. This would be another achievement of Mahmud II's reign (1808–1839).[273] Once Britain achieved its definitive hegemonic status, it replaced France as the protector of Ottoman integrity, which it saw as both checking Austrian and Russian ambitions and ensuring the lifeline to India, which had by then become a prime British concern.[274] But most importantly, Great Britain was now able to impose its terms on the Ottomans as the price for its protection of the Empire. The terms were high. At the very end of Mahmud II's rule, in 1838, Britain and the Ottoman Empire signed the Anglo–Turkish Commercial Convention (ATCC) of Balta Limann. The immediate prelude to the signing of this Convention in August had been the proclamation of Egyptian (plus Syrian) independence by Mohamed Ali. Britain would help the Empire to negate this proclamation.[275] In return, ATCC confirmed all previous capitulatory privileges "forever" and limited the rights of the Ottomans to impose *ad valorem* customs duties higher than 3% for imports and transit trade and 12% for exports. All monopolies were ended and British was given most-favored-nation status.[276] British importers also agreed to pay 2% in lieu of other internal duties. This had the effect of supporting the Ottoman center against potential secessionists like Egypt.

As all observers agree, this treaty represented the "virtual adoption of free trade" by the Ottomans.[277] The negative impact of the treaty was

[269] Shaw (1971, 178–179).

[270] In 1784, Vergennes instructed the French Ambassador, the Comte de Choiseul-Gouffier, to offer the Turks military missions to aid them in "a renovation of their armies" (Roche, 1985, 84–85).

[271] "The most immediate result of Bonaparte's expedition was the loss of the Porte to France's enemies, Great Britain and Russia. . . . Thus did Bonaparte's rash gamble cost France its Middle Eastern position and assets, which had been built up for centuries" (Shaw, 1971, 262–263).

[272] So would the United States. See Earle (1927).

[273] See Findley (1980, 126–140). Findley (1972, 399–400) nonetheless gives credit to Selim's "short-lived" innovations as having laid the groundwork.

On Mahmud II's contributions, which "have yet to be given their due," see Berkes (1964, 92).

[274] See Jelavich & Jelavich (1977, 22).

[275] By so doing, they also eliminated any further need of the Ottomans to seek aid from Russia and thus undermined the Treaty of Hünkâr-İskelesı of 1833 which had granted the Russians their demand that, in the event of war, the Dardanelles be closed. See Puryear (1935, ch. 3).

[276] See Puryear (1935, 123–125).

[277] Findley (1980, 341). İnalçık (1971, 1187) speaks of it turning the Ottoman Empire into "an entirely open market just at the time when the European mechanized industry was seeking outlets for its production. In the next ten years, local

great.[278] In addition to its impact on the composition of production (the decline of Ottoman manufactures), it also seriously cut into Ottoman state revenues, leading in 1854 to the Ottoman state's becoming a borrowing power, which ultimately culminated in the debacle of 1878 and the consequent debt tutelage.[279] After 1838, Turkey became Britain's fourth best customer and by 1846 Lord Palmerston could tell Parliament that there was "no foreign country with which we carried on commercial intercourse in which the tariff was so low and so liberal as that of Turkey."[280]

The political and administrative reforms of the Tanzimat in the Gulhane Rescript of 1839 at the onset of the new sultanate of Abdülmecid I marked the last stage in this process. "The doors to the West were thrown wide open."[281] The incorporation became so complete that by 1872, the British subject, J. Lewis Farley, who was serving as the Consul of the Sublime Porte in Bristol, could argue that *since* Turkey "has fairly entered the community of nations," and *since* her administrative system has been "remodeled" and *since* she recognized the paramountcy of universalism over the claims of sect, therefore, perhaps now, some of the capitulations might be revised.[282] In short, they were no longer needed.

The reconstruction of the political mechanisms on the Indian sub-continent followed a quite different trajectory than that of the Ottoman Empire. In the case of the Ottoman Empire, the outcome by 1850 was a state internally stronger than in 1750, but externally weaker and geographically reduced in scope. Ultimately, the territory would be subdivided even more, but with all the successor states fully participating in and constrained by the interstate system. By contrast, in 1750, the Mughal Empire was at the end of a political disintegrative process that was much further advanced than that of the Ottoman Empire (and no doubt the Mughals had never been as internally cohesive and georgaphically extensive as the Ottomans). The result of incorporation would be the total abolition by 1857 of the Mughal Empire as well as all the other smaller political structures that had existed on the Indian subcontinent and their

industry collapsed." Karpat speaks (1972, 247) of its giving Britain "undisputed competitive superiority with respect to domestic manufactures," thereby bringing about the virtual collapse of the Ottoman state economy. Issawi reminds us that the establishment of this "substantially free trade area" was part of a pattern: "The British government, and more particularly Lord Palmerston, was . . . eager to cut Mehmet Ali down to size. Moreover, it was applying in Turkey the economic policy it was to follow in Iran in 1841, in China in 1842 and in Morocco in 1856, the so-called 'Imperialism of Free Trade' " (1980b, 125).

[278] See Kançal (1983), but see Kurmus (1983) who is skeptical.

[279] See Puryear (1935, 104–105), who asserts: "Mehmet Ali was right; in the long run, the Anglo–Turkish Commercial Convention hurt Turkey more than Egypt."

[280] Cited in Köymen (1971, 50).

[281] Berkes (1964, 137). See also Findley: "The reformers seem by the end of the 1830s to have had a rather clear grasp of the extent to which innovative reform implied movement towards a rational-legal order. . . . [Witness] Mustafa Reşid's contemporary perception of European support of the empire against Mohammed Ali as a matter of the entry of the Ottoman state 'dans le droit européen' "(1980, 163).

[282] Farley (1872, 161).

collective replacement by a single (but complex) administrative unit, India, which was however nonsovereign. It is this entity which would go forward to independence in the twentieth century in the form of two (later three) sovereign states. Nonetheless, the historical evolution of the two zones between 1750 and 1850 show certain clear parallels in the (re)construction of state structures, neither too strong nor too weak, fully ensconced in the interstate system.

The explanation of the weaknesses of the Mughal Empire of the seventeenth and eighteenth centuries has been much debated in Indian historiography. Two major accounts are those of Irfan Habib and Satish Chandra. Essentially, Habib argues that the central administration sought to raise enough revenue from the peasantry to secure its military strength but not so much as to make impossible the subsistence of the peasantry. However, the Mughal Empire, as all such structures, had to rely on some intermediary cadres, in this case, the *jagirdars*, to collect the revenue. The interests of the intermediaries being quite different from that of the central administration, they tended over time to raise steadily the level of surplus extraction in order to retain more for themselves. In Habib's words, this was "reckless," since it led (in the Mughal Empire as it had elsewhere, it should be added) to flights from the land, armed resistance, and a decline in cultivation, undermining in the long run the economic base of the imperial structure.[283]

Satish Chandra words his explanation somewhat differently. He says that the system was up against the "basic problem" that the available surplus was "insufficient to defray the cost of administration, pay for wars of one type or another, and to give the ruling class a standard of life in keeping with its expectations."[284] Athar Ali affects to see a contradiction between Chandra's argument and that of Habib, asserting that the latter argues that the *mansabdar* system worked too well, and that Chandra argues that it didn't work well enough. I do not myself see the contradiction. The process which Habib describes led to the situation that Chandra describes. The only question is whether this process was significantly precipitated by the European presence in Asia. Athar Ali's own answer is that, given the nonexpansion of production, European demand for Asian goods served to increase the real prices of those products on Asian markets, thereby causing a "serious disturbance" in their economies and intensifying "the financial difficulties" of the ruling classes.[285] This would then partially explain the increased squeeze of which Habib speaks, and would affect not only the direct producers but those one level up in the structure. It thereby led in effect, says Gupta, to a drain of local capital such that, unable to pay the "exorbitant revenues" to the Empire, local land controllers were often

---

[283] See Habib (1963, 319–338).
[284] S. Chandra (1972, xlvi).

[285] Athar Ali (1975, 388).

led to transfer their rights to collect revenues by sale or mortgage, despite this being illegal. Thus, he argues, "the pre-conditions for the functioning of a land market in India . . . came into existence in the last days of Mughal rule."[286]

The military disintegration of the Mughal Empire, the extensive warfare on the subcontinent, and the rise of new autonomous zones no doubt made the European trading companies aware, by the 1740s of "the political opportunities which lay open to further their own economic interests."[287] But simply because "opportunities" exist does not mean they are seized. For such "opportunities" have their cost. Political conquest and direct administration have many advantages but they require a significant financial disbursement. In general, if the same or more profit can be made without them, the states representing strong economic actors will seek to sidestep such disbursements. It is clear that, not only in the 1740s but for a half-century or even a century, therefore, there were many powerful persons in Great Britain who thought it prudent to sidestep such disbursements. Yet, as we know, they were made.

The Seven Years' War, during which India was an important locus of Franco–British warfare, played its role. As Spear says, it gave the Europeans a new "confidence in the superiority of their armed forces in Indian conditions,"[288] and the Clive period may, in addition, have propagated or expanded a myth of India as a "land of abundant wealth"[289] which eclipsed the reality of the costs of military and administrative expenditures. That a link between increasing involvement in the production networks of the world-economy and a consequent restructuring of the political networks was perceived by local rulers at the time is illustrated by the anecdote related by a merchant from Malabar traveling to Calicut in

[286] Gupta (1963, 28).

[287] K. N. Chaudhuri (1982, 395). Of course Perlin is quite right to underline the degree to which these "opportunities" were themselves the doing of the Europeans. "Those conditions of anarchy and disarray, both on frontiers and in recently acquired territories, which stimulated the British to so much moral ire, and which justified ultimate military action, were the result of the aggressive movement of which they were part, both in the long run and in the short" (1974, 181). See also Watson (1978, 63–64).

[288] Spear (1965, 79), who continues: "Thus the power of the main Indian arm was centralized and the balance restored, as in classical times, to small numbers of highly trained infantry." Of course, European naval power had long predominated in the Indian Ocean trade. The Portuguese had broken the Muslim monopoly in the sixteenth century by their superior naval force. See Boxer (1969, 46) and Chaudhuri (1981, 230) who insists on "the violence of the methods used by Lusitanian explorers." Sir Josiah Child in the seventeenth century explained that the Moghuls could not go to war with the English because the English could then "obstruct their trade with all the Eastern nations" and thus bring starvation and death upon themselves (cited in Woodruff, 1953, 73). Prakash points out that the Dutch could impose upon Indian traders a system of "passports" (permission to trade in given ports and immunity from naval attacks) because of "the almost total absence of naval power in Mughal India" (1964, 47). But all this naval power was insufficient to transform either the production or the political structures of the Indian subcontinent.

[289] Butel (1978b, 102).

1784. It is told that he

> saw on his way that all sandal trees and pepper vines were being cut down. People told him that the Nawab [i.e., Tipu Sultan] had given strict orders for their destruction as it was because of these commodities that the Europeans sought to make war on him.[290]

As Marshall insists, and as this anecdote shows, India was by no means "an inert victim ripe for conquest by any European state that chose to assert its irresistible power."[291] And furthermore, in the eighteenth century, neither the British government nor the Court of Directors of the East India Company manifested any strong desire for the use of military force.[292] Yet, "paradoxically," as Harlow says,[293] the actual result was the acquisition of the largest, most populated land mass to be colonized either before or since.

One reason for this colonization was that there were not two but three major British actors on the Indian scene. In addition to the British government and the Court of Directors of the East India Company, there were the private traders. Furthermore, there were at least two kinds of private traders, those who were themselves servants of the Company and those who were not.[294] Obviously those who were employees of the Company had conflicts of interest; their private interests were given latitude by the realities of distance and the extreme difficulties of effective centralized control. It seems clear, furthermore, that the pursuit of these private economic interests frequently led the Company's servants to use their authority to pressure Indian states in political ways. As Marshall puts it, "they were willing to use [their military ascendancy] to extract concessions from Indian rulers whose cumulative effect was to weaken and eventually destroy those states."[295]

This drive for political control did not happen without considerable debate within the framework of the Company. This was the heart of the disagreements in the 1770s and 1780s between the so-called Hastings and Francis factions.[296] But the fact is that the attitude of even the anti-

---

[290] Das Gupta (1967, 113). Furthermore, Tipu was absolutely right. When Tipu attacked Travancore in 1789, Lord Cornwallis, who had been for peace and the dissolution of the Bombay Presidency (that is, the abandonment of western India), changed his position and, by 1790, "these rather vague ideas [of Cornwallis] of restoring western India to its condition before the rise of Mysore had given place to a firm and definite policy of annexation" (Nightingale, 1970, 58).

[291] Marshall (1975b, 30).

[292] "Political or imperial adventures in India were frowned upon by the Company at home for the same reason that the opening of new factories was disliked in the earlier period. They tended to increase the overhead costs without bringing immediate financial returns" (K. N. Chaudhuri, 1978,

56). Furthermore, as Rothermund says: "The interference of the European factories within the Indian economy was effective enough without territorial rule" (1981, 88).

[293] Harlow (1964, 1).

[294] The picture in reality was more complicated. Watson (1980a, 81) distinguishes five types of private traders: the company's servants, commanders and seamen of Indo–European route ships, free merchants resident in the East, interlopers, and Indian bankers and merchants employed by the company.

[295] Marshall (1975b, 43).

[296] See Embree (1962, 62). The Hastings faction, of course, had political strength not only in India but in Britain. See Philips (1961, 23–24).

involvement forces was not unambiguous. The two factions, for example, argued, to be sure, about the annexation of Oudh which was inland, and which was finally annexed by Wellesley in 1801. But the anti-involvement forces had economic designs no less clear than those who wished to annex. As Marshall puts it:

> Free trade is a game which requires more than one player. If Europeans were to give up their political influence to support their trade, they felt that the Wazir [of Oudh] must be persuaded to remedy the conditions which, in their view, made the use of political influence necessary.[297]

Ultimately, there was a give and take relationship between the Company and the traders. The latter needed to fall back often on the "protection of nationality," as well as on the credit rating afforded by the fact of the Company's presence. Conversely, however, they utilized the Company's commercial infrastructure. They paid duties; they stimulated trade. "The benefit received from such 'invisibles' as discounts on remitted estates, payments for permissions, stated damages, freights and fines on prohibited goods, would all have helped to nullify the occasional outrage." All this added up to a "difficult" and "ambivalent" relationship.[298] Thus, these private trade interests could get away with overcommitting first the Company and then the British government.

Still, one has to wonder why, at certain crucial points, the brakes were not more sternly applied. I think we have to take this question at two points in time, from 1757 to 1793, and from 1793 on. The fact is that the political acquisition of Bengal turned out to be quite profitable in the immediate period under discussion. The bullion outflows from Britain ceased, and since the cotton piece goods and other items were still arriving in Britain, it is clear that something was paying for them. The state revenues must have been this something. Indeed, as we know, Bengal silver began to flow out to the other Presidencies and finance their conquest and administration as well.[299] Since this was occurring at a moment of great financial strain for the British state (as for the French) in the aftermath of the American Revolution, the inward flow of revenues from the Indian subcontinent could not have been unwelcome or unnoticed. Cain and Hopkins summarize this situation quite well: "Plassey plunder did not start the Industrial Revolution, but it did help Britain to buy back the National Debt from the Dutch."[300] In short, there was a short-run justification for direct colo-

---

[297] Marshall (1975a, 470).

[298] Watson (1980a, 179, 189). Watson further points out that an English "national interest was always present" in the commerce of the East India Company from the beginning. "The great public involvement in the East India Company after 1708 reflected the strength of this belief in England" (p. 361).

[299] See Bagchi (1976c, 248), Ganguli (1965), and Arasaratnam (1979, 27). N. K. Sinha says: "The stock of silver in Bengal in 1757 was not only not replenished but much of it was drained away in various ways" (1956, 14).

[300] Cain & Hopkins (1980, 471).

nization which tended to outweigh the middle-run negatives which might otherwise have governed the policy-making in London.

The rivalry with France was crucial. In part, no doubt, this was rivalry in the direct manner one usually suggests, that is, a competition for control of a new peripheral zone of the world-economy; though here one should exmpasize this was more true for Britain than for France in view of their differing geopolitical strategies in the world-economy, especially after 1763.[301] But in greater part, probably, it was crucial indirectly in that it enabled Britain to resolve the state financial crisis of the 1780s which France was precisely unable to surmount, a fact we have already discussed in terms of its link with the French Revolution. As we have seen, the ultimate outcome of the third round of Anglo–French rivalry led to the final consecration of the British economic lead.

The dilemma posed to both the Court of Directors and the British government was therefore clear. Unhappy as they may have been about the creeping political dominion into which they were being led, they were constrained from applying the brakes. They came to feel that the British government had really only one choice, which was to take over the operation more directly. This was the Pitt solution, which eventually was imposed. As Harlow puts it, the Company's employees, having gotten out of hand, represented "a menace to the Company" and had therefore to be "transformed into quasi-civil servants."[302] Like it or not, and the Court of Directors did not like it, the Court of Directors could not really do this alone. The British state had to become involved. Lord Stormont stated the objective clearly at the time: "a strong government in India, subject to the check and control of a still stronger government at home."[303] And this they got. With Pitt's India Act in 1784[304] and the reforms of Lord Cornwallis in the decade following it, the Company's servants disappeared from the picture as independent actors.[305]

[301] Lüthy catches this difference in describing the relationship of the Compagnie des Indes to the French government: "For French politics India represented merely a diversion, easily given up when it did not succeed or became too costly. . . . To be sure, from the War of the Austrian Succession to the Napoleonic wars, when the game had long since been lost for France, each new conflict saw French agents, officers, and *condottieri* conclude alliances with Indian princes, and revive the wars in India. It was precisely this constantly renewed menace which made English conquest irreversible by keeping the English from ever letting go, even when they had a wish to do so. . . . For England, it was the engagements on the continent of Europe which were the diversion" (1960, 860–861). See also Mukherjee (1955, 85).

[302] Harlow (1964, 18). See Bolton: "The nabobs of the East India Company proved as great an embarassment to successive British governments as the Anglo–Irish and American colonists. Seeking British connivance at their ascendancy in an overseas community, they could be curbed only by extension of Whitehall's powers which they fought every step of the way" (1966, 196).

[303] Cited in Harlow (1940, 142).

[304] In his speech on the India Act, Pitt was most explicit about his objectives: "The first and principal object would be to take care to prevent the Government from being ambitious and bent on conquest. . . . Commerce was our objective, and with a new to its extension, a pacific system should prevail, and a system of defence and conciliation." Therefore, the Board of Control should supervise the Court of Directors. "The days of buccaneering in India insofar as legislation could decide, are over" (cited in Nightingale, 1970, 8).

[305] See Sinha (1956, 219).

Of course, as the wise and prudent had anticipated, the costs of government, direct and indirect, turned out to be greater than anticipated. The "balance of payments" issue returned, and a renewed silver outflow began. Furthermore, there was the continuing silver outflow to the other great trade zone in the East, China. To solve this problem, Britain could now turn its emerging political dominion to good use. The situation at the end of the eighteenth century is summarized thus by Spear:

> The Company's trade in India was no longer profitable, for its profits, instead of being augmented by the revenues of Bengal, were in fact absorbed by the costs of administration. Its profits came from China. . . . . A cogent economic argument for the hegemony of India was the preservation of the China trade.[306]

Because it controlled India, it could create the export crops which would find a market in China, where it could not yet force a restructuring of production processes.

The compromise involved in the modality of renewing the Company's charter in 1793 served these interests well. The British government increased its control over the Company. The Company, however, retained its monopoly over the China trade and some monopolies in India. But the private traders got new statutory claims on a certain amount of shipping. This compromise combined stability as Britain was entering the long wars with France,[307] a stability from which the private traders themselves would benefit,[308] with assurances that the China trade would be pursued aggressively by the Company. Meanwhile, 1793 was also the year of the Permanent Settlement of Cornwallis, the culmination of a process of legal and administrative reform that had the effect of removing barriers to considering land to be "a commodity to be bought and sold in a market."[309]

With the ending of the Napoleonic Wars approaching in 1813, the British government could go further in asserting direct control when the Company again came up for Charter revewal. In the meantime, the private

---

[306] Spear (1965, 113). Spear adds two other motives for pursuing dominion: "the hope of more to come," and vested interests. As Chung puts it, "tea provided the Indian interests with a good instrument for converting British money in India into British money at home" (1974, 416).

[307] Tripathi calls this "the only possible [attitude] in 1793," that is, "on the brink of the largest of wars that Britain had ever waged." He adds: "A new system might well have jeopardized the existence of the Company for as yet a chimerical advantage" (1956, 32–33).

[308] See Philips: "The outbreak of war with France in 1793 created an upheaval in the world of commerce. . . . In the Eastern seas French privateers, operating from the islands of Bourbon and Mau-

ritius, captured the greater number of India-built private ships, particularly between 1803 and 1809, and there can be no doubt that, had the Indian trade been open to British private traders in 1793, they would have suffered heavy losses" (1961, 99). The Company's trade was safeguarded by convoys.

[309] Cohn (1961, 621). On the provisions of the Settlement, see Wright (1954, 212), who cites the Minutes: "in order to simplify the demand of the landholder upon the ryots or cultivators of the soil, we must begin by fixing the demand of Government upon the former." Gupta says that the most important objective, aside from assuring revenue, was "to promote the extension of cultivation to the vast stretches of waste land and thereby to promote the trade of the province" (1963, 72).

traders had successfully expanded their trade and were chafing at the constraints as well as at the losses on remittances made via the Company. The Lancashire manufacturers now also entered the fray, anxious to expand their own markets in India. Hence, the new Charter ended all monopoly in India but extended the China monopoly of the Company for 20 years. The Charter also provided for the total separation of territorial and commercial accounts, thereby preparing the way for a proper fully colonial administration.[310] "By the year 1837 the British were no longer simply *a* power in India. They were *the* power over India."[311]

The incorporation of Russia was quite another story still. Whether Russia was a part of Europe (and, therefore, of the European interstate system) in the sixteenth and seventeenth centuries was and is a matter of scholarly (and popular) doubt. Whether Russia is part of "Europe" remains a question for some even in the twentieth century, but there can be no doubt that the U.S.S.R. is today a full participant in the (now worldwide) interstate system. It shall be my contention that Russia only became a fully integrated member of the (then European) interstate system in the eighteenth century.

As Dehio reminds us, on the one hand, "the Russians, unlike the Turks, were distant cousins of the Western peoples both ethnically and in mentality," yet on the other hand, "the young Leibniz still spoke of Russia, Persia, and Abyssinia in the same breath."[312] In any case, if one use the criterion of the existence of reciprocal diplomacy, it is only with the reign of Peter the Great (1689–1725) that we find its beginnings.[313] This was coordinate with the significant expansion of foreign trade and "the gradual elimination of Russia's political and cultural isolation from the rest of Europe."[314]

Peter presented himself as the great "Westernizer" or, in today's language, as the great "modernizer," and many, in Russia and elsewhere, then

[310] See Tripathi (1956, 132–136). This was reinforced, of course, by what Nightingale calls the "imperialism of the private trader" (1970, 127). As for the interests of the manufactures, see Nightingale (1970, 236–237).

[311] Frykenberg (1965, 24).

[312] Dehio (1962, 94–95; see also 93–107, passim).

[313] See Sumner (1949, 59) and Anderson (1978, 77–78).

[314] Kahan (1974a, 222). Kahan argues that "one of the most outstanding factors in the expansion of foreign trade [was] the need to support the active foreign policy of Peter the Great that resulted in almost uninterrupted warfare, including the Northern War with Sweden and the wars with the Ottoman Empire and Persia" (p. 223). Thus Kahan implies a sequence: war needs lead to increased taxes lead to increased cash cropping. But where did these "war needs" come from? Surely the Northern War involved some Swedish concern to see that Peter's attempts to integrate into the world-economy would not be at Sweden's long-term expense. See Wallerstein (1980, 218–222). And the wars with the Ottoman Empire and Persia were aimed at ensuring a stronger role for Russia in this world-economy. Kahan indicates (see pp. 224–225) one of the constraints on this attempt. Russian merchants were unable to compete for credit with west European merchants in the carrying trade between them. The latter had easier access to capital markets, lower insurance and shipping rates, etc. However, in the trade with the Ottoman Empire, Persia, and China, Russian merchants flourished. Russia is emerging in a typically semiperipheral position. See Foust (1961).

and now, accept this description. This is the same role, *mutatis mutandis*, claimed for Mohamed Ali of Egypt or, with less éclat, for Sultan Mahmud II. Peter undoubtedly launched the process of creating a centralized bureaucracy with the creation of the Ruling Senate in 1711–1722.[315] He also transformed the army by making the nobleman's service in it both compulsory and permanent.[316] And it is generally agreed that it was the performance of this modernized army that established "Russia's status as an important part of the European political system."[317]

Still, recent scholarship has been more skeptical of how much Peter the Great achieved, as distinguished from what he hoped or claimed to achieve. Cracraft argues that the Petrine myth may perhaps be "of greater historical significance than any achievements of the Petrine regime."[318] And Torke calls the administrative changes Peter effected "greatly over-rated" and asserts that he accomplished "almost nothing" in this regard. The true "turning-point," he says, was 1762, that is, the accession of Catherine II to the throne.[319]

Peter's work was in some sense transitional work. He put the nobility into the army on a regular basis and put the army into the administration as well. He thereby curbed the decentralizing tendencies by absorbing the time of the nobility and using them to force each other into ensuring better internal flows of surplus. It was left to Catherine (1762–1796) to end compulsory lifetime military service for the nobility, creating in its place a civilian apparatus, which in addition had the virtue of allowing the nobility the time to become the cash-crop entrepreneurs. Catherine abolished the old provinces and divided Russia into some 50 *guberniyas* (subdivided into *uezds*), each of which had collegial administrative structures composed partly of centrally appointed officials and partly of locally elected representatives.[320] She thus transformed Russia's government fundamentally,

[315] See Yaney (1973, 7) who spells out the subsequent steps under Catherine II and then in the nineteenth century.

[316] See Raeff (1966, 38–47). This step is credited with changing more than the army. Raeff argues: "Service in the modernized rational and bureaucratic establishment indoctrinated the nobleman with the idea that a clear chain of command, hierarchical subordination, and absolute obedience were the essence of good administration" (p. 49). See also Yaney: "In the army Russian gentry could work with Russian peasants within the framework of a *systematic* organization" (1973, 61).

Portal draws the most important implication of this experience: "[The Noble] brought to the administration of the demesne these military and police ideas. It was a policy of guardianship that he imposed on the peasantry, deforming relatively free institutions of which the theoretical symbol is

the *mir*. The chosen leaders of this community became the agents of the seignior" (1963, 10).

[317] Anderson (1978, 6). Seton-Watson puts it even more strongly: "But that the Russian empire [a title Peter invented] was now one of the Great Powers of Europe there can be no doubt" (1967, 10); see also Fedorov (1979, 137).

[318] Cracraft (1980, 544).

[319] Torke (1971, 457–458). Keep (1972) criticizes the views of Torke, who responds (1972). The majority of Soviet scholars argue that it is in the 1760s that "the capitalist system was established" in Russia (Druzhinina, 1975, 219). See also Baron (1972, 717) on the important 1965 document, *Perekhod ot feodolizma k kapitalizmu v Rossii.*

[320] See Yaney (1973, 69). Griffiths insists on the perceptions by Catherine and her advisors that Russia "lagged substantially behind" the advanced nations of western Europe and that by wise legisla-

"from a tribute-collecting hierarchy to a civil administration whose servitors, like those of the army, were aware of general purposes. . . ."[321] In 1766, Catherine signed the Anglo–Russian Commercial Treaty providing low duties on the exports of raw materials, which served Britain well.[322] It is in this context that we should evaluate Catherine's somewhat aggressive military policy, triumphing over the Ottoman Empire, participating in the partition of Poland, and giving an "overwhelming impression . . . of Russian dynamism."[323] But it was as though this external policy were to compensate the external trade policy and allow Catherine the possibility to take up in earnest, through her administrative reforms, "the organization of [Russia's] internal space."[324]

This internal reorganization meant, of course, among other things, an increasingly effective oppression of the work force, as we have seen.[325] And this repression led both to a "massive flight" of the Russian peasantry eastward across the Volga, to the Urals and even Siberia[326] and to popular rebellions linked to "deterioriating . . . economic conditions."[327] As the involvement in the world-economy grew, this "development" impinged increasingly on the once remote and free Cossack frontiersmen.[328] Their complaints, linked to those of the new industrial serfs and those of the intensified serfdom on cash-crop estates (which we have already explained) plus the opposition of the Old Believers,[329] created an explosive mix which reached its apogee in Pugachev's revolt, precisely in Catherine's days. The underlying ideological theme was that of peasant memories, "hark[ing] back to times when their forefathers were free men,"[330] or at least freer men than under the conditions of incorporation into a capitalist world-economy.

Catherine nevertheless held strong. She suppressed the peasants and maintained free trade. This policy had sufficiently negative effects to induce her successors to take the advice of "frankly protectionist" advisors like M.D. Chulkov who pushed for greater reciprocity in Russian–British relations. The onslaught of the Protectionists against "the long-resented British traders" reached a point where Tsar Paul broke relations with Britain in 1800, embargoed British goods, and confiscated British vessels.[331]

But Russia found herself caught up in the constraints of the interstate

---

tion one could bridge the gap and make the backwardness "transitory" (1979, 471).

[321] Yaney (1973, 59).

[322] See Clendenning (1979, 145–148, 156).

[323] Dyck (1980, 455).

[324] This phrase of Garrett Mattingly is applied by Le Donne (1983, 434) to Catherine's policies. To be fair, Catherine did devote "a great deal of energy . . . to encourage national mercantile shipping" (Ahlström, 1983, 156).

[325] Gerschenkron dates this from Peter the Great, whose policies "in a very real sense increased the effectiveness of the system of serfdom" (1970, 91).

[326] Portal (1966, 37).

[327] Longworth (1975b, 68).

[328] See Longworth (1969, 26–27, 88).

[329] See Gerschenkron (1970, 28–29).

[330] Longworth (1979, 269).

[331] Macmillan (1979, 171, 176–177).

system and discovered that her freedom of action was very limited. Already in the 1780s, Russia's attempts to increase her margin of maneuver with Britain by developing commercial links with France foundered on the contrary interests of the two countries vis-à-vis the Ottoman Empire.[332] Russia counted on her expansionist role in the "East"—both politically and economically—to ensure that her incorporation would be as a semiperipheral state and not as a peripheralized zone. And indeed the triumph over the Ottomans in the Treaty of Küçük Kaynarca did signal a "quantum leap forward in Russia's international position."[333] Her ability to achieve this was undoubtedly due to the fact that, in 1783, France and Great Britain were absorbed in their struggles related to the American War of Independence and could do little to implement "their professed opposition to the Russian annexation of the Crimea."[334]

But there was a price to this game. Russia needed the benevolent neutrality of at least one of the western European great powers in the Middle East. Since France in the late eighteenth century supported the Ottomans diplomatically, Russia felt she had to maintain her links with Britain. Thus Paul's gestures in 1800–1801 could not be satisfied, especially given Napoleon's long-term thrust, and Russia was forced back into Britain's camp. Russia was caught between and bound by her attempts to consolidate her domain and influence in southeastern Europe, the Black Sea, and the Caucasus region on the one hand and to carve out a stronger position vis-à-vis western Europe on the other.[335] To do the former, she sacrificed the latter, and thus was incorporated into the capitalist world-economy in ways that guaranteed and promoted the famous "backwardness" of which later authors would write. But Russia still enjoyed a less weak interstate position than other incorporated zones, and this fact would result eventually in her ability to pursue the Russian Revolution.

West Africa was different from all the other three zones in that there was, as of 1750, no world-empire in the area comparable in scope of organization to the Ottoman, Mughal, or Russian Empires. There were instead a number of strong, largely slave-selling states, and a plenitude of small entities which were militarily and politically weak.

We have been arguing that incorporation into the world-economy requires states that are neither too strong nor too weak, but ones that are responsive to the "rules of the game" of the interstate system. It is often asserted that one of the reasons for the political pressures of western European states in these zones was to restore "order" in areas where "anarchy" made pacific trade impossible. We have already indicated we thought this a dubious explanation for the Indian subcontinent, where much of the "order" restored by the British after 1750 served as a remedy

---

[332] See Sirotkin (1970, 71).
[333] Davison (1976, 464).

[334] Fisher (1970, 137).
[335] See Dojnov (1984, 62–63).

for an "anarchy" in the very creation of which the Western intrusion had played a significant role in the previous 100 years. The point is that capitalism needs not "order" but rather what might be called "favorable order." The promotion of "anarchy" often serves to bring down "unfavorable order," that is, order that is capable of resisting incorporation.

In the historiography of West Africa, one familiar theme is the so-called slave–gun cycle. The evidence for the link between the acquisition of firearms and the acquisition of slaves seems in general quite strong. "For the professional slave gatherers the firearms represented important inputs."[336] Richards insists this "high correlation" was already found in the 1658–1730 period, and led then to the "most dramatic changes" in the West African political scene.[337] For it was precisely in that period that the great slave-selling states, such as Dahomey and Asante, took form. No doubt these states thought they were creating insulation from the impact of the world market, as Polanyi argues. But it is also true that "once caught up in the vicious cycle of slave-raiding warfare the dependency could only intensify."[338] From the point of view of the economic forces of the world-economy, however, these growing slave-selling structures were creating "anarchy" in other zones, thereby breaking down "unfavorable order." That is, the source of what Akinjogbin calls the "greatest paradox" of the slave trade.

> At the beginning of the eighteenth century, Aja politics had become chaotic because of the increase of trade. At the end of the century, instability was about to set into the kingdom of Dahomey because the trade was declining.[339]

The now "favorable order" of the slave-selling states depended, however, on too restricted a definition of economic activity. As the central focus of West African involvement in the world-economy shifted from a period primarily of slave-export trade to a period of mixed exports to a still later period of virtually no slave exports—a process we have already described—the rather small pockets of slave-selling states amid a larger, more "anarchic" zone became less useful. What was needed were new states, larger in most cases than the existing states, but states which were once again neither too weak nor too strong.

Thus the British merchants on the Gold Coast sided strongly with the Fanti states which were resisting Asante expansion because they "were convinced that if Asante power could be destroyed, a vast field of commerce would be opened to them."[340] The Islamic thrust of the nineteenth century was, as we have seen, one toward the "large-scale political integration of

[336] Inikori (1977, 351), who points out: "Not only did the Bonny trading area import [in the period 1750–1807] more guns absolutely than other parts of West Africa but also, it imported far more guns for every slave exported" (p. 361).
[337] Richards (1980, 57).
[338] A. Norman Klein (1968, 221).

[339] Akinjogbin (1967, 209).
[340] Fynn (1971, 28). The major accomplishment of the 1831 Treaty of the Asantehene and George MacLean (representing the Committee of Merchants on Cape Coast) was that the Asantehene was required "to pronounce the allied [Fanti] tribes independent of his control" (Metcalfe, 1962, 140).

several small states and petty principalities."[341] And where no state form existed, as in Ibo country, a "partial state formation" in the guise of the Aro Chuku grew up.[342]

Among other things, one can interpret the British drive against the slave trade as a drive to break down the "unfavorable order" of the smaller units in the interests of recreation of larger units. It was, of course, aimed also at weakening the positions of French and other economic competitors.[343] If we cannot yet talk of reciprocal diplomacy in this period, we do see the emergence of more structured political entities who began to guarantee the flows of the emergent cash-crop production for the world-economy.

We have insisted on dating this incorporation process as roughly 1750–1850 (or in the case of West Africa perhaps 1750–1880). Is this the only possible periodization? Obviously not, and the empirical debate is widespread on this issue of dating. Unfortunately, many of the participants do not have a clear model of the process, or at least they have not been using the same model we have been using: external arena–incorporation–peripheral (or semiperipheral) zone. In terms of this model, what we see is that some authors move the dating of incorporation back to the time when a zone becomes part of the external arena. Some authors, on the other hand, will not consider a zone incorporated until it begins functioning as a peripheral zone of the world-economy. Neither of these two sets of authors perceive of "incorporation" as a distinctive process in the way we have been arguing.

A standard way of formulating this debate is to argue about the date at which "capitalism" began. Some authors insist that with the widespread development of long-distance trade in the earlier period of the "external arena," we already have capitalism, or at least protocapitalism. This is often accompanied by an argument about the "indigenous" roots of capitalism, or the "interruption" of this process by European intrusion. Other authors insist that the very earliest "capitalist" period occurs much later. In extreme cases, some argue that it barely exists even today. We have insisted that there are not multiple capitalist states but one capitalist world-system, and that to be part of it one has minimally to be integrated into its production networks or commodity chains, and be located in states that participate in the interstate system which forms the political superstructure of this capitalist world-economy. Incorporation is then defined as precisely the period of such integration.

[341] Oloruntimehin (1971–1972, 34).

[342] Stevenson (1968, 190; cf. Dike, 1956, 38). But Northrup (1978, 141–142) is reserved on such a designation.

[343] "Once the British, who had handled the largest share of the trade in the eighteenth century, decided to give it up, it was in their interest to persuade others to give it up as well" (Ajayi & Oloruntimehin, 1976, 207).

Gorée, which had been France's major trade base in West Africa, was so weakened in the post-1815 period that it could only survive by transforming itself into a free-trade port. See Zuccarelli (1959). In general, the *Exclusif,* though restored with fanfare in 1817, was dismantled by 1868. See Schnapper (1959, 150–151, 198).

4

THE SETTLER DECOLONIZATION OF THE AMERICAS: 1763–1833

The French artist and lithographer, Francisque-Martin-François Grenier de Saint-Martin (1793–1867), student of David, specialized in historical topics. This print, executed in 1821, shows General Toussaint l'Ouverture handing over two letters to the general commanding the English forces that were in Haiti in 1798. The letters indicate the request of the French Commissioners that Toussaint seize the English general and Toussaint's refusal to do so on the grounds that he would not dishonor himself by reneging on his word. "A noble refusal," says Grenier. At the bottom we see Haiti's seal, with the inscription "Liberté Egalité."

In the middle of the eighteenth century, more than half the territory of the Americas was, in juridical terms, composed of colonies of European states, primarily of Great Britain, France, Spain, and Portugal. The remaining territory was outside the interstate system of the capitalist world-economy. By the middle of the nineteenth century, virtually all of these colonies had been transformed into independent sovereign states (after some combinations of and divisions among previous administrative entities). Furthermore, these new states had, by this time, laid claim to jurisdiction over the remaining land area in the hemisphere.

This was a remarkable reshaping of the physiognomy of the interstate system. This "decolonization" of the Americas occurred under the aegis of their European settlers, to the exclusion not only of the Amerindian populations but also of the transplanted Africans, despite the fact that, in many of these newly sovereign states, Amerindians and Blacks constituted a substantial proportion (even a majority) of the population. To be sure, there was one exception, Haiti, and this exception was to play an important historical role, as we shall see. In any case, this decolonization differed strikingly from the second great "decolonization" of the modern world-system, that which occurred in the twentieth century, the difference being precisely in terms of the populations who would control the resulting sovereign states.

The story is conventionally and correctly said to begin in 1763, "a great turning point."[1] The outcome of the Seven Years' War was that Great Britain had effectively ousted France from the Western Hemisphere. And this fact alone would be enough to make it impossible for the Spanish and Portuguese to attempt to take advantage of the renewed expansion of the world-economy and to (re)assert true economic control over their American colonies. But this very triumph of Great Britain acutely posed, for the first time in the Americas, the question of the intra-elite disposition of the rewards. As we know, this dispute would lead the settlers, first those of British North America, then those of Hispanic America and Brazil, to found separate state structures.

The issues facing Great Britain in 1763 are well illustrated in an important diplomatic event. In the discussions leading to the Treaty of Paris, one major question was whether Great Britain would obtain territorial control from the French over Canada or over Guadeloupe. It was accepted from the outset that Britain could not have both, but that Britain had the choice. Those Britons who argued for the retention of Guadeloupe pointed out that the small sugar island was far richer than bleak Canada, and that its acquisition would be both a boon for Britain and a great loss for France. This, of course, was precisely the fear of the sugar planters of the

[1] Andrews (1924, 122).

existing British West Indian territories who saw Guadeloupe sugar as
unwanted competition. Their views ultimately prevailed.[2]

In addition to this strictly economic argument, there was a geopolitical
debate. Proponents of the retention of Guadeloupe pointed out that the
defense of Canada posed a continuing and draining burden on France
whose navy was not strong enough for such imperial warfare. But even
more important than Canada's impact on French strategy was its potential
impact on the attitudes of British settlers in North America. Already, on
May 9, 1761, the Duke of Bedford wrote to the Duke of Newcastle:

> I do not know whether the neighborhood of the French to our Northern Colonies
> was not the greatest security of their dependence on the Mother Country who I
> fear will be slighted by them when their apprehensions of the French are
> removed.[3]

The argument was very prescient. Furthermore, there was a British settler
counterpart to this argument: "[The colonies] seem to wish Canada as
French, it made them of some consequence [to the British]."[4]

If this geopolitical argument for leaving Canada to the French did not
prevail, it was because, in addition to the weight of the West Indian sugar
interests in London, there existed a certain British pride in territorial
conquest and a British insouciance about the settlers, whose "mutual
jealousies" were thought to be a guarantee of continued dependence upon
the mother country. But no doubt the strongest argument was that of state
finances:

> It would save a vast expense to Britain in not being obliged to keep up a great
> number of regular forces which must be maintained if the smallest spot is left with
> the French upon that Continent.[5]

As we have already argued, the ability of the British to keep their state
finances under better control than the French was to be a crucial element in
the last phase of their struggle for hegemony. So perhaps this was as
prescient an argument as the other.

[2] See Nicolas (1967); see also Whitson (1930, 74) and Hacker (1935, 289–290).

[3] Cited in Namier (1930, 320). General Murray in Quebec was voicing the same views at this time: "If we are wise we won't keep [Canada]. New England needs a bit to chomp on and we'll give one to keep her busy by not keeping this country." Cited in Ryerson (1960, 197). Later scholars agreed: "The conquest of Canada severed the chief material bond attaching these colonies to Great Britain, and made their independence a political possibility" (Beer, 1907, 172–173).

A Frenchman, Pierre Kolm, expressed the very same view already in 1749: "Without the French next door, the Americans would quickly break the ties that unite them to England." Cited in Vignols (1928b, 790). By 1758, a senior official in France's Ministry of Marine was actually advocating the end of France's role in Canada in order to achieve this objective. See Eccles (1971, 21, fn. 96). It is well known that Choiseul predicted this as a consequence of the Treaty of Paris.

[4] John Watts to General Monckton on May 16, 1764, cited in Namier (1930, 327).

[5] Letter of the Earl of Morton to the Earl of Hardwicke, January 15, 1760, cited in Namier (1930, 323).

Britain's problem had long been how to create a very strong state, both inside its frontiers and within the interstate system without incurring the negative consequences of too heavy a public finance burden. This problem had been greatly exacerbated by the Seven Years' War.[6] The "bloated Leviathan of government" erected by Walpole on the basis of the "broad consensus" of the Glorious Revolution had already been under attack for being "fat with corruption, complaisant, and power-engrossing."[7] The new *rapport de force* in the world after the Treaty of Paris seemed to offer the British two benefits in this regard: a lowered military expenditure because of the weakening of France and the possibility of shifting part of the tax base outside of the metropole to British settlers in North America.

Seen, however, from the standpoint of these British settlers, the Treaty of Paris had an almost opposite meaning. They were now "freed" from their fears of the French (and the Spaniards) and could therefore devote their energies and resources to the prospect of "a vast growth of power and wealth with . . . westward expansion."[8] Thus, while both the British at home and the settlers in North America "rolled the sweets of victory under their tongues,"[9] they drew from it opposite expectations. The British anticipated a "rationalization" of empire, and therefore sought to "tighten controls." The settlers, on the other hand, were expecting a "loosening of constraints."[10] What seemed merely a sensible objective to the British, the need for "a more highly-keyed . . . imperial organization"[11] to secure their successes, seemed to the settlers to be "a fundamental attack upon the extant moral order within the empire."[12] A clash was inevitable, although secession was not.

A good deal of the historiography of the revolution in British North America is concerned with explaining its roots in prior long-term tendencies—economic, social, and/or ideological—which culminated, say the various historians, in the events of 1765–1776, and which therefore enable us to characterize what the "American Revolution" was really about. Much of what is said is true, but a good deal of it is irrelevant as explanation. All major political events have long-term roots, although these are often easier to discern ex post facto than at the time. But it is seldom the case that these long-term trends could have led only to the particular outcome (even broadly defined) that did in fact occur. It is not that the outcome was logically accidental. It is rather that, as we specify more and more the particular outcome, we need to include more and more specific factors in

---

[6] "The [British] national debt had been doubled by the Seven Years' War and the annual cost of the American establishment had been quintupled" (Brebner, 1966, 44).

[7] Bailyn (1973, 8–9).

[8] Gipson (1950, 102).

[9] Brebner (1966, 32).

[10] Meinig (1986, 295).

[11] Christie & Labaree (1976, 274).

[12] Greene (1973a, 79).

the accounting, and many of these are inevitably conjunctural[13] rather than structural.

The most important general conjunctural change was the renewed expansion of the capitalist world-economy in the eighteenth century, and Britain's ability to win the struggle with France for hegemony. But there were conjunctural trends more specific to the situation in British North America. The general economic conditions of British North America had been improving since 1720, at first gradually, then, after 1745, more rapidly.[14] But expansion, of course, did not mean an even distribution of rewards. On the one hand, it led to a "sudden increase in concentration of wealth"[15] in the colonies, which easily explains the apparent paradox that colonial society became "less coherent and more rigid at the same time."[16] On the other hand, it also led to a sharpened rivalry between private business interests in England and those in the colonies. The role of English capital was increasing to the detriment of even the wealthier merchants and planters of the colonies. The "agents" of British firms were displacing colonial merchants. Over a half century, "profit margins were lessened, and possibilities for local development sacrificed."[17]

The increasing difficulties of colonial merchants in this period brings us to that "hardy perennial,"[18] the question of how much of a burden the

---

[13] In the sense that this term is used by Braudel (1958) and, more generally, by economic historians writing in European languages other than English.

In his classical lectures on the American revolution, Charles M. Andrews (1924, 28) gave what I consider a structural rather than conjunctural explanation of its origins: "Thus the leading features of British history can be summed up in the words 'expansion' and 'centralizing' processes which manifested themselves in ever widening spheres of commerce, colonies, and ocean supremacy. Britain's policy in regard to her plantations was to secure a more closely knit and efficient colonial administration in the interest of the trade of her merchants; whereas the colonials, though they accepted their obligations as loyal subjects of the crown, early began to strive for greater freedom of action than that which they had as colonists in the strictly legal sense of the term."

Nettels, however, insists that before 1763, "the colonists as a whole were not seriously antagonized by British imperium . . . , [but that] after 1763 the story is different" (1952, 113–114). The rewards to the colonists went down, and the exigencies of the British (taxes, enforcement of restraints, etc.) went up significantly.

[14] See Egnal & Ernst (1972, 11). Klingaman finds a 35% increase, for example, in the tobacco colonies between 1740 and 1770 coming from a combination of tobacco and wheat exports (1969, 278). Shepherd and Walton insist that the increased income from shipping and other merchandising

activities is even more important than from "commodity production" (1972, 158). See, however, the dissenting voice of Terry L. Anderson who argues that, in the long growth trend of North America from initial colonization to today, "the one bleak period . . . was the first eighty years of the eighteenth century" (1979, 256).

[15] Lockridge (1973, 416). The other side of concentration of wealth is the growth of poverty. Nash claims there was chronic poverty for 20% of the households in seaport cities at this time, (1976b, 574) and that this led to "a rising tide of class antagonism and political consciousness" (1976a, 18). Alice Hanson Jones, in her study of wealth inequality over the 150 years preceding the Revolution, argues that inequality did increase "but not dramatically" (1980, 269). For still greater skepticism about the significance of wealth inequality, see Brown (1955b) and Warden (1976).

Berthoff and Murrin, on the other hand, suggest an analogy to the contemporaneous "feudal revival" in Europe. "By 1730 the older colonies had become populous enough to make the old feudal claims incredibly lucrative. . . . Old charters . . . were revived only because they had been profitable. In the colonies, as in France, these claims aroused resentment precisely because they divorced the pursuit of profit from any larger sense of community welfare" (1973, 265–267).

[16] Greene (1973b, 10).

[17] Egnal & Ernst (1972, 3).

[18] Egnal (1975, 192).

Navigation Acts constituted for the North American colonists. Hardy perennial it has been to subsequent historians of colonial North America, but was it a hardy perennial to people of the time? Greene asserts that "the extent of colonial compliance" with the mercantilist regulations of Great Britain suggests a "very high degree of accommodation" to the system. This is a plausible argument provided we consider the degree of compliance high. He adds that, given the degree of prosperity, many persons had a "strong vested interest" in maintaining their ties with the British. Again, this is plausible presuming the degree of prosperity remained high.[19] The presumed "burden" of mercantilist regulations has been a matter of continued quantitative debate since figures were first offered by Lawrence Harper and, as in most such debates, it is a question of what to count and how much is too much. Harper's original conclusion was that, even if the mercantile laws were administered in "perfect fairness" by an administration balancing equities, decisions were being made in far-off England and "the colonies were at a disadvantage."[20] Aside from the subsequent acerbic debate on the quality of Harper's data,[21] a good deal of the discussion has centered upon calculations of whether or not it would have made a difference had independence been achieved earlier, the so-called counterfactual premise.

This counterfactual premise literature started with Robert Paul Thomas in 1965 and has continued ever since. Thomas purported to demonstrate that "the largest burden would be slightly more than 1 percent of national income,"[22] and therefore insignificant. Price thought that even Thomas's low figure was overstated since the "meaningful unit of economic life" was the firm and not the transaction, and firms take into account more than sales prices on single transactions. Firms consider something Price called the balance of "overall exchange" (for example, calculating costs of credit) and thus they might have found "sound business reasons" for sticking to the traditional entrepôts even had there been no mercantilist constraints.[23] Price's argument was intended to weaken the Harper argument even more, but in fact it strengthened it by reminding us (and especially the cliometricians) that real economic calculations of profit have to be done in wider space and longer time.[24]

Ransom proceeded to point out that aggregate North American calculations might hide differential regional effects of the Navigation Acts and

[19] Greene (1973a, 47, 50).

[20] Harper (1939, 31). See also the calculations and judicious assessment in Harper (1942). Dickerson's polemic against Harper far overstates the accusation, suggesting that Harper believed that the Navigation Acts "were steadily reducing the Americans to a condition of hopeless poverty" (1951, 55).

[21] "By no stretch of generosity can Harper's measurement techniques be labeled anything but nonsensical" (McClelland, 1973, 679).

[22] Thomas (1965, 638).

[23] Price (1965, 659).

[24] In his critique of Thomas, McClelland says correctly (1969, 376): "As long as [the counterfactual hypothesis] remains confined to thirteen years [1763–1775], the possibility of dynamic influences seriously magnifying the . . . percentage [of colonial gross national product sacrificed because of British interference with overseas trade] seems quite remote."

that the Southern states' exports were particularly negatively affected.[25] Thomas agreed in reply, and admitted such arguments might justify an "economic interpretation" of the origins of the American Revolution since such disparities might lead to the creation of a "passionate minority" who would champion such a political outcome. He even noted that many of the events of the time, such as protests about the Currency Act and the Stamp Act, lend credence to such an interpretation.[26] And this then is perhaps the point. As Broeze remarked in his commentary on this debate, while the New Economic History may contribute to the calculation of real economic growth (and Broeze himself is not at all hostile to such undertakings), it cannot tell us anything about a "subjective notion" such as the "burden" people feel. The historian's perceptions about the actors' feelings "can only be gathered and understood from their writings and actions."[27] The subject of the real cost of the Navigation Acts may have become "a great bore,"[28] but the subject of collective motivations remains central.

We thus come to the economic conjuncture of the 1760s and how it was perceived in the Americas. The end of the Seven Years' War brought on a postwar slump[29] which followed the "unprecedented prosperity"[30] of the Seven Years' War and negatively affected almost all the sectors of the North American economy—merchants, planters, small farmers, and laborers.

Schlesinger, in his classic disquisition on the North American merchants, starts from the premise that the century preceding the Treaty of Paris had been their "Golden Age."[31] When, therefore, the normal postwar downturn and readjustments were "substantially prolonged" by the attempts of the British to reorganize the empire and "bring the colonials into a more subordinate status,"[32] this gave the merchant classes "food for sober reflection."[33] It was the merchants more than anyone else who were surprised and aggrieved by the "new rules to the game after 1763."[34] In

---

[25] He argues that exports of Southern planters might have been "67 percent higher without the restrictions," and the South's overall income 2.5% higher, "not an inconsequential amount" (Ransom, 1968, 433–434). Remember, that for Thomas, 1% was considered without significance.

[26] Thomas (1968a, 438).

[27] Broeze (1973, 678).

[28] Krooss (1969, 385).

[29] Actually, Bridenbaugh dates it as of 1760, the "peak" year for the merchant classes of the colonial towns (1955, 282). See also Rothenberg on price indexes for British North America (1979, 981).

[30] Hacker (1935, 293), who points out that "the expanding market in the West Indies, the great expenditures of the British quartermasters, the illegal and contraband trade with the enemy forces,

all had furnished steady employment for workers and lucrative outlets for the produce of small farmers." The end of the war led to unemployment, bankruptcy of small tradesmen, and a diminished market for small farmers. "Into the bargain, escape into the frontier zones—always the last refuge of this dispossessed—was shut off" (pp. 293–294).

[31] Schlesinger (1917, 15).

[32] Bridenbaugh (1955, 251).

[33] Schlesinger (1917, 91).

[34] Walton & Shepherd (1979, 175). Somehow these authors feel that this demonstrates that the issues were not economic but threats to an "already established freedom" (p. 153), but the rhetoric of freedom is often confounded with the realities of the pocketbook.

self-protection, they moved to seek relief by nonimportation of British goods.[35]

At the same time, southern planters came into problems because of their chronic indebtedness to Scots factors. In 1762 there was a collapse of credit which shook the planters of Maryland and Virginia.[36] The colonial governments had been financing their current expenditures by a system called "currency finance," which involved issuing notes in anticipation of future tax returns.[37] The expansion of this process led to British merchant concern with the security of debts and the passage of the Currency Act of 1764 which offered the compromise that paper currency would continue as legal tender for public but no longer for private debts. The main losers here were the colonial planters who thereupon "turned to politics."[38] The 1762 crisis was followed by the worse one of 1772. In the context of general metropole–settler strained relations, the "psychological effects" of the Currency Act were very important, serving as a "constant reminder"[39] of colonial dependency on the economic priorities of the imperial government to the detriment of the colonists.

The general situation exacerbated relations between small farmers and the elite planters. At the very time the larger planters were challenging the British government in one way or another, small farmers were undertaking rural action whose effect was "to challenge and undermine the authority of provincial institutions"[40] controlled by the local elites. As small farmers became involved in the political agitation, in some localities they radicalized "patriot" activities,[41] but in some localities they turned against the patriot activities.[42] It was clear that the small farmers were at least as concerned with their struggles against the planters as they were with a struggle against the British.

[35] This, argue Egnal and Ernst, was "only incidentally designed to compel Parliament to repeal obnoxious legislation" (1972, 17). Perhaps, but fixating on a political claim would at least give a concrete realizable goal for their agitation.

[36] See Egnal & Ernst (1972, 28).

[37] See Ernst (1973a, 22); see also Ferguson (1953).

[38] Ernst (1973a, 360). Ernst speaks of a "quantum leap in American debt" (p. 356), but Walton and Shepherd (1979, 108) say that debt was "not widespread on the eve of the Revolution." Andrews agrees the problem was not serious before 1770, at which point, however, an "orgy" of buying in the colonies and selling in England increased indebtedness by some 3 million pounds and "ushered in a short period of extravagance and inflation. The fall was rapid" (1924, 109). This then led to the severe balance of payments crisis of 1772 and a period of severe "credit stringency" which was explosive (Sheridan, 1960, 186).

[39] Greene & Jellison (1961, 518). Ernst (1976) argues that the 1772 crisis marks the shift from the protest movement being reformist to it being an independence movement.

[40] Countryman (1976a, 57). Barker says of the struggle against the proprietary system of Maryland that it was "the schooling for the Revolution" (1940, 375).

[41] "The Revolution was no longer [the] exclusive property [of the city intellectuals and merchants who had earned the title of radicals], if ever it had been. And because it was not, it was all the more a revolution" (Countryman, 1976a, 61).

[42] See the ambivalent role of the Regulators in the western parts of North Carolina (Greene, 1943; Kay, 1976) and of the other "reluctant revolutionaries" (Hoffman, 1976). On the other hand, Schlebecker argues that the support of small farmers for the Revolution was demonstrated by the necessity for the British during the Revolutionary War to send food and fodder to their armies (1976, 21).

Finally, the urban poor were not quiescent. In the post-1763 period, "inequality rapidly advanced"[43] in the urban centers, and especially in Boston, the "major town least enjoying prosperity" from 1765 to 1775. Thus it was no accident that Boston was "the most radical town" during these years.[44] For Nash, it was out of these grievances that came "much of the social force that saw in Revolution the possibility of creating a new social order."[45]

For Great Britain, however, 1763 marked a turning point more significant than a mere postwar slump. It marked the end of Phase II of the Franco–British struggle for hegemony. Nonetheless, this struggle, while won in principle by Great Britain in 1763, would require one last immense spasm going from 1763 to 1815 before the issue would no longer be contested by France. We have sought above to place this final British triumph in the context of the renewed economic expansion of the capitalist world-economy (the A-phase of a logistic) which we have dated as going approximately from the 1730s to (conventionally) 1817.

Hegemony, as we have already seen from the Dutch example in the seventeenth century (Vol. II, Chapter 2), is a state in which the leading power fears no economic competition from other core states. It, therefore, tends to favor maximal openness of the world-economy. This policy is one which some historians have called informal empire (that is, noncolonial and eventually even anti-colonial imperialism). In the specific situation of British imperial institutions this is the structural basis of what Vincent Harlow has termed the founding of the "second" British empire. Harlow notes that, following the Treaty of Paris in 1763, Britain undertook a "sustained outburst of maritime exploration" whose only prior parallel was in the Tudor days. The object was to create a "network of commercial exchange" throughout the Pacific and Indian oceans, based on a chain of trading ports and naval bases, but *not* on colonies. The exception to this pattern was to be India, and we have already discussed why India was an exception.

Where did the "old" colonies, those of the "first" British empire, fit in this schema? These "old" colonies were primarily in the Americas. As Harlow notes, in the course of the late eighteenth century, as the quarrel with the American colonists became acute, "radical economists in England preached the startling doctrine that political separation was a consummation to be wished."[46] But was such a view really widespread among policy makers? We have little evidence that this is so, particularly at the beginning of the

[43] Kulikoff (1971, 409). See also Nash (1979, 253) who says that in Boston, New York, and Philadelphia, the economic distress that commenced in 1763 led to the "rapid growth of a class of truly impoverished persons" among the laboring classes.
[44] Price (1976, 708–709).

[45] Nash (1984, 250). Price is more skeptical. "Whether the dependent poor . . . had much to do with revolutionary activity is [a] question" (1976, 709).
[46] Harlow (1952, 3–5).

process. Perhaps a thin case could be made that such a view underlay Edmund Burke's arguments concerning the American revolution.[47] But, in general, politicians are rarely bold and farsighted innovators. Nor are most capitalists. Investors at the time showed few signs of being "aware of a need to choose" between an Oriental trade empire and a Western hemispheric colonial system. Rather, they invested "wherever a profit seemed likely."[48]

Foresight is not, however, the issue. Structural changes will, of their own accord, slowly but decisively change attitudes and policies. The cause of the restiveness of the American settlers was no doubt complex. But the British government, when it responded, found itself in a situation where the growth of its power in the world-economy forced it to take into account a wider set of interests than previously. This posed dilemmas, and in this case, as Peter Marshall notes, "dilemmas were antecedent to disasters,"[49] or at least what seemed at first to be disasters.

The first dilemma was that of finding political solutions that could reconcile the demands which distant White settler populations would now begin to put forward with what was required for maintaining internal political balances at home. We previously discussed the political importance of the Glorious Revolution of 1688–1689 as the basis of a consensus among the powerful forces in England, and after the Act of Union in 1707, of Great Britain.[50] The institutional key to the compromise was the constitutional supremacy of parliament with a circumscribed role for the monarch, one that has become ever more circumscribed in the centuries that have gone by. Any demand by White settlers for legitimating the decentralization of legislative power not only threatened the central control of the British state over the colonies but also threatened the internal constitutional compromise in Great Britain, a compromise that had already been taxed "by the addition of Scotland in 1707 and the corruption of parliament under Walpole and George III."[51] Asking the king to exercise any

[47] Felix Cohen, in a 1949 British colonial commission report, posed the question this way: "Why is it that force of reaction in domestic politics (Edmund Burke and W. R. Hearst, to take two notable examples) often throw their support to independence movements of subject peoples? The answer to both questions is to be found, I think, in a recognition of the fact that economic imperialism is not necessarily dependent upon, and is sometimes even hindered by, political imperialism. Where such hindrances arise it will be to the interest of the economic imperialists to eliminate the political phase of colonialism" (1949, 103). On the other hand, Namier's observation (1930, 45) is at least worth considering. "Had Burke been in office during the American Revolution, we might merely have had to antedate his counter-revolutionary Toryism by some twenty years."

[48] Marshall (1964a, 21).
[49] Marshall (1964b, 145).
[50] See Wallerstein (1980, chaps. 3, 6). Greene (1968a, 168) speaks of the "remarkable agreement upon fundamentals" of eighteenth-century British political culture, based on the sanctity of the Settlement of 1688–1714. This was all the more true since the Seven Years' War had just accomplished the final end of Jacobitism. "By 1760 the *Scots Magazine* was calculating that one in four Scots of military age were serving with the British army and navy: many of these recruits stayed on in England after the war, often acquiring English wives before returning home"(Colley, 1986, 100).
[51] Innis (1943, 321).

powers outside of the British parliament seemed, in Namier's phase, "a dangerous and unconstitutional reversion to 'prerogative' "[52]—the monarch's prerogative.

It was still too early for Britain to think of, much less adopt, the Commonwealth solution of the nineteenth and twentieth centuries, precisely because the British monarch was still too strong internally in Britain. And to the extent that Britain was now entering into an "age of interests" in which parliament was expected to respond, in the exercise of its power, to multiple pressure groups, the settlers in British North America were less powerful than many rival interests. "North America's political influence in no way equalled its economic importance."[53]

Seen from the angle of British settlers in North America, this was precisely the problem. One of the very first things the British government did after 1763 was to implement a treaty obligation it had incurred in 1758 vis-à-vis the Ohio Valley Indians. The treaty provided that if the Indians deserted the French they would be "secure in their lands."[54] On October 7, 1763, the British issued a proclamation decreeing that the Ohio Valley was to be maintained as an Indian preserve and therefore to be closed to settlers. But the immense growth of the settler population in the preceding two decades had been premised on "cheap land [being] readily available."[55] The creation of the "proclamation line" seemed to close that door.

Why did the British create the proclamation line? Yes, they had signed a treaty with the Indians, but this was scarcely enough in itself to explain the act. The British victory over the French seemed to open the "Northwest" to two groups eager to exploit the area: most immediately, New England fur trappers previously excluded by the French, and behind them, potential settlers and land speculators. The immediate "harshness"[56] of the new trappers to the Indians and the Indians' general fears concerning the Treaty of Paris[57] led to a major uprising, the Conspiracy of Pontiac, which involved a militarily significant organization of various Indian groups. The rising was crushed by a "war of complete extermination,"[58] but the British drew a quick lesson therefrom.

---

[52] Namier (1930, 42).

[53] Kammen (1970, 95, 113). "Contemporaries regarded the West India holdings, not the continental ones, as the jewels of empire" (Ragatz, 1935, 8). See also Palmer (1959, 173): "It must be admitted that the British government had many interests to consider, which the Americans dismissed as foreign"—such as West Indian sugar planters, French Canadians, American Indians, and the East India Company, not to speak of the British taxpayer.

As Bolton adds, similar demands for privileges without taxation were being made everywhere in the empire at this time. "Seen in this context, the American Revolution represents merely the least successful attempt to reconcile these issues" (1966, 200).

[54] Gipson (1950, 94).

[55] Meinig (1986, 289).

[56] Chaunu (1964, 170).

[57] "The news that the trans-Appalachian west had been ceded stunned the Indians" (Jennings, 1976, 334).

[58] Rich (1960, II, 4), who says that General Amherst, the British commander-in-chief "was thinking . . . even of spreading smallpox among the disaffected tribes, and was treating the Indians more as brutes than as human beings."

The Royal Proclamation divided up New France. It constituted in the north a new government called Quebec (but attached Labrador and Anticosti to Newfoundland). However, it made all the zones west of the Alleghenies into reserves under the protection of an Indian Service.[59] British merchants rapidly took over the role of the French in Montreal, developing within ten years "an organization which had features strikingly similar to those of the French regime."[60] Indeed, as British practice evolved, the fur trade became, in effect, "a subsidized industry"[61] because the Indians now received supplies from two sources: purchase from the traders paid for by furs and free presents of identical items offered by the British government.

- Thus, the Proclamation underlined a "far-reaching divergence of interest" between the British and their settlers in North America. The British were attempting "to call a halt to the westward expansion of her colonies" and to utilize trans-Appalachia as a source of extraction via peaceful trade with secure indigenous populations, a policy dictated both by "commercial reasons [and] considerations of economy."[62]

At the same time, the British moved to make the settlers begin to pay for the costs of empire and to enforce vigorously the mercantilist commercial regulations. This led to a decade of controversy in which colonial opposition brought about repeated de facto backdowns by the British government—for example, imposition then repeal of the Stamp Act, imposition then repeal of the Townshend duties—always followed by new British attempts to pursue the same policies. In the process, both sides became more "principled" or more ideological. In 1766, when Parliament repealed the Stamp Act, they simultaneously passed the Declaratory Act affirming the abstract right to tax the colonies. Over a 10-year period, colonists who objected to particular acts became transformed into persons denying the British parliament this abstract right—"no taxation without representation."

It was a kind of acceleration of conflict, or raising of the decibels. "The decade of controversy had failed to resolve a single basic issue."[63] But the issues themselves do not seem, in retrospect, all that intractable, nor were they all that new. Knollenberg argues they date from 1759,[64] and Greene

[59] See Ryerson (1960, 201); see also Chaunu (1964, 171), who argues that the British "adopted a policy of safeguarding the Indians, thereby dilapidating the immense capital of sympathy they had acquired in the West" through the Seven Years' War.

[60] Innis (1956, 176). That is, the mercantile houses in Montreal linked London houses with smaller merchants in western towns like Michilimackinac and Detroit, who in turn dealt with small mobile traders who traveled with the Indians, what the French had called *coureurs de bois*. The British

continued to use French traders, although now various English, Scots, and Irish persons also entered the circuit. This group were essentially engaged in a credit operation to the Indians who repaid with returns from the hunts. See Stevens (1926, 122–124, 145).

[61] Stevens (1926, 161).

[62] Harlow (1952, 179, 184).

[63] Smith (1964, 6).

[64] Knollenberg (1960, 1) speaks of the reaction to the Stamp Act as the "colonial uprising of 1765–1766," to whose brink the colonists had been

from 1748.[65] There seems little reason to doubt that, in the absence of the acute economic downturn, the whole controversy might have been reduced to a momentary tempest.[66]

There is another point of view, of which Bernard Bailyn has become the prime expositor, that the fundamental concerns of the colonists were not economic but "ideological," which Bailyn defines as a struggle between power and liberty.[67] In this vision,

> Unconstitutional taxing, the invasion of placemen, the weakening of the judiciary, plural officeholding, Wilkes, standing armies—these were major evidences of a deliberate assault of power upon liberty.[68]

And it was the Tea Act, he says, which was the turning point for the colonists whose anger cannot be "lightly dismissed as mere window dressing for the more fundamental economic questions."[69]

But Bailyn undermines his own case for the primacy of ideological motivations when he turns to fight on another front. Against those who would contend that the importance of the American Revolution was that it was socially revolutionary, a struggle that achieved the overthrow of an "ancien régime," Bailyn wishes to insist that de facto the great revolutionary objective of "equality of status before the law" had long since been won in practice in British North America. In practice, he argues, but not, he admits, in theory. "Many felt the changes . . . represented deviance; that they lacked, in a word, legitimacy." This represented a "divergence between habits of mind and belief on the one hand," which habits he says remained "aristocratic" in the sense that the colonists "conceded to the classes of the well-born and rich the right to exercise public office," and "experience and behavior on the other." This divergence ended with the Revolution; "this lifting into consciousness and endowment with high

brought by a number of "provocative British measures" between 1759 and 1764: disallowances by the Privy Council in 1759 of the Virginia Act, general writs of assistance to the customs service in 1761, prohibition in 1761 of governors issuing commissions not revocable by the King, and the attempts of Church of England officials to strengthen their position.

[65] The decision by colonial authorities in Britain "to abandon Walpole's policy of accommodation and to attempt to bring the colonies under much more rigid controls . . . was taken, not abruptly in 1763 . . . but gradually in the decade beginning in 1748" (Greene, 1973a, 65). Thus, for Greene, what Knollenberg sees as new measures were "merely a renewal and an extension of the earlier reform program" (p. 74).

[66] What Barker says of Maryland seems to me to be true more widely: "Without persistent depression in the tobacco trade, neither political discontent nor intercolonial connection would have been so prominent. Constitutional struggle could not have grown from English tradition alone, nor from legal-mindedness; its great dynamic was economic need" (1940, 376).

[67] It is not I, but Bailyn, who anthropomorphizes the issue: "What gave transcendent importance to the aggressiveness of power was the fact that its natural prey, its necessary victim, was liberty, or law, or right" (1967, 57).

[68] Bailyn (1967, 117).

[69] A statement of Merrill Jensen in 1963 cited approvingly by Bailyn (1967, 118, fn. 26).

moral purpose [of] inchoate, confused elements of social and political change . . . was the American Revolution."[70]

But Bailyn cannot have it both ways. If the motivations that impelled the colonists were more than anything else, ideological, they cannot have been largely unconscious of them; they cannot have been driven merely by "inchoate confused elements of social and political change."[71] First of all, as Arthur Schlesinger says, the view that the Revolution was "a great forensic controversy over abstract governmental rights will not bear close scrutiny," and that for the very simple reason that the ideological case was never put forward consistently:

> At best, an exposition of the political themes of the anti-Parliamentary party is an account of their retreat from one strategic position to another. Abandoning a view that based their liberties on charter rights, they appealed to their constitutional rights as Englishmen; and when that position became untenable, they invoked the doctrine of the rights of man.[72]

Of course, the colonists were ideologically jumping from claim to claim. In the middle of serious political strife, we all tend to use whatever arguments are at hand, and sometimes, no doubt, we come to believe passionately in their validity. Later we like to think that we always felt the way we ended up feeling, but it is dubious practice for the analyst to do more than acknowledge the *a posteriori* utility of ideological positions. The fact is that the colonists were not rebellious as long as they continued to experience "the tangible benefits of empire," but when "the conclusion of the Seven Years' War radically altered the situation,"[73] their political and, hence, their ideological stance evolved.

Still, why weren't they more "patient"? Christie and Labaree argue that their worries about "the establishment of imperial precedents seems to reveal a curious blindness to the implications of current population trends," asserting that if they'd waited less than two generations, the settlers would have been in a position "to conduct arguments with Great Britain from a position of material superiority."[74] But "curious blindness"

---

[70] Bailyn (1962, 348, 350–351).

[71] For a generally perceptive critique of Bailyn's views on ideology and its role in the American Revolution, see Ernst (1973b). Strangely, Bailyn's insistence on the ideological implications of the American Revolution are echoed by Herbert Aptheker, who writes as an historical materialist: "The promulgation of popular sovereignty . . . as the only legitimate basis for governmental power was a basically revolutionary event. . . . the Revolution represented . . . a fundamental break in the theory of government" (1960, 233–234).

[72] Schlesinger (1919, 76).

[73] Ernst (1976, 172).

[74] Christie & Labaree (1976, 276). Interestingly, the population trends to which they allude are basically the numbers of white settlers. They ignore another population trend. From 1670 to 1770, Blacks went from 4% to 20% of the population of British North America, and between 1700 and 1775, the number of African slaves brought in equalled the number of European migrants. See Walton & Shepherd (1979, 56–57). This too was an "inchoate, confused element of social . . . change" which may have formed part of the latent consciousness of the settlers.

is an analyst's arrogance. Why not go for the simpler explanation? The opposition to the Stamp Act in 1765 and the Townshend duties in 1767 had first of all to do with their immediate financial impact, both directly as taxes and indirectly in terms of their effects on the balance of trade; and both colonists and their friends in Great Britain feared it as "a killing of the goose that was laying the golden eggs."[75] And, as in most economic crises, the negatives cumulated. For example, a series of poor crops in England beginning in 1764 led to an increased demand for grain exports from the middle colonies. Good for some, no doubt, but given the high rate of unemployment and poverty in the towns, the consequent sharp rise in food prices in British North America led to demands to forbid the exports.[76] The cumulation of grievances reached a point where a small spark seemed enough to push each side to even more militant positions. We have traced reasons why the British were getting less and less flexible as their White settler colonists were getting more and more irritated. The "radical" elements who bruited independence demands seemed less and less unreasonable. In this atmosphere, the British came up with a brilliant but unwise maneuver, the Quebec Act, enacted on June 22, 1774, as a constitution for the province.

There were two aspects to the Quebec Act. One was the question of the form of government Quebec would have, which was an issue involving a conflict between the older French-speaking (and Catholic) settlers and the newer English-speaking Protestant settlers. The second was the extension of the boundaries of Quebec to include the Ohio Valley, which involved the conflict between the fur interest and the agricultural settlers for the control of the Ohio Valley.[77]

The English-speaking Protestant settlers in Quebec had been seeking an autonomous local government since the conquest by Great Britain, but one from which the French-speaking "Papists" would be excluded. The British authorities, and in particular Governor Carleton, had been resisting their demands under counterpressure from the French-speakers. The debate had been going on since 1764. The British administrators finally persuaded a reluctant George III to give the French-speakers the essence of their demands: liberty of Catholic worship within the framework of a loosely interpreted "supremacy" of the Church of England; reinstitution of French (that is, Roman–Dutch) civil law; permission for the Catholic Church to collect the tithe; and elimination of the requirement that civil servants take an antipapist oath.[78]

At the same time, the Ohio Valley became part of the territory of Quebec. This was of no special interest to the French-speaking peasantry in Quebec. But it was crucial to the fur interest. Of course, one may wonder

---

[75] Andrews (1924, 139).

[76] See Sachs (1953, 284–290), Ernst (1976, 180–181), and Nash (1979, viii).

[77] The Quebec Act also restored to the province Labrador, the Iles de la Madeleine, and the Ile d'Anticosta.

[78] See Lanctot (1965, 21–38).

why the system of an Indian reserve established in 1763 did not suffice. Neatby argues that the very success of the fur trade, its expansion "involving complicated relations with the Indians," created the need for some direct regulation. This could be done either out of Montreal or Albany, the two fur-trading entrepôts. Given the choice, "it was inevitable that Quebec should be chosen." But for the land seekers the situation had now become even more "oppressive,"[79] not to speak of the alienation of the Albany-based fur merchants.[80]

The decision upset the seaboard colonies on multiple grounds. First, "the fruit of the Seven Years' War [seemed to be] sacrificed, and the terror of being hemmed in by Indians and French from the north and west was easily revived."[81] Second, the colonists "feared an absolutist government formed in their neighborhood [and] a Catholic religion they identified with intolerance and the Inquisition."[82] Third, they were particularly dismayed that the laws governing the Ohio Valley would have "so un-English a form of land tenure."[83] Finally, the Quebec Act was passed at the same time as the Intolerable Acts and was, therefore, "tainted by this association." The colonists, therefore, regarded the Act "naturally, if uncritically, . . . as the systematic recreation of the old northern threat to the coastal colonies, this time for British ends."[84]

The delegates at the Continental Congress in Philadelphia were thereupon placed before a dilemma—how to win over Quebec to their cause while simultaneously denouncing the Quebec Act. The resolution was that the Continental Congress pursued a "subtle" campaign in which they emphasized the taxation issue and argued that the Quebec Act was essentially the triumph of an alliance of the clergy and the landed seigniors.[85] This was not without resonance among ordinary French-speaking persons in the countryside.[86]

As for the merchants, although the Continental Congress was "willing to

---

[79] Neatby (1966, 134–135).

[80] "The Quebec Act . . . recognized the predominance of furs in the Canadian economy as well as Montreal's control over the West. . . . [It] laid the basis for a new effort to expand" (Ouellet, 1971, 102). He notes that up to then the Montreal-based beaver merchants had only made "slow conquests" but now a wealthy elite could emerge. At the same time "the years 1774–75 mark the decline of Albany both in fur exporting and in redistributing trade items westward."

[81] Van Alstyne (1960, 38). Innis (1956, 178) observes: "To a very large extent the American Revolution and the fall of New France were phases of the struggle of settlement against furs." He sees a parallel between the French occupation of the Ohio Valley in 1754 as the immediate precipitant of the French and Indian War of 1754–1763, and the Quebec Act in relation to 1776.

[82] Trudel (1949b, 16).

[83] Knollenberg (1975, 124).

[84] Brebner (1966b, 54).

[85] This was not incorrect. As Ouellet notes: "Everything in 1774 led the clergy and the seigniors to be on the side of the government. The belief in an absolute monarchy based on divine right took on even greater significance since the bourgeoisie was not demanding parliamentary rule and proposing a new system of values for society" (1971, 118).

[86] Lanctot (1965, 87–88). Ouellet points out that the reaction of the French-speaking peasantry was "more complex than was believed at the time." It included fear for their security because of the military weakness of the British authorities. But at the same time the peasantry resisted voluntary military service because they had become convinced, ever since 1760, that "the English government wanted to sign [them] up only the better to organize a massive deportation" (1971, 122).

make every possible concession in order to win over the Canadian trading class,"[87] the latter reacted with great prudence. On the one hand, they were upset with the Quebec Act which took away from them English civil and commercial law (as well as trial by jury and *habeas corpus*); on the other hand, they were in direct competition with the New England merchants.[88]

In September 1774, the Continental Congress sent a "message to the Canadian People" emphasizing the absence of democratic government in the provisions of the Quebec Act, citing Montesquieu on popular liberty, and lauding the example of the Swiss confederation of Protestant and Catholic cantons. They even printed the message in French and had 2,000 copies widely circulated.[89] However, they simultaneously sent an Address to Great Britain protesting the Quebec Act, in which they spoke of Catholics having brought blood to England and being impious and bigoted. Governor Carleton distributed this letter in Quebec, where the double language was not appreciated.[90] Nonetheless, when the Continental Army invaded the province in the autumn of 1775 it was regarded by many of the French-speaking peasants as "indeed an army of liberation,"[91] despite the threats of the clergy, who rallied to the British cause, and threatened those who refused to fight the invaders with the refusal of sacraments, even excommunication.[92]

The military action at first succeeded (Montreal fell), and then failed. The rebellious colonists were still indecisive. The Declaration of Independence was still in the future.[93] The Protestant merchant class determined that their "deepest necessities," that is, "close connection with London and unrestricted trade with the Indians in the far west" were precisely what the rebellious colonists could not grant.[94] And the French-speaking *habitants* realized that they were being asked to subscribe to still more radical ends than were the American colonists. For the objectives of the latter were "liberal and *Protestant* in character." It was not only the authority of the state that was being challenged but "an authoritarian ecclesiastical order" as well. Thus the initial sympathy of the *habitants* shifted to greater antagonism.[95] In the end, as Dehio says, Britain kept Canada "for the very reason

[87] Stevens (1926, 49).

[88] Ouellet (1971, 120). In addition they had the fear that the "fur trade would pass into the hands of the [French-speaking] Canadians" (Lanctot, 1969, 51). As a consequence, "there can be little doubt that their interests caused those who went engaged in the fur industry to remain loyal to Great Britain" (Stevens, 1926, 49). See also Clark (1959, 118): "It had been the reluctance of the Montreal merchants to give up the British market that had led them to turn down [the] proposal to send delegates to the Continental Congress."

[89] Ryerson (1960, 208–209).

[90] See Trudel (1949b, 25–31).

[91] Clark (1959, 101).

[92] See Ryerson (1960, 208–210).

[93] Ryerson thinks this made the difference: "The main issue on which the Canadians *might* have risen in alliance with the Americans was that of national independence from alien rule. But the American colonists had not yet taken a stand for outright independence. Their Declaration of Independence was adopted only *after* the invasion of Canada. 'If this declaration had been made nine months earlier,' ruefully commented . . . Samuel Adams, 'Canada would be ours today'" (1960, 214).

[94] Creighton (1937, 64).

[95] Clark (1959, 117).

that there were no English settlers there." The local Catholics thought their Puritan neighbors more fanatical than the "negligently tolerant regime of London."[96]

As the American colonists became more militant, the social basis of support of the movement began to shift somewhat, as happens frequently in revolutionary situations. Socially conservative elements often became a bit frightened of the momentum their own self-interested protests create. What Schlesinger notes of the merchants of the northern colonies was probably true more generally:

> The experience of the years 1764–1766 gave the merchant class food for other reflection. Intent on making out a complete case for themselves they had, in their zeal, overreached themselves in calling to their aid the unruly elements of the population. . . . Dimly, the merchants began to perceive the danger of an awakened self-conscious group of radical elements.[97]

Thus although, as Jensen notes, before 1774 or 1775, the revolutionary movement was not a democratic or radical movement "except by inadvertance," popular mobilization transformed the situation somewhat and brought popular objectives more to the forefront.[98] Did the situation change to the point that the struggle could not be said to be primarily a "popular war,"[99] one in which "the strength of the revolutionary party lay most largely in the plain people, as distinguished from the aristocracy"?[100]

Perhaps! What seems clear is that "contemporaries had no doubt the War for Independence was accompanied by a struggle over who should rule at home."[101] But there were two kinds of conservative reactions to such a developing radicalization. One was to withdraw support altogether; some did this.[102] But a second was to rush to resume leadership of the struggle in order to deflect class objectives into purely national ones.[103] Both reactions occurred, which is what accounts for the revolutionary–loyalist split among the wealthier strata. Those who sought to moderate the political outcome of the independence movement by joining with it were

[96] Dehio (1962, 122).

[97] Schlesinger (1917, 91–92).

[98] Jensen (1957, 326). Jensen concludes from this that "the American Revolution was a democratic movement, not in origin, but in result" (p. 341).

[99] Aptheker (1960, 59).

[100] Jameson (1926, 25).

[101] Lynd (1961, 33), who continues: "Fear of just such an internal revolution made Robert R. Livingston hesitate long on the brink of independence."

[102] "Many merchants . . . , actuated by a broader understanding of class interest, frankly cast their lot [in 1775–1776] with the mother country" (Schlesinger, 1917, 604).

[103] "Most of the Whig leaders outside New England seemed to regard war with Britain, not as a means to independence, but as alternative to, even security against, revolution. The war . . . gave a temporary unity of purpose to all Americans except outright Tories, and also directed against the British energies that might otherwise turn against the established social order in the colonies" (Nelson, 1961, 117).

See also Hoerder: "By sanctioning some of the spontaneous rioting en post facto, the Whig elite appeared as leadership even when it was trying to catch up with the crowds. . . . Popular demands were deflected by rhetoric about united interests and by the condescension of leaders" (1976, 265–266).

historically more significant than the Tories and were able in the long run to achieve their objectives because the situation remained one in which "in fact . . . the radical elements were a minority of the colonial population."[104]

Still, it is important to note that the groups ready to pursue their grievances with the British government did not win out everywhere. There were 30 British colonies in the Americas after 1763, all subject to the trade and navigation acts. As Harper says, a valid explanation of the American War for Independence "must show why thirteen colonies joined in the revolt while seventeen remained loyal."[105] This is especially true since the Thirteen Colonies made various kinds of efforts to secure the adherence of the other colonies.

The attempt to pull Quebec into the revolution was abortive. But Quebec was a special case, given the fact that most inhabitants had come under British rule only recently and did not think of themselves as "British." East Florida too was a similar special case.[106] There was, however, another British colony on the North American continent which was a possible recruit since it was settled largely by New Englanders. This was Nova Scotia. Brebner points out that if, on the continent of North America, there was a geographical core of colonies where the "fires of imminent revolution" blew hot in 1774, the heat seemed to grow less as one moved to the margins. Georgia, Vermont, Maine, and Nova Scotia all "hung in the balance,"[107] but only Nova Scotia didn't come along in the end.

At this time, there were close economic (and indeed family) ties beween Nova Scotia and New England. Furthermore, like the Southern planters, the Nova Scotians were "debt-ridden" at this time and might have been tempted to rebel for the sake of debt repudiation.[108] Despite this, they showed "apathy"[109] to the proposal of active solidarity and affirmed

[104] Schlesinger (1919, 75).

[105] Harper (1942, 24). Harper's figure of 30 is possible inaccurately low. By using the New Cambridge Modern History's *Atlas*, I come up with 39. It's no doubt a question of how you count various West Indian units.

[106] East Florida was acquired from Spain in 1763. There were a few British settlers who sought to replicate the South Carolina structure of a plantation economy, but the failure of rice and the slow development of indigo were "obvious inhibitors to settlement" (Chesnutt, 1978, 14). These plantations utilized servant labor from southern Europe. Some 1400 laborers were recruited to come to New Smyrna, mostly Minorcans, with about 100 Italians from Leghorn, and some Greeks. "The heterogeneous group overtaxed the slender resources of the colony, and within two months after landing [in 1768], a revolt broke out, led by the Greeks and Italians." Although the revolt

was suppressed and its two leaders executed, disturbances continued. "With the outbreak of the American Revolution the Minorcans, hitherto the most pacific element in the colony, were believed to have conspired with the Spaniards at Havana" (Morris, 1946, 178–180). Between the loyalist planters and the Spanish-oriented Minorcans, there seemed little space for recruits to the cause of the American Revolution.

[107] Brebner (1966b, 56–57). Newfoundland was too underpopulated and economically weak even to consider rebellion; it was "as yet unable to pursue a self-directed course."

[108] Brebner (1937, 293).

[109] Brebner (1937, 353) who says it "can be attributed to poverty about as much as topographical barriers between the settlements. . . . [Nova Scotia] could not even afford to be properly represented in her own Assembly." See also Kerr (1932a, 101): "That the Nova Scotian New Englanders

instead a position of "neutrality."[110] In part, their military weakness as an exposed peninsula with very scattered settlements was a major factor in their reluctance to contemplate rebellion.[111] In part, New England had reserved its "expansionist" energy for Quebec and didn't think Nova Scotia of sufficient importance to risk its military input.[112]

Still Nova Scotians were a frontier people, and "like all frontier peoples, the Nova Scotians were separatists."[113] However, they found themselves too weak to resist politically, that is, militarily. Consequently, or so it seems, they found their outlet in a religious movement, the Great Awakening. The small settlements of Nova Scotia were peopled largely by Congregationalists who feared the recurring "threat of episcopacy" being pressed upon them from London and Halifax (the capital city). When, in addition, they found themselves pressed and unwilling to choose between their kin in New England and loyalty to the Crown, the revival of religion "offered at once an escape and a vindication."[114]

The so-called New Light revival movement grew out of the "same conditions of social unrest and dissatisfaction"[115] as did the revolutionary movements elsewhere, but was obviously more politically acceptable to the British. In addition, it gave to Nova Scotians "a new sense of identity" such that by 1783 it seemed as if Nova Scotia had become a "vital centre of the Christian world."[116] Nova Scotia thus removed itself from the orbit of the United States in creation. This was unimportant economically to the future United States and perhaps beneficial to Nova Scotia in the short run.[117] But it was of great geopolitical consequence in the long run since, had Nova Scotia become the fourteenth state, there seems little doubt that England would have found it difficult to hold on to Canada, and probable that England would thus have been "driven out" of America.[118] Had this happened, the whole process of settler decolonization might have taken a different turn.

entertained a passive sympathy for their relations in insurrection is not to be doubted; but it is also clear that they did not seriously contemplate action for themselves."

[110] The claim to a position of neutrality afforded a means of protecting ties with the neighboring revolutionary colonies while avoiding an open break with Britain" (Clark, 1959, 105).

[111] "In 1776 only the British navy and army stood in the way of the successful joining of Nova Scotia . . . with the revolutionary colonies. . . . The failure of revolution was largely determined by Britain's military advantages in carrying on of war in areas which could be encircled or blockaded by naval forces. The American revolutionary movement was a continental movement" (Clark, 1959, 102). See also Rawlyk (1963, 380) who finds that Nova Scotia's unwillingness to join rebellion, despite "widespread sympathy for Revolutionary

principles," is explained most satisfactorily by the fact that it had no navy.

[112] Rawlyk (1973, 230). He argues that Massachusett's thrust into Nova Scotia in 1776 failed because of its weakness. "It is difficult to imagine how Massachusetts could have cared less in 1776 about Nova Scotia" (p. 240).

[113] Clark (1959, 70).

[114] Armstrong (1946, 54).

[115] Clark (1959, 111).

[116] Rawlyk (1973, 250–251).

[117] "With the break of trade relations with New England, . . . Halifax's strategic military position gave it a new importance as a commercial centre . . . . Gradually the economic advantages enjoyed by the colony as a member of the British Empire, with the old colonies excluded from trade, asserted themselves" (Clark, 1959, 110–111).

[118] Weaver (1904, 52).

In the Caribbean, the relationship of the colonies to Britain presented itself differently. Unlike British North America which was suffering a period of economic depression, the West Indies entered into a boom period for its major export produce, sugar.[119] And in addition, the Free Port Act of 1766 successfully counteracted the trade depression for the West Indies, one whose roots went back to 1751. West Indian commerce had had, for over a century, a large contraband component. This was in effect the major modality of trade between Great Britain and Hispanic America. Circa 1751, a "radical change" occurred in this trade.[120] Instead of British ships trading in Spanish ports, Spanish ships began to frequent British ports. This, of course, was totally illegal under the Navigation Acts, but the local British authorities at first connived in this. In 1763–1764, as part of the general tightening of enforcement launched by Grenville, new acts were passed making foreign ships hovering near British ports liable to seizure.[121]

With the Rockingham ministry in 1765, the Stamp Act was repealed to appease the North Americans, and the Free Port Act was passed to appease the West Indian merchants. The initial motivation had to do with French island sugar. The British colonists had opposed the acquisition of Guadeloupe because they feared the competition. However, British island production, while sufficient to supply Great Britain, could not meet the demand for reexport to the continent. By opening the British West Indian ports to illicit export from the French islands, whose sugar would then pass through Britain and be sold on the continent, Britain could in effect have its cake and eat it too, garnering both trade and shipping profits without the political costs of colonial administration.

The act, as passed, was aimed not only at acquiring French island sugar; it was intended also to revive trade with the Spanish Indies, particularly via Jamaica. If the revival was slow at first, it would be very successful in the longer run. In any case, it precipitated an immediate Spanish reaction.[122] The Spanish reaction to the Free Port Act was, however, only a small part of a larger dilemma posed for Spain. The Treaty of Paris was in the long run as consequential for Hispanic America as for the British colonies for one very simple reason. With France eliminated as a major actor on the

---

[119] Pares (1960, 40) calls the years between the Peace of Paris and the outbreak of the American Revolution "the silver age of sugar."

[120] Armytage (1953, 22).

[121] The Sugar Act (4 Geo. III, c. 15) provided in Clause XXIII for the confiscation of foreign vessels in British ports. "It was to these words . . . that Jamaica merchants ascribed the decay of the Spanish trade" (Christelow, 1942, 320). On the Free Port Act as an effort to redeem the effect of having seized Spanish vessels, see Williams (1972, 378–379).

[122] "Both Spanish and French took umbrage, as well they might, at the methods used by the British to break down the monopoly which each nation practiced in its colonial empire. In the case of the Spaniards, the opening of the British free ports was followed by several attempts to strengthen the barricade which protected the Spanish monopoly" (Armytage, 1953, 48). See also Hammett (1971, 27). The Spanish reaction merely reinforced British efforts to make the West Indies "an entrepôt for trade with the forbidden areas" (Goebel, 1938, 289).

American scene, "Spain was left to face the English menace for the next two decades alone."[123] Spain's basic problem remained what it had been for more than a century at least. In the gibe of the seventeenth-century German publicist, Samuel Pufendorf, "Spain kept the cow and the rest of Europe drank the milk."[124] But now, even keeping the cow seemed to be put into question.

The threat, of course, predated the Treaty of Paris. The British merchants operating out of Jamaica were, already in the 1740s, seeking to bypass wholly the Cádiz entrepôt.[125] In 1762, the British had seized Havana (and Manila) and threatened Veracruz. Although the Treaty of Paris restored Havana to the Spanish, and even though, in addition, France ceded Louisiana to Spain as compensation for its assistance during the Seven Years' War, the British menace was nonetheless still very real, and in 1765 Charles III of Spain initiated the famous reforms associated with his reign, the institution of *comercio libre*, free trade.

Free trade was no doubt Charles III's "strategy,"[126] but it should be borne clearly in mind that in this situation free trade had quite a restricted meaning. The Spanish policy was in reality "only a liberalization of trade *within* the imperial framework."[127] The successive decrees of 1765, 1778, and 1789 basically provided for three things: considerable freedom for intercolonial trade among Spain's colonies, elimination of the peninsular Spanish monopoly of the parts of Seville and Cádiz, and permission for Spain's colonists to transport goods themselves from Spanish colonies to Spanish ports.[128] The essential object of this intraimperial liberalization of trade was to "achieve revenge over Great Britain."[129]

The revenge was to be achieved via two routes. One was that, by making the trade of the colonists with peninsular Spain more profitable to the Spanish colonists, the widespread contraband trade with the British (and others) would become less attractive. It would thus undermine exactly what the Free Port Act of Great Britain had been designed to enhance. But the second measure was to be more direct. The counterpart of liberalization of intraimperial trade was to be greater real administration of the empire by the metropole. The spirit of the Spanish colonial bureaucracy under the Hapsburgs had been said to be: "Obedezco pero no cumplo." "I obey but I do not execute the commands." The Bourbons, beginning with Charles III, were determined to try to change this. So "liberalization," which on the surface seemed to mean more freedom, really meant "less *de facto* freedom

[123] Brown (1928, 187). See also Savelle (1939, 162).
[124] Cited in Christelow (1947, 3).
[125] See Stein & Stein (1970, 95–96).
[126] Avelino (1978, 83).
[127] Stein & Stein (1970, 100).
[128] See Arcila (1955, 94–95). The second of these aspects of the reforms, was, of course, an issue internal to peninsular Spain as well and represented "the triumph of the Spanish peripheral zones over the monopolistic centralism of Cádiz." But, as Vázquez de Prada adds (1968, 220), this triumph was "even more that of the American economy over the Spanish economy."
[129] Navarro García (1975, 137).

. . . as [the Americans] were now subject to a more efficient monopoly and specifically excluded from benefits extended to Spaniards."[130] This seeming paradox came from the fact that, as the Spanish government reduced the differences in commercial rights of persons resident in peninsular Spain and those resident in the colonies, they at the same time increased the *de facto* differences in rights between peninsular Spaniards resident in the colonies and Creoles in the colonies.

It is crucial to observe that, as of 1763, the British and the Spanish faced parallel problems in two fields. First, their laws governing colonial trade were being violated by their own citizens "almost with impunity" and, when they were not, it was due more to "convenience and complaisance [than] to fear of coercion."[131] After 1763, in response, both the British and the Spanish governments moved toward a great increase in the use of coercion.[132]

The second parallel problem for the two governments was the increasing financial burden of the state-machinery. They both, therefore, sought to increase taxes in the colonies after 1763. The colonists of both countries reacted in similar ways. British colonists dumped tea into the harbor of Boston in 1770 and Spanish colonists dumped aguardiente (and also burned tobacco) in Socorro in 1781. These reactions nonetheless did not stop the British/Spanish drive to impose order, which evoked parallel resentment in both colonial zones, in both cases in the name of a prior tradition of decentralization. The only difference, as Phelan remarks, was that the prior decentralization of the British empire had been largely legislative, whereas that of the Spanish had been largely bureaucratic.[133]

Portugal too was set back by the Seven Years' War. The Marquis of Pombal, who became Secretary of Foreign Affairs in 1750, had initiated a policy of seeking greater economic independence for Portugal by creating situations in which "the profits of the American dominions would accrue largely if not exclusively" to Portuguese nationals.[134] The primary mechanism was an increase in "state control" of the colonial economy. This was indeed seen by Pombal as the "foundation" of his conception of political economy.[135] His attempts were no doubt aided considerably by the means placed at the country's disposal with the dramatic rise of gold mining in Brazil.[136] Indeed, as a result, Portugal had a higher per capita revenue at

[130] Lynch (1973, 13).

[131] Christie and Labaree (1976, 27) say this of the British, but it was equally true of Hispanic America. Chaunu estimates that contraband trade was *exceeding* that of Cádiz's legal monopoly trade throughout the eighteenth century, although toward the end of the century, because of liberalization, "monopoly trade was growing more rapidly than contraband trade" (1963, 409, fn. 14).

[132] There was a difference, however, in the degree to which they used cooptation. "What Britain in

part proposed to effect by tightening up the acts of trade, Spain in part proposed to effect by the relaxation" (Humphreys, 1952, 215).

[133] See Phelan (1978, 34).

[134] Christelow (1947, 9).

[135] Reis (1960, I[2], 327). See Novais on why Portuguese internal reforms inspired by Enlightenment ideas and increased mercantilism in the colonies was "only apparently a contradiction: it was the backwardness itself which inflicted it." (1979, 223).

[136] See Navarro García (1975, 249).

this time than France. Braudel suggests an analogy to Kuwait in the second half of the twentieth century.[137]

Pombal was not trying to place Portugal's historic alliance with Britain into question. He was merely trying to take advantage of the "large room for maneuver" which the new situation in the world-economy offered Portugal. But Spain's invasion of Portugal in 1762 was a "shattering challenge to [Pombal's] basic assumptions," and the continuing Spanish threat in the Americas after 1763 "made the retention of British goodwill by Portugal essential."[138] Britain's price was to be the abandonment of Portugal's pretensions, and Pombal's successors would reverse his policies. Still, this would not fully happen until later.[139] In the meantime, the Pombaline policy reduced Portuguese (and therefore Brazilian) trade with Britain considerably,[140] and elicited a serious negative reaction from merchants in Brazil.[141]

Thus it was that, as of 1763, not only Great Britain but Spain and Portugal as well had to begin to deal with the increasing disaffection of their settlers in the Americas. One should in fact say that the latter provoked the serious disaffection of their settlers by their somewhat successful efforts to reestablish Spanish and Portuguese strength in the world-system, which they did by reinforcing the administrative cohesion of the two empires, by reinforcing the armies, and by putting the central governments on far firmer financial bases.

Charles III moved on many fronts to strengthen the ability of the Spanish state to deal with the metropole (peninsular Spain), with its colonial territories in the Americas, and with the world. Although informed by Spain's version of Enlightenment ideology, the *Ilustración*, the actual policies were designed to (re)create in Spain the absolutist state, to diminish the role of the aristocracy, to weaken the power of the Church, and to base his administration on a more professional salaried bureaucracy,

[137] See Braudel (1984, 304). It was a Kuwait, however, whose source of income was located primarily in the colonies. "It is in function of the export of Brazilian products that the Portuguese balance of trade managed to be [in this period] positive" (Novais, 1979, 293). Already in 1738 the Portuguese ambassador to Paris, Dom Luis da Cunha, had written: "in order to preserve Portugal, the king needs the wealth of Brazil more than that of Portugal itself." (Cited in Silva, 1984, 469.) For a view that this far overstates the "disarticulation" of the Portuguese economy in the eighteenth century and was true only of the post-1808 phase, see Pereira (1986).

[138] Maxwell (1973, 22, 33, 38). See Silva (1984, 484–485) on Pombal's call for English assistance after Portuguese defeats by Spain in South America in 1763.

[139] "The swing of the pendulum back [of British

trade with Portugal] was accelerated by the French Revolution. War with France, as of old, drove England and Portugal together" (Manchester, 1933, 53).

[140] Trade with Portugal "fell from being 'the most advantageous trade' England 'drove anywhere' to an humble sixth place among the foreign nations buying from England" (Manchester, 1933, 46).

[141] "The strongest reaction by the colonists was against the Pombaline policy of nationalizing the Luso–Brazilian trade. All too often it was the Brazilian merchant who felt that his interests were being sacrificed to those of the crown and the metropolitan merchants as was the case with Pombal's policy of establishing monopolistic 'chartered companies' for Brazil" (Russell-Wood, 1975, 28–29).

both civil and military. The object was to obtain an expansion in economic activity by reforms in commercial regulation and the encouragement of colonial exports, and then, via this new effective bureaucracy "reap [the] fiscal harvest." At first, the economic (and fiscal) success was "extraordinary,"[142] but this great upsurge of Spanish strength turned out to rest on "a fragile equipoise"[143] that could not be maintained because of forces in the world-economy that were beyond the control of the Spanish state. It is to this story we must now turn.

Since the "catalyst of change" was the Seven Years' War, in which Spain suffered unpleasant military reverses (the fall of Havana being the most notable but not the only one), the first step in Charles III's reforms were military ones, and soldiers were to play a central role in the administrative revolution, which has even been termed the "Reconquest of the Americas."[144] But the most radical changes were in civil administration. This involved the revival of the institution of the *visita general*, the dispatching from Madrid of an official with powers to enquire and act at the highest level. The key individual in the process of reform, Don José de Gálvez, originally appears on the scene as the first of these Visitors-General, to New Spain from 1765 to 1767.

But the most important reform was the introduction of intendants, that classical Colbertian mechanism of state centralization. Intendants were to replace the district magistrates called *alcaldes mayores* and *corregidores* (collectors of Indian tribute, recruiters, and assigners of Indian labor), whose posts had been sold for over a century and who had been using their posts (and tax power) for private commercial profit. In 1768, Gálvez, along with Viceroy Croix of New Spain, proposed the outright abolition of this category of officials who simultaneously oppressed the Indians and kept the largest part of the Crown's fiscal revenue. When Gálvez became Minister of the Indies in 1776 he came to personify the "reformist zeal of the Bourbon government,"[145] and finally, in 1786, he pushed through his reform. This can be interpreted as the reward of persistence; it can equally be interpreted as the proof of how difficult it was to reform in the climate of "metropolitan immobility."[146]

---

[142] Brading (1984, 408). Since the sixteenth century, the reign of Charles III was that "least wounding to national pride" (Whitaker, 1962a, 2). See also Chaunu, who calls the period 1770–1800 that of the "recovery of Spain" (1963, 417). Finally, García-Baquero speaks of the period after 1778 as a "phase of spectacular expansion" of Cádiz trade (1972, 127). But this is equally true of Catalonia; see Delgado (1979, 25–26). Finally, Fisher calls the free trade policy of Charles III a "striking success, particularly in its impact on the economic life of Spanish America. Its effects upon the peninsular economy were somewhat more modest" (1985, 62).

[143] Brading (1984, 439). See also Humphreys (1952, 213): "Under Charles III and during the early years of Charles IV, [Spain] enjoyed what seems in retrospect to have been an Indian summer of prosperity. What was true of Spain was also true of her empire."

[144] Brading (1984, 399–400).

[145] Navarro García (1975, 160).

[146] Stein (1981, 28). Stein's view of Gálvez's success is somewhat acerbic: "Eighteen years after Gálvez offered a plan for intendants in New Spain, ten years after he was appointed Minister of the Indies, six years after the massive Indian uprising

Gálvez's lasting impact was in the transformation of the political geography that he effectuated, a transformation which was to have an important impact on the future process of decolonization. In 1776, one of his first acts as Minister of the Indies was to establish the Viceroyalty of La Plata. In the sixteenth century there had only been two Viceroyalties, New Spain and Peru. A third, New Granada, was carved out in 1739. Why did Gálvez create a fourth in 1776 (as well as a number of lesser units as Capitanerías Generales and Audiencias)? 1776 was not a fortuitous date. The War of Independence in British North America had started. It seemed a golden moment to move against Great Britain and its ally, Portugal, who, among other things, were economically penetrating the Indian zones of South America under Spanish rule via illicit trade on the Sacramento–Buenos Aires route. Charles III sought to create a strong government that would cut short this penetration. This was to be La Plata which included present-day Argentina, Uruguay, Paraguay, and Bolivia. "In normal circumstances, England would not have tolerated carrying out such intentions."[147] But these were not normal circumstances. The reinvigoration of the military forces paid off. An expedition of 8,500 men crossed the Rio de la Plata in 1776 and captured Sacramento "for the third and last time."[148] This Spanish victory would be ratified at the Treaty of San Ildefonso in 1778 and Portugal's aspirations over La Banda Oriental (today Uruguay) were forever at an end.

The struggle in North America provided a continuous pressure on Hispanic America. It gave "a character of urgency"[149] to the reform movement which led to the second set of free trade decrees of 1778. Spain was under great pressure to join the war against Britain in 1779, following upon France which had already done so in 1777. The French decision was quite obvious in a sense. They had been seeking to reduce Great Britain's power in the Americas ever since 1763. Upon his retirement in 1770, the Duc de Choiseul left a memo in which he reiterated the five necessary elements in such a policy: avoid war, ally with Spain and Holland, weaken British financial credit, promote the independence of Britain's American colonies, and reduce commerce between Britain and the colonies of Spain and Portugal. When Vergennes took office in 1774, he revived Choiseul's policies.[150] The American colonies had now, however, forced the French hand by starting a war.

of Tupac-Amaru began in the central Andes, and two years after Peru received its ordinance, on December 4, 1786, Gálvez finally managed to push through his long-cherished ordinance for New Spain. Within months he was dead" (p. 13). And almost immediately his co-author of the original plan, Croix, now Viceroy of Peru, recommended reinstating in Peru the *repartimiento de mercancias*, the chief evil of the old system of corregidores.

[147] Céspedes del Castillo (1946, 865).

[148] Brading (1984, 401). The reinvigoration of the military would continue to show its fruits a few years later when Spain entered the North American war and invaded Pensacola. In 1783 Britain ceded both Pensacola and East Florida to Spain. It was at this same time that the Spanish finally evicted the British from the Mosquito Coast (presently in eastern Nicaragua).

[149] Rodríguez (1976, 23).

[150] See Savelle (1939, 164–165).

At first the French restricted themselves to secret aid to the North American revolutionaries. The French cabinet was divided, Turgot believing that war should be avoided as "the greatest of evils."[151] And it was far from sure that the North Americans could hold out very long. They had, after all, lost the Battle of Long Island on August 27, 1776. Thus the defeat of General Burgoyne at Saratoga on October 16, 1777 had an immense impact on France, and on Spain.[152] France suddenly began to fear something even worse than a British victory—a victory of the rebel forces unaided by France, that is, the possibility of an independent and unfriendly United States.[153] France signed a treaty with the United States on February 6, 1778 and joined openly in the war.

Now the pressure was on Spain, and the Spanish were very reluctant. Spain was hesitant to do anything that might seem to legitimate colonial revolt. Furthermore, Spain was bargaining her neutrality against a cession by Britain of Gibraltar and Minorca, a deal the British felt no need to make. The French were more anxious to get Spanish support and paid the Spanish price in the Treaty of Aranjuez in 1779. This price was the promise of a joint invasion of England, which Spain conceived to be the way of ending the war before her "overextended and vulnerable colonial empire" was attacked.[154] Spain signed its treaty with France, not the United

---

[151] Van Tyne (1916, 530).

[152] "On October 16th, 1777, General Burgoyne surrendered in Saratoga to General Gates. It is difficult for us to realise what this news meant then. Till then the war had been seen in Europe, in the words of an English pamphleteer of 1776, as 'the insolence' of 'the leaders of the infatuated colonists, ambitious demagogues' who had 'led forward an ignorant populace, step by step till their retreat from ruin is difficult, if not impossible.' Suddenly this ignorant populace beat one of the best armies in the Old World, one of the richest in military history" (Madariaga, 1948, 300).

[153] "Vergennes had been haunted with the bogey from 1776 on, that as a result of America's struggle for independence, France and Spain would lose their West Indian possessions" (Van Tyne, 1916, 534). In 1776, Silas Deane, the delegate of the Continental Congress in Paris, "warned the French that without sufficient help the Americans would be forced to reunite with the British. An independent America, on the other hand, would make France a successor to Britain in the domination of world commerce" (Kaplan, 1977, 138–139). On July 23, 1777, Vergennes sent a memo to King Louis XVI in which he said: "If England could not speedily crush the American revolt she must make terms with it. Those whom she had failed to retain as subjects she could make allies, in a joint assault upon the riches of Peru and Mexico and the French Sugar Islands." (Cited in Corwin, 1915, 34.)

France's distrust of United States's real intentions remained and was a major factor in France's pressure during the later peace negotiations in Paris in 1782–1783 that Britain be permitted to retain Canada. Already in 1778, the Continental Congress had asked the French to commit themselves to favor the conquest of Canada (as well as Nova Scotia and the Floridas) by the colonists. Vergennes, however, in his instructions to his diplomat in the United States, Conrad-Alexandre Gérard, on March 29, 1778, wrote that British "possession of these three territories (*contrées*), or at least Canada, would be a useful principle of uncertainty and vigilance for the Americans. It will make them feel a greater need for the friendship and alliance of the King, and it is not in his interest that this be destroyed" (Reprinted in Frégault & Trudel, 1963, 153). In 1779, at Luzerne, Vergennes asserted that France had no interest "in seeing North America play the role of a power and be in a position to create disquiet among its neighbors." When it came to the Paris negotiations, Britain was actually ready to concede more than the French wished they would (for example, fishing rights in the St. Lawrence, and even more importantly, boundaries greater than the colonists had in 1775). Needless to say, France's attitude was not appreciated by the Americans. See Trudel (1949b, 213–214).

[154] Dull (1985, 108).

States.[155] Its object was quite explicitly to regain Minorca and Gibraltar, of course, but it was also to "dislodge the English from all their positions in the Caribbean—Louisiana, the Mosquito Coast, Jamaica, the Lesser Antilles."[156]

Spain paid a high price "in blood and treasure."[157] The war resulted in the first of successive de facto cuts in the links between Hispanic America and Spain. The Company of Caracas was ruined. The state treasury did not receive income from the Americas. The Catalan cotton industry suffered.[158] And the trade of the Cádiz merchants, still the most important group, "fell into the greatest confusion, which inevitably redounded to the benefit of contraband which now knew its period of greatest development."[159]

The greatest damage of all was probably the inflationary cycle that was now launched. As late as 1774, the Count of Campomanes had been citing Spain's freedom from paper money inflation as a "great national asset." But the war expenditures combined with diminished intake exhausted the royal treasury. This pattern was to be repeated after 1793. Since the costs were real, the Spanish state had to recoup somehow. In effect, "the American colonists were taxed for [the] redemption" of the paper currency.[160] So, of course, were the people at home. Ultimately, this inflation became a factor both in the Napoleonic conquest of Spain and in the independence movements.

Spain's "halfhearted" involvement in the War of American Independence was thus to have "reverberations in and for Spanish America."[161] Two major revolts occurred precisely at this moment, that of Túpac Amaru in Peru, and that of the Comuneros in New Granada.[162] The Túpac Amaru revolt so shook the Americas that its very objective remains a subject of great controversy. Was it the first clarion call of the independence movement or was it almost the opposite?

There are those who see the Indian uprising in the Andes led by Túpac Amaru—which was, let us remember, merely the culmination of a long series but the one with greatest impact[163]—as "the last major effort of the unsubdued Indians."[164] This was clearly the view of many administrators at the time, at worst a primitive refusal to accept civilized ways, at best a

---

[155] "During the Anglo–American Revolution, Spain [was] the ally of France but never of the United States, whose independence she would not recognize until Great Britain had done so" (Bemis, 1943, 16).

[156] Navarro García (1975, 141). In fact, all Spain got was the Floridas and the Mosquito Coast, and for that they had in effect to trade Belize. Spain also got Minorca but not Gibraltar.

[157] Hamilton (1944, 40).

[158] See Herr (1958, 145–146).

[159] García-Baquero (1972, 43). The favorite

mode of contraband was to "hacerse el sueco," that is, adopt Swedish neutral colors.

[160] Hamilton (1944, 41, 48).

[161] Liss (1983, 137).

[162] As Madariaga remarks pertinently: "Rebellions are apt to be contagious. . . . At any rate, it is significant that the revolutionary movements connected with the Tupac Amaru-Condorcanqui rising lasted till 1783, i.e., till the Peace of Versailles" (1948, 302–303).

[163] See Bonilla (1972, 17).

[164] Harlow (1964, 636).

"social scream"[165] which therefore can be understood if not approved or tolerated. This camp places itself in opposition to those who have tried to coopt the history of the Indian revolts of the Andes as a "prodrome of independence." That effort of some later Peruvian historians is denounced by Chaunu, who says it is a "total misconception (*contresens*)." He argues that, far from these Indian revolts involving a revolt of America against Europe, they were a revolt by the Indians against "their unique enemy, . . . Creole oppression."[166] In this version of the events, great emphasis is placed on the fact that Túpac Amaru asserted that his movement was "loyalist"[167]—to the King, albeit not to the King's servants. But loyalism worked both ways. One result of the Túpac Amaru uprising was to make a part of the White population feel that the colonial order was "the best defense of its own hegemony, and the only guarantee against extermination at the hands of the more numerous indigenous and mixed-blood castes."[168]

There is, however, a third position. It is to see Túpac Amaru neither as loyalist whose quarrel was with the Creoles, nor as the first fighter for independence, but as the social revolutionary. These revolts make sense only if we place them inside the cyclical phase (or *conjoncture*) of the world-economy. There are three considerations. First, we know of the general economic downturn after 1763, which by 1776 has produced the events of the revolution of British North America, and Spain's involvement against the British as of 1779. Second, we know of the reform movement launched by Charles III and which got a second major push in 1778. Third, there was the effect of the decline of agricultural prices in the Andean region. It turns out that the years 1779–1780 "correspond, quite exactly, to one of the deepest drops in the century." The prices were at their lowest since 1725–1727. Furthermore, the years 1779–1780 were only the dramatic low point of a cycle that had been downward since 1759.[169]

Far from being primitive resistance, the revolts were caused first of all by the involvement of the Indians in the capitalist world-economy, which had, only recently, been made more efficacious by the various attempts "to strengthen the arm of the central administration."[170] Peru was proverbial for the corruption and abuses of its corregidores. When José Gabriel Condorcanqui, claiming to be Túpac Amaru II Inca, rose up in 1780, he

[165] Valcárcel (1960, 358). The only alternative Valcárcel envisages is that we consider it a "movement for political independence set on establishing a new State," and this would be "senseless," he says.

[166] Chaunu (1964, 194).

[167] Valcárcel (1957, 241).

[168] Halperín-Donghi (1972, 118). See also Chaunu himself (1963, 406), who sees the revolt of

Túpac Amaru as "one of the essential causes of Peru's loyalism."

[169] Tandeter & Wachtel (1983, 231–232). They point out the parallels here to the scenario Labrousse sketches for the French Revolution.

[170] Cornblit (1970, 131). As he argues, "the decisive project of modernization . . . had the consequence of generalizing the conflicts (p. 133)."

used as his main theme the "bad government" which was oppressing the Indians through taxes far too high and ruining the economy.

It is really not to the point to try to decipher Túpac Amaru's personal social motivations. What is significant is the social response he evoked. The heart of the rebellion was to be found in the Indian rural population, but not to the same degree everywhere. Golte does some crude but persuasive calculations. He created an index for each province of the per capita total income (which varied obviously with the soil conditions, the amount of export production, and the opportunities for wages from mine employment). He deducted from that the average level of tribute actually levied, legally and illegally. He found an almost exact correlation of the lowness of the sum remaining and the degree of participation in the uprising.[171] Piel correctly points out the many parallels between the Túpac Amaru uprising and the almost simultaneous Pugachev uprising (1773–1775) which we discussed above: the claim to be a "tsar" or an "Inca"; peasants on large landholdings rebelling; and a large mining operation, based partly on forced labor—in short, a great deal of labor coercion for market-oriented activity.[172]

Túpac Amaru sought the support of the Creoles. Indeed, at first, the authorities suspected that corregidores, angry with reforms in prospect, had inspired Túpac Amaru, and there was perhaps some evidence of this.[173] But the interests of the two groups went in opposite directions. The "pride of blood" of the Creole vis-à-vis Indians, Blacks, mestizos, and mulattoes, was not merely a social fact of Hispanic America from the outset but had actually increased during the eighteenth century.[174] The sentiment of social distance was reciprocated.[175]

The demographics were clear. In 1780, 60% of the population of Peru was Indian, but few lived in Lima. Only 12% were Spanish (Creole or peninsular). The rest were so-called castes—principally Blacks, mestizos, and mulattoes.[176] For the Indians their most immediate enemy was those who controlled economic and social life and "in general these were Creoles," and not peninsulars.[177] Furthermore, Túpac Amaru promised to free slaves, and put forward "suspect" views on property, destroying Creole-owned *obrajes* (textile manufacturing units), for example. Faced with this kind of revolt, "Creoles soon made common cause with

[171] See Golte (1980, 176–179).
[172] See Piel (1975, 205, fn. 22).
[173] See Fisher (1971, 409–410).
[174] Konetzke (1946, 232).
[175] "The Creole, White son of Spaniards and Europeans, wished to have nothing to do with the Indian, and the Indian, devoted to his race and his tradition, had no contact with the Creole, whom he ignored or hated" (Gandia, 1970, 10).
[176] See Golte (1980, 42–43). This, of course, was not the only demographic pattern in the Americas.

The proportions were similar in Mexico, Guatemala, and Bolivia. But in New Granada the mestizo element was much larger than the Indians. In Brazil, and the Caribbean, Blacks were numerically dominant, and in North America, Whites. See Humboldt's 1820 charts reproduced in Chaunu (1964, 196). On the categorizations utilized in the race system of Hispanic America, see McAlister (1963).

[177] Fisher (1971, 421).

Spaniards."[178] In general, in Hispanic America, as Lewin puts it, there were at the time two different revolutionary movements, the Creole and the Indian. "Sometimes their paths crossed, . . . and sometimes they went their separate ways."[179]

The rebellion of Túpac Amaru was overcome by a combination of concessions—the suppression of the repartimentos[180]—and military force. But the importance of the rebellion lay in its political consequences for Hispanic America. The Indians "lost definitively any initiative in conducting any more significant rebellions."[181] And the reason was that the extent, early successes, and fierceness of the Túpac Amaru rebellion thoroughly frightened the Whites. There would be no more "adhesion" of Whites and near-Whites to such rebellions after 1780.[182] Instead, the Creoles were to assume from this point on the leadership of revolutions. Still, even after this became so, as a general rule, the depth of commitment to separatism and independence remained "inversely proportional to the percentage of Indians and Blacks under domination."[183] And in the wars of independence, particularly in Peru, the Indians were made to suffer from both sides. "They were plundered by all the armies."[184]

The initial successes of Túpac Amaru inspired a movement known as the Comuneros in the neighboring Viceroyalty of New Granada.[185] It too was a manifestation of the "great revolutionary process" set off by (but not caused by) the process of Bourbon reform.[186] The successes of Túpac Amaru also kept the Creoles of Santa Fé de Bogotá, the capital of New Granada, and those in the other urban centers, in a state of "constant anxiety."[187]

The immediate cause of the uprising of the *comuneros* on March 16, 1781 was outrage at the harsh new procedures and increased *alcabala* (sales tax) of the new Visitor-General, Juan Francisco Gutiérrez de Pinedes. The central issue was "who had the authority to levy new fiscal exactions."[188] Thus, the issue was a constitutional one and parallel to the issue that had been raised by the British North American settlers. The difference was that, in New Granada, there was a significant Indian population who were less interested in devolution of central fiscal power and far more interested

[178] Humphreys & Lynch (1965a, 28). "The manumission of Black slaves of Tungasua, the destruction of Creole obrajes in the course of the rebellion, and above all the potential danger inherent in the independent mobilization of the Indian population were more than sufficient reasons to part company and later to turn the Creoles against the Indians" (Bonilla, 1972, 19).

[179] Lewin (1957, 143–144).

[180] See Golte (1980, 202), and Fisher (1971, 411).

[181] Bonilla (1972, 16).

[182] Campbell (1981, 693).

[183] Chaunu (1963, 408). The percentage of

Whites was highest in Venezuela and La Plata, the two centers of revolution, next in New Granada, followed by New Spain and Peru (p. 408, fn. 13).

[184] Lynch (1973, 276).

[185] "The Socorranos [Socorro was the locality of the insurrection] were intoxicated by the alleged success of Tupac Amaru" (Phelan, 1978, 68).

[186] Liévano Aguirre (1968, 467), who also notes that the Túpac Amaru revolt "had a decisive resonance on the course of the Revolution of the Comuneros" (p. 470).

[187] Cárdenas Acosta (1960, I, 88).

[188] Phelan (1978, xviii).

in the abuses of this power, such as excessive tribute and the invasion of the *Resguardos*, the community lands of the Indians, which were being auctioned off to Creole large landowners (*hacendados*) as well as to smaller purchasers who were largely mestizos. The situation was worsened by the fact that the local textile industry was in decline, again a result of the general economic problems of the world-economy.[189]

Whereas in Peru the social tinderbox, when ignited, fell into the hands of Indian leadership (albeit Indians who were *caciques* and claimed descent from the old Inca aristocracy), in New Granada, the insurrection had a very large mestizo element from the outset and the leadership was assumed by a Creole, Juan Francisco Berbeo, who was a *hacendado* (albeit a modest one). There were thus, in New Granada, virtually two revolts, more or less under one heading—a mestizo–Creole one centered in Socorro and an Indian one in the *llanos* of Casanare.

The rebels marched on Santa Fé, where, in the confusion, power had been assumed temporarily by the Archbishop, Antonio Caballero y Góngora, whose line was subtle and conciliatory. Berbeo "held back the rebel army"[190] and entered into negotiations with Caballero. The result was a compromise, the capitulations of Zipaquirá (June 8, 1781), which reduced taxes, assured greater access to office by nonpeninsular Spaniards, and offered some improvements to the Indians. The latter, however, basically saw the capitulations as a "betrayal,"[191] a way to keep the Indians from entering Santa Fé (by appeasing the Creole and mestizo elements of the revolt). The Indians sought to continue the struggle alone but were crushed with the help of their former allies.

In the end, the temporary alliance of a part of the elite, unhappy with Spain and the "plèbe," the "disinherited," was an impossible alliance.[192] The former were inspired by the revolt of their counterparts, the North American settlers.[193] The latter were inspired by the example of Túpac Amaru, and in the end, the Creole landowners "not only did not support them, but openly rebuffed them and collaborated with the authorities."[194] However, in New Granada, the elites (sustained by somewhat different demographics) had quickly learned the lesson of Túpac Amaru. By assuming the leadership of the revolt and sapping it from within, they preserved their options for the future far better in terms of pursuing their

[189] See Loy (1981, 255).

[190] Lynch (1985, 34).

[191] Lynch (1985, 36); see also Arciniegas (1973) whose chapter XIX is entitled, "The Betrayal."

[192] Liévano Aguirre (1968, 447).

[193] See Cárdenas Acosta (1960, I, 88).

[194] Izard (1979, 134). There was another factor to consider—Black slaves. Túpac Amaru had frightened the Creoles by proclaiming an end to slavery. While the issue did not arise directly during the Comunero uprising, it lay in the background.

Venezuela had long been a zone in which significant communities of escaped slaves, so-called *cimarrones*, had flourished. Many were engaged in "social banditry" and maintained a collusive relationship with slaves on plantations, enabling the latter to use the threat of *cimarrón* reprisals as bargaining weapons with their masters. "Venezuela was not an idyllic, peaceful place" (Dominguez, 1980, 48). A prolonged Indian revolt might surely have sparked one by Black slaves.

own interests vis-à-vis Spain. Bolívar was to emerge in New Granada, and to suffer a very mixed reception in Peru in the 1820s.

The Creole drive to independence thus now found its double spur—the grievances of Creole against peninsular, and the fear that both had of the non-White lower strata. It is the first, the subject of Creole–peninsular rivalry, that has virtually dominated the historiography of the late colonial period of Hispanic America (and to a lesser degree of Brazil). A Creole was, by definition, the descendant of a peninsular. At all moments in Hispanic America, as in almost all settler colonies, a segment of the settlers were born in the colony, and a segment were migrants from the metropole. Among the latter, some were new settlers, and others were persons who migrated temporarily to hold office of some kind with the intention of returning to the metropole. Some fulfilled this intent and others did not. In any case, even if a peninsular returned to the metropole, it was perfectly possible that he had children born in the colony who opted to remain.

The discussion has in a sense gone through two phases. The classic position is that the Creoles were being excluded from office in the eighteenth century in favor of peninsulars, and this was the source of their discontent.[195] Beginning in the 1950s this position came under attack. Eyzaguirre, for example, argues that Creoles still maintained "unquestioned predominance in the bureaucracy," and what was at issue was a Creole drive to transform its majority into an "exclusivity" of access to official posts.[196] The revisionists argue that the sequence—Bourbon reforms leading to Creole discontent—was, in fact, the reverse. Creole control caused "alarm" to Spanish officialdom.[197] Bourbon reform was "a consequence rather than a cause of Creole assertion."[198]

It seems clear that whatever the sequence of development of the issue, and whatever the degree of reality in perceptions, the subject of the "place" of peninsulars in Hispanic America had become "more acute," that is, more public and that, in the dispute, the colonial administration placed "all its weight" on the side of the peninsulars.[199] This was less a matter of new legislation than of enforcing old ones.[200] The issue became more acute also because, on the one hand, there was a significant numerical growth in the number of Creoles.[201] And on the other hand, there was a significant new influx of immigrants precisely because of the Spanish effort at "reconquest" of the Americas and economic expansion.[202]

[195] This was the position of the nineteenth-century liberal historians. It was still being echoed by Diffie (1945, 488) and Haring (1947, 136, 194). Collier (1963, 19) says it's an exaggerated but nonetheless real view. Bonilla (1972, 58) argues it is true as of 1776–1787. For a discussion of the historiography, see Campbell (1972a, 7) and Burkholder (1972, 395).
[196] Eyzaguirre (1957, 54, 57). The emphasis on

the preponderant role of Creoles in the administration is shared by Barbier (1972, 434).
[197] Campbell (1972a, 20).
[198] Marzahl (1974, 637).
[199] Halperín-Donghi (1972, 127).
[200] See Konetzke (1950).
[201] See the figures in Chaunu (1964, 195).
[202] "Bureaucrats and merchants flooded to the colonies in search of a new world, a world fit for

No doubt the situation was exacerbated by the "arbitrariness' of the metropolitan authorities as viewed by the Creoles,[203] and by the "ineptitude and suspected disloyalty" of the Creoles as seen by the Spanish authorities.[204] Precisely as in British North America, the mutual suspicions grew, slowly perhaps but steadily. But there was a further complication—racism. In British North America, the situation was relatively clearcut. There were Whites and there were Blacks. The racial barrier was strong. Indians were disdained but they were largely outside the economic system. Mulattoes were Blacks. And among Whites, the distinctions were largely on straight class lines, uncomplicated by too much ethnicity. There were sure to be settlers whose origins were not British but rather, for example, German. But whatever antagonisms existed in this regard played almost no role in the political turmoil. There were loyalists and patriots, but no peninsulars nor Creoles.

Racial lines were far more complex in Hispanic America (as well as in Portuguese and French colonies). Instead of a simple bifurcation of White–Black (or non-White), there was a complex graded hierarchy. The realities of sexual habits over three centuries meant that peninsulars were "pure white" but Creoles were "more or less white." As Lynch points out, in fact, many Creoles had dark skins, thick lips, coarse skin, "rather like Bolívar himself."[205]

No doubt the fact of being in fact of mixed blood (two out of three, according to Chaunu[206]) in a structure where "whiteness" was prized led many Creoles to translate their high status as "descendants" (albeit tinged with racial ambiguity) into a class superiority over the newly arrived. The Creole group, largely composed of persons whose ancestors had arrived from Andalucia, Extremadura, and Castile in the sixteenth and seventeenth centuries, saw in the eighteenth-century arrivals not Spaniards but persons disproportionally from the Cantabrian Mountains and Galicia. "The 'anti-*gachupin*' folklore [*gachupin* was out of the derisory expressions for peninsulars] is quite reminiscent of the 'anti-Cantabrian' and even more the 'anti-Galician' folklore of Seville."[207] Creoles also called peninsulars *godos*, that is Goths, presumably implying a parallel to the descent of the "barbarian" Goths into Roman Spain.[208] The peninsulars retorted by classifying the Creoles as "idle."[209] The peninsulars who were settlers were in fact often poor persons who were upwardly mobile.[210] The Creoles seemed often to be "trapped on a downwardly mobile economic escala-

---

Spaniards, where they were still preferred in the higher administration, and where *comercio libre* had built-in safeguards for peninsular monopolists" (Lynch, 1973, 16).

[203] Liévano Aguirre (1968, 439).

[204] Campbell (1976, 55). Campbell is referring specifically to the reaction of Gálvez to the role of the Creole militia in the Túpac Amaru uprising.

[205] Lynch (1973, 19).

[206] Chaunu (1964, 197).

[207] Chaunu (1963, 412–413). Chaunu notes that these tensions persist during the Carlist wars in the nineteenth century.

[208] See Chaunu (1964, 197).

[209] Brading (1971, 213).

[210] See Congreso Hispánoamericano (1953, 273).

tor."[211] The fact is that Creoles and peninsulars took these statuses seriously, but only up to a point. Gandia reminds us that, when the crunch of political struggle finally arrived, the labels often reflected not family history but current political option. "The curious thing is that these supposed Creoles were often not Creoles but Spaniards, and the Spaniards were not Spaniards but Creoles."[212] And economic locus was often the crucial consideration. As Izard says of Venezuela, "the confrontation between merchants and landowners did not take place between metropolitans and Creoles, but between producers and buyers."[213] The proof, he says, is that the conflicts continued after independence when all the peninsular merchants disappeared from the scene.

What comes through clearly is that the Bourbon reforms crystallized the issues. The attempt to reassert central authority, so necessary if Spain were to limit the impending final thrust forward of British economic interests in Hispanic America—a "desperate rearguard action,"[214] was a no-win game. Had Charles III and his agent Gálvez failed, the British would have won. But Charles III and Gálvez did not fail. They were, for example, quite successful in reining in the Church. The expulsion of the Jesuits was achieved with remarkable ease and resolved various financial and authority problems for the Spanish state. But, in the process, the loyalty of the Creoles was sorely strained, for the over 1,000 American Jesuits who sailed off to Europe were in fact "the very flower of the Creole elite."[215] The price of this policy was to be the "alienation" of those who remained.[216] And this "alienation"—because of the Jesuits, because of the substitution of intendants for corregidores, because of the higher taxes more effectively collected—was to lead the elites in the direction of independence, especially given the evolving political climate of the world-system. By 1781, Marcos Marrero Valenzuela wrote a memo to Charles III predicting that this had to happen.[217]

Thus it was that, following the Treaty of Paris of 1763, in less than 20 years the Americas—all the Americas—seemed inescapably headed down the path of the establishment of a series of independent settler states. The next 50 years was merely the unfolding of a pattern whose general lines, if not detailed etching, had been drawn. Why this was so probably lies less in the heroics of some devotion to "liberty" on the part of the settlers or in some "errors" of judgment of the metropolitan powers—two favorite lines of argument—as in the cumulation of successive evaluations of costs and benefits (on all sides) in the context of the newly emerging British world

[211] Brading (1973b, 397).
[212] Gandia (1970, 27).
[213] Izard (1979, 54).
[214] Brading (1984, 438).
[215] Brading (1984, 402). See also Bauer (1971, 80–85). The expulsion of the Jesuits marked an-

other turning point from Hapsburg to Bourbon policies. "Where the Habsburgs used priests the Bourbons employed soldiers" (Brading, 1971, 27).
[216] Brading (1984, 403).
[217] See Muñoz Oraá (1960).

order. This was not all cool calculation, to be sure. Once launched, the settler thrust for independence would build its own momentum which led to results that often went beyond narrower calculations of collective interests. The final outcome was beneficial in different ways simultaneously to the British and to the settlers in the Americas, both north and south. Of course, the degree and quality of the benefits varied. The principal losers were the Iberian states and the non-White populations of the Americas. It was an unequal contest, and in hindsight the outcome may seem evident. The de facto long-term alliance of those who gained was the one that provided the most immediate political stability to the world-system, and was, therefore, optimal for the worldwide accumulation of capital.

In 1781, the United States forces defeated the British at Yorktown. This seemed a great defeat for Great Britain, and no doubt it was sobering for the British. Yet peace was not made until the Treaty of Versailles in 1783. Why this was so places the real world military situation into some perspective. For Great Britain was not only fighting its colonies. It was at war with France, Spain, and the Netherlands as well, and most of Europe was de facto aligned against her. In the two years between 1781 and 1783, the British fleet decisively defeated the French fleet in the West Indies in the Battle of the Saints. And the Franco–Spanish attack on Gibraltar proved fruitless. These British successes against her European enemies outweighed the defeat at Yorktown and meant that, following 1783, Britannia would continue to rule the waves even though she had lost her thirteen Continental colonies."[218]

From the British point of view, 1783 marked not peace but a truce in warfare. There was no interruption in her drive to hegemony. We have already discussed (in Chapter 2) how the French sought next to deal with the British—the Eden Treaty, the Revolution, the revolutionary wars, Napoleonic expansion, and the Continental Blockade. We must now return to the story of how the settler populations sought to defend their interests. After 1783, there were three key "moments" that shook the balance of forces in the struggle of the settlers: the revolution in Haiti, the Napoleonic invasion of Spain, and the final collapse of the French in 1815. We shall seek to trace the story from the perspective of the Americas in terms of these markers.

After 1783, the newly independent United States sought to realize the fruits of its victory. It turned out to be harder than it had expected. In particular, two of its central economic objectives—obtaining a significant expansion of its exports, to Europe, to the Caribbean, and elsewhere; and obtaining access to and control over the frontier lands of the North American continent—were by no means guaranteed simply by ending

[218] Gottschalk (1948, 7). See also Anderson (1965, 267–268).

British overrule. Furthermore, the Revolutionary War had stirred up many internal social conflicts, which threatened the stability of the new state and hence its possibility of achieving the economic objectives the settlers had set for themselves.

During the War for Independence, the Continental Congress had, of course, cut economic ties with Great Britain. Internationally, the Continental Congress took a strong free trade position as early as 1776, a position it maintained throughout the war.[219] The cutoff from British manufactures was partially compensated for by an increase in home manufactures and increased imports from France, the Netherlands, and Spain. The latter were paid for in small part by exports, and in larger part by subsidies and loans as well as by the fact that the French expeditionary forces shored up the productive sector by its own expenditures. In general, however, the war did not have "revolutionary effects" in the economy and in particular on the manufacturing sector.[220]

Furthermore, in the immediate postwar trade depression, Great Britain (the loser) seemed to fare better than the United States and France (the winners). Essentially, the United States remained in a quite dependent relation on Great Britain,[221] a matter of some frustration to both the United States and France. With our present knowledge, the reasons seem obvious enough. For the United States, British entrepôts were strong and inexpensive in their offerings. Above all, United States merchants had "long established commercial connections" with them, which meant that long-term credits were available. Nor should one forget the value of a common language and culture.[222] Moreover, after 1783, British merchants "bestirred themselves to recapture the American trade." The British government assisted them by offering these merchants the same drawbacks, exemptions, and bounties they had been getting when the United States were still British colonies.[223] By contrast, for French merchants, developing trade with the United States involved creating new channels of trade and, given the losses port merchants had suffered during the war, in 1783 they couldn't "permit themselves the luxury of much innovation."[224]

Thus, the United States found its commerce back in the hands of the

---

[219] See Bemis (1935, 45–46) and Nettels (1962, 1–6).

[220] Nettels (1962, 44); see also Walton & Shepherd (1979, 181–182). By contrast, the American War of Independence seemed to have served Scotland well in this regard. By destroying Glasgow's role as an entrepôt, it forced a restructuring of economic priorities. "As long as Glasgow retained its monopoly of the traffic in tobacco with America, manufactures—even the cotton manufacture—would have tended to remain subordinate to trade" (Robertson, 1956, 131).

[221] "For Britain the loss [of the war] was greater in terms of prestige than of material interests: the economic independence of the United States lagged far behind the winning and use of national sovereignty" (Marshall, 1964a, 23).

[222] Clauder (1932, 16).

[223] Nettels (1962, 47), who also notes that "British merchants, having abundant capitals, advanced goods on credits running from twelve to eighteen months" (p. 231).

[224] Meyer (1979b, 181). See also Fohlen (1979) on why the French merchants missed their "unique chance to expel the British from the North American market" (p. 98).

British, though at a lower overall level[225] and with the two countries "in an unequal position." This was because "however valuable American trade was to England, English trade was vital to America."[226] It is no wonder that Arthur Young could reflect in a conversation with the Abbé Raynal in 1789 that it was "a most extraordinary event in world politics" for people to lose an empire "and to gain by the loss."[227]

The most obvious zone in which the United States could hope to expand its trade was the Caribbean with which it had long been trading. But here too, the 1780s proved to be a difficult period. None of the British West Indian islands had joined in the American War of Independence, despite various declarations of sympathy throughout the islands and some measure of covert support.[228] The reason was probably twofold: demographics, that is, the fact that Blacks (mostly slaves) were about seven-eighths of the population;[229] and the military vulnerability of small islands to British seapower.[230]

However, the link of the mainland colonies and the British West Indies had grown strong in the decades before the outbreak of the Revolution, precisely because the increasingly monocultural production of sugar had led to a great need for food imports by the West Indian islands. The disruptions of the war caused "severe short-term dislocations" in this trade link and thereby raised the cost of sugar production[231] giving the West Indians great motivation to resume ties as soon as possible. Yet, after 1783, United States ships were excluded by the British from their West Indian colonies (as they were from Spanish colonies).[232] This was bad news as well

---

[225] "Foreign trade, as measured by exports to Britain throughout the 1780s failed to reach two-thirds of its pre-Revolutionary level" (Jeremy, 1981, 14).

[226] Benians (1940, 16). Bemis also argues that, at this time, Anglo–American commerce "was vitally necessary for the national existence of the United States. . . . Ninety percent of American imports [1789] came from Great Britain and the American revenues came mostly from the tariff on imports. Suddenly to have upset commercial relations with Great Britain . . . would have meant the destruction of three-quarters of American foreign commerce. To use a later expression of Alexander Hamilton, it would have cut out credit by the roots" (1923, 35–36).

Furthermore, the British were conscious of their advantage at the time. Lord Sheffield argued against relaxing the Navigation Laws saying: "Friendly indeed we may yet be, and well disposed to them; but we should wait events rather than endeavor to force them . . . and with prudent management [Great Britain] will have as much of [United States] trade as it will be her interest to wish for." (Cited in Stover, 1958, 405.)

[227] Young went on in the vein of a sophisticated twentieth-century imperial decolonizer, expressing doubts that colonizing states could ever bring themselves to abandon colonies voluntarily, even though "to renounce them would be wisdom." He sighed: "France clung to St. Domingue; Spain to Peru; and England to Bengal." (Cited in Lokke, 1932, 155.) As we know, the first two powers were on the verge of losing their ability to cling to these colonies.

[228] See Brathwaite (1971, 68–71) and Kerr (1936, 61).

[229] See the figures in Knollenberg (1960, 298). The two colonies which most actively abetted the Thirteen Colonies were Bermuda and the Bahamas, the only places with a White settler majority.

[230] See Brown (1974, 20). This is, of course, one of the major explanations also offered for why Nova Scotia failed to support the War of Independence.

[231] Knight (1983, 243, 246–247).

[232] See Walton & Shepherd (1979, 183). Williams explains the reasoning behind the order-in-council of December 1783 barring United States ships as based on an arrogance about United States inability to retaliate: "It was the shipping interest . . . whose

for the sugar plantation owners. "From 1783 onward marginal plantations began to collapse."[233]

If external trade prospects seemed momentarily dim for the new settler state, they thought that at least they could expand their economic development on the continent by colonizing the "frontier" zones. But neither Great Britain nor Spain had any intention of facilitating this ambition which ran directly opposite to their own interests. One can think of the eastern half of the North American continent as forming a rectangle in which, in 1783, the new United States constituted a box within the box. Though its border to the east was the same as that of the larger box, the Atlantic Ocean, it was surrounded to the north by Canada which was excluded from its jurisdiction; to the south where the whole northern border of the Gulf of Mexico (from Louisiana to Florida) was under Spanish jurisdiction; and to the west by a vast zone between the Mississippi and the Appalachians, the jurisdiction over which was contested.

There was no question during the peace discussion at Versailles of whether the United States would get Canada. They had failed militarily or politically to secure it during the war. And they certainly had no French diplomatic support in this regard.[234] The British were, if anything, more casual about Canada than the French.[235] The bigger question was whether the United States should be allowed to expand westward. The treaty of 1783 provided that Great Britain turn over the so-called Western ports, eight frontier posts on the American side of the boundary line from Lake Michigan to Lake Champlain. The British dragged their feet. The excuse

views had prevailed. They insisted that Britain need not fear foreign competition nor domestic in the American market for manufactured goods. . . . "The assumption that British command of the American market was secure seemed quickly to be justified by events" (1972, 220, 222).

They also lost the protection of British warships for their Mediterranean trade, which would lead to their problems with the Barbary pirates. As for trade with Ireland, direct trade had been "insignificant during the colonial period" and did not expand now (Nash, 1985, 337).

The one bright spot, but only significant in the longer run, was the opening of the China trade, "a direct consequence of the Revolution" (Ver Steeg, 1957, 366).

[233] Craton (1974, 240), who goes onto argue that even "the 70 percent increase [of sugar production] between 1783 and 1805 was not indicative of great profitability, rather the reverse: it represented an attempt to restore profits by increased production, with inflationary results" (pp. 245–246).

The loss of food imputs from the United States was compounded by an unprecedented series of hurricanes from 1780–1786, denuding vegetation.

The result, says Sheridan (1976a, 615) was a "subsistence crisis."

[234] On the continuity of French policy in this regard from Choiseul to Vergennes, see Trudel (1949b, 131). In 1778, Choiseul, in retirement, wrote a memo to Vergennes, arguing that France should seek an outcome of the war with the United States independent but with Canada, Nova Scotia, and the Carolinas in British hands. Vergennes, in turn, explained to Gérard that such an outcome would ensure that the colonies, once independent, would "prolong indefinitely their rupture with England to the profit of France."

[235] "The casual way in which Lord Shelburne and his agent Richard Oswald seemed prepared, during the spring of 1782, to throw in all Canada as a gratuitous addition to an independent United States can be explained [by their views on free trade]. Roughly their idea was that Great Britain possessed such a commanding lead over the United States in industry and commerce that the formerly British North America must continue to be a rich and expanding market, whether independent or not. The real objective was to exclude France as thoroughly as possible" (Brebner, 1966b, 62).

was that the United States refused to restitute confiscated property of the Loyalists, the United States retorting that the British had permitted thousands of Blacks who were slaves to emigrate to Canada (thus not "restituting property"). In reality, the British merely sought to give Canadian fur traders enough time "to reorganize their businesses and withdraw their property."[236] The matter would not be settled until the Jay Treaty of 1796. Yet the quarrel would eventually be settled with the British, precisely because the British counted on maintaining the United States as a sort of economic satellite.[237] In addition, it is likely that the British were skeptical that the new United States government could solve the real obstacle to its westward expansion, the strong drive to separatism on the part of the frontiersmen.[238]

The situation in the northwest was complex. In addition to the United States and Great Britain, the individual states of the United States had varying interests, as did fur traders and land speculators, as did the White frontiersmen and the Native Americans (the so-called Indians).

The problem, seen from the perspective of the new country, involved two successive issues: first, straightening out the claims of the various thirteen east coast colonies among themselves; then, straightening out the disputes between the east coast (in some zones called the "Tidewater") and the frontier (largely but not entirely trans-Appalachia).

The first issue revolved around presumed ancient rights. Six states—Massachusetts and Connecticut (in the North) and Virginia, North Carolina, South Carolina, and Georgia (in the South)—claimed that their charters going "from sea to sea" allowed them indefinite westward expansion. The states in between—and notably Pennsylvania, Maryland, Delaware, and New Jersey—had no such clause in their founding documents, and would, therefore, be excluded from the land speculation rush. They sought to organize private companies (e.g., the Indiana Company and the

[236] Jones (1965, 508). See also Burt (1931). Rippy suggests another motive for British reluctance to cede the ports, the fear that this would enable the United States "to menace Canada" (1929, 23–24).

The French were not unhappy about British foot dragging. See Trudel (1949a, 195). Canada was not a united force on this issue. The great merchants felt that the Treaty of 1783 had destroyed the old commercial empire of the St. Lawrence and maintained pressure right up to 1815 for a revision of the frontiers. But 1783 also marked the arrival in Canada of the Loyalists from the now-independent colonies. These loyalists were primarily farmers and brought "production for export into the heart of the primitive fur-trading state" (Creighton, 1937, 89).

As for the United States, access to the West seemed a sort of "pay-off" which would allow it both to absorb the public debt and to give opportu-

nities to large numbers of persons "to repair their fortunes" (Henderson, 1973, 187). Hence, British delay seemed unconscionable.

[237] "During the first two decades after 1783, England's economic partnership with the United States reduced the role of [Canada and Newfoundland] to one of minor importance" (Graham, 1941, 56). See also Brebner (1966, 85) who observes the "contrast between British intransigence [to the United States] on maritime issues and complaisance on continental ones."

[238] Harlow (1964, 603) argues that the prevailing opinion in British government circles at this time was that "it seemed probable that the western frontier of the United States would remain at the Allegheny and Appalachian Mountains. It did not seem practicable that a federal government near the Atlantic coast could extend its authority over a vast ultramontane wilderness."

Illinois-Wabash Company), and turned to the new United States to help them, as they had in earlier times turned to the British.[239] The outcome was a compromise, the Northwest Ordinance of 1787. The states with "sea to sea" claims ceded these claims to the United States, allowing the land to be sold off (and thereby reduce United States debt), but only in lots of 640 acres (thereby satisfying the large land speculators in "democratic" fashion).

The Ordinance had, however, another provision, the possibility of creating new states in the region. This clause, again excluding equally all east coast "imperialism," would eventually be the solution for the tidewater–backwoodsmen tension which plagued the Continental Congress throughout the revolution—the hostility of the "Regulators" in North Carolina and the ambivalence of Vermont to the revolutionary cause.[240] In general, "westerners," particularly those in the new territories of Kentucky and Tennessee saw Congressional control as "deliverance from the role of the coast counties in the legislatures."[241] The frontiersmen thought of themselves as continuing the battle of 1776, with themselves as the "oppressed colonists," and with the east coast state governments in the role of "tyrant formerly filled by George III."[242] Furthermore, the economic geography of the situation was such that it was easier to ship their products by inland navigation northeast into British zones and southwest into Spanish zones than overland to the east coast states.[243]

The Northwest Ordinance deflected this resentment by creating a distinction between the central United States government and the eastern states. But there was a second issue which pushed the frontier zones away from the separatism which tempted them, the Indians. The British were playing the traditional game of trying to create a "neutral Indian barrier state" inside the United States,[244] and the frontiersmen basically coveted the "unceded" Indian lands. This is where the United States could help

---

[239] See Jensen (1936, 28–30; see also 1939). Expansion plans had been aborted by the War of American Independence. Just before it, the Vandalia Company had been formed incorporating the Indiana and Ohio Companies. In 1773, the Company had gained from the Lords Commissioners of Trade and Planations a report recommending the grant of territory approximately including today's West Virginia and eastern Kentucky to be called Vandalia. "Although all of the processes of transfer, excepting a few formalities, had been effected, the outbreak of the American Revolution put a stop to the grant" (Turner, 1895, 74).

[240] In the United States textbooks, Ethan Allen is a revolutionary hero. In reality, he and his brothers set up an independent commonwealth in 1777 and were bargaining with the British for the recognition of the independence of Vermont, bargaining that

was continuing as late as 1789 when Levi Allen went to London to offer a deal to George III. After some further bargaining with the state of New York (which relinquished some land claims in 1790), Vermont "entered" the United States as the four- teenth state in 1791. See Brebner (1966b, 66–67). The "independence" of Maine from Massachusetts involved similar issues. See Greene (1943, 408– 409).

[241] Turner (1896, 268).

[242] Whitaker (1962a, 92).

[243] See Bemis (1916, 547).

[244] Bemis (1923, 109) Stevens (1926, 14–15) argues that the British success with the Indians allowed them to maintain commercial supremacy in the Northwest until after the War of 1812. See also Wright (1975, 35).

them, especially after 1789 with the formal creation of a federal government, and the simultaneous distraction of Great Britain because of the French Revolution and its aftermath. "Europe's distresses were America's advantage."[245] That is, it was to the advantage of the White settlers, not the Native Americans. For the latter,

> the American president was a man to be feared, the direct analogue of czar, emperor, and sultan; for Creeks and Cherokees, Chickasaws, Shawnees, Winnebagos, and many others, the new city of Washington was what St. Petersburg was for the Finns, Peking for the Miao, or Constantinople for the Serbs: the seat of a capricious, tyrannical power.[246]

Whereas Great Britain's attitude towards United States frontier expansion was that of a hegemonic power handling an essentially minor, if troubling, problem, the Spanish had to take the issue more seriously. They were defending an American empire that was already under attack and could not afford either United States economic success or the spread of the United States political example. The British–United States treaties of peace and the British–Spanish treaty of peace were both signed on September 3, 1783. Yet they contradicted each other on a crucial issue affecting the entire Mississippi Valley. The treaty with the United States granted the United States free navigation of the Mississippi River and fixed the southern boundary at the 30° parallel. The treaty with Spain made no mention of navigation on the Mississippi. It provided, however, that Spain should retain West Florida which, according to a British order-in-council of 1764, included the Mississippi river port of Natchez and all territory north to a point about 32°26'.[247]

At first the Spanish found it hard to distinguish between their traditional enemy, England, and its offshoot, the United States, whom they referred to as "Anglo–Americans."[248] But the distinction began to take hold, and not to the favor of the United States. Perhaps the Spanish read the astute forecast of Jacques Accarias de Sérionne in 1766:

> New England is perhaps more to be feared than the old one, with regard to Spain's losing its colonies. The population and the liberty of the Anglo–Americans seem a distant announcement of the conquest of the richest zones of America, and the establishment of a new empire of Englishmen, independent of Europe.[249]

The Spanish found that the British merchants in the newly acquired ports of St. Augustine, Mobile, and Pensacola favored them over the United

---

[245] Bemis (1943, 18).
[246] Meinig (1986, 369–370). Chaunu (1964, 183) sees the fur traders and the settlers as constituting a one-two operation of spatial conquest against the Indians. "A forward line of trappers preceded the true frontier, that of farmers (with fire and ax)

pushing back the Indians already conquered by whiskey, rum, and more surely still, by firearms."
[247] See Whitaker (1962a, 11).
[248] Whitaker (1962a, 33–34).
[249] Accarias de Sérionne (1766, I, 73).

States traders with whom they had "bitter feuds." There was, however, a price for the Spanish resulting from their own economic weakness. "In order to prevent [United States] Americans from trading with her Indian neighbors, [Spain] had to permit Englishmen to trade with them through her own ports."[250]

Spain as defender of the fur trader in the southwest against the United States land speculator was even less able to succeed than Britain in this role in the northwest, especially given the large role of non-Spaniards in the local economy of Louisiana and the Floridas. Spain was never able to integrate these zones (all recently acquired) into its own colonial system and this foreshadowed the loss of the two colonies (in 1815 and 1819, respectively) to the United States.[251]

The new United States was not only a new power in the Americas with economic interests to pursue. It was also a symbol of settler independence. It espoused a principle of republicanism. But what was a republic? It seemed to many to be an ideology of free trade, free men, and equality. We have just seen that in the 1780s the United States did not do so well promoting free trade. Indeed, as McCoy observes, the commercial crisis of the 1780s had a "profoundly unsettling effect on the way in which Americans viewed themselves and their society."[252] The failure in foreign trade was no doubt one of the elements that created the constitutional crisis of 1783–1791, the moment where the survival of the new state as a unified political entity was in question. But, in the long run, what was more important for the world-system, insofar as the United States presented itself and was thought of as a model of settler independence, was how it resolved the questions of free men and equality in this period.

The question of free men did not revolve around the Native Americans. They were outside the realm (and constitutionally remained so in the United States until 1924). The settlers wanted to displace the Indians from their land, not incorporate them as a work force in their economic activities.[253] The Blacks, largely slaves, were not outside the realm.

---

[250] Whitaker (1962a, 37, 43). See also Williams (1972, 57–59). This had a precedent. When the Spanish assumed effective control of Louisiana from the French with the arrival of General O'Reilly in New Orleans in 1769, they ejected the English merchant establishment. But when, in 1770, O'Reilly, back in Havana, prohibited the export of inferior Louisiana tobacco as a threat to Cuban export, the English returned de facto as clandestine traders. See Clark (1970, 170–180).

[251] See Whitaker (1928, 198) and Clark (1970, 220).

[252] McCoy (1980, 105).

[253] On the limited meaning for Indians even of the Citizenship Act of 1924, see Lacy (1985, 91 ff.) The debates over the Articles of Confederation

about Indians revolved around the role of the central government versus those of the states. The victory of the Center was in fact a victory for the ideological exclusion of the Indians from the body politic. "The concept of the Indian Country was strengthened. Not only was the Indian Country that territory lying beyond the boundary lines and forbidden to settlers and to unlicensed traders; but it was also the area over which federal authority extended. Federal laws governing the Indians and the Indian trade took effect in the Indian Country only; outside they did not hold" (Prucha, 1970, 31).

This attitude of exclusion marked a shift from an early colonial period attitude when it was thought the Indians might "incorporate [European ways] into their own lives" (McNickle, 1957, 8).

They were an integral, indeed a central part, of the productive process. In 1774, the population of the Thirteen Colonies (excluding Indians), was 2.3 million. Of these, 20% were Black slaves and another 1% free Blacks.[254] The eighteenth century saw a steady increase of slave imports into the Americas.[255] One of the main reasons for this was the sharp decline and eventual elimination of the system of indentured labor. In the case of British North America, the indentured laborers had been mostly English in the seventeenth century, but the ethnic pattern changed in the eighteenth century, a large percentage now being Germans, Swiss, Scots, Scotch–Irish, Irish, etc.[256] The last two decades of the colonial era saw the "rapid abandonment of bound labor" in the major northern cities. This was of course in part because of the economic difficulties, and indeed even led to "resentment of slave labor competition" by artisans and attacks on slavery.[257] But the longer term reason was that, with the growing demand for labor, the elasticity of the supply of slaves was much greater than that of indentured workers, and hence the costs of the latter rose with respect to the costs of the former.[258]

When Jefferson sought to include in the Declaration of Independence a section denouncing George III for curtailing efforts to ban the slave trade, he met with "heated objections" not only from the delegates from Georgia and South Carolina where slaves were plentiful but from delegates from Massachusetts, Connecticut, and Rhode Island, in which states the slave trade remained an important business.[259] Slavery existed even in the northern states where, if "relatively small" in numbers, it remained a "common and accepted practice."[260] The American War of Independence opened the question up, as both the British and the colonists considered the possibility of using Blacks as soldiers. Although the idea was unpopular, even in England, "the war brought realities of its own." First the British recruited, and then with greater reluctance the Continental Congress and most of the northern states recruited, granting freedom as "the reward for faithful service."[261]

[254] A. H. Jones (1980, 39, Table 2.4). Main's figures for 1760 show 23% of the population as Black slaves, of which four-fifths were in the southern states (1965, 271).

[255] See Curtin (1969, 216, Table 6.5) for one estimate which shows a doubling over the century.

[256] See Morris (1946, 315–316).

[257] Nash (1979, 320–321).

[258] See Galenson (1981b, 175). Among the reasons given in Georgia at the time in public defense of slavery was that "slaves could be fed, clothed and housed at about one-quarter of the cost of maintaining white servants." Furthermore, slaves were said to work better than the White servants "selected from the dregs of white society, unused to farm work, repelled by the thought of hard work,

vulnerable to the 'heats' and 'colds' of Georgia, and likely to abscond successfully from their masters" (Gray & Wood, 1976, 356).

In 1774, the French formally abolished the system of *engagés* (indentured labor), henceforth relying on slave labor as "the unique solution of the problem of colonial labor" (Vignols, 1928a, 6).

[259] Aptheker (1960, 101). The slave trade was particularly concentrated in the hands of Rhode Island merchants, who controlled between 1725 and 1807 from 60% rising to 90% of the trade. See Coughtry (1981, 6, 25).

[260] Zilversmit (1967, 7).

[261] Quarles (1961, 100, 198). See also Berlin (1976, 352–353). The British–colonist competition for Black support was probably initiated by Lord

The Blacks (freemen and slaves) maneuvered as best they could. Those who became Loyalists were "less pro-British than they were pro-Black." They saw themselves as "advocates of Black liberation."[262] Others joined the Revolutionary cause and thereby contributed to a process of eradicating slavery which, by the end of the war, had been launched in all the northern states except New York and New Jersey.[263] The message was clearly mixed at best. And the postwar pattern remained mixed. The Northwest Ordinance of 1787 did ban slavery from this region. And the matter of the slave trade was much debated in the Constitutional Convention. The famous compromise, a total abolition of the slave trade to come into effect 20 years later (in 1808), had the important side effect of pushing slavery "deeper into the South."[264] Seventy years later, in 1857, Chief Justice Roger Taney would declare in the Dred Scott decision that, as of 1787, the Blacks "had no rights which man was bound to respect." As Litwack says, this was "less a sign of moral callousness than an important historical truth."[265] The "inalienable rights" of the colonists did not yet include Blacks.

Well then, were at least all White settlers equal? Not quite. We know that there was growing inequality in the period leading up to the War of Independence. The question is whether the war itself and its immediate aftermath had any significant impact on the degree of economic polarization and on the political ideology that was in formation. What originally split empire loyalists and rebels in British North America was less the perception of British policy (widely considered to be misguided) as the attitude to take toward it. The Whigs thought they were rebelling on behalf of British national ideals; the Tories thought loyalty to the Crown had to be maintained despite ministerial folly. The positive act of creating a new nation came later. It was the "march of events of the Revolution [that] were inexorably pushing the Americans toward the formation of the image of a nation."[266] This is important to remember, because the dynamic of a nationalism in creation had a lot of impact upon the social perception of inequality.

Dunmore, Governor of Virginia, who in November 1775 promised freedom to slaves who rallied to the kind and bore arms. "The British were trying, not to initiate a revolution, but to end a rebellion. *Status quo ante bellum* was their basic policy" (Robinson, 1971, 105). When the British troops left the United States at the end of the war, they took with them "thousands" of Blacks—to Great Britain, Canada, the West Indies, and even Africa (Berlin, 1976, 355). This actually became, as we previously noted, a source of contention with the United States government.

[262] Walker (1975, 53, 66).

[263] See Zilversmit (1967, 137, 146–152) and Litwack (1961, 3–4). The process was nonetheless

slow. Only two states had totally abolished slavery— Vermont in 1777 and Massachusetts in 1783. Others took partial steps in a process that dragged on in the northern states until 1846 when New Jersey, bringing up the rear, finally abolished slavery totally.

[264] Freehling (1972, 89). It should further be noted that Indian exclusion was closely tied to the expansion of Black slave inclusion. "The American Revolution freed southern slaveholders from various imperial restraints, opening the way for Indian removal and for a westward expansion of slavery" (Davis, 1983, 273).

[265] Litwack (1987, 316).

[266] Savelle (1962, 916).

To understand what was happening, we have to look at who was cool to revolution. We must always bear in mind that here, as in most revolutionary situations, at the beginning, only a minority were strongly committed either way. The majority were "dubious, afraid, uncertain, indecisive."[267] There seemed to be three zones where Toryism (or at least Loyalism) had its strongest foothold. One zone was constituted by the maritime regions of the middle colonies. This was the Toryism of social conservatism. These were the people who feared New England activists as "radical levellers."[268] These were the people who saw themselves in a great battle with other colonists over "what kind of institutions America ought to have." If one looks at these Tories vis-à-vis the Patriots, one can talk of a "civil war," in which the Patriots were the party of movement against the Tories as the party of order.[269] This is the basis of the mythology, plausible up to a point, of the American Revolution as a social revolution.

But there were other Tories. A second major group were the frontiersmen from Georgia to Vermont, most notable in the Regulator Movement in western North Carolina. "Wherever sailors and fishermen, trappers and traders outnumbered farmers and planters, there Tories outnumbered Whigs."[270] These were the Loyalists who looked to the British government as a check on the rapacious land speculators of the east coast. As we have just seen, the fear was real and justified and the victory of the settler Patriots doomed these frontiersmen. Perhaps they were "doomed" in any case, but the American Revolution no doubt accelerated the pace. For these Loyalists, the Patriots represented a conservative not a radical force.

There was a third node of resistance, the "cultural minorities," all of whom seemed to show a higher rate of Loyalism. This group, who overlapped with the group of frontiersmen, were more beset by poverty. From Pennsylvania to Georgia, inland counties were "largely peopled" by Scots, Irish, and Germans. The differences of origin between inlanders and those on the coast were most marked in the Carolinas, where the most serious clashes in fact occurred.[271] Religious as well as ethnic minorities (of course, often they were the same) also inclined toward Loyalism. Episcopalians in the northern colonies, Presbyterians in the southern ones, Pietists and Baptists everywhere, were not leaning toward the Revolutionary cause.[272] All of these people seemed skeptical that the new national and nationalist majority would consider their interests. They feared that the emphasis on individual interests would eradicate their group interests.

---

[267] Shy (1973, 143).
[268] Henderson (1973, 180).
[269] Nelson (1961, 1).
[270] Nelson (1961, 88).
[271] Greene (1943, 158).
[272] Nelson (1961, 90). Catholics and Jews were, however, an "exception." Was it that they felt "obliged to follow what seemed majority opinion for their own safety" or was it because they had no reason to believe the British would protect them? Catholics in Ireland behaved differently.

In terms, therefore, of the defense of social privilege, there were Loyalists who were Loyalists because they feared egalitarian tendencies and there were Loyalists who were Loyalists for exactly the opposite reason. In the end, Palmer's evaluation seems quite just: "the patriots were those who saw an enlargement of opportunity in the break with Britain, and the loyalists were in large measure those who had benefited from the British connection," or at least, one might add, who saw no reason to presume they would benefit from the break.[273]

One last consideration. Why was not what might be called the Toryism of the left, those who were not Patriots precisely because they feared inegalitarian majorities, not stronger than it was? For had it been politically stronger, it is probable the settlers would never have won the war with the British. Morgan notes how different the intensity of this class conflict was between the atmosphere in 1676 at the time of Bacon's Rebellion[274] and in 1776. In between, he says, "the growth of slavery had curbed the growth of a free, depressed lower class and correspondingly magnified the social and economic opportunities of whites."[275]

The ambivalence about the social implications of the War of American Independence maintained itself after 1783. The reality of polarization in fact grew. If Boston, for example, heartland of the radical thrust of the revolution, had been intensely unequal before the Revolution, "an even more unequal society" developed after the Revolution.[276] When, in the post-1783 period, New England merchants found themselves excluded from the West Indies by British retribution, they translated their economic difficulties into "debt collection." When small farmers in western Massachusetts grumbled, repressive legislation ensued which "spurred many farmers to direct action," the insurrection known as Shay's Rebellion in 1786.[277] It was suppressed.

This ambivalence was the context within which the Constitution was drafted in 1787. It is in this sense that the Beardian interpretation,[278] much contested in the American celebration of the 1950s and 1960s, has merit. If the social revolutionaries played a large role in launching the Revolution, and some of their radical thrust had gained strength by the very process of the Revolution, it seems clear that the Constitutional Convention represented an attempt to turn back this thrust. The conspicuous popular leaders of 1776 were all absent from the 1787 Convention, most of whose members "deplored democracy and agreed that a powerful central govern-

---

[273] Palmer (1959, I, 201).
[274] See the documents in Middlekauff (1964).
[275] Morgan (1973, 296).
[276] Kulikoff (1971, 376).
[277] Szatmary (1980, 92).
[278] See Beard (1913; 1915). For a recent sophisticated defense of Beard, see McGuire and Ohsfeldt (1984, 577), who suggest that the voting patterns of

the Constitutional Convention support a narrow Beardian interpretation "that the only economic interests that would matter would be those in which a significant financial interest is directly at stake," but that the votes of the ratifying conventions give support to a "broad Beardian interpretation" that all economic interests would matter regardless of the scale of their impact.

ment was needed to remedy the evils which had beset the nation because of it."[279] This was so marked that it almost torpedoed the ratification process, which led to the concession of 1791 with the adoption of the first Ten Amendments to the Constitution, the Bill of Rights.[280]

If the peace of 1783 opened a period of great uncertainty for the United States, it was even more serious in the long run for Spanish America, precisely because Spain not only had to deal with her own populations and her European rivals as before, but now with the United States as well.[281] At one level this was a golden period for the Spanish colonial economy. The average annual exports from Spain to Spanish America between 1782 and 1796 (the year that war began again between Spain and Great Britain and hence a British naval blockade disrupted trade) were four times higher than in 1778 (just before Spain and Great Britain went to war). In particular, there was a "massive expansion" of trade in 1784–1785.[282] This was in part due to the ability of Spain to reduce seriously the amount of contraband trade, an ability that had been steadily growing since 1760.[283]

To be sure, the golden age was only to be "brief" and the commercial expansion of Spain between the declaration of *comercio libre* in 1778 to the British naval blockade of 1796 seems "far less impressive" if placed in the context of the overall growth of the world-economy.[284] The Steins even speak of the "meager returns" for Spanish (and Portuguese) efforts at economic nationalism. Iberian colonial trade merely "shored up the 'gothic edifice,' which was not precisely the way to ready it for the great crisis."[285] Local artisanal and manufacturing production in Spanish America was "jeopardized"[286] by Spanish liberalization of trade. But this was to metropolitan Spain's advantage only momentarily because of Spain's inability to compete with Great Britain as a producer of goods and as an exporter of capital. Thus, precisely where foreign penetration was deepest, Caracas and La Plata, some colonists began to think that perhaps "a golden prospect was in store for them if they could but shake off the Spanish yoke."[287] In the meantime, the position of British merchants located in Cádiz (and Lisbon) "seemed particularly fortunate and happy," since they

[279] Jensen (1974, 172).

[280] Nor did this conservative attempt to counter the "destabilizing" effects of the Revolution stop then. The "older entrenched elite" continued to try to erect "bulwarks . . . to secure vested property rights and to maintain the status quo" (Bruchey, 1987, 309).

[281] "If ever a peace failed to pacify, it was the peace of 1783. . . . For no treaty defined the relations or restrained the rivalry of the oldest and newest empires in America, Spain, and the United States" (Whitaker, 1962a, 1).

[282] Fisher (1981, 32). Navarro García (1975, 173) speaks of New Spain reaching "levels of prosperity never before known" during this period.

[283] "It seems that in 1792–95, contraband trade had become less than a third of the official trade between the metropole and the colonies, which constituted a total reversal of the situation compared to earlier periods (except for the sixteenth century)" (Bousquet, 1974, 21).

[284] Brading (1984, I, 413, 418).

[285] Stein & Stein (1970, 104). And Whitaker (1962a, 16) uses the phrase, the "sick man of America."

[286] Bousquet (1974, 42). On the decline of the *obrajes* in Mexico in this period, see Greenleaf (1967, 240) and Salvucci (1981, 199).

[287] Whitaker (1928, 202).

could immediately benefit from the abolition of the monopolies.[288] Furthermore, it may even be that the relative success of the Spanish against the interlopers was itself negative for Spain politically, since previously these British interlopers, "by supplying the needs of the Spanish–American colonies, kept them from rebelling earlier against the rule of Spain."[289]

Still, during this brief interlude of the 1780s, matters were quiet in Spanish America, and the United States was absorbed in its own difficulties. The outbreak of the French Revolution in 1789 was unsettling. But even more unsettling was the fact that the outbreak of the Revolution in France set in motion a process in St.-Domingue that would lead to the creation of the first Black republic in the modern world-system. The violent birth of Haiti was a more critical factor in the history of the Americas than we usually suggest. It should be given credit for hastening and clarifying the pattern of settler independence everywhere else. For the Haitian Revolution was indeed, as that scholarly racist T. Lothrop Stoddard put it, "the first great shock between the ideals of white supremacy and race equality."[290]

The difficulties began in the economic arena. St.-Domingue had been a jewel in France's crown, the leading sugar exporter of the Americas, and all to the profit of France. Then the Eden Treaty of 1786 and the Franco–American convention of 1787 "broke a wide breach" in the *Pacte Colonial*,[291] and hence made French planters aware that they now needed actively to look after their economic interests in the political arena. Thus, when Louis XVI convened the Estates-General in 1787, there was an immediate debate about whether St.-Domingue should claim representation. The advocates won the day, and in this way, St.-Domingue was drawn into the vortex of the Paris events.[292]

The White settlers found almost immediately a resistance to their interests in the French National Assembly on two quite different grounds: resistance to the idea of colonial autonomy; and resistance by some who wished to accord individual rights (and hence share in control of any potential autonomy) to the so-called "free colored" (a legal category) and even thought of emancipating slaves.[293] The reaction was swift. On April

[288] Christelow (1947, 8).

[289] Pantaleão (1946, 275). This would imply that it was less desirable than it seemed that Spain's trade with Spanish America in this period "enjoyed an incredible scope" (Villalobos, 1965, 10).

[290] Stoddard (1914, vii). Stoddard's book, however biased, is a clear, step-by-step, detailed exposition of the whole political history of the Haitian revolution.

[291] Stoddard (1914, 18). Debien (1953, 52) explains the attitudes of the White settlers in 1786 as refusing to play any longer the role of Cinderella. "They sensed simultaneously the incompetence of the metropole and their own competence to run their own affairs and first of all their commercial affairs."

[292] This claim to colonial representation was not envisaged by Louis XVI and hence constituted "a revolutionary act" (Césaire, 1961, 37).

[293] The official census of 1788 showed the White population as 28,000, the "free colored" as 22,000, and slaves as 405,000. Two estimates of intendants in 1789 give slightly higher figures for the first two categories, and are possibly more accurate, but the difference was not great. See Stoddard (1914, 8–9).

15, 1790, at Saint-Marc, the General Assembly of the French Sector of St.-Domingue met and refused the title of colony. Its President, Bacon de la Chevalerie, posed the following question: "By what subtle reasoning has one arrived at a situation in which one puts free and independent conquerers under the most astonishing despotic yoke?"[294] (shades of 1776). He promptly announced to the "colored" populations that they would be put back behind their demarcation line (shades of 1787).

The difference was that, in France, the revolution proclaimed the aim of ending legal privilege, while the White settlers of St.-Domingue made claims for autonomous authority on the basis for "the political nonexistence of other free persons and . . . the political and civil nonexistence of the slaves." In short, instead of ending legal privilege, they wanted to given permanent legal status to "a dominant caste."[295] They were not successful in this objective.

France's Constituent Assembly in 1790 ambiguously gave the vote to propertied mulattoes in St.-Domingue. When a political leader of the mulattoes returned to St.-Domingue and sought by rebellion to enforce this right, he was captured, tortured, and executed. The National Assembly, upset, passed another, less ambiguous decree. The White settlers rose up against the French and against the mulattoes. And suddenly, in the midst of this, we have the first Black uprising of slaves. Instead of the "class alliance" of the government, the planters, and the rich mulattoes against poor Whites, mulattoes, and Black slaves, as occurred in other French colonies, such as Isle-de-France and Isle de Bourbon, the "race war" had begun.[296]

The race war was not what the White settlers had wanted when seeking their racially pure autonomy. Nor was it what the French Revolutionaries in Paris wanted, since, for them, the principle of "territorial conservation" remained strong.[297] Nor was it what the "free coloreds"—often rich, slave-owning mulattoes—had wanted when they laid claim to their equal rights. But it was imposed by the Black slaves themselves, in what can only be seen as the most successful slave rebellion in the history of the capitalist world-economy. Now began the period of the "three-way civil war"[298] in St.-Domingue, the fruit of the three successive uprisings—"the fronde of the important Whites, the mulatto revolt, and the Negro revolution."[299]

The situation alarmed, appalled, and discontented all four powers in the

[294] Cited in Debien (1953, 215). On the background of this sentiment of "American patriotism" among the White settlers prior even to 1786, see Debien (1954). On the earlier White revolt of the coffee growers in 1769, see Trouillot (1981). On French perceptions of and ambivalences about "decolonization" tendencies prior to 1789, see Sée (1929) and Lokke (1932).

[295] Saintoyant (1930, II, 75–76, 423).

[296] See Stoddard (1914, 97–99).

[297] Saintoyant (1930, I, 376), who also argues that the Convention could only regard the Haitian revolution as "more menacing for the existence, not only of the new régime, but of France itself" than all the various hexagonal insurrections, including the Vendée (I, 233).

[298] Ott (1973, 51).

[299] Césaire (1961).

region—France, Great Britain, the United States, and Spain. The views in the National Assembly and then in the Convention were mixed and perhaps confused. But overall, the Convention tended to be on the side of the mulattoes, as the guarantors of a civilized transition. As Césaire put it, the famous Société des Amis des Noirs in Paris was "first and foremost the Society of the mulattoes."[300]

As for the British, as soon as the war broke out between Great Britain and France in February, 1793, the White settlers appealed for British assistance and entered into secret accords with the British.[301] The British saw this as a good opportunity to ruin the commerce of France. The British sent an expedition, but their occupation of St.-Domingue backfired badly, ranking "among the greatest disasters in British military history."[302] Indeed, their intervention, by creating a competition among French, Spanish, and British troops for slave support, "dramatically broadened the scope of the then languishing [slave] revolt and rescued it from what might have been extinction."[303]

The United States, which feared as much as Great Britain, that "the virus of freedom would infect slaves in their own possessions," was, however, "by no means enthusiastic" about the British intervention, which threatened to place their trading partner, St.-Domingue, "behind the bars of the Navigation System."[304] The United States therefore tried very hard to maintain and extend its role as food supplier to St.-Domingue, while avoiding all political relations.[305]

[300] Césaire (1961, 85). In a chapter entitled "The Limits of the French Revolution," Césaire says: "Let's face it, the French assemblies talked profusely about the Negroes and did very little on their behalf" (p. 159). As Sala-Molins notes: "The Convention did not abolish slavery for Blacks [on February 4, 1794] because of their lovely eyes, but because the rebels forced them to do it; and because of the English and Spanish policies of the time threatened, in those far-off Windward Islands, to undermine the unity and indivisibility of the Republic" (1987, 262).

[301] See Debien (1954, 53–54).

[302] Geggus (1981, 285). "No regimental banner bears the words 'St. Domingo.' No minister or general wished to preserve in his memoirs the history of occupation. It was an episode best forgotten and which the nineteenth century had no need to remember" (Geggus, 1982, 387).

[303] Geggus (1982, 389). Momentarily, this was all very good for British West Indian prosperity. Between the civil war in St.-Domingue and the capture of the Dutch colonies in 1796, "Britain suddenly became almost the sole supplier [of sugar] to Europe" (Checkland, 1958, 461). This "final phase" of prosperity lasted only to 1799.

The British also drew the lessons of St.-Domingue for their own Black West Indian possess-

ions. They armed Blacks in West India Regiments beginning in 1795. They thereby won control over the White settlers and over the Black slaves, for now the British had slaves "who would police the huge slave empire in the Caribbean" (Buckley, 1979, 140).

[304] Perkins (1955, 106). Jordan observes that, for the United States "St. Domingo assumed the character of a terrifying volcano of violence," threatening to reopen the "closed subject" of slavery. Furthermore, settler refugees from Haiti brought slaves to the United States, who were "vectors of insurrectionary plague." It was considered, he says, "from the very first . . . a threat to American security" (1968, 380–386).

But this was balanced, as Ott notes, by a second line, "sometimes at loggerheads" with the line defending Southern slave society. The second line of interest to New England merchants, was "the maintenance of Saint-Domingue as a trading base," a line which "usually meant support of the government in power" (1973, 53–54). In the period 1798–1800, when the United States was waging a "quasi-war" with France, John Adams even entered into a "quasialliance" with both Great Britain and Toussaint L'Ouverture, to whom was extended a "quasi-recognition" (Logan, 1941, 68).

[305] See Trendley (1961).

The Spaniards, of course, were equally wary. The eastern half of the island was their colony of Santo Domingo. The Black revolution did not really spread there, except by conquest. The economy was different (cattle and subsistence farming instead of sugar plantations). The demography was therefore different—Whites, *libertos* (mostly mulatto, but some Black), and Black slaves in equal proportions. Finally, the social structure was different. The *libertos* were not an important economic force, like the mulattoes in St.-Domingue, and the Spanish administration was able to keep them under stricter control.[306] The initial Spanish intervention in St.-Domingue was no more successful then the British.

Toussaint L'Ouverture was able to take advantage of the Franco–British war to consolidate his administration and to create a disciplined army. He kept the plantations going, confining the Black workers to them but giving them a fourth of the produce. But as the Europeans temporarily stopped fighting among themselves, they turned their anxiety about the Black republic into a new attempt to decapitate it. Napoleon's troops arrested Toussaint in 1802. And Spain, the United States, and Great Britain all tacitly collaborated with France in this attempt at recolonization.[307] Though the island remained independent with, after a while, two governments in existence, recognition on the part of the four powers remained "unthinkable" for quite a while.[308]

[306] See Franco (1968). Still the Spanish authorities had been worried. In 1791, the Conde de Floridablanca instructed the Viceroys of Mexico and Santa Fé, the governors of La Habana, Puerto Rico, Santo Domingo, Trinidad, and Cartagena to make sure that "the contagion of insurrection is not communicated to Spanish possessions, and specifically in pursuit of this objective the Government of Santo Domingo shall establish a *cordon* of troops at the frontier." (Cited by Verna, 1984, 747.) On the effects of the revolution in St.-Domingue on Santo Domingo, see Dilla Alfonso (1982, 83–90). The Spanish government put down antislavery conspiracies in Louisiana in 1795, in Martinique and Guadeloupe in 1794, in Tierra Firma in 1795, and in Guatemala in 1797.

[307] See Lokke (1928). At the time, President Thomas Jefferson spoke of trying "to reduce Toussaint to starvation" and called Haiti "another Algiers" (p. 324).

Bonaparte's expedition, despite the death of Toussaint L'Ouverture, was a disaster. The greatest beneficiary was not France but the United States. It is generally conceded that this experience led Napoleon to cede (sell) Louisiana to the United States. See Léger (1934, 17), Sloane (1904, 514), Logan (1941, 142–144), and Whitaker (1962b, 234–236). On the previous extensive social links of Louisiana and St.-Domingue, see Baur (1970, 401–404). On why, therefore, Jefferson feared danger in Louisiana as a result of Napoleon's victory, see

pp. 411–412. But as Jordan observes: "The United States was not then nor afterward overwhelmed with gratitude for Haitian assistance, for by 1804 American would see in the new Republic of Haiti little else than a sample of Negro rule" (1968, 377).

[308] Logan (1941, 152). Liévano Aguirre speaks of a "*cordon* of security that was erected to isolate Haiti" (1968, 954). France recognized Haiti only in 1825, Great Britain in 1833 (the year of slave emancipation), the United States only much later in 1862. See Logan (1941, 76–77), and Jordan (1968, 378, fn. 2). Even the Spanish American republics would hold Haiti at a distance. Colombia took the lead of excluding Haiti from the Congress of Panama in 1824. See Verna (1969, 477–495), and Baur (1970, 410). No Latin America country would recognize Haiti until Brazil did so in 1865. Mexico was to recognize Haiti only in 1934.

The "Blackness" of Haiti seemed to get even greater emphasis after the death of Toussaint. His immediate successor, Dessalines, forbade non-Blacks to hold property, making an exception only for Frenchmen who had supported independence, and for German and Polish deserters to the Haitian cause (Verna, 1969, 64; Nicholls, 1978, 179). On the Poles, see Pachoński & Wilson (1986). It was after Dessalines's assassination that Haiti was divided into a Black-ruled kingdom in the north under Henri Christophe and a mulatto-dominated republic in the west and south under Alexandre Pétion, later the friend of Bolívar. The two sections were

In retrospect, we can probably say that the Black revolution in St.-Domingue slowed down the drive for independence in Hispanic America, despite the friendly but ambiguous links of Simón Bolívar and Alexandre Pétion, president of one of the two successor states in Haiti, the mulatto-dominated southern part. The effect of St.-Domingue was to instill a great deal of prudence not only in the European powers but, above all, among the White settlers of the Americas.[309]

It was in this same period that the prospects of an Irish revolution, which initially seemed to be carried along by the same wave that swept up British North America, but then began to assume the shape of a social revolution, came to an end. Ireland had played a role in precipitating the British imperial crisis of the 1760s in the first place. In some ways, in North America, Great Britain was repeating attitudes and carrying out policies already invented for the Irish situation.[310] Ireland itself was actually in many ways worse off than British North America. British Protestant settlers had imposed their rule on a dense Irish Catholic peasant population, not on a scattered group of largely hunting tribes. It was a situation structurally more akin to Peru or central Mexico than to the Thirteen Colonies.[311]

The absence of all political rights for Catholics (as of 1691) meant, however, that it was the Protestant settlers who felt "the full force of English commercial jealousy." It was, therefore, this "trusted 'garrison' [that] was [being] treated as a commercial menace."[312] The Protestant settlers were not even allowed to have a shipping industry (which the New England settlers had), and Ireland was not permitted to be an entrepôt between the Americas and Europe. Indeed, one of the explicit North American fears of the time was that they might be reduced to "the unhappy condition of northern Ireland."[313]

---

rejoined in 1811. On this period, and in particular on land reform in Haiti, see Lacerte (1975); see also Lundhal (1984). Trouillot (1971) considers that the end of the process was the triumph of what he calls the Black Creoles. See for a similar view Joachim (1970).

[309] See Madariaga (1948, 324–325) and Sheridan (1976b, 237). It had a particular impact on Cuba, which could now replace St.-Domingue as a sugar supplier. The slave insurrection in St.-Domingue served as a "terrible warning" to Creoles and Spaniards alike in Cuba (Humphreys & Lynch, 1965a, 19). It was a warning great enough, adds Thomas, "to keep Cuban planters from giving an inch to their slaves for nearly a hundred years" (1971, 77). See also Knight (1970, 25) and Corwin (1967, 22), who also observes that: "When the news arrived in November 1791, of the great slave rebellion in Haiti, [Francisco de] Aranga [y Parreno,

spokesman for sugar interests in Cuba] saw this not as a threatening example to Cuba, where slaves were still relatively few, but as Cuba's golden opportunity at French Haiti's expense" (pp. 13–14).

[310] For example, Rockingham's Declaratory Act adopted after the Repeal of the Stamp Act in 1766, and which so irritated the North Americans, was "modeled almost word for word on the Irish Act of 1720, with which both British and colonial leaders were familiar" (James, 1973, 296).

[311] For this specific comparison, see Harlow (1952, 503) who notes that in the sixteenth century, "Ireland and the Irish were seen in much the same light as the Teutonic Knights had regarded the wild natives living between the Oder and the Vistula." See also James (1973, 289–290).

[312] Harlow (1952, 505–506).

[313] Savelle (1953, 207).

Hence, with the defeat of the French in the Seven Years' War, an "Anglo–Irish colonial nationalism"[314] developed, and for the same reasons as in North America. In the Irish Parliament, a reform group known as the Patriots emerged. At the very moment that Charles Townshend was trying to impose the Stamp Act on British North America, he sent his elder brother George as Lord Lieutenant to Ireland "to tighten up direct British control and get the Irish too to pay for a larger share of imperial defense."[315] It is obvious why the North American and Irish settlers felt they shared constitutional grievances and objectives. And thus many Irishmen "naturally sympathized" in 1775 with the North Americans— many Protestant Irishmen, that is, since the Catholics tended to support Britain's American policy.[316]

The American Revolution, in fact, worsened the economic situation in Ireland. The British defeat spurred on Irish demands, and the British in 1782 were willing to give some greater political autonomy. Pitt even proposed economic concessions, but on the condition the Irish share in imperial defense expenditures.[317] As soon as a peace treaty was signed with France in 1783, the British line hardened further.[318] Still, the Irish Patriots were not ready to press for independence, because they were not ready to create "an inclusive party," and were not "a fully national movement."[319] The fear of internal social revolution held them back (then as in the twentieth century).

The French Revolution had a big impact on Ireland, opening up new possibilities. Catholics and Presbyterian Dissenters began to draw together in rebellious republican intent. The Catholics were demanding Emancipation. Catholic tenants also began to rebel against their oppression by landlords (who were Protestants). It was at this point in 1795 that the Orange Society was formed as a secret Protestant society to resist Catholic demands. In 1796, Wolfe Tone, leader of the United Irishmen, the nationalist movement, went from the United States to Paris to help plan an expedition to Ireland. He convinced the Directory that Ireland was "ripe for revolution."[320] He counted on support not only from Catholics but from the Presbyterians of Ulster who had a long republican tradition and whose leaders justified their appeal to French assistance by the "precedent" of 1688.[321]

---

[314] Palmer (1959, I, 165).

[315] Doyle (1981, 152).

[316] McDowell (1979, 241). On British recruiting among Catholics for soldiers to send North America, see Kraus (1939, 343–344).

[317] See Kraus (1939, 346) and Harlow (1952, 495).

[318] See Godechot (1965, 145).

[319] Doyle (1981, 157). And thus they could not even profit from the limited autonomy they had achieved. On Ireland's inability to control her com-

mercial life, as illustrated in the futile attempt to negotiate a trade treaty with Portugal between 1770 and 1790, see Lammey (1986, 40).

The Protestants did seek support of the Catholics. However they were unwilling to grant them representation in the Irish Parliament. "The Catholics would be 'virtually' represented. That is where the Irish Revolution fell short" (Harlow, 1952, 511).

[320] Lecky (1972, 309).

[321] Lecky (1972, 388).

The invasion failed. The weather was bad. The seamanship was bad. The French had chosen the region of landing, Bantry Bay, badly. It was a zone where the United Irishmen had the least support. But they almost made it. British dominion in Ireland rested at this point on an "extremely precarious tenure."[322] But Bantry Bay was the turning point. And its consequences for the world-system were great. As Thompson says: It is arguable that France lost Europe, not before Moscow, but in 1797, when only the Navy in mutiny stood between them and an Ireland on the eve of rebellion."[323]

The rebellion of the United Irishmen went forward in 1798. By this time the faith of Ulster Presbyterians in the French Revolution had cooled and the Orange lodges had grown stronger. The rebels were given no quarter by the British. Napoleon decided against a second invasion, diverting his troops to the conquest of Egypt, a decision he is said later to have regretted. The failure of the revolutionaries hurt as well the position of the moderate reformers in the Irish Parliament, like Arthur Grattan. The British decided to press to abolish the reforms of 1782. Pitt pushed through the Act of Union in 1800. The Irish Parliament was no more. The Protestant settlers in effect gave up (were pressed to give up) all perspectives of autonomy, because they feared that it was an autonomy they could not control, an autonomy that would be too democratic.[324]

Thus the 1790s saw two major defeats of White settlers—in St. Domingue and in Ireland. The historic situations were different. The final outcomes were different—an ostracized Black republic in Haiti and a reintegration into the metropole in Ireland. But both served as a signal, warning the White settlers of the Americas that the road to a settler republic was a difficult one and strewn with hazards, and that the example of the Thirteen Colonies would be difficult to emulate if one wanted to have the desired outcome. And Haiti and Ireland in the 1790s came after Túpac Amaru and the Comuneros in the 1780s. Independence was decidedly a risky affair.

It was no wonder then that those like Miranda and Bolívar who preached settler revolution were received cautiously for the most part. Then one event transformed the world political situation: Napoleon's invasion of Spain in 1808. Before, however, we discuss why this event could crystallize

[322] Lecky (1972, 313). General Lake, chief commander in Ulster, said in his report to the Viceroy, Lord Camden, in the spring of 1797: "The lower order of the people and most of the middle class are determined Republicans, have imbibed the French principles, and will not be contented with anything short of a Revolution" (p. 315). He recommended "coercive measures in the strongest degree."

[323] Thompson (1968, 470).

[324] "The ascendancy [the Protestant establishment in Ireland] were then cajoled, frightened, beguiled and persuaded—some bought—into the extinction of the achievements of 1782. In 1800, an Act of Union determined that Ireland and Britain become one kingdom, its parliament in London. In the years after 1782, the ascendancy had demonstrated its incapacity, in a sense, to understand the meaning of its own victory: that nationality must become policy" (Doyle, 1981, 179).

and give renewed life to the cause of settler independence in the Americas, we must observe what had been happening in the one existent settler republic until then.

The years 1793–1807 were "extraordinarily prosperous ones" for the young United States. In what in retrospect seems a long-run pattern of United States economic growth, this period was a particular "bulge" in which the United States was able to take advantage of their "neutral" position in the Franco–British wars by gaining a substantial share of the trans-Atlantic commerce.[325]

What made this possible was a strategic decision by the United States in 1794, to tilt their "neutrality" toward the eventual victor and hegemonic power, their ex-colonial master, Great Britain. It was in fact the outbreak of war in 1793 that precipitated the decision which took the form of Jay's Treaty in 1794. Great Britain had refused to recognize the United States' claims to full rights of wartime trade to the French West Indian islands. The United States tacitly ceded the issue in return for the return of the western ports (at last! they had been legally the possession of the United States since 1783), and some new trading rights in the British West Indies.[326] The terms were basically poor for the United States, but the United States feared war with Great Britain more than the latter did. Essentially, Jay's Treaty "served to postpone hostilities" to 1812, a moment that would be more favorable to the United States.[327] The British, meanwhile, saw the treaty as guaranteeing a freedom of commerce with the United States for the benefit of British industry.[328]

There seemed to be two great economic pressures on the United States which lay behind this strategic choice. The economics of transport still condemned the United States to earn a large part of its income from foreign trade, though this would later change after 1820.[329] The second factor was the opportunity for agricultural revival offered to the Southern

[325] North (1974, 69, 73). See also Nettels (1962). Goldin and Lewis have reservations about how much the "considerable fillip" to the United States shipping and export industries deriving from neutrality actually increased the per capita rate of growth (1980, 22). See similar views in David (1967, 154, 188–194) and Adams (1980, 714, 734). Cuenca, however, gives considerable support to North, laying particular emphasis on the importance of the trade with the Spanish world which was "a timely windfall and a vital redress in a period when . . . international indebtedness would grow to a point of default" (1984, 540). See also George Rogers Taylor (1964, 437).

[326] See Nettels (1962, 324–325). This resulted in a "quasiwar" with France.

[327] Bemis (1923, 270). Beard argues that an interruption of trade relations in 1794 with Great Britain would have meant "irreparable loss to American merchants" and impairment of public and private credit. Peace on the other hand involved "at least a temporary relief for Southern creditors and no serious difficulties for the farmers anywhere" (1915, 274–275). See also Williams (1972, 228).

[328] See Graham (1941, 91).

[329] "At the time of the American Revolution a ton of goods could be moved 3000 miles from Europe to America by water as cheaply as it could move 30 miles overland in the New Nation" (North, 1965, 213). United States internal transport costs would drop dramatically with the introduction of the steamboat in 1816 and the construction of the canal system from 1825 on. See also Cochran (1981, 44–48).

United States by the invention of the cotton gin in 1793. The Revolutionary War had been quite destructive of agriculture in the Lower South and there seemed to be no expanding markets for their principal staples of indigo and rice.[330] The South in the 1790s "urgently needed a new crop."[331] Cotton was it, and cotton needed Great Britain as a customer.[332]

To be sure, this geopolitical–economic deal of the United States with Great Britain would have its negative side for the weaker partner. It slowed down the development of United States manufactures, which could not compete as a locus of investment given the "high profits to be won in foreign commerce" in the period after 1793.[333] In 1808, an American author, James Cheetham, was boasting of the fact that the United States had become, "as by enchantment, the successful rival of the greatest commercial nation on earth."[334] It was perhaps fortunate for the United States that renewed hostilities in Europe burst this naive bubble. On November 11, 1807, Great Britain placed a total ban on United States trade with European ports under Napoleon's control. President Thomas Jefferson sought to pressure both Great Britain and France by an embargo on both. The Embargo Act of 1808 lasted only one year and turned out to be self-defeating,[335] but it eventually led to the renewal of conflict with Great Britain in 1812, to which we will return. What it did do was renew the role of the United States, as a rival as well as collaborator with Great Britain in the decolonization of the Americas.[336]

Much has been written about the ideological inspiration of the American and above all of the French Revolution on the thinking of the Creoles in Spanish America. No doubt it is true, at least for certain strata. Yet it is too easy to exaggerate the importance of such diffusion of ideas *ex post facto* in cases where the ultimate political outcome makes the importance of such diffusion plausible. What Eyzaguirre concludes for Chile may in fact be more widely true: "It cannot be demonstrated that the French Revolution was a catalyst for separatist ideas; it may even have been on the contrary the occasion for the Creoles to reaffirm their fidelity to the monarchy."[337]

Spain was at war with revolutionary France from 1793 to 1796. But in

[330] See Bjork (1964, 557).
[331] Nettels (1962, 184).
[332] In 1787 over half of Britain's import of cotton came from the West Indies (under all European powers) and another quarter from the Ottoman Empire. By 1807, the United States provided 171,000 out of 282,000 bales. See North (1966, 41).
[333] Bruchey (1965, 90–91). On the economic obstacles to creating in the United States a textile industry that would be competitive on the world market, see Jeremy (1981, 34–35). The upsurge in manufacturers caused by the trade depression of 1786–1792 was squelched by the trade boom after 1793. See Nettels (1962, 125).

[334] Cheetham wrote this in a book, *Peace or War* (p. 20), cited in Clauder (1932, 134).
[335] "The Embargo Act broke down through its own severity" (Fitton, 1958, 313). Though it hurt Britain economically more than the United States, it led to acute internal political divisions. See Frankel (1982, 309), who insists on the degree to which the Embargo was "well-enforced" and "effective."
[336] See Rippy (1929, vi–vii).
[337] Eyzaguirre (1957, 79). See Brading (1983) on the two views of Spanish American independence, one as the third act of the Atlantic Revolution, one as precipitated by 1808.

1796, the Spanish Minister Manuel de Godoy led Spain into an alliance with France in the Treaty of San Ildefonso. Great Britain retaliated by cutting Spain's maritime links with the Americas.[338] But Great Britain at this point hesitated to give any serious support to the burgeoning settler independence movement.[339]

In any case, the entire economic impact of the economic reforms of Charles III, the neoprotectionism combined with intraimperial liberalism that had led to the revived prosperity of Spain, was "completely overturned" between 1797 and 1814.[340] The impact was equally great on some zones of Spanish America. Venezuela in particular entered into economic difficulties as of 1797. One response was the legalization of contraband.[341] The sharp price inflation in Mexico increased economic polarization and led to discontent among the less-privileged classes.[342] But these difficulties reappeared cyclically and under other geopolitical conditions would have had few major political consequences.

In 1806, an unauthorized British expeditionary force occupied Buenos Aires. But the local population proved loyal to Spain and successfully defeated them; they proved "unwilling to exchange on imperial master for another."[343] Miranda's tiny expedition to liberate Venezuela failed that same year, undone at least in part by the semblance of Haitian support.[344] The lack of enthusiasm for independence, even in Venezuela and Argentina (shortly to be the pacemakers), was evident.

All this would change abruptly. In 1807, Napoleon induced Spain to join in conquering Portugal. Dom João fled to Brazil. Godoy's permission for French troops to enter Spain en route to Portugal led to a Spanish nationalist reaction and Godoy's unseating. Charles IV was deposed by his son Ferdinand VII. Summoned to Bayonne by Napoleon, Ferdinand then

---

[338] See Chaunu (1964, 193, 205).

[339] "As Britain had formerly wavered between plundering the Spanish American colonies and trading with them, so now [1796–1808] she hesitated between their conquest and their emancipation" (Humphreys, 1952, 225). Neither was really necessary because, as Chaunu says, from 1797 to 1810, "Iberian America became . . . the most beautiful of British colonies" (1964, 210). To be sure, there were some British personalities, like Thomas Pownall, who advocated the creation of an independent group of American nations united to Britain in an Atlantic federation. See Schutz (1946, 264). And already in 1785, the French Ambassador in Spain was reporting that Floridablanca, the Spanish Foreign Minister, expressed fear that British would seek to compensate its loss of the thirteen colonies with a parallel loss by Spain. See Ségur-Depeyron (1873, 376, fn.). But Great Britain in fact moved most prudently.

[340] Bousquet (1974, 14). "The tendency to fi-

nancial collapse in Spain was accelerated after the French Revolution in 1789" (Rodriguez, 1976, 23). This had great internal consequences. Spain's conflicts first with France (1793–1795), then with Great Britain (1796–1808), were costly. In order to secure enough revenue "to stave off bankruptcy," Spain in 1801 opened her ports to neutral shipping, so-called *comercio neutral* (Barbier, 1980, 37). This involved the "abandonment of the nationalistic principles underlying the 1778 *reglamento*" (Fisher, 1985, 63). "In the process, that unified economy which the Bourbons had sought to create had to be sacrificed, thus starting under royal auspices a disintegration which was to be sanctioned by independence" (Barbier, 1980, 21–22).

[341] See Izard (1979, 27–41).

[342] See Garner (1972) and Florescano (1969, 188–194).

[343] Lynch (1985, 25).

[344] See Lubin (1968, 304–305) and Lynch (1985, 48–49).

returned the throne to Charles who promptly abdicated in favor of Joseph
Bonaparte. Ferdinand also renounced his rights. Suddenly, there was no
legitimate authority in the Spanish Empire. A central junta assumed
authority in Seville, and signed an alliance with the British. It declared
American lands not to be colonies and invited them to participate in the
cortés. But the French forced the junta to flee to Cádiz. It then dissolved.
Confusion spread everywhere in Spanish America. Regional and local
juntas took over in the name of Ferdinand VII, in many cases ousting
Spanish authorities. Creoles were now exercising de facto self-government
in the name of loyalism.[345] In Caracas, in 1810, the local junta went
further. In the name of loyalism to Ferdinand VII, it explicitly denied the
authority of the new Spanish Council of Regency (successor to the junta in
Cádiz). This was followed by revolts in Argentina, Chile, and Mexico. They
all declared their ports open to free trade. Bolívar went to London in 1810
and was received by the Foreign Secretary Lord Wellesley, who "advised a
continuing allegiance to Spain as the best avenue to British assistance."[346]

The Mexican revolution proved the most socially radical. When a local
parish priest, Miguel Hidalgo y Castillo in 1810 called for an end to
viceroys forever in his *Grito de Dolores* (did he copy the name from the
Cahiers de doléance?), he united all the Creole establishment against him as
well as the Spanish authorities. The Hidalgo uprising swept through
central Mexico, "spreading terror and shock." The "virtually unarmed"
Indians managed to reach the capital city, acquiring 20,000 men in the
process and executing some 2,000 *gachupines* (Spaniards) out of an estimated total population of 15,000. Hidalgo was put down by the overwhelmingly Creole Regiment of New Spain. One of Hidalgo's lieutenants,
José Maria Morelos, also a priest, took up the struggle and this time created
a "superbly organized and effective army" and a clear political program
including radical social reforms. This second phase of the revolt was
supported more by *mestizos* than by Indians. Morelos was not as easily
crushed, but his military power declined rapidly once the Creole congress
preempted his program by proclaiming independence in 1813.[347]

Three elements now entered to set the stage for the final phase of the
Spanish American settler independences: the War of 1812 (actually 1812–
1814) between the United States and Great Britain, the restoration of

---

[345] These new juntas claimed to be peaceful and
to base themselves on their legitimacy. "How sin-
cere was this self-image of the revolutionaries?"
asks Halperín-Donghi. He says we should not forget that they "did not consider themselves [in 1810]
to be rebels, but heirs of a power that had fallen,
perhaps forever. There was no reason to indicate
dissidence from a political–administrative patri-
mony that they now considered theirs and that they
intended to use for their own purposes" (1972,
129).

[346] Kaufmann (1951, 50–51). Meanwhile, Great
Britain used this moment of Spain's weakness to
establish "firm commercial relations" with several of
Spain's principal colonial ports (Cuenca, 1981,
419). See also Rippy (1959, 18–19)..

[347] See Anna (1978a, 64, 76, and ch. 3, passim)
and Anna (1985, 67–68). Chaunu speaks of Mexico
knowing "its Tupac Amaru revolt with a 30-year
lag" (1964, 207).

Ferdinand VII to the throne of Spain in 1813, and the Congress of Vienna in 1815.

The War of 1812 was more or less the last act of the settler decolonization of the United States. Relations of the United States with Great Britain had been difficult ever since 1783, but there had never been a real break. Great Britain wanted the United States as a market but not as a competitor. The United States was seeking to improve its standing in the world-economy. The Franco–British wars were both an opportunity and an exasperation for the United States. As the British maritime position grew uncontested, United States anger against British constraints on its trade grew greater. When fighting broke out again on the continent, the United States' opportunity to press Great Britain, and perhaps to conquer Canada, arrived.[348] In a sense, the United States did badly in the war. There was now little enthusiasm either among English-speaking or French-speaking Canadians for incorporation into the United States.[349] Canada remained British. The importance of the fur trade had declined.[350] The British made no real concessions about the constraints of their navigation code on the carrying trade.[351] All that Great Britain surrendered at the Treaty of Ghent was an intangible recognition of a United States right to its own westward and southern expansion,[352] and a say (at least a junior say) in the developments to come in the decolonization of the Americas. But, of course, this was crucial.[353]

The war between Great Britain and the United States came at a critical moment for Spain. With the defeat of Napoleon, Ferdinand VII would return to the throne in 1814. He abrogated the liberal constitution of 1812 and sought to restore the *status quo ante* including in Hispanic America. Within a year, most of the uprisings in Hispanic America were put down by

[348] "If England and France had maintained peace . . . it seems unlikely that there would have been war between England and America in 1812" (Horsman, 1962, 264). See also Gibbs: "According to J.Q. Adams it was the [British] insistence on the right of search [of neutral ships] which was the principal cause of the war of 1812–14, though the root of the trouble probably lay in the demand for the conquest of Canada" (1969, 88–89).

[349] The Maritime provinces of Canada found common cause with New England in "resisting the anti-British policy of the [United States] federal governments" (Clark, 1959, 240). As for the French speakers, their sympathy for the French Revolution and their "revolutionary ardor" having cooled, it was not reawakened by this new alliance between the United States and France (p. 244). On the latter group, see also Ouellet (1971, 230).

[350] See Ouellet (1971, 37).

[351] See Graham: "In all the ups and downs of British policy after the American Revolution, mo-

nopoly of carriage—that fundamental principle of the navigation code—was never forsaken. . . . When Great Britain emerged triumphant from the long Napoleonic struggle, the principle of colonial monopoly remained fundamentally unimpaired" (1941, 197, 218).

[352] The British de facto withdrew their support of Spain in the Floridas. As late as 1811, the United States Congress was passing the No-Transfer resolution, looking toward the annexation of West Florida (accomplished in 1813) and warning Great Britain against attempting to reacquire East Florida from Spain. See Bemis (1943, 28–30) and Nettels (1962, 322–324). By 1819, the United States achieved the great "diplomatic victory" of getting Spain to cede Florida (if not Texas) and to recognize the "undisputed right of the United States to territory clear through to the Pacific Coast" (Bemis, 1943, 37–38).

[353] See the analysis of who got what at the Treaty of Ghent in Perkins (1964, 137–138).

his armies. Bolívar himself wrote that, but for the War of 1812, "Venezuela singlehandedly would have triumphed, and South America would not have been devastated by Spanish cruelty nor destroyed by revolutionary anarchy."[354]

Bolívar may have been right about the very short run. But actually the Spanish restoration guaranteed the only slightly delayed independences of Hispanic America. The return of Ferdinand VII liberated both the United States and Great Britain to pursue their penchant to support the settler movements.[355] And the Treaty of Ghent reduced the United States–British mutual sense of need to be fearful that these independences would favor the other.

Finally the Congress of Vienna, by establishing peace in Europe on the basis of the support of legitimacy and absolutism, in a perverse way, weakened the Spanish claim to Hispanic America. The major European powers feared that Spain's repressive measures were "unlikely to be effective," and that revolutions leading to independence in Hispanic America would "encourage liberal revolutionaries" in Europe. Hence they much preferred that Spain grant "concessions" to the colonies.[356] This further freed Great Britain's hand to pursue her commercial interests in Latin America, especially now that it had become a major zone of expansion of cotton textile sales for Great Britain.[357]

All that remained for the settlers was to make sure that the independence to which there was now no major obstacle would truly fall into their hands, and not into the hands of other groups. The second round of struggles began. Much of the difference between the form of the struggle in the different colonies was a consequence of the different *rapport de force* between Creole elements and Blacks, Indians, and mestizo–*pardo* (mulatto) groups. Indeed, the degree to which Creole elites were for, against, or ambivalent on the question of immediate independence was to a considerable degree their assessment of the "conditions necessary for containing the actual or potential rebelliousness of the masses."[358] Once the process of

[354] Cited in Liss (1983, 209).

[355] See Halperín-Donghi: "The British government, which had maintained up to [Spanish restoration] a cautious ambiguity [to the independence movements], if it was not now going to come out in favor of the revolutionary cause, would be less vigilant about the flow of volunteers (and more importantly of arms) for the Armies fighting against [the Spanish]. For its part, the U.S. . . . from this point on showed a more benevolent face to the patriots: it consequently became ever easier to buy armaments there and recruit corsairs" (1972, 144). In fact, this last element of assistance by the United States to the Hispanic American movements, the easing of the recruitment of corsairs, redounded against the United States itself. Between

1810 and 1823, there was in consequence widespread piracy in the West Indies, which became the "chief interference with trade" between the United States and the West Indies (Chandler, 1924, 482).

[356] Waddell (1985, 205).

[357] See Bousquet (1978, 57). In the first quarter of the nineteenth century, only Latin America and western Europe saw a significant expansion of British textile exports.

[358] Andrews (1985, 128). See Fisher: "The Cuzco rebellion of 1814–1815 was a revolution for independence which enjoyed widespread support for both Whites and Indians in southern Peru. Had the inhabitants of Lima and the coast supported it, it would almost certainly have succeeded. Their failure to do so is to be explained by their ingrained

disintegration of the Spanish empire started, many Creoles who formerly were skeptical of independence felt obliged to jump on the bandwagon, not primarily in order to take power from the Spanish but, "above all, to prevent the *pardos* from taking it."[359] We do not have to look to the reluctant, belated, and somewhat conservative independence movements of Peru and Mexico to verify this. It can be seen with some clarity in the radical, avant-garde independence movements of La Plata and Venezuela.

La Plata was a colony with a particularly high percentage of Creoles, perhaps half the population. It could easily sustain a Creole-based revolution, and one that was "liberal" in attitudes to Indians and Blacks, mestizos and *pardos*. In La Plata, as previously in British North America, both colonial ruler and settler revolutionary sought, "hesitantly at first," to recruit Black and *pardo* soldiers into their armies, promising ultimate liberation.[360] And as in British North America, the Blacks got some small advantage out of it, but at the cost of heavy casualties. The Indians were freed from *encomienda*, but only to be recruited as peons on sugar plantations. The mestizo gauchos were to be tamed to work on the estancias.

In Venezuela, with its great latifundias, the problem of slavery and peonage was still greater than in La Plata. Whites were only 20% of the population and many of these were the *blancos de orilla*, poor Whites often of Canarian origin. When Bolívar relaunched the struggle in 1816, he arrived from Haiti, and saw "the need of fusing the creole, pardo and slave rebellions into one great movement."[361] Bolívar promised to liberate the slaves in Venezuela and elsewhere.[362] But he was unable to impose abolition on his fellow *hacendados*, and the Black slaves became less enthusiastic about independence, lapsing into neutrality.[363] Full abolition

conservatism and their fear of the Indian" (1979, 257). By 1821, there would be "few signs of a popular mobilization" for Creole-led independence in Peru (Bonilla & Spalding, 1972, 108). See also Ladd on Mexico: "Fear of the masses was a crucially important factor in the disciplining of elite grievances" (1976, 89).

Of course, this was not the only factor. For a careful analysis of the combinations of economic factors (presence of specialized agricultural export zones, capacity to expand, nature of competition) which account for differential support of Creole elites for independence movements, see Bousquet (1974).

[359] Humphreys & Lynch (1965a, 24).

[360] Rout (1976, 165). The attitudes of the Creole leaders was far from welcoming. The commander of the second Argentine expedition to Upper Peru, General Belgrano, remarked that "the Negroes and mulattos are a rabble, as cowardly as they are blood thirsty . . . ; the only consolation is that White

officers are on the way" (cited in Lynch, 1973, 85).

[361] Lynch (1973, 210).

[362] See Bierck (1953, 365). The Spaniards used this promise against him and exaggerated the degree of Haitian military help. See Verna (1983, 146).

[363] In 1953, a Venezuelan historian, Cristóbal Mendoza, downplayed the independence role of the mestizos (and Blacks), suggesting that it was "the upper classes, the Creoles who launched the movement" for independence. No doubt he was right, but why? (Congresso Hispánoamericano, 1953, 51). On why the Creoles could not get mass support, see Liévano Aguirre (1968, 947–948). On the role of the *mantuanos*, the great landlords, see Izard (1979, 50–51). On the independence struggle as a "civil war," see Bagú (1979, 13). On the survival of the latifundias, if not of all the *latifundistas*, see Brito (1966, I, 219–220), and Izard (1979, 163).

would only come much later, in 1854.[364] And Bolívar himself would repay his early Haitian support by refusing later to recognize Haiti or to support its invitation to the Panama Congress in 1826. Indeed "the fear of creating another Haiti . . . entered into the decision not to invade Cuba."[365]

The Spanish-American states now went forward to independence one after the other, in ambiguous, or violent, or conservative revolutions.[366] They went forward one by one. Bolívar's dream of replicating the formula of unity achieved by the Thirteen Colonies failed. The area involved was, of course, far more dispersed, and hence there was no possibility of unifying the military struggle, an important factor in the creation of the United States. Bolívar's Congress of Panama in June 1826 failed completely.

The year 1823 sealed the issue. Britain's Secretary of State, George Canning, and United States President James Monroe competed to see who could get the credit for giving the definitive blessing to Hispanic-American independence.[367] Meanwhile, in Spain, the French invasion of April 1823 permitted Ferdinand VII to free himself from the "constitutionalists" and to pursue a policy of "unrelieved reaction." The decade from 1823 to 1833 became known as the "ominous decade."[368] This triumph at home for Ferdinand meant, however, that all hope of Spain in the Americas was now doomed.[369]

The story in Brazil basically parallelled that of Hispanic America. It was the story of simultaneous decolonization (1789–1831) and of British penetration of its economy (1810–1827).[370] The post-Pombaline era in Brazil gave rise to two "conspiracies," the so-called *Inconfidência mineira* of Minas Gerais in 1788–1789 and the *Conjuracão Bahia* in 1798.[371] They were both early attempts at independence. The first, led by Creole elites protesting against taxation, was a "precursor."[372] The second was urban and more radical, "aiming at an armed uprising of mulattoes, free Blacks,

[364] Lombardi (1971, 46).

[365] Ott (1973, 194). The United States was very worried about Cuba. Calhoun advocated annexation in 1822. The two fears of the United States were that Cuba might "fall into the hands of Great Britain" or "be revolutionized by the negroes" (Rippy, 1929, 80–81).

[366] These are the adjectives used by Lynch (1973) to describe Peru, Venezuela, and Mexico, respectively.

[367] See Rippy (1929, 112–124) and Temperley (1925a, 53). On United States recognitions of independences, see Robertson (1918b, 261).

[368] Carr (1969, 452).

[369] "The Fernandine system . . . played a major role in the loss of America" (Anna, 1978b, 357). Halperín-Donghi makes clear the link between events in Spain and the Canning-Monroe position: "Thanks to the restoration of absolutism in Spain

[in 1823], British neutrality inclined more definitely on the side of the Spanish-American revolution. . . . At the same time, the United States with the purchase of Spanish Florida in 1822 [the treaty was signed in 1819 but only ratified by Spain in 1822], having lost the last reasons to take care not to offend the Spain of Fernando, noisily aligned its policy with that of Britain" (1972, 146). See also Waddell (1985, 213–223).

[370] See Mota (1973, 76). On British preeminence in Brazil, see Manchester (1933, chs. IX & X).

[371] Two others—in Rio de Janeiro in 1794 and in Pernambuco in 1801—were crushed immediately.

[372] Luz (1960, I, Part 2, 405). In this conspiracy, the issue of slavery was seen as a "possible obstacle," the solution to which might be to free the mulattoes (sic!) (p. 399). Novais (1979, 170) also uses the word, "precursor."

and slaves."[373] It was particularly inspired by the French Revolution seeking "a complete revolution," in order to create a society "without distinction between Whites, Blacks (*preta*) and mulattoes (*parda*)."[374]

In Brazil, too, Napoleon precipitated matters by causing the flight of Prince Regent Dom João to Brazil. This, of course, created a different situation than the abdications in Spain. The Portuguese king could provide the legitimate transition to eventual independence. In 1815, instead of returning to Portugal, Dom João raised Brazil to the status of a coequal kingdom, with the center of the now dual monarchy in Brazil. The result was that Portugal was in effect governed in Lisbon by a Council of Regency (and it in turn was presided over by an Englishman, Marshal Beresford, who had been the commander-in-chief of the Portuguese army which had reoccupied the country, and remained afterwards).

In 1820–1821, a liberal revolt erupted and a new constitution was adopted. The revolt spread to Brazil. There the "Brazilian party," representing the Creole elites, "won supremacy," while the popular classes could not "obtain their demands."[375] The Portuguese helped the Brazilian Creoles in this effort. A Portuguese deputy, José Joaquim Ferreira de Moura, defended sending troops to Bahia in 1821 by the argument that the Brazilian people, "composed of Negros, mulattoes, & White Creoles, and Europeans of various sorts" are under the impulse of "passions in effervescence" and need help in restoring order.[376] Dom João returned to Portugal, and now the Brazilians feared they were faced with less than full equality. They transferred allegiance from King João VI to the Prince Regent Dom Pedro, who was persuaded to remain. Soon thereafter, in 1822, Dom Pedro I became Emperor of Brazil, with the blessing and under the protection of Great Britain.[377]

Thus, slowly, over 50 years, the White settlers created states throughout the Western Hemisphere that became members of the interstate system. They all, in one way or another, came under the politico–economic tutelage of the new hegemonic power, Great Britain, although the United States was able to carve itself out a role as lieutenant and, therefore, potential and eventual rival to Britain.

The one exception was Haiti, and Haiti was ostracized. France, Spain, and Portugal were effectively eliminated from any role. But so were the Blacks and the Indians. The dream of Morelos, that he could found a republic modeled on European constitutional theories but which proclaimed "Aztec antiquity as the true origin of the nation," remained a

---

[373] Bethell (1985, 166). See also Mota (1967, 103–194) on the difference between the two revolts. Maxwell points out that the Creole fears of a racial upheaval led to "a remarkable cohesion of views . . . [with] the British government" (1973, 238).

[374] Phraseology cited by Novais (1979, 171).
[375] Prado (1957, 48).
[376] Cited in Tavares (1977, 57).
[377] See Mota (1972, 71–72).

dream that was quashed.[378] The new nationalism was "almost entirely devoid of social content."[379]

None of the great revolutions of the late eighteenth century—the so-called industrial revolution, the French Revolution, the settler independences of the Americas—represented fundamental challenges to the world capitalist system. They represented its further consolidation and entrenchment. The popular forces were suppressed, and their potential in fact constrained by the political transformations. In the nineteenth century, these forces (or rather their successors) would reflect on their failures and construct a totally new strategy of struggle, one that was far more organized, systematic, and self-conscious.

[378] Phelan (1960, 768). See also Griffin (1962,   [379] Lynch (1973, 340).
20).

BIBLIOGRAPHY

Abel, Wilhelm. (1973). *Crises agraires en Europe (XIIIe–XXe siècle)*. Paris: Flammarion.

Aberdam, Serge. (1975). "La Révolution et la lutte des métayers," *Etudes rurales*, No. 59, 73–91.

Abir, M. (1977). "Modernisation, Reaction and Muhammad Ali's 'Empire,'" *Middle Eastern Studies*, **XIII**, 3, 295–313.

Abou-el-Haj, Rifa'at Ali. (1967). "Ottoman Diplomacy at Karlowitz," *Journal of the American Oriental Society*, **LXXXVII**, 4, 498–512.

Abou-el-Haj, Rifa'at Ali. (1969). "The Formal Closure of the Ottoman Frontier in Europe: 1699–1703," *Journal of the American Oriental Society*, **LXXXIX**, 3, 467–475.

Abou-el-Haj, Rifa'at Ali. (1974). "Ottoman Attitudes toward Peace Making: The Karlowitz Case," *Der Islam*, **LI**, 1, 131–137.

Abray, Jane. (1975). "Feminism in the French Revolution," *American Historical Review*, **LXXX**, 1, 43–62.

Accarias de Sérionne, Jacques. (1766). *Intérêts des nations de l'Europe développés relativement au commerce*, **I**. Paris: Desain.

Acomb, Frances. (1939). "Unemployment and Relief in Champagne, 1788." *Journal of Modern History*, **XI**, 1, 41–48.

Adams, Donald R., Jr. (1970). "Some Evidence on English and American Wage Rates," *Journal of Economic History*, **XXX**, 3, 499–520.

Adams, Donald R., Jr. (1980). "American Neutrality and Prosperity, 1793–1808: A Reconsideration," *Journal of Economic History*, **XL**, 4, 713–737.

Adamu, Mahdi. (1979). "The Delivery of Slaves from the Central Sudan to the Bight of Benin in the Eighteenth and Nineteenth Centuries," in H. A. Gemery & J. S. Hogendorn, eds., *The Uncommon Market*. New York: Academic Press, 163–180.

Ado, A. (1977). "Le mouvement paysan et le problème de l'égalité (1789–1794)," in A. Soboul, dir., *Contribution à l'histoire paysanne de la Révolution française*. Paris: Ed. Sociales, 119–138.

Aguessy, Honorat. (1970). "Le Dan-Homê du XIXe siècle était-il une société esclavagiste?" *Revue française d'études politiques africaines*, No. 50, 71–91.

Agulhon, Maurice. (1980). "1830 dans l'histoire du XIXe siècle français," *Romantisme*, **X**, 28/29, 15–27.

Ahlström, G. (1983). "Aspects of the Commercial Shipping between St. Petersburg and Western Europe, 1750–1790," in W. J. Weringa *et al.*, eds., *The Interactions of Amsterdam and Antwerp with the Baltic Region, 1400–1800*. Leiden: Martinus Nijhoff, 153–160.

Aiton, Arthur S. (1932). "Spanish Colonial Reorganization under the Family Compact." *Hispanic American Historical Review*, **XII**, 3, 269–280.

Ajayi, J. F. Ade. (1965). "West African States at the Beginning of the Nineteenth Century," in J. F. Ade Ajayi & I. Espie, eds., *A Thousand Years of West African History*. London: Nelson, 248–261.

Ajayi, J. F. Ade & Oloruntimehin, B. O. (1976). "West Africa in the Anti-Slave Trade Era," in *Cambridge History of Africa*, **V**: John. E. Flint, ed., *From c. 1790 to c. 1870*. Cambridge, Engl.: Cambridge University Press, 200–221.

Akinjogbin, I. A. (1967). *Dahomey and Its Neighbours, 1708–1818*. Cambridge, Engl.: At the University Press.

Albion, Robert Greenhalgh. (1926). *Forest and Sea Power: The Timber Problem of The Royal Navy, 1652–1852*, Harvard Economic Studies, Vol. XXIX. Cambridge, MA: Harvard University Press.

Alden, Dauril. (1961a). "The Undeclared War of 1773–1777: Climax of Luso-Spanish Platine Rivalry," *Hispanic American Historical Review*, **XLI**, 1, 55–74.

Alden, Dauril. (1961b). "The Marquis of Pombal and the American Revolution," *The Americas*, **XVII**, 4, 369–382.

Alden, Dauril. (1976). "The Significance of Cacao Production in the Amazon Region During the Late Colonial Period: An Essay in Comparative Economic History," *Proceedings of the American Philosophical Society*, **CXX**, 2, 103–135.

Aldrich, Robert. (1987). "Late-Comer or Early Starter? New Views on French Economic History," *Journal of European Economic History*, **XVI**, 1, 89–100.

Alexander, John T. (1970). "Recent Soviet Historiography on the Pugachev Revolt: A Review Article," *Canadian–American Slavic Studies*, **IV**, 3, 602–617.

Almeida Wright, Antoñia Fernanda P. de. (1973). "Os Estados Unidos e a independencia do Brasil (revendo a posiçao norte-americana," *Revista de Historia*, **XLVI**, 94, 369–382.

Almquist, Eric L. (1929). "Pre-famine Ireland and the Theory of European Proto-industri-alization: Evidence from the 1841 Census," *Journal of Economic History*, **XXXIX**, 3, 699–718.

Ambrose, Gwilym. (1931). "English Traders at Aleppo (1658–1756)," *Economic History Review*, **III**, 2, 246–266.

Amin, Samir. (1971). "La politique coloniale française à l'égard de la bourgeoisie commer-çante sénégalaise (1820–1960)," in C. Meillassoux, ed., *The Development of Indigenous Trade and Markets in West Africa*. London: Oxford University Press, 361–376.

Amin, Samir. (1972a). "Préface" to B. Barry, *Le Royaume de Waalo*. Paris: Maspéro, 7–54.

Amin, Samir. (1972b). "Underdevelopment and Dependence in Black Africa—Origins and Contemporary Forms," *Journal of Modern African Studies*, **X**, 4, 503–524.

Anderson, B. L. & Richardson, David. (1983). "Market Structure and Profits of the British African Trade in the Late Eighteenth Century: A Comment," *Journal of Economic History*, **XLIII**, 3, 713–721.

Anderson, B. L. & Richardson, David. (1985). "Market Structure and the Profits of the British Africa Trade in the Late Eighteenth Century: A Rejoinder Rebutted," *Journal of Economic History*, **XLV**, 3, 705–707.

Anderson, J. L. (1972). "Aspects of the Effects on the British Economy of the War Against France, 1793–1815," *Australian Economic History Review*, **XII**, 1, 1–20.

Anderson, J. L. (1974). "A Measure of the Effect of British Public Finance, 1793–1815," *Economic History Review*, 2nd ser., **XXVII**, 4, 610–619.

Anderson, M. S. (1952). "Great Britain and the Russian Fleet, 1769–70," *Slavonic and East European Review*, **XXXI**, No. 16, 148–163.

Anderson, M. S. (1954). "Great Britain and the Russo-Turkish War of 1768–74," *English Historical Review*, **LXIX**, No. 270, 39–58.

Anderson, M. S. (1965). "European Diplomatic Relations, 1763–1790," in *New Cambridge Modern History*, **VIII**: A. Goodwin, ed., *The American and French Revolutions, 1763–93*. Cambridge, Engl.: At the University Press, 252–278.

Anderson, M. S. (1967). "The Continental System and Russo-British Relations During the Napoleonic Wars," in K. Bourne & D. C. Watt, eds., *Studies in International History*. London: Longmans, 68–80.

Anderson, M. S., ed. (1970). *The Great Powers and the Near East, 1774–1923*. London: Edward Arnold.

Anderson, M. S. (1978). *Peter the Great*. London: Thames & Hudson.

Anderson, M. S. (1979). *Historians and Eighteenth-Century Europe, 1715–1789*. Oxford: Clarendon Press.

Anderson, M. S. (1984). "Preface" to A. I. Bağiş, *Britain and the Struggle for the Integrity of the Ottoman Empire*. Istanbul: Isis.

Anderson, Perry. (1964). "Origins of the Present Crisis," *New Left Review*, No. 23, 26–54.

Anderson, Perry. (1980). *Arguments Within English Marxism*. London: New Left Books.

Anderson, R. L. & Richardson, David. (1983). "Market Structure and Profits of the British African Trade in the Late Eighteenth Century: A Comment," *Journal of Economic History*, **XLIII**, 3, 713–721.

Anderson, Terry L. (1979). "Economic Growth in Colonial New England: 'Statistical Renais-sance,'" *Journal of Economic History*, **XXXIX**, 1, 243–257.

Andrews, Charles M. (1924). *The Colonial Background of the American Revolution: Four Essays in American Colonial History*. New Haven, CT: Yale University Press.

Andrews, Charles M. (1926). "The American Revolution: An Interpretation," *American Historical Review*, **XXXI**, 2, 219–232.

Andrews, George Reid. (1985). "Spanish American Independence: A Structural Analysis," *Latin American Perspectives*, **XII**, 1, 105–132.

Anisson-Dupéron, Etienne-Alexandre-Jacques. (1847). "Essai sur les traités de commerce de Methuen et de 1786 dans leur rapports avec la liberté commerciale," *Journal des économistes*, 6e année, **XVII**, 1–17.

Anna, Timothy E. (1974). "Economic Causes of San Martin's Failure at Lima," *Hispanic American Historical Review*, **LIV**, 4, 657–681.

Anna, Timothy E. (1975). "The Peruvian Declaration of Independence: Freedom by Coercion," *Journal of Latin American Studies*, **VII**, 2, 221–248.

Anna, Timothy E. (1978a). *The Fall of the Royal Government in Mexico City*. Lincoln, NE: University of Nebraska Press.

Anna, Timothy E. (1978b). "The Buenos Aires Expedition and Spain's Secret Plan to Conquer Portugal, 1814–1820," *The Americas*, **XXXIV**, 3, 356–379.

Anna, Timothy E. (1983). *Spain and the Loss of America*. Lincoln, NE: University of Nebraska Press.

Anna, Timothy E. (1985). "The Independence of Mexico and Central America," in *Cambridge History of Latin America*, **III**: L. Bethell, ed., *From Independence to c. 1870*. Cambridge, Engl.: Cambridge University Press, 51–94.

Anon. (1810). "Cotton," *Encyclopedia Britannica*, 4th ed., Edinburgh.

Anstey, Roger. (1968) "Capitalism and Slavery: A Critique," *Economic History Review*, 2nd ser., **XXI**, 2, 307–320.

Anstey, Roger. (1974). "The Volume and Profitability of the British Slave Trade, 1761–1807," in S. L. Engerman & E. D. Genovese, eds., *Race and Slavery in the Western Hemisphere: Quantitative Studies*. Princeton, NJ: Princeton University Press, 3–31.

Anstey, Roger. (1975). *The Atlantic Slave Trade and British Abolition, 1760–1810*. London: Macmillan.

Anstey, Roger. (1976a). "The Historical Debate on the Abolition of the British Slave Trade," in R. Anstey & P. E. H. Hair, eds., *Liverpool, The Slave Trade, and Abolition*. Bristol, Engl.: Western Printing Service, 157–166.

Anstey, Roger. (1976b). "The British Slave Trade, 1751–1807: A Comment," *Journal of African History*, **XVII**, 4, 606–607.

Anstey, Roger. (1977). "The Slave Trade of the Continental Powers, 1760–1810," *Economic History Review*, 2nd ser., **XXX**, 2, 259–268.

Appleby, Joyce. (1984). *Capitalism and a New Social Order: The Republican Vision of the 1790s*. New York: New York University Press.

Aptheker, Herbert. (1960). *The American Revolution, 1763–1783*. New York: International Publ.

Arasaratnam, S. (1978). "Indian Commercial Groups and European Traders, 1600–1800: Changing Relationships in Southeastern India," *South Asia*, n.s., **I**, 2, 42–53.

Arasaratnam, S. (1979). "Trade and Political Dominion in South India, 1750–1790. Changing British–Indian Relationships," *Modern Asian Studies*, **XIII**, 1, 19–40.

Arasaratnam, S. (1980). "Weavers, Merchants and Company: The Handloom Industry in South-eastern India, 1750–1790," *Indian Economic and Social History Review*, **XVII**, 3, 257–281.

Arbellot, Guy. (1973). "La grande mutation des routes en France au milieu du XVIIIe siècle," *Annales E.S.C.*, **XXVIII**, 2, 764–791.

Archer, Christon I. (1974). "Pardos, Indians and the Army of the New Spain: Inter-relationships and Conflicts, 1780–1810," *Journal of Latin American Studies*, **VI**, 2, 231–255.

Archer, Christon I. (1977). *The Army in Bourbon Mexico, 1760–1810*. Albuquerque, NM: University of New Mexico Press.

Archer, Christon I. (1981). "The Royalist Army in New Spain: Civil–Military Relationships, 1810–1821," *Journal of Latin American Studies*, **XIII**, 1, 57–82.

Archer, Christon I. (1982). "The Officer Corps in New Spain: The Martial Career, 1759–1821," *Jahrbuch für Geschichte von Staat, Wirtschaft und Gesellschaft Lateinamerikas*, **XIX**, 137–158.

Archives de la Ministère des Affaires Etrangères (France). (1788–1789, 1797). *Mémoires et Documents, Angleterre*, No. 46: *Mémoires sur le Commerce, le Finance, etc., 1713 à 1811* (Arch. A.E. 46): 21. f°239–243 [ca. 1788–1789], 3e mémoire, Recherche sur ce qui est relatif aux étoffes de laines; 29. f°287–297, may 1797, Remarques sur le traité de commerce entre la France et l'Angleterre de l'an 1786, par Theremin; 37. f°326–328, Brumaire an VIII, Moyens d'attaquer l'Angleterre dans la source de sa prospérité; 38. f°329–334, Paris, 29 nivose an 8, Arnould, membre du tribunal au ler consul Bonaparte, sur la Paix: De la Paix avec l'Angleterre sous les rapports de la marine et du commerce de la France.

Arcila Farias, Eduardo. (1955). *El siglo ilustrado en América. Reformas economicas del siglo XVIII en Nueva España*. Caracas: Ed. del Ministerio de Educación.

Arciniegas, Germán. (1973). *Los Comuneros*. Medellín: Ed. Bedout.

Ardant, Gabriel. (1975). "Financial Policy and Economic Infrastructure of Modern States and Nations," in Charles Tilly, ed., *The Formation of National States in Western Europe*. Princeton, NJ: Princeton University Press, 164–242.

Argyle, W. J. (1966). *The Fon of Dohomey: A History and Ethnography of the Old Kingdom*. Oxford: Clarendon Press.

Armengaud, André. (1973). "Population in Europe, 1700–1914," in C. M. Cipolla, ed., *Fontana Economic History of Europe*, **III**: *The Industrial Revolution*. London: Collins/Fontana, 22–76.

Armstrong, Maurice W. (1946). "Neutrality and Religion in Revolutionary Nova Scotia," *New England Quarterly*, **XIX**, 1, 50–62.

Armytage, Frances. (1953). *The Free Port System in the British West Indies: A Study in Commercial Policy, 1766–1822*, Imperial Studies Series, Vol. XX. London: Longmans, Green.

Arnold, Rosemary. (1957a). A Port of Trade: Whydah of the Guinea Coast," in K. Polanyi *et al.*, eds., *Trade and Market in the Early Empires*. New York: Free Press, 154–176.

Arnold, Rosemary. (1957b). "Separation of Trade and Market: Great Market of Whydah," in K. Polanyi *et al.*, eds., *Trade and Market in the Early Empires*. New York: Free Press, 177–187.

Arnould, Ambroise-Marie. (1791). *De la balance du commerce et les relations commerciales extérieures de la France dans toutes les parties du globe, particulierement à la fin du règne de Louis XIV et au moment de la Révolution*, 2 vols. Paris: Buisson.

Artola, Miguel. (1952). "Campillo y las reformas de Carlos III," *Revista de Indias*, **XII**, 50, 685–714.

Ascherson, Neal, ed. (1975). *The French Revolution: Extracts from The Times, 1789–1794*. London: Times Books.

Asdrubal Silva, Hernán. (1978). "The United States and the River Plate: Interrelationships and Influences Between Two Revolutions," in S. Tulchin, ed., *Hemispheric Prospectives on the United States*. Westport, CT: Greenwood Press, 22–36.

Ashton, T. S. (1924). *Iron and Steel in the Industrial Revolution*. Manchester, Engl.: Manchester University Press.

Ashton, T. S. (1948). *The Industrial Revolution, 1760–1830*. London: Oxford University Press.

Ashton, T. S. (1949). "The Standard of Life of the Workers in England, 1790–1830," *Journal of Economic History*, Suppl. IX, 19–38.

Ashton, T. S. (1959). *Economic Fluctuations in England 1700–1800*. Oxford: Clarendon Press.

Asiegbu, Johnson U. J. (1969). *Slavery and the Politics of Liberation, 1787–1861*. London: Longmans.

Athar Ali, M. (1975). "The Passing of Empire: The Mughal Case," *Modern Asian Studies*, **IX**, 3, 385–396.

Auckland, William. (1861–1862). *The Journal and Correspondence of William, Lord Auckland,* 4 vols. London: Richard Bentley.

Auffray, Danièle, Baudouin, Thierry, Collin, Michèle & Guillerm, Alain. (1980). *Feux et lieux: Histoire d'une famille et d'un pays face à la société industrielle.* Paris: Galilée.

Aufhauser, R. Keith. (1974). "Profitability of Slavery in the British Caribbean," *Journal of Interdisciplinary History,* **V**, 1, 45–67.

Augé, Marc. (1971). "L'organisation du commerce pré-colonial en Basse Côte d'Ivoire et ses effets sur l'organisation sociale des populations côtières," in C. Meillassoux, ed., *The Development of Indigenous Trade and Markets in West Africa.* London: Oxford University Press, 153–167.

Aulard, A. (1913). "La nuit du 4 août," *La Révolution française,* **XLIV**, 200–215.

Austen, Ralph A. (1970). "The Abolition of the Overseas Slave Trade: A Distorted Theme in West African History," *Journal of the Historical Society of Nigeria,* **V**, 2, 257–274.

Austen, Ralph A. (1979). "The Trans-Saharan Slave Trade: A Tentative Census," in H. A. Gemery & J. S. Hogendorn, eds., *The Uncommon Market.* New York: Academic Press, 23–76.

Avelino, Ivone Días. (1978). "Instituição do 'comercio livre' na mudança estrutural do sistema colonial espanhol," *Revista de historia do América,* No. 85, 59–83.

Avrich, Paul. (1973). *Russian Rebels, 1600–1800.* London: Allen Lane.

Ayandele, E. A. (1967). "Observations in Some Social and Economic Aspects of Slavery in Pre-colonial Northern Nigeria," *Nigerian Journal of Economic and Social Studies,* **IX**, 3, 329–338.

Azevedo, João Lucio d' (1922). *O Marques de Pombal e a sua época,* 2a ed. con emendas. Rio de Janeiro: Anuario do Brasil.

Bã, Amadou Hampaté & Daget, Jacques. (1962). *L'empire peul de Macina,* **I**: *(1818–1853).* Paris & La Haye: Mouton. (Originally published in *Etudes Soudanaises,* **III**, 1955.)

Baer, Gabriel. (1983). "Landlord, Peasant and the Government in the Arab Provinces of the Ottoman Empire in the 19th and Early 20th Century," in J. L. Bacqué-Grammont & P. Dumont, dirs., *Economie et sociétés dans l'Empire ottomane (fin du XVIIIe–début du XXe siècle),* Colloques Internationaux du CNRS, No. 601. Paris: Ed. du CNRS, 261–274.

Bagchi, Amiya Kumar. (1976a). "De-Industrialization in India in the Nineteenth Century: Some Theoretical Implications," *Journal of Development Studies,* **XII**, 2, 135–164.

Bagchi, Amiya Kumar. (1976b). "De-Industrialization in Gangetic Bihar, 1809–1901," in *Essays in Honour of Professor Susobhan Chandra Sarkar.* New Delhi: People's Publ. House, 499–522.

Bagchi, Amiya Kumar. (1976c). "Reflections in Patterns of Regional Growth in India During the Period of British Rule," *Bengal Past and Present,* **XCV**, Part 1, No. 180, 247–289.

Bagchi, Amiya Kumar. (1979). "A Reply," *Indian Economic and Social History Review,* **XVI**, 2, 147–161.

Bağiş, A. I. (1984). *Britain and the Struggle for the Integrity of the Ottoman Empire: Sir Robert Ainslie's Embassy to Istanbul, 1776–1794.* Istanbul: Isis.

Bagú, Sergio. (1979). "Prólogo," in M. Izard, *El miedo a la revolución.* Madrid: Ed. Tecnos, 13–17.

Bagwell, Philip S. (1974). *The Transport Revolution from 1770.* London: B. T. Batsford.

Baillargeon, Georges E. (1968). *La survivance du régime seigneurial à Montréal. Un régime qui ne veut pas mourir.* Ottawa: Le Cercle du Livre de France.

Bailyn, Bernard. (1962). "Political Experience and Enlightenment Ideas in Eighteenth-Century America," *American Historical Review,* **LXVII**, 2, 339–351.

Bailyn, Bernard. (1967). *Ideological Origins of the American Revolution.* Cambridge, MA: Belknap Press of Harvard University Press.

Bailyn, Bernard. (1969). "A Comment," *American Historical Review,* **LXXV**, 2, 361–363.

Bailyn, Bernard. (1973). "The Central Themes of the American Revolution: An Interpretation," in S. G. Kurtz & J. H. Hutson, eds., *Essays on the American Revolution.* Chapel Hill, NC: University of North Carolina Press, 3–31.

Bailyn, Bernard. (1986a). *The Peopling of British North America: An Introduction*. New York: Knopf.

Bailyn, Bernard. (1986b). *Voyagers to the West: A Passage in the Peopling of America on the Eve of the Revolution*. New York: Knopf.

Bairoch, Paul. (1973a). "Agriculture and the Industrial Revolution, 1700–1914," in C. M. Cipolla, ed., *Fontana Economic History of Europe*, **III:** *The Industrial Revolution*. London: Collins/Fontana, 452–506.

Bairoch, Paul. (1973b). "Commerce international et genèse de la révolution industrielle anglaise," *Annales E.S.C.*, **XXVIII**, 2, 545–553.

Bairoch, Paul. (1974). *Révolution industrielle et sous-développement*, 4ᵉ ed. Paris & La Haye: Mouton.

Bairoch, Paul. (1983). "La place de l'énergie hydraulique dans les sociétés traditionelles et au cours des XIXe et XXe siècles," paper delivered at XV Settimana di Studio, Ist. Int. di Storia Economica "Francesco Datini," Prato, 15–20 apr., mimeo.

Ballot, Charles. (1923). *L'introduction du machinisme dans l'industrie française*. Paris: Comité des travaux historiques, section d'histoire moderne (depuis 1715) et d'histoire contemporaine, fasc. IX. Lille: O. Marquant.

Bamford, Paul Walden. (1952). "France and the American Market in Naval Timber and Masts, 1776–1786," *Journal of Economic History*, **XII**, 1, 21–34.

Barber, Elinor. (1955). *The Bourgeoisie in Eighteenth-Century France*. Princeton, NJ: Princeton University Press.

Barbier, Jacques A. (1972). "Elites and Cadres in Bourbon Chile," *Hispanic American Historical Review*, **LII**, 3, 416–435.

Barbier, Jacques A. (1977). "The Culmination of the Bourbon Reforms, 1787–1792," *Hispanic American Historical Review*, **LVII**, 1, 51–68.

Barbier, Jacques A. (1980). "Peninsular France and Colonial Trade: The Dilemma of Charles IV's Spain," *Journal of Latin American Studies*, **XII**, 1, 21–37.

Barel, Yves. (1968). *Le développement de la Russie tsariste*. Paris & La Haye: Mouton.

Barkan, Ömer Lütfi. (1954). "La 'Méditerranée' de F. Braudel vue d'Istamboul," *Annales E.S.C.*, **IX**, 2, 189–200.

Barkan, Ömer Lütfi. (1956). "Le Servage existait-t-il en Turquie?" *Annales E.S.C.*, **XI**, 1, 54–60.

Barker, Charles Albro. (1940). *The Background of the Revolution in Maryland*. New Haven, CT: Yale University Press.

Barnave, Antoine. (1960). *Introduction à la Révolution française, Cahiers des Annales*, No. 15. Texte établi sur la manuscrit original et présenté par Fernand Rude. Paris: Armand Colin.

Baron, Samuel H. (1972). "The Transition from Feudalism to Capitalism in Russia: A Major Soviet Historical Controversy," *American Historical Review*, **LXXVII**, 3, 715–729.

Baron, Samuel H. (1973). "The Fate of the *gosti* in the Reign of Peter the Great," *Cahiers du monde russe et soviétique*, **XIV**, 4, 488–512.

Baron, Samuel H. (1974). "Who were the *Gosti*?" *California Soviet Studies*, **VII**, 1–40.

Barr, Stringfellow. (1949). *The Pilgrimage of Western Man*. New York: Harcourt, Brace.

Barrow, Thomas C. (1968). "The American Revolution as a Colonial War for Independence," *William and Mary Quarterly*, 3rd ser., **XXV**, 3, 452–464.

Barry, Boubacar. (1972). *Le royaume de Waalo: Le Sénégal avant la conquête*. Paris: Maspéro.

Barthélemy, Edouard. (1848). *Notice historique sur les établissements des Côtes occidentales d'Afrique*. Paris: Arthus Bertrand.

Bartlett, Roger P. (1979). *Human Capital: The Settlement of Foreigners in Russia, 1792–1804*. Cambridge, Engl.: Cambridge University Press.

Bathily, Abdoulaye. (1986). "La traite atlantique des esclaves et ses effets économiques et sociaux en Afrique: Le cas de Galam, royaume de l'hinterland sénégambien au dix-huitième siècle," *Journal of African History*. **XXVII**, 2, 269–293.

Bauer, Arnold J. (1971). "The Church and Spanish American Agrarian Structure, 1765–1865," *The Americas*, **XXVIII**, 1, 78–98.

Bauer, Arnold J. (1983). "The Church in the Economy of Spanish America: *Censos* and *Depósitas* in the Eighteenth and Nineteenth Centuries," *Hispanic American Historical Review*, **LXIII**, 4, 707–734.

Bauer, John E. (1970). "International Repercussions of the Haitian Revolution," *The Americas*, **XXVI**, 4, 394–418.

Baykov, Alexander. (1974). "The Economic Development of Russia," in W. Blakewell, ed., *Russian Economic Development from Peter the Great to Stalin*. New York: New Viewpoints, 5–20. (Originally published in *Economic History Review*, n.s., **VII**, 1954.)

Bayly, C. A. (1975). "Town Building in North India, 1740–1830," *Modern Asian Studies*, **IX**, 4, 483–504.

Bayly, C. A. (1985). "State and Economy in India Over Seven Hundred Years," *Economic History Review*, 2nd ser., **XXXVIII**, 4, 583–596.

Bayly, C. A. (1986). "The Middle East and Asia during the Age of Revolutions, 1760–1830," *Itinerario*, **X**, 2, 69–84.

Bazant, Jan. (1964). "Evolución de la industria textil poblana (1544–1845)," *Historia Mexicana*, **XII**, 4, 473–516.

Beales, H. S. (1929). "Historical Revisions: The 'Industrial Revolution,'" *History*, n.s., **XIV**, No. 54, 125–129.

Bean, Richard. (1974). "A Note on the Relative Importance of Slaves and Gold in West African Exports," *Journal of African History*, **XV**, 3, 351–356.

Beard, Charles A. (1913). *An Economic Interpretation of the Constitution of the United States*, New York: Macmillan.

Beard, Charles A. (1915). *Economic Origins of Jeffersonian Democracy*. New York: Macmillan.

Béaur, Gérard. (1984). *Le marché foncier à la veille de la révolution*. Paris: Ed. de l'E.H.E.S.S.

Beck, Thomas. (1981). "The French Revolution and Nobility: A Reconsideration," *Journal of Social History*, **XV**, 2, 219–233.

Becker, Charles & Martin, Victor. (1975). "Kayor et Baol, royaumes sénégalais et traite des esclaves au XVIIIe siècle," *Revue française d'histoire d'Outre-Mer*, **LXII**, 226/227, 270–300.

Beckett, J. V. (1977). "English Landownership in the Later Seventeenth and Eighteenth Centuries: The Debate and the Problems," *Economic History Review*, 2nd ser., **XXX**, 4, 567–581.

Beer, George Louis. (1907). *British Colonial Policy, 1754–1765*. New York: Macmillan.

Behrens, Betty. (1965). "'Straight History' and 'History in Depth': The Experience of Writers on Eighteenth-Century France," *Historical Journal*, **VIII**, 1, 117–126.

Behrens, Betty (C. B. A.). (1967). *The Ancien Regime*. New York: Harcourt, Brace, Jovanovich.

Behrens-Abouseif, Doris. (1982). "The Political Situation of the Copts, 1798–1923," in B. Braude & B. Lewis, eds., *Christians and Jews in the Ottoman Empire*, **II**: *The Arabic-Speaking Lands*. New York: Holmes & Meier, 185–205.

Belaunde, Victor Andrés. (1938). *Bolivar and the Political Thought of the Spanish American Revolution*. Baltimore, MD: Johns Hopkins University Press.

Bell, Herbert C. (1916). "British Commercial Policy in the West Indies, 1785–93, *English Historical Review*, **XXXI**, No. 123, 429–441.

Bemis, Samuel Flagg. (1916). "Relations Between the Vermont Separatists and Great Britain, 1789–1791," *American Historical Review*, **XXI**, 3, 547–560.

Bemis, Samuel Flagg. (1923). *Jay's Treaty: A Study in Commerce and Diplomacy*. New York: Macmillan.

Bemis, Samuel Flagg. (1935). *The Diplomacy of the American Revolution*. New York: Appleton-Century.

Bemis, Samuel Flagg. (1943). *The Latin American Policy of the United States: An Historical Interpretation*. New York: Harcourt, Brace.

Bemis, Samuel Flagg. (1949). *John Quincy Adams and the Foundations of American Foreign Policy.* New York: Knopf.

Bemis, Samuel Flagg. (1956). *John Quincy Adams and the Union.* New York: Knopf.

Bendjebbar, André. (1987). "Les problèmes des alliances politiques, sociales et économiques dans la Contre-Révolution angevine (1787–1799)," in F. Lebrun & R. Dupuy, eds., *Les résistances à la Révolution.* Paris: Imago, 87–96.

Benians, E. A. (1940). "The Beginnings of the New Empire, 1783–1793," in J. H. Rose *et al.,* eds., *The Cambridge History of the British Empire,* **II:** *The Growth of the New Empire, 1783–1870.* Cambridge, Engl.: At the University Press, 1–35.

Ben-Shachar, Ari Y. (1984). "Demand versus Supply in the Industrial Revolution: A Comment," *Journal of Economic History,* **XLIV,** 3, 801–805.

Bent, J. Theodore. (1890). "The English in the Levant," *English Historical Review,* **V,** No. 20, 654–664.

Berend, Iván T. & Ranki, György. (1982). *The European Periphery and Industrialization, 1780–1914.* Cambridge, Engl.: Cambridge University Press.

Bergeron, Louis. (1970). "Problèmes économiques de la France napoléonienne," *Revue d'histoire moderne et contemporaine,* **XVII,** 3, 469–505 ("Discussion," 630–638).

Bergeron, Louis. (1978a). "Introduction," in Pierre Léon, dir., *Histoire économique et sociale du monde,* **III:** Louis Bergeron, dir., *Inerties et révolutions, 1730–1840.* Paris: Lib. Armand Colin, 7–9.

Bergeron, Louis. (1978b). "Les réseaux de la finance internationale," in Pierre Léon, dir., *Histoire économique et sociale du monde,* **III:** Louis Bergeron, dir., *Inerties et révolutions, 1730–1840.* Paris: Lib. Armand Colin, 119–135.

Bergeron, Louis. (1978c). "La révolution agricole en Angleterre," in Pierre Léon, dir., *Histoire économique et sociale du monde,* **III:** Louis Bergeron, dir., *Inerties et révolutions, 1730–1840.* Paris: Lib. Armand Colin, 226–232.

Bergeron, Louis. (1978d). "La révolution industrielle anglaise," in Pierre Léon, dir., *Histoire économique et sociale du monde,* **III:** Louis Bergeron, dir., *Inerties et révolutions, 1730–1840.* Paris: Lib. Armand Colin, 317–345.

Bergeron, Louis. (1978e). "L'économie française sous le feu de la révolution politique et sociale," in Pierre Léon, dir., *Histoire économique et sociale du monde,* **III:** Louis Bergeron, dir., *Inerties et révolutions, 1730–1840.* Paris: Lib. Armand Colin, 347–369.

Bergeron, Louis. (1978f). *Banquiers, négociants et manufacturiers parisiens du Directoire à l'Empire.* Paris & La Haye: Mouton.

Bergier, J. F. (1973). "The Industrial Bourgeoisie and the Rise of the Working Class, 1700–1914," in C. M. Cipolla, ed., *Fontana Economic History of Europe,* **III:** *The Industrial Revolution.* London: Collins/Fontana, 397–451.

Berkes, Niyazi. (1964). *The Development of Secularism in Turkey.* Montreal: McGill University Press.

Berlin, Ira. (1976). "The Revolution in Black Life," in A. F. Young, ed., *The American Revolution: Explanations in the History of American Radicalism.* DeKalb, IL: Northern Illinois University Press, 349–382.

Bernstein, Harry. (1945). *Origins of Inter-American Interest, 1700–1812.* Philadelphia, PA: University of Pennsylvania Press.

Berov, Ljuben. (1974). "Changes in Price Conditions in Trade Between Turkey and Europe in the 16th–19th Centuries," *Etudes balkaniques,* **II,** 2/3, 168–178.

Berrill, K. E. (1960). "International Trade and the Rate of Economic Growth," *Economic History Review,* 2nd ser., **XII,** 3, 351–359.

Bertaud, Jean-Paul. (1975). "Voies nouvelles pour l'histoire militaire de la révolution, *Annales historiques de la Révolution française,* **XXVII,** No. 219, 66–94.

Berthoff, Rowland & Murrin, John M. (1973). "Feudalism, Communalism, and the Yeoman Freeholder: The American Revolution Considered as a Social Accident," in S. G. Kurtz & J. H. Hutson, eds., *Essays on the American Revolution.* Chapel Hill, NC: University of North Carolina Press, 256–288.

Besset, Giliane. (1982). "Les relations commerciales entre Bordeaux et la Russie au XVIIIe siècle," *Cahiers du monde russe et soviétique*, **XXIII**, 2, 197–219.

Bethell, Leslie. (1969). "The Independence of Brazil and the Abolition of the Brazilian Slave Trade: Anglo-Brazilian Relations, 1822–1826," *Journal of Latin American Studies*, **I**, 2, 115–147.

Bethell, Leslie. (1985). "The Independence of Brazil," in *Cambridge History of Latin America*, **III**: L. Bethell, ed., *From Independence to c. 1870*. Cambridge, Engl.: Cambridge University Press, 157–196.

Bezanson, Anna. (1922). "The Early Use of the Term Industrial Revolution," *Quarterly Journal of Economics*, **XXXVI**, 2, 343–349.

Bhattacharya, Neeladri. (1986). "Colonial State and Agrarian Society," in S. Bhattacharya & R. Thapar, eds., *Situating Indian History*. Delhi: Oxford University Press, 106–145.

Bhattacharya, Sabyasachi. (1983). "Regional Economy: Eastern India," in D. Kumar, ed., *Cambridge Economic History of India*, **II**: *c. 1757–c. 1970*. Cambridge, Engl.: Cambridge University Press, 270–332.

Bhattacharya, Sukumar. (1954). *The East India Company and the Economy of Bengal from 1704 to 1740*. London: Luzac.

Bien, David D. (1974). "La réaction aristocratique avant 1789: l'example de l'armée," *Annales E. S. C.*, **XXIX**, 1. 23–48; **XXIX**, 2, 505–534.

Bierck, Harold C., Jr. (1953). "The Struggle for Abolition in Gran Colombia," *Hispanic American Historical Review*, **XXXIII**, 3, 365–386.

Bils, Mark. (1984). "Tariff Protection and Production in the Early U. S. Cotton Textile Industry," *Journal of Economic History*, **XLIV**, 4, 1033–1045.

Birch, Alan. (1967). *The Economic History of the British Iron and Steel Industry, 1784–1879*. London: Frank Cass.

Birmingham, David. (1966). *Trade and Conflict in Angola: The Mbundu and their Neighbours under the Influence of the Portuguese*. Oxford: Clarendon Press.

Birmingham, David. (1970). "Early African Trade in Angola and Its Hinterland," in R. Gray & D. Birmingham, eds., *Pre-Colonial African Trade*. London: Oxford University Press, 163–173.

Bjork, Gordon C. (1964). "The Weaning of the American Economy: Independence, Market Changes, and Economic Development," *Journal of Economic History*, **XXIV**, 4, 541–560.

Blanc, Simone. (1964). "Aux origines de la bourgeoisie russe," *Cahiers du monde russe et soviétique*, **X**, 3, 294–301.

Blanc, Simone. (1969). Tatiščev et la pratique du mercantilisme," *Cahiers du monde russe et soviétique*, **X**, 3/4, 353–370.

Blanc, Simone. (1974). "The Economic Policy of Peter the Great," in W. Blakewell, ed., *Russian Economic Development from Peter the Great to Stalin*. New York: New Viewpoints, 23–49. (Transl. from *Cahiers du monde russe et soviétique*, **III**, 1962.)

Blaug, Mark. (1963). "The Myth of the Old Poor Law and the Making of the New," *Journal of Economic History*, **XXIII**, 2, 151–184.

Blaug, Mark. (1964). "The Poor Law Report Reexamined," *Journal of Economic History*, **XXIV**, 2, 229–245.

Bloch, Camille. (1900). "Le traité de commerce de 1786 entre la France et l'Angleterre," in *Etudes sur l'histoire économique de la France (1760–89)*. Paris: Alphonse Picard et fils, 239–269.

Bloch, Camille. (1901). *Memoire sur le Traité de Commerce de 1786 entre la France et l'Angleterre, d'après la correspondance du plenipotentiaire anglais*. Paris: Imprimerie Nationale. (Extract from *Bulletin des sciences économiques et sociaux du Comité des Travaux historiques et scientifiques*, 1900, 257–269.)

Bloch, Marc. (1930). "La lutte pour l'individualisme agraire dans la France du dix-huitième siècle," *Annales d'histoire économique et sociale*, **II**. 329–383; 511–556.

Bloch, Marc. (1952, 1956). *Les caractères originaux de l'histoire rurale française*, 2 vols. Paris: A. Colin.

Bloch, Marc. (1966). *French Rural History.* Berkeley & Los Angeles: University of California Press.

Bloch, Raymond (1970). "Préface," in Albert Soboul, ed., *La civilisation et la Révolution française,* **I:** *Crise de l'Ancien Régime.* Paris: Arthaud, 11–13.

Blum, Jerome, (1960). "Russian Agriculture in the Last 150 Years of Serfdom," *Agricultural History,* **XXXIV,** 1, 3–12.

Blum, Jerome. (1961). *Lord and Peasant in Russia from the Ninth to the Nineteenth Century.* Princeton, NJ: Princeton University Press.

Boahen, A. Adu. (1964). *Britain, the Sahara, and the Western Sudan, 1788–1861.* Oxford: Clarendon Press.

Bois, Paul. (1971). *Paysans de l'Ouest.* Paris: Flammarion.

Bolton, G. C. (1966). "The Founding of the Second British Empire," *Economic History Review,* 2nd ser., **XIX,** 1, 195–200.

Bondois, Paul-M. (1933). "L'organisation industrielle et commerciale sous l'Ancien Régime: Le privilège exclusif au XVIIIe siècle," *Revue d'histoire économique et sociale,* **XXI,** 2/3, 140–189.

Bonilla, Heraclio.(1972). "Clases populares y Estado en el contexto de la crisis colonial," in *La Independencia en el Perú,* Perú Problema, No. 7. Lima: Institute de Estudios Peruanos, 13–69.

Bonilla, Heraclio & Spalding, Karen. (1972). "La Independencia en el Perú: las palabras y los hechos," in *La Independencia en el Perú,* Perú Problema, No. 7. Lima: Instituto de Estudios Peruanos, 70–114.

Bosher, J. F. (1965). "French Administration and Public Finance in Their European Setting," in *New Cambridge Modern History,* **VIII:** A. Goodwin, ed., *The American and French Revolutions, 1763–93.* Cambridge, Engl.: At the University Press, 565–591.

Bosher, J. F. (1970). *French Finances 1770–1795: From Business to Bureaucracy.* Cambridge, Engl.: Cambridge University Press.

Boulègue, Jean. (1972). *Les Luso-africains de Sénégambie, XVIe–XIXe siècles.* Dakar: Université de Dakar, Faculté des Lettres et Sciences Humaines, Département d'Histoire.

Boulle, Pierre H. (1972). "Slave Trade, Commercial Organization and Industrial Growth in Eighteenth-Century Nantes," *Revue française d'histoire d'outre-mer,* **LIX,** 1er trimestre, No. 214, 70–112.

Boulle, Pierre H. (1975). "Marchandises de traite et développement industriel dans la France et l'Angleterre du XVIIIe siècle," *Revue française d'histoire d'outre-mer,* **LXII,** 1e et 2e trimestres, Nos. 226/227, 309–330.

Bouloiseau, Marc. (1956). "Aspects sociaux de la crise cotonnière dans les campagnes rouennaises en 1788–1789," in *Actes du 81ᵉ Congrès national des Sociétés savantes Rouen–Caen: Section d'histoire moderne et contemporaine.* Paris: Imprimerie Nationale, 403–428.

Bouloiseau, Marc. (1957). *Cahiers de doléances du Tiers Etat du Baillage de Rouen pour les Etats généraux de 1789.* **I:** *La Ville.* Paris: Presses Universitaires de France.

Bouloiseau, Marc. (1960). *Cahiers de doléances du Tiers Etats du Baillage de Rouen pour les Etats généraux de 1789.* **II:** *La baillage principal.* Rouen: Imprimerie administrative de la Seine-Maritime.

Bouloiseau, Marc. (1983). *The Jacobin Republic, 1792–94.* Cambridge, Engl.: Cambridge University Press.

Bourde, André J. (1953). *The Influence of England on the French Agronomes, 1750–1789.* Cambridge, Engl.: At the University Press.

Bourde, André J. (1967). *Agronomie et agronomes en France au XVIIIe siècle,* 3 vols. Paris: S. E. V. P. E. N.

Bourgin, Georges. (1908). "Les communaux et la Révolution française," *Nouvelle revue historique de droit français et étranger,* 3e sér., **XXXII,** 6, 690–751.

Bourgin, Georges. (1911). "L'agriculture, la classe paysanne et la Révolution française (1789–an IV)," *Revue d'histoire économique et social,* **IV,** 155–228.

Bourgin, Hubert. (1904–1905). "L'histoire économique de la France de 1800 à 1830," *Revue d'histoire moderne et contemporaine*, **VI**, 22–37.

Bousquet, Nicole. (1974). "La dissolution de l'empire espagnol au XIXe siècle et son contexte économique," unpublished M. A. thesis, McGill University.

Bousquet, Nicole, (1978). "La carrière hégémonique de l'Angleterre au sein de l'économie-monde et le démantèlement des empires espagnol et portugais en Amérique au début du XIXe siècle," unpublished Ph.D. thesis, McGill University.

Boutier, Jean. (1979). "Jacquerie en pays croquant: les Révoltes paysannes en Aquitaine (décembre 1789–mars 1790)," *Annales E. S. C.,* **XXXIV**, 4, 760–786.

Bouvier, Jean. (1970). "A propos de la crise dite de 1805. Les crises économiques sous l'Empire," *Revue d'histoire moderne et contemporaine*, **XVII**, juil.–sept. 506–513.

Bowden, Witt. (1919). "The English Manufacturers and the Commercial Treaty with France," *American Historical Review*, **XXV**, 1, 18–35.

Boxer, C. R. (1969). *The Portuguese Seaborne Empire, 1415–1825*. New York: Knopf.

Boyetet, M. (1789). *Receuil de divers memoires relatifs au traité de commerce avec l'Angleterre, faits avant, pendant et après les négotiations*. Versailles: Baudouin.

Brading, David A. (1970). "Mexican Silver-Mining in the Eighteenth Century: The Revival of Zacatecas," *Hispanic American Historical Review*, **L**, 4, 665–681.

Brading, David A. (1971). *Miners and Merchants in Bourban Mexico, 1763–1810*. Cambridge, Engl.: At the University Press.

Brading, David A. (1973a). "La estructura de la producción agricola en el Bajío de 1700 a 1850," *Historia Mexicana*, **XXIII**, 2, 197–237.

Brading, David A. (1973b). "Government and Elites in Late Colonial Mexico," *Hispanic American Historical Review*, **LIII**, 3, 389–414.

Brading, David A. (1983). *Classical Republicanism and Creole Patriotism: Simon Bolivar (1783–1830) and the Spanish American Revolution*. Cambridge, Engl.: Centre of Latin American Studies, Cambridge University.

Brading, David A. (1984). "Bourbon Spain and its American Empire," in *Cambridge History of Latin America*, **I**: Leslie Bethell, ed., *Colonial Latin America*. Cambridge, Engl.: Cambridge University Press, 389–439.

Brading, David A. & Wu, Celia. (1973). "Population Growth and Crisis: León, 1720–1860," *Journal of Latin American Studies*, **V**, 1, 1–36.

Brathwaite, Edward, (1971). *The Development of Creole Society in Jamaica, 1770–1820*. Oxford: Clarendon Press.

Braude, Benjamin. (1979). "International Competition and Domestic Cloth in the Ottoman Empire, 1500–1650: A Study in Underdevelopment," *Review*, **II**, 3, 437–451.

Braude, Benjamin & Lewis, Bernard. (1982). "Introduction," in B. Braude & B. Lewis, eds., *Christians and Jews in the Ottoman Empire*, **I**: *The Central Lands*. New York: Holmes & Meier, 1–34.

Braudel, Fernand. (1958). "Histoire et sciences sociales: La longue durée," *Annales E. S. C.,* **XIII**, 4, 725–753.

Braudel, Fernand. (1979). *Civilisation matérielle, économie et capitalisme, XVe–XVIIIe siècle*, **I**: *Les structures du quotidien*, **II**: *Les jeux de l'échange*, **III**: *Le temps du monde*. Paris: Lib. Armand Colin.

Braudel, Fernand. (1980). "L'empire turc est-il une économie-monde?," in *Memorial Ömer Lütfi Barkan*, Bibliothèque de l'Institut Françqis d'Etudes Anatoliennes d'Istanbul, Vol. XXVIII. Paris: Lib. d'Amérique et d'Orient A. Maisonneuve, 39–51.

Braudel, Fernand. (1982). *Civilization and Capitalism, 15th–18th Century*, **II**: *The Wheels of Commerce*. New York: Harper & Row.

Braudel, Fernand. (1984). *Civilization and Capitalism, 15th–18th Century*, **III**: *The Perspective of the World*. New York: Harper & Row.

Brebner, John Bartlett. (1937). *The Neutral Yankees of Nova Scotia: A Marginal Colony During the Revolutionary Years*. New York: Columbia University Press.

Brebner, John Bartlett. (1966a). "Laissez-faire and State Intervention in Nineteenth-Century Britain," in E. M. Carus-Wilson, ed., *Essays in Economic History,* Vol. III. New York: St. Martin's Press, 252–262. (Originally published in *Journal of Economic History,* 1948.)

Brebner, John Bartlett. (1966). *North Atlantic Triangle: The Interplay of Canada, the United States and Great Britain.* Toronto: McClelland & Stewart.

Briavoinne, Natalis. (1838). "Sur les inventions et perfectionnemens dans l'industrie, depuis la fin du XVIIIe siècle jusqu'à nos jours," Mémoire couronné le 8 mai 1837. *Mémoires couronnés par l'academie royale des Sciences et Belles-Lettres de Bruxelles,* **XIII,** 5–187.

Briavoinne, Natalis. (1839). *De l'industrie en Belgique, causes de décadence et de prosperité, sa situation actuelle,* Vol. I. Bruxelles: Eugene Dubois.

Bridenbaugh, Carl. (1955). *Cities in Revolt: Urban Life in America, 1743–1776.* New York: Oxford University Press.

Briggs, Asa. (1960). "The Language of 'Class' in Early Nineteenth-Century England," in A. Briggs & J. Saville, eds., *Essays in Labour History.* London: Macmillan, 43–73.

British Parliamentary Papers (BPP), Reports from Committees. (1832). X, Parts I & II. *Minutes of Evidence taken before the Select Committee on the Affairs of the East India Company, II: Finance and Accounts–Trade,* ordered by the House of Commons to be printed on August 16.

British Parliamentary Papers (BPP), Reports from Committees. (1840a). VII. *Report from the Select Committee on East India Produce,* ordered by the House of Commons to be printed on July 21.

British Parliamentary Papers (BPP), Reports from Committees. (1840b). VII. *Report from the Select Committee of the House of Lords appointed to consider the petition of the East India Company for Relief,* ordered by the House of Commons to be printed on June 4.

British Parliamentary Papers (BPP), Reports from Committees. (1848a). IX. *Report from the Select Committee on the Growth of Cotton in India,* ordered by the House of Commons to be printed on July 17.

British Parliamentary Papers (BPP), Reports from Committees. (1848b). XXIII, Part IV. *Supplement No. 1 to the Eighth Report from the Select Committee on Sugar and Coffee Planting,* ordered by the House of Commons to be printed on May 29 (361—II—Suppl. No. 1).

British Parliamentary Papers (BPP), Accounts and Papers. (1861). XLIV. *Report of the Indigo Commission,* ordered by the House of Commons to be printed on March 4.

Brito Figueroa, Federico. (1966). *Historia económica y social de Venezuela,* 2 vols. Caracas: Universidad Central de Venezuela.

Broder, Albert. (1976). "Le commerce extérieur: L'échec de la conquête d'une position internationale," in Fernand Braudel & Ernest Labrousse, dirs., *Histoire économique et social de la France,* **III:** *L'avènement de l'ère industriel (1789-années 1880).* Paris: Presses Universitaires de France, 305–346.

Broeze, Frank J. A. (1973). "The New Economic History, the Navigation Acts, and the Continental Tobacco Market, 1770–90," *Economic History Review,* 2nd ser., **XXVI,** 4, 668–678.

Brooks, George E. (1975). "Peanuts and Colonialism: Consequences of the Commercialization of Peanuts in West Africa, 1830–70," *Journal of African History,* **XVI,** 1, 29–54.

Brooks, Philip Coolidge. (1936). "Spanish Royalists in the United States, 1809–1821," in A. C. Wilgus, ed., *Colonial Hispanic America.* Washington, DC: George Washington University Press, 559–572.

Brown, Jonathon C. (1979). *A Socioeconomic History of Argentina, 1776–1860.* Cambridge, Engl.: Cambridge University Press.

Brown, Murray. (1965). "Towards an Endogenous Explanation of Industrialization," *Social Research,* **XXXIII,** 2, 295–313.

Brown, Robert E. (1955a). "Economic Democracy Before the Constitution," *American Quarterly,* **VII,** 3, 257–274.

Brown, Robert E. (1955b). *Middle-Class Democracy and the Revolution in Massachusetts, 1691–1780*. Ithaca, NY: Cornell University Press.

Brown, Vera Lee. (1922). "Anglo-Spanish Relations in America in the Closing Years of the Colonial Era," *Hispanic American Historical Review*, **V**, 3, 325–483.

Brown, Vera Lee. (1928). "Contraband Trade: A Factor in the Decline of Spain's Empire in America," *Hispanic American Historical Review*, **VIII**, 2, 178–189.

Brown, Vera Lee. (1929–1930). "Studies in the History of Spain in the Second Half of the Eighteenth Century," *Smith College Studies in History*, **XV**, 1/2, 3–92.

Brown, Wallace. (1974). "The American Colonies and the West Indies," *American History Illustrated*, **IX**, 2, 12–23.

Browning, Oscar. (1885). "The Treaty of Commerce between England and France in 1786," *Transactions of the Royal Historical Society, n.s.*, **II**, 349–364.

Browning, Oscar, ed. (1909, 1910). *Despatches from Paris, 1784–1790*, **I**: *(1784–1787)*, Camden Third Series, XVI, 1909; **II**: *(1788–1790)*, Camden Third Series, XIX, 1910. London: Offices of the Royal Historical Society.

Bruchey, Stuart. (1958). "Success and Failure Factors: American Merchants in Foreign Trade in the Eighteenth and Early Nineteenth Centuries," *Business History Review*, **XXXII**, 3, 272–292.

Bruchey, Stuart. (1965). *The Roots of American Economic Growth, 1607–1861: An Essay in Social Causation*. New York: Harper & Row.

Bruchey, Stuart. (1987). "Economy and Society in an Earlier America," *Journal of Economic History*, **XLVII**, 2, 299–319.

Brugière, Michel. (1986). *Gestionnaires et profiteurs de la Révolution: L'administration des finances françaises de Louis XVI à Bonaparte*. Paris: Olivier Orban.

Brunet, Michel. (1959). "The British Conquest: Canadian Social Scientists and the Fate of the *Canadiens*," *Canadian Historical Review*, **XL**, 2, 93–107.

Buckley, Roger Norman. (1979). *Slaves in Red Coats: The British West India Regiments, 1795–1815*. New Haven, CT: Yale University Press.

Buda, Aleks. (1972). "Problèmes de l'histoire de l'Albanie des VIIIe–XVIIIe siècles dans les recherches de la nouvelle historiographie albanaise," in *Actes du IIe Congrès International des Etudes du Sud-Est Européen*, Athènes, 7–13 mai 1970, **I**: *Chronique du Congrès, Rapports*. Athènes: Comité Hellénique d'Organisation, 87–103.

Bullion, John L. (1983). *A Great and Necessary Measure: George Greenville and the Genesis of the Stamp Act, 1763–1765*. Columbia, MO: University of Missouri Press.

Burckhardt, Jacob. (1965). *Fragments historiques*. Genève: Lib. Droz.

Burkholder, Mark A. (1972). "From Creole to *Peninsular:* The Transformation of the Audiencia de Lima," *Hispanic American Historical Review*, **LII**, 3, 395–415.

Burkholder, Mark A. (1976). "The Council of the Indies in the Late Eighteenth Century: A New Perspective," *Hispanic American Historical Review*, **LVI**, 3, 404–423.

Burstin, Haim. (1986). "'I sanculotti: un dossier da riaprire," *Passato e presente*, No. 10, genn.–apr., 23–52.

Burt, A. L. (1931). "A New Approach to the Problem of the Western Posts," *Report of Annual Meeting of Canadian Historical Association*, Ottawa, May 26–27. Ottawa: Department of Public Archives, 61–75.

Busch-Zantner, R. (1938). *Agrarverfassung, Gesellschaft und Siedlung in Südosteuropas in besonderer Berücksichtigung der Türkenzeit*. Leipzig: Otto Harrasowitz.

Bushnell, David. (1985). "The Independence of Spanish South America," in *Cambridge History of Latin America*, **III**: L. Bethell, eds., *From Independence to c. 1870*. Cambridge, Engl.: Cambridge University Press, 95–156.

Butel, Paul. (1970). "Crise et mutation de l'activite économique à Bordeaux sous le Consulat et l'Empire," *Revue d'histoire moderne et contemporaine*, **XVII**, juil.–sept., 540–558.

Butel, Paul. (1978a). "Les Amériques et l'Europe," in Pierre Léon, dir., *Histoire économique et sociale du monde,* **III:** *Louis Bergeron, dir., Inerties et révolutions, 1730–1840.* Paris: Lib. Armand Colin, 53–92.

Butel, Paul. (1978b). "La richesse des Indes," in Pierre Léon, dir., *Histoire économique et sociale du monde,* **III:** *Louis Bergeron, dir., Inerties et révolutions, 1730–1840.* Paris: Lib. Armand Colin, 93–109.

Butel, Paul. (1978c). "Marchés europeens, traditions et renouvellements," in Pierre Léon, dir., *Histoire économique et sociale du monde,* **III:** *Louis Bergeron, dir., Inerties et révolutions, 1730–1840.* Paris: Lib. Armand Colin, 109–119.

Cadot, Michel & Van Regemorter, Jean-Louis. (1969). "Le commerce extérieur de la Russie en 1784, d'après le journal de voyage de Baert du Hollant," *Cahiers du monde russe et soviétique,* **X,** 3/4, 371–391.

Cahen, Léon. (1939). "Une nouvelle interpretation du traité franco-anglais de 1786–1787," *Revue historique,* 64 année, **CLXXXV,** 2, 257–285.

Cain, P. J. & Hopkins, A. J. (1980). "The Political Economy of British Expansion Overseas, 1750–1914," *Economic History Review,* 2nd ser., **XXXIII,** 4, 463–491.

Cain, P. J. & Hopkins, A. G. (1986). "Gentlemanly Capitalism and British Expansion Overseas. I. The Old Colonial System, 1688–1850," *Economic History Review,* 2nd ser., **XXXIX,** 4, 501–525.

Calhoun, Craig. (1982). *The Question of Class Struggle: Social Foundations of Popular Radicalism during the Industrial Revolution.* Chicago, IL: University of Chicago Press.

Callahan, William J. (1968). "A Note on the Real y General Junta de Comercio, 1679–1814," *Economic History Review,* 2nd ser., **XXI,** 3, 519–528.

Callender, Guy S. (1902). "The Early Transportation and Banking Enterprises of the States in Relation to the Growth of the Corporation," *Quarterly Journal of Economics,* **XVII,** 1, 111–162.

Cameron, Rondo E. (1956). "Some French Contributions to the Industrial Development of Germany, 1840–1870," *Journal of Economic History,* **XVI,** 3, 281–321.

Cameron, Rondo E. (1958). "Economic Growth and Stagnation in France, 1815–1914," *Journal of Modern History,* **XXX,** 1, 1–13.

Cameron, Rondo. (1982). "The Industrial Revolution: A Misnomer," *The History Teacher,* **XV,** 3, 377–384.

Cameron, Rondo. (1985). "A New View of European Industrialization," *Economic History Review,* 2nd ser., **XXXVIII,** 1, 1–23.

Cameron, Rondo. (1986). "Was England Really Superior to France?" *Journal of Economic History,* **XLVI,** 4, 1031–1039.

Cameron, Rondo & Freedeman, Charles E. (1983). "French Economic Growth: A Radical Revision," *Social Science History,* **VII,** 1, 3–30.

Campbell, Leon G. (1972a). "A Colonial Establishment: Creole Domination of the Audiencia of Lima During the Late Eighteenth Century," *Hispanic American Historical Review,* **LII,** 1, 1–25.

Campbell, Leon G. (1972b). "Black Power in Colonial Peru: The 1779 Tax Rebellion of Lambayeque," *Phylon,* **XXXIII,** 2, 140–152.

Campbell, Leon G. (1976). "The Army of Peru and the Túpac Amaru Revolt, 1780–1783," *Hispanic American Historical Review,* **LVI,** 1, 31–57.

Campbell, Leon G. (1979). "Recent Research on Andean Peasant Revolts, 1750–1820," *Latin America Research Review,* **XIV,** 1, 3–49.

Campbell, Leon G. (1981). "Social Structure of the Túpac Amaru Army in 1780–81," *Hispanic American Historical Review,* **LXI,** 4, 675–693.

Campbell, R. H. (1967). "The Industrial Revolution in Scotland: A Revision Article," *Scottish Historical Review,* **XLVI,** 1, 141, 37–55.

Cannadine, David. (1984). "The Past and the Present in the English Industrial Revolution, 1880–1980," *Past and Present,* No. 103, May, 131–172.

Cárdenas Acosta, Pablo E. (1960). *El movimiento comunal de 1781 en el Nuevo Reino de Granada (Reivindicaciones históricas)*, 2 vols. Bogotá: Ed. Kelly.

Carr, Raymond. (1969). "Spain and Portugal, 1793 to c.1840," in *New Cambridge Modern History*, **IX**: C. W. Crawley, ed., *War and Peace in an Age of Upheaval, 1793–1830*. Cambridge, Engl.: At the University Press, 439–461.

Carrera Damas, Germán. (1963). "A propósito de los hipótesis de Charles C. Griffin: Cuestiones económicos–sociales de la emancipación," *Crítica contemporanea*, No. 10, marzo–abril, 13–21.

Carrière, Charles. (1973). *Négociants marseillais au XVIIIe siècle*. Marseilles: Institut Historique de Provence.

Carus-Wilson, E. M. (1954). "An Industrial Revolution of the Thirteenth Century," in E. M. Carus-Wilson, ed., *Essays in Economic History*, Vol. I. London: Edward Arnold, 41–60. (Originally published in *Economic History Review*, 1941.)

Castañeda, C. E. (1929). "The Corregidor in Spanish Colonial Administration," *Hispanic American Historical Review*, **IX**, 4, 446–470.

Catchpole, Brian & Akinjogbin, I. A. (1984). *A History of West Africa in Maps and Diagrams*. London: Collins Educational.

Cavanaugh, Gerald J. (1972). "The Present State of French Revolutionary Historiography: Alfred Cobban and Beyond," *French Historical Studies*, **VII**, 4, 587–606.

Cazals, Rémy. (1983). *Les révolutions industrielles à Mazamet, 1750–1900*. Paris & Toulouse: La Découverte-Maspéro, Privat.

Césaire, Aimé. (1961). *Toussaint Louverture: La Révolution française et le problème colonial*. Paris: Présence africaine.

Céspedes del Castillo, Guillermo. (1946). "Lima y Buenos Aires: repercusiones económicos y políticas de la creación del Virreinato del Rio de la Plata," *Anuario de Estudios Americanos*, **III**, 667–874.

Chabert, Alexandre. (1945). *Essai sur les mouvement des prix et des revenus en France de 1798 à 1820*. Paris: Lib. de Médicis.

Chabert, Alexandre. (1949). *Essai sur le mouvement des revenus et de l'activité économique en France de 1798 à 1820*. Paris: Lib. de Médicis.

Chalmin, Pierre. (1968). "La querelle des Bleus et des Rouges dans l'Artillerie française à la fin du XVIIIe siècle," *Revue d'histoire économique et sociale*, **XLVI**, 4, 465–505.

Chaloner, W. H. (1957). "The Agriculture Activities of John Wilkinson, Ironmaster," *Agriculture History Review*, **V**, 1, 48–51.

Chaloner, W. H. (1964). "Hazards of Trade with France in Time of War, 1776–1783," *Business History*, **VI**, 2, 79–92.

Chamberlin, Christopher. (1979). "Bulk Exports, Trade Tiers, Regulation, and Development: An Economic Approach to the Study of West Africa's 'Legitimate Trade,'" *Journal of Economic History*, **XXXIX**, 2, 419–438.

Chambers, J. D. (1940). "Enclosure and the Small Landowner," *Economic History Review*, **X**, 2, 118–127.

Chambers, J. D. (1953). "Enclosure and Labour Supply in the Industrial Revolution," *Economic History Review*, 2nd ser., **V**, 3, 319–343.

Chambers, J. D. (1957). "The Vale of Trent, 1670–1800, a Regional Study of Economic Change," *Economic History Review*, Suppl. No. 3. London: Cambridge University Press.

Chambers, J. D. (1972). *Population, Economy, and Society in Pre-Industrial England*. London: Oxford University Press.

Chambers, J. D. & Mingay, G. E. (1966). *The Agricultural Revolution, 1750–1880*. London: B. T. Batsford.

Chambre, Henri. (1964). "Pososkov et le mercantilisme," *Cahiers du monde russe et soviétique*, **IV**, 4, 335–365.

Champion, Edne. (1897). *La France d'après les cahiers de 1789*. Paris: Armand Colin.

Chandler, Charles Lyon. (1924). "United States Commerce with Latin America at the Promulgation of the Monroe Doctrine," *Quarterly Journal of Economics,* **XXXVIII,** 3, 466–486.

Chandra, Bipan. (1968). "Reinterpretation of Nineteenth Century Indian Economic History," *Indian Economic and Social History Review,* **V,** 1, 35–75.

Chandra, Satish. (1966). "Some Aspects of the Growth of a Money Economy in India during the Seventeenth Century," *Indian Economic and Social History Review,* **III,** 4, 321–331.

Chandra, Satish. (1972). *Parties and Politics at the Mughal Court, 1707–1740,* 2nd ed. New Delhi: People's Publishing House.

Chandra, Satish. (1974). "Some Aspects of Indian Village Society in Northern India during the 18th Century—The Position and Role of the *Khud-kásht* and *páhi-kásht,*" *Indian Historical Review,* **I,** 1, 51–64.

Chapman, Stanley D. (1965). "The Transition to the Factory System in the Midlands Cotton-Spinning Industry," *Economic History Review,* 2nd ser., **XVIII,** 3, 526–543.

Chapman, Stanley D. (1970). "Fixed Capital Formation in the British Cotton Industry, 1770–1815," *Economic History Review,* 2nd ser., **XXIII,** 2, 235–266.

Chapman, Stanley D. (1971). "Fixed Capital Formation in the British Cotton Manufacturing Industry," in J. P. P. Higgins & S. Pollard, eds., *Aspects of Capital Investment in Great Britain, 1750–1850: A Preliminary Survey.* London: Methuen, 57–107.

Chapman, Stanley D. (1972). *The Cotton Industry in the Industrial Revolution.* London: Macmillan.

Chapman, Stanley D. (1979). "Financial Restraints on the Growth of Firms in the Cotton Industry, 1790–1850," *Economic History Review,* 2nd ser., **XXXII,** 1, 50–69.

Chaptal, Jean-Antoine. (1819). *De l'industrie françoise,* 2 vols. Paris: A. A. Renouard.

Chaptal, Jean-Antoine-Claude (1893). "Un projet de traité de commerce avec l'Angleterre sous le Consulat," *Revue d'économie politique,* **VII,** 2, 83–98.

Charles, Eunice A. (1977). *Precolonial Senegal: The Jolof Kingdom, 1800–1890.* Boston, MA: African Studies Center, Boston University.

Chassagne, Serge. (1978). "L'industrie lainière en France à l'époque révolutionnaire et impériale (1790–1810)," in A. Soboul, dir., *Voies nouvelles pour l'histoire de la Révolution française,* Commission d'histoire économique et sociale de la Révolution française, Mémoires et Documents, Vol. XXXV. Paris: Bibliothèque Nationale, 143–167.

Chassagne, Serge. (1979). "La diffusion rurale de l'industrie cotonnière en France (1750–1850)," *Revue du Nord,* **LXI,** No. 240, 97–114.

Chassagne, Serge. (1980). *Oberkampf: Un entrepreneur capitaliste au Siècle des Lumières.* Paris: Aubier Montaigne.

Chassagne, Serge. (1981). "Aspects des phénomènes d'industrialisation et de désindustrialisation dans les campagnes françaises au XIXe siècle," *Revue du Nord,* **LXIII,** No. 248, 35–58.

Chaudhuri, Binoy Bhushan. (1976). "Agricultural Growth in Bengal and Bihar, 1770–1860. Growth of Cultivation since the Famine of 1770," *Bengal Past and Present,* **XCV,** 1, No. 180, 290–340.

Chaudhuri, K. N. (1966). "India's Foreign Trade and the Cessation of the East India Company's Trading Activities, 1828–1840," *Economic History Review,* 2nd ser., **XIX,** 2, 345–363.

Chaudhuri, K. N. (1968). "India's International Economy in the Nineteenth Century: A Historical Survey," *Modern Asian Studies,* **II,** 1, 31–50.

Chaudhuri, K. N. (1971). "Introduction," in K. N. Chaudhuri, ed., *the Economic Development of India under the East India Country, 1814–58. A Selection of Contemporary Writings.* Cambridge, Engl.: At the University Press, 1–50.

Chaudhuri, K. N. (1974). "The Structure of the Indian Textile Industry in the Seventeenth and Eighteenth Centuries," *Indian Economic and Social History Review,* **XI,** 2/3, 127–182.

Chaudhuri, K. N. (1978). *The Trading World of Asia and the English East India Company, 1660–1760.* Cambridge, Engl.: Cambridge University Press.

Chaudhuri, K. N. (1979). "Markets and Traders in India during the Seventeenth and Eighteenth Centuries," in K. N. Chaudhuri & Clive J. Dewey, eds., *Economy and Society: Essays in Indian Economic and Social History.* Delhi: Oxford University Press, 143–162.

Chaudhuri, K. N. (1981). "The World-System East of Longitude 20°: The European Role in Asia, 1500–1750," *Review,* **V,** 2, 219–245.

Chaudhuri, K. N. (1982). "Foreign Trade: European Trade in the India," in T. Raychaudhuri & I. Habib, eds., *Cambridge Economic History of India,* **I.** *c.1200–c.1700.* Cambridge, Engl.: Cambridge University Press, 382–407.

Chaudhuri, K. N. (1983a). "Foreign Trade and Balance of Payments (1757–1947)," in D. Kumar, ed., *Cambridge Economic History of India,* **II:** *c.1757–c.1970.* Cambridge, Engl.: Cambridge University Press, 804–877.

Chaudhuri, K. N. (1983b). "The Trading World of Asia and the English East India Company, 1660–1760: A Review of Reviews," *South Asia Research,* **III,** 1, 10–17.

Chaunu, Pierre. (1954). "Pour une histoire sociale de l'Amérique espagnole coloniale," *Revue historique.* 78ᵉ année, **CCXI,** 2, 309–316.

Chaunu, Pierre. (1963). "Interprétation de l'indépendance de l'Amérique latine," *Bulletin de la Faculté des Lettres de Strasbourg,* **LXI,** 8, TILAS III, 403–421.

Chaunu, Pierre. (1964). *L'Amérique et les Amériques.* Paris: Lib. Armand Colin.

Chaunu, Pierre. (1966). *La civilisation de l'Europe classique.* Paris: Arthaud.

Chaunu, Pierre. (1972a). "Les enquêtes du Centre de Recherches d'Histoire Quantitative de Caen: Réflexions sur l'échec industriel de la Normandie," in Pierre Léon *et al.,* dirs., *L'industrialisation en Europe au XIXe siècle,* Colloques Internationaux du CNRS, No. 540. Paris: Ed. du CNRS, 285–299 (with "Discussion," 300–304).

Chaunu, Pierre. (1972b). "Interpretación de la independencia de América," in *La Independencia en el Perú,* Perú Problema, No. 7. Lima: Instituto de Estudios Peruanos, 167–194.

Chaussinand-Nogaret, Guy. (1970). *Les financiers du Languedoc au XVIIIe siècle,* Paris: S.E.V.P.E.N.

Chaussinand-Nogaret, Guy. (1975). "Aux origines de la Révolution: noblesse et bourgeoisie," *Annales E.S.C.,* **XXX,** 2/3, 265–278.

Chaussinand-Nogaret, Guy. (1981). "La ville jacobine et balzacienne," in G. Duby, dir., *Histoire de la France urbaine,* **III:** E. Le Roy Ladurie, dir., *La ville classique de la Renaissance aux Révolutions.* Paris: Seuil, 537–621.

Chaussinand-Nogaret, Guy. (1985). "L'identité nationale et le problème des élites: la France du XVIIIe siècle," *Commentaire,* No. 31, aut., 856–863.

Checkland, S. G. (1958). "Finance for the West Indies, 1780–1815," *Economic History Review,* 2nd ser., **X,** 3, 461–469.

Chesnutt, David R. (1978). "South Carolina's Impact Upon East Florida, 1763–1776," in S. Proctor, ed., *Eighteenth-Century Florida and the Revolutionary South.* Gainesville, FL: University Presses of Florida, 5–14.

Chevallier, Dominique. (1968). "Western Development and Eastern Crisis in the Mid-Nineteenth Century: Syria Confronted with the European Economy," in W. R. Polk & R. L. Chambers, eds., *Beginnings of Modernization in the Middle East.* Chicago, IL: University of Chicago Press, 205–222.

Chicherov, A. I. (1971). *India, Economic Development in the 16th-18th Centuries.* Moscow: Nauka.

Choulgine, Alexandre. (1922). "L'organisation capitaliste de l'industrie éxistait-elle en France à la veille de la Révolution?," *Revue d'histoire économique et social,* **X,** 2, 184–218.

Christelow, Allan. (1942). "Contraband Trade Between Panama and the Spanish Main, and the Free Port Act of 1766," *Hispanic American Historical Review,* **XXII,** 2, 309–343.

Christelow, Allan. (1947). "Great Britain and the Trades from Cadiz and Lisbon to Spanish America and Brazil, 1759–1783," *Hispanic American Historical Review,* **XXVII,** 1, 2–29.

Christie, Ian R. & Labaree, Benjamin W. (1976). *Empire or Independence, 1760–1776.* New York: W. W. Norton.

Chung, Tan. (1974). "The British–China–India Trade Triangle (1771–1840)," *Indian Economic and Social History Review,* **XI**, 4, 411–431.

Cipolla, Carlo. (1961). "Sources d'énergie et histoire de la humanité," *Annales E.S.C.,* **XVI**, 3, 521–534.

Cipolla, Carlo M. (1973). "Introduction," in C. M. Cipolla, ed., *Fontana Economic History of Europe,* **III:** *The Industrial Revolution.* London: Collins/Fontana, 7–21.

Clapham, J. H. (1917). "Loans and Subsidies in Time of War, 1793–1914," *Economic Journal,* **XXVII**, No. 108, 495–501.

Clapham, J. H. (1920). "Europe After the Great Wars, 1816 and 1920," *Economic Journal,* **XXX,** No. 120, 423–435.

Clapham, J. H. (1923). "The Growth of an Agrarian Proletariat, 1688–1832: A Statistical Note," *Cambridge Historical Journal,* **I**, 1, 92–95.

Clapham, J. H. (1940). "Industrial Revolution and the Colonies, 1783–1822," in J. Holland Rose, A. P. Newton & E. A. Benians, eds., *The Cambridge History of the British Empire,* **II:** *The Growth of the New Empire, 1783–1870.* Cambridge, Engl.: At the University Press, 217–240.

Clapham, J. H. (Sir John). (1944). *The Bank of England: A History.* Cambridge, Engl.: At the University Press.

Clapham, J. H. (1966). "The Last Years of the Navigation Acts," in E. M. Carus-Wilson, ed., *Essays in Economic History,* Vol. III. New York: St. Martin's Press, 144–178. (Originally published in *English Historical Review,* 1910.)

Clark, Edward C. (1974). "The Ottoman Industrial Revolution," *International Journal of Middle East Studies,* **V**, 1, 65–76.

Clark, G. N. (1953). *The Idea of the Industrial Revolution.* Glasgow: Jackson, Son & Co., 1953.

Clark, J. C. D. (1985). *English Society, 1688–1832: Ideology, Social Structure, and Political Practice during the Ancien Regime.* Cambridge, Engl.: Cambridge University Press.

Clark, J. C. D. (1986). *Revolution and Rebellion: State and Society in England in the Seventeenth and Eighteenth Centuries.* Cambridge, Engl.: Cambridge University Press.

Clark, John G. (1970). *New Orleans, 1718–1812: An Economic History.* Baton Rouge, LA: Louisiana State University Press.

Clark, John G. (1981). *La Rochelle and the Atlantic Economy during the Eighteenth Century.* Baltimore & London: Johns Hopkins University Press.

Clark, S. D. (1959). *Movements of Political Protest in Canada, 1640–1840.* Toronto: University of Toronto Press.

Clark, Victor S. (1916). *History of Manufactures in the United States, 1607–1800.* Washington, DC: Carnegie Institution.

Clarkson, Jesse Dunsmore. (1970). "Some Notes on Bureaucracy, Aristocracy, and Autocracy in Russia, 1500–1800," in G. A. Ritter, hrsg., *Entstehung and Wandel der modernen Gesellschaft.* Berlin: Walter de Gruyter, 187–220.

Clauder, Anna C. (1932). *American Commerce as Affected by the Wars of the French Revolution and Napoleon, 1793–1812.* Philadelphia: University of Pennsylvania Thesis.

Clendenning, P. H. (1972). "Eighteenth Century Russian Translation of Western Economic Works," *Journal of European Economic History,* **I**, 3, 745–753.

Clendenning, P. H. (1979). "The Background and Negotiations for the Anglo-Russian Commercial Treaty of 1766," in A. G. Cross, ed., *Great Britain and Russia in the Eighteenth Century: Contrasts and Comparisons.* Newton, MA: Oriental Research Partners, 145–163.

Clère, Jean-Jacques. (1982). "La vaine pâture au XIXe siècle: un anachronisme?" *Annales historiques de la Révolution française,* LIV année, No. 244, 113–128.

Clogg, Richard. (1973). "Aspects of the Movement for Greek Independence," in R. Clogg, ed., *The Struggle for Greek Independence.* London: Macmillan, 1–40.

Clough, Shepard B. (1957). "The Diffusion of Industry in the Last Century and a Half," in *Studi in onore di Armando Sapori,* Vol. II. Milano: Istituto Ed. Cisalpino, 1341–1357.

Coale, A. J. & Hoover, E. M. (1969). "The Effects of Economic Development on Population Growth," in Michael Drake, ed., *Population in Industrialization*. London: Methuen, 11–20. (Originally published 1958.)

Coats, A. W. (1958). "Changing Attitudes of Labour in Mid-Eighteenth Century," *Economic History Review*, 2nd ser., **XI,** 1, 35–51.

Cobb, Richard. (1959). "The People in the French Revolution," *Past and Present*, No. 15, 60–72.

Cobb, Richard & Rudé, George. (1955). "Le dernier mouvement populaire de la Révolution à Paris: Les journées de germinal et de prairial, an III," *Revue historique*, **LXXIX,** No. 219, 250–281.

Cobban, Alfred. (1954). "British Secret Service in France, 1784–1792," *English Historical Review*, **LXIX,** No. 271, 226–261.

Cobban, Alfred. (1956). "The Vocabulary of Social History," *Political Science Quarterly*, **LXXI,** 1, 1–17.

Cobban, Alfred. (1958). *Historians and the Causes of the French Revolution*, Historical Association, Pamphlet No. 2. London: Routledge & Kegan Paul.

Cobban, Alfred. (1963). *A History of Modern France, I: Old Regime and Revolution, 1715–1799,* 3rd ed. Hammondsworth, Engl.: Penguin.

Cobban, Alfred. (1964). *The Social Interpretation of the French Revolution.* Cambridge Engl.: Cambridge University Press.

Cobban, Alfred. (1965). *A History of Modern France, II: From the First Empire to the Second Empire, 1799–1871,* 2nd ed. Hammondsworth, Engl.: Penguin.

Cobban, Albert. (1967). "The French Revolution, Orthodox & Unorthodox: A Review of Reviews," *History*, **LII,** No. 175, 149–159.

Cobban, Alfred. (1968a). "The Enlightenment and the French Revolution," in *Aspects of the French Revolution*. New York: George Braziller, 18–28. (Originally published 1965.)

Cobban, Alfred. (1968b). "Historians and the Causes of the French Revolution," in *Aspects of the French Revolution*. New York: George Braziller, 29–67. (Originally published 1958.)

Cobban, Alfred. (1968c). "The *Parlements* of France in the Eighteenth Century," in *Aspects of the French Revolution*. New York: George Braziller, 68–82. (Originally published in *History*, 1950.)

Cobban, Alfred. (1968d). "The Myth of the French Revolution," in *Aspects of the French Revolution*. New York: George Braziller, 90–111. (Originally published 1955.)

Cobbett, William, ed. (1816). *The Parliamentary History of England from the Earliest Period to the Year 1803*, **XXVI:** *15 May 1786 to 8 Feb. 1788.* London: T. C. Hansard.

Cochran, Thomas C. (1981). *Frontiers of Change: Early Industrialism in America*. New York: Oxford University Press.

Coelho, Philip R. P. (1973). "The Profitability of Imperialism: The British Experience in the West Indies, 1768–1772," *Explorations in Economic History*, **X,** 3, 253–280.

Cohen, Felix. (1949). Appendix XIV to United Kingdom, Colonial Office, Gold Coast: *Report to His Excellency the Governor by the Committee on Constitutional Reform*, Colonial No. 250. London: HMSO, 100–104.

Cohen, Jon S. & Weitzman, Martin L. (1975). "A Marxian Model of Enclosures," *Journal of Development Economics*, **I,** 4, 287–336.

Cohn, Bernard S. (1961). "From Indian Status to British Contract," *Journal of Economic History*, **XXI,** 4, 613–628.

Cole, Arthur H. (1959). "The Tempo of Mercantile Life in Colonial America," *Business History Review*, **XXXIII,** 3, 277–299.

Cole, G. D. H. (1952). *Introduction to Economic History, 1750–1950.* London: Macmillan.

Cole, W. A. (1969). "Trends in Eighteenth-Century Smuggling," in W. E. Minchinton, ed., *The Growth of English Overseas Trade in the Seventeenth and Eighteenth Centuries*. London: Methuen, 1969, 121–143. (Originally published in *Economic History Review*, 1958.)

Cole, W. A. (1973). "Eighteenth-Century Economic Growth Revisited," *Explorations in Economic History*, **X**, 4, 327–348.

Cole, W. A. (1981). "Factors in Demand, 1700–80," in R. Floud & D. N. McCloskey, eds., *The Economic History of Britain Since 1700*, **I**. *1700–1860*. Cambridge, Engl.: Cambridge University Press, 36–65.

Cole, W. A. & Deane, Phyllis. (1966). "The Growth of National Incomes," in H. J. Habakkuk & M. Postan, eds., *Cambridge Economic History of Europe*, **VI**: *The Industrial Revolutions and After: Incomes, Population and Technological Change*. Cambridge, Engl.: Cambridge University Press, 1–55.

Coleman, D. C. (1956). "Industrial Growth and Industrial Revolutions," *Economica*, n.s., **XXIII**, No. 89, 1–22.

Coleman, D. C. (1964). "Industrial Revolution," in Julius Gould & William L. Kolb, eds., *A Dictionary of the Social Sciences*. London: Tavistock, 326–327.

Coleman, D. C. (1966). "Industrial Growth and Industrial Revolutions," in E. M. Carus-Wilson, eds., *Essays in Economic History*, Vol. III. New York: St. Martin's Press, 334–352. (Originally published in *Economica*, 1956.)

Coleman, D. C. (1983). "Proto-Industrialization: A Concept Too Many," *Economic History Review*, 2nd ser., **XXXVI**, 3, 435–448.

Colley, Linda. (1984). "The Apotheosis of George III: Loyalty, Royalty and the British Nation, 1760–1820," *Past and Present*, No. 102, 94–129.

Colley, Linda. (1986). "Whose Nation? Class and National Consciousness in Britain, 1750–1830," *Past and Present*, No. 113, 97–117.

Collier, Simon. (1963). *Ideas and Politics of Chilean Independence, 1808–1833*. Cambridge, Engl.: At the University Press.

Collins, E. J. T. (1975). "Dietary Change and Cereal Consumption in Britain in the Nineteenth Century," *Agricultural History Review*, **XXIII**, Part II, 97–115.

Colvin, Lucie G. (1971). "The Commerce of Hausaland, 1780–1833," in D. McCall & N. Bennett, eds., *Aspects of West African Islam*, Boston University Papers on Africa, Vol. V. Boston, MA: Boston University African Studies Center, 101–135.

Comadrán Ruiz, Jorge. (1955). "En torno al problema del indio en el Rio de la Plata," *Anuario de Estudios Americanos*, **XII**, 39–74.

Comninel, George C. (1985). "The Political Context of the Popular Movement in the French Revolution," in F. Krantz, ed., *History From Below: Studies in Popular Protest and Popular Ideology in Honour of George Rudé*. Montreal: Concordia University, 143–162.

Comninel, George C. (1987). *Rethinking the French Revolution*. London: Verso.

Confino, Michael. (1960a). "Maîtres de forge et ouvriers dans les usines métallurgiques de l'Oural aux XVIIIe–XIXe siècles," *Cahiers du monde russe et soviétique*, **I**, 2, 239–284.

Confino, Michael. (1960b). "La politique de tutelle des seigneurs russes envers leurs paysans vers la fin du XVIIIe siècle," *Revue des études slaves*, **XXXVII**, fasc. 1-4, 39–69.

Confino, Michael. (1961a). "La compatabilité des domaines privés en Russie dans la seconde moitié du 18 de siècle (d'après les 'Travaux de Société Libre d'Economie' de St. Petersbourg)," *Revue d'histoire moderne et contemporaine*, **VIII**, 1, 5–34.

Confino, Michael. (1961b). "Problèmes agraires, le système des redevances mixtes: Dans les domaines privés en Russie (XVIIIe–XIXe siècles)" *Annales E.S.C.*, **XVI**, 6, 1066–1095.

Confino, Michael. (1963). *Domaines et seigneurs en Russie vers la fin du XVIIIe siècle: Etude de structure agraires et de mentalités économiques*. Paris: Institut d'Etudes Slaves de l'Université de Paris.

Confino, Michael. (1969). *Systèmes agraires et progrès agricole: L'assolement triennal en Russie aux XVIIIe-XIXe siècles*. Paris & La Haye: Mouton.

Confino, Michael. (1986). "The Limits of Autocracy: Russia's Economy and Society in the Age of Enlightenment," *Peasant Studies*, **XIII**, 3, 149–170.

Congreso Hispánoamericano de Historia. (1953). *Causas y caracteres de la independencia hispanoamericano*. Madrid: Ed. Cult. Hispánica.

Connell, K. H. (1950). "The Colonization of Waste Land in Ireland, 1780–1845," *Economic History Review*, 2nd ser., **III**, 1, 44–71.

Connell, K. H. (1969). "Some Unsettled Problems in English and Irish Population History, 1750–1845," in Michael Drake, ed., *Population in Industrialization*. London: Methuen, 30–39. (Originally published in *Irish Historical Studies*, 1951.)

Conrotte, Manuel. (1920). *La intervención de España en la Independencia de los Estados Unidos de la America del Norte*. Madrid: Lib. General de Victoriano Suarez.

Cooper, Frederick. (1979). "The Problem of Slavery in African Studies," *Journal of African History*, **XX**, 1, 103–125.

Coquery-Vidrovitch, Catherine. (1971). "De la traite des esclaves à l'exportation de l'huile de palme et des palmistes au Dahomey: XIXe siècle," in C. Meillassoux, ed., *The Development of Indigenous Trade and Markets in West Africa*. London: Oxford University Press, 107–123.

Coquery-Vidrovitch, Catherine & Moniot, Henri. (1974). *L'Afrique noire de 1800 à nos jours*, Nouvelle Clio, No. 46. Paris: Presses Universitaires de France.

Coquin, François-Xavier (1978). "En Russie: l'initiative étatique et seigneuriale," in Pierre Léon, dir., *Histoire économique et sociale du monde*, **III**: Louis Bergeron, dir., *Inerties et révolutions, 1730–1840*. Paris: Lib. Armand Colin, 39–50.

Cornblit, Oscar. (1970). "Levantimiento de masas en Perú y Bolivia durante el siglo dieciocho," *Revista latinoamericana de sociología*, **VI**, 1, 100–141.

Corwin, Arthur F. (1967). *Spain and the Abolition of Slavery in Cuba, 1817–1886*. Austin, TX: University of Texas Press.

Corwin, Edward S. (1915). "The French Objective in the American Revolution," *American Historical Review*, **XXI**, 1, 33–61.

Corwin, Edward S. (1916). *French Policy and the American Alliance of 1778*. Princeton, NJ: Princeton University Press.

Costeloe, Michael P. (1981). "Spain and the Latin American Wars of Independence: The Free Trade Controversy, 1810–1820," *Hispanic American Historical Review*, **LXI**, 2, 209–234.

Cottret, Monique. (1986). *La Bastille à prendre: Histoire et mythe de la forteresse royale*. Paris: Presses Universitaires de France.

Coughtry, Jay. (1981). *The Notorious Triangle: Rhode Island and the African Slave Trade, 1700–1807*. Philadelphia, PA: Temple University Press.

Countryman, Edward. (1976a). " 'Out of the Bounds of the Law': Northern Land Rioters in the Eighteenth Century," in A. F. Young, ed., *The American Revolution: Explorations in the History of American Radicalism*. DeKalb, IL: Northern Illinois University Press, 36–69.

Countryman, Edward. (1976b). "Consolidating Power in Revolutionary America: The Case of New York, 1775–1783," *Journal of Interdisciplinary History*, **VI**, 4, 645–677.

Coupland, (Sir) Reginald. (1964). *The British Anti-Slavery Movement*. London: Frank Cass. (Original edition 1933.)

Cracraft, James. (1980). "More 'Peter the Great,' " *Canadian–American Slavic Studies*, **XIV**, 4, 535–544.

Craeybeckx, Jan. (1968). "Les débuts de la révolution industrielle en Belgique et les statistiques de la fin de l'Empire," in *Mélanges offerts à G. Jacquemyns*. Bruxelles: Université Libre de Bruxelles, Ed. de l'Institut de Sociologie, 115–144.

Crafts, N. F. R. (1976). "English Economic Growth in the Eighteenth Century: A Re-Examination of Deane and Cole's Estimates," *Economic History Review*, 2nd ser., **XXIX**, 2, 226–235.

Crafts, N. F. R. (1977). "Industrial Revolution in England and France: Some Thoughts on the Question, 'Why was England First?' " *Economic History Review*, 2nd ser., **XXX**, 3, 429–441.

Crafts, N. F. R. (1978). "Entrepreneurship and a Probabilistic View of the British Industrial Revolution," *Economic History Review*, 2nd ser., **XXXI**, 4, 613–614.

Crafts, N. F. R. (1981). "The Eighteenth Century: A Survey," in R. Floud & D. N. McCloskey, eds., *The Economic History of Britain Since 1700*, **I**. *1700–1860*. Cambridge, Engl.: Cambridge University Press, 1–16.

Crafts, N. F. R. (1983). "British Economic Growth, 1700–1831: A Review of the Evidence," *Economic History Review,* 2nd ser., **XXXVI**, 2, 177–199.

Crafts, N. F. R. (1984). "Economic Growth in France and Britain, 1830–1910: A Review of the Evidence," *Journal of Economic History,* **XLIV**, 1, 49–67.

Crafts, N. F. R. (1985). "English Workers' Real Wages During the Industrial Revolution: Some Remaining Problems," *Journal of Economic History,* **XLV**, 1, 139–144.

Craton, Michael. (1974). *Sinews of the Empire: A Short History of British Slavery.* New York: Anchor Press.

Creighton, Donald. (1937). *The Commercial Empire of the St. Lawrence, 1760–1850.* Toronto: Ryerson Press.

Crosby, Alfred W. (1965). *America, Russia, Hemp., and Napoleon: American Trade with Russia and the Baltic, 1783–1812.* Columbus: Ohio State University Press.

Crouzet, François. (1958). *L'économie britannique et le blocus continental (1806–1813),* 2 vols. Paris: Presses Universitaires de France.

Crouzet, François. (1959). "Las origines du sous-développement économique du Sud-Ouest," *Annales du Midi,* **LXXI**, No. 45, 71–79.

Crouzet, François. (1962). "Les conséquences économiques de la Révolution: A propos d'un inédit de Sir Francis d'Ivernois," *Annales historiques de la Révolution française,* **XXXIV**, 2, 168, 182–217; No. 169, 336–362.

Crouzet, François. (1964). "Wars, Blockade, and Economic Change in Europe, 1792–1815," *Journal of Economic History,* **XXIV**, 4, 567–590.

Crouzet, François. (1965). "Bilan de l'économie britannique pendant les guerres de la Révolution et de l'Empire," *Revue historique,* 92ᵉ année, **CCXXXIV**, 1, No. 234, 71–110.

Crouzet, François. (1966). "Le charbon anglais en France au XIXe siècle," in L. Trenard, dir., *Charbon et Sciences humaines, Actes du colloque,* Lille, mai 1963. Paris & La Haye: Mouton, 173–206.

Crouzet, François. (1967a). "Agriculture et Révolution industrielle: quelques réflexions," *Cahiers d'histoire,* **XII**, 1/2, 67–85.

Crouzet, François. (1967b). "England and France in the Eighteenth Century: A Comparative Analysis of Two Economic Growth," in R. M. Hartwell, ed., *The Causes of the Industrial Revolution in England.* London: Methuen, 139–174. (Translated from *Annales E.S.C.,* 1966.)

Crouzet, François. (1970). "Essai de construction d'un indice annuel de la production industrielle française au XIXe siècle," *Annales E.S.C.,* **XXV**, 1, 56–99.

Crouzet, François. (1971). "Discussion" of paper by Albert Soboul, in *L'abolition de la "feoautité" dans le monde occidental,* Colloque de Toulouse, 12–16 nov. 1968, 2 vols. Paris: Ed. du CNRS, **II**, 556–558.

Crouzet, François. (1972a). "Introduction," in F. Crouzet, ed., *Capital Formation in the Industrial Revolution.* London: Methuen, 1–69.

Crouzet, François. (1972b). "Capital Formation in Great Britain during the Industrial Revolution," in F. Crouzet, ed., *Capital Formation in the Industrial Revolution.* London: Methuen, 162–222. (Originally published in *Second International Conference of Economic History,* **II**, 1965.)

Crouzet, François (1972c). "Encore la croissance économique française au XIXe siècle," *Revue du Nord,* **LIV**, No. 214, 271–288.

Crouzet, François. (1980). "Toward an Export Economy: British Exports During the Industrial Revolution," *Explorations in Economic History,* **XVII**, 1, 48–93.

Crouzet, François. (1981). "The Sources of England's Wealth: Some French Views in the Eighteenth Century," in P. L. Cottrell & D. H. Aldcroft, eds., *Shipping, Trade and Commerce: Essays in memory of Ralph Davis.* Leicester, Engl.: Leicester University Press, 61–79.

Crouzet, François. (1985). *De la supériorité de l'Angleterre sur la France—L'économique et l'imaginaire, XVIIe–XXe siècles.* Paris: Lib. Académique Perrin.

Crummey, Robert O. (1977). "Russian Absolutism and the Nobility," *Journal of Modern History,* **XLIX**, 3, 456–468.

Cuenca Esteban, Javier. (1981). "Statistics of Spain's Colonial Trade, 1792–1820: Consular Duties, Cargo Inventories, and Balances of Trade," *Hispanic American Historical Review*, **LXI**, 3, 381–428.

Cuenca Esteban, Javier. (1984). "Trends and Cycles in U. S. Trade with Spain and the Spanish Empire," *Journal of Economic History*, **XLIV**, 2, 521–543.

Cunningham, Audrey. (1910). *British Credit in the Last Napoleonic War*. Cambridge, Engl.: At the University Press.

Cuno, Kenneth M. (1984). "Egypt's Wealthy Peasantry, 1740–1820: A Study of the Region of al-Mansūra," in T. Khalidi, ed., *Land Tenure and Social Transformation in the Middle East*. Beirut: American University of Beirut, 303–332.

Currie, R. & Hartwell, R. M. (1965). "The Making of an English Working Class?" *Economic History Review*, 2nd ser., **XVIII**, 3, 633–643.

Curtin, Philip D. (1950). "The Declaration of the Rights of Man in Saint-Domingue, 1788–1791," *Hispanic American Historical Review*, **XXX**, 2, 157–175.

Curtin, Philip D. (1969). *The Atlantic Slave Trade: A Census*. Madison, WI: University of Wisconsin Press.

Curtin, Philip D. (1974). "Measuring the Atlantic Slave Trade," in S. L. Engerman & E. D. Genovese, eds., *Race and Slavery in the Western Hemisphere: Quantitative Studies*. Princeton, NJ: Princeton University Press, 104–128.

Curtin, Philip D. (1975a). *Economic Change in Precolonial Africa: Senegambia in the Era of the Slave Trade*. Madison, WI: University of Wisconsin Press.

Curtin, Philip D. (1975b). *Economic Change in Precolonial Africa: Supplementary Evidence*. Madison, WI: University of Wisconsin Press.

Curtin, Philip D. (1976). "Measuring the Atlantic Slave Trade Once Again: A Comment," *Journal of African History*, **XVII**, 4, 595–605.

Curtin, Philip & Vansina, Jan. (1964). "Sources of the Nineteenth-Century Atlantic Slave Trade," *Journal of African History*, **V**, 2, 185–208.

Cvetkova, Bistra A. (1960). "L'évolution du régime féodal turc de la fin du XVIe jusqu'au milieu du XVIIIe siècle," in *Etudes historiques*, à l'occasion du XIe Congrès International des Sciences Historiques—Stockholm, août. Sofia: Académie des Sciences de Bulgarie, 171–206.

Cvetkova, Bistra. (1969). "Quelques problèmes du féodalisme ottomane à l'époque du XVIe–XVIIIe siècles," in *Actes du Premier Congrès International des Etudes Balkaniques et Sud-est Européennes*, Sofia, 26 août-1 septembre 1966, **III**: *Histórie (Ve–XVe ss.; XVe–XVIIe ss.)*. Sofia: Ed. de l'Académie Bulgare des Sciences, 709–721.

Cvetkova, Bistra. (1970). "Les *celep* et leur rôle dans la vie économique des Balkans à l'époque ottomane (XVe–XVIIIe siècles)," in M. A. Cook, ed., *Studies in the Economic History of the Middle East*. London: Oxford University Press, 172–192.

Daget, Serge. (1971). "L'abolition de la traite des noirs en France de 1814 à 1831," *Cahiers d'études africaines*, **XI**, 1, 14–58.

Daget, Serge. (1975). "Long cours et négriers nantais du trafic illégal (1814–1833)," *Revue française d'histoire d'outre-mer*, **LXII**, 1ᵉ et 2ᵉ trimestres, Nos. 226/227, 90–134.

Daget, Serge. (1979). "British Repression of the Illegal French Slave Trade: Some Considerations," in H. A. Gemery & J. S. Hogendorn, eds., *The Uncommon Market*. New York: Academic Press, 419–442.

Dahlman, Carl J. (1980). *The Open Field System and Beyond*. Cambridge, Engl.: Cambridge University Press.

Dakin, Douglas. (1973). "The Formation of the Greek State, 1821–33," in R. Clogg, ed., *The Struggle for Greek Independence*. London: Macmillan, 156–181.

Daniel, Norman. (1966). *Islam, Europe and Empire*. Edinburgh: Edinburgh University Press.

Daniels, George W. (1915–1916). "The Cotton Trade During the Revolutionary and Napoleonic Wars," *Transactions of the Manchester Statistical Society*, 53–84.

Daniels, George W. (1917–1918). "The Cotton Trade at the Close of the Napoleonic War," *Transactions of the Manchester Statistical Society*, 1–29.

Danière, Andre. (1958a). "Feudal Incomes and Demand Elasticity for Bread in Late Eighteenth-Century France," *Journal of Economic History*, **XVIII**, 3, 317–331.

Danière, Andre. (1958b). "Rejoinder," *Journal of Economic History*, **XVIII**, 3, 339–341.

Darby, H. C. & Fullard, Harold. (1970). *New Cambridge Modern History*, **XIV:** *Atlas*. Cambridge, Engl.: At the University Press.

Dardel, Pierre. (1948). "Crises et faillites à Rouen et dans la Haute-Normandie de 1740 à l'an V," *Revue d'histoire économique et sociale*, **XXVII**, 1, 53–71.

Dardel, Pierre. (1963). *Navires et marchandises dans les ports de Rouen et du Havre au XVIIIe siècle*. Paris: S.E.V.P.E.N.

Darity, William, Jr. (1985). "The Numbers Game and the Profitibility of the British Trade in Slaves," *Journal of Economic History*, **XLV**, 3, 693–703.

Das Gupta, Ashin. (1967). *Malabar in Asian Trade, 1740–1800*. Cambridge, Engl.: At the University Press.

Das Gupta, Ashin. (1970). "Trade and Politics in 18th-Century India," in D. S. Richards, ed., *Islam and the Trade of Asia: A Colloquium*. Oxford, Engl.: Bruno Cassirer & Philadelphia, PA: University of Pennsylvania Press, 181–214.

Das Gupta, Ashin. (1974). "Presidential Address" ("The Maritime Merchant, 1500–1800"), *Proceedings of the Indian History Congress*, Thirty-Fifth Session, Jadavpur (Calcutta), 99–111.

Das Gupta, Ashin. (1979). *Indian Merchants and the Decline of Surat c. 1700–1750*. Wiesbaden: Franz Steiner Verlag.

Datta, K. K. (1959). "India's Trade in the Europe and America in the Eighteenth Century," *Journal of the Economic and Social History of the Orient*, **II,** Part 3, 313–323.

Daumard, Adeline. (1976). "L'état libéral et le libéralisme économique," in F. Braudel & E. Labrousse, dirs., *Histoire économique et social de la France*, **III:** *L'avènement de l'ère industriel (1789–années 1880)*. Paris: Presses Universitaires de France, 137–159.

Daumard, Adeline & Furet, François. (1961). *Structures et relations sociales à Paris au milieu du XVIIIe siècle*, Cahier des Annales, No. 18. Paris: Armand Colin.

Daumas, Maurice (1963). "Le mythe de la révolution technique," *Revue d'histoire des sciences et de leurs applications*, **XVI**, 4, 291–302.

Daumas, Maurice. (1965). "Introduction," in M. Daumas, dir., *Histoire générale des techniques*, **II:** *Les premières étapes du machinisme*. Paris: Presses Universitaries de France, v–xix.

Daumas, Maurice & Garanger, André. (1965). "Le machinisme industriel," in M. Daumas, dir., *Histoire générale des techniques*, **II:** *Les premières étapes du machinisme*. Paris: Presses Universitaires de France, 251–288.

David, Paul A. (1967). "The Growth of Real Product in the United States Before 1840: New Evidence, Controlled Conjectures," *Journal of Economic History*, **XXVII**, 2, 151–197.

Davidson, Basil. (1961). *Black Mother: The Years of the African Slave Trade*. London: Victor Gollancz.

Davidson, Basil. (1971). "Slaves or Captives? Some Notes on Fantasy and Fact," in D. I. Huggins *et al.*, eds., *Key Issues in the Afro-American Experience*, Vol. I. New York: Harcourt, Brace, Jovanovich, 54–73.

Davies, Alan. (1958). "The New Agriculture in Lower Normandy, 1750–1789," *Transactions of the Royal Historical Society*, 5th ser., **VIII**, 129–146.

Davies, K. G. (1957). *The Royal African Company*. London: Longmans, Green.

Davis, David Brion. (1975). *The Problem of Slavery in the Age of Revolution, 1770–1823*. Ithaca, NY: Cornell University Press.

Davis, David Brion. (1983). "American Slavery and the American Revolution," in I. Berlin & R. Hoffman, eds., *Slavery and Freedom in the Age of the American Revolution*. Charlottesville, VA: University of Virginia Press, 262–280.

Davis, Ralph. (1969). "English Foreign Trade, 1700–1774," in W. E. Minchinton, ed., *The*

Growth of English Overseas Trade in the Seventeenth and Eighteenth Centuries. London: Methuen, 99–120. (Originally published in *Economic History Review,* 1962.)

Davis, Ralph. (1970). "English Imports from the Middle East, 1580–1780," in M. A. Cook, ed., *Studies in the Economic History of the Middle East.* London: Oxford University Press, 193–206.

Davis, Ralph. (1973). *The Rise of the Atlantic Economies.* London: Weidenfeld & Nicolsen.

Davis, Ralph. (1979). *The Industrial Revolution and British Overseas Trade.* Leicester, Engl.: Leicester University Press.

Davison, Roderic H. (1976). " 'Russian Skill and Turkish Imbecility': The Treaty of Kuchuk Kainardji Reconsidered," *Slavic Review,* **XXXV,** 3, 463–483.

De, Barun. (1964). "Some Implications and Political and Social Trends in 18th Century India," in O. P. Bhatnagar, ed., *Studies in Social History (Modern India).* Allahabad, India: St. Paul's Press Training School, 203–271.

Deane, Phyllis. (1957). "The Output of the British Woolen Industry in the Eighteenth Century," *Journal of Economic History,* **XVII,** 2, 207–223.

Deane, Phyllis. (1972). "Capital Formation in Britain before the Railway Age," in F. Crouzet, ed., *Capital Formation in the Industrial Revolution.* London: Methuen, 94–118. (Originally published in *Economic Development and Cultural Change,* 1961.)

Deane, Phyllis. (1973a). "Great Britain," in Carlo Cipolla, ed., *Fontana Economic History of Europe,* **IV:** *The Emergence of Industrial Societies.* London: Collins/Fontana, Part One, 161–227.

Deane, Phyllis. (1973b). "The Role of Capital in the Industrial Revolution," *Explorations in Economic History,* **X,** 3, 349–364.

Deane, Phyllis. (1979). *The First Industrial Revolution,* 2nd ed. Cambridge, Engl.: Cambridge University Press.

Deane, Phyllis & Cole, W. A. (1967). *British Economic Growth, 1688–1959,* 2nd ed. Cambridge, Engl.: At the University Press.

Deane, Phyllis & Hubakkuk, H. J. (1963). "The Take-Off in Britain," in W. W. Rostow, ed., *The Economics of Take-Off into Sustained Growth.* London: Macmillan, 63–82.

Debbasch, Yvan. (1961). "Poésie et traite, l'opinion française sur le commerce négrier au début du XIXe siècle," *Revue française d'histoire d'outre-mer,* **XLVIII,** Nos. 172/173, 3ᵉ et 4ᵉ trimestres, 311–352.

Debien, Gabriel. (1953). *La Société coloniale aux XVIIe et XVIIIe siècles.* **II:** *Les colons de Saint-Domingue et la Révolution. Essai sur le club Massia (Août 1789–Août 1792).* Paris: Lib. Armand Colin.

Debien, Gabriel. (1954). *Esprit colon et esprit d'autonomie à Saint-Domingue an XVIIIe siècle,* 2e éd., Notes d'histoire coloniale, XXV. Paris: Larose.

DeClercq, Jules. (1864). *Receuil des Traités de la France,* **I:** *1713–1802.* Paris: Aymot.

De Gregori, Thomas R. (1969). *Technology and the Economic Development of the Tropical African Frontier.* Cleveland, OH: Press of Case Western Reserve University.

Dehio, Ludwig. (1962). *The Precarious Balance.* New York: Knopf.

Delcourt, André. (1952). *La France et les établissements française au Sénégal entre 1713–1763: La compagnie des Indes et de Sénégal.* Dakar: Institut français d'Afrique noire.

Delgado, José Maria. (1979). "Comerç colonial i reformisme borbònic: els decrets de lliure comerç," *L'Avenç,* No. 15, 24–28.

Desai, Ashok V. (1972). "Population and Standards of Living in Akbar's Time," *Indian Economic and Social History Review,* **IX,** 1, 42–62.

Desai, Ashok V. (1978). "Population and Standards Living in Akbar's Time. A Second Look," *Indian Economic and Social History Review,* **XV,** 1, 53–79.

Devine, T. M. (1976). "The Colonial Trades and Industrial Investment in Scotland, c. 1700–1815." *Economic History Review,* 2nd ser., **XXIX,** 1, 1–13.

Devlashouwer, Robert. (1970). "Le Consulat et l'Empire, période de 'take off' pour l'economie belge?" *Revue d'histoire moderne et contemporaine,* **XVII,** 610–619.

Deyon, Pierre & Guignet, Phillippe. (1980). "The Royal Manufactures and Economic Progress in France before the Industrial Revolution," *Journal of European Economic History*, **IX**, 3, 611–632.

Dhondt, Jean. (1955). "L'industrie cotonnière gantoise à l'époque française," *Revue d'histoire moderne et contemporaine*, **II**, 4, 233–279.

Dhondt, Jean & Bruwier, Marinette. (1973). "The Industrial Revolution in the Low Countries, 1700–1914," in C. Cipolla, ed., *The Fontana Economic History of Europe*, **IV**: *The Emergence of Industrial Societies*, Part 1. London: Collins, 329–366.

Dickerson, Oliver M. (1942). "Discussion of Professor Harper's and Professor Root's Papers," *Canadian Historical Review*, **XXIII**, 1, 29–34.

Dickerson, Oliver M. (1951). *The Navigation Acts and the American Revolution*. Philadelphia: University of Pennsylvania Press.

Diffie, Bailey W. (1945). *Latin American Civilization: Colonial Period*. Harrisburg, PA: Stackpole Sons.

Digby, Simon. (1982). "The Maritime Trade of India," in T. Raychaudhuri & I. Habib, eds., *Cambridge Economic History of India*, **I**. *c. 1200–c. 1700*. Cambridge, Engl.: Cambridge University Press, 125–159.

Dike, K. Onwika. (1956). *Trade and Politics in the Niger Delta, 1830–1885*. Oxford: Clarendon Press.

Dilla Alfonso, Haroldo. (1982). "La evolución histórica dominicana y sus relaciones con Haiti, 1492–1844," *Santiago*, No. 48, 65–119.

Dipper, Christof. (1971). "Die Bauern in der Französischen Revolution: Zu einer aktuellen Kontroverse," *Geschichte und Gesellschaft*, **VII**, 1, 119–133.

Disney, Anthony. (1978). "Commentary on the Papers by S. Arasaratnam and I. Bruce Watson," *South Asia*, n.s., **I**, 2, 65–66.

Dmytryshyn, Basil. (1960). "The Economic Content of the 1767 *Nakaz* of Catherine II," *American Slavonic & East European Review*, **XIX**, 1, 1–9.

Dobb, Maurice, (1946). *Studies in the Development of Capitalism*. London: Routledge & Kegan Paul.

Dobb, Maurice. (1961). "Alcune considerazioni sulla rivoluzione industriale," *Studi Storici*, **II**, 3/4, 457–464.

Dodgshon, Robert A. (1976). "The Economics of Sheep Farming in the Southern Uplands during the Age of Improvement, 1750–1833," *Economic History Review*, 2nd ser., **XXIX**, 4, 551–569.

Doerflinger, Thomas M. (1976). "The Antilles Trade of the Old Regime: A Statistical Overview," *Journal of Interdisciplinary History*, **VI**, 3, 397–415.

Dojnov, Stefan. (1984). "La Russie et le Mouvement de Libération Nationale Bulgare au XVIIIe siècle," in *Etudes historiques*, **XII**, à l'occasion du Vème Congrès International des Etudes Balkaniques du Sud-Est Européennes—Belgrade. Sofia: Ed. de l'Académie Bulgare des Sciences, 37–67.

Dominguez, Jorge F. (1980). *Insurrection or Loyalty, the Breakdown of the Spanish American Empire*. Cambridge, MA: Harvard University Press.

Doniol, Henri. (1886–1899). *Histoire de la participation de la France à l'établissement des Etats-Unis d'Amérique*, 6 vols. Paris: Imprimerie Nationale.

Doubout, Jean-Jacques. (1974). "Problèmes d'une période de transition. De Saint-Domingue à Haiti—1793–1806," *La Pensée*, No. 174, 67–80.

Dovring, Folke. (1966). "The Transformation of European Agriculture," in H. J. Habakkuk & M. Postan, eds., *Cambridge Economic History of Europe*, **VI**: *The Industrial Revolutions and After: Incomes, Population and Technological Change*. Cambridge, Engl.: At the University Press, 604–672.

Dovring, Folke. (1969). "Eighteenth-Century Changes in European Agriculture: A Comment," *Agricultural History*, **XLIII**, 1, 181–186.

Doyle, David Noel. (1981). *Ireland, Irishmen and Revolutionary America, 1760–1820.* Dublin: Mercier Press.

Doyle, William. (1972). "Was There an Aristocratic Reaction in Pre-Revolutionary France?," *Past and Present,* No. 57, 97–122.

Doyle, William. (1980). *Origins of the French Revolution.* London: Oxford University Press.

Drake, B. K. (1976). "The Liverpool–African Voyage c. 1790–1807: Commercial Problems," · in R. Anstey & P. E. H. Hair, eds., *Liverpool, The Slave Trade, and Abolition.* Bristol, Engl.: Western Printing Service, 126–156.

Drake, Michael. (1963). "Marriage and Population Growth in Ireland, 1750–1845," *Economic History Review,* 2nd ser., **XVI,** 2, 301–313.

Drake, Michael. (1969). "Introduction," in Michael Drake, ed., *Population in Industrialization.* London: Methuen, 1–10.

Drescher, Seymour D. (1976a). "Capitalism and Abolition: Values and Forces in Britain, 1783–1814," in R. Anstey & P. E. H. Hair, eds., *Liverpool, The Slave Trade, and Abolition,* Bristol, Engl.: Western Printing Service, 167–195.

Drescher, Seymour. (1976b). "Le 'declin' du système esclavagiste britannique et l'abolition · de la traite," *Annales E.S.C.,* **XXXI,** 2, 414–435.

Drew, Ronald F. (1959). "The Emergence of an Agricultural Policy for Siberia in the XVII and XVIII Centuries," *Agricultural History,* **XXXIII,** 1, 29–39.

Dreyfus, François-G. (1978). "Le nouveau démarrage industriel des Allemagnes," in Pierre Léon, dir., *Histoire économique et sociale du monde,* **III:** Louis Bergeron, dir., *Inerties et révolutions, 1730–1840.* Paris: Lib. Armand Colin, 36–39.

Druzhinin (Družinin), Michail Nikolaevic. (1973). "Besonderheiten der Genesis des Kapitalismus in Russland," in P. Hoffmann & H. Lemke, hrsg., *Genesis und Entwicklung des Kapitalismus in Russland.* Berlin: Akademie Verlag, 26–62.

Druzhinina (Droujinina), E. I. (1975). "Les rapports agraires en Russie aux XVIIe et XVIIIe siècles," in *Le Village en France et en URSS: des origines à nos jours,* Colloque franco-soviétique organisé à Toulouse du 24 au 29 mai 1971. Toulouse: Université de Toulouse-Le Mirail, Service des Publications, 209–221.

Dubinovsky de Bueno, Adela. (1985). "Los origenes de la República en Chile," *Cuadernos Hispanoamericanos,* No. 418, 111–120.

Dubois, Marcel & Terrier, Auguste. (1902). *Un siècle d'expansion coloniale, 1800–1900,* Collection, les Colonies français, Tome I. Paris: Augustin Challamel.

Dubuc, Alfred. (1967). "Les classes sociales au Canada," *Annales E. S. C.,* **XXII,** 4, 829–844.

Duckham, Baron F. (1969). "Serfdom in Eighteenth-Century Scotland," *History,* **LIV,** No. 181, 178–197.

Duignan, Peter & Clendennen, Clarence. (1963). *The United States and the African Slave Trade, 1619–1862.* Stanford, CA: Hoover Institution on War, Revolution, and Peace, Stanford University.

Dukes, Paul. (1967). *Catherine the Great and the Russian Nobility.* Cambridge, Engl.: At the University Press.

Dukes, Paul. (1971). "Russia and the Eighteenth Century Revolution," *History,* **LVI,** No. 188 371–386.

Dukes, Paul. (1977). "Catherine II's Enlightened Absolutism and the Problem of Serfdom," in W. E. Butler, ed., *Russian Law: Historical and Political Perspectives.* Leiden: A. W. Sijthoff, 93–115.

Dukes, Paul. (1984). *The Making of Russian Absolutism, 1613–1800,* 2nd impr. London & New York: Longman.

Dull, Jonathan R. (1983). "France and the American Revolution Seen as Tragedy," in N. L. Roelker & C. K. Warner, eds., *Two Hundred Years of Franco-American Relations.* Worcester, MA: Hefferman Press, 1–22.

Dull, Jonathan R. (1985). *A Diplomatic History of the American Revolution.* New Haven, CT: Yale University Press.

Dumas, François. (1904). *Etude sur le Traité de Commerce de 1786 entre la France et l'Angleterre.* Toulouse: E. Privat.

Dumbell, Stanley. (1923). "Early Liverpool Cotton Imports and the Organization of the Cotton Market in the Eighteenth Century," *Economic Journal,* **XXXIII,** No. 131, 362–373.

Dunham, Arthur Louis. (1955). *The Industrial Revolution in France, 1815–1848.* New York: Exposition Press.

Dupâquier, Jacques. (1970). "Problèmes démographiques de la France napoléonienne," *Revue d'histoire moderne et contemporaine,* **XVII,** 339–358.

Dupâquier, Jacques. (1972). "La non-révolution agricole du XVIIIe siècle," *Annales E.S.C.,* **XXVII,** 1, 80–84.

Dupin, Baron Charles. (1858, 1859, 1860). *Force productive des nations, depuis 1800 jusqu'à 1851,* Introduction aux rapports de la commission française instituée par la jury international de l'exposition universelle à Londres, en 1851. 4 vols. Paris: Imprimerie Impériale, I : 1 : 1–2, 1858; I : 2, 1859; I : 3, 1860.

Dupont de Nemours. (1786). "Observations sur la Note concernant la Base du Traité de Commerce, communiqué par Monsieur le Comte de Vergennes à Monsieur le controlleur Général," in *Archives des Affaires Etrangères (Paris): Angelterre,* No. 65: *1786: Mémoires sur le projet de traité de Commerce. Dix pièces,* 34–234.

Dupont de Nemours. (1788). *Lettre à la Chambre de Commerce de Normandie sur le Mémoire qu'elle a publié relativement au traité de commerce avec l'Angleterre.* Rouen & Paris: Moutard.

Dutt, Romesh Chunder. (1956). *The Economic History of India under the Early British Rule,* 8th impr. London: Routledge & Kegan Paul. (Originally published 1901.)

Dyck, Harvey L. (1980). "Pondering the Russian Fact: Kaunitz and the Catherinian Empire in the 1770s," *Canadian Slavonic Papers,* **XXII,** 4, 451–469.

Eagly, Robert V. & Smith, V. Kerry. (1976). "Domestic and International Integration of the London Money Market, 1731–1789," *Journal of Economic History,* **XXXVI,** 1, 198–212.

Earle, Edward Meade. (1927). "American Interest in the Greek Cause, 1821–1827," *American Historical Review,* **XXXIII,** 1, 44–63.

East, Robert A. (1946). "The Business Entrepreneur in a Changing Colonial Economy, 1763–1795," *Journal of Economic History,* Suppl. VI, 16–27.

Eça, Raul d'. (1936). "Colonial Brazil as an Element in the Early Diplomatic Negotiations Between the United States and Portugal, 1776–1808," in A. A. Wilgus, ed., *Colonial Hispanic America.* Washington, DC: George Washington University Press, 551–558.

Eccles, W. J. (1971). "The Social, Economic, and Political Significance of the Military Establishment in New France," *Canadian Historical Review,* **LII,** 1, 1–22.

Edwards, Michael M. (1967). *The Growth of the British Cotton Trade, 1780–1815.* Manchester, Engl.: Manchester University Press.

Eeckante, Denise. (1965). "Les brigands en Russie du XVIIe au XIXe siècle: mythe et réalité," *Revue d'histoire moderne et contemporaine,* **XII,** 3, 161–202.

Egnal, Mark. (1975). "The Economic Development of the Thirteen Continental Colonies, 1720–1775," *William and Mary Quarterly,* 3d ser., **XXXII,** 2, 191–222.

Egnal, Mark & Ernest, Joseph A. (1972). "An Economic Interpretation of the American Revolution," *William and Mary Quarterly,* 3d ser., **XXIX,** 1, 3–32.

Egret, Jean. (1962). *La pré-Révolution française (1787–1788).* Paris: Presses Universitaires de France.

Ehrman, John. (1962). *The British Government and Commercial Negotiations with Europe, 1783–1793.* Cambridge, Engl.: At the University Press.

Eisenstein, Elizabeth L. (1965). "Who Intervened in 1788? A Commentary on *The Coming of the French Revolution,*" *American Historical Review,* **LXXI,** 1, 77–103.

Eisenstein, Elizabeth L. (1967). "A Reply," *American Historical Review,* **LXXII,** 2, 514–522.

Ellis, Geoffrey. (1978). "Review Article: The 'Marxist Interpretation' of the French Revolution," *English Historical Review*, **XCIII**, No. 367, 353–376.

Ellis, Geoffrey. (1981). *Napoleon's Continental Blockade: The Case of Alsace*. Oxford: Clarendon Press.

Ellison, Thomas. (1862, 1863). "The Great Crises in the History of the Cotton Trade: A Retrospect of Prices and Supply, 1790 to 1862," *Exchange, a home and colonial review of commerce, manufactures, and general politics* (London), **I**, 306–315 (1862); **II**, 45–54 (1863).

Eltis, David. (1977). "The Export of Slaves from Africa, 1821–1843," *Journal of Economic History*, **XXXVII**, 2, 409–433.

Elwert, Georg. (1973). *Wirtschaft und Herrschaft von 'Dāxome' (Dahomey) im 18. Jahrhundert: Ökonomie des Sklavenraubs und Gesellschaftsstruktur, 1724 bis 1818*. München: Kommissionsverlag Klaus Renner.

Embree, Ainslee T. (1962). *Charles Grant and British Rule in India*. New York: Columbia University Press.

Embree, Ainslee T. (1964). "Landholding in India and British Institutions," in R. E. Frykenberg, ed., *Land Control and Social Structure in Indian History*. Madison, WI: University of Wisconsin Press, 33–52.

Emsley, Clive. (1981). "An Aspect of Pitt's 'Terror': Prosecutions for Sedition During the 1790s," *Social History*, **VI**, 2, 155–184.

Endrei, Walter. (1983). "Energie hydraulique et révolution industrielle," paper delivered at XV Settimana di Studio, Ist. Int. di Storia Economica "Francesco Datini," Prato, 15–20 apr., mimeo.

Engels, Frederick. (1971). "The Position of England: The Eighteenth Century," in Karl Marx & Frederick Engels, *Articles on Britain*. Moscow: Progress Publishers, 9–31. (Originally published 1844.)

Engerman, Stanely L. (1972). "The Slave Trade and British Capital Formation in the Eighteenth Century: A Comment on the Williams Thesis," *Business History Review*, **XLVI**, 4, 430–443.

Engerman, Stanley L. (1975). "Comments on Richardson and Boulle and the 'Williams Thesis,'" *Revue française d'histoire d'outre-mer*, **LXII**, 1ᵉ et 2ᵉ trimestres, Nos. 226/227, 331–336.

Engerman, Stanley L. (1976). "Some Economic and Demographic Comparisons of Slavery in the United States and the British West Indies," *Economic History Review*, 2nd ser., **XXIX**, 2, 258–275.

Engerman, Stanley L. (1981). "Notes on the Patterns of Economic Growth in the British North American Colonies in the Seventeenth, Eighteenth and Nineteenth Centuries," in P. Bairoch & M. Lévy-Leboyer, eds., *Disparities in Economic Development since the Industrial Revolution*. New York: St. Martin's Press, 46–57.

Engerman, Stanley L. (1986). "Slavery and Emancipation in Comparative Perspective: A Look at Some Recent Debates," *Journal of Economic History*, **XLVI**, 2, 317–339.

Ernst, Joseph Albert. (1973a). *Money and Politics in America, 1755–1775: A Study in the Currency Act of 1764 and the Political Economy of Revolution*. Chapel Hill, NC: University of North Carolina Press.

Ernst, Joseph Albert. (1973b). "Ideology and the Political Economy of Revolution," *Canadian Review of American Studies*, **IV**, 2, 137–148.

Ernst, Joseph Albert. (1976). "'Ideology' and an Economic Interpretation of the Revolution," in A. F. Young, ed., *The American Revolution: Explorations in the History of American Radicalism*. DeKalb, IL: Northern Illinois University Press, 159–185.

Escoffier, Maurice. (1907). "La Restauration, l'Angleterre et les colonies," *Revue d'histoire diplomatique*, **XXI**, 40–56.

Evans, Laurence. (1983). "Gulliver Bound: Civil Logistics and the Destiny of France," *Historical Reflections*, **X**, 1, 19–44.

Eversley, D. E. C. (1967). "The Home Market and Economic Growth in England, 1750–80," in E. L. Jones & G. E. Mingay, eds., *Land, Labour and Population in the Industrial Revolution.* London: Edward Arnold, 206–259.

Eyzaguirre, Jaime. (1957). *Ideario y ruta de la emancipación Chilena.* Santiago, Chile: Editorial Universitaria.

Fage, J. D. (1969). "Slavery and the Slave Trade in the Context of West African History," *Journal of African History,* **X**, 3, 393–404.

Fage, J. D. (1975). "The Effect of the Export Slave Trade on African Populations," in R. P. Moss & J. A. R. Rathbone, eds., *The Population Factor in African Studies,* 15–23.

Fage, J. D. (1980). "Slaves and Society in Western Africa, c. 1445–c. 1700," *Journal of African History,* **XXI**, 3, 289–310.

Falkner, S. A. (1919). *Bumazhnia djengi frantzuzkoj revoljucii (1789–1797).* Moscow: Redakcionno-Izdatelskogo Otdjela V.S.N.H.

Falkus, M. E. (1972). *The Industrialisation of Russia, 1700–1914.* London: Macmillan.

Fanfani, Amintore. (1963). "Osservazione sul significato del '700 nella storia economica," *Economia e storia,* **X**, 1, 9–20.

Farley, J. Lewis. (1862). *The Resources of Turkey Considered with Especial Reference to the Profitable Investment of Capital in the Ottoman Empire.* London: Longman, Green, Longman, & Roberts.

Farley, J. Lewis. (1872). *Modern Turkey.* London: Hurst & Blackett.

Faucheux, Marcel. (1964). *L'insurrection vendéenne de 1793: Aspects économiques et sociaux,* Commission d'histoire économique et sociale de la Révolution, Mémoires et Documents, XVII. Paris: Imprimerie Nationale.

Fay, C. R. (1940). "The Movement Towards Free Trade, 1820–1853," in J. Holland Rose, A. P. Newton, & E. A. Benians, eds., *The Cambridge History of the British Empire,* **II**: *The Growth of the New Empire, 1783–1870.* Cambridge, Engl.: Cambridge University Press, 388–414.

Feavearyear, A. E. (1931). *The Pound Sterling: A History of English Money.* Oxford: Clarendon Press.

Febvre, Lucien. (1962). "Civilisation: Evolution d'un mot et d'un groupe d'idées," in *Pour une Histoire à part entière.* Paris: S.E.V.P.E.N., 481–528. (Originally published 1930.)

Fedorov, A. S. (1979). "Russia and Britain in the Eighteenth Century: A Survey of Economic and Scientific Links," in A. G. Cross, ed., *Great Britain and Russia in the Eighteenth Century: Contrasts and Comparison.* Newton, MA: Oriental Research Partners, 137–144.

Fehér, Ferenc. (1987). *The Frozen Revolution: An Essay on Jacobinism.* Cambridge, Engl.: Cambridge University Press.

Feinstein, C. H. (1981). "Capital Accumulation and the Industrial Revolution," in R. Floud & D. N. McCloskey, eds., *The Economic History of Britain Since 1700.* **I**: *1700–1860.* Cambridge, Engl.: Cambridge University Press, 128–142.

Felix, David. (1956). "Profit Inflation and Industrial Growth: The Historic Record and Contemporary Analogies," *Quarterly Journal of Economics,* **LXX**, 3, 441–463.

Ferguson, E. James. (1953). "Currency Finance: An Interpretation of Colonial Monetary Practices," *William and Mary Quarterly,* 3rd ser., **X**, 2, 153–180.

Ferguson, E. James. (1954). "Speculation in the Revolutionary Debt: The Ownership of Public Securities in Maryland, 1790," *Journal of Economic History,* **XIV**, 1, 35–45.

Fernández de Avila, Rafael Camón. (1975). "La emancipación y el comercio catalán con América," *Revista de Indias,* **XXXV**, Nos. 139/142, 229–260.

Ferro, Marc. (1981). "Tentation et peur de l'histoire," *Le monde diplomatique,* 28e année, No. 323, 32.

Findley, Carter V. (1970). "The Legacy of Tradition to Reform: Origins of the Ottoman Foreign Ministry," *International Journal of Middle East Studies,* **I**, 4, 334–357.

Findley, Carter V. (1972). "The Foundation of the Ottoman Foreign Ministry: The Beginnings of Bureaucratic Reform under Selîm III & Mahmûd II," *International Journal of Middle East Studies,* **III**, 4, 388–416.

Findley, Carter V. (1980). *Bureaucratic Reform in the Ottoman Empire: The Sublime Porte, 1789–1922.* Princeton, NJ: Princeton University Press.

Finer, Samuel E. (1975). "State- and Nation-Building in Europe: The Role of the Military," in Charles Tilly, ed., *The Formation of National States in Western Europe.* Princeton, NJ: Princeton University Press, 84–163.

Firminger, W. K. (1962). *Historical Introduction to the Bengal Portion of the Fifth Report.* Calcutta: Indian Studies, Past and Present. (Originally published 1917.)

Fisher, Alan W. (1970). *The Russian Annexation of the Crimea, 1772–1783.* Cambridge, Engl.: At the University Press.

Fisher, Colin M. (1978). "Planters and Peasants: The Ecological Context of Agrarian Unrest on the Indigo Plantations of North Bihar, 1820–1920," in C. Dewey & A. G. Hopkins, eds., *The Imperial Impact: Studies in the Economic History of Africa and India.* London: Athlone, 114–131.

Fisher, H. E. S. (1969). "Anglo-Portuguese Trade, 1700–1770," in W. E. Minchinton, ed., *The Growth of English Overseas Trade in the Seventeenth and Eighteenth Centuries.* London: Methuen, 144–164. (Originally published in *Economic History Review*, 1963.)

Fisher, J. R. (1971). "La rebelión de Túpac Amaru y el programa de la Reforma Imperial de Carlos III," *Anuario de estudios americanos*, **XXVIII**, 405–421.

Fisher, John. (1979). "Royalism, Regionalism, and Rebellion in Colonial Peru, 1808–1815," *Hispanic American Historical Review*, **LIX**, 2, 232–257.

Fisher, John. (1981). "Imperial 'Free Trade' and the Hispanic Economy, 1778–1796," *Journal of Latin American Studies*, **XIII**, 1, 21–56.

Fisher, John. (1985). "The Imperial Response to 'Free Trade': Spanish Imports from Spanish America, 1778–1796," *Journal of Latin American Studies*, **XVII**, 1, 33–78.

Fisher, Lillian Estelle. (1966). *The Last Inca Revolt, 1780–1783.* Norman, OK: University of Oklahoma Press.

Fitton, R. S. & Wadsworth, A. P. (1958). *The Strutts and the Arkwrights, 1758–1830.* Manchester, Engl.: Manchester University Press. (Part Two by R. S. Fitton alone.)

Flinn, M. W. (1958). "The Growth of the English Iron Industry, 1660–1760," *Economic History Review*, 2nd ser., **XI**, 1, 144–153.

Flinn, M. W. (1961). "The Poor Employment Act of 1817," *Economic History Review*, 2nd ser., **XIV**, 1, 82–92.

Flinn, M. W. (1970). *British Population Growth, 1700–1850.* London: Macmillan.

Flinn, M. W. (1974). "Trends in Real Wages, 1750–1850," *Economic History Review*, 2nd ser., **XXVII**, 3, 395–413.

Flinn, M. W. (1978). "Technical Change as an Escape from Resource Scarcity: England in the Seventeenth and Eighteenth Centuries," in A. Mączak & W. N. Parker, eds., *Natural Resources in European History*, Research Paper R-13. Washington, DC: Resources for the Future, 139–159.

Flinn, M. W. (1981). *The European Demographic System, 1500–1820.* Baltimore, MD: Johns Hopkins University Press.

Flint, J. E. (1974). "Economic Change in West Africa in the Nineteenth Century," in J. F. A. Ajayi & M. Crowder, eds., *History of West Africa*, Vol. II. London: Longman, 380–401.

Florescano, Enrique. (1969). *Precios del maíz y crisis agrícolas en México (1708–1810).* México: El Colegio de México.

Floyd, Troy S. (1961). "The Guatemalan Merchants, the Government, and the *Provincianos*, 1750–1800," *Hispanic American Historical Review*, **XLI**, 1, 90–110.

Foblen, Claude. (1973). "France, 1700–1914," in C. M. Cipolla, ed., *Fontana Economic History of Europe*, **IV**: *The Emergence of Industrial Societies*, Part 1. London: Collins/Fontana, 7–75.

Fohlen, Claude. (1979). "The Commercial Failure of France in America," in N. L. Roelker & C. K. Warner, eds., *Two Hundred Years of Franco-American Relations.* Worcester, MA: Hefferman Press, 93–119.

Foner, Laura. (1970). "The Free People of Color in Louisiana and St. Domingue," *Journal of Social History*, **III**, 4, 406–430.

Forbes, R. J. (1958). "Power to 1850," in C. Singer *et al.*, *A History of Technology*, **IV:** *The Industrial Revolution, c. 1750 to c. 1850*. Oxford: Clarendon Press, 148–167.

Ford, Franklin L. (1953). *Robe and Sword: The Regrouping of the French Aristocracy after Louis XIV*. Cambridge, MA: Harvard University Press.

Ford, Franklin L. (1963). "The Revolutionary Napoleonic Era: How Much of a Watershed?," *American Historical Review*, **LXIX**, 1, 18–29.

Ford, Lacy K. (1985). "Self-Sufficiency, Cotton, and Economic Development in the South Carolina Upcountry, 1800–1860," *Journal of Economic History*, **XLV**, 2, 261–275.

Forrest, Alan. (1981). *The French Revolution and the Poor*. Oxford: Basil Blackwell.

Forster, Robert. (1957). "The Noble as Landlord in the Region of Toulouse at the End of the Old Regime," *Journal of Economic History*, **XVII**, 2, 224–244.

Forster, Robert. (1960). *The Nobility of Toulouse in the Eighteenth Century: A Social and Economic Study*, Johns Hopkins University, Studies in the Historical and Political Sciences, **LXXVIII.**

Forster, Robert. (1961). "The Noble Wine Producers of the Bordelais in the Eighteenth Century," *Economic History Review*, 2nd ser., **XIV**, 1, 18–33.

Forster, Robert. (1963). "The Provincial Noble: A Reappraisal," *American Historical Review*, **LXVIII**, 3, 681–691.

Forster, Robert. (1967). "The Survival of the Nobility during the French Revolution," *Past and Present*, No. 37, 71–86.

Forster, Robert. (1970). "Obstacles to Agricultural Growth in Eighteenth-Century France," *American Historical Review*, **LXXV**, 6, 1600–1615.

Foster, John. (1974). *Class Struggle and the Industrial Revolution: Early Industrial Capitalism in Three English Towns*. London: Weidenfeld & Nicolson.

Foust, Clifford M. (1961). "Russian Expansion to the East Through the Eighteenth Century," *Journal of Economic History*, **XXI**, 4, 469–482.

Foust, Clifford M. (1969). *Muscovite and Mandarin: Russia's Trade with China and Its Setting, 1727–1805*. Chapel Hill, NC: University of North Carolina Press.

Franco, Franklin J. (1968). "Gérmenes de una burguesía colonial en Santo Domingo, siglos XVI al XVIII," *Revista de ciencias sociales*, **XII**, 4, 527–539.

Frangakis, Helen. (1985). "The Commerce of Izmir in the Eighteenth Century (1695–1820)," unpublished Ph.D. dissertation, King's College, London University.

Frank, André Gunder. (1978). *World Accumulation, 1492–1789*. New York: Monthly Review Press.

Frankel, Jeffrey A. (1982). "The 1807–1809 Embargo Against Great Britain," *Journal of Economic History*, **XLII**, 2, 291–308.

Freehling, William W. (1972). "The Founding Fathers and Slavery," *American Historical Review*, **LXXVII**, 1, 81–93.

Frégault, Guy & Trudel, Marcel. (1963). *Histoire du Canada par les textes*, **I:** *1534–1854*, ed. revue et augmentée. Ottawa: Ed. Fides.

Freudenberg, Herman & Redlich, Fritz. (1964). "The Industrial Development of Europe: Reality, Symbols, Images," *Kyklos*, **XVII**, 3, 372–403.

Froidevaux, Henri. (1918). "Desintéressement de la France à l'égard du Canada entre 1775 et 1782," *Revue de l'histoire des colonies françaises*, **VI**, 4ᵉ trimestre, 485–491.

Frykenberg, Robert Eric. (1965). *Guntur District, 1788–1848: A History of Local Influence and Central Authority in South India*. Oxford: Clarendon Press.

Fugier, André. (1954). *La Révolution française et l'empire napoléonien*, Vol. IV of Pierre Renourin, dir., *Histoire des relations internationales*. Paris: Hachette.

Furber, Holden. (1938). "The Beginnings of American Trade with India, 1784–1812," *New England Quarterly*, **XI**, 235–265.

Furber, Holden. (1951). *John Company at Work: A Study of European Expansion in India in the Late Eighteenth Century*. Cambridge, MA: Harvard University Press.

Furber, Holden. (1965). *Bombay Presidency in the Mid-Eighteenth Century*. London: Asia Publ. House.

Furber, Holden. (1976). *Rival Empires of Trade in the Orient, 1600–1800*. Minneapolis, MN: University of Minnesota Press.

Furet, François. (1963). "Pour une définition des classes inférieures à l'epoque moderne," *Annales E.S.C.*, **XVIII**, 3, 459–474.

Furet, François. (1978). *Penser la Révolution française*. Paris: Gallimard. (Includes, pp. 113–172, expanded version of "Le catéchisme révolutionnaire," originally in *Annales E.S.C.*, 1971.)

Furet, François. (1983). "Entretien: Faut-il célébrer le bicentenaire de la Révolution française?" *L'Histoire*, No. 52, 71–77.

Furet, François. (1986a). *La gauche et la Révolution française au milieu du XIXe siècle: Edgar Quinet et la question du Jacobinisme (1865–1870)*. Paris: Hachette.

Furet, François. (1986b). *Marx et la Révolution française*, Textes de Marx présentés, réunis, traduits par Lucien Calvié. Paris: Flammarion.

Furet, François & Ozouf, Jacques. (1977). *Lire et écrire: L'alphabétisation des français*. Paris: Minuit.

Furet, François & Richet, Denis. (1973). *La Révolution française*, nouv. éd. Paris: Fayard.

Fussell, G. E. (1958). "Agriculture: Techniques of Farming," in C. Singer *et al.*, *A History of Technology, c. 1750 to c. 1850*. Oxford: Clarendon Press, 13–43.

Fussell, G. E. & Compton, M. (1939). "Agricultural Adjustments After the Napoleonic Wars," *Economic History Review*, **X**, 14, 184–204.

Fyfe, Christopher. (1976). "Freed Slave Colonies in West Africa," in *Cambridge History of Africa*, **V**: J. E. Flint, ed., *From c. 1790 to c. 1870*. Cambridge, Engl.: Cambridge University, Press, 170–199.

Fynn, J. K. (1971). "Ghana-Asante (Ashanti)," in M. Crowder, ed., *West African Resistance*. London: Hutchison, 19–52.

Gaillardon, Charles. (1908, 1909). "L'industrie et les industriels en Normandie, au moment de la convocation des Etats-Généraux de 1789," *Revue d'études normandes*, 3e année, 1, 22–33 (1908); 3e année, 3/4, 138–153 (1909); 3e année, 7, 258–269 (1909).

Gaissinovitch, A. (1938). *La révolte de Pougatchev*. Paris: Payot.

Galenson, David W. (1981a). "White Servitude and the Growth of Black Slavery in Colonial America," *Journal of Economic History*, **XLI**, 1, 39–48.

Galenson, David W. (1981b). *White Servitude in Colonial America: An Economic Analysis*. Cambridge, Engl.: Cambridge University Press.

Galenson, David W. & Menard, Russell R. (1980). "Approaches to the Analysis of Economic Growth in Colonial British America," *Historical Methods*, **XIII**, 1, 3–18.

Gallagher, John & Robinson, Ronald. (1953). "The Imperialism of Free Trade," *Economic History Review*, 2nd ser., **VI**, 1, 1–15.

Gandev, Christo. (1960). "L'apparition des rapports capitalistes dans l'économie rurale de la Bulgarie du nord-ouest au cours du XVIIIe siècle," in *Etudes historiques*, à l'occasion du XIe Congrès International des Sciences Historiques—Stockholm, août, 1960. Sofia: Académie des Sciences de Bulgarie, 207–220.

Gandia, Enrique de. (1970). "Genesis y descubrimiento de la conciencia nacional en América," in *Dos Ensayos de Enrique de Gandia*. Carcas: Tip. Vargas, 3–59.

Ganguli, B. N. (1965). *Dadabhai Naoroji and the Drain Theory*. Bombay: Asia Publ. House.

Garavaglia, Juan Carlos. (1985). "Economic Growth and Regional Differentiation: The River Plate Region at the End of the Eighteenth Century." *Hispanic American Historical Review*, **LXV**, 1, 51–89.

García-Baquero González, Antonio. (1972). *Comercio colonial y guerras revolucionarias. La decadencia económica de Cádiz a raíz de la emancipación americana*. Sevilla: Publ. de la Escuela de Estudios Hispano-Americanos de Sevilla.

Garden, Maurice. (1970). *Lyon et les Lyonnais au XVIIIe siècle*. Paris: Société d'Edition "Les Belles Lettres."

Garden, Maurice. (1978a). "Rappel du système économique pré-industriel," in Pierre Léon, dir., *Histoire économique et sociale du monde,* **III:** Louis Bergeron, dir., *Inerties et révolutions, 1730–1840.* Paris: Lib. Armand Colin, 13–20.

Garden, Maurice. (1978b). "Un exemple régional: l'industrie textile des Pays-Bas autrichiens," in Pierre Léon, dir., *Histoire économique et sociale du monde,* **III:** Louis Bergeron, dir., *Inerties et révolutions, 1730–1840.* Paris: Lib. Armand Colin, 20–27.

Garden, Maurice. (1978c). "Images industrielles dans l'Europe occidentale," in Pierre Léon, dir., *Histoire économique et sociale du monde,* **III:** Louis Bergeron, dir., *Inerties et révolutions, 1730–1840.* Paris: Lib. Armand Colin, 28–36.

Garden, Maurice. (1978d). "L'évolution démographique," in Pierre Léon, dir., *Histoire économique et sociale du monde,* **III:** Louis Bergeron, dir., *Inerties et révolutions, 1730–1840.* Paris: Lib. Armand Colin, 137–171.

Garner, Richard L. (1972). "Problemes d'une ville minière mexicaine à la fin de l'époque coloniale: Prix et salaires à Zacatecas (1760–1821)," *Cahiers des Amériques Latines,* No. 6, 75–112.

Garner, Richard L. (1985). "Price Trends in Eighteenth-Century Mexico," *Hispanic American Historical Review,* **LXV,** 2, 279–325.

Garrett, Mitchell Bennett. (1918). "The French Colonial Question, 1789–1791," Ph.D. dissertation, University of Michigan.

Gaski, John F. (1982). "The Cause of the Industrial Revolution: A Brief 'Single-Factor' Argument," *Journal of European Economic History,* **XI,** 1, 227–233.

Gauthier, Florence. (1977). *La voie paysanne dans la Révolution française: L'exemple de la Picardie.* Paris: Maspéro.

Gayer, Arthur D., Rostow, W. W. & Schwartz, Anna Jacobson. (1975). *The Growth and Fluctuation of the British Economy, 1790–1850,* 2 vols., new ed. New York: Barnes & Noble.

Geary, Frank. (1984). "The Cause of the Industrial Revolution and 'Single-Factor' Arguments: an Assessment," *Journal of European Economic History,* **XIII,** 1, 167–173.

Geggus, David. (1981). "The British Government and the Saint Domingue Slave Revolt, 1791–1793," *English Historical Review,* **XCVI,** No. 379, 285–305.

Geggus, David. (1982). *Slavery, War, and Revolution: The British Occupation of Saint Domingue, 1793–1798.* Oxford: Clarendon Press.

Geggus, David. (1987). "The Enigma of Jamaica in the 1790s: New Light on the Causes of Slave Rebellions," *William and Mary Quarterly,* 3rd ser., **XLIV,** 2, 274–299.

Gemery, Henry A. & Hogendorn, Jan S. (1974). "The Atlantic Slave Trade: A Tentative Economic Model," *Journal of African History,* **XV,** 2, 223–246.

Gemery, Henry & Hogendorn, Jan S. (1978). "Technological Change, Slavery and the Slave Trade," in C. Dewey & A. G. Hopkins, eds., *The Imperial Impact: Studies in the Economic History of Africa and India.* London: Athlone, 243–258.

Gemery, Henry A. & Hogendorn, Jan S. (1979). "The Economic Costs of West African Participation in the Atlantic Slave Trade: A Preliminary Sampling for the Eighteenth Century," in H. A. Gemery & J. S. Hogendorn, eds., *The Uncommon Market.* New York: Academic Press, 143–161.

Genç, Mehmet. (1976). "A Comparative Study of the Life Term Tax Farming Data and the Volume of Commercial and Industrial Activities in the Ottoman Empire during the Second Half of the 18th Century," in N. Todorov *et al.,* dirs., *La révolution industrielle dans le Sud-est Europe—XIXe siècle.* Sofia: Institut d'Etudes Balkaniques, 243–280.

Georgescu, Valentin. (1976). "La terminologie: modernisation et européanisation de l'Empire ottoman et du sud-est de l'Europe, à la lumière de l'experience roumaine," in N. Todorov *et al.,* dirs., *La révolution industrielle dans le Sud-est Europe—XIXe siècle.* Sofia: Institut d'Etudes Balkaniques, 113–139.

Georgiades, Dimitrios. (1885). *Smyrne et l'Asie Mineure au point de vue économique et commerciale.* Paris: Impr. Chaix.

Gerschenkron, Alexander. (1952). "An Economic History of Russia," *Journal of Economic History*, **XII**, 2, 146–159.

Gerschenkron, Alexander. (1955). "Comment" in National Bureau of Economic Research, *Capital Formation and Economic Growth*. Princeton, NJ: Princeton University Press, 373–378.

Gerschenkron, Alexander. (1962). *Economic Backwardness in Historical Perspective*. Cambridge, MA: Harvard University Press.

Gerschenkron, Alexander. (1970). *Europe in the Russian Mirror: Four Lectures in Economic History*. Cambridge, Engl.: At the University Press.

Gerschenkron, Alexander. (1971). "Soviet Marxism and Absolutism," *Slavic Review*, **XXX**, 4, 853–869.

Gibb, H. A. R. & Bowen, Harold. (1950, 1957). *Islamic Society and the West*, Vol. I, 2 Parts. London: Oxford University Press.

Gibbs, N. H. (1969). "Armed Forces and the Art of War, A: Armies," in *New Cambridge Modern History*, **IX**: C. W. Crawley, ed., *War and Peace in an Age of Upheaval, 1793–1830*. Cambridge, Engl.: At the University Press, 60–76.

Gilboy, Elizabeth Waterman. (1930). "Wages in Eighteenth-Century England," *Journal of Economic and Business History*, **II**, 4, 603–629.

Gilboy, Elizabeth Waterman. (1932). "Demand as a Factor in the Industrial Revolution," in A. H. Cole *et al.*, *Facts and Factors in Economic History*. Cambridge, MA: Harvard University Press, 620–639.

Gilboy, Elizabeth Waterman (1975). "The Cost of Living and Real Wages in Eighteenth-Century England," in Arthur J. Taylor, ed., *The Standard of Living in Britain in the Industrial Revolution*. London: Methuen, 1–20. (Originally published in *Review of Economic Statistics*, 1936.)

Gill, Conrad. (1961). *Merchants and Marines of the Eighteenth Century*. London: Edward Arnold.

Gille, Bertrand. (1947). *Les origines de la grande industrie métallurgique en France*. Paris: Ed. Domat Montchrestien.

Gille, Bertrand. (1949). *Histoire économique et sociale de la Russie du moyen age au XXe siècle*. Paris: Payot.

Gille, Bertrand. (1959). *Recherches sur la formation de la grande enterprise capitaliste (1815–1848)*. Paris: S.E.V.P.E.N.

Gille, Bertrand. (1961). "Recherches sur le problème de l'innovation. Perspectives historiques dans le cas français," *Cahiers de l'I.S.E.A.*, Suppl. No. 111 (Série AD, No. 1), 134–168.

Gille, Bertrand. (1973). "Banking and Industrialisation in Europe, 1730–1914," in C. M. Cipolla, ed., *Fontana Economic History of Europe*, **III**: *The Industrial Revolution*. London: Collins/Fontana, 255–300.

Gillespie, Charles C. (1972). "The Natural History of Industry," in A. E. Musson, ed., *Science, Technology, and Economic Growth in the Eighteenth Century*. London: Methuen, 121–135. (Originally published in *Isis*, 1957.)

Gipson, Lawrence Henry. (1950). "The American Revolution as an Aftermath of the Great War for the Empire, 1754–1763," *Political Science Quarterly*, **LXV**, 1, 86–104.

Girard, L. (1966). "Transport," in *Cambridge Economic History of Europe*, **VI**: H. J. Habakkuk & M. Postan, eds., *The Industrial Revolution and After: Incomes, Population and Technological Change*. Cambridge, Engl.: At the University Press, 212–273.

Gleave, M. B. & Prothero, R. M. (1971). "Population Density and 'Slave Raiding'—A Comment," *Journal of African History*, **XII**, 2, 319–324.

Godechot, Jacques. (1956). *La grande nation: L'expansion révolutionnaire de la France dans le monde, 1789–1799*, 2 vols. Paris: Aubier.

Godechot, Jacques. (1958a). "The Business Classes and the Revolution Outside France," *American Historical Review*, **LXIV**, 1, 1–13.

Godechot, Jacques. (1958b). "Les relations économiques entre la France et les Etats-Unis de 1778 à 1789," *French Historical Studies*, **I**, 1, 26–39.

Godechot, Jacques. (1959). "Mes souvenirs d'Albert Mathiez," *Annales historiques de la Révolution française*, **XXI**, No. 156, 97–109.

Godechot, Jacques. (1965). *Les révolutions (1770–1799)*, Nouvelle Clio, No. 36. Paris: Presses Universitaires de France.

Godechot, Jacques. (1967a). *L'Europe et l'Amerique à l'epoque napoléonienne*, Nouvelle Clio, No. 37. Paris: Presses Universitaires de France.

Godechot, Jacques. (1967b). "L'historiographie française de Robespierre," in *Actes du Colloque Robespierre*, XIIe Congrès International des Sciences Historiques, Vienne, 3 sept. 1965. Paris: Société des Etudes Robespierristes, 167–189.

Godechot, Jacques. (1970). "Sens et importance de la transformation des institutions révolutionnaires à l'époque napoléonienne," *Revue d'histoire moderne et contemporaine*, **XVII**, 795–813.

Godechot, Jacques. (1972). "L'industrialisation en Europe à l'époque révolutionnaire," in Pierre Léon *et al.*, dirs., *L'industrialisation en Europe au XIXe siècle*, Colloques Internationaux du CNRS, No. 540, Lyon, 7–10 oct. 1970. Paris: Ed. du CNRS, 359–371 (with "Discussion," 371–377).

Godechot, Jacques. (1974). *Un jury pour la Révolution*. Paris: Ed. Robert Laffont.

Godechot, Jacques. (1980a). "La France et les problèmes de l'Atlantique à la veille de la Révolution," in *Regards sur l'epoque révolutionnaire*. Paris: Privat, 69–83. (Originally published in *Revue du Nord*, 1954.)

Godechot, Jacques. (1980b). "Sens et importance de la transformation des institutions revolutionnaires à l'epoque napoléonienne," in *Regards sur l'époque révolutionnaire*. Paris: Privat, 182–196. (Originally published in *Annales historiques de la Révolution française*, 1970.)

Godechot, Jacques. (1980c). "Révolution 'française' ou Révolution occidentale?," in *Regards sur l'époque révolutionnaire*. Paris: Privat, 199–217. (Originally published in *Information historique*, 1960.)

Godechot, Jacques. (1980d). "Les relations économiques entre la France et les Etats-Unis de 1778 à 1789," in *Regards sur l'époque révolutionnaire*. Paris: Privat, 409–418. (Originally published in *French Historical Studies*, 1958.)

Godechot, Jacques & Palmer, R. R. (1955). "Le problème de l'Atlantique du XVIIIe au XXe siècles," in *X Congresso Internazionale di Scienze Storiche*, Roma, 4–11 sett., 1955. *Relazioni*, **V**: *Storia contemporanea*. Firenze: G. G. Sansoni, 173–239.

Goebel, Dorothy Burne. (1938). "British Trade to the Spanish Colonies, 1796–1823," *American Historical Review*, **XLIII**, 2, 288–320.

Goetzmann, William H. (1978). "The United States: Revolution, Independence and Interdependence," in T. S. Tolchin, ed., *Hemispheric Perspectives in the United States*. Westport, CT: Greenwood Press, 3–13.

Gokhale, B. G. (1964–1965). "Capital Accumulation in XVIII Century Western India," *Journal of the Asiatic Society of Bombay*, n.s., **XXXIX/XL**, 51–60.

Goldin, Claudia D. & Lewis, Frank D. (1980). "The Role of Exports in American Economic Growth during the Napoleonic Wars, 1793–1807," *Explorations in Economic History*, **XVII**, 1, 6–25.

Goldman, Marshall. (1956). "The Relocation and Growth of the Pre-Revolutionary Russian Ferrous Metal Industry," *Explorations in Entrepreneurial History*, **IX**, 1, 19–36.

Goldstone, J. A. (1986). "The Demographic Revolution in England: A Re-examination," *Population Studies*, **XLIX**, 1, 5–33.

Golte, Jürgen. (1980). *Repartos y rebeliones: Túpac Amaru y las contradicciones de la economia colonial*. Lima: Instituto de Estudios Peruanos.

Gongora, Mario. (1975). *Studies in the Colonial History of Spanish America*. Cambridge, Engl.: Cambridge University Press.

Goodwin, Albert. (1965a). "The Social Structure and Economic and Political Attitudes of the French Nobility in the Eighteenth Century," in *XIIe Congrès International des Sciences*

Historiques, Vienne, 29 août–5 sept., 1965. *Rapports*, **I:** *Grands thèmes*. Horn/Wien: Verlag Ferdinand Berger & Sohne, 356–368.

Goodwin, Albert. (1965b). "The Landed Aristocracy as a Governing Class in XIX Century Britain," in *XIIe Congrès International des Sciences Historiques*, Vienne, 29 août–5 sept. 1965, *Rapports*, **I:** *Grands thèmes*. Horn/Wien: Ferdinand Berger & Sohne, 368–374.

Goodwin, Albert. (1979). *The Friends of Liberty: The English Democratic Movement in the Age of the French Revolution*. Cambridge, MA: Harvard University Press.

Gottschalk, Louis. (1948). *The Place of the American Revolution in the Causal Pattern of the French Revolution*, Easton, PA: The American Friends of Lafayette.

Goubert, Pierre. (1969, 1973). *L'Ancien Régime*, **I:** *La société*. Paris: Lib. Armand Colin, 1969; **II:** *Les pouvoirs*. Paris: Lib. Armand Colin, 1973.

Goubert, Pierre. (1974). "Sociétés rurales françaises du XVIIIe siècle: vingt paysanneries contrastées, quelques problèmes," in *Conjoncture économique, structures sociales*. Paris & La Haye: Mouton, 378–387.

Gough, Kathleen. (1978). "Agrarian Relations in Southeast India, 1750–1976," *Review*, **II**, 1, 25–53.

Gourvish, T. R. (1972). "The Cost of Living in Glasgow in the Early Nineteenth Century," *Economic History Review*, 2nd ser., **XXV**, 1, 65–80.

Goy, Joseph & Head-König, Anne-Lise. (1969). "Une expérience: les revenus décimaux en France méditerranéenne, XVIe–XVIIIe siècles," in J. Goy & E. LeRoy Ladurie, dirs., *Les fluctuations du produit de la dîme*. Paris & La Haye: Mouton, 255–272.

Graham, Gerald S. (1941). *Sea Power and British North America, 1783–1820: A Study in British Colonial Policy*. Cambridge, MA: Harvard University Press.

Graham, Gerald S. (1966). "The British Empire in Relation to the European Balance of Power at the End of the Napoleonic Wars," in *Bilan du Monde en 1815: Rapports Conjoints*, XIIe Congrès International des Sciences Historiques, Vienne, 29 août–5 sept. 1965. Paris: Ed. du CNRS, 5–13.

Gran, Peter. (1979). *Islamic Roots of Capitalism: Egypt, 1760–1840*. Austin, TX: University of Texas Press.

Grange, Henri. (1957). "Turgot et Necker devant le problème des salaires," *Annales historiques de la Révolution française*, **XXIX**, No. 146, 19–33.

Grant, William L. (1912). "Canada versus Guadeloupe: An Episode of the Seven Years' War," *American Historical Review*, **XVII**, 4, 735–743.

Grantham, George W. (1978). "The Diffusion of the New Husbandry in Northern France, 1815–1840," *Journal of Economic History*, **XXXVIII**, 2, 311–337.

Grantham, George W. (1980). "The Persistence of Open-Field Farming in Nineteenth Century France," *Journal of Economic History*, **XL**, 3, 515–531.

Gray, Ralph & Wood, Betty. (1976). "The Transition from Indentured to Involuntary Servitude in Colonial Georgia," *Explorations in Entrepreneurial History*, **XIII**, 4, 353–370.

Green, W. A. (1973). "The Planter Class and Production, Before and After Emancipation," *Economic History Review*, 2nd ser., **XXVI**, 448–463.

Greenberg, Michael. (1951). *British Trade and the Opening of China, 1800–42*. Cambridge, Engl.: At the University Press.

Greene, Evarts B. (1943). *The Revolutionary Generation, 1763–1790*. New York: Macmillan.

Greene, Jack P. (1962). "The Flight from Determinism: A Review of Recent Literature on the Coming of the American Revolution," *South Atlantic Quarterly*, **LXI**, 2, 235–259.

Greene, Jack P. (1968a). "The Plunge of Lemmings: A Consideration of Recent Writings on British Policies and the American Revolution," *South Atlantic Quarterly*, **LXVII**, 1, 141–175.

Greene, Jack P. (1968b). "The Reappraisal of the American Revolution in Recent Historical Literature," in J. P. Greene, ed., *The Reinterpretation of the American Revolution, 1763–1789*. New York: Harper & Row, 2–74.

Green, Jack P. (1969a). "Political Nemesis: A Consideration of the Historical and Cultural

Roots of Legislative Relations in the British Colonies in the Eighteenth Century," *American Historical Review*, **LXXV**, 2, 337–360.

Greene, Jack P. (1969b). "Reply," *American Historical Review*, **LXXV**, 2, 364–367.

Greene, Jack P. (1973a). "An Uneasy Connection: An Analysis of the Preconditions of the American Revolution," in S. G. Kurtz & J. H. Hutson, eds., *Essays on the American Revolution*. Chapel Hill, NC: University of North Carolina Press, 32–80.

Greene, Jack P. (1973b). "The Social Origins of the American Revolution: An Interpretation," *Political Science Quarterly*, **LXXXVIII**, 1, 1–22.

Greene, Jack P. & Jellison, Richard M. (1961). "The Currency Act of 1764 in Imperial-Colonial Relations, 1764–1766," *William and Mary Quarterly*, 3rd ser., **XVIII**, 4, 485–518.

Greenleaf, Richard E. (1967). "The Obraje in the Late Mexican Colony," *The Americas*, **XXIII**, 3, 227–250.

Green-Pedersen, Svend E. (1979). "The Economic Considerations behind the Danish Abolition of the Negro Slave Trade," in H. A. Gemery & J. S. Hogendorn, eds., *The Uncommon Market*. New York: Academic Press, 399–418.

Grenon, Michel & Robin, Regine. (1976). "A propos de la polémique sur l'Ancien Régime et la Révolution: pour une problématique de la transition," *La Pensée*, No. 187, 5–30.

Griffin, Charles C. (1937). *The United States and the Disruption of the Spanish Empire, 1810–1822*. New York: Columbia University Press.

Griffin, Charles C. (1949). "Economic and Social Aspects of the Era of Spanish–American Independence," *Hispanic American Historical Review*, **XXIX**, 2, 170–187.

Griffin, Charles C. (1962). *Las temas sociales y económicos en la época de la Independencia*. Caracas: Publicación de la Fundación John Boulton y la Fundación Eugenio Mendoza.

Griffiths, David M. (1979). "Eighteenth-Century Perceptions of Backwardness: Projects for the Creation of a Third Estate in Catherinean Russia," *Canadian–American Slavic Studies*, **XIII**, 4, 452–472.

Grochulska, Barbara. (1980). "Programme de modernisation de la République dans le seconde moitié du XVIIIe siècle," paper delivered at 1er Colloque Franco-Polonais, Antibes, 6–9 novembre.

Grubb, Farley. (1985a). "The Market For Indentured Immigrants: Evidence on the Efficiency of Forward Labor Contracting in Philadelphia, 1745–1773," *Journal of Economic History*, **XLV**, 4, 855–868.

Grubb, Farley. (1985b). "The Incidence of Servitude in Trans-Atlantic Migration, 1771–1804," *Explorations in Economic History*, **XXII**, 3, 316–339.

Gruder, Vivian R. (1968). *The Royal Provincial Intendants. A Governing Elite in Eighteenth-Century France*. Ithaca, NY: Cornell University Press.

Gruder, Vivian R. (1984). "A Mutation in Elite Political Culture: The French Notables and the Defense of Property and Participation, 1787," *Journal of Modern History*, **LVI**, 4, 598–634.

Guerci, Luciano. (1980). "Furet e la Rivoluzione francese," *Studi storici*, **XXI**, 2, 227–240.

Guérin, Daniel. (1958). "Bataille autour de notre mère," *La nouvelle réforme*, **I**, 2, 195–217.

Guérin, Daniel. (1968). *La lutte de classes sous la Première République: Bourgeois et "bras nus" (1793–1797)*, nouv. ed. revue et augmentée, 2 vols. Paris: Gallimard.

Guéry, Alain. (1978). "Les finances de la monarchie française sous l'Ancien Régime," *Annales E.S.C.*, **XXXIII**, 2, 216–239.

Guha, Amalendu. (1972). "Raw Cotton of Western India: Output, Transport, and Marketing, 1750–1850," *Indian Economic and Social History Review*, **IX**, 1, 1–42.

Guha, Amalendu. (1976). "Imperialism of Opium: Its Ugly Face in Assam (1773–1921)," in *Proceedings of the Indian History Congress*, Thirty-Seventh Session, Calicut, 338–346.

Guibert-Sledziewski, E. (1977). "Du féodalisme au capitalisme. Transition révolutionnaire ou système transitoire?," in A. Soboul, dir., *Contribution à l'histoire paysanne de la Révolution française*. Paris: Ed. Sociales, 47–71.

Guilhaumou, Jacques. (1980). "Les discours jacobins (1792–1794)," *Mots*, No. 1, 219–225.

Guillerm, Alain. (1981). "L'Etat et l'espace de la guerre: Fortifications et marine," 2 vols., unpublished Ph.D. dissertation, Université de Paris-VIII.

Gupta, Sulekh Chandra. (1963). *Agrarian Relations and Early British Rule in India.* Bombay: Asia Publ. House.

Guttridge, G. H. (1933). "Adam Smith on the American Revolution: An Unpublished Memorial [Feb., 1778]," *American Historical Review,* **XXXVIII**, 4, 714–720.

Guy, Camille. (1900). *La mise en valeur de notre domaine colonial.* Collection, les Colonies françaises, Tome III. Paris: Augustin Challamel.

Habakkuk, H. J. (1953). "English Population in the Eighteenth Century," *Economic History Review,* 2nd ser., **VI**, 2, 117–133.

Habakkuk, H. J. (1955). "The Historical Experience of the Basic Conditions of Economic Progress," in L. H. Dupriez, ed., *Economic Progress: Papers and Proceedings of a Round Table held by the International Economic Association.* Louvain: Institut de Recherches Economiques.

Habakkuk, H. J. (1958). "The Economic History of Modern Britain," *Journal of Economic History,* **XVIII**, 4, 486–501.

Habakkuk, H. J. (1965). "Population, Commerce and Economic Ideas," in *New Cambridge Modern History,* **VIII**: A. Goodwin, ed., *The American and French Revolutions, 1763–93.* Cambridge, Engl.: At the University Press, 25–54.

Habakkuk, H. J. (1971). *Population Growth and Economic Development Since 1750.* Leicester, Engl.: Leicester University Press.

Habib, Irfan. (1963). *The Agrarian System of Mughal India (1556–1702).* New York: Asia Publ. House.

Habib, Irfan. (1969). "Potentialities of Capitalistic Development in the Economy of Mughal India," *Journal of Economic History,* **XXIX**, 1, 32–78.

Habib, Irfan. (1985). "Studying a Colonial Economy—Without Perceiving Colonialism," *Modern Asian Studies,* **XIX**, 3, 355–381.

Hacker, Louis M. (1935). "The First American Revolution," *Columbia University Quarterly,* Part I, 259–295.

Hague, D. C. (1963). "Summary Record of the Debate," in W. W. Rostow, ed., *The Economics of Take-Off into Sustained Growth.* London: Macmillan, 301–476.

Hair, J. E. H. (1965). "The Enslavement of Koelle's Informants," *Journal of African History,* **VI**, 2, 193–203.

Hajnal, J. (1965). "European Marriage Patterns in Perspective," in D. V. Glass & D. C. E. Eversley, eds., *Population in History.* London: Edward Arnold, 101–143.

Hall, Gwendolyn M. (1971). *Social Control in Plantation Societies: A Comparison of St. Domingue and Cuba.* Baltimore, MD: Johns Hopkins University Press.

Halperín-Donghi, Tulio. (1972). "La crisis de Independencia," in *La independencia en el Perú,* Perú Problema, No. 7. Lima: Instituto de Estudios Peruanos, 115–166.

Halperín-Donghi, Tulio. (1975). *Politics, Economics, and Society in Argentina in the Revolutionary Period, 1776–1860.* Cambridge, Engl.: Cambridge University Press.

Hamill, Hugh M., Jr. (1966). *The Hidalgo Revolt: Prelude to Mexican Independence.* Gainesville, FL: University of Florida Press.

Hamilton, Earl J. (1940). "Growth of Rigidity in Business during the Eighteenth Century," *American Economic Review, Supplement,* **XXX**, 1, 298–305.

Hamilton, Earl J. (1944). "Monetary Problems in Spain and Spanish America, 1751–1800," *Journal of Economic History,* **IV**, 1, 21–48.

Hamilton, Earl J. (1953). "Profit Inflation and the Industrial Revolution, 1751–1800" in Frederic C. Lane & Jelle C. Riemersma, eds., *Enterprise and Secular Change.* Homewood, IL: Richard D. Irwin, 322–336. (Originally published in *Quarterly Journal of Economics,* 1942.)

Hamnett, Brian R. (1971). *Politics and Trade in Southern Mexico, 1750–1821.* Cambridge, Engl.: At the University Press.

Hamnett, Brian R. (1980) "Mexico's Royalist Coalition: The Response to Revolution, 1808–1821," *Journal of Latin American Studies,* **XII**, 1, 55–86.

Hampson, Norman. (1963). *A Social History of the French Revolution.* Toronto: Toronto University Press.

Hancock, W. K. (1942). *Survey of British Commonwealth Affairs,* **II:** *Problems of Economic Policy, 1918–1939,* Part 2. London: Oxford University Press.

Hardy, Georges. (1921). *La mise en valeur du Sénégal de 1817 à 1854.* Paris: Emile Larose.

Haring, Clarence H. (1947). *The Spanish Empire in America.* New York: Harcourt, Brace & World.

Harley, C. Knick. (1982). "British Industrialization before 1841: Evidence of Slower Growth during the Industrial Revolution," *Journal of Economic History,* **XLII,** 2, 267–289.

Harlow, Vincent T. (1940). "The New Imperial System, 1783–1815," in J. Holland Rose, A. P. Newton & E. A. Benians, eds., *The Cambridge History of the British Empire,* **II:** *The Growth of the New Empire, 1783–1870.* Cambridge, Engl.: At the University Press, 129–187.

Harlow, Vincent T. (1952). *The Founding of the Second British Empire, 1763–1793,* **I:** *Discovery and Revolution.* London: Longmans, Green.

Harlow, Vincent T. (1964). *The Founding of the Second British Empire, 1763–1793,* **II:** *New Continents and Changing Values.* London: Longmans, Green.

Harper, Lawrence A. (1939). "The Effects of the Navigation Acts on the Thirteen Colonies," in R. B. Morris, ed., *The Era of the American Revolution.* New York: Columbia University Press, 3–39.

Harper, Lawrence A. (1942). "Mercantilism and the American Revolution," *Canadian Historical Review,* **XXIII,** 1, 1–15.

Harris, Charles H., III. (1975). *A Mexican Family Empire: The Latifundo of the Sánchez Navarros, 1765–1867.* Austin, TX: University of Texas Press.

Harris, J. R. (1976a). "Skills, Coal and British Industry in the Eighteenth Century," *History,* **LXI,** No. 202, 167–182.

Harris, J. R. (1976b). "Technological Divergence and Industrial Development in Britain and France Before 1800," in *Fifth International Conference of Economic History,* Leningrad, 1970. The Hague: Mouton, **VII,** 31–41.

Harris, Robert D. (1976). "French Finances and the American War, 1777–1783," *Journal of Modern History,* **XLVIII,** 2, 233–258.

Harsin, Paul. (1930). "De quand date le mot industrie?" *Annales d'histoire économique et sociale,* **II,** 6, 235–242.

Harsin, Paul. (1954). *La révolution liégoise de 1789.* Bruxelles: La Renaissance du Livre.

Hartmann, Peter Clause. (1978). "Die Steuersysteme in Frankreich und England am Vorabend der Französischen Revolution," in E. Hinrichs *et al.,* hrsg., *Vom Ancien Regime zur Französischen Revolution.* Göttingen: Vanderhoeck & Ruprecht, 43–65.

Hartwell, R. M. (1961). "The Rising Standard of Living in England, 1800–1850," *Economic History Review,* 2nd ser., **XIII,** 3, 397–416.

Hartwell, R. M. (1963). "The Standard of Living," *Economic History Review,* 2nd ser., **XVI,** 1, 135–146.

Hartwell, R. M. (1967a). "Introduction," in R.M. Hartwell, ed., *The Causes of the Industrial Revolution in England.* London: Methuen, 1–30.

Hartwell, R. M. (1967b). "The Causes of the Industrial Revolution: An Essay in Methodology," in R. M. Hartwell, ed., *The Causes of the Industrial Revolution in England.* London: Methuen, 53–79. (Originally published in *Economic History Review,* 1965.)

Hartwell, R. M., ed. (1968). *The Industrial Revolution in England,* rev. ed. London: The Historical Association.

Hartwell, R. M. (1970a). "The Standard of Living Controversy: A Summary," in R. M. Hartwell, ed., *The Industrial Revolution.* Oxford: Basil Blackwell, 167–179.

Hartwell, R. M. (1970b). "The Great Discontinuity: Interpretations of the Industrial Revolution," *Historical Journal* (New South Wales), **I,** 3–16.

Hartwell, R. M. (1972). "Discussion of J. Godechot, 'L'industrialisation en Europe à l'époque révolutionnaire,'" in Pierre León, *et al.,* dirs., *L'industrialisation en Europe du XIXe siècle,*

Colloques Internationaux du CNRS, No. 540, Lyon, 7-10 oct. 1970. Paris: Ed. du CNRS, 372–373.

Hartwell, R. M. & Engerman, S. (1975). "Modes of Immiseration: the Theoretical Basis of Pessimism," in Arthur J. Taylor, ed., *The Standard of Living in Britain in the Industrial Revolution.* London: Methuen, 189–213.

Hartwell, R. M. & Higgs, Robert. (1971). "Good Old Economic History," *American Historical Review,* **LXXVI**, 2, 467–474.

Haskett, Richard C. (1954). "Prosecuting the Revolution," *American Historical Review,* **LIX**, 3, 578–587.

Hasquin, Hervé. (1971). *Une mutation: le "Pays de Charleroi" aux XVIIe et XVIIIe siècles: Aux origines de la Révolution industrielle en Belgique.* Bruxelles: Ed. de l'Institut de Sociologie.

Hauser, Henri. (1923). "Avant-propos" to Charles Ballot, *L'introduction du machinisme dans l'industrie française.* Lille: O. Marquant, v–ix.

Hawke, G. R. & Higgins, J. P. P. (1981). "Social Overhead Capital," in R. Floud & D. N. McCloskey, eds., *The Economic History of Britain Since 1700,* **I:** *1700–1860.* Cambridge, Engl.: Cambridge University Press, 227–252.

Heaton, Herbert. (1932). "Industrial Revolution," *Encyclopedia of the Social Sciences,* Vol. VIII. New York: Macmillan, 3–13.

Heaton, Herbert. (1941). "Non-Importation, 1806–1812," *Journal of Economic History,* **I**, 2, 178–198.

Heaton, Herbert. (1972). "Financing the Industrial Revolution," in F. Crouzet, ed., *Capital Formation in the Industrial Revolution.* London: Methuen, 84–93. (Originally published in *Bulletin of Business History Society,* 1937.)

Heavner, Robert O. (1978). "Indentured Servitude: The Philadelphia Market, 1771–1773," *Journal of Economic History,* **XXXVIII**, 3, 701–713.

Heckscher, Eli P. (1922). *The Continental System: An Economic Interpretation.* Oxford: Clarendon Press.

Heckscher, Eli F. (1934). *Mercantilism,* 2 vols. London: George Allen & Unwin.

Helleiner, Karl F. (1965). "The Vital Revolution Reconsidered," in D. V. Glass & D. C. E. Eversley, eds., *Population in History.* London: Edward Arnold, 79–86. (Originally published in *Canadian Journal of Economical and Political Science,* 1957.)

Hellie, Richard. (1967). "The Foundations of Russian Capitalism," *Slavic Review,* **XXVI**, 1, 148–154.

Hellie, Richard. (1971). *Enserfment and Military Change in Muscovy.* Chicago, IL: University of Chicago Press.

Henderson, Archibald. (1914). "The Creative Forces in Westward Expansion: Henderson and Boone," *American Historical Review,* **XX**, 1, 86–107.

Henderson, H. James. (1973). "The Structure of Politics in the Continental Congress," in S. G. Kurtz & J. H. Hutson, eds., *Essays on the American Revolution.* Chapel Hill, NC: University of North Carolina Press, 157–196.

Henderson, W. O. (1957). "The Anglo-French Commercial Treaty of 1786," *Economic History Review,* 2nd ser., **X**, 1, 104–112.

Henderson, W. O. (1961). *The Industrial Revolution on the Continent.* London: Frank Cass. (Also entitled *The Industrial Revolution in Europe.*)

Henderson, W. O. (1972). *Britain and Industrial Europe, 1750–1870,* 3rd ed. Leicester, Engl.: Leicester University Press.

Henderson, W. O. (1976). "The Labour Force in the Textile Industries," *Archiv für Sozialgeschichte,* **XVI**, No. 76, 283–324.

Herr, Richard. (1958). *The Eighteenth-Century Revolution in Spain.* Princeton, NJ: Princeton University Press.

Hertzberg, Arthur. (1968). *The French Enlightenment and the Jews. The Origins of Modern Anti-Semitism.* New York: Columbia University Press & Philadelphia, PA: Jewish Publ. Society of America.

Hess, Andrew C. (1970). "The Evolution of the Ottoman Seaborne Empire in the Age of the Oceanic Discoveries, 1453–1525," *American Historical Review*, **LXXV**, 7, 1892–1919.

Heston, Alan W. (1977). "The Standard of Living in Akbar's Time: A Comment," *Indian Economic and Social History Review*, **XIV**, 3, 391–396.

Heuvel, Gerd van den. (1982). *Grundprobleme der französischen Bauernschaft, 1730–1794*. München & Wien: Oldenbourg.

Heyd, Uriel, (1961). "The Ottoman 'Ulemâ and Westernization in the Time of Selîm III and Mahmûd II," *Scripta Hierosolymitana*, **IX**: U. Heyd, ed., *Studies in Islamic History and Civilization*, 63–96.

Heyd, Uriel. (1970). "The Later Ottoman Empire in Rumelia and Anatolia," in P. M. Holt *et al.*, *The Cambridge History of Islam*, **I**: *The Central Islamic Lands*. Cambridge, Engl.: At the University Press, 354–373.

Heywood, Colin. (1981). "The Launching of an 'Infant Industry'? The Cotton Industry of Troyes Under Protectionism, 1793–1860," *Journal of European Economic History*, **X**, 3, 553–581.

Higonnet, Patrice. (1979). "Babeuf: Communist or Proto-Communist?" *Journal of Modern History*, **LI**, 4, 773–781.

Higonnet, Patrice. (1980). "The Politics of Linguistic Terrorism and Grammatical Hegemony During the French Revolution," *Social History*, **V**, 1, 41–69.

Higonnet, Patrice. (1981). *Class, Ideology, and the Rights of Nobles during the French Revolution*. Oxford: Clarendon Press.

Higonnet, Patrice. (1986). "Le sens de la Terreur dans la Révolution française," *Commentaire*, No. 35, 436–445.

Hill, Christopher. (1967). *Reformation to Industrial Revolution*, Pelican Economic History of Britain, Vol. II. London: Penguin.

Hill, Christopher. (1980). "A Bourgeois Revolution?," in J. G. A. Pocock, ed., *Three British Revolutions: 1641, 1688, 1776*. Princeton, NJ: Princeton University Press, 109–139.

Hirsch, Jean-Pierre, ed., (1978). *La nuit du 4 août*, Collection Archives. Paris: Gallimard-Juilliard.

Hirsch, Jean-Pierre. (1979). "Un fil rompu? A propos du crédit à Lille sous la Révolution et l'Empire," *Revue du Nord*, **LXI**, No. 240, 181–192.

Hirsch, Jean-Pierre. (1980). "Note critique: Pensons la Révolution française," *Annales E.S.C.*, **XXXV**, 2, 320–333.

Hirschman, Albert. (1957). "Investment Policies and 'Dualism' in Underdeveloped Countries," *American Economic Review*, **XLVII**, 5, 550–570.

His de Butenval, Charles Adrien (Comte). (1869). *Précis historique et économique du traité du commerce entre la France et la Grande-Bretagne signé à Versailles, le 26 septembre 1786*. Paris: Dentu.

Hiskett, Mervyn. (1962). "An Islamic Tradition of Reform in the Western Sudan from the Sixteenth to the Eighteenth Century," *Bulletin of SOAS*, **XXV**, 3, 577–596.

Hiskett, Mervyn. (1976). "The Nineteenth-Century Jihads in West Africa," in J. E. Flint, ed., *Cambridge History of Africa*, **V**: *From c. 1790 to c. 1870*. Cambridge, Engl.: Cambridge University Press, 125–169.

Hobsbawm, E. J. (1952). "The Machine-Breakers," *Past and Present*, No. 1, Feb., 57–70.

Hobsbawm, E. J. (1957). "The British Standard of Living, 1790–1850," *Economic History Review*, 2nd ser., **X**, 1, 46–68.

Hobsbawm, E. J. (1962). *The Age of Revolution, 1789–1848*. New York: Mentor.

Hobsbawm, E. J. (1963). "The Standard of Living during the Industrial Revolution: A Discussion," *Economic History Review*, 2nd ser., **XVI**, 1, 120–134.

Hobsbawm, E. J. (1968). *Industry and Empire*, The Pelican Economic History of Britain, Volume III. Harmondsworth, Engl.: Penguin.

Hobsbawm, E. J. (1975). "Essays in Postscript: The Standard of Living Debate," in Arthur J.

Taylor, ed., *The Standard of Living in Britain in the Industrial Revolution.* London: Methuen, 179–188.

Hodgkin, Thomas. (1960). "Uthman dan Fodio," *Nigeria Magazine,* A Special Independence Issue, Oct., 75–82.

Hodgson, Marshall. (1974). *The Venture of Islam: Conscience and History in a World Civilization,* 3 vols. Chicago: IL: University of Chicago Press.

Hoerder, Dirk. (1976). "Boston Leaders and Boston Crowds, 1765–1776," in A. F. Young, ed., *The American Revolution: Explorations in the History of American Radicalism.* DeKalb, IL: Northern Illinois University Press, 233–271.

Hoffman, Ronald. (1976). "The 'Disaffected' in the Revolutionary South," in A. F. Young, ed., *The American Revolution: Explorations in the History of American Radicalism.* DeKalb, IL: Northern Illinois University Press, 273–316.

Hoffmann, Peter. (1973). "Zur Problematik der sogenannten ursprünglichen Akkumulation in Russland," in P. Hoffman & H. Lemke, hrsg., *Genesis and Entwicklung des Kapitalismus in Russland,* Berlin: Akademie-Verlag, 154–177.

Hoffmann, Walther G. (1955). *British Industry, 1700–1950.* Oxford: Basil Blackwell.

Hoffmann, Walther G. (1958). *The Growth of Industrial Economies.* Manchester, Engl.: Manchester University Press.

Hogendorn, Jan S. (1977). "The Economics of Slave Use on Two 'Plantations' in the Zaria Emirate of the Sokoto Caliphate," *International Journal of African Historical Studies,* **X**, 3, 369–383.

Hogendorn, Jan S. (1980). "Slave Acquisition and Delivery in Precolonial Hausaland," in B. K. Schwartz, Jr. & R. Dumett, eds., *West African Culture Dynamics: Archaeological and Historical Perspectives.* The Hague: Mouton, 477–494.

Holderness, B. A. (1971). "Capital Formation in Agriculture," in J. P. P. Higgins & S. Pollard, eds., *Aspects of Capital Investment in Great Britain, 1750–1850: A Preliminary Survey.* London: Methuen, 159–183.

Holderness, B. A. (1974). "The English Land Market in the Eighteenth Century: The Case of Lincolnshire," *Economic History Review,* 2nd ser., **XXVII**, 4, 557–576.

Hone, J. Ann (1982). *For the Cause of Truth: Radicalism in London 1796–1821.* Oxford: Clarendon Press.

Hopkins, A. G. (1973). *An Economic History of West Africa.* London: Longmans.

Hoppit, Julian. (1986). "Financial Crises in Eighteenth-Century England," *Economic History Review,* 2nd ser., **XXXIX**, 1, 39–58.

Horsman, Reginald. (1962). *The Cause of the War of 1812.* Philadelphia, PA: University of Pennsylvania Press.

Horton, W. R. G. (1954). "The Ohu System of Slavery in a Northern Ibo Village-Group," *Africa,* **XXIV**, 4, 311–336.

Hoselitz, Bert F. (1955a). "Entrepreneurship and Capital Formation in France and Britain since 1700," in National Bureau of Economic Research, *Capital Formation and Economic Growth.* Princeton, NJ: Princeton University Press, 291–337.

Hoselitz, Bert F. (1955b). "Reply" in National Bureau of Economic Research, *Capital Formation and Economic Growth.* Princeton, NJ: Princeton University Press, 385–393.

Hossain, Hameeda. (1979). "The Alienation of Weavers: Impact of the Conflict Between the Revenue and Commercial Interests of the East India Company, 1750–1800," *Indian Economic and Social History Review,* **XVI**, 3, 323–345.

Hourani, Albert. (1957). "The Changing Face of the Fertile Crescent in the XVIIIth Century," *Studia Islamica,* **VIII**, 89–122.

Hourani, Albert. (1968). "Ottoman Reform and the Politics of Notables," in W. R. Polk & R. L. Chambers, eds., *Beginnings of Modernization in the Middle East.* Chicago, IL: University of Chicago Press, 41–68.

Houtte, François-Xavier van. (1949). *L'évolution de l'industrie textile en Belgique et dans le monde de*

1800 à 1939, Université de Louvain, Collection de l'Ecole des Sciences Politiques et Sociales, No. 141. Louvain: E. Nauwelaerts.

Hueckel, Glenn. (1973). "War and the British Economy, 1793–1815: A General Equilibrium Analysis," *Explorations in Economic History,* **X,** 4, 365–396.

Hueckel, Glenn. (1976a). "English Farming Profits during the Napoleonic Wars, 1793–1815," *Explorations in Economic History,* **XIII,** 3, 331–345.

Hueckel, Glenn. (1976b). "Relative Prices and Supply Response in English Agriculture during the Napoleonic Wars," *Economic History Review,* 2nd ser., **XXIX,** 3, 401–414.

Hueckel, Glenn. (1981). "Agriculture During Industrialisation," in R. Floud & D. N. McCloskey, eds., *The Economic History of Britain Since 1700,* **I.** *1700–1860.* Cambridge, Engl.: Cambridge University Press, 182–203.

Hufton, Olwen. (1980). *Europe: Privilege and Protest, 1730–1789,* Vol. X of Fontana History of Europe. London: Harvester.

Hufton, Olwen. (1983). "Social Conflict and the Grain Supply in Eighteenth-Century France," *Journal of Interdisciplinary History,* **XIV,** 2, 303–331.

Hughes, H. B. L. (1944). "British Policy Towards Haiti, 1801–1805," *Canadian Historical Review,* **XXV,** 4, 397–408.

Hughes, J. R. T. (1968). "Industrialization: I. Economic Aspects," *International Encyclopedia of the Social Sciences,* Vol. VII. New York: Macmillan & Free Press, 252–263.

Hughes, J. R. T. (1969). "Discussion," *American Economic Review,* **LIX,** 2, Papers and Proceedings, 382–384.

Humboldt, Alexander von. (1972). *Political Essay on the Kingdom of New Spain,* the John Black translation (abridged). New York: Knopf.

Humphreys, R. A. (1952). "The Fall of the Spanish American Empire," *History,* n.s., **XXXVII,** 213–227.

Humphreys, R. A. (1965). *Tradition and Revolt in Latin America, and other essays.* London: Weidenfeld & Nicolson.

Humphreys, R. A. & Lynch, John. (1965a). *The Origins of the Latin American Revolutions, 1808–1826.* New York: Alfred A. Knopf, 3–27.

Humphreys, R. A. & Lynch, John. (1965b). "The Emancipation of Latin America," in *XIIe Congrès International des Sciences Historiques, Rapports,* **III:** *Commissions,* Vienne, 29 août– 5 sept., 1965. Wien: Ferdinand Berger & Sohne, 39–56.

Hunecke, Volker. (1978). "Antikapitalistische Strömungen in der Französischen Revolution. Neuere Kontroversen der Forschung," *Geschichte und Gesellschaft,* **IV,** 3, 291–323.

Hunt, David. (1979). "The People and Pierre Dolivier: Popular Uprisings in the Seine-et-Oise Department (1791–1792), *French Historical Studies,* **XI,** 2, 184–214.

Hunt, David, (1983). "Theda Skocpol and the Peasant Route," *Socialist Review,* **XIII,** 4, 121– 144.

Hunt, David. (1984). "Peasant Politics in the French Revolution," *Social History,* **IX,** 3, 277–299.

Hunt, E. W. & Bothan, E. W. (1987). "Wages in Britain during the Industrial Revolution," *Economic History Review,* 2nd ser., **XL,** 3, 380–399.

Hunt, H. G. (1959). "Landownership and Enclosure, 1750–1850," *Economic History Review,* 2nd ser., **XI,** 3, 497–505.

Hunt, Lynn. (1984). *Politics, Culture, and Class in the French Revolution.* Berkeley, CA: University of California Press.

Hurewitz, J. C. (1956). *Diplomacy in the Near and Middle East,* **I:** *A Documentary Record, 1535–1914.* Princeton, NJ: Van Nostrand.

Hurewitz, J. C. (1961a). "The Europeanization of Ottoman Diplomacy: The Conversion from Unilateralism to Reciprocity in the Nineteenth Century," *Türk Tarih Kurumu Belleten,* **XXV,** No. 99, 455–466.

Hurewitz, J. C. (1961b). "Ottoman Diplomacy and the European State System," *Middle East Journal,* **XV,** 2, 141–152.

Huttenback, R. A. (1961). "The French Threat to India and British Relations with Sind, 1799–1809," *English Historical Review*, **LXXVI**, No. 301, 590–599.

Hyam, Ronald. (1967). "British Imperial Expansion in the Late 18th Century," *Historical Journal*, **X**, 1, 113–124.

Hyde, Charles K. (1973). "The Adoption of Coke-Smelting by the British Iron Industry, 1709–1790," *Explorations in Economic History*, **X**, 3, 397–418.

Hyde, Francis E., Parkinson, Bradbury B. & Marriner, Sheila. (1953). "The Nature and Profitability of the Liverpool Slave Trade. *Economic History Review*, 2nd ser., **V**, 3, 368–377.

Hyslop, Beatrice Fry. (1934). *French Nationalism in 1789 According to the General Cahiers*. New York: Columbia University Press.

Imbart de la Tour, J., Dorvault, F., & Lecomte, H. (1900). *Régime de la propriété; Régime de la main d'oeuvre; L'agriculture aux colonies*, Collection, les Colonies françaises, Tome V. Paris: Augustin Challamel.

Imlah, Albert H. (1958). *Economic Elements in the Pax Britannica*. Cambridge, MA: Harvard University Press.

İnalçık, Halil. (1955). "Land Problems in Turkish History," *The Muslim World*, **XLV**, 3, 221–228.

İnalçık, Halil. (1969). "Capital Formation in the Ottoman Empire," *Journal of Economic History*, **XXIX**, 1, 97–140.

İnalçık, Halil. (1971). "Imtiyāzāt, ii–The Ottoman Empire," in B. Lewis *et al.*, eds., *The Encyclopaedia of Islam*, new ed., Vol. III. Leiden: E. J. Brill, 1179–1189.

İnalçık, Halil. (1980). "Military and Fiscal Transformations in the Ottoman Empire, 1600–1700," *Archivum Ottomanicum*, **VI**, 283–337.

İnalçık, Halil. (1983). "The Emergence of Big Farms, *Çiftlik*s: State Landlords and Tenants," in J. L. Bacqué-Grammont & P. Dumont, eds., *Contribution à l'histoire économique et sociale de l'Empire ottoman*, Collection Turcica, Vol. III. Leuven: Ed. Peeters, 104–126.

Indova, E. I. (1964). "Les activités commerciales de la paysannerie dans les villages de la région de Moscou (première moitié du XVIIIe siècle)," *Cahiers du monde russe et soviétique*, **V**, 2, 206–228.

Inikori, J. E. (1976a). "Measuring the Atlantic Slave Trade: An Assessment of Curtin and Anstey," *Journal of African History*, **XVII**, 2, 197–223.

Inikori, J. E. (1976b). "Measuring the Atlantic Slave Trade: A Rejoinder," *Journal of African History*, **XVII**, 4, 607–627.

Inikori, J. E. (1977). "The Import of Firearms into West Africa, 1750–1807: A Quantitative Analysis," *Journal of African History*, **XVIII**, 3, 339–368.

Inikori, J. E. (1981). "Market Structures and the Profits of the British African Trade in the Late Eighteenth Century," *Journal of Economic History*, **XLI**, 4, 745–776.

Inikori, J. E. (1983). "Market Structure and the Profits of the British African Trade in the Late Eighteenth Century: A Rejoinder," *Journal of Economic History*, **XLIII**, 3, 723–728.

Inikori, J. E. (1985). Market Structure and Profits: A Further Rejoinder," *Journal of Economic History*, **XLV**, 3, 708–711.

Innis, Harold A. (1943). "Decentralization and Democracy," *Canadian Journal of Economics and Political Science*, **IX**, 3, 317–330.

Innis, Harold A. (1956). *The Fur Trade in Canada: An Introduction to Canadian Economic History*, rev. ed. Toronto: University of Toronto Press.

Ippolito, Richard A. (1975). "The Effect of the 'Agricultural Depression' on Industrial Demand in England: 1730–1750," *Economica*, n.s., **XLII**, No. 167, 298–312.

Issawi, Charles. (1961). "Egypt Since 1800: A Study in Lopsided Development," *Journal of Economic History*, **XXI**, 1, 1–25.

Issawi, Charles. (1966). *The Economic History of the Middle East, 1800–1914: A Book of Readings*, edited and with introductions. Chicago, IL: University of Chicago Press.

Issawi, Charles. (1980a). *The Economic History of Turkey, 1800–1914.* Chicago, IL: University of Chicago Press.

Issawi, Charles. (1980b). "Notes on the Negotiations Leading to the Anglo-Turkish Commercial Convention of 1828," In *Mémorial Ömer Lûtfi Barkan,* Bibliothèque de l'Institut Français des Etudes Anatoliennes d'Istanbul, Vol. XXVIII. Paris: Lib d'Amérique et d'Orient A. Maisonneuve, 119–134.

Issawi, Charles. (1982). "The Transformation of the Economic Position of the *Millets* in the Nineteenth Century," in B. Braude & B. Lewis, eds., *Christians and Jews in the Ottoman Empire,* I: *The Central Lands.* New York: Holmes & Meier, 261–285.

Itzkowitz, Norman. (1962). "Eighteenth Century Ottoman Realities," *Studia Islamica,* **XVI,** 73–94.

Izard, Miguel. (1979). *El miedo a la revolución. La lucha para la libertad en Venezuela (1777–1830).* Madrid: Ed. Tecnos.

James, C. L. R. (1963). *The Black Jacobins; Toussaint L'Ouverture and the San Domingo Revolution.* New York: Vintage Books.

James, Francis Goodwin. (1973). *Ireland in the Empire, 1688–1770.* Cambridge, MA: Harvard University Press.

James, James Alton. (1917). "Spanish Influence in the West During the American Revolution," *Mississippi Valley Historical Review,* **IV,** 2, 193–208.

Jameson, J. Franklin. (1926). *The American Revolution Considered as a Social Movement.* Princeton, NJ: Princeton Univ. Press.

Jeannin, Pierre. (1980). "La protoindustrialisation: développement ou impasse? (Note critique)," *Annales E.S.C.,* **XXXV,** 1, 52–65.

Jelavich, Charles & Jelavich, Barbara. (1977). *The Establishment of the Balkan National States, 1804–1920.* Seattle, WA: University of Washington Press.

Jennings, Francis. (1975). *The Invasions of America: Indians, Colonization, and the Cant of Conquest.* Chapel Hill, NC: University of North Carolina Press.

Jennings, Francis. (1976). "The Indians' Revolution," in A. F. Young, ed., *The American Revolution: Explorations in the History of American Radicalism.* DeKalb, IL: Northern Illinois University Press, 319–348.

Jensen, Merrill. (1936). "The Cession of the Old Northwest," *Mississippi Valley Historical Review,* **XXIII,** 1, 27–48.

Jensen, Merrill. (1939). "The Creation of the National Domain, 1781–1784," *Mississippi Valley Historical Review,* **XXVI,** 3, 323–342.

Jensen, Merrill. (1957). "Democracy and the American Revolution," *Huntington Library Quarterly,* **XX,** 4, 321–341.

Jensen, Merrill. (1974). *The American Revolution Within America.* New York: New York University Press.

Jeremy, David J. (1977). "Damming the Flood: British Efforts to Check the Outflow of Technicians and Machinery, 1780–1843," *Business History Review,* **LI,** 1, 1–34.

Jeremy, David J. (1981). *Transatlantic Industrial Revolution: The Diffusion of Textile Technologies Between Britain and America, 1790–1830s.* Cambridge, MA: M.I.T. Press.

Joachim, Bénoît. (1970). "La structure sociale en Haïti et le mouvement d'indépendance au dix-neuvième siècle," *Cahiers d'histoire mondiale,* **XII,** 3, 452–465.

Joachim, Bénoît. (1971). "Le néo-colonialisme à l'essai: La France et l'indépendance d'Haïti," *La Pensée,* No. 156, 35–51.

John, A. H. (1967). "Farming in Wartime: 1793–1815," in E. L. Jones & G. E. Mingay, eds., *Land, Labour, and Population in the Industrial Revolution.* London: Edward Arnold, 28–47.

Johnson, Christopher H. (1983). "Response to J. Rancière, 'The Myth of the Artisan,'" *International Labor and Working Class History,* No. 24, 21–25.

Johnson, Marion. (1970). "The Cowrie Currencies of West Africa," *Journal of African History,* **XI,** 1, 17–49; **XI,** 3, 331–353.

Johnson, Marion. (1976). "The Atlantic Slave Trade and the Economy of West Africa," in R. Anstey & P. E. H. Hair, eds., *Liverpool, The Slave Trade, and Abolition.* Bristol: Western Printing Service, 14–38.

Johnson, Marion. (1978). "Technology Competition and African Crafts," in C. Dewey & A. G. Hopkins, eds., *The Imperial Impact: Studies in the Economic History of Africa and India.* London: Athlone, 259–270.

Johnson, Marion. (1980). "Polanyi, Peukert and the Political Economy of Dahomey," *Journal of African History,* **XXI,** 3, 395–398.

Jones, Alice Hanson. (1980). *Wealth of a Nation to Be: The American Colonies on the Eve of the Revolution.* New York: Columbia University Press.

Jones, E. H. Stuart. (1950). *The Invasion that Failed: The French Expedition to Ireland, 1796.* Oxford: Basil Blackwell.

Jones, E. L. (1967). "Industrial Capital and Landed Investment: The Arkwrights in Herefordshire, 1809–43," in E. L. Jones & G. E. Mingay, eds., *Land, Labour, and Population in the Industrial Revolution.* London: Edward Arnold, 48–71.

Jones, E. L. (1968a). *The Development of English Agriculture, 1815–1873.* London: Macmillan.

Jones, E. L. (1968b). "Agricultural Origins of Industry," *Past and Present,* No. 40, 58–71.

Jones, E. L. (1970). "English and European Agricultural Development, 1650–1750," in R. M. Hartwell, ed., *The Industrial Revolution.* Oxford: Basil Blackwell, 42–76.

Jones, E. L. (1974a). "Agriculture and Economic Growth in England, 1660–1750: Agricultural Change," in *Agriculture and the Industrial Revolution.* Oxford: Basil Blackwell, 67–84. (Originally published in *Journal of Economic History,* 1965.)

Jones, E. L. (1974b). "Agriculture and Economic Growth in England, 1750–1815," in *Agriculture and the Industrial Revolution.* Oxford: Basil Blackwell, 85–127. (Originally published in 1967.)

Jones, E. L. (1974c). "The Agricultural Labour Market in England, 1793–1872," in *Agriculture and the Industrial Revolution.* Oxford: Basil Blackwell, 211–233. (Originally published in *Economic History Review,* 1964.)

Jones, E. L. (1974d). "The Constraints on Economic Growth in Southern England, 1650–1850," *Third International Conference of Economic History,* Munich, 1965. Paris & La Haye: Mouton, **V,** 423–430.

Jones, E. L. (1977). "Environment, Agriculture, and Industrialization in Europe," *Agricultural History,* **LI,** 3, 491–502.

Jones, E. L. (1981). "Agriculture, 1700–80," in R. Floud & D. N. McCloskey, eds., *The Economic History of Britain Since 1700,* **I:** *1700–1860,* Cambridge, Engl.: Cambridge University Press, 66–86.

Jones, G. I. (1963). *The Trading States of the Oil Rivers: A Study of Political Development in Eastern Nigeria.* London: Oxford University Press.

Jones, Gareth Stedman. (1974). "Working-Class Culture and Working-Class Politics in London, 1870–1890: Notes on the Remaking of a Working Class," *Journal of Social History,* **VIII,** 4, 460–508.

Jones, Gareth Stedman. (1975). "Class Struggle and the Industrial Revolution," *New Left Review,* No. 90, 35–69.

Jones, J. R. (1980). *Britain and the World, 1649–1815.* Glasgow: Fontana.

Jones, M. A. (1965). "American Independence in its Imperial, Strategic and Diplomatic Aspects," in A. Goodwin, ed., *New Cambridge Modern History,* **VIII:** *The American and French Revolutions, 1763–93.* Cambridge, Engl.: At the University Press, 480–508.

Jones, Robert Leslie. (1946). "Agriculture in Lower Canada, 1792–1815," *Canadian Historical Review,* **XXVII,** 1, 33–51.

Jones, Stuart. (1981). "The First Currency Revolution," *Journal of European Economic History,* **X,** 3, 583–618.

Jordan, Winthrop D. (1968). *White Over Black: American Attitudes Toward the Negro, 1550–1812.* Chapel Hill, NC: Univ. of North Carolina Press.

Jouvenel, Bertrand de. (1942). *Napoléon et l'économie dirigée. Le Blocus Continental.* Bruxelles & Paris: La Toison d'Or.

Juglar, Clément. (1891). *Des crises commerciales et de leur retour périodique en France, en Angleterre, et aux Etats-Unis.* Paris: A. Picard.

Kahan, Arcadius. (1962). "Entreprenenship in the Early Development of Iron Manufacturing in Russia," *Economic Development and Cultural Change,* **X**, 4, 395–422.

Kahan, Arcadius. (1966). "The Costs of 'Westernization' in Russia: The Gentry and the Economy in the Eighteenth Century," *Slavic Review,* **XXV**, 1, 40–66.

Kahan, Arcadius. (1974a). "Continuity in Economic Activity & Policy During the Post-Petrine Period in Russia," in W. Blakewell, ed., *Russian Economic Development from Peter the Great to Stalin.* New York: New Viewpoints, 53–70. (Originally in *Journal of Economic History,* **XXV**, 1965.)

Kahan, Arcadius. (1974b). "Observations on Petrine Foreign Trade," *Canadian-American Slavic Studies,* **VIII**, 2, 222–236.

Kahan, Arcadius. (1979). "Eighteenth-Century Russian-British Trade: Russia's Contribution to the Industrial Revolution in Great Britain," in A. G. Cross, ed., *Great Britain and Russia in the Eighteenth Century: Contrasts and Comparisons.* Newton, MA: Oriental Research Partners, 181–189.

Kahan, Arcadius, with the editorial assistance of Richard Hellie. (1985). *The Plow, the Hammer, and the Knout—An Economic History of Eighteenth-Century Russia.* Chicago, IL: University of Chicago Press.

Kamendrowsky, Victor & Griffiths, David M. (1978). "The Fall of the Trading Nobility Controversy in Russia: A Chapter in the Relationship between Catherine II and the Russian Revolution," *Jahrbücher für Geschichte Osteuropas,* **XXVI**, 2, 198–221.

Kammen, Michael. (1970). *Empire and Interest: The American Colonies and the Politics of Mercantilism.* Philadelphia, PA: J.P. Lippincott.

Kançal, Salgur. (1983). "La conquête du marché interne ottoman par le capitalisme industriel concurrentiel (1838–1881), in J. L. Bacqué-Grammont & P. Dumont, dirs., *Economie et Sociétés dans l'Empire Ottoman (fin du XVIIIe–Début du XXe siècle),* Colloques Internationaux du CNRS, No. 601. Paris: Ed. du CNRS, 355–409.

Kaplan, Lawrence S. (1972). *Colonies into Nation: American Diplomacy, 1763–1801.* New York: Macmillan.

Kaplan, Lawrence S. (1977). "Towards Isolationism: The Rise and Fall of the Franco-American Alliance, 1775–1801," in L. S. Kaplan, ed., *The American Revolutions and "A Candid World."* Kent, OH: Kent State University Press, 134–160.

Kaplan, Steven L. (1976). *Bread, Politics, and Political Economy in the Reign of Louis XV,* 2 vols. The Hague: Martinus Nijhoff.

Kaplan, Steven L. (1979). "Réflexions sur la police du monde du travail, 1700–1815," *Revue historique,* **CCLXI**, 1, No. 529, 17–77.

Kaplan, Steven L. (1982). "The Famine Plot Persuasion in Eighteenth-Century France," *Transactions of the American Philosophical Society,* **LXXII**, 3.

Kaplow, Jeffry. (1967). "On 'Who Intervened in 1788?'," *American Historical Review,* **LXXII**, 2, 497–502.

Kaplow, Jeffry. (1972). *The Names of Kings.* New York: Basic Books.

Karpat, Kemal H. (1972). "The Transformation of the Ottoman State, 1789–1908," *International Journal of Middle East Studies,* **III**, 3, 243–281.

Karpat, Kemal H. (1974). "The Social and Economic Transformation of Istanbul in the Nineteenth Century. Part I: Istanbul During the First Half of the Century," *Bulletin de l'Association International d'Etudes du Sud-Est Européen,* **XII**, 2, 269–308.

Kaufmann, William W. (1951). *British Policy and the Independence of Latin America, 1804–1828.* New Haven, CT: Yale University Press.

Kay, Marvin L. Michael. (1965). "An Analysis of a British Colony in Late Eighteenth Century America in the Light of Current American Historiographical Controversy," *Australian Journal of Politics and History,* **XI**, 2, 170–184.

Kay, Marvin L. Michael. (1976). "The North Carolina Regulation, 1766–1776: A Class Conflict," in A.F. Young, ed., *The American Revolution: Explorations in the History of American Redicalism.* DeKalb, IL: Northern Illinois University Press, 71–123.

Keene, Charles A. (1978). "American Shipping and Trade, 1798–1820: The Evidence from Leghorn," *Journal of Economic History,* **XXXVIII**, 3, 681–700.

Keep, John. (1972). "Light and Shade in the History of the Russian Administration," *Canadian-American Slavic Studies,* **VI**, 1, 1–9.

Kellenbenz, Hermann. (1970, 1971). "Marchands en Russie aux XVIIe et XVIIIe siècles," *Cahiers du monde russe et soviétique,* **XI**, 4, 516–620 (1970); **XII**, 1/2, 76–109 (1971).

Kellenbenz, Hermann. (1973). "The Economic Significance of the Archangel Route (from the late 16th to the late 18th Century)," *Journal of European Economic History,* **II**, 3, 541–581.

Kemp, Tom. (1962). "Structural Factors in the Retardation of French Economic Growth," *Kyklos,* **XV**, 2, 325–352.

Kennedy, Michael L. (1984). "The Best and the Worst of Times: The Jacobin Club Network from October 1791 to June 2, 1793," *Journal of Modern History,* **LVI**, 4, 635–666.

Kenyon, Cecelia M. (1962). "Republicanism and Radicalism in the American Revolution: An Old-Fashioned Interpretation," *William and Mary Quarterly,* **XIX**, 2, 153–182.

Kenyon, Gordon. (1961). "Mexican Influence in Central America, 1821–1823," *Hispanic American Historical Review,* **XLI**, 1, 175–205.

Kerr, Wilfred Brenton. (1932a). "The Merchants of Nova Scotia and the American Revolution," *Canadian Historical Review,* **XIII**, 1, 20–36.

Kerr, Wilfred Brenton. (1932b). "Nova Scotia in the Critical Years, 1775–6," *Dalhousie Review,* **XII**, 97–107.

Kerr, Wilfred Brenton. (1936). *Bermuda and the American Revolution: 1760–1783.* Princeton, NJ: Princeton University Press.

Kerridge, Eric. (1967). *The Agricultural Revolution.* London: George Allen & Unwin.

Kerridge, Eric. (1969). "The Agricultural Revolution Reconsidered," *Agricultural History,* **XLIII**, 4, 463–475.

Kessel, Patrick. (1969). *La nuit du 4 août 1789.* Paris: Arthaud.

Kessinger, Tom G. (1983). "Regional Economy: North India," in D. Kumar, ed., *Cambridge Economic History of India,* **II:** *c. 1757–c. 1970.* Cambridge, Engl.: Cambridge University Press, 242–270.

Keyder, Çağlar. (1976). The Dissolution of the Asiatic Mode of Production," *Economy and Society,* **V**, 2, 178–196.

Keyder, Çağlar & İslamoğlu, Huri. (1977). "Agenda for Ottoman History," *Review,* **I**, 1, 31–55.

Kicza, John E. (1982). "The Great Families of Mexico: Elite Maintenance and Business Practices in Late Colonial Mexico City," *Hispanic American Historical Review,* **LXII**, 3, 429–457.

Kiernan, Victor. (1952). "Evangelicism and the French Revolution," *Past and Present,* No. 1, Feb., 44–56.

Kilson, Marion Dusser de Barenne. (1971). "West African Society and the Atlantic Slave Trade, 1441–1865," in N.I. Huggins *et al.,* eds., *Key Issues in the Afro-American Experience,* Vol. I. New York: Harcourt, Brace, Jovanovich, 39–53.

Kindleberger, Charles. (1975). "Commercial Expansion and the Industrial Revolution," *Journal of European Economic History,* **IV**, 3, 613–654.

Kirchner, Walther. (1966). *Commercial Relations Between Russia and Europe, 1400–1800: Collected Essays.* Bloomington, IN: Indiana University Press.

Kisch, Herbert. (1959). "The Textile Industries in Silesia and the Rhineland: A Comparative Study in Industrialization," *Journal of Ecnomic History,* **XIX**, 4, 541–564.

Kisch, Herbert. (1962). "The Impact of the French Revolution on the Lower Rhine Textile Districts—Some Comments on Economic Development and Social Change," *Economic History Review,* 2nd ser., **XV**, 2, 304–327.

Kizevetter, M. (1932). "Paul Ier et l'état intérieur de la Russie à la fin du XVIIIe siècle," in Paul

Milioukov, dir., *Histoire de la Russie*, **II:** *Les successeurs de Pierre le Grand: de l'autocratie appuyée sur la noblessa à l'autocratie bureaucratique.* Paris: E. Leroux, 629–655.

Klein, A. Norman. (1968). "Karl Polanyi's Dahomey: To Be or Not to Be a State? A Review Article," *Canadian Journal of African Studies*, **II**, 2, 210–223.

Klein, Herbert S. (1978). "The English Slave Trade to Jamaica, 1782–1808," *Economic History Review*, 2nd ser., **XXXI**, 1, 25–45.

Klein, Martin A. (1968). *Islam and Imperialism in Senegal: Sine-Saloum, 1847–1914.* Stanford, CA: Stanford University Press.

Klein, Martin A. (1972). "Social and Economic Factors in the Muslim Revolution in Senegambia," *Journal of African History*, **XIII**, 3, 419–441.

Klein, Martin & Lovejoy, Paul E. (1979). "Slavery in West Africa," in H.A. Gemery & J.S. Hogendorn, eds., *The Uncommon Market.* New York: Academic Press, 181–212.

Klingaman, David. (1969). "The Significance of Grain in the Development of the Tobacco Colonies," *Journal of Economic History*, **XXIX**, 2, 268–278.

Knight, Franklin W. (1970). *Slave Society in Cuba During the Nineteenth Century.* Madison, WI: University of Wisconsin Press.

Knight, Franklin W. (1977). "Origins of Wealth and the Sugar Revolution in Cuba, 1750–1850," *Hispanic American Historical Review*, **LVII**, 2, 231–253.

Knight, Franklin W. (1983). "The American Revolution and the Caribbean," in I. Berlin & R. Hoffman, eds., *Slavery and Freedom in the Age of the American Revolution:* Charlottesville, VA: University of Virginia Press, 237–261.

Knollenberg, Bernhard. (1960). *Origin of the American Revolution: 1759–1766.* New York: Macmillan.

Knollenberg, Bernhard. (1975). *Growth of the American Revolution, 1766–1775.* New York: Free Press.

Kochanowicz, Jacek. (1980). "Le paysan et la modernisation: Le Royaume de Pologne dans la première moitié du XIXe siècle," paper delivered at Ier Colloque Franco-Polonais, Antibes, 6-9 novembre.

Konetzke, Richard. (1946). "El mestizaje y su importancia en el desarollo de la población hispano-americana durante la época colonial," *Revista de Indias*, **VII**, No. 23, 7–44; **VII**, No. 24, 216–237.

Konetzke, Richard. (1950). "La condición legal de los criollos y las causes de la Independencia," *Estudios americanos*, **II**, 5, 31–54.

Kopytoff, Igor. (1979). "Commentary One [on Lovejoy]," in M. Craton, ed., *Roots and Branches: Current Directions in Slave Studies.* Toronto: Pergamon, 62–77.

Kopytoff, Igor & Miers, Suzanne. (1977). "African 'Slavery' as an Institution of Marginality," in S. Miers & I. Kopytoff, eds., *Slavery in Africa: Historical and Anthropological Perspectives.* Madison, WI: University of Wisconsin Press, 3–81.

Koulischer, Joseph. (1931). "La grande industrie aux XVIIe et XVIIIe siècles: France, Allemagne, Russie," *Annales d'historie économique et sociale*, **III**, No. 9, 11–46.

Koutaissoff, E. (1951). "The Ural Metal Industry in the Eighteenth Century," *Economic History Review*, 2nd ser., **IV**, 2, 252–255.

Köymen, Oya. (1971). "The Advent and Consequences of Free Trade in the Ottoman Empire," *Etudes balkaniques*, **VII**, 2, 47–55.

Kranzberg, Melvin. (1969). "Industrial Revolution," *Encyclopedia Britannica*, Vol. XII. Chicago & London: Encyclopedia Britannica, 210–215.

Kraus, Michael. (1939). "America and the Irish Revolutionary Movement in the Eighteenth Century," in R.B. Morris, ed., *The Era of the American Revolution.* New York: Columbia University Press, 332–348.

Krause, John T. (1958). "Changes in English Fertility and Mortality, 1781–1850," *Economic History Review*, 2nd ser., **XI**, 1, 52–70.

Krause, John T. (1967). "Some Aspects of Population Change, 1690–1770," in E.C. Jones & G.E. Mingay, eds., *Land, Labour and Population in the Industrial Revolution.* London: Edward Arnold, 187–205.

Krause, John T. (1969). "Some Neglected Factors in the English Industrial Revolution," in Michael Drake, ed., *Population in Industrialization*. London: Methuen, 103–117. (Originally published in *Journal of Economic History*, 1959.)

Kriedte, Peter. (1983). *Peasants, Landlords and Merchant Capitalists: Europe and the World Economy, 1500–1800*. Cambridge, Engl.: Cambridge University Press.

Kriedte, Peter, Medick, Hans & Schlumbohm, Jürgen. (1977). *Industrialisierung vor der Industrialisierung*. Göttingen: Vanderhoeck & Ruprecht.

Kroeber, Clifton B. (1957). *The Growth of the Shipping Industry in the Rio de la Plata Region, 1794–1860*. Madison, WI: University of Wisconsin Press.

Krooss, Herman E. (1969). "Discussion," *American Economic Review*, **LIX**, 2, Papers and Proceedings, 384–385.

Kulikoff, Allan. (1971). "The Progress of Neutrality in Revolutionary Boston," *William and Mary Quarterly*, 3rd ser., **XXVIII**, 3, 375–412.

Kulshreshtha, S.S. (1964). *The Development of Trade and Industry under the Mughals (1526 to 1707 A.D.)*. Allahabad, India: Kitab Mahal.

Kumar, Dharma. (1965). *Law and Caste in South India*. Cambridge, Engl.: At the University Press.

Kumar, Dharma. (1985). "The Dangers of Manichaeism," *Modern Asian Studies*, **XIX**, 3, 383–386.

Kurmuş, Orhan. (1983). "The 1838 Treaty of Commerce Reexamined," in J.-L. Bacqué-Grammont & P. Dumont, dirs., *Economie et Sociétés dans l'Empire Ottoman (fin du XVIIIe–Début du XXe siècle)*, Colloques Internationaux du CNRS, No. 601. Paris: Ed. du CNRS, 411–417.

Labrousse, C.-E. (1933). *Esquisse de mouvement des prix et des revenus en France au XVIIIe siècle*, 2 vols. Paris: Lib. Dalloz.

Labrousse, C.-E. (1944). *La crise de l'économie française à la fin de l'Ancien Régime et au début de la révolution*, Vol. I. Paris: Presses Universitaires de France.

Labrousse, C.-E. (1945). "Préface," in A. Chabert, *Essai sur les mouvements des prix et des revenus en France 1798 à 1820*. Paris: Lib. des Médicis, i–ix.

Labrousse, C.-E. (1948). "Comment naissent les revolutions," in *Actes du Congres historique du Centenaire de la Révolution de 1848*. Paris: Presses Universitaires de France, 1–29.

Labrousse, C.-E. [Ernest]. (1954). "Préface" to Pierre Léon, *La naissance de la grande industrie en Dauphiné (fin du XVIIe siècle–1869)*. Paris: Presses Universitaires de France, v–xiv.

Labrousse, C.-E. [Ernest]. (1955). "Voies nouvelles vers une histoire de la bourgeoisie occidentale aux XVIIIe et XIXe siècles (1700–1850)," in X Congresso Internazionale di Scienze Storiche, Roma, 4–11 settembre, 1955. *Relazioni*, **IV**: *Storia moderna*. Firenze: G.C. Sansoni, 365–396.

Labrousse, C.-E. (1965). "Eléments d'un bilan économique: La croissance dans la guerre," in XIIe Congrès International des Sciences Historiques, Vienne, 29 août–5 sept. *Rapports*, **I**: *Grands thèmes*. Horn/Wein: Ferdinand Berger & Sohne, 473–497.

Labrousse, C.-E. [Ernest]. (1966). "The Evolution of Peasant Society in France from the Eighteenth Century to the Present," in E.M. Acomb & M.L. Brown, Jr., eds., *French Society and Culture Since the Old Regime*. New York: Holt, Rinehart & Winston, 44–64.

Labrousse, C.-E. (1970). "Dynamismes économiques, dynamismes sociaux, dynamismes mentaux," in Fernand Braudel & Ernest Labrousse, dirs., *Histoire économique et social de la France*, **II**: *Des derniers temps de l'age seigneurial aux préludes de l'age industriel (1660–1789)*. Paris: Presses Universitaires de France, 691–740.

Lacerte, Robert K. (1975). "The First Land Reform in Latin America: The Reforms of Alexandre Pétion, 1809–1814," *Inter-American Economic Affairs*, **XXVIII**, 4, 77–85.

Lacy, Michael G. (1985). "The United States and American Indians: Political Relations," in V. Deloria, Jr., ed., *American Indian Policy in the Twentieth Century*. Norman, OK: University of Oklahoma Press, 83–104.

Ladd, Doris M. (1976). *The Mexican Nobility at Independence, 1780–1826*. Austin, TX: University of Texas Press.

Lamb, D.P. (1976). "Volume and Tonnage of the Liverpool Slave Trade, 1772–1807," in R.

Anstey & P.E.H. Hair, eds., *Liverpool, The Slave Trade, and Abolition.* Bristol, Engl.: Western Printing Service, 91–112.

Lammey, David. (1986). "The Irish–Portuguese Trade Dispute, 1770–90," *Irish Historical Studies*, **XXV**, No. 97, 29–45.

Lanctot, Gustave. (1965). *Le Canada et la Révolution américaine.* Montréal: Lib. Beauchemin.

Landes, David S. (1949). "French Entrepreneurship and Industrial Growth in the Nineteenth Century." *Journal of Economic History*, **IX**, 1, 45–61.

Landes, David S. (1950). "The Statistical Study of French Crises," *Journal of Economic History*, **X**, 2, 195–211.

Landes, David S. (1958a). "Reply to Mr. Danière and Some Reflections on the Significance of the Debate," *Journal of Economic History*, **XVIII**, 3, 331–338.

Landes, David S. (1958b). "Second Reply," *Journal of Economic History*, **XVIII**, 3, 342–344.

Landes, David S. (1969). *The Unbound Prometheus: Technological Change and Industrial Development in Western Europe from 1750.* Cambridge, Engl.: At the University Press.

Langer, W.L. (1975). "American Foods and Europe's Population Growth, 1750–1850," *Journal of Social History*, **VIII**, 2, 51–66.

Lanning, John Tate. (1930). "Great Britain and Spanish Recognition of the Hispanic American States," *Hispanic American Historical Review*, **X**, 4, 429–456.

Laran, Michael. (1966). "Nobles et paysans en Russie, de 'l'âge d'or' du servage à son abolition (1762–1861)," *Annales E.S.C.*, **XXI**, 1, 111–140.

Laslett, Peter. (1965). *The World We Have Lost.* London: Methuen.

Last, Murray. (1974). "Reform in West Africa: The Jihad Movements of the Nineteenth Century," in J.F.A. Ajayi & M. Crowder, eds., *History of West Africa*, Vol. II. London: Longman, 1–29.

Latham, A.J.H. (1971). "Currency, Credit and Capitalism on the Cross River in the Pre-Colonial Era," *Journal of African History*, **XII**, 4, 599–605.

Latham, A.J.H. (1973). *Old Calabar, 1600–1891: The Impact of the International Economy Upon a Traditional Economy.* Oxford: Clarendon Press.

Latham, A.J.H. (1978). "Price Fluctuations in the Early Palm Oil Trade," *Journal of African History*, **XIX**, 2, 213–218.

Laufenberger, Henri. (1925). "L'industrie cotonnière du Haut Rhin et la France," *Revue politique et parlementaire*, **CXXV**, 387–415.

Laurent, Robert. (1976a). "Les cadres de la production agricole: propriété et modes de production," in Fernand Braudel & Ernest Labrousse, dirs., *Histoire économique et social de la France*, **III**: *L'avènement de l'ère industrielle (1789–années 1880).* Paris: Presses Universitaires de France, 629–661.

Laurent, Robert. (1976b). "L'utilisation du sol: La rénovation des methodes de culture," in Fernand Braudel & Ernest Labrousse, dirs., *Histoire économique et social de la France*, **III**: *L'avènement de l'ère industriel (1789–années 1880).* Paris: Presses Universitaires de France, 663–684.

Law, Robin. (1977). "Royal Monopoly and Private Enterprise in the Atlantic Trade: The Case of Dahomey," *Journal of African History*, **XVIII**, 4, 555–577.

Law, Robin. (1986). "Dahomey and the Slave Trade: Reflections on the Historiography of the Rise of Dahomey," *Journal of African History*, **XXVII**, 2, 237–267.

Lazonick, William. (1974). "Karl Marx and Enclosures in England," *Review of Radical Political Economics*, **VI**, 2, 1–59.

Lebrun, Pierre. (1948). *L'industrie de la laine à Verviers pendant le XVIIIe et le début du XIXe siècles: Contribution à l'étude des origines de la révolution industrielle.* Liège: Faculté de Philosophie et Lettres, fasc. CXIV.

Lebrun, Pierre. (1960). "Croissance et industrialisation: L'Expérience de l'industrie drapière verviétoise, 1750–1850," in *First International Conference of Economic History: Contributions and Communications*, Stockholm, August. Paris & La Haye: Mouton, 531–568.

Lebrun, Pierre. (1961). "La rivoluzione industriale in Belgio: Strutturazione e destruttura-zione delle economie regionali," *Studi storici,* **II**, 3/4, 548–658.

Lecky, W.E.H. (1972). *A History of Ireland in the Eighteenth Century.* Chicago, IL: University of Chicago Press, 1972. (Originally published 1892.)

Le Donne, John P. (1982, 1983). "The Territorial Reform of the Russian Empire, 1775–1796. I: Central Russia, 1775–1784," *Cahiers du monde russe et soviétique,* **XXIII**, 2, 147–185 (1982); "II: The Borderlands, 1777–1796," **XXIV**, 4, 411–457 (1983).

Lee, R.D. & Schofield, R.S. (1981). "British Population in the Eighteenth Century," in R. Floud & D.N. McCloskey, eds., *The Economic History of Britain Since 1700,* **I.** *1700–1860.* Cambridge, Engl.: Cambridge University Press, 17–35.

Leet, Don R. & Shaw, John A. (1978). "French Economic Stagnation, 1700–1960: Old Economic History Revisited," *Journal of Interdisciplinary History,* **VIII**, 3, 531–544.

Lefebvre, Georges. (1929). "La place de la Révolution dans l'histoire agraire de la France," *Annales d'histoire économique et sociale,* **I**, 4, 506–523.

Lefebvre, Georges. (1932). *La grande peur de 1789.* Paris: Lib. Armand Colin.

Lefebvre, Georges. (1937). "Le mouvement des prix et les origines de la Révolution française," *Annales historiques de la Révolution française,* **XIV**, No. 82, 288–329.

Lefebvre, Georges. (1939). *Quatre-vingt-neuf.* Paris: Maison du Livre Français.

Lefebvre, Georges. (1947a). "Review of Daniel Guérin, *La lutte de classes sous la première République,"* in *Annales historiques de la Révolution française,* **XIX**, No. 106, 173–179.

Lefebvre, Georges. (1947b). *The Coming of the French Revolution.* Princeton, NJ: Princeton University Press.

Lefebvre, Georges. (1956). "Le mythe de la Révolution française," *Annales historiques de la Révolution française,* **XXVIII**, No. 145, 337–345.

Lefebvre, Georges. (1963). "La Révolution française et les paysans," in *Etudes sur la Revolution française,* 2e ed. revue. Paris: Presses Universitaires de France, 338–367. (Originally published in *Cahiers de la Révolution française,* 1933.)

Lefebvre, Georges. (1968). *La Révolution française,* Vol. XIII of *Peuples et civilisations,* 6th ed. Paris: Presses Universitaires de France.

Lefebvre, Georges. (1969). *Napoleon from 18 Brumaire to Tilsit, 1799–1807.* New York: Columbia University Press.

Lefebvre, Georges. (1972). *Les paysans du nord pendant la Révolution française,* nouv. éd. Paris: Lib. Armand Colin.

Lefebvre, Georges. (1973). *The Great Fear of 1789.* New York: Pantheon.

Lefebvre, Georges. (1978). "Les historiens de la Révolution française," in *Réflexions sur l'histoire.* Paris: Maspéro, 223–243. (Originally in *Bulletin de la faculté des lettres de Strasbourg,* 1929–1930.)

Lefebvre, Henri. (1975). "What is the Historical Past?" *New Left Review,* No. 90, 27–34.

Lefort, Claude. (1980). "Penser la Révolution dans la Révolution française," *Annales E.S.C.,* **XXXV**, 2, 334–352.

Léger, Jacques. (1934). "Le rôle de Toussaint Louverture dans la cession de la Louisiane aux Etats-Unis," *La Relève,* **II**, 16–18.

LeGoff, T. J. A. (1981). *Vannes and its Region: A Study of Town and Country in Eighteenth-Century France.* Oxford: Clarendon Press.

LeGoff, T. J. A. & Sutherland, D. M. G. (1974). "The Revolution and the Rural Community in Eighteenth-Century Brittany," *Past and Present,* No. 62, 96–119.

LeGoff, T. J. A. & Sutherland, D. M. G. (1983). "The Social Origins of Counter-Revolution in Western France," *Past and Present,* No. 99, 65–87.

Leleux, Fernand. (1969). *A l'aube du capitalisme et de la révolution industrielle: Liévin Bauwens, industriel Gaulois,* Paris: S.E.V.P.E.N.

Léon, Pierre. (1954). *La naissance de la grande industrie en Dauphiné fin du XVII siècle–1869,* 2 vols. Paris: Presses Universitaires de France.

Léon, Pierre. (1960). "L'industrialisation en France, en tant que facteur de croissance économique du début de XVIIIe siècle à nos jours," in *First International Conference of Economic History*, Stockholm, August. Paris & La Haye: Mouton, 163–205.

Léon, Pierre. (1966). "Introduction générale: Les structures rurales de la France du Sud-Est, problèmes et premières interprètations," in P. Léon, dir., *Structures économiques et problèmes sociaux du Sud-Est (fin du XVIIe siècle–1835)*. Paris: Soc. d'Ed. "Les Belles Lettres," 7–32.

Léon, Pierre. (1974). "Structure du commerce extérieur et évolution industrielle de la France à la fin du XVIIIe siècle," in *Conjoncture économique, structures sociales: Hommage à Ernest Labrousse*. Paris & La Haye: Mouton, 407–432.

Léon, Pierre. (1976a). "L'impulsion technique," in Fernand Braudel & Ernest Labrousse, dirs., *Histoire économique et social de la France*, **III:** *L'avènement de l'ère industriel (1789–années 1880)*. Paris: Presses Universitaires de France, 475–501.

Léon, Pierre. (1976b). "Les nouvelles repartitions," in Fernand Braudel & Ernest Labrousse, dirs., *Histoire économique et social de la France*, **III:** *L'avènement de l'ère industriel (1789–années 1880)*. Paris: Presses Universitaires de France, 543–580.

Léon, Pierre. (1976c). "La dynamisme industriel," in Fernand Braudel & Ernest Labrousse, dirs., *Histoire économique et social de la France*, **III:** *L'avènement de l'ère industriel (1789–années 1880)*. Paris: Presses Universitaires de France, 581–616.

Le Roy Ladurie, Emmanuel. (1969). "L'Aménorrhée de famine (XVIIe–XXe siècles)," *Annales E.S.C.*, **XXIV**, 6, 1589–1601.

Le Roy Ladurie, Emmanuel. (1974). "Révoltes et contestations rurales en France de 1675 à 1788," *Annales E.S.C.*, **XXIX**, 1, 6–22.

Le Roy Ladurie, Emmanuel. (1975). "De la crise ultime à la vraie croissance, 1660–1789," in Georges Duby, dir., *Histoire de la France rurale*, **II:** E. LeRoy Ladurie, dir., *L'Age classique des paysans, 1340–1789*. Paris: Seuil, 355–599.

Le Roy Ladurie, Emmanuel. (1976). "La crise et l'historien," *Communications*, No. 24, 19–33.

Le Roy Ladurie, Emmanuel. (1978). "L'histoire immobile," in *Le territoire de l'historien*, Vol. II. Paris: Gallimard, 7–34. (Originally published in *Annales E.S.C.*, 1974.)

Le Roy Ladurie, Emmanuel. (1983–1984). "Sur la Révolution française: Les 'fevisions' d'Alfred Cobban," *Commentaire*, **VI**, No. 24, 834–837.

Le Roy Ladurie, Emmanuel & Goy, Joseph. (1969a). "Présentation" in J. Goy & E. Le Roy Ladurie, eds., *Les fluctuations du produit de la dîme*. Paris & La Haye: Mouton, 9–24.

Le Roy Ladurie, Emmanuel, with Goy, Joseph. (1969b). "Première esquisse d'une conjoncture du produit décimal et domanial, fin du Moyen Age–XVIIIe siècle," in J. Goy & E. Le Roy Ladurie, eds., *Les fluctuations de la dîme*. Paris & La Haye: Mouton, 334–374.

Le Roy Ladurie & Goy, Joseph. (1982). *Tithe and Agrarian History from the Fourteenth to the Nineteenth Centuries*. Cambridge, Engl.: Cambridge University Press & Paris: Ed. de la Maison des Sciences de l'Homme.

Le Roy Ladurie, Emmanuel, with Quilliet, Bernard. (1981). "Baroque et lumières," in G. Duby, dir., *Histoire de la France urbaine*, **III:** E. Le Roy Ladurie, dir., *La ville classique de la Renaissance aux Révolutions*. Paris: Seuil, 287–535.

Letaconnoux, J. (1908, 1909). "Les transports intérieurs en France au XVIIIe siècle," *Revue d'histoire moderne et contemporaine*, **XI**, 97–114 (1908); 269–292 (1909).

LeVeen, E. Phillip. (1974). "A Quantiative Analysis of the Impact of British Suppression Policies on the Volume of the Nineteenth Century Atlantic Slave Trade," in S. L. Engerman & E. D. Genovese, eds., *Race and Slavery in the Western Hemisphere: Quantitative Studies*. Princeton, NJ: Princeton University Press, 51–81.

Levene, Ricardo, ed. (1941). *Historia de la Nación Argentina*, 2a ed., **V:** *La Revolución de Mayo hasta la Asamblea General Constitugente*, 2 secciones. Buenos Aires: Lib. y Ed. "El Ateneo."

Levy, Avigdor. (1971). "The Officer Corp in Sultan Mahmud's New Army, 1826–39," *International Journal of Middle East Studies*, **II**, 1, 21–39.

Lévy-Bruhl, Henri. (1933). "La Noblesse de France et le commerce à la fin de l'ancien régime," *Revue d'histoire moderne*, n.s., **II**, No. 8, 209–235.

Lévy-Leboyer, Maurice. (1964). *Les banques européennes et l'industrialisation internationale, dans la première moitié du XIXe siècle.* Paris: Presses Universitaires de France.

Lévy-Leboyer, Maurice. (1968). "Les processus d'industrialisation: Le cas de l'Angleterre et de la France," *Revue historique,* 92e année, **CCXXXIX**, 2, 281–298.

Lewin, Boleslao. (1957). *La rebelion de Túpac Amaru y los origenes de la emancipación americana.* Buenos Aires: Lib. Hachette.

Lewis, Bernard. (1953). "The Impact of the French Revolution in Turkey: Some Notes on the Transmission of Ideas," *Cahiers d'histoire mondiale,* **I**, 1, 105–125.

Lewitter, L. R. (1973). "Ivan Tikhonovich Pososhkov (1652–1726) and 'The Spirit of Capitalism,' " *Slavonic and East European Review,* **II**, No. 125, 524–553.

Liévano Aguirre, Indalecio. (1968). *Los grandes conflictos sociales y económicos de nuestro historia,* 3a ed. Bolivia: Ed. Tercer Mundo.

Lilley, Samuel. (1973). "Technological Progress and the Industrial Revolution, 1700–1914," in C. M. Cipolla, ed., *Fontana Economic History of Europe,* **III:** *The Industrial Revolution.* London: Collins/Fontana, 187–254.

Lindert, Peter H. & Williamson, Jeffrey G. (1983). "English Workers' Living Standards during the Industrial Revolution: A New Look," *The Economic History Review,* **XXXVI**, 1, 1–25.

Lindert, Peter H. & Williamson, Jeffrey G. (1985). "English Workers' Real Wages: Reply to Crafts," *Journal of Economic History,* **XLV**, 1, 145–153.

Lingelbach, W. E. (1914). "Historical Investigation and the Commercial History of the Napoleonic Era," *American Historical Review,* **XIX**, 2, 257–281.

Lipski, Alexander. (1959). "Some Aspects of Russia's Westernization during the Reign of Anna Ioannova, 1730–1740," *American Slavonic and East European Review,* **XVIII**, 1, 1–11.

Lis, C. & Soly, H. (1977). "Food Consumption in Antwerp between 1807 and 1859: A Contribution to the Standard of Living Debate," *Economic History Review,* 2nd ser., **XXX**, 3, 460–486.

Liss, Peggy K. (1983). *Atlantic Empires: The Network of Trade and Revolution, 1713–1826.* Baltimore, MD: Johns Hopkins University Press.

Little, Anthony. (1976). *Deceleration in the Eighteenth-Century British Economy.* London: Croom Helm.

Littlefield, Daniel C. (1981). "Plantations, Paternalism, and Profitability: Factors Affecting African Demography in the Old British Empire," *Journal of Southern History,* **XLVIII**, 2, 167–182.

Litwack, Leon F. (1961). *North of Slavery: The Negro in the Free States, 1790–1860.* Chicago, IL: University of Chicago Press.

Litwack, Leon F. (1987). "Trouble in Mind: The Bicentennial and the Afro-American Experience," *Journal of American History,* **LXXIV**, 2, 315–337.

Lloyd, Christopher. (1965). "Armed Forces and the Art of War, 1: Navies," in *New Cambridge Modern History,* **VIII:** A. Goodwin, ed., *The American and French Revolutions, 1763–93.* Cambridge, Engl.: Cambridge University Press, 174–190.

Lloyd, Peter C. (1971). *The Political Development of Yoruba Kingdoms in the Eighteenth and Nineteenth Centuries.* London: Royal Anthropological Institute of Great Britain and Ireland, Occasional Paper, No. 31.

Locke, Robert R. (1981). "French Industrialization: The Roehl Thesis Reconsidered," *Explorations in Economic History,* **XVIII**, 4, 415–433.

Lockridge, Kenneth A. (1973). "Social Change and the Meaning of the American Revolution," *Journal of Social History,* **VI**, 4, 403–449.

Logan, Rayford W. (1941). *The Diplomatic Relations of the United States with Haiti, 1776–1891.* Chapel Hill, NC: University of North Carolina Press.

Logan, Rayford W. (1968). *Haiti and the Dominican Republic.* New York: Oxford University Press.

Lokke, Carl Ludwig. (1928). "Jefferson and the Leclerc Expedition," *American Historical Review*, **XXXIII**, 2, 322–328.
Lokke, Carl Ludwig. (1930). "French Dreams of Colonial Empire under Directory and Consulate," *Journal of Modern History*, **II**, 2, 237–250.
Lokke, Carl Ludwig. (1932). *France and the Colonial Question: A Study of Contemporary French Opinion, 1763–1801.* New York: Columbia University Press.
Lombardi, John V. (1971). *The Decline and Abolition of Negro Slavery in Venezuela, 1820–1854.* Westport, CT: Greenwood.
Longworth, Philip. (1969). *The Cossacks.* New York: Holt, Rinehart & Winston.
Longworth, Philip. (1973). "The Last Great Cossack Peasant Rising," *Journal of European Studies*, **III**, 1, 1–35.
Longworth, Philip. (1974). "The Pugachev Revolt. The Last Great Cossack Peasant Rising," in H. A. Landsberger, ed., *Rural Protest: Peasant Movements and Social Change.* London: Macmillan, 194–256.
Longworth, Philip. (1975a). "The Pretender Phenomenon in Eighteenth-Century Russia," *Past and Present*, No. 66, 61–83.
Longworth, Philip (1975b). "Peasant Leadership and the Pugachev Revolt," *Journal of Peasant Studies*, **II**, 2, 183–205.
Longworth, Philip. (1979). "Popular Protest in England and Russia: Some Comparisons and Suggestions," in A. G. Cross, ed., *Great Britain and Russia in the Eighteenth Century: Contrasts and Comparisons.* Newton, MA: Oriental Research Partners, 263–278.
Loschky, David J. (1973). "Studies of the Navigation Acts: New Economic Non-History?" *Economic History Review*, 2nd ser., **XXVI**, 4, 689–691.
Lotté, Sophie A. (1962). "A propos de l'article de George Rudé," *Critica storica*, **I**, 4, 387–391.
Lough, John. (1987). *France on the Eve of Revolution: British Travellers' Observations, 1763–1788.* Chicago, IL: Dorsey Press.
Lovejoy, Paul E. (1978). "Plantations in the Economy of the Sokoto Caliphate," *Journal of African History*, **XIX**, 3, 341–368.
Lovejoy, Paul E. (1979). "Indigenous African Slavery," in M. Craton, ed., *Roots and Branches: Current Directions in Slave Studies.* Toronto: Pergamon, 19–61.
Lovejoy, Paul E. (1982). "The Volume of the Atlantic Slave Trade: A Synthesis," *Journal of African History*, **XXIII**, 4, 473–501.
Lovejoy, Paul E. & Hogendorn, Jan S. (1979). "Slave Marketing in West Africa," in H. A. Gemery & J. S. Hogendorn, eds., *The Uncommon Market.* New York: Academic Press, 213–235.
Lowenthal, David. (1952). "Colonial Experiments in French Guiana, 1760–1800," *Hispanic American Historical Review*, **XXXII**, 1, 22–43.
Loy, Jane M. (1981). "Forgotten Comuneros: The 1781 Revolt in the Llanos of Casanare," *Hispanic American Historical Review*, **LXI**, 2, 235–257.
Lubin, Maurice A. (1968). "Les premiers rapports de la nation haïtienne avec l'étranger," *Journal of Interamerican Studies*, **X**, 2, 277–305.
Lucas, Colin. (1973). "Nobles, Bourgeois and the Origins of the French Revolution," *Past and Present*, No. 60, Aug., 84–126.
Lucas, Colin. (1979). "Violence thermidorienne et société traditionnelle," *Cahiers d'histoire*, **XXXIV**, 4, 3–43.
Ludden, David. (1985). *Peasant History in South India.* Princeton, NJ: Princeton University Press.
Lundahl, Mats. (1984). "Defense and Distribution: Agricultural Policy in Haiti During the Reign of Jean-Jacques Dessalines, 1804–1806," *Scandinavian Economic History Review*, **XXXII**, 2, 77–103.
Lutfalla, Michel. (1966). "Saint-Just, analyste de l'inflation révolutionnaire," *Revue d'histoire économique et sociale*, **XLIV**, 2, 242–255.
Lüthy, Herbert. (1960). "Necker et la Compagnie des Indes," *Annales E.S.C.*, **XV**, 5, 852–881.

Lüthy, Herbert. (1961). *La banque protestante en France de la Révocation de l'Edit de Nantes à la Révolution,* **II:** *De la banque aux finances (1730–1794).* Paris: S.E.V.P.E.N.

Luz, Nicia Vitela. (1960). "Inquietações revolucionarias no sul: conjuração mineira," in S. Buarque de Holanda, dir., *Historia Geral da Civilização Brasieira,* Tomo I, 2° Vol. São Paulo: Difusão Européia do Livro, 394–405.

Lyashchenko, Peter I. (1970). *History of the National Economy of Russia to the 1917 Revolution.* New York: Octagon.

Lynch, John. (1969). "British Policy and Spanish America, 1783–1808," *Journal of Latin American Studies,* **I,** 1, 1–30.

Lynch, John. (1973). *The Spanish American Revolutions, 1808–1826.* New York: W. W. Norton.

Lynch, John. (1985). "The Origins of Spanish American Independence," in *Cambridge History of Latin America,* **III.** L. Bethell, ed. *From Independence to c. 1870.* Cambridge, Engl.: Cambridge University Press, 3–50.

Lynd, Staughton. (1961). "Who Shall Rule at Home? Dutchess County, New York, in the American Revolution," *William and Mary Quarterly,* 3d ser., **XVIII,** 3, 330–359.

Lynd, Staughton. (1967). *Class Conflict, Slavery, and the United States Constitution: Ten Essays.* Indianapolis, IN: Bobbs-Merrill.

McAlister, L. N. (1963). "Social Structure and Social Change in New Spain," *Hispanic American Historical Review,* **XLIII,** 3, 349–379.

McCallum, John. (1980). *Unequal Beginnings: Agriculture and Economic Development in Quebec and Ontario until 1870.* Toronto: University of Toronto Press.

McCary, B. D. (1928). *The Causes of the French Intervention in the American Revolution.* Toulouse: Edward Privat.

McClelland, Peter D. (1969). "The Cost to America of British Imperial Policy," *American Economic Review,* **LIX,** 2, Papers & Proceedings, 370–381.

McClelland, Peter D. (1970). "On Navigating the Navigation Acts with Peter McClelland: Reply," *American Economic Review,* **LX,** 5, 956–958.

McClelland, Peter D. (1973). "The New Economic History and the Burdens of the Navigation Acts: A Comment," *Economic History Review,* 2nd ser., **XXVI,** 4, 679–686.

McCloskey, Donald N. (1972). "The Enclosure of Open Fields: Preface to a Study of Its Impact on the Efficiency of English Agriculture in the Eighteenth Century," *Journal of Economic History,* **XXXII,** 1, 15–35.

McCloskey, Donald N. (1981). "The Industrial Revolution, 1780–1860: A Survey," in R. Floud & D. N. McCloskey, eds., *The Economic History of Britain Since 1700,* **I:** *1700–1860.* Cambridge, Engl.: Cambridge University Press, 103–127.

McCloy, Shelby T. (1952). *French Inventions of the Eighteenth Century.* Lexington, KY: University of Kentucky Press.

McCoy, Drew R. (1974). "Republicanism and American Foreign Policy: James Madison and the Political Economy of Commercial Discrimination, 1789–1794." *William and Mary Quarterly,* 3rd ser., **XXXI,** 4, 633–646.

McCoy, Drew R. (1980). *The Elusive Republic: Political Economy in Jeffersonian America.* Chapel Hill, NC: University of North Carolina Press.

McCulloch, J. R. (1827). "Rise, Progress, Present State, and Prospects of the Cotton Manufacture," *Edinburgh Review,* **XLVI,** No. 91, 1–39.

McDonald, Forrest. (1960). "Rebuttal," *William and Mary Quarterly,* 3rd ser., **XVII,** 1, 102–110.

Macdonald, Stuart. (1980). "Agricultural Response to a Changing Market during the Napoleonic Wars," *Economic History Review,* 2nd ser., **XXXIII,** 1, 59–71.

McDowell, R. B. (1979). *Ireland in the Age of Imperialism and Revolution, 1760–1801.* Oxford: Clarendon Press.

Macedo, Jorge de. (1954). Portugal e a economia 'pombalina': temas e hipóteses," *Revista de Historia,* **IX,** 81–99.

McEvedy, Colin. (1972). *The Penguin Atlas of Modern History (to 1815).* London: Penguin.

McGowan, Bruce. (1981a). *Economic Life in Ottoman Europe.* Cambridge, Engl.: Cambridge University Press.

McGowan, Bruce. (1981b). "The Study of Land and Agriculture in the Ottoman Provinces Within the Context of an Expanding World Economy in the 17th and 18th Centuries," *International Journal of Turkish Studies,* **II,** 1, 57–63.

McGuire, Robert A. & Ohsfeldt, Robert L. (1984). "Economic Interests and the American Constitution: A Qualitative Rehabilitation of Charles A. Beard," *Journal of Economic History,* **XLIV,** 2, 509–519.

Mackay, D. L. (1974). "Direction and Purpose in British Imperial Policy, 1793–1801," *Historical Journal,* **XVII,** 3, 487–501.

McKeown, Thomas. (1976). *The Modern Rise of Population.* New York: Academic Press.

McKeown, Thomas C. & Brown, R. G. (1969). "Medical Evidence Related to English Population Changes in the Eighteenth Century," in M. Drake, ed., *Population in Industrialization.* London: Methuen, 40–72. (Originally published in *Population Studies,* 1955.)

McKeown, T., Brown, R. G. & Record, R. G. (1972). "An Interpretation of the Modern Rise of Population in Europe," *Population Studies,* **XXVI,** Part 3, 345–382.

McKeown, T. & Record, R. G. (1962). "Reasons for the Decline of Mortality in England and Wales During the Nineteenth Century," *Population Studies,* **XVI,** Part 2, 94–122.

Mackesy, Piers. (1964). *The War for America, 1775–1783.* Cambridge, MA: Harvard University Press.

Mackrell, J. Q. C. (1973). *The Attack on 'Feudalism' in Eighteenth-Century France.* London: Routledge & Kegan Paul.

Macmillan, David S. (1970). "The Scottish–Russian Trade: Its Development, Fluctuations, and Difficulties, 1750–1796," *Canadian–American Slavic Studies,* **IV,** 3, 426–442.

Macmillan, David S. (1973). "Paul's 'Retributive Measures' of 1800 Against Britain: The Final Turning-Point in British Commercial Attitudes towards Russia," *Canandian-American Slavic Studies,* **VII,** 1, 68–77.

Macmillan, David S. (1979). "Problems in the Scottish Trade with Russia in the Eighteenth Century: A Study in Mercantile Frustration," in A. G. Cross, ed., *Great Britain and Russia in the Eighteenth Century: Contrasts and Comparisons.* Newton, MA: Oriental Research Partners, 164–180.

McNeill, William H. (1964). *Europe's Steppe Frontier, 1500–1800.* Chicago, IL: University of Chicago Press.

McNeill, William H. (1976). *Plagues and Peoples.* Garden City, NY: Anchor Press.

McNeill, William H. (1982). *The Pursuit of Power.* Chicago, IL: University of Chicago Press.

McNickle, D'Arcy (1957). "Indian and European: Indian–White Relations from Discovery to 1887," *Annals of the A.A.P.S.S.,* **CCCXI,** May, 1–11.

McPhee, Allan. (1926). *The Economic Revolution in British West Africa.* London: Geo. Routledge & Sons.

Madariaga, Isabel de. (1962). *Britain, Russia, and the Armed Neutrality of 1780.* New Haven, CT: Yale University Press.

Madariaga, Isabel de. (1974). "Catherine II and the Serfs: A Reconsideration of Some Problems," *Slavonic and East European Review,* **LII,** No. 126, 34–62.

Madariaga, Salvador de. (1948). *The Fall of the Spanish American Empire.* New York: Macmillan.

Mahan, Capt. Alfred T. (1893). *The Influence of Sea Power upon the French Revolution and Empire, 1793–1812,* 2 vols. London: Sampson Low, Marston.

Maier, Pauline. (1971). "Revolutionary Violence and the Relevance of History," *Journal of Interdisciplinary History,* **II,** 1, 119–136.

Maier, Pauline. (1972). *From Resistance to Revolution: Colonial Radicals and the Development of American Opposition to Great Britain, 1765–1776.* New York: Alfred A. Knopf.

Main, Gloria L. (1983). "The Standard of Living in Colonial Massachusetts," *Journal of Economic History,* **XLIII,** 1, 101–108.

Main, Jackson Turner. (1960). "Charles A. Beard and the Constitution: A Critical Review of Forrest McDonald's *We the People,*" *William and Mary Quarterly,* 3rd ser., **XVIII,** 1, 86–102.

Main, Jackson Turner. (1961). *The Antifederalists: Critics of the Constitution, 1781–1788.* Chapel Hill, NC: University of North Carolina Press.

Main, Jackson Turner. (1965). *The Social Structure of Revolutionary America.* Princeton, NJ: Princeton University Press.

Manchester, Alan K. (1931). "The Rise of the Brazilian Aristocracy," *Hispanic American Historical Review,* **XI,** 2, 145–168.

Manchester, Alan K. (1933). *British Preëminence in Brazil: Its Rise and Decline.* Chapel Hill, NC: University of North Carolina Press.

Manchester, Alan K. (1957). "The Recognition of Brazilian Independence," *Hispanic American Historical Review,* **XXXI,** 1, 80–96.

Manfred, Alfred Z. (1961). *La Grande Révolution française du XVIIIe siècle.* Moscow: Ed. en langues étrangères.

Mann, Julia de Lacy. (1958). "The Textile Industry: Machinery for Cotton, Flax, Wool, 1760–1850," in C. Singer *et al., A History of Technology,* **IV:** *The Industrial Revolution, c. 1750 to c. 1850.* Oxford: Clarendon Press, 277–307.

Manning, Patrick. (1969). "Slaves, Palm-Oil, and Political Power on the West African Coast," *African Historical Studies,* **II,** 2, 279–288.

Manning, Patrick. (1979). "The Slave Trade in the Bight of Benin, 1640–1890," in H. A. Gemery & J. S. Hogendorn, eds., *The Uncommon Market.* New York: Academic Press, 107–141.

Manning, Patrick. (1981). "The Enslavement of Africans: A Demographic Model," *Canadian Journal of African Studies,* **XV,** 3, 499–526.

Manning, Patrick. (1982). *Slavery, Colonialism and Economic Growth in Dahomey, 1640–1960.* Cambridge, Engl.: Cambridge University Press.

Mansuy, Andie. (1974). "L'impérialisme britannique et les relations coloniales entre le Portugal et le Brésil: un rapport de l'Amiral Campbell au Foreign Office (14 août 1804)," *Cahiers des Amériques Latines,* Nos. 9/10, 131–191.

Mantoux, P. (1928). *The Industrial Revolution in the Eighteenth Century,* 2nd rev. ed. London: Jonathan Cape.

Mantran, Robert. (1959). "L'évolution des relations entre la Tunisie et l'empire ottoman du XVIe du XIXe siècle," *Cahiers de Tunisie,* **VII,** 2ᵉ–3ᵉ trimestres, Nos. 26/27, 319–333.

Mantran, Robert. (1962). *Istanbul dans la seconde moitié du XVIIe siècle,* Bibliothèque Archéologique et Historique de l'Institut Français d'Archéologie d'Istanbul. Paris: Lib. A. Maisonneuve.

Mantran, Robert. (1984). *L'empire ottoman du XVIe au XVIIIe siècle. Administration, économie, société.* London: Variorum Reprints.

Manuel, Frank E. (1938). "The Luddite Movement in France," *Journal of Modern History,* **X,** 2, 180–211.

Marczewski, Jean. (1961a). "Y a-t-il eu un "take off" en France?," *Cahiers de l'I.S.E.A.,* Suppl. au No. 111, (Série A-D, No. 1), 69–94.

Marczewski, Jean. (1961b). "Some Aspects of the Economic Growth of France, 1660–1958," *Economic Development and Cultural Change,* **IX,** 2, 369–386.

Marczewski, Jean. (1963). "The Take-Off Hypothesis and French Experience," in W. W. Rostow, ed., *The Economics of Take-Off into Sustained Growth.* London: Macmillan, 119–138.

Marczewski, Jean. (1965). "Le produit physique de l'économie française de 1789 à 1913 (comparaison avec l'Angleterre)," *Cahiers de l'I.S.E.A.,* AF (4), No. 163, vii-cliv.

Mardin, Şerif. (1969). "Power, Civil Society and Culture in the Ottoman Empire," *Comparative Studies in Society and History,* **XI,** 3, 258–281.

Margadant, Ted W. (1983). "Local Elites and the Revolutionary Reconstruction of the French State," paper delivered at Fourth International Conference of Europeanists, Washington, DC, Oct. 13–15, mimeo.

Markov, Walter. (1960). "Les 'Jacquesroutins'," *Annales historique de la Révolution française,* **XXXII,** avr.–juin, 163–182.

Markovitch, Tihomir J. (1965, 1966a–c). "L'industrie francaise de 1789 à 1964," *Cahiers de l'I.S.E.A.,* AF, 4, No. 163, juil. (1965); AF, 5, No. 171, mars (1966a); AF, 6, No. 174, juin (1966b); AF, 7, No. 179, nov. (1966c).

Markovitch, Tihomir J. (1968). "L'industrie française au XVIIIe siècle: L'industrie lainiere à la fin du règne de Louis XIV et sous la Régence," *Economies et sociétés,* **II,** 8, 1517–1697.

Markovitch, Timohir J. (1974). "La révolution industrielle: le cas de la France," *Revue d'histoire économique et sociale,* **LII,** 1, 115–125.

Markovitch, Timohir J. (1976a). "La croissance industrielle sous l'Ancien Régime," *Annales E.S.C.,* **XXXI,** 3, 644–655.

Markovitch, Tihomir J. (1976b). *Histoire des industries françaises, I: Les industries lainières de Colbert à la Révolution,* Travaux de Droit, d'Economie, de Sociologie et de Sciences Politiques, No. 104. Genève: Lib. Droz.

Marshall, J. D. (1968). *The Old Poor Law, 1795–1834.* London: Macmillan.

Marshall, Peter J. (1962). "Radicals, Conservatives, and the American Revolution," *Past and Present,* No. 23, 44–56.

Marshall, Peter J. (1964a). "The First and Second British Empires: A Question of Demarcation," *History,* **XLIX,** No. 165, 13–23.

Marshall, Peter J. (1964b). "The British Empire and the American Revolution," *Huntington Library Quarterly.* **XXVII,** 2, 135–145.

Marshall, Peter, J., ed. (1968). *Problems of Empire: Britain and India, 1757–1813.* London: George Allen & Unwin.

Marshall, Peter J. (1975a). "Economic and Political Expansion: The Case of Oudh," *Modern Asian Studies,* **IX,** 4, 465–482.

Marshall, Peter J. (1975b). "British Expansion in India in the Eighteenth Century: A Historical Revision," *History,* **LX,** No. 198, 28–43.

Marshall, Peter J. (1976). *East Indian Failures: The British in Bengal in Eighteenth Century.* Oxford: Clarendon Press.

Marshall, Peter J. (1980). "Western Arms in Maritime Asia in the Early Phases of Expansion," *Modern Asian Studies,* **XIV,** 1, 13–28.

Martin, Bradford G. (1976). *Muslim Brotherhoods in Nineteenth-Century Africa.* Cambridge, Engl.: Cambridge University Press.

Martin, Gaston. (1930). "Capital et travail à Nantes au cours du XVIIIe siècles," *Revue d'histoire économique et social,* **XVIII,** 1, 52–85.

Martin, Gaston. (1931). *Nantes au XVIIIe siècle: L'ère des négriers (1714–1774).* Paris: Lib. Felix Alcan.

Martin, Gaston. (1948). *Histoire de l'esclavage dans les colonies françaises.* Paris: Presses Universitaires de France.

Martin, Phyllis M. (1972). *The External Trade of the Loango Coast, 1576–1870: The Effects of Changing Commercial Relations on the Vili Kingdom of Loango.* Oxford: Clarendon Press.

Marwick, W. H. (1924). "The Cotton Industry and the Industrial Revolution in Scotland," *Scottish Historical Review,* **XXI,** 207–218.

Marx, Karl (1967). *Capital,* 3 vol. New York: International Publishers. (Originally published 1894).

Marzahl, Peter. (1974). "Creoles and Government: The Cabildo of Popayán," *Hispanic American Historical Review,* **LIV,** 4, 636–656.

Mason, Michael. (1969). "Population Density and 'Slave Raiding'—The Case of the Middle Belt of Nigeria," *Journal of African History,* **X,** 4, 551–564.

Mason, Michael. (1971). "Population Density and 'Slave Raiding'—A Reply," *Journal of African History,* **XII,** 2, 324–327.

Masson, Paul. (1911). *Histoire du commerce français dans le Levant au XVIIIe siècle.* Paris: Lib. Hachette.

Mathias, Peter. (1969). *The First Industrial Nation*. London: Methuen.

Mathias, Peter. (1973). "Capital, Credit and Enterprise in the Industrial Revolution," *Journal of European Economic History*, **II**, 1, 121–143.

Mathias, Peter. (1979a). "British Industrialization: "Unique or Not?," in *The Transformation of England*. London: Methuen, 3–20. (Originally published in *Annales E.S.C.*, 1972.)

Mathias, Peter. (1979b). "Skills and the Diffusion of Innovations from Britain in the Eighteenth Century," in *The Transformation of England*. London: Methuen, 21–44. (Originally published in *Transactions of the Royal Historical Society*, 1975.)

Mathias, Peter. (1979c). "Who Unbound Prometheus? Science and Technical Change, 1600–1800," in *The Transformation of England*. London: Methuen, 45–71. (Originally published 1972.)

Mathias, Peter. (1979d). "The Social Structure in the Eighteenth Century: A Calculation by Joseph Massie," in *The Transformation of England*. London: Methuen, 171–189. (Originally published 1957.)

Mathias, Peter. (1986). "British Trade and Industry, 1786–1986," in S. Foreman, ed., *Striking a Balance . . . The Board of Trade, 1786–1986*, London: HMSO, 1–21.

Mathias, Peter & O'Brien, Patrick. (1976). "Taxation in Britain and France, 1715–1810," *Journal of European Economic History*, **V**, 3, 601–650.

Mathiez, Albert. (1923–1924). *La Révolution française*. Paris: Armand Colin.

Mathiez, Albert. (1931). "Les corporations ont-elles été supprimés en principe dans la nuit du 4 août 1989?" *Annales historiques de la Révolution française*, **VIII**, No. 45, 252–257.

Matsui, Toru. (1968). "On the Nineteenth-Century Indian Economic History—A Review of a 'Reinterpretation,' " *Indian Economic and Social History Review*, **I**, 1, 17–33.

Matthewson, Timothy M. (1979). "George Washington's Policy Toward the Haitian Revolution," *Diplomatic History*, **III**, 3, 321–336.

Mattoso, Katia M. de Queiros. (1970). "Conjoncture et société au Brésil à la fin du XVIIIe siècle," *Cahiers des Amériques Latines*, Série "Sciences de l'Homme," No. 5, janv.–juin, 33–53.

Mauro, Frédéric. (1972). "A conjuntura atlântica e a Independência do Brasil," in C. G. Mota, org., *1822: Dimensões*, São Paulo: Ed. Perspectiva, 38–47.

Maxwell, Kenneth R. (1968). "Pombal and the Nationalization of the Luso-Brazilian Economy," *Hispanic American Historical Review*, **XLVIII**, 4, 608–631.

Maxwell, Kenneth R. (1973). *Conflicts and Conspiracies: Brazil and Portugal, 1750–1808*. Cambridge, Engl.: At the University Press.

Mayer, Margit & Fay, Margaret A. (1977). "The Formation of the American Nation-State," *Kapitalistate*, No. 6, Fall, 39–90.

Mazauric, Claude. (1965). "Vendée et chouannerie," *La Penseé*, n.s., No. 124, 54–85.

Mazauric, Claude. (1967). "Réflexions sur une nouvelle conception de la Révolution française," *Annales historiques de la Révolution française*, **XXXIX**, No. 189, 339–368.

Mazauric, Claude. (1969). "Bilan et perspectives de recherches: L'histoire du XVIIIe siècle et de la Révolution française," *Annales historiques de la Révolution française*, **XLI**, 4, No. 198, 667–685.

Mazauric, Claude. (1970). *Sur la Révolution française. Contributions à la révolution bourgeoise.* Paris: Ed. Sociales.

Mazauric, Claude. (1975). "Quelques voies nouvelles pour l'histoire politique de la Révolution française," *Annales historiques de la Révolution française*, **XLVII**, No. 219, 134–173.

Mazauric, Claude. (1985). "Autopsie d'un échec: La résistance à l'anti-Révolution et la défaite de la Contre-Révolution," in F. Lebrun & R. Dupuy, eds., *Les résistances à la Révolution*. Paris: Imago, 237–244.

M'Bokolo, Elikia. (1980). *De l'abolition de la traite à la conquête continentale, 1800–1870*. Paris: Centre d'études africaines, mimeo.

Meillassoux, Claude. (1971a). "Introduction," in *The Development of Indigenous Trade and Markets in West Africa*. London: Oxford University Press, 3–86.

Meillassoux, Claude. (1971b). "Le commerce pré-colonial et le développement de l'esclavage à Gūbu du Sahel (Mali)," in C. Meillassoux, ed., *The Development of Indigenous Trade and Markets in West Africa.* London: Oxford University Press, 182–195.

Meinig, D. W. (1986). *The Shaping of America: A Geographical Perspective on 500 Years of History, I: Atlantic America, 1492–1800.* New Haven, CT: Yale University Press.

Mendels, Franklin. (1972). "Proto-industrialization: The First Phase of the Industrialization Process," *Journal of Economic History.* **XXXII**, 1, 241–261.

Metcalf, George. (1987). "A Microcosm of Why Africans Sold Slaves: Akan Consumption Patterns in the 1770s," *Journal of African History,* **XXVIII**, 3, 377–394.

Metcalfe, G. E. (1962). *MacLean of the Gold Coast: The Life and Times of George MacLean, 1801–1847.* London: Oxford University Press.

Mettas, Jean. (1975). "La traite portugaise en Haute Guinée, 1758–1797: Problèmes et méthodes," *Journal of African History,* **XVI**, 3, 343–363.

Meuvret, Jean. (1971a). "Les oscillations das prix des céréales aux XVIIe et XVIIIe siècles en Angleterre et dans les pays du bassin parisien," in *Etudes d'histoire économique.* Paris: Lib. Armand Colin, 113–124. (Originally published in *Revue d'histoire moderne et contemporaine,* 1969.)

Meuvret, Jean. (1971b). "L'agriculture en Europe aux XVIIe et XVIIIe siècles," in *Etudes d'histoire économique.* Paris: Lib. Armand Colin, 163–181. (Originally published in *Relazioni del X Congresso Internazionale di Scienze Storiche,* 1955.)

Meuvret, Jean. (1971c). "Domaines ou ensembles territoriaux?" in *Etudes d'histoire économique.* Paris: Lib. Armand Colin, 183–191. (Originally published in *Première conférence internationale d'histoire économique,* 1960.)

Meuvret, Jean. (1971d). "La vaine pâture et le progrès agronomique avant la Révolution," in *Etudes d'histoire économique.* Paris: Lib. Armand Colin, 193–196. (Originally published in *Revue d'histoire moderne et contemporaine,* 1969.)

Meuvret, Jean. (1971e). "Les crises de subsistance et la démographie de la France d'Ancien Régime," in *Etudes d'histoire économique.* Paris: Lib. Armand Colin, 271–278. (Originally published in *Population,* 1946.)

Meyer, Jean. (1960). "Le commerce négrier nantais (1774–1792)," *Annales E.S.C.,* **XV**, 1, 120–129.

Meyer, Jean. (1966). *La noblesse bretonne au XVIIIe siècle,* 2 vols. Paris: S.E.V.P.E.N.

Meyer, Jean. (1969). *L'armement nantais dans la deuxième moitié du XVIIIe siècle.* Paris: S.E.V.P.E.N.

Meyer, Jean. (1979a). "La guerre d'indépendence américaine et les problèmes navals européens. Rapports de force et influence sur le conflit," in *la Révolution américaine et l'Europe,* Colloques Internationaux du CNRS, No. 577. Paris: Ed. du CNRS, 187–217.

Meyer, Jean. (1979b). "Les difficultés de commerce franco-américain vues de Nantes (1776–1790)," *French Historical Studies,* **XI**, 2, 159–183.

Meyers, Allan. (1971). "Slavery in the Hausa-Fulani Emirates," in D. McCall & W. Bennett, eds., *Aspects of West African Islam,* Boston University Papers on Africa, Vol. V. Boston, MA: Boston University African Studies Center, 173–184.

Michalet, Charles-Albert. (1968). "Economie et politique chez Saint-Just. L'exemple de l'inflation," *Annales historiques de la Révolution française,* **LV**, No. 191, 60–110.

Michoff, Nicolas V. (1970). *Contribution à l'histoire du commerce de la Turquie et de la Bulgarie, VI: Auteurs français, allemands et anglais.* Sofia: Bulg. Akad. na nauike.

Middlekauff, Robert, ed. (1964). *Bacon's Rebellion,* Berkeley Series in American History. Chicago, IL: Rand McNally.

Miller, Alexandre. (1926). *Essai sur l'histoire des institutions agraires de la Russie centrale du XVIe au XVIIIe siècles.* Paris: Marcel Giard.

Milward, Alan S. & Saul, S.B. (1973). *The Economic Development of Continental Europe, 1780–1870.* London: George Allen & Unwin.

Minchinton, Walter, E. (1969). "Introduction," in Walter E. Minchinton, ed., *The Growth of English Overseas Trade in the Seventeenth and Eighteenth Centuries.* London: Methuen, 1–63.

Minchinton, Walter, E. (1973). "Patterns of Demand, 1750–1914," in C.M. Cipolla, ed., *Fontana Economic History of Europe,* **III:** *The Industrial Revolution.* London: Collins/Fontana, 77–186.

Minchinton, Walter, E. (1979). "The Trangular Trade Revisted," in H.A. Gemery & J.S. Hogendorn, eds., *The Uncommon Market.* New York: Academic Press, 331–352.

Mingay, G. É. (1956). "The Agricultural Depression, 1730–1750," *Economic History Review,* 2nd ser., **VIII,** 3, 323–338.

Mingay, G. E. (1960). "The Large Estate in Eighteenth-Century England," in *First International Conference of Economic History,* Stockholm. Paris & La Haye: Mouton, 367–383.

Mingay, G. E. (1963). "The 'Agricultural Revolution' in English History: A Reconsideration," *Agricultural History* **XXXVII,** 3, 123–133.

Mingay, G. E. (1969). "Dr. Kerridge's 'Agricultural Revolution': A Comment," *Agricultural History,* **XLIII,** 4, 477–481.

Mingay, G. E., ed. (1977). *The Agricultural Revolution: Changes in Agriculture, 1650–1880.* London: Adam & Charles Black.

Misra, B. B. (1959). *The Central Administration at the East India Company, 1773–1834.* Manchester, Engl.: Manchester University Press.

Mitchell, Harvey. (1968). "The Vendée and Counter-Revolution: A Review Essay," *French Historical Studies,* **V,** 4, 405–429.

Mitchell, Harvey. (1974). "Resistance to the Revolution in Western France," *Past and Present,* No. 63, 94–131.

Mitchison, Rosalind. (1959). "The Old Board of Agriculture (1793–1822)," *English Historical Review,* **LXXIV,** No. 290, 41–69.

Mokyr, Joel. (1974). "The Industrial Revolution in the Low Countries in the First Half of the Nineteenth Century: A Comparative Case Study," *Journal of Economic History,* **XXXIV,** 2, 365–391.

Mokyr, Joel. (1977). "Demand vs. Supply in the Industrial Revolution," *Journal of Economic History,* **XXXVII,** 4, 981–1008.

Mokyr, Joel. (1984). "Demand versus Supply in the Industrial Revolution: A Reply," *Journal of Economic History,* **XLIV,** 3, 806–809.

Mokyr, Joel & Savin, N. Eugene. (1976). "Stagflation in Historical Perspective: The Napoleonic Wars Revisited," in P. Uselding, ed., *Research in Economic History,* Vol. I. Greenwich, CT: Greenwood Press, 198–259.

Montgolfier, Bernard de. (1980). *Il y a cent cinquante ans . . . Juillet 1830.* Paris: Musée Carnavalet.

Moore, Barrington, Jr. (1966). *Social Origins of Dictatorship and Democracy.* Boston: Beacon Press.

Moosvi, Shireen. (1973). "Production, Consumption, and Population in Akbar's Time," *Indian Economic and Social History Review,* **X,** 2, 181–195.

Moosvi, Shireen. (1977). "Note on Professor Alan Heston's 'The Standard of Living in Akbar's Time: A Comment,' " *Indian Economic and Social History Reveiw,* **XIV,** 3, 359–374.

Morgan, Edmund S. (1967). "The Puritan Ethic and the American Revolution," *William and Mary Quarterly,* 3rd ser., **XXIV,** 1, 3–43.

Morgan, Edmund S. (1973). "Conflict and Consensus in the American Revolution," in S. G. Kurtz & J. H. Hutson, eds., *Essays on the American Revolution.* Chapel Hill, NC: University of North Carolina Press, 289–309.

Morgan, Edmund S. (1977). *The Birth of the Republic, 1763–1789,* rev. ed. Chicago, IL: University of Chicago Press.

Morgan, Edmund S. & Helen M. (1953). *The Stamp Act Crisis: Prelude to Revolution.* Chapel Hill, NC: University of North Carolina Press.

Morgan, Valerie. (1971). "Agricultural Wage Rates in Late Eighteenth-Century Scotland," *Economic History Review*, 2nd ser., **XXIV**, 2, 181–201.

Morin, Victor. (1949). "La 'république canadienne' de 1838," *Revue d'histoire de l'Amérique française*, **II**, 4, 483–512.

Morineau, Michel. (1965). "Le balance du commerce franco-néerlandais et le resserrement économique des Provinces-Unies au XVIIIe siècle," *Economisch–Historisch Jaarboek*, **XXX**, 170–233.

Morineau, Michel. (1969a). "Histoire sans frontière: Prix et 'révolution agricole,'" *Annales E.S.C.*, **XXIV**, 2, 403–423.

Morineau, Michel. (1969b). "Réflexions tardives et conclusions prospectives," in J. Goy & E. LeRoy Ladurie, eds., *Les fluctuations de la dîme*. Paris & La Haye: Mouton, 320–333.

Morineau, Michel. (1971). *Les faux-semblants d'un démarrage économique: agriculture et démographie en France au XVIIIe siècle*. Paris: Lib. Armand Colin.

Morineau, Michel. (1972a). "L'ankylose de l'économie méditerranéenne au XVIIIe et au début de XIXe siècles: le rôle de l'agriculture," in *Cahiers de la Méditerranée*, sér. spéc., No. 1, journées d'études des 12 et 13 mai, Nice, 95–105.

Morineau, Michel. (1972b). "Budgets populaires en France au XVIIIe siècle," *Revue d'histoire économique et sociale*, **L**, 2, 203–237; **L**, 4, 449–481.

Morineau, Michel. (1974a). "A la Halle de Charleville: Fourniture et prix des grains ou les mécanismes du marché (1647–1821)," in *Actes du 95e Congrès National des Sociétés Savantes, Reims, 1970, Section d'histoire moderne et contemporaine*. Paris: Bibliothèque Nationale, II, 159–222.

Morineau, Michel. (1974b). "Révolution agricole, Révolution alimentaire, Révolution démographique," *Annales de démographie historique*, 335–371.

Morineau, Michel. (1976a). "Le rose et le vert," *Annales E.S.C.*, **XXXI**, 2, 467–510.

Morineau, Michel. (1976b). "Les problèmes de la modernisation des structures économiques et sociales dans une économie multisectorielle," in *Fifth International Conference of Economic History*, Leningrad, 1970. The Hague: Mouton, VII, 42–72.

Morineau, Michel. (1978). "Trois contributions au colloque de Göttingen," in E. Hinrichs *et al.*, eds., *Von Ancien Regime zur Französischen Revolution*. Göttingen: Vandenhoeck & Ruprecht, 374–419.

Morineau, Michel. (1980a). "La dîme et l'enjeu," *Annales historiques de la Révolution française*, **LII**, 2, No. 240, 161–180.

Morineau, Michel. (1980b). "Budgets de l'Etat et gestion des finances royales en France au dix-huitième siècle," *Revue historique*, **CCLXIV**, 2, No. 536, 289–336.

Morineau, Michel. (1985). "Raison, Révolution et Contre-Révolution," in F. Lebrun & R. Dupuy, eds., *Les résistances à la Révolution*. Paris: Imago, 284–291.

Morris, Morris David. (1968). "Towards a Re-interpretation of the 19th Century Indian Economic History," *Indian Economic and Social History Review*, **V.**, 1, 1–16.

Morris, Morris David & Stein, Burton. (1961). "The Economic History of India: A Bibliographic Essay," *Journal of Economic History*, **XXI**, 2, 179–207.

Morris, Richard B. (1946). *Government and Labor in Early America*. New York: Columbia University Press.

Morris, R. J. (1979). *Class and Class Consciousness in the Industrial Revolution, 1780–1850*. London: Macmillan.

Mota, Carlos Guilherme. (1967). *Idéia de revolução no Brasil no final do século XVIII*. São Paulo: Universidade de São Paulo.

Mota, Carlos Guilherme. (1972). "Europeus no Brasil à Epoca da Independência: Um Estudo," in C.G. Mota, ed., *1822: Dimensões*. São Paulo: Ed. Perspectiva, 56–73.

Mota, Carlos Guilherme. (1973). "Efectos dos movimentos sociais brasileiros no política metropolitana: a 'revolução' nordestina de 1817," *Luso-Brazilian Review*, **X**, 1, 76–85.

Moreaux, Philippe. (1968). "Truck-System et revendications sociales dans la sidérurgie luxembourgeoise du XVIIIe siècle," *Mélanges offerts à G. Jacquemyns*. Bruxelles: Université Libre de Bruxelles, 527–530.

Mourlot, F. (1911). "La Crise de l'industrie drapière à Sedan, en 1788," *Revue historique ardennaise*, **XVIII**, mai–juin, 104–106.

Mouser, Bruce L. (1973). "Trade, Coasters, and Conflict in the Rio Pongo from 1790–1808," *Journal of African History*, **XIV**, 1, 45–64.

Mouyabi, Jean. (1976). "La Piste des Esclaves et des Portages," Mémoire de D.E.A., Dép. d'Histoire, Université de Brazzaville.

Mouyabi, Jean. (1979). "Essai sur le commerce précolonial et protocolonial au Congo méridional (XVIIe–début XXe siècle)," Thèse 3e cycle, E.H.E.S.S., Paris.

Mui & Mui, Lorna H. (1963). "The Commutation Act and the Tea Trade in Britain, 1784–1793," *Economic History Review*, 2nd ser., **XVI**, 2, 234–253.

Mui & Mui, Lorna H. (1975). " 'Trends in Eighteenth Century Smuggling' Reconsidered," *Economic History Review*, 2nd ser., **XXVIII**, 1, 28–43.

Mukherjee, Nolmani. (1962). *The Ryotwari System in Madras, 1792–1827*. Calcutta: Firma K. L. Mukhopadhyay.

Mukherjee, Nolmani & Frykenberg, Robert Eric. (1969). "The Ryotwari System and Social Organization in the Madras Presidency," in R.E. Frykenberg, ed., *Land Control and Social Structure in Indian History*. Madison, WI: University of Wisconsin Press, 217–226.

Mukherjee Ramkrishna. (1955). *The Rise and Fall of the East India Company*. Berlin: VEB Deutscher Verlag der Wissenschaften.

Mukherjee, Rudrangshu. (1982). "Trade and Empire in Awadh, 1765–1804," *Past and Present*, No. 94, 85–102.

Müller, Birgit. (1985). "Commodities as Currencies: The Integration of Overseas Trade into the Internal Trading Structure of the Igbo of South-East Nigeria," *Cahiers d'études africaines*, **XXV**, 1, No. 97, 57–77.

Mullet, Ch. F. (1946). "The Cattle Distemper in Mid-Eighteenth Century England," *Agricultural History*, **XX**, 3, 144–165.

Munger, Frank. (1981). "Contentious Gatherings in Lancashire, England, 1750–1830," in Louise A. Tilly & Charles Tilly, eds., *Class Conflict and Collective Action*. Beverly Hills, CA: Sage, 73–109.

Muñoz Oraá, Carlos E. (1960). "Pronóstico de la independencia de América, y un proyecto de Monarquías en 1781," *Revista de historia de América*, No. 50, 439–473.

Munro, J. Forbes. (1976). *Africa and the International Economy, 1800–1960*. London: J. M. Dent & Sons.

Murphy, James & Higonnet, Patrice. (1973). "Les députés de la noblesse aux Etats généraux de 1789," *Revue d'histoire moderne et contemporaine*, **XX**, 2, 230–247.

Murphy, Orville T. (1966). "DuPont de Nemours and the Anglo-French Commcerial Treaty of 1786," *Economic History Review*, 2nd ser., **XIX**, 3, 569–580.

Musson, A. E. (1972). Introduction," in A.E. Musson, ed., *Science, Technology and Economic Growth in the Eighteenth Century*. London: Methuen, 1–68.

Musson, A. E. (1976). "Industrial Motive Power in the United Kingdom, 1800–70," *Economic History Review*, 2nd ser., **XXIX**, 3, 415–439.

n.a. (1960). "Conference Report: The Origins of the Industrial Revolution," *Past and Present*, No. 17, 71–81.

Naff, Thomas. (1963). "Reform and the Conduct of Ottoman Diplomacy in the Reign of Selim III, 1789–1807," *Journal of the American Oriental Society*, **LXXXIII**, 3, 295–315.

Nairn, Tom. (1964). "The English Working Class," *New Left Review*, No. 24, 43–57.

Namier, Lewis B. (1930). *England in the Age of the American Revolution*. London: Macmillan.

Namier, Lewis B. (1957). *The Structure of Politics at the Accession of George III*, 2nd ed., London: Macmillan.

Naqui, H. K. (1968). *Urban Centres and Industries in Upper India, 1556–1803*. New York: Asia Publ. House.

Nash, Gary B. (1976a). "Social Change and the Growth of Prerevolutionary Urban Radicalism," in A. F. Young, ed., *The American Revolution: Explorations in the History of American Radicalism.* DeKalb, IL: Northern Illinois University Press, 3–36.

Nash, Gary B. (1976b). "Urban Wealth and Poverty in Pre-Revolutionary America," *Journal of Interdisciplinary History,* **VI,** 4, 545–584.

Nash, Gary B. (1979). *The Urban Crucible: Social Change, Political Consciousness, and the Origins of the American Revolution.* Cambridge, MA: Harvard University Press.

Nash, Gary B. (1984). "Social Development," in Jack P. Greene & J.R. Pole, eds., *Colonial British America: Essays in the New History of the Early Modern Era.* Baltimore, MD: Johns Hopkins University Press, 233–261.

Nash, Gary B. (1986). *Race, Class, and Politics: Essays on American Colonial Revolutionary Society.* Urbana, IL: University of Illinois Press.

Nash, R. C. (1985). "Irish Atlantic Trade in the Seventeenth and Eighteenth Centuries," *William and Mary Quarterly,* 3rd ser., **XLII,** 3, 329–356.

Nathan, James A., (1980). "The Heyday of the Balance of Power: Frederick the Great and the Decline of the Old Regime," *Naval War College Review,* **XXXIII,** 4, Seq. 280, 53–67.

Navarro García, Luis. (1975). *Hispanoamérica en el siglo XVIII.* Sevilla: Publ. de la Universidad de Sevilla.

Neale, R. S. (1966). "The Standard of Living, 1780–1844: A Regional and Class Study," *Economic History Review,* 2nd ser., **XIX,** 3, 590–606.

Neale, Walter, C. (1962). *Economic Change in Rural India: Land and Tenure and Reform, 1800–1955.* New Haven, CT: Yale University Press.

Neatby, Hilda. (1966). *Quebec: The Revolutionary Age, 1760–1791.* Toronto: McClelland & Stewart.

Nef, John U. (1943). "The Industrial Revolution Reconsidered," *Journal of Economic History,* **III,** 1, 1–31.

Nef, John U. (1954). "The Progress of Technology and the Growth of Large-Scale Industry in Great Britain, 1540–1640," in E.M. Carus-Wilson, ed., *Essays in Economic History,* Vol. I. London: Edward Arnold, 88–107. (Originally published in *Economic History Review,* 1934.)

Nef, John U. (1957). "'Coal Mining and Utilization," in C. Singer *et al., A History of Technology.* **III:** *From the Renaissance to the Industrial Revolution, c. 1500–c. 1750.* Oxford: Clarendon Press, 72–88.

Nef, John U. (1968). "Industrie: l. la civilisation industrielle," *Encyclopedia Universalis,* Vol. VIII. Paris: Encyclopedia Universalis France, 966–972.

Nelson, William H. (1961). *The American Tory.* Oxford: Clarendon Press.

Nelson, William H. (1965). "The Revolutionary Character of the American Revolution," *American Historical Review,* **LXX,** 4, 998–1014.

Nettels, Curtis P. (1952). "British Mercantilism and the Economic Development of the Thirteen Colonies," *Journal of Economic History,* **XII,** 2, 105–114.

Nettels, Curtis P. (1962). *The Emergence of a National Economy 1775–1815,* Vol. 11 of *The Economic History of the United States.* New York: Holt, Rinehart, & Winston.

Neumann, William L. (1947). "United States Aid to the Chilean Wars of Independence," *Hispanic American Historical Review,* **XXVII,** 2, 204–219.

Newbury, Colin W. (1961). *The Western Slave Coast and Its Rulers: European Trade and Administration Among the Yoruba and Adja-speaking peoples of South-Western Nigeria, Southern Dahomey and Togo.* Oxford: Clarendon Press.

Newbury, Colin, W. (1966). "North African and Western Sudan Trade in the Nineteenth Century: A Re-evaluation," *Journal of African History,* **VII,** 2, 233–246.

Newbury, Colin, W. (1969). "Trade and Authority in West Africa From 1850 to 1880," in L.H. Gann & P. Duignan, eds., *Colonialism in Africa,* **I:** *The History and Politics of Colonialism, 1870–1914.* Cambridge, Engl.: At the University Press, 66–99.

Newbury, Colin W. (1971). "Price and Profitability in Early 19th Century West African

Trade," in C. Meillassoux, ed., *The Development of Indigenous Trade and Markets in West Africa.* London: Oxford University Press, 91–106.

Newbury, Colin W. (1972). "Credit in Early Nineteenth Century West African Trade," *Journal of African History,* **XIII,** 1, 81–95.

Newman, K. (1983). "Anglo-Dutch Commercial Co-operation and the Russian Trade in the Eighteenth Century," in W. T. Wieringa *et al., The Interactions of Amsterdam and Antwerp with the Baltic Region, 1400–1800.* Leiden: Martinus Nijhoff, 95–104.

Nicholls, David. (1978). "Race, couleur et indépendance en Haïti (1804–1825)," *Revue d'histoire moderne et contemporaine,* **XXV,** 2, 177–212.

Nicholas, Maurice. (1967). "A propos du traité de Paris, 1763: Arpents de neige ou îles à sucre?" *Revue Historique de l'Armée,* **XXIII,** 3, 73–77.

Nightingale, Pamela. (1970). *Trade and Empire in Western India, 1784–1806.* Cambridge: Engl. At the University Press.

Nolde, Boris. (1952–1953). *La formation de l'empire Russe; études, notes et documents,* Collection historique de l'institut d'études slaves, XV, 2 vols. Paris: Institut d'Etudes Slaves.

Nolte, Hans–Heinrich. (1981). *Der Aufsteig Russlands zur europäischen Grossmacht.* Stuttgart: Ernst Klett.

Nolte, Hans-Heinrich. (1982). "The Position of Eastern Europe in the International System in Early Modern Times," *Review,* **IV,** 1, 25–84.

Nørregård, Georg. (1966). *Danish Settlements in West Africa, 1658–1850.* Boston, MA: Boston University Press.

North, Douglass C. (1960). "The United States Balance of Payments, 1790–1860," in National Bureau of Economic Research, *Trends in the American Economy in the Nineteenth Century: Studies in Income and Wealth,* Vol. XXIV of the Conference on Research in Income and Wealth. Princeton, NJ: Princeton University Press, 573–627.

North, Douglass C. (1965). "The Role of Transportation in the Economic Development of North America," in *Les grandes voies maritimes dans le monde, XVe–XIXe siècles.* Paris: S.E.V.P.E.N., 209–246.

North, Douglass C. (1966). *The Economic Growth of the United States, 1790–1860.* New York: W. W. Norton.

North, Douglass, C. (1968). "Sources of Productivity Changes in Ocean Shipping, 1600–1850," *Journal of Political Economy,* **LXXVI,** 5, 953–970.

North, Douglass C. (1974). *Growth and Welfare in the American Past: A New Economic History,* 2nd ed. Englewood Cliffs, NJ: Prentice-Hall.

North, Douglass C. (1985). "Transaction Costs in History," *Journal of European Economic History,* **XIV,** 3, 557–576.

Northrup, David. (1972). "The Growth of Trade Among the Igbo Before 1800," *Journal of African History,* **XIII,** 2, 217–236.

Northrup, David. (1976). "The Compatibility of the Slave and Palm Oil Trades in the Bight of Biafra," *Journal of African History,* **XVII,** 3, 353–364.

Northrup, David. (1978). *Trade Without Rulers: Pre-colonial Economic Development in South-Eastern Nigeria.* Oxford: Clarendon Press.

Novais, Fernando A. (1979). *Portugal e Brasil na Crise do Antigo Sistema Colonial (1777–1808).* São Paulo: Ed. Hucitec.

Nussbaum, Frederick L. (1925). "American Tobacco and French Politics, 1783–89," *Political Science Quarterly,* **XL,** 4, 497–516.

Nussbaum, Frederick L. (1933). "The Formation of the New East India Company of Calonne," *American Historical Review,* **XXXVII,** 3, 475–497.

O'Brien, Bickford. (1955). "Ivan Pososhkov: Russian Critic of Mercantilist Principles," *American Slavonic and East European Review,* **XIV,** 4, 503–511.

O'Brien, Patrick K. (1959). "British Incomes and Property in the Early Nineteenth Century," *Economic History Review,* 2nd ser., **XII,** 2, 255–267.

O'Brien, Patrick K. (1977). "Agriculture and Industrial Revolution," *Economic History Review,* 2nd ser., **XXX**, 1, 166–181.

O'Brien, Patrick K. (1983). "The Impact of the Revolutionary and Napoleonic Wars, 1793–1815, on the Long Run Growth of the British Economy," Princeton University, Davis Center Seminar, mimeo.

O'Brien, Patrick K. (1988). "The Political Economy of British Taxation: 1660 to 1815," *Economic History Review,* 2nd ser., **XLI**, 1, 1–32.

O'Brien, Patrick K. & Engerman, S. L. (1981). "Changes in Income and Its Distribution During the Industrial Revolution," in R. Floud & D. N. McCloskey, eds., *The Economic History of Britain Since 1700,* **I:** *1700–1860.* Cambridge, Engl.: Cambridge University Press, 164–181.

O'Brien, Patrick K. & Keyder, Caglar. (1978). *Economic Growth in Britain and France, 1780–1914.* London: George Allen & Unwin.

O'Brien, Patrick K. & Keyder, Caglar. (1979). "Les voies de passage vers la société industrielle en Grande-Bretagne et en France (1780–1914)," *Annales E. S. C.,* **XXXIV**, 6, 1284–1303.

Okoye, F. Nwabueze. (1980). "Chattel Slavery as the Nightmare of the American Revolutionaries," *William and Mary Quarterly,* 3rd ser., **XXXVII**, 1, 3–28.

Okyar, Osman. (1987). "A New Look at the Problem of Economic Growth in the Ottoman Empire," *Journal of European Economic History,* **XVI**, 1, 7–49.

Oliver, Roland & Atmore, Anthony. (1981). *The African Middle Ages, 1400–1800.* Cambridge, Engl.: Cambridge University Press.

Olivier, Pierre. (1936). *Les antécédents d'une révolution: Etudes sur le développement de la Société française de 1715 à 1789.* Paris: Lib. Marcel Rivière.

Oloruntimehin, B. Olatunji. (1971–1972). "The Impact of the Abolition Movement on the Social and Political Development of West Africa in the Nineteenth and Twentieth Centuries," *African Notes,* **VII**, 1, Third Term, 33–58.

Oloruntimehin, B. Olatunji. (1974). "The Western Sudan and the Coming of the French, 1800–1893," in J. F. A. Ajayi & M. Crowder, eds., *History of West Africa,* Vol. II. London, Longman, 344–379.

Osler, Pierre, dir. (1978). *Dictionnaire de citations français.* Paris: Usuels de Robert.

Ospina Vasquez, Luis. (1955). *Industria y protección en Colombia, 1810–1930.* Medellín: Bibl. Colombiana de Ciencias Sociales FAES.

Ott, Thomas O. (1973). *The Haitian Revolution, 1789–1804.* Knoxville, TN: University of Tennessee Press.

Ouellet, Fernand. (1971). *Histoire économique et sociale du Québec, 1760–1850: Structures et conjoncture,* 2 vols. Montréal: Ed. Fides.

Ouellet, Fernand & Hamelin, Jean. (1962). "La crise agricole dans le Bas-Canada (1802–1837)," *Etudes rurales,* No. 7, 36–57.

Owen, David Edward. (1934). *British Opium Policy in China and India.* New Haven, CT: Yale University Press.

Owen, Roger. (1981). *The Middle East in the World Economy, 1800–1914.* London: Methuen.

Ozouf, Mona. (1984). "War and Terror in French Revolutionary Discourse (1792–1794)," *Journal of Modern History,* **LVI**, 4, 579–597.

Pachoński, Jan & Wilson, Reuel K. (1986). *Poland's Caribbean Tragedy: A Study of Polish Legions in the Haitian War of Independence, 1802–1803.* Boulder, CO: East European Monographs.

Palmer, R. R. (1954). "The World Revolution of the West, 1763–1801," *Political Science Quarterly,* **LXIX**, 1, 1–14.

Palmer, R. R. (1959, 1964). *The Age of the Democratic Revolution: A Political History of Europe and America, 1760–1800,* 2 vols. Princeton, NJ: Princeton University Press.

Palmer, R. R. (1967). "Polémique américaine sur le rôle de la bourgeoisie dans la Révolution française," *Annales historiques de la Révolution française,* **XXXIX**, No. 189, 369–380.

Palmer, R. R. (1971). *The World of the French Revolution.* New York: Harper & Row.

Pandey, Gyan. (1981). *Economic Dislocation in Nineteenth Century Eastern U.P.: Some Implications of the Decline of Artisanal Industry in Colonial India*, Occasional Paper No. 37. Calcutta: Centre for Studies in Social Sciences.

Panikkar, Kavalam Madhava. (1953). *Asia and Western Dominance: A Survey of the Vasco da Gama Epoch of Asian History, 1498–1945*. London: George Allen & Unwin.

Pantaleão, Olga. (1946). *A penetração commercial da Inglaterra na América Espanhola de 1773–1783*, Boletim LXII. Univ. de São Paulo, Faculdade de Filosofia, Ciencias e Letras.

Pares, Richard. (1953). Review of V. T. Harlow, *The Founding of the Second British Empire, 1763–1793*, Vol. I, in *English Historical Review*, **LXVIII**, No. 266, 282–285.

Pares, Richard. (1960). *Merchants and Planters*, Economic History Review, Suppl. 4. Cambridge, Engl.: At the University Press.

Paret, Peter. (1964). "Colonial Experience and European Military Reform at the End of the Eighteenth Century," *Bulletin of the Institute of Historical Research*, **XXXVII**, No. 95, 47–59.

Paris, Robert. (1957). *Le Levant de 1660 à 1789*, Vol. V of G. Rambert, dir., *Histoire du Commerce de Marseille*. Paris: Plon.

Parker, Harold T. (1979). *The Bureau of Commerce in 1781 and Its Policies with Respect to French Industry*. Durham, NC: Carolina Academic Press.

Parker, R. A. C. (1955). "Coke of Norfolk and the Agrarian Revolution," *Economic History Review*, 2nd ser., **VII**, 2, 156–166.

Parker, W. H. (1959). "A New Look at Unrest in Lower Canada in the 1830's," *Canadian Historical Review*, **XL**, 3, 209–218.

Parkinson, C. Northcote. (1937). *Trade in the Eastern Seas, 1793–1813*. Cambridge, Engl.: At the University Press.

Paskaleva, Virginia. (1965). "Einige Probleme auf der Geschichte der Orientfrage in der Ersten Halfte des 19. Jahrhunderts," in *Etudes historiques*, à l'occasion du XIIe Congrès International de Sciences Historiques—Vienne, août–septembre. Sofia: Académie des Sciences de Bulgarie, II, 185–205.

Paskaleva, Virginia. (1968). "Contribution aux relations commerciales des provinces balkaniques de l'Empire ottoman avec les états européens au cours du XVIIIe et la première moitié du XIXe s.," in *Etudes historiques*, à l'occasion du VIe Congrès International des Etudes Slaves—Prague. Sofia: Académie des Sciences de Bulgarie, IV, 265–292.

Patch, Robert W. (1985). "Agrarian Change in Eighteenth-Century Yucatan," *Hispanic American Historical Review*, **LXV**, 1, 21–49.

Patterson, R. (1957). "Spinning and Weaving," in C. Singer *et al.*, eds., *A History of Technology*, **III**: *From the Renaissance to the Industrial Revolution, c. 1500–c. 1750*. Oxford: Clarendon Press, 151–180.

Payen, Jacques. (1969). *Capital et machine à vapeur au XVIIIe siècle: Les frères Périer et l'introduction en France de la machine à vapeur de Watt*. Paris & La Haye: Mouton.

Pearson, M. N. (1972). "Political Participation in Mughal India," *Indian Economic and Social History Review*, **IX**, 2, 113–131.

Pereira, Miriam Halpern. (1986). "Portugal and the Structure of the World Market in the XVIIIth & XIXth Centuries," in W. Fischer *et al.*, eds., *The Emergence of a World Economy, 1500–1914, Part I: 1500–1850*. Wiesbaden: Franz Steiner Verlag, 279–300.

Pereira Sales, Eugenio. (1971). *Los primeros contactos entre Chile y los Estados Unidos, 1778–1809*. Santiago: Ed. Andres Bello.

Pérez Rojas, Reyes Antonio. (1978). "The Impact of the American Revolution on the Independence of Guatemala," in J. S. Tulchin, ed., *Hemispheric Perspectives on the United States*. Westport, CT: Greenwood Press, 14–21.

Perkin, H. J. (1968). "The Social Causes of the British Industrial Revolution," *Transactions of the Royal Historical Society*, 5th ser., **XVIII**, 123–143.

Perkin, H. J. (1969). *The Origins of Modern English Society, 1780–1880*. London: Routledge & Kegan Paul.

Perkins, Bradford. (1955). *The First Rapprochement: England and the United States, 1795–1805.* Philadelphia, PA: University of Pennsylvania Press.

Perkins, Bradford. (1963). *Prologue to War: England and the United States, 1805–1812.* Berkeley, CA: University of California Press.

Perkins, Bradford. (1964). *Castlereagh and Adams: England and the United States, 1812–1823.* Berkeley, CA: University of California Press.

Perkins, Dexter. (1927). *The Monroe Doctrine, 1823–1826.* Cambridge, MA: Harvard University Press.

Perlin, Frank. (1974). "Society in Crisis: Early 19th Century Western India in Demographic and Institutional Perspective," paper delivered at IVth European Conference on Modern South Asian Studies, Sussex, England, 173–193.

Perlin, Frank. (1978). "Of White Whale and Countrymen in the Eighteenth Century Maratha Deccan: Extended Class Relations, Rights, and the Problem of Rural Autonomy Under the Old Regime," *Journal of Peasant Studies,* **V**, 2, 172–237.

Perlin, Frank. (1979). "To Identify Change in an Old Regime Polity: Agrarian Transaction and Institutional Mutation in 17th to Early 19th Century Maharashtra," in *Asie du Sud: Traditions et changements,* Sèvres, 8–13 juillet 1978, Colloques Internationaux du CNRS, No. 582. Paris: Ed. du CNRS, 197–204.

Perlin, Frank. (1980a). "Precolonial South Asia and Western Penetraton in the Seventeenth to Nineteenth Centuries: A Problem of Epistemological Status," *Review,* **IV**, 2, 267–306.

Perlin, Frank. (1980b). "A History of Money in Asian Perspective," *Journal of Peasant Studies,* **VII**, 2, 235–244.

Perlin, Frank. (1981). "The Precolonial State in History and Epistemology: A Reconstruction of Societal Formation in the Western Deccan from the Fifteenth to the Early Nineteenth Centuries," in H. Claessen & P. Skonik, eds., *The Study of the State.* The Hague: Mouton, 275–302.

Perlin, Frank. (1983). "Proto-industrialization and Pre-colonial South Asia," *Past and Present,* No. 98, 30–95.

Perlin, Frank. (1984). "Growth of Money Economy and Some Questions of Transition in Late Pre-colonial India," *Journal of Peasant Studies,* **VI**, 3, 96–107.

Pérotin-Dumon, Anne. (1986). "Ambiguous Revolution in the Caribbean: The White Jacobins, 1789–1800," *Historical Reflections,* **XIII**, 2/3, 499–516.

Perrot, Jean-Claude. (1975a). "Voies nouvelles pour l'histoire économique de la Révolution," *Annales historiques de la Révolution française,* **XLVII**, No. 219, 30–65.

Perrot, Jean-Claude. (1975b). *Genèse d'une ville moderne. Caen au XVIIIe siècle,* 2 vols. Paris & La Haye: Mouton.

Perrot, Jean-Claude. (1976). "L'âge d'or de la statistique régionale (an IV-1804)," *Annales historiques de la Révolution française,* **XLVII**, No. 224, 215–276.

Perrot, Jean-Claude. (1981). "Le présent et la durée dans l'oeuvre de F. Braudel," *Annales E.S.C.,* **XXXVI**, 1, 3–15.

Petrosian, Juri. (1976). "Die Ideen 'Der Europäisierung' in dem sozialpolitischen Leben des Osmanischen Reiches in der Neuzeit (ende des 18. Anfang des 20. Jh.),", in N. Todorov, *et al.,* réd., *La révolution industrielle dans le sud-est Europe XIXe siècle.* Sofia: Institut d'Etudes Balkaniques, 61–75.

Peukert, Werner. (1978). *Der atlantische Slavenhandel von Dahomey, 1740–1797.* Wiesbaden: Franz Steiner Verlag.

Phelan, John Leddy. (1960). "Neo-Aztecism in the Eighteenth Century and the Genesis of Mexican Nationalism," in S. Diamond, ed., *Culture in History: Essays in Honor of Paul Radin.* New York: Columbia University Press, 760–770.

Phelan, John Leddy. (1978). *The People and the King: The Comunero Revolution in Colombia, 1781.* Madison, WI: University of Wisconsin Press.

Philips, C. H. (1961). *The East India Company, 1784–1834,* 2nd ed., reprinted with minor corrections. Manchester, Engl.: Manchester University Press.

Piault, Marc-Henri. (1975). "Captifs de pouvoir et pouvoir des captifs," in C. Meillassoux, ed., *L'esclavage en Afrique précoloniale*. Paris: Maspéro, 321–350.

Picard, Roger. (1910). *Les Cahiers de 1789 au point de vue industriel et commercial*. Paris: Marcel Rivière.

Piel, Jean. (1970). "The Place of the Peasantry in the National Life of Peru in the Nineteenth Century," *Past and Present*, No. 46, 108–133.

Piel, Jean. (1975). *Capitalisme agraire au Pérou, I: Originalité de la société agraire péruvienne au XIX siècle*. Paris: Ed. Anthropos.

Pietraszek, Bernardine. (1955). "British and Direct Spanish American Trade, 1815–1825," *Mid-America*, **XXXVII** (n.s. XXVI), 2, 67–100.

Pinchbeck, Ivy. (1930). *Women Workers and the Industrial Revolution, 1750–1850*. London: Routledge. (Reprinted Frank Cass, 1977).

Pinkney, David. (1950). "Paris, capitale du coton sous la Premier Empire," *Annales E.S.C.*, **V**, 1, 56–60.

Pinter, Walter McKenzie. (1967). *Russian Economic Policy under Nicholas I*. Ithaca, NY: Cornell University Press.

Pinter, Walter McKenzie. (1980). "The Evolution of Civil Officialdom, 1755–1855," in W. M. Pinter & D. K. Rowney, eds., *Russian Officialdom from the 17th to 20th Century: The Bureaucratization of Russian Society*. Chapel Hill, NC: University of North Carolina Press, 190–226.

Pluchon, Pierre. (1979). *Toussaint Louverture de l'esclavage au pouvoir*. Paris: Ed. de l'Ecole.

Plumb, J. H. (1950). *England in the Eighteenth Century*, Pelican History of England, Vol. 7. Harmondsworth, Engl.: Penguin.

Plumb, J. H. (1956). *The First Four Georges*. London: Fontana/Collins.

Plumb, J. H. (1982). "Commercialization and Society," in N. McKendrick, J. Brewer, & J. H. Plumb, *The Birth of a Consumer Society*. London: Europa Publications Ltd., 265–335.

Pocock, J. G. A. (1972). "Virtue and Commerce in the Eighteenth Century," *Journal of Interdisciplinary History*, **III**, 1, 119–134.

Polanyi, Karl. (1957). *The Great Transformation*. Boston, MA: Beacon Press. (Originally published 1944.)

Polanyi, Karl, in collaboration with Abraham Rotstein. (1966). *Dahomey and the Slave Trade*. Seattle, WA: University of Washington Press.

Polk, William R. (1963). *The Opening of South Lebanon, 1788–1840*. Cambridge, MA: Harvard University Press.

Pollard, Sidney. (1963). "Factory Discipline in the Industrial Revolution," *Economic History Review*, 2nd ser., **XVI**, 2, 254–271.

Pollard, Sidney. (1964). "The Factory Village in the Industrial Revolution," *English Historical Review*, **LXXIX**, No. 312, 513–531.

Pollard, Sidney. (1965). *The Genesis of Modern Management. A Study of the Industrial Revolution in Great Britain*. Cambridge, MA: Harvard University Press.

Pollard, Sidney. (1972a). "Capital Accounting in the Industrial Revolution," in F. Crouzet, ed., *Capital Formation in the Industrial Revolution*. London: Methuen, 119–144. (Originally published in the *Yorkshire Bulletin of Social and Economic Research*, 1962.)

Pollard, Sidney. (1972b). "Fixed Capital in the Industrial Revolution in Britain," in F. Crouzet, ed., *Capital Formation in the Industrial Revolution*. London: Methuen, 145–161. (Originally published in *Journal of Economic History*, 1964.)

Pollard, Sidney. (1973). "Industrialization and the European Economy," *Economic History Review*, 2nd ser., **XXVI**, 4, 636–648.

Pollard, Sidney. (1981). *The Integration of the European Economy since 1815*. London: George Allen & Unwin.

Portal, Roger. (1949). "Manufactures et classes sociales en Russie au XVIIIe siècle," *Revue historique*, 73ᵉ année, **CCI**, avr.–juin, 161–185; **CCII**, juil.–sept., 1–23.

Portal, Roger. (1950). *L'Oural au XVIIIe siècle: Etude d'histoire économique et sociale*, Collection historique de l'institut d'etudes slaves, Vol. XIV. Paris: Inst. d'Etudes Slaves.

Portal, Roger. (1961). "Aux origines d'une bourgeoisie industrielle en Russie," *Revue d'historie moderne et contemporaine,* **VIII,** 1, 35–60.

Portal, Roger. (1963). "Préface," in M. Confino, *Domaines et seigneurs en Russie vers la fin du XVIIIe siècle.* Paris: Inst. d'Etudes Slaves, 9–13.

Portal, Roger. (1966). *L'Empire russe de 1762 à 1855.* Paris: Centre du Documentation Universitaire.

Post, John D. (1976). "Famines, Mortality, and Epidemic Disease in the Process of Modernization," *Economic History Review,* 2nd ser., **XXIX,** 1, 14–37.

Postan, M. (1972). "The Accumulation of Capital," in F. Crouzet, ed., *Capital Formation in the Industrial Revolution.* London: Methuen, 70–83. (Originally published in *Economic History Review,* 1935.)

Postma, Johannes. (1972). "The Dimension of the Dutch Slave Trade from Western Africa," *Journal of African History,* **XIII,** 2, 237–248.

Poulantzas, Nicos. (1971). *Pouvoir politique et classes sociales,* 2 vols. Paris: Maspéro (Petite Collection 77).

Poulantzas, Nicos. (1973). *Political Power and Social Classes.* London: New Left Books.

Prado, Caio, Jr. (1957). *Evolução política do Brasil e outros estudos,* 2a ed. São Paulo: Ed. Brasilense.

Prakash, Om. (1964). "The European Trading Companies and Merchants of Bengal, 1650–1725," *Indian Economic and Social History Review,* **I,** 3, 37–63.

Pratt, E. J. (1931). "Anglo-American Commercial and Political Rivalry on the Plata, 1820–1830," *Hispanic American Historical Review,* **XI,** 3, 302–335.

Pratt, Julius W. (1935). "Fur Trade Strategy and the American Left Flank in the War of 1812," *American Historical Review,* **XL,** 2, 246–273.

Pressnell, L. S. (1953). "Public Monies and the Development of English Banking," *Economic History Review,* 2nd ser., **V,** 3, 378–397.

Pressnell, L. S. (1960). "The Rate of Interest in the Eighteenth Century," in L. S. Pressnell, ed., *Studies in the Industrial Revolution: Presented to T. S. Ashton.* London: University of London, Athlone Press, 178–214.

Price, Jacob M. (1965). "Discussion," *Journal of Economic History,* **XXV,** 4, 655–659.

Price, Jacob M. (1973). *France and the Chesapeake: A History of the French Tobacco Monopoly, 1674–1791, and of its Relationship to the British and American Tobacco Trades,* 2 vols. Ann Arbor, MI: University of Michigan Press.

Price, Jacob M. (1976). "Quantifying Colonial America: A Comment on Nash and Warden," *Journal of Interdisciplinary History,* **VI,** 4, 701–709.

Priestly, Herbert Ingram. (1916). *José de Galvez, Visitor-General of New Spain (1765–1771).* Berkeley, CA: University of California Press.

Priestley, Margaret. (1969). *West African Trade and Coast Society: A Family Study.* London: Oxford University Press.

Prothero, I. J. (1979). *Artisans and Politics in Early Nineteenth Century London: John Gast and His Times.* Folkestone, Engl.: Dawson.

Prucha, Francis Paul. (1970). *American Indian Policy in the Formative Years: The Indian Trade and Intercourse Acts, 1790–1834.* Lincoln, NE: University of Nebraska Press.

Pugh, Wilma J. (1939). "Calonne's 'New Deal,'" *Journal of Modern History,* **XI,** 3, 289–312.

Puryear, Vernon J. (1935). *International Economics and Diplomacy in the Near East.* Stanford, CA: Stanford University Press.

Quarles, Benjamin. (1961). *The Negro in the American Revolution.* Chapel Hill, NC: University of North Carolina Press.

Quimby, Robert S. (1957). *The Background of Napoleonic Warfare: The Theory of Military Tactics in Eighteenth-Century France,* Columbia Studies in the Social Sciences, No. 596. New York: Columbia University Press.

Quinney, Valerie. (1972). "The Problem of Civil Rights for Free Men of Color in the Early French Revolution," *French Historical Studies,* **VII,** 4, 544–557.

Rae, J. (1883). "Why Have the Yeomanry Perished?" *Contemporary Review,* **XXXIV,** 2, 546–556.

Raeff, Marc. (1966). *Origins of the Russian Intelligentsia: The Eighteenth-Century Nobility.* New York: Harcourt, Brace & World.

Raeff, Marc. (1971a). *Imperial Russia, 1682–1825: The Coming of Age of Modern Russia.* New York: Knopf.

Raeff, Marc. (1971b). "Pugachev's Rebellion," in R. Forster & J. P. Greene, eds., *Preconditions of Revolution in Early Modern Europe.* Baltimore, MD: Johns Hopkins University Press, 161–202.

Raeff, Marc. (1975). "The Well-Ordered Police State and the Development of Modernity in Seventeenth- and Eighteenth-Century Europe: An Attempt at a Comparative Approach," *American Historical Review,* **LXXX,** 5, 1221–1244.

Raeff, Marc. (1979). "The Bureaucratic Phenomena of Imperial Russia, 1700–1905," *American Historical Review,* **LXXXIV,** 2, 399–411.

Ragatz, Lowell J. (1928). *The Fall of the Planter Class in the British Caribbean, 1763–1833.* New York: Century.

Ragatz, Lowell J. (1935). "The West Indian Approach to the Study of American Colonial History," *American Historical Association,* pamphlet series. London: Arthur Thomas.

Ragsdale, Hugh. (1970). "A Continental System in 1801: Paul I and Bonaparte," *Journal of Modern History,* **XLII,** 1, 70–89.

Ram, N. (1972). "Impact of Early Colonisation on Economy of South India," *Social Scientist,* **I,** 4, 47–65.

Ramsey, John Fraser. (1939). *Anglo-French Relations, 1763–1770: A Study of Choiseul's Foreign Policy,* University of California Publications in History, Vol. XVII, No. 3. Berkeley, CA: University of California Press, i-x & 143–264.

Rancière, Jacques. (1983). "The Myth of the Artisan: Critical Reflections on a Category of Social History," *International Labor and Working Class History,* No. 24, Fall, 1–16.

Ransom, Roger L. (1968). "British Policy and Colonial Growth: Some Implications of the Burden from the Navigation Acts," *Journal of Economic History,* **XXVIII,** 3, 427–435.

Rao, G. N. (1977). "Agrarian Relations in Coastal Andhra under Early British Rule," *Social Scientist,* **VI,** I, No. 61, 19–29.

Rasch, Aage. (1965). "American Trade in the Baltic, 1783–1807," *Scandinavian Economic History Review,* **XIII,** 1, 31–64.

Rawley, James A. (1980). "The Port of London and the Eighteenth Century Slave Trade: Historians, Sources, and a Reappraisal," *African Economic History,* No. 9, 85–100.

Rawley, James A. (1981). *The Transatlantic Slave Trade: A History.* New York: W. W. Norton.

Rawlyk, George A. (1963). "The American Revolution and Nova Scotia Reconsidered," *Dalhousie Review,* **XLIII,** 3, 379–394.

Rawlyk, George A. (1968). *Revolution Rejected, 1774–1775.* Scarborough, Ont.: Prentice-Hall of Canada.

Rawlyk, George A. (1973). *Nova Scotia's Massachusetts: A Study of Massachusetts–Nova Scotia Relations, 1630–1784.* Montreal: McGill–Queen's University Press.

Ray, Indrani. (1980). *The Multiple Faces of the Early 18th Century Indian Merchants,* Occasional Paper No. 29, Calcutta: Centre for Studies in Social Sciences.

Ray, Ratnalekha. (1979). *Change in Bengal Agrarian Society, 1760–1850.* New Delhi: Manohar.

Raychaudhuri, Tapan. (1962). *Jan Company in Coromandel, 1605–1690,* Verhandelingen van het Koninklijk Instituut voor Taal-, Land-, en Volkenkunde, Vol. XXXVIII. 'S-Gravenhage: Martinus Nijhoff.

Raychaudhuri, Tapan. (1965). "Some Patterns of Economic Organization and Activity in Seventeenth Century India: A Comparative Study," in *Second International Conference of Economic History,* Aix-en-Provence, 1962, **II:** *Middle Ages and Modern Times.* Paris: Mouton, 751–760.

Raychaudhuri, Tapan. (1968). "A Re-interpretation of Nineteenth Century Indian Economic History?" *Indian Economic and Social History Review,* **V,** 1, 77–100.

Raychaudhuri, Tapan. (1969). "Permanent Settlement in Operation: Bakarkanj District, East Bengal," in R. E. Frykenberg, ed., *Land Control and Social Structure in Indian History.* Madison, WI: University of Wisconsin Press, 163–174.

Raychaudhuri, Tapan. (1982a). "Non-Agricultural Production: Mughal India," in T. Raychaudhuri & I. Habib, eds., *Cambridge Economic History of India,* **I:** *c. 1200–c. 1700.* Cambridge, Engl.: Cambridge University Press, 261–307.

Raychaudhuri, Tapan. (1982b). "Inland Trade," in T. Raychaudhuri & I. Habib, eds., *Cambridge Economic History of India,* **I,** *c. 1200–c. 1700.* Cambridge, Engl.: Cambridge University Press, 325–359.

Rayneval, Gérard de. (1784). "Aperçu sur le Traité de Commerce à conclûre avec la Cour de Londres," Envoyé copie à M. de Calonne le 29 avril 1784, in *Archives des Affaires Etrangères (Paris): Angleterre,* No. 46: *Mémoires sur le Commerce, le Finance, etc. 1713 à 1811,* 202–220.

Razzell, P. E. (1969). "Population Change in Eighteenth Century England: A Re-Appraisal," in M. Drake, ed., *Population in Industrialization.* London: Methuen, 128–156. (Originally published in *Economic History Review,* 1965.)

Razzell, P. E. (1974). "An Interpretation of the Modern Rise of Population in Europe—a Critique," *Population Studies,* **XXVIII,** Part I, 5–17.

Rebérioux, Madeline. (1965). "Jaurès et Robespierre," in *Actes du Colloque Robespierre,* XIIe Congrès international des Sciences historiques, Vienne, 3 septembre. Paris: Société des Robespierristes, 191–204.

Recht, Pierre. (1950). *Les biens communaux du Namurois et leur partage à la fin du XVIIIe siècle.* Bruxelles: E. Bruylant.

Regemorter, J.L. Van. (1963). "Commerce et politique: préparation et négociation du traité franco-russe de 1787," *Cahiers du monde russe et soviétique,* **IV,** 3, 230–257.

Regemorter, Jean-Louis Van. (1971). *Le déclin du servage, 1796–1855,* Vol. I of R. Portal, dir., *Histoire de la Russie.* Paris: Hatier.

Reid, Joseph D., Jr. (1970). "On Navigating the Navigation Acts with Peter D. McClelland: Comment," *American Economic Review,* **LX,** 5, 949–955.

Reid, Marjorie G. (1925). "The Quebec Fur Traders and Western Policy, 1763–1774," *Canadian Historical Review,* **VI,** 1, 15–32.

Reinhard, Marcel. (1946). "La Révolution française et le problème de la population," *Population,* **I,** 3, 419–427.

Reinhard, Marcel. (1965). "Bilan démographique de l'Europe: 1789–1815," in *XIIe Congrès International des Sciences Historiques,* Vienne, 29 août–5 sept., *Rapports,* **I:** *Grands thèmes.* Horn/Wein: Ferdinand Berger & Sohne, 451–471.

Rémond, André. (1957). "Trois bilans de l'économie française au temps des théories physiocratiques," *Revue d'histoire économique et sociale,* **XXXV,** 4, 416–456.

Reis, Arthur Cézar Ferreira. (1960). "O Comércio colonial e as companhias privilegiadas," in S. Buarque de Holanda, dir., *Historia Geral da Civilização Brasileira,* Tomo I, 2 vols. São Paulo: Difusão Européia do Livro, 311–339.

Resnick, Daniel P. (1972). "The Société des Amis des Noirs and the Abolition of Slavery," *French Historical Studies,* **VII,** 4, 558–569.

Reubens, E. P. (1955). "Comment," in National Bureau of Economic Research, *Capital Formation and Economic Growth.* Princeton, NJ: Princeton University Press, 378–380.

Reynolds, Edward. (1973). "Agricultural Adjustments on the Gold Coast after the End of the Slave Trade, 1807–1874," *Agricultural History,* **XLVII,** 4, 308–318.

Rich, E. E. (1955). "Russia and the Colonial Fur trade," *Economic History Review,* 2nd ser., **VII,** 3, 307–328.

Rich, E. E. (1960). *Hudson's Bay Company, 1670–1870,* 3 vols. Toronto: McClelland & Stewart.

Richards, Alan. (1977). "Primitive Accumulation in Egypt, 1798–1882," *Review,* **I,** 2, 3–49.

Richards, E. S. (1973). "Structural Change in a Regional Economy: Sutherland and the Industrial Revolution, 1780–1830," *Economic History Review*, 2nd ser., **XXVI**, 1, 63–76.

Richards, J. F. (1981). "The Indian Empire and Peasant Production of Opium in the Nineteenth Century," *Modern Asian Studies*, **XV**, I, 59–82.

Richards, W. A. (1980). "The Import of Firearms into West Africa in the Eighteenth Century," *Journal of African History*, **XXI**, 1, 43–59.

Richardson, David. (1975). "Profitability in the Bristol–Liverpool Slave Trade," *Revue française d'histoire d'outre-mer*, **LXII**, 1ᵉ et 2ᵉ trimestres, Nos. 226/227, 301–308.

Richardson, David. (1979). "West African Consumption Patterns and Their Influence on the Eighteenth-Century English Slave Trade," in H. A. Gemery & J. S. Hogendorn, eds., *The Uncommon Market*, New York: Academic Press, 303–330.

Richardson, Thomas L. (1969). Review of W. E. Tate, *The Enclosure Movement*, in *Agricultural History*, **XLIII**, 1, 187–188.

Richet, Denis. (1968). "Croissance et blocages en France du XVᵉ au XVIIIᵉ siècles," *Annales E.S.C.*, **XXIII**, 4, 759–787.

Richet, Denis. (1969). "Autour des origines idéologiques lointaines de la Révolution française: Elites et despotisme," *Annales E.S.C.*, **XXIV**, 1, 1–23.

Richet, Denis. (1973). *La France moderne: L'esprit des institutions*. Paris: Flammarion.

Ridings, Eugene W. (1985). "Foreign Predominance among Overseas Traders in Nineteenth-Century Latin America," *Latin America Research Review*, **XX**, 2, 3–27.

Riley, James C. (1973). "Dutch Investment in France, 1781–1787," *Journal of Economic History*, **XXXIII**, 4, 732–760.

Riley, James C. (1986). *The Seven Years' War and the Old Regime in France: The Economic and Financial Toll*. Princeton, NJ: Princeton University Press.

Riley, James C. (1987). "French Finances, 1727–1768," *Journal of Modern History*, **LIX**, 2, 209–243.

Rippy, J. Fred. (1929). *United States and Great Britain over Latin America (1808–1830)*. Baltimore, MD: Johns Hopkins Press.

Rippy, J. Fred. (1959). *British Investments in Latin America, 1822–1949*. Minneapolis, MN: University of Minnesota Press.

Rippy, J. Fred & Debo, Angie. (1924). "The Historical Background of the American Policy of Isolation," *Smith College Studies in History*, **IX**, 3/4, 69–165.

Roberts, J. M. (1978). *The French Revolution*. Oxford: Oxford University Press.

Roberts, M. W. (1966). "Indian Estate Labour in Ceylon during the Coffee Period (1830–1880)," *Indian Economic and Social History Review*, **III**, 1, 1–52; **III**, 2, 101–136.

Roberts, P. E. (1968). "The East India Company and the State, 1772–86," in *Cambridge History of India*, **V**: H. H. Dodwell, ed., *British India, 1497–1858*, third Indian reprint. Delhi: S. Chand, 181–204.

Roberts, Richard. (1980). "Long Distance Trade and Production: Sinsani in the Nineteenth Century," *Journal of African History*, **XXI**, 2, 169–188.

Robertson, M. L. (1956). "Scottish Commerce and the American War of Independence," *Economic History Review*, 2nd ser., **IX**, 1, 123–131.

Robertson, William Spence. (1915). "South America and the Monroe Doctrine, 1824–1828," *Political Science Quarterly*, **XXX**, 1, 82–105.

Robertson, William Spence. (1918a). "The Recognition of the Spanish Colonies by the Motherland," *Hispanic American Historical Review*, **I**, 1, 70–91.

Robertson, William Spence. (1918b). "The Recognition of the Hispanic American Nations by the United States," *Hispanic American Historical Review*, **I**, 3, 239–269.

Robertson, William Spence. (1926). "The Policy of Spain Toward Its Revolted Colonies, 1820–1823," *Hispanic American Historical Review*, **VI**, 1/3, 21–46.

Robertson, William Spence. (1939). *France and Latin-American Independence*. Baltimore, MD: Johns Hopkins Press.

Robertson, William Spence. (1941). "Russia and the Emancipation of Spanish America, 1816–1826," *Hispanic American Historical Review,* **XXI,** 2, 196–221.

Robin, Régine. (1970). *La sociéte française en 1789: Semur-en-Auxois.* Paris: Plon.

Robin, Régine. (1971). "Fief et seigneurie dans le droit et l'idéologie juridique à la fin du XVIIIe siècle," *Annales historiques de la Révolution française,* **LIII,** 4, No. 206, 554–602.

Robin, Régine. (1973). "La nature de l'Etat à la fin de l'Ancien Régime: Formation sociale, Etat et Transition," *Dialectiques,* Nos. 1/2, 31–54.

Robinson, Cedric J. (1987). "Capitalism, Slavery and Bourgeois Historiography," *History Workshop,* No. 23, Spring, 122–140.

Robinson, Donald L. (1971). *Slavery in the Structure of American Policies, 1768–1820.* New York: Harcourt, Brace, Jovanovich.

Robinson, Eric H. (1974). "The Early Diffusion of Steam Power," *Journal of Economic History,* **XXXIV,** 1, 91–107.

Roche, Max. (1985). "La présence française en Turquie (1764–1866)," *Annales du Levant,* No. 1, 83–95.

Roche, Patrick A. (1975). "Caste and the British Merchant Government in Madras, 1639–1748," *Indian Economic and Social History Review,* **XIII,** 4, 381–407.

Rodney, Walter. (1966). "African Slavery and Other Forms of Social Oppression on the Upper Guinea Coast in the Context of the Atlantic Slave Trade," *Journal of African History,* **VII,** 3, 431–443.

Rodney, Walter. (1967). *West Africa and the Atlantic Slave-Trade,* Historical Assn. of Tanzania, Paper No. 2. Nairobi: East African Publ. House.

Rodney, Walter. (1968). "Jihad and Social Revolution in Futa Djalon in the Eighteenth Century," *Journal of the Historical Society of Nigeria,* **IV,** 2, 269–284.

Rodney, Walter. (1970). *A History of the Upper Guinea Coast, 1545–1800.* London: Oxford University Press.

Rodney, Walter. (1975a). "The Guinea Coast," in *Cambridge History of Africa,* **IV:** Richard Gray, ed., *From c. 1600 to c. 1790.* Cambridge, Engl.: Cambridge University Press, 223–324.

Rodney, Walter. (1975b). "Africa in Europe and the Americas," in *Cambridge History of Africa,* **IV:** Richard Gray, ed., *From c. 1600 to c. 1790.* Cambridge, Engl.: Cambridge University Press, 578–622.

Rodrigues, José Honório. (1977). "A revolução americana e a revolução brasileira da independéncia (1776–1822)," *Revista de história de America,* No. 83, enero–junio, 69–91.

Rodríguez, Mario. (1976). *La revolución americana de 1776 y el mundo hispánico: Ensayos y documentos.* Madrid: Ed. Tecnos.

Roehl, Richard. (1976). "French Industrialization: A Reconsideration," *Explorations in Economic History,* **XIII,** 3, 233–281.

Roehl, Richard. (1981). "French Industrialization: A Reply," *Explorations in Economic History,* **XVIII,** 4, 434–435.

Rogers, James E. Thorold. (1884). *Six Centuries of Work and Wages,* with a new preface by G. D. H. Cole in 1949. London: George Allen & Unwin.

Rogger, Hans. (1960). *National Consciousness in Eighteenth-Century Russia.* Cambridge, MA: Harvard University Press.

Romano, Ruggiero. (1960). "Movements des prix et développement économique. L'Amérique du sud au XVIIIᵉ siècle," *Annales E.S.C.,* **XVIII,** 1, 63–74.

Root, Hilton Lewis. (1985). "Challenging the Seigneurie: Community and Contention on the Eve of the French Revolution," *Journal of Modern History,* **LVII,** 4, 652–681.

Root, Hilton Lewis. (1987). *Peasants and King in Burgundy: Agrarian Foundations of French Absolutism.* Berkeley, CA: University of California Press.

Root, Winfred Trexler. (1942). "The American Revolution Reconsidered," *Canadian Historical Review,* **XXIII,** 1, 16–29.

Roover, Raymond de. (1968). "Un contraste: La structure de la banque anglaise et celle de la banque continentale au XVIIIe siècle," in *Third International Congress of Economic History*, Munich, 1965. Paris & La Haye: Mouton, **V**, 623–627.

Rose, J. Holland. (1893). "Napoleon and English Commerce," *English Historical Review*, **VIII**, No. 32, 704–725.

Rose, J. Holland. (1908). "The Franco-British Commercial Treaty of 1786," *English Historical Review*, **XXIII**, No. 92, 709–724.

Rose, J. Holland. (1929a). "The Political Reactions of Bonaparte's Eastern Expedition," *English Historical Review*, **XLIV**, No. 173, 48–58.

Rose, J. Holland. (1929b). "British West India Commerce as a Factor in the Napoleonic War," *Cambridge Historical Journal*, **III**, 1, 34–46.

Rose, M. E. (1981). "Social Change and the Industrial Revolution," in R. Floud & D. N. McCloskey, eds., *The Economic History of Britain Since 1700*, **I**: *1700–1860*. Cambridge, Engl.: Cambridge University Press, 253–275.

Rose, R. B. (1956). "The French Revolution and the Grain Supply: Nationalization Pamphlets in the John Rylands Library," *Bulletin of The John Rylands Library*, **XXXIX**, 1, 171–187.

Rose, R. B. (1959). "18th-century Price-riots, the French Revolution, and the Jacobin Maximum," *International Review of Social History*, **IV**, 3, 432–445.

Rose, R. B. (1961). "Eighteenth Century Price Riots and Public Policy in England," *International Review of Social History*, **VI**, 2, 277–292.

Rose, R. B. (1965). *The Enragés: Socialists of the French Revolution?* Melbourne: Melbourne University Press.

Rose, R. B. (1972). "Babeuf, Dictatorship and Democracy," *Historical Studies*, **XV**, No. 58, 223–236.

Rose, R. B. (1978). *Gracchus Babeuf, the First Revolutionary Communist*. Stanford, CA: Stanford University Press.

Rose, R. B. (1984). "The 'Red Scare' of the 1790s: The French Revolution and the 'Agrarian Law,'" *Past and Present*, No. 103, 113–130.

Rosen, Howard. (1975). "Le système Gribauval et la guerre moderne," *Revue historique des armées*, **II**, 1/2, 29–36.

Rosenberg, Nathan. (1967). "Anglo-American Wage Differences in the 1820's," *Journal of Economic History*, **XXVII**, 2, 221–229.

Rostow, W. W. (1941). "Business Cycles, Harvests, and Politics, 1790–1850," *Journal of Economic History*, **I**, 2, 206–221.

Rostow, W. W. (1971). *The Stages of Economic Growth*, 2nd ed. Cambridge, Engl.: At the University Press.

Rostow, W. W. (1973). "The Beginnings of Modern Growth in Europe: An Essay in Synthesis," *Journal of Economic History*, **XXXIII**, 3, 547–580.

Rostow, W. W. (1978). "No Random Walk: A Comment on 'Why was England First?'" *Economic History Review*, 2nd ser., **XXXI**, 4, 610–612.

Rothenberg, Winifred B. (1979). "A Price Index For Rural Massachusetts, 1750–1855," *Journal of Economic History*, **XXXIX**, 4, 975–1001.

Rothenberg, Winifred B. (1981). "The Market and Massachusetts Farmers, 1750–1855," *Journal of Economic History*, **XLI**, 2, 283–314.

Rothenberg, Winifred B. (1985). "The Emergence of a Capital Market in Rural Massachusetts, 1730–1838," *Journal of Economic History*, **XLV**, 4, 781–808.

Rothermund, Dietmar. (1981). *Asian Trade in the Age of Mercantilism*. New Delhi: Manohar.

Rousseau, Jean-Jacques. (1947). *The Social Contract*. New York: Hafner. (Originally published 1762.)

Rousseaux, Paul. (1938). *Les mouvements de fond de l'économie anglaise, 1800–1913*. Bruxelles: Ed. Universelle & Paris: Desclée, De Brouwer & Cie.

Rout, Leslie B., Jr. (1976). *The American Experience in Spanish America: 1502 to the Present Day*. Cambridge, Engl.: Cambridge University Press.

Roux, René. (1951). "La Révolution française et l'idée de lutte de classes," *Revue d'histoire économique et sociale*, **XXIX**, 3, 252–279.

Rozman, Gilbert. (1976). *Urban Networks in Russia 1750–1800, and Pre-Modern Periodization*. Princeton, NJ: Princeton University Press.

Rudé, George. (1954). "The French Revolution," *Marxist Quarterly*, **I**, 1, 242–251.

Rudé, George. (1956). "La taxation populaire de mai 1775 à Paris et dans la région parisienne," *Annales historiques de la Révolution française*, **XXVIII**, No. 143. 139–179.

Rudé, George. (1961a). *Interpretations of the French Revolution*. London: The Historical Association.

Rudé, George. (1961b). "La taxation populaire de mai 1775 en Picardie, en Normandie, et dans le Beauvaisis," *Annales historique de la Révolution française*, **XXXIII**, No. 165, 305–326.

Rudé, George. (1962). "Quelques réflexions sur la composition, le rôle, les idées et les formes d'action des sans-culottes dans la Révolution française," *Critica storica*, **I**, 4, 369–383.

Rudé, George. (1964). *Revolutionary Europe, 1783–1815*. New York: Harper & Row.

Rudé, George. (1967). *The Crowd in the French Revolution*. Oxford: Oxford University Press.

Russell-Wood, A. J. R. (1974). "Local Government in Portugese America: A Study in Cultural Divergence," *Comparative Studies in Society and History*, **XVI**, 2, 187–231.

Russell-Wood, A. J. R. (1975). "Preconditions and Precipitants of the Independence Movement in Portugese America," in A. J. R. Russell-Wood, ed., *From Colony to Nation: Essays on the Independence of Brazil*. Baltimore, MD: Johns Hopkins University Press, 3–40.

Rustow, Dankwart A. (1970). "The Political Impact of the West," in P. M. Holt *et al.*, eds., *The Cambridge History of Islam*, **I**: *The Central Islamic Lands*. Cambridge, Engl.: At the University Press, 673–697.

Ruwet, Joseph. (1967). *Avant les révolutions: Le XVIIIe siècle*, Etudes d'histoire wallonne, Vol. IX. Bruxelles: Fondation Charles Plisnier.

Ryan, A. N. (1959). "The Defense of British Trade with the Baltic, 1808–1813," *English Historical Review*, **LXXIV**, No. 292, 443–466.

Ryan, A. N. (1958). "Trade with the Economy in the Scandinavian and Baltic Ports during the Napoleonic War: For and Against," *Transactions of the Royal Historical Society*, 5th ser., **XII**, 123–140.

Rydjord, John. (1941). "British Mediation Between Spain and Her Colonies: 1811–1813," *Hispanic American Historical Review*, **XXI**, 1, 29–50.

Ryerson, Stanley B. (1960). *The Founding of Canada: Beginnings to 1815*. Toronto: Progress Books.

Ryerson, Stanley B. (1973). *Unequal Union: Roots of Crisis in the Canadas, 1815–1873*, 2nd ed. Toronto: Progress Books.

Sachs, William A. (1953). "Agricultural Conditions in the Northern Colonies before the Revolution," *Journal of Economic History*, **XIII**, 3, 274–290.

Saint-Jacob, Pierre de. (1960). *Les paysans de la Bourgogne du Nord au dernier siècle de l'Ancien Régime*. Paris: Les Belles-Lettres.

Saint Lu, André. (1970). *Condition coloniale et conscience créole au Guatémala (1524–1821)*. Paris: Presses Universitaires de France.

Saintoyant, J. (1929). "La représentation coloniale pendant la Révolution," *Revue de l'histoire des colonies françaises*, **XVII**, 4, 353–380.

Saintoyant, J. (1930). *La colonisation française pendant la Révolution (1789–1799)*, 2 vols. Paris: La Renaissance du Livre.

Salaman, Redcliffe N. (1949). *The History and Social Influence of the Potato*. Cambridge, Engl.: At the University Press.

Sala-Molins, Louis. (1987). *Le Code noir, ou le calvaire de Canaan*. Paris: Presses Universitaires de France.

Salvucci, Richard J. (1981). "Enterprise and Economic Development in Colonial Mexico: the Case of the Obrajes," *Journal of Economic History*, **XLI**, 1, 197–199.

Samuel, Raphael. (1977). "Workshop of the World: Steam Power and Hand Technology in Mid-Victorian Britain," *History Workshop*, No. 3, Spring, 6–72.

Savelle, Max. (1939). "The American Balance of Power and European Diplomacy, 1713–78," in R. B. Morris, ed., *The Era of the American Revolution*. New York: Columbia University Press, 140–169.

Savelle, Max. (1953). *United States: Colonial Period*. Instituto Panamericano de Geografía e Historia, Publ. No. 159. Mexico: Ed. Cultura S.A.

Savelle, Max. (1962). "Nationalism and Other Loyalties in the American Revolution," *American Historical Review*, **LXVII**, 4, 901–923.

Savelle, Max. (1974). *Empires to Nations: Expansionism in America, 1713–1824*. Minneapolis, MN: University of Minnesota Press.

Saville, John. (1969). "Primitive Accumulation and Early Industrialization in Britain," in *The Socialist Register, 1969*. London: Merlin Press, 247–271.

Schellenberg, T. R. (1934). "Jeffersonian Origins of the Monroe Doctrine," *Hispanic American Historical Review*, **XIV**, 1, 1–32.

Schlebecker, John T. (1976). "Agricultural Marketing and Markets in the North, 1774–1777," *Agricultural History*, **L**, 1, 21–36.

Schlesinger, Arthur M., Sr. (1917). *The Colonial Merchants and the American Revolution, 1763–1776*. New York: Columbia University Press.

Schlesinger, Arthur M., Sr. (1919). "The American Revolution Reconsidered," *Political Science Quarterly*, **XXXIV**, 1, 61–78.

Schlote, Werner. (1952). *British Overseas Trade from 1700 to the 1930's*. Oxford: Basil Blackwell.

Schmidt, Charles. (1908). "La crise industrielle de 1788 en France," *Revue historique*, 33e année, **XCVII**, 1, fasc. 192, 78–94.

Schmidt, Charles. (1913, 1914). "Les debuts de l'industrie cotonnière en France, 1706–1806," *Revue d'histoire économique et sociale*, **VI**, 3, 261–298; **VII**, 1, 26–55.

Schmidt, S. O. (1966). "La politique intérieure du tsarisme au milieu du XVIIIe siècle," *Annales E.S.C.*, **XXI**, 1, 95–110.

Schmitt, Eberhard. (1976). *Einführung in die Geschiechte der Französischen Revolution*. München: Verlag C. H. Beck.

Schnapper, Bernard. (1959). "La fin du régime de l'Exclusif: Le commerce étranger dans les possessions français d'Afrique tropicale (1817–1870)," *Annales africaines*, **VI**, 149–200.

Schnapper, Bernard. (1961). *La politique et le commerce français dans le Golfe de Guinée de 1838 à 1871*. Paris & La Haye: Mouton.

Schremmer, Eckart. (1981). "Proto-Industrialization: A Step Towards Industrialization?" *Journal of European Economic History*, **X**, 3, 653–670.

Schumpeter, Elizabeth Brody. (1938). "English Prices and Public Finance, 1660–1822," *Review of Economic Statistics*, **XX**, 1, 21–37.

Schumpeter, Joseph. (1939). *Business Cycles*, 2 vols. New York: McGraw-Hill.

Schutz, John A. (1946). "Thomas Pownall's Proposed Atlantic Federation," *Hispanic American Historical Review*, **XXVI**, 2, 263–268.

Schuyler, Robert L. (1945). *The Fall of the Old Colonial System: A Study in British Free Trade, 1770–1870*. New York: Oxford University Press.

Schwartz, Stuart D. (1970). "Magistracy and Society in Colonial Brazil," *Hispanic American Historical Review*, **L**, 4, 715–730.

Scott, James Brown. (1928). "Introduction," in G. Chinard, ed., *The Treaties of 1778 and Allied Documents*. Baltimore, MD: Johns Hopkins Press, x–xxv.

Scott, Samuel F. (1970). "The Regeneration of the Line Army during the French Revolution," *Journal of Modern History*, **XLII**, 3, 307–330.

Scott, Samuel F. (1978). *The Response of the Royal Army to the French Revolution: The Role and Development of the Line Army, 1787–93*. Oxford: Clarendon Press.

Seckinger, Ron L. (1976). "South American Power Politics During the 1820's," *Hispanic American Historical Review*, **LVI**, 2, 241–267.

Sédillot, Rene. (1987). *Le coût de la Révolution française.* Paris: Lib. Académique Perrin.

Sée, Henri. (1908). "La portée du régime seigneurial au XVIIIe siècle," *Revue d'histoire moderne et contemporaine*, **X**, 171–191.

Sée, Henri. (1913). "Une enquête sur la vaine pâture et le droit de parcours à la fin du règne de Louis XV," *Revue du dix-huitième siècle*, **I**, 3, 265–278.

Sée, Henri. (1923a). "Les origines de l'industrie capitaliste en France à la fin de l'Ancien Régime," *Revue historique*, 48e année, **CXLVIII**, No. 287, 187–200.

Sée, Henri. (1923b). "Le partage des biens communaux à la fin de l'Ancien Régime," *Nouvelle revue historique du droit française et étranger*, 4e sér., **II**, l, 47–81.

Sée, Henri. (1923c). "La mise en valeur des terres incultes à la fin de l'Ancien Régime," *Revue d'histoire économique et sociale*, **XI**, 1, 62–81.

Sée, Henri. (1926). "Commerce between France and the United States," *American Historical Review*, **XXXI**, 1, 732–737.

Sée, Henri. (1929). "Les économistes et la questions coloniale an XVIIIe siècle," *Revue de l'histoire des colonies françaises*, **XVII**, 4, 381–392.

Sée, Henri. (1930). "The Normandy Chamber of Commerce and the Commercial Treaty of 1786," *Economic History Review*, **II**, 2, 308–313.

Sée, Henri. (1931a). "Introduction et notes," in Arthur Young, *Voyages en 1787–1788–1789*, 3 vols. Paris: Armand Colin.

Sée, Henri. (1931b). "The Economic Origins of the French Revolution," *Economic History Review*, **III**, 1, 1–15.

Sée, Henri. (1933). "Préface," to C.-E. Labrousse, *Esquisse du mouvement des prix et des revenus en France au XVIIIe siècle.* Paris: Lib. Dalloz, vii–xi.

Ségur-Dupeyron, P. de. (1873). *Histoire des négotiations commerciales et maritimes de la France aux XVIIe et XVIIIe siècles*, **III**: *Fragments historiques: Negotiation du traité de commerce conclu en 1786 entre la France et l'Angleterre.* Paris: Ernest Thorin.

Semmel, Bernard. (1973). *The Methodist Revolution.* New York: Basic Books.

Serajuddin, A. M. (1978). "The Salt Monopoly of the East India Company's Government in Bengal," *Journal of the Economic and Social History of the Orient*, **XXI**, Part 3, 304–322.

Seton-Watson, Hugh. (1967). *The Russian Empire, 1801–1917.* Oxford: Clarendon Press.

Sewell, William H., Jr. (1980). *Work and Revolution in France: The Language of Labor from the Old Regime to 1848.* Cambridge, Engl.: Cambridge University Press.

Sewell, William H., Jr. (1983). "Response to J. Rancière, 'The Myth of the Artisan,'" *International Labor and Working Class History*, No. 24, Fall, 17–20.

Sewell, William H., Jr. (1985). "Ideologies and Social Revolutions: Reflections on the French Case," *Journal of Modern History*, **LVII**, 1, 57–85.

Shalhope, Robert E. (1972). "Toward a Republican Synthesis: The Emergence of an Understanding of Republicanism in American Historiography," *William and Mary Quarterly*, 3d ser., **XXIX**, 1, 49–50.

Shapiro, Gilbert. (1967). "The Many Lives of Georges Lefebvre," *American Historical Review*, **LXXII**, 2, 502–514.

Shapiro, Seymour. (1974). "The Structure of English Banking and the Industrial Revolution," in *Third International Conference of Economic History*, Munich, 1965. Paris & La Haye: Mouton, **V**, 229–235.

Shaw, A. G. L. (1970). "Introduction," in A.G.L. Shaw, ed., *Great Britain and the Colonies, 1815–1868.* London: Methuen, 1–26.

Shaw, Stanford J. (1962). *The Financial and Administrative Organization and Development of Ottoman Egypt, 1517–1798.* Princeton, NJ: Princeton University Press.

Shaw, Stanford J. (1963). "The Ottoman View of the Balkans," in Charles Jelavich & Barbara Jelavich, eds., *The Balkans in Transition.* Berkeley, CA: University of California Press, 56–80.

Shaw, Stanford J. (1971). *Between Old and New: The Ottoman Empire under Sultan Selim III, 1789–1807.* Cambridge, MA: Harvard University Press.

Shelton, Walter J. (1973). *English Hunger and Industrial Disorders.* Toronto: University of Toronto Press.

Shepherd, James F. & Walton, Gary M. (1969). "Estimates of 'Invisible' Earnings in the Balance of Payments of the British North American Colonies, 1768–1772," *Journal of Economic History*, **XXIX**, 2, 230–263.

Shepherd, James F. & Walton, Gary M. (1972) *Shipping, Maritime Trade, and the Economic Develoment of Colonial North America.* Cambridge, Engl.: At the University Press.

Sheridan, Richard B. (1958). "The Commercial and Financial Organization of the British Slave Trade, 1750–1807," *Economic History Review*, 2nd ser., **XI**, 2, 249–263.

Sheridan, Richard B. (1960). "The British Credit Crisis of 1772 and the American Colonies," *Journal of Economic History*, **XX**, 2, 155–186.

Sheridan, Richard B. (1965). "The Wealth of Jamaica in the Eighteenth Century," *Economic History Review*, 2nd ser., **XVIII**, 2, 292–311.

Sheridan, Richard B. (1968). "The Wealth of Jamaica in the Eighteenth Century: A Rejoinder," *Economic History Review*, 2nd ser., **XXI**, 1, 46–61.

Sheridan, Richard B. (1976a). "The Crisis of Slave Subsistence in the British West Indies during and after the American Revolution," *William and Mary Quarterly*, 3d ser., **XXXIII**, 4, 615–664.

Sheridan, Richard B. (1976b). " 'Sweet Malefactor': The Social Costs of Slavery and Sugar in Jamaica and Cuba, 1807–54," *Economic History Review*, 2nd ser., **XXIX**, 2, 236–257.

Sherwig, John M. (1969). *Guineas and Gunpowder: British Foreign Aid in the War with France, 1793–1815.* Cambridge, MA: Harvard University Press.

Shy, John. (1973). "The American Revolution: The Military Conflict Considered as a Revolutionary War," in S. G. Kurtz & J. H. Hutson, eds., *Essays on the American Revolution.* Chapel Hill, NC: University of North Carolina Press, 121–156.

Siddiqi, Asiya. (1973). *Agrarian Change in a North Indian State: Uttar Pradesh, 1819–1833.* Oxford: Clarendon Press.

Siddiqi, Asiya. (1981). "Money and Prices in the Earlier Stages of Europe: India and Britain, 1760–1840," *Indian Economic and Social History Review*, **XVIII**, 3/4, 231–262.

Silberling, Norman J. (1923). "British Prices and Business Cycles, 1779–1850," *Review of Economic Statistics*, **V**, Suppl. 2, 219–261.

Silberling, Norman J. (1924). "Financial and Monetary Policy in Great Britain During the Napoleonic Wars," *Quarterly Journal of Economics*, **XXXVII**, 2, 214–233; 3, 397–439.

Silva, Andrée Mansuy-Diniz. (1984). "Portugal and Brazil: Imperial Re-organization, 1750–1808," in *Cambridge History of Latin America*, **I**: Leslie Bethell, ed., *Colonial Latin America.* Cambridge, Engl.: Cambridge University Press, 469–508.

Singh, N. P. (1974). "The Deplorable Conditions of Saltpetre Manufacturers of Bihar (1773–1833)," *Proceedings of the Indian History Congress*, Thirty-Fifth Session, Jadavpur (Calcutta), 280–285.

Sinha, Narendra Krishna. (1956, 1962a). *The Economic History of Bengal from Plassey to the Permanent Settlement*, 2 vols. Calcutta: Firma K. L. Mukhopadhyay.

Sinha, Narendra Krishna. (1962b). "Foreword," in N. Mukerjee, *The Ryotwari System in Madras, 1792–1827.* Calcutta: Firma K. L. Mukhopadhyay, iii–iv.

Sinha, Narendra Krishna. (1970). *The Economic History of Bengal*, **III**: *1793–1848.* Calcutta: Firma K. L. Mukhopadhyay.

Sinzheimer, G. P. G. (1967). "Les industries 'kustar': un chapitre de la révolution industrielle en Russie," *Cashiers du monde russe et soviétique*, **VII**, 2, 205–222.

Sirotkin, V. G. (1970). "Le renouvellement en 1802 du traité de commerce franco-russe de 1787," in *La Russie et l'Europe, XVIe-XXe siècles.* Paris: S.E.V.P.E.N., 69–101.

Sivakumar, S.S. (1978). "Transformation of the Agrarian Economy in Tandaimandalam, 1760–1900," *Social Scientist*, **VI**, 10, No. 70, 18–39.

Six, G. (1929). "Fallait-il quatre quartiers de noblesse pour être officier à la fin de l'ancien régime?" *Revue d'histoire moderne*, **IV**, No. 19, 47–56.

Skempton, A. W. (1957). "Canals and River Navigation Before 1750," in C. Singer *et al.*, eds., *A History of Technology*, **III:** *From the Renaissance to the Industrial Revolution, c. 1500–c. 1750.* Oxford: Clarendon Press, 438–470.

Skiotis, Dennis. (1971). "From Bandit to Pasha: First Steps in the Rise to Power of Ali of Tepelen, 1750–1784," *International Journal of Middle East Studies*, **II**, 3, 219–244.

Skocpol, Theda. (1979). *States and Social Revolutions.* Cambridge, Engl.: Cambridge University Press.

Skocpol, Theda. (1985). "Cultural Idioms and Political Ideologies in the Reconstruction of State Power: A Rejoinder to Sewell," *Journal of Modern History*, **LVII**, 1, 86–96.

Slavin, Morris. (1984). *The French Revolution in Miniature: Section Droits-de-l'Homme, 1789–1795.* Princeton, NJ: Princeton University Press.

Slicher van Bath, B. H. (1963). *The Agrarian History of West Europe, A.D. 500–1850.* London: Edward Arnold.

Slicher van Bath, B. H. (1969). "Eighteenth-Century Agriculture on the Continent of Europe: Evolution or Revolution, *Agricultural History*, **XLIII**, 1, 169–179.

Sloane, William M. (1904). "The World Aspects of the Louisiana Purchase," *American Historical Review*, **IX**, 3, 507–521.

Smelser, Neil. (1959). *Social Change and the Industrial Revolution.* Chicago, IL: University of Chicago Press.

Smith, H. F. C. (1961). "A Neglected Theme of West African History: The Islamic Revolutions of the 19th Century," *Journal of the Historical Society of Nigeria*, **II**, 1, 169–185.

Smith, Paul H. (1964). *Loyalists and Redcoats: A Study in British Revolutionary Policy.* Chapel Hill, NC: University of North Carolina Press.

Smith, Robert S. (1959). "Indigo Production and Trade in Colonial Guatemala," *Hispanic American Historical Review*, **XXXIX**, 2, 181–211.

Smith, Walter B. & Cole, Arthur. (1935). *Fluctuations in American Business, 1790–1860.* Cambridge, MA: Harvard University Press.

Soboul, Albert. (1954). "Classes et luttes de classes sous la Révolution française," *La Pensée*, No. 53, janv.–févr., 39–62.

Soboul, Albert. (1956). "The French Rural Community in the Eighteenth and Nineteenth Centuries," *Past and Present*, No. 10, 78–95.

Soboul, Albert. (1958a). *Les sans-culottes parisiens en l'An II.* La Roche-sur-Yon, Fr.: Imp. Henri Potier.

Soboul, Albert. (1958b). "Classi e lotte delle classi durante la Rivoluzione francese," in A. Saitta, a cura di, *Sanculotti e contadini nella Rivoluzione francese.* Bari: Laterza. (Originally published in *Movimento Operaio*, 1953.)

Soboul, Albert. (1962). "A propos des réflexions de George Rudé sur la sans-culotterie," *Critica storica*, **I**, 4, 391–395.

Soboul, Albert. (1963). "Personnel sectionnaire et personnel babouviste," in *Babeuf et les problèmes de babouvisme*, Colloque International de Stockholm. Paris: Ed. Sociales, 107–131.

Soboul, Albert. (1965). "Esquisse d'un bilan social en 1815," in *XIIe Congrès International des Sciences Historiques*, Vienne, 29 août–5 sept., *Rapports*, **I:** *Grands thèmes.* Horn/Wien: Verlag Ferdinand Berger & Sohne, 517–545.

Soboul, Albert. (1968). "Aux origines de la classe ouvrière industrielle française (fin XVIIIe–début XIXe siècle)," *Third International Conference of Economic History*, Munich, 1965. Paris & La Haye: Mouton, 187–192.

Soboul, Albert. (1970a). "Le héros et l'histoire," *Revue d'histoire moderne et contemporaine*, **XVII**, 333–338.

Soboul, Albert. (1970b). *La Civilisation de la Révolution française*, **I:** *La crise de l'Ancien Régime.* Paris: Arthaud.

Soboul, Albert. (1973). "Sur le mouvement paysan dans la Révolution française," *Annales historiques de la Révolution française*, **XLV**, 1, No. 211, 85–101.

Soboul, Albert. (1974). "L'historiographie classique de la Révolution française. Sur des controverses récentes," *La Pensée*, No. 177, oct., 40–58.

Soboul, Albert. (1976a). "Le choc revolutionnaire, 1789–1797," in Fernand Braudel & Ernest Labrousse, dirs., *Histoire économique et social de la France*, **III**: *L'avènement de l'ère industrielle (1789–années 1880)*. Paris: Presses Universitaires de France, 3–64.

Soboul, Albert. (1976b). "La reprise économique et la stabilisation sociale, 1797–1815," in Fernand Braudel & Ernest Labrousse, dirs., *Histoire économique et social de la France*, **III**: *L'avènement de l'ère industrielle (1789–années 1880)*. Paris: Presses Universitaires de France, 65–133.

Soboul, Albert. (1976c). "Sur l'article de Michel Grenon et Robin," *La Pensée*, No. 187, juin, 31–35.

Soboul, Albert. (1976d). *Problèmes paysans de la Révolution (1789–1848). Etudes d'histoire révolutionnaire*. Paris: Maspéro.

Soboul, Albert. (1977a). *A Short History of the French Revolution, 1789–1799*. Berkeley & Los Angeles, CA: University of California Press. (Original publication in French, 1965.)

Soboul, Albert. (1977b). "Problèmes agraires de la Révolution française," in A. Soboul, dir., *Contributions à l'histoire paysanne de la Révolution française*. Paris: Ed. Sociales, 9–43.

Soboul, Albert. (1979). "Alla luce della Rivoluzione: problema contadino e rivoluzione borghese," in A. Groppi *et al.*, *La Rivoluzione francese*. Milano: Franco Angeli Ed., 99–128.

Soboul, Albert. (1981a). "Le maximum des salaires parisiens et le 9 thermidor," in *Comprendre la Révolution*. Paris: Maspéro, 127–145. (Originally published in *Annales historiques de la Révolution française*, 1954.)

Soboul, Albert. (1981b). "La Révolution française dans l'histoire du monde contemporain," in *Comprendre la Révolution*. Paris: Maspéro, 349–380. (Originally in *Studien über die Revolution*, 1969.)

Soboul, Albert. (1981c). "Trois notes pour l'histoire de l'aristocratie (Ancien Régime–Révolution)," in B. Köpeczi & E. H. Balaźs, eds., *Noblesse française, noblesse hongroise, XVIe–XIXe siècles*. Budapest: Akadémiai Kiadó & Paris: Ed. du C.N.R.S., 77–92.

Socolow, Susan Migden. (1978). *The Merchants of Buenos Aires, 1778–1810: Family and Commerce*. Cambridge, Engl.: Cambridge University Press.

Sonenscher, Michael. (1984). "The *sans-culottes* of the Year II: Rethinking the Language of Labour in Pre-revolutionary France," *Social History*, **IX**, 3, 301–328.

Sorel, Albert. (1885–1904). *L'Europe et la Révolution française*, 8 vols. Paris: Plon.

Sovani, N. V. (1954). "British Import in India before 1850–57," *Cahiers d'histoire mondiale*, **I**, 4, 857–882.

Spear, Percival. (1965). *History of India*, Vol. II. Harmondsworth, Engl.: Penguin.

Spodek, Howard. (1974). "Rulers, Merchants, and Other Groups in the City-States of Saurashtra, India, around 1800," *Comparative Studies in Society and History*, **XVI**, 4, 448–470.

Stagg, J. C. A. (1981). "James Madison and the Coercion of Great Britain: Canada, the West Indies, and the War of 1812," *William and Mary Quarterly*, 3d ser., **XXXVIII**, 1, 3–34.

Stanley, George F. G. (1968). *New France: The Last Phase, 1744–1760*. Toronto: McClelland & Stewart.

Stavrianos, L. S. (1952). "Antecedents to the Balkan Revolutions of the Nineteenth Century," *Journal of Modern History*, **XXIX**, 4, 335–348.

Stearns, Peter. (1965). "British Industry Through the Eyes of French Industrialists (1820–1848)," *Journal of Modern History*, **XXXVII**, 1, 50–61.

Stein, Robert Louis. (1978). "Measuring the French Slave Trade, 1713–1792/3," *Journal of African History*, **XIX**, 4, 515–521.

Stein, Robert Louis. (1979). *The French Slave Trade in the Eighteenth Century: An Old Regime Business*. Madison, WI: University of Wisconsin Press.

Stein, Robert Louis. (1983). "The State of French Colonial Commerce on the Eve of the Revolution," *Journal of European Economic History*, **XII**, 1, 105–117.

Stein, Stanley J. (1981). "Bureaucracy and Business in the Spanish Empire, 1759–1804: Failure of a Bourbon Reform in Mexico and Peru," *Hispanic American Historical Review*, **LXI**, 1, 2–28.

Stein, Stanley J. & Stein, Barbara H. (1970). *The Colonial Heritage of Latin America: Essays on Economic Dependence in Perspective*. New York: Oxford University Press.

Stern, Walter M. (1964). "The Bread Crisis in Britain, 1795–96," *Economica*, n.s., **XXXI**, No. 122, 168–187.

Stevens, Wayne Edson. (1926). *The Northwest Fur Trade, 1763–1800*. University of Illinois Studies in the Social Sciences, Vol. XIV, No. 3. Urbana, IL: University of Illinois Press.

Stevenson, John. (1971) "The London 'Crimp' Riots of 1794," *International Review of Social History*, **XVI**, 40–58.

Stevenson, John. (1974). "Food Riots in England, 1792–1818," in J. Stevenson & R. Quinault, eds., *Popular Protest and Public Order*, London: George Allen & Unwin, 33–74.

Stevenson, Robert F. (1968). *Population and Political Systems in Tropical Africa*. New York: Columbia University Press.

Stewart, John Hall, ed. (1967). *The French Revolution: Some Trends in Historical Writing, 1945–1965*. Washington, DC: American Historical Association.

Stewart, Watt. (1930). "Argentina and the Monroe Doctrine, 1824–1828," *Hispanic American Historical Review*, **X**, 1, 26–32.

Stoddard, T. Lothrop. (1914). *The French Revolution in San Domingo*. Boston, MA: Houghton-Mifflin.

Stoianovich, Traian. (1953). "Land Tenure and Related Sectors of the Balkan Economy, 1600–1800," *Journal of Economic History*, **XIII**, 4, 398–411.

Stoianovich, Traian. (1960). "The Conquering Balkan Orthodox Merchant," *Journal of Economic History*, **XX**, 2, 234–313.

Stoianovich, Traian. (1962). "Factors in the Decline of Ottoman Society in the Balkans," *Slavic Review*, **XXI**, 4, 623–632.

Stoianovich, Traian. (1963). "The Social Foundations of Balkan Politics, 1750–1941," in C. Jelavich & B. Jelavich, eds., *The Balkans in Transition*. Berkeley, CA: University of California Press, 297–345.

Stoianovich, Traian. (1976). "Balkan Peasants and Landlords and the Ottoman State: Familial Economy, Market Economy and Modernization," in N. Todorov *et al.*, eds., *La Révolution industrielle dans le Sud-Est Européen—XIXe siècle*. Sofia: Institut d'Etudes Balkaniques, Musée National Polytechnique, 164–204.

Stoianovich, Traian. (1983). "Commerce et industrie ottomans et maghrébins: pôles de diffusion, aires d'expansion," in J. L. Bacqué-Grammont & P. Dumont, eds., *Contributions à l'histoire économique et sociale de l'Empire ottoman*, Collection Turcica, Vol. III. Leuven: Ed. Peeters, 329–352.

Stoianovich, Traian & Haupt, Georges C. (1962). "Le maïs arrive dans les Balkans," *Annales E.S.C.*, **XVII**, 1, 84–93.

Stokes, Eric. (1975). "Agrarian Society and the Pax Britannica in Northern India in the Early Nineteenth Century," *Modern Asian Studies*, **IX**, 4, 505–528.

Stourm, Rene. (1885). *Les Finances de l'ancien régime et de la Révolution*, Vol. II. Paris: Guillaumin.

Stover, John F. (1958). "French-American Trade during the Confederation, 1781–1789," *North Carolina Historical Review*, **XXXV**, 4, 399–414.

Sućeska, Avdo. (1966). "Bedeutung und Entwicklung des Begriffes A'yân in Osmanischen Reich," *Südost-Forschungen*, **XXV**, 3–26.

Sugar, Peter F. (1977). *Southeastern Europe under Ottoman Rule, 1354–1804*. Seattle, WA: University of Washington Press.

Sumner, B. H. (1949). *Peter the Great and the Ottoman Empire*. Oxford: Basil Blackwell.

Sumner, B. H. (1951). *Peter the Great and the Emergence of Russia*. London: English Universities Press.

Sundström, Lars. (1974). *The Exchange Economy of Pre-Colonial Tropical Africa.* London: C. Hurst. (Previously published as *The Trade of Guinea,* 1965).

Supple, Barry. (1973). "The State and the Industrial Revolution, 1700–1914," in C. M. Cipolla, ed., *Fontana Economic History of Europe,* **III:** *The Industrial Revolution.* London: Collins/Fontana, 301–357.

Suret-Canale, Jean. (1961). *Afrique noire occidentale et centrale,* 2ᵉ éd. revue et mise à jour, **I:** *Géographie, Civilisations, Histoire.* Paris: Ed. Sociales.

Suret-Canale, Jean. (1980a). "Contexte et conséquences sociales de la traite africaine," *in Essais d'histoire africaine (de la traite des Noirs au néo-colonialisme).* Paris: Ed. Sociales, 73–96. (Originally in *Présence africaine,* 1964).

Suret-Canale Jean. (1980b). "La Sénégambie à l'ère de la traite," in *Essais d'histoire africaine (de la traite des Noirs au néo-colonialisme).* Paris: Ed. Sociales, 97–112. (Originally in *Canadian Journal of African Studies,* 1977).

Sutherland, Donald. (1982). *The Chouans: The Social Origins of Popular Counter-Revolution in Upper Brittany, 1770–1796.* Oxford: Clarendon Press.

Sutton, Keith. (1977). "Reclamations of Wasteland During the Eighteenth and Nineteenth Centuries," in H. D. Clout, ed., *Themes in the Historical Geography of France.* New York: Academic Press, 247–300.

Svoronos, Nicolas G. (1956). *Le commerce de Salonique au XVIIIe siècle.* Paris: Presses Universitaires de France.

Swai, Bonaventure. (1979). "East India Company and Moplah Merchants of Tellichery: 1694–1800," *Social Scientist,* **VIII,** 1, No. 85, 58–70.

Sweezy, Paul M. (1938). *Monopoly and Competition in the English Coal Trade, 1550–1850,* Harvard Economic Studies, Vol. LXVII. Cambridge, MA: Harvard University Press.

Szatmary, David P. (1980). *Shay's Rebellion: The Making of an Agrarian Insurrection.* Amherst, MA: University of Massachusetts Press.

Szeftel, Mark. (1975). "La monarchie absolue dans l'Etat Moscovite et l'Empire russe (fin XVe s.–1905)," in *Russian Institutions and Culture up to Peter the Great.* London: Variorum Reprints, 737–757. (Originally in *Recueils de la Société Jean Bodin,* **XXII,** 1969.)

Szeftel, Mark. (1980). "Two Negative Appraisals of Russian Pre-Revolutionary Development," *Canadian–American Slavic Studies,* **XIV,** 1, 74–87.

Tambo, David C. (1976). "The Sokoto Caliphate Slave Trade in the Nineteenth Century," *International Journal of African Historical Studies,* **IX,** 2, 187–217.

Tandeter, Enrique. (1901). "Trabajo forzado y trabajo libre en el Potosí colonial tardío," *Desarrollo Económico,* **XX,** No. 80, 511–548.

Tandeter, Enrique & Watchel, Nathan. (1983). "Precios y producción agraria. Potosí y Charcas en el siglo XVIII," *Desarrollo Económico,* **XXIII,** No. 90, 197–232.

Tanguy de La Boissière, C.-C. (1796). *Mémoire sur la situation commerciale de la France avec les Etats-Unis d'Amérique depuis l'année 1775 jusques et y compris 1795. Suivi d'un sommaire d'observations sur les Etats-Unis de l'Amérique.* Paris.

Tann, Jennifer. (1978). "Marketing Methods in the International Steam Engine Market: The Case of Boulton and Watt," *Journal of Economic History,* **XXXVIII,** 2, 363–391.

Tansill, Charles Callan. (1938). *The United States and Santo Domingo, 1798–1873: A Chapter in Caribbean Diplomacy.* Baltimore, MD: Johns Hopkins Press.

Tarle, Eugne. (1926). "Napoleon 1ᵉʳ et les intérêts économiques de la France," *Napoléon: La revue du XIXe siècle,* 15ᵉ année, **XXVI,** 1/2, 117–137.

Tarrade, J. (1972). *Le commerce colonial de la France à la fin de l'Ancien Régime. L'évolution du régime de "L'Exclusif" de 1763 à 1789.* 2 vols. Paris: Presses Universitaires de France.

Tate, W. E. (1945). "Opposition to Parliamentary Enclosure in Eighteenth-Century England," *Agriculture History,* **XIX,** 3, 137–142.

Tavares, Luís Henrique Dias. (1973). "A Independencia como decisão da Unidade do Brasil," *Revista brasileira de cultura,* **V,** No. 17, 89–96.

Tavares, Luís Henrique Dias. (1977). *A Independencia do Brasil na Bahia*. São Paulo: Civilização Brasileira.

Taylor, Arthur J. (1960). "Progress and Poverty in Britain, 1780–1850: A Reappraisal," *History*, **XLV**, No. 153, 16–31.

Taylor, Arthur J. (1972). *Laissez-faire and State Intervention in Nineteenth-century Britain*. London: Macmillan.

Taylor, George Rogers. (1964). "American Economic Growth before 1840: An Exploratory Essay," *Journal of Economic History*, **XXIV**, 4, 427–444.

Taylor, George V. (1961). "The Paris Bourse on the Eve of the Revolution, 1781–1789," *American Historical Review*, **LXVII**, 4, 951–977.

Taylor, George V. (1963). "Some Business Partnerships at Lyon, 1785–1793," *Journal of Economic History*, **XXIII**, 1, 46–70.

Taylor, George V. (1964). "Types of Capitalism in Eighteenth-Century France," *English Historical Review*, **LXXIX**, No. 312, 478–497.

Taylor, George V. (1967). "Noncapitalist Wealth and the Origins of the French Revolution," *American Historical Review*, **LXXII**, 2, 469–496.

Taylor, George V. (1972). "Revolutionary and Nonrevolutionary Content in the *Cahiers* of 1789: An Interim Report," *French Historical Studies*, **VII**, 4, 479–502.

Temperley, Harold. (1925a). "French Designs on Spanish America in 1820–5," *English Historical Review*, **XL**, No. 157, 34–53.

Temperley, Harold. (1925b). *The Foreign Policy of Canning, 1822–1827*. London: G. Bell & Sons.

Thomas, Hugh. (1971). *Cuba: The Pursuit of Freedom*. New York: Harper & Row.

Thomas, Robert Paul. (1965). "A Quantitative Approach to the Study of the Effects of British Imperial Policy upon Colonial Welfare: Some Preliminary Findings," *Journal of Economic History*, **XXV**, 4, 615–638.

Thomas, Robert Paul. (1968a). "British Imperial Policy and the Economic Interpretation of the American Revolution," *Journal of Economic History*, **XXVIII**, 3, 436–440.

Thomas, Robert Paul. (1968b). "The Sugar Colonies of the Old Empire: Profit or Loss for Great Britain?" *Economic History Review*, 2nd ser., **XXI**, 1, 30–45.

Thomas, Robert Paul & Bean, Richard Nelson. (1974). "The Fishers of Men: The Profits of the Slave Trade," *Journal of Economic History*, **XXXIV**, 4, 885–914.

Thomas, Robert Paul & McCloskey, D. N. (1982). "Overseas Trade and Empire, 1700–1860," in R. Floud & D. N. McCloskey, eds., *The Economic History of Britain Since 1700*, **I**: 1700–1860. Cambridge, Engl.: Cambridge University Press, 87–102.

Thomas, William I., & Thomas, Dorothy Swaine. (1928). *The Child in America*. New York: Knopf.

Thomis, Malcolm I. (1972). *The Luddites: Machine-Breaking in Regency England*. New York: Schocken.

Thompson, Edward P. (1968). *The Making of the English Working Class*, rev. ed. Harmondsworth, Engl.: Pelican.

Thompson, Edward P. (1971). "The Moral Economy of the English Crowd in the Eighteenth Century," *Past and Present*, No. 50, 76–136.

Thompson, Edward P. (1978a). "Eighteenth-Century English Society: Class Struggle without Class?" *Social History*, **III**, 2, 133–165.

Thompson, Edward P. (1978b). "The Peculiarities of the English," in *The Poverty of Theory and Other Essays*. London: Merlin Press, 35–91. (Originally published in *The Socialist Register*, 1965.)

Thuillier, Guy. (1967). "Pour une histoire monétaire du XIXe siècle: la crise monétaire de l'automne 1810," *Revue historique*, 91e année, **CCXXXVIII**, juil.–sept., 51–84.

Tilly, Charles. (1968). *The Vendée*, 2nd printing with preface. Cambridge, MA: Harvard University Press.

Tilly, Charles. (1982). "Proletarianization and Rural Collective Action in East Anglia and Elsewhere, 1500–1900," *Peasant Studies*, **X**, 1, 5–34.

Tilly, Charles. (1983). "Flows of Capital and Forms of Industry in Europe, 1500–1900," *Theory and Society*, **XII**, 2, 123–142.

Tilly, Charles & Tilly, Richard. (1971). "Agenda for European Economic History in the 1970s," *Journal of Economic History*, **XXXI**, 1, 184–198.

Tilly, Louise A. (1971). "The Food Riot as a Form of Political Conflict in France," *Journal of Interdisciplinary History*, **II**, 1, 23–57.

Timmer, C. Peter. (1969). "The Turnip, the New Husbandry, and the English Agricultural Revolution," *Quarterly Journal of Economics*, **LXXXIII**, 3, 375–395.

Tinker, Hugh. (1978). *A New System of Slavery. The Export of Indian Labour Overseas, 1830–1920*. London: Oxford University Press.

Tocqueville, Alexis de. (1953). *L'Ancien Régime et la Révolution: Fragments et notes inédites sur la Révolution*, texte établi et annoté par Andre Jardin. Paris: Gallimard.

Tocqueville, Alexis de. (1955). *The Old Regime and the French Revolution*. Garden City, NY: Doubleday Anchor.

Todorov, Nikolai. (1963). "Sur quelques aspects du passage du féodalisme au capitalisme dans les territoires balkaniques de l'Empire ottoman," *Revue des études sud-est européennes*, Nos. 1/2, 103–136.

Todorov, Nikolai. (1965). "La coopération interbalkanique dans de mouvement grec de libération nationale à la fin du XVIIIe et au début du XIXe siècle—Son idéologie et son action," *Etudes historiques*, à l'occasion du XIIe Congrès International des Sciences Historiques—Vienne, août–sept. Sofia: Académie des Sciences de Bulgarie, II, 171–184.

Todorov, Nikolai. (1977). *La ville balkanique sous les Ottomans (IX–XIXe s.)*. London: Variorum Reprints.

Todorova, Maria. (1976). "The Europeanization of the Ruling Elite of the Ottoman Empire during the Period of Reforms," in N. Todorov *et al.*, réds., *La révolution industrielle dans le sud-est Europe—XIXe siècle*, Sofia: Institut d'Etudes Balkaniques, 103–112.

Tolles, Frederick B. (1954). "The American Revolution Considered as a Social Movement: A Re-Evaluation," *American Historical Review*, **LX**, 1, 1–12.

Tønnesson, Kåre D. (1959). *La défaite des sans-culottes: Mouvement populaire et réaction bourgeoise en l'an III*. Oslo: Presses Universitaires & Paris: Lib. R. Clavreuil.

Torke, Hans J. (1971). "Continuity and Change in the Relations Between Bureaucracy and Society in Russia, 1613–1861," *Canadian Slavic Studies*, **V**, 4, 457–476.

Torke, Hans J. (1972). "More Shade than Light," *Canadian–American Slavic Studies*, **VI**, 1, 10–12.

Toutain, J.-C. (1961). "Le produit de l'agriculture française de 1700 à 1958. I. Estimation du produit au XVIIIe siècle," *Cahiers de l'I.S.E.A.*, sér. AF, no. 1, No. 115, 1–216; "II. La Croissance," sér. AF, no. 2, Suppl. No. 115.

Toutain, J.-C. (1963). "La population de la France de 1700 à 1959," *Cahiers de l'I.S.E.A.* sér. AF, 3, no. Suppl. No. 133.

Toynbee, Arnold. (1956). *The Industrial Revolution*. Boston: Beacon Press. (Originally published 1884.)

Tranter, N.L. (1981). "The Labour Supply, 1780–1860," in R. Floud & D.N. McCloskey, eds., *The Economic History of Britain Since 1700*, **I**: *1700–1860*. Cambridge, Engl.: Cambridge University Press, 204–226.

Trendley, Mary. (1916). "The United States and Santo Domingo, 1789–1866," *Journal of Race Development*, **VII**, 1, 83–145; 2, 220–274.

Tribe, Keith. (1981). *Genealogies of Capitalism*. London: Macmillan.

Tripathi, Amales. (1956). *Trade and Finance in the Bengal Presidency, 1793–1833*. Calcutta: Orient Longmans.

Tripathi, Dwijendra. (1967). "Opportunism of Free Trade: Lancashire Cotton Famine and Indian Cotton Cultivation," *Indian Economic and Social History Review*, **IV**, 3, 255–263.

Trouillot, Hénock. (1971). "La guerre de l'indépendance d'Haïti: Les grandes prêtres du Vodou contre l'armée française," *Revista de Historia de América*, No. 72, julio–dic., 259–327.

Trouillot, Hénock. (1972). "La guerre de l'indépendance d'Haïti: II. Les hommes des troupes coloniales contre les grands prêtres de Vodou," *Revista de Historia de América*, Nos. 73/74, enero–dic., 75–130.

Trouillot, Michel-Rolph. (1981). "Peripheral Vibrations: The Case of Saint-Domingue's Coffee Revolution," in R. Robinson, ed., *Dynamics of World Development*, Political Economy of the World-System Annuals, Vol. 4. Beverly Hills, CA: Sage, 27–41.

Trouillot, Michel-Rolph. (1982). "Motion in the System: Coffee, Color, and Slavery in Eighteenth-Century Saint-Domingue," *Review*, **V**, 3, 331–388.

Trudel, Marcel. (1949a). "Le traité de 1783 laisse le Canada à l'Angleterre," *Revue d'histoire de l'Amérique française*, **III**, 2, 179–199.

Trudel, Marcel. (1949b). *Louis XIV, le Congrès Américain et le Canada, 1774–1789*. Québec: Publ. de l'Université Laval.

Tscherkassowa, A.S. (1986). "Quellen der Arbeitskraftebildung des Urals im XVIII. Jahrhundert. Grossmetallurgie," paper delivered at XVIIIa Settimana di Studio, Ist. Int. di Storia Economica "Francesco Datini," Prato, mimeo.

Tucker, G.S.L. (1963). "English Pre-Industrial Population Trends," *Economic History Review*, 2nd ser., **XVI**, 2, 205–218.

Tucker, R.S. (1975). "Real Wages of Artisans in London, 1729–1935," in Arthur J. Taylor, ed., *The Standard of Living in Britain in the Industrial Revolution*. London: Methuen, 21–35. (Originally published in *Journal of the American Statistical Association*, 1936.)

Tulard, Jean. (1970). "Problèms sociaux de la France napoléonienne," *Revue d'histoire moderne et contemporaine*, **XVII**, juil.–sept., 639–663.

Turgay, A. Üner. (1983). "Ottoman–British Trade Through Southeastern Black Sea Ports During the Nineteenth Century," in J.L. Bacqué-Grammont & P. Dumont, réds., *Economie et Sociétés dans l'Empire Ottomane (fin du XVIIIe–Début du XXe siècle)*, Colloques Internationaux du CNRS, No. 601. Paris: Ed. du C.N.R.S. 297–315.

Turner, Frederick J. (1895, 1896). "Western State-Making in the American Revolutionary Era," *American Historial Review*, **I**, 1, 70–87 (1895); **I**, 2, 251–269 (1896).

Turner, Michael. (1982). "Agricultural Productivity in England in the Eighteenth Century: Evidence from Crop Yields," *Economic History Review*, 2nd ser., **XXXV**, 4, 489–510.

Unwin, G. (1922). "Transition to the Factory System," *English Historical Review*, **XXXVI**, No. 146, 206–218; **XXXVI**, No. 147, 383–397.

Uzoigwe, G.N. (1973). "The Slave Trade and African Societies," *Transactions of the Historical Society of Ghana*, **XIV**, 2, 187–212.

Valcárcel, Carlos Daniel. (1957). "Túpac Amaru, fidelista y precursor," *Revista de Indias*, **XVII**, 68, 241–253.

Valcárcel, Carlos Daniel. (1960). "Perú Borbónico y emancipación," *Revista de Historia de América*, No. 50, dic., 315–438.

Valensi, Lucette. (1969). *Le Maghreb avant la prise d'Alger (1790–1830)*. Paris: Flammarion.

Van Alstyne, Richard W. (1960). *The Rising American Empire*. Oxford: Basil Blackwell.

Van Dantzig, Albert. (1975). "Effects of the Atlantic Slave Trade on Some West African Societies," in *Revue française d'histoire d'outre-mer*, **LXII**, 1e et 2e trimestres, Nos. 226/227, 252–269.

Vandenbroeke, C. & Vanderpijpen, W. (1978). "The Problem of the 'Agricultural Revolution' in Flanders and in Belgium: Myth or Reality?" in H. van der Wee & E. van Cauwenberghe, eds., *Productivity of Land and Agricultural Innovation in the Low Countries (1250–1800)*. Leuven: Leuven University Press, 163–170.

Van Tyne, Claude H. (1916). "Influences Which Determined the French Government to

Make the Treaty with America, 1778," *American Historical Review,* **XXI**, 3, 528–541.

Van Tyne, Claude H. (1925). "French Aid Before the Alliance of 1778," *American Historical Review,* **XXXI**, 1, 20–40.

Vargas Ugarte, Rubén. (1971). *Historia General del Perú,* 2a ed., **V:** *Postrimerías del poder español (1776–1815);* **VI:** *Emancipación (1816–1825).* Lima: Ed. Carlos Milla Batrès.

Vázquez de Prada, Valentín. (1968). "Las rutas comerciales entre España y América en el siglo XVIII," *Anuario de estudios americanos,* **XXV**, 197–241.

Venturi, Franco. (1979). "From Scotland to Russia: An Eighteenth Century Debate in Feudalism," in A.G. Cross, ed., *Great Britain and Russia in the Eighteenth-Century: Contrasts and Comparisons.* Newton, MA: Oriental Research Partners, 2–24.

Verhaegen, Paul. (1922–1929). *La Belgique sous la domination française, 1792–1814,* 5 vols. Bruxelles: Goemaere & Paris: Plon.

Verna, Paul. (1969). *Pétion y Bolivar.* Caracas: Oficina Central de Información.

Verna, Paul. (1983). "Bolivar 'El Haitiano': Revolucionario integral y libertador social," *Revista nacional de cultura,* **XLIV**, No. 250, 145–159.

Verna, Paul. (1984). "La revolución haitiana y sus manifestaciones socio-juridicas en el Caribe y Venezuela," *Boletín de la Academia Nacional de la Historia,* **LXVII**, No. 268, 741–752.

Vernadsky, George. (1945). "On Some Parallel Trends in Russian and Turkish History," *Transactions of the Connecticut Academy of Arts and Sciences,* **XXXVI**, July, 25–36.

Ver Steeg, Clarence L. (1957). "The American Revolution Considered as an Economic Movement," *Huntington Library Quarterly,* **XX**, 4, 361–372.

Vicziany, Marika. (1979). "The Deindustrialization of India in the Nineteenth Century: A Methodological Critique of Amiya Kumar Bagchi," *Indian Economic and Social Hsitory Review,* **XVI**, 2, 105–146.

Vidalenc, Jean. (1969). "La traite négrière en France, 1814–1830," *Actes du 91ᵉ Congrès National des Sociétés Savantes,* Rennes, 1966, Section d'histoire moderne et contemporaine, Tome I: *Histoire maritime et coloniale.* Paris: Bibliothèque Nationale, 197–229.

Vidotto, Vittorio. (1979). "Il recente dibattito storiografico sulla Rivoluzione francese," in A. Groppi *et al., La Rivoluzione francese: problemi storici e metodologici.* Milano: Franco Angeli Ed., 11–68.

Viennet, Odette. (1947). *Napoléon et l'industrie française; la crise de 1810–1811.* Paris: Plon.

Vignols, Léon. (1928a). "Etudes négrières de 1774 à 1928. Introduction. Pourquoi la date de 1774," *Revue d'histoire économique et sociale,* **XVI**, 1, 5–11.

Vignols, Léon. (1928b). "La mise en valeur du Canada à l'epoque française," *Revue d'histoire économique et sociale,* **XVI**, 4, 720–795.

Vilar, Pierre. (1974). "Réflexions sur la 'crise de l'ancien type': 'inégalité des récoltes' et 'sous-développement,'" in *Conjoncture économique, structure sociales.* Paris & La Haye: Mouton, 37–58.

Viles, Perry. (1972). "The Slaving Interest of the Atlantic Ports, 1763–1792," *French Historical Studies,* **VII**, 4, 529–543.

Villalobos R., Sergio. (1962). "El comercio extranjero a fines de la dominación española," *Journal of Inter-American Studies,* **IV**, 4, 517–544.

Villalobos R., Sergio. (1965). *Comercio y contrabando en el Rio de la Plata y Chile.* Buenos Aires: Eudeba.

von Tunzelmann, G.N. (1978). *Steam Power and British Industrialization to 1860.* Oxford: Clarendon Press.

von Tunzelmann, G.N. (1979). "Trends in Real Wages, 1750–1850, Revisited," *Economic History Review,* 2nd ser., **XXXII**, 1, 33–49.

von Tunzelmann, G.N. (1981). "Technical Progress During the Industrial Revolution," in R. Floud & D.N. McCloskey, eds., *The Economic History of Britain Since 1700,* **I:** *1700–1860.* Cambridge, Engl.: Cambridge University Press, 143–163.

Vovelle, Michel. (1972). *La chute de la monarchie, 1787–1792.* Paris: Seuil.

Vovelle, Michel. (1980). *Ville et campagne au 18e siècle (Chartres et la Beauce).* Paris: Ed. Sociales.
Vovelle, Michel. (1984). *The Fall of the French Monarchy, 1787–1792.* Cambridge, Engl.: Cambridge University Press.
Vovelle, Michel & Roche, David. (1965). "Bourgeois, Rentiers, and Property Owners," in Jeffry Kaplan, ed., *New Perspectives on the French Revolution.* New York: Wiley, 25–46. (Translated from *Actes du Quatre-Vingt-Quatrième Congrès National des Sociétés Savantes,* 1959.)
Waddell, D.A.G. (1985). "International Politics and Latin American Independence," in L. Bethell, ed., *Cambridge History of Latin America,* **III:** *From Independence to c. 1870.* Cambridge, Engl.: Cambridge University Press, 197–228.
Wadsworth, Alfred P. & Mann, Julia de Lacy. (1931). *The Cotton Trade and Industrial Lancashire, 1600–1780.* Manchester, Engl.: Manchester University Press.
Waldman, Marilyn Robinson. (1965). "The Fulani *Jihad:* A Reassessment," *Journal of African History,* **VI,** 3, 333–355.
Walker, James W. St. G. (1975). "Blacks as American Loyalists: The Slaves' War for Independence," *Historical Reflections,* **II,** 1, 51–67.
Wallerstein, Immanuel. (1974). *The Modern World-System,* **I:** *Capitalist Agriculture and the Origins of the European World-Economy in the Sixteenth Century.* New York: Academic Press.
Wallerstein, Immanuel. (1980). *The Modern World-System,* **II:** *Mercantilism and the Consolidation of the European World-Economy, 1600–1750.* New York: Academic Press.
Wallerstein, Immanuel & Kasaba,Reşat. (1983). "Incorporation into the World-Economy: Changes in the Structure of the Ottoman Empire, 1750–1839," in J. L. Bacqué-Grammont & P. Dumont, eds., *Economie et société dans l'empire ottoman.* Paris: Ed. du C.N.R.S., 335–354.
Walsh, Lorena S. (1983). "Urban Amenities and Rural Sufficiency: Living Standards and Consumer Behavior in the Colonial Chesapeake, 1643–1777," *Journal of Economic History,* **XLIII,** 1, 109–117.
Walton, Gary M. (1967). "Sources of Productivity Change in American Colonial Shipping, 1675–1775," *Economic History Review,* 2nd ser., **XX,** 1, 67–78.
Walton, Gary M. (1971). "The New Economic History and the Burdens of the Navigation Acts," *Economic History Review,* 2nd ser., **XXIV,** 4, 533–542.
Walton, Gary M. (1973). "The Burdens of the Navigation Acts: A Reply," *Economic History Review,* 2nd ser., **XXVI,** 4, 687–688.
Walton, Gary M. & Shepherd, James F. (1979). *The Economic Rise of Early America.* Cambridge, Engl.: Cambridge University Press.
Ward, J.R. (1978). "The Profitability of Sugar Planting in the British West Indies, 1650–1834," *Economic History Review,* 2nd ser., **XXXI,** 2, 197–213.
Ward, W.R. (1965). "The Beginning of Reform in Great Britain: Imperial Problems: Politics and Administration, Econonic Growth," in *New Cambridge Modern History,* **VIII:** A. Goodwin, ed., *The American and French Revolutions, 1762–1793.* Cambridge, Engl.: At the University Press, 537–564.
Warden, G. B. (1976). "Inequality and Instability in Eighteenth-Century Boston: A Reappraisal," *Journal of Interdisciplinary History,* **VI,** 4, 585–620.
Warner, Charles K. (1975). "Soboul and the Peasants," *Peasant Studies Newsletter,* **IV,** 1, 1–5.
Watson, Ian Bruce. (1978). "Between the Devil and the Deep Blue Sea: Commercial Alternatives in India, 1707–1760," *South Asia,* n.s., **I,** 2, 54–64.
Watson, Ian Bruce. (1980a). *Foundation for Empire: English Private Trade in India, 1659–1760.* New Delhi: Vikas.
Watson, Ian Bruce. (1980b). "Fortifications and the 'Idea' of Force in Early English East India Company Relations with India," *Past and Present,* No. 88, 70–88.
Weaver, Emily P. (1904). "Nova Scotia and New England during the Revolution," *American Historical Review,* **X,** 1, 52–71.
Webster, C. K. (1912). "Castlereagh and the Spanish Colonies. I. 1815–1818," *English Historical Review,* **XXVII,** No. 105, 78–95.

Wee, Herman van der. (1980). "La dette publique aux XVIIIe et XIXe siècles," in *Actes du 9e Colloque International,* Spa, 12–16 Sept. 1978. Bruxelles: Credit Commercial de Belgique, 13–21.

Weiss, Roger W. (1970). "The Issue of Paper Money in the American Colonies, 1720–1774," *Journal of Economic History,* **XXX,** 4, 770–784.

Weiss, Roger W. (1974). "The Colonial Monetary Standard of Massachusetts," *Economic History Review,* 2nd ser., **XXVII,** 4, 577–592.

Western, J. R. (1956). "The Volunteer Movement as an Anti-Revolutionary Force, 1793–1801," *English Historical Review,* **LXXI,** No. 281, 603–614.

Western, J. R. (1965). "Armed Forces and the Art of War. 2: Armies," in *New Cambridge Modern History,* **VIII:** A. Goodwin, ed., *The American and French Revolutions, 1763–93.* Cambridge, Engl.: Cambridge University Press, 190–217.

Weulersse, Georges. (1985). *La Physiocratie à l'aube de la Révolution, 1781–1792.* Paris: Ed. de l'E.H.E.S.S.

Whitaker, Arthur P. (1928). "The Commerce of Louisiana and the Floridas at the End of the Eighteenth Century," *Hispanic American Historical Review,* **VIII,** 2, 190–203.

Whitaker, Arthur P. (1941). *The United States and the Independence of Latin America, 1800–1830.* Baltimore, MD: Johns Hopkins Press.

Whitaker, Arthur P. (1960). "Causes of Spanish American Wars of Independence: Economic Factors," *Journal of Inter-American Studies,* **II,** 2, 132–139.

Whitaker, Arthur P. (1962a). *The Spanish-American Frontier: 1783–1795. The Westward Movement and the Spanish Retreat in the Mississippi Valley.* Gloucester, MA: Peter Smith. (Originally published 1927.)

Whitaker, Arthur P. (1962b). *The Mississippi Question, 1795–1803: A Study in Trade, Politics, and Diplomacy.* Gloucester, MA: Peter Smith. (Originally published 1932.)

Whitehead, Donald. (1964). "History to Scale? The British Economy in the Eighteenth Century," *Business Archives and History,* **IV,** 1, 72–83.

Whitehead, Donald. (1970). "The English Industrial Revolution as an Example of Growth," in R. M. Hartwell, ed., *The Industrial Revolution.* Oxford: Basil Blackwell, 3–27.

Whitson, Agnes M. (1930). "The Outlook of the Continental American Colonies on the British West Indies, 1760–1775," *Political Science Quarterly,* **XLV,** 1, 56–86.

Wicker, Elmus. (1985). "Colonial Monetary Standards Contrasted: Evidence from the Seven Years War," *Journal of Economic History,* **XLV,** 4, 869–884.

Wilks, Ivor. (1971). "Asante Policy Towards the Hausa Trade in the Nineteenth Century," in C. Meillassoux, ed., *The Development of Indigenous Trade and Markets in West Africa.* London: Oxford University Press, 124–141.

Wilks, Ivor. (1975). *Asante in the Nineteenth Century: The Structure and Evolution of a Political Order.* London: Cambridge University Press.

Williams, Eric. (1944). *Capitalism and Slavery.* London: André Deutsch. (1966 reprint.)

Williams, Gwyn A. (1968). *Artisans and Sans-culottes: Popular Movements in France and Britain During the French Revolution.* London: Edward Arnold.

Williams, J. E. (1966). "The British Standard of Living, 1750–1850," *Economic History Review,* 2nd ser., **XIX,** 3, 581–589.

Williams, Judith Blow. (1934). "The Establishment of British Commerce with Argentine," *Hispanic American Historical Review,* **XV,** 1, 43–64.

Williams, Judith Blow. (1972). *British Commercial Policy and Trade Expansion, 1750–1850.* Oxford: Clarendon Press.

Williams, Raymond. (1976). *Keywords.* New York: Oxford University Press.

Williams, William Appleman. (1962). "Fire in the Ashes of Scientific History," *William and Mary Quarterly,* 3d ser., **XIX,** 2, 274–287.

Williamson, Jeffrey G. (1984). "Why Was British Growth So Slow During the Industrial Revolution?" *Journal of Economic History,* **XLIV,** 3, 687–712.

Wilson, Charles. (1977). "The British Isles," in C. Wilson & G. Parker, eds., *An Introduction to the Sources of European Economic History, 1500–1800*, **I:** *Western Europe*. London: Weidenfeld & Nicolson, 115–154.

Wilson, R. G. (1966). "Transport Dues as Indices of Economic Growth, 1775–1820," *Economic History Review*, 2nd ser., **XIX**, 1, 110–123.

Winsor, Justin. (1896). "Virginia and the Quebec Bill," *American Historical Review*, **I**, 3, 436–443.

Wood, A. C. (1925). "The English Embassy at Constantinople, 1660–1762," *English Historical Review*, **XL**, No. 160, 533–561.

Wood, Gordon S. (1966). "Rhetoric and Reality in the American Revolution," *William and Mary Quarterly*, 3d ser., **XXIII**, 1, 3–32.

Woodruff, Philip. (1953). *The Men Who Ruled India*, **I:** *The Founders*. London: Jonathan Cape.

Woodward, Margaret L. (1968). "The Spanish Army and the Loss of America, 1810–1824," *Hispanic American Historical Review*, **XLVIII**, 4, 586–607.

Woodward, Ralph Lee, Jr. (1968). "The Merchants and Economic Development in the Americas, 1750–1850: A Preliminary Study," *Journal of Inter-American Studies*, **X**, 1, 134–153.

Woodward, Robert Lee, Jr. (1965). "Economic and Social Origins of the Guatemalan Political Parties (1773–1823)," *Hispanic American Historical Review*, **XLV**, 4, 544–566.

Wordie, J. R. (1974). "Social Change on the Leveson–Gower Estates, 1714–1832," *Economic History Review*, 2nd ser., **XXVII**, 4, 593–606.

Woronoff, Denis. (1984a). *L'industrie sidérurgique en France pendant la Révolution et l'Empire*. Paris: Ed. de l'E.H.E.S.S.

Woronoff, Denis. (1984b). *The Thermidorean Regime and the Directory, 1794–1799*. Cambridge, Engl.: Cambridge University Press.

Wright, H. R. C. (1954). "Some Aspects of the Permanent Settlement in Bengal," *Economic History Review*, 2nd ser., **VII**, 2, 204–215.

Wright, H. R. C. (1955). *Free Trade and Protection in the Netherlands, 1816–30: A Study of the First Benelux*. Cambridge, Engl.: At the University Press.

Wright, H. R. C. (1959). "The Abolition by Cornwallis of the Forced Cultivation of Opium in Bihar," *Economic History Review*, 2nd ser., **XII**, 1, 112–119.

Wright, J. F. (1965). "British Economic Growth, 1688–1959," *Economic History Review*, 2nd ser., **XVIII**, 2, 397–412.

Wright, J. Leitch, Jr. (1975). *Florida in the American Revolution*. Gainesville, FL: University of Florida Press.

Wrigley, C. C. (1971). "Historicism in Africa: Slavery and State Formation," *African Affairs*, **LXX**, No. 279, 113–124.

Wrigley, E. A. (1967). "The Supply of Raw Materials in the Industrial Revolution," in R. M. Hartwell, ed., *The Causes of the Industrial Revolution in England*. London: Methuen, 97–120. (Originally published in *Economic History Review*, 1962.)

Wrigley, E. A. (1969). "Family Limitation in Pre-Industrial England," in M. Drake, ed., *Population in Industrialization*. London: Methuen, 157–194. (Originally published in *Economic History Review*, 1966.)

Wrigley, E. A. (1972). "The Process of Modernization and the Industrial Revolution in England," *Journal of Interdisciplinary History*, **III**, 2, 225–259.

Wrigley, E. A. & Schofield, R. S. (1981). *The Population History of England, 1541–1871: A Reconstruction*. Cambridge, MA: Harvard University Press.

Wyczański, Andrzej & Topolski, Jerzy. (1974). "Peasant Economy Before and During the First State of Industrialization: General Report," in *Sixth International Congress of Economic History, Copenhagen, 19–23 August, Five Themes*. Copenhagen: Institute of Economic History, University of Copenhagen, 11–31.

Yaney, George L. (1973). *The Systematization of Russian Government: Social Evolution in the*

Domestic Administration of Imperial Russia, 1711–1905. Urbana, IL: University of Illinois Press.

Yanov, Alexander. (1978). "The Drama of the Time of Troubles, 1725–30," *Canadian–American Slavic Studies,* **XII,** 1, 1–59. (Corrigenda: **XII,** 4, 593.)

Yaresh, Leo. (1956). "The Problem of Periodization," in C. E. Black, ed., *Rewriting Russian History.* New York: Vintage Books, 32–77.

Yelling, J. A. (1977). *Common Field and Enclosure in England, 1450–1850.* London: Macmillan.

Yoder, John C. (1974). "Fly and Elephant Parties: Political Polarization in Dahomey," *Journal of African History,* **XV,** 3, 417–432.

Youngson, A. J. (1966). "The Opening Up of New Territories," in H. J. Habakkuk & M. Postan, eds., *Cambridge Economic History of Europe,* **VI:** *The Industrial Revolutions and After: Incomes, Population and Technological Change.* Cambridge, Engl.: At the University Press, 139–211.

Zacker, Jacques. (1962). "Quelques mots sur les sans-culottes de la Révolution française à propos de l'article de George Rudé)," *Critica storica,* **I,** 4, 384–387.

Zaozerskaja, E. I. (1965). "Le salariat dans les manufactures textiles russes au XVIIIe siècle," *Cahiers du monde russe et soviétique,* **VI,** 2, 188–222.

Zapperi, Roberto. (1972). "Siéyès et l'abolition de la féodalité en 1789," *Annales historiques de la Révolution française,* **XLIV,** No. 209, 321–351.

Zapperi, Roberto. (1974). *Per la critica del concetto di rivoluzione borghese.* Bari: De Donato.

Závala, Silvio. (1967). *El mundo americano en la época colonial,* 2 vols. Mexico: Ed. Porrua.

Zeller, Gaston. (1955). *Les temps modernes,* **II:** *De Louis XIV à 1789,* Vol. III of Pierre Renouvin, dir., *Histoire des relations internationales.* Paris: Hachette.

Zilversmit, Arthur. (1967). *The First Emancipation: The Abolition of Slavery in the North.* Chicago, IL: University of Chicago Press.

Zimmerman, A. F. (1931). "Spain and its Colonies, 1808–1820," *Hispanic American Historical Review,* **XI,** 4, 439–463.

Zuccarelli, François. (1959). "L'entrepôt fictif de Gorée entre 1822 et 1852: Une exception au régime de l'Exclusif," *Annales africaines,* **VI,** 261–282.

INDEX

In this index, items dealing with particular political jurisdictions have been grouped together, despite name changes over time, under the appellations in use at the end of the period under consideration. Thus, for example, New France is to be found under Quebec, La Plata under Argentina, and the Austrian Netherlands under Belgium. Of course, the boundaries were not always identical. An effort has been made to maximize coherence of grouping while minimizing dispersion of entries. The references to a people (an ethnic group) are to be found grouped with references to the country of origin. Thus, "Greeks" is located under "Greece," and "Irish" under "Ireland." Proper names with prefixes are catalogued according to the rules of the American Library Association.